Hungry for Ecstasy

Hungry for Ecstasy

Trauma, the Brain, and the Influence of the Sixties

Sharon Klayman Farber, PhD

JASON ARONSON
Lanham • Boulder • New York • Toronto • Plymouth, UK

Published by Jason Aronson
A wholly owned subsidiary of The Rowman & Littlefield Publishing Group, Inc.
4501 Forbes Boulevard, Suite 200, Lanham, Maryland 20706
www.rowman.com

10 Thornbury Road, Plymouth PL6 7PP, United Kingdom

British Library Cataloguing in Publication Information Available

Library of Congress Cataloging-in-Publication Data

Farber, Sharon Klayman.
Hungry for ecstasy : trauma, the brain, and the influence of the sixties / Sharon Klayman Farber.
p. cm.
Includes bibliographical references and index.
ISBN 978-0-7657-0858-8 (hardback : alk. paper) -- ISBN 978-0-7657-0859-5 (e-ISBN)
[DNLM: 1. Dissociative Disorders--psychology. 2. Euphoria. 3. Mind-Body Relations, Metaphysical. 4. Self-Injurious Behavior.
WM 173.6]
616.85'23--dc23
2012012907

The paper used in this publication meets the minimum requirements of American National Standard for Information Sciences Permanence of Paper for Printed Library Materials, ANSI/NISO Z39.48-1992.

Printed in the United States of America

I dedicate this book to my family: my husband Stuart, my son David, daughter-in-law Rebecca, and my grandchildren Sam, Jake, and Ava. You make my life a joy.

This book is dedicated as well to my patients, and the many people who have contacted me either from my dissertation study or elsewhere, to tell me something of their story. I wish you all health, hope, and healing.

And once again, I dedicate this book to the memory of my neighbor, Kathy, who killed herself at age eighteen when life became too hard.

Contents

Acknowledgments

The writer E. L. Doctorow said "Writers are not just people who sit down and write. They hazard themselves. Every time you compose a book your composition of yourself is at stake." He knew what he was talking about. Writing a book and getting it published are not for the faint of heart. It can take over your life, sometimes in wonderful ways, sometimes in terrible ways.

When I published my first book, *When the Body Is the Target: Self-Harm, Pain, and Traumatic Attachments*, Carol Tosone, PhD, Associate Professor of Social Work at New York University School of Social Work, played a key part in my becoming the author of a published book. When I was awarded my PhD. in 1995, we had never met until she approached me right after the graduation ceremony, She told me that she had heard such interesting things about my dissertation and that I really ought to consider writing a book on the subject. She had no way of knowing that writing a book had always been a daydream of mine. I never imagined that the fantasy might actually become a reality. I needed just that kind of encouragement to get me to start to imagine it. She provided me with the contact information for various publishers. And that's how *When the Body Is the Target* was born. And once I had written the book and knew that I could do it, it gave me the courage to try another one. Thank you, Carol, for your support and generosity.

To William James, because he was interested in many of the same things that have captured my imagination in this book. He was interested in consciousness, influenced modern ideas of consciousness, and in fact, coined the term *stream of consciousness,* which had a great impact on modern psychology and on authors such as James Joyce and others and me. James' ideas on science and spirituality, *The Varieties of Religious Experience* in particular, may be the most revealing investigation into the psychology of religion ever attempted.

To Charles Raphael, a wonderful English teacher at Hunter College High School, who introduced me to the wonders of *stream of consciousness* writing, which opened up worlds to me. He gave the creative writing class the assignment of writing in this mode. I began to write that way, which I came to know later was akin to the process of free association, and so was part of my attraction not only to writing but to psychoanalysis.

Before I had any professional training at all, I worked with drug addicts at Manhattan General Hospital's detoxification program. Knowing them has taught me so much about the nature of addiction and dissociative processes that has served me well in understanding the nature of addictions of all kinds. They may not have realized it but they were teaching me. I am grateful for that.

To my patients and colleagues who have trusted me enough to tell me their stories and allowed me to include them here, I could not have done it without you.

There were so many people who were helpful to me in different ways in writing this book and inevitably, I am afraid I will forget to thank some of them. I took an outstanding course on how to write a non-fiction book proposal from Melinda Marshall, who helped me shape a book proposal that got my publisher, Jason Aronson, interested enough to decide to publish it. Julie Kirsch, editorial director at Jason Aronson, provided the direction for me to shape my book so that it appealed to mental health clinicians and related professionals as well as to a serious non-fiction readership of the general public. Julie, Samantha Kirk, Amy King, and Lindsey Porambo were my midwives, helping me through labor and delivery.

Over the years I have been privileged to have the critical attention of David M. Krueger, MD, a wonderful writer and thinker. A number of people read certain chapters. To those who read my chapter on the brain and ecstasy, I owe you such a debt of gratitude for keeping me from embarrassing myself by writing incorrectly about the brain. Thanks to Richard Chefetz, MD, Karen Hopenwasser, MD, and Robert Scaer, MD.

I have come to know some brave and talented people through the International Cultic Studies Association, who have helped me with my understanding of cult involvement, and some have been kind enough to review my chapter on the subject. They include Gina Catena, MS, Lorna Goldberg, MSW, Bill Goldberg, MSW, Michael Langone, PhD, Patrick Ryan, Kristen Skedgell, MSW, Dan Shaw, MSW, Ann Stamler, Joe Stamler, Joe Szimhart, and Vanessa Weber, MSW.

When I inquired of other mental health professionals about creativity in their personal lives and work, the response exceeded anything I had ever expected. I am proud to be part of such a group of creative mental health professionals. Thanks to Gemma Marangoni Ainslee, Penelope Andrew, LCSW, Liz Baring, MSc, Lisa Bartoletto, Ann Beckett, Claudia Behr, LCSW, John R. Brauer, PsyD, Pamela Brewer, PhD, Nancy Burke, Dan Buccino, Gloria Cardey, Joseph A. Cattano, PhD, Jan Chess, PhD, Maggie Chubb, Lynne Clements, LCSW, Penny Cohen, LCSW, Lynn Crook, Susan Deane-Miller, LCSW, Molly Donovan, Ruth Eichenstein, MSW, John F. Elliott, MA, Jody Bowle-Evans, MD, Katie Fallin, Al Frankel, LCSW, Arlene Gellman, John Gerson PhD, Michael M. Gindi, PhD, Ruth Greer, DSW, Ruth Grill, MSW, Robin Halpern, LCSW, Celia Harrisson, William Henkin, PhD, Sheila Henoch, LCSW, Karen Hopenwasser, MD, Katie Keech, Libby Kessman, LCSW, Kathleen Kosche, LCSW, Lee Kraemer, Patricia Kuusisto, Beatriz E Ledesma PhD, Deborah Levine, PhD, Judith Schweiger Levy, PhD, Dan Mackler, LCSW, Nancy McWilliams, PhD, Mark McGonigle, LCSW, Lori Kalman-McCartney, MSN, Clancy McKenzie, MD, Pamela Meek, PhD, Marilyn N. Metzl, PhD, Lauren Miller, PsyD, Kevin Nelson, MD, Dr. Randy Noblitt, Jane Parker, Tony Patterson, LMHC, Lisa Pelton, LCSW, Joanna Poppink, MFT, Laura Pontrelli, Michael Ramseur, Karyn Reader, MSW, Karen Redding, Deborah Rubin, PhD, Marty Saeman, MSW, Roberta Shafter, PhD, Marjorie Scheer, Jonathan Schiff, LICSW, Betti Schleyer, PhD, Mark Singer, MD, Angelica Smith, LCSW, Mark Steinberg, PhD, Kathie Talbot, Mila Ruiz Tecala, LICSW, Barbara Tholfsen, LCSW, Robin Ticic, Dr. Robert C. Twigg, Wendy West, LPC, Larry Wetzler, PhD, Lee Miriam Whitman-Raymond, PhD, Ann Wilkens, and Julie Willstatter, LCSW.

The Dissociative Disorders listserv has been a remarkable resource for me. Presentations on ecstasy at conferences of the International Society for the Study of Trauma and Dissociation and the New York State Society of Clinical Social Workers have yielded unusual material, included in the book.

Thanks go to Vincent D'Amico, MD, Martin Katchen, Daniel Merkur, PhD, Andrew Newberg, MD, Robert Schavrien, MSW, and Tony Smith, MD.

There were times when I wanted to throw my computer out the window. Kish Melawi and Oscar Lopez have always magically known how to make a misbehaving computer sit up and act like an adult.

Mike McCoy, librarian at the Hastings-on-Hudson Public Library, came through on what must have seemed endless requests for journal articles and books. Thanks so much.

Becoming a grandmother has been one of the best things that has ever happened in my life. I regret that writing this book has taken so much of my time away from Sammy, Jake, Ava and my son David and daughter-in-law Rebecca. It has taken so much time away from my husband Stuart, who has been a rock of Gibraltar during this long, difficult process. My family keeps teaching me so much about what is most important in life.

Preface

While writing this book, I tried to do it as if I were having a conversation with someone who may be concerned about someone else who takes great risks with his life or who just enjoys reading about what is happening in our culture and in the human mind. This includes intelligent readers of non-fiction, psychotherapists, psychoanalysts, human resource and school counselors, professionals in related fields such as the neurosciences, as well as in cultural studies, religion, sexuality, history, creativity, and cultic studies.

I like to make the psychoanalytic concepts which I find so useful accessible and understandable to those who have not been trained in psychoanalysis. British psychoanalyst Adam Phillips (1994) said that when psychoanalysis works the way it should, there is nothing mystical or esoteric about it; it is a form of conversation that helps some people feel better. In that spirit, I hope that you will find this book quite accessible, readable, straight-forward, and engaging.

I did not choose to become an independent scholar; it just happened that way. The best thing about it is that I write what I want to write without the constraints of academic politics. I do not have to live with the *publish or perish* dilemma that academic scholars must contend with. This freedom comes with a price; , there is no university providing a salary, health benefits, paid vacations, holidays, and sick days. I write because I want to, because I loved writing and wanted to be a writer long before I even knew that I wanted to be a psychotherapist. When I get interested in something, I can be like a dog on a bone, pursuing it obsessively. I'll read not only journal articles but books related to the topic, centrally or tangentially. A newspaper horoscope put it like this: "Your passion for learning grows exponentially as you enjoy getting into the more nuanced layers of a subject. The joy of learning is its own reward." (Horoscope and fortune cookie messages sometimes speak to me, sometimes they don't.)

When my first book was published in 2000, a number of people who were not mental health clinicians read it and a few left very positive comments on Amazon.com. One even called it a page-turner! A few contacted me to thank me for the book. They were people who had the trauma-related problems with eating disorders and self-mutilation I had written about. They had found that I wrote in a way that expressed the turmoil that they experienced better than they could express it themselves. One woman said that while reading it, it felt as if I had written the book for her. Hearing this was very gratifying for me, and so when I started to write my second book, I realized that I wanted it to be published by a trade publisher, in order to reach not only mental health professionals but also to reach larger numbers of thoughtful readers of serious non-fiction.

I learned that to get a book published as a trade book, it is best to write a book proposal and find a literary agent to represent you, something very different from that which I experienced with getting my first book published. At that time, once I had decided that I wanted to write and publish a book, I telephoned the acquisitions editors at several publishing houses, and two were interested enough to ask me to submit a proposal. Looking back, I laugh at how naïve and how fortunate I was. I wrote letters to two of them, saying that I proposed to write a book based on the exciting findings of my doctoral dissertation. Both editors apparently realized that I did not know what a book proposal was and were too polite to tell me, and each of them asked me to send them a copy of my dissertation. I was delighted to do it, because it meant that more than the three people on my dissertation committee would read it. John Kerr at the Analytic Press was also an author of a dissertation that was turned into a book, *A Most Dangerous Method* (Kerr 1993) and even into a film. He was very helpful in pointing me in the direction of attachment theory, which I have found is central to understanding and helping those pursuing high-risk behavior. Ultimately I was sent a book contract by Michael Moskowitz at Jason Aronson, Inc., only two months after making that initial phone call.

Based on that experience, I was not at all prepared for how much more difficult it would be to get my second book published. In the fall of 2002, two years after publishing the first book, I enrolled in a six session class in how to write the non-fiction book proposal offered by a writing center. There I learned far more about writing a book proposal, the publishing business in general, and the importance of enlisting the help of a literary agent to intercede between the author and the publishing houses. The woman who taught the course thought that with significant revision of my sample proposal written for the course, I would readily find an agent to help me find a publisher. She was wrong about that. By the winter of 2009, I had accumulated quite a hefty collection of rejection letters from literary agencies. Although several agents found my proposal quite compelling, they did not think there would be a large enough readership to justify publishing it. A few recommended appealing to a publisher of "crossover" books. Although I had developed a thicker skin that tolerated so much rejection, after almost seven years of trying, I became quite discouraged and was ready to call it quits.

I had learned the hard way that in today's harsh economy, having a book published in the old form we are accustomed to, a hard copy with bound pages that you can hold in your hand, is no small feat. Today most books are being published as e-books, electronic books to be downloaded to a portable electronic reading device. I discovered that there was little in the way of non-fiction being published at all, and very little of it electronically. A friend who writes children's books told me that even more and more children's books are being published as e-books. Borders, a large bookstore chain, has closed. This leaves the author of serious non-fiction up a creek.

I did not have the emotional energy to continue to pursue what was clearly a dead end, so I did nothing about it for several months. I needed time to lick my wounds. But nonetheless, I still wanted so much to get it published. After talking with two colleagues who had some experience in getting their books published, I finally decided to appeal to Jason Aronson again. This time, I knew what a book proposal was. And this time, Jason Aronson was a different company from the one that published my first book. It had been acquired as an imprint of the Rowman & Littlefield Publishing Group, which, as stated on their website "provides innovative, high-quality college texts, provocative and timely titles for general readers, and professional and scholarly books throughout the humanities and social sciences" (Rowman & Littlefield 2011). I appealed to the editorial director, Julie Kirsch, that this could be marketed as a "crossover" book, not only to mental health professionals, but also to those in related disciplines, and to intelligent thoughtful laymen.

While writing this book, I found it was necessary to disclose more personal information than I am accustomed to doing. But by now, I have done this work of psychotherapy and psychoanalysis long enough that I have little need to cloak myself in the anonymity for which psychoanalysts, deservedly or undeservedly, are known. I am as real and human as the patients I see, and with them too, I disclose as much personal information as I think might be helpful in understanding certain experiences or accepting certain aspects of themselves. Last but not least, I write for the same reasons others write—to communicate my thoughts and feelings to others.

Introduction

> There are more things in heaven and earth, Horatio,
> Than are dreamt of in your philosophy.
> —William Shakespeare, *Hamlet*

I love writing and exploration of new territory. I am very curious about people, and consider myself to be open-minded as well as skeptical. In writing this book, I have done what I enjoy doing. I did not have a clear-cut plan to begin with. I followed my nose and sniffed out the way, much as I do in the treatment of my patients. I rediscovered books I had had in my own library for years, and discovered others I knew nothing about. I wrote and read, and read and wrote, enjoying this back and forth process, resulting in the development of some thoughts about what ecstasy is and why people search for it. I have arrived at no final conclusions, only speculations and questions.

"The last thing one settles on in writing a book is what one should put in first," said Oliver Sacks (Sacks 1987, p.vii). Julie Kirsch told me the same thing. It was not until I was in the midst of writing my eleventh chapter that I thought about what I should write in my introduction. And while writing the introduction, it occurred to me to write a preface.

For a long time I have been drawn to that which is mysterious and uncanny, to paradoxes and that which is ambiguous, and so it makes sense that I have been drawn to the late Robert Stoller, who was drawn to the same things. He said that "We never know what clues may help solve puzzles of behavior . . . . There is value, then—beyond the impulse to capture rare specimens for humanity's zoo—in searching out oddities that can spotlight forces too muffled to be perceived in ordinary conduct (Stoller 1985, p. 157)." Oliver Sacks has studied neurological oddities, and in the telling, made them human. This book is something of an oddball book. The subject, ecstasy, is something that, oddly enough, scientific study tends to ignore.

HOW THIS BOOK BEGAN

After submitting the manuscript for my first book, Jason Aronson, my publisher, called me and said he had edited out several whole chapters because they were superfluous, and would make an already big book much too big. He thought that they really constituted the subject of a second book. Puzzled, I asked him what the second book was about. He said that he would leave that for me to figure out. So that is what I tried to do. It took awhile before it dawned on me that an underlying theme running through these chapters was a search for ecstatic experience.

I came to realize that much of what was omitted had to do with individuals who cannot live comfortably in their own skins, who harm themselves through disordered eating, self-mutilation of one kind or another and the most bizarre body modifications, way beyond tattooing and body piercing. These practices are derived from the Modern Primitives movement, which is the indiscriminate adoption of tribal practices of primitive cultures. The term *body suspension* might make you think about automobiles, but the body suspensions I am referring to have nothing to do with automobiles. The practice of body suspension was adopted from both Hindu and Native American cultures. It involves a process in which a person voluntarily allows others to insert large hooks, the kind fishermen use for catching very large fish, through his flesh, attach them to wire cables, then hoist and suspend his body a foot or two off the ground. During this process, which can last an hour or more, and can result in great harm and even death, all sensibility, voluntary motion, and mental power is suspended. I found that here I was again, with a sustained interest in the theme begun in my first book, the attraction to destruction and self-destruction.

ECSTASY AND THAT WHICH IS STRANGE AND UNCANNY

Learning about body suspension brought to mind an image I had seen of Bernini's 1652 marble sculpture *The* Ecstasy *of St. Teresa*, in which St. Teresa of Avila seemed to be in a state in which her sensibility, voluntary motion, and mental power were all suspended. Was it possible that some of the people who had their bodies suspended went into ecstatic states as St. Teresa and other medieval mystics did? My research confirmed that this was the case for some of them. It was also striking to me that the image of St. Teresa in ecstasy was an undeniably erotic image, in which she appeared to be in the throes of orgasm. I began to wonder if ecstatic experience, arising from very different experiences such as religion, spirituality, sexual arousal, and pain were phenomenologically the same.

After letting my mind run free with these and other thoughts, I knew that my second book would be about ecstatic experience. I took the content of those omitted chapters and reworked them, and so the book started to take shape. While writing the eleventh chapter, I compared the psychotherapy of someone looking for ecstatic experience to the treatment of someone with a perversion, and referred to Stoller's work with the perversions. In a nutshell, those with perversions, like those seeking ecstasy, usually do not seek treatment for their perversion because this behavior is so dear to them that they do not want to give it up. But we *do* see individuals, however, whose high-risk behavior can lead them in the direction of seeking ecstasy. With them, we have an opportunity to intervene whether we are a psychotherapist, school counselor, teacher, family member, or just someone who cares. This opportunity is addressed in the eleventh chapter. The twelfth chapter is meant specifically for psychotherapists and describes how such intervention and treatment can not only literally save someone's life but can help turn it into a life that is enjoyable and worth living. Stoller was a psychoanalyst and on faculty at University of California Medical School at Los Angeles. While chatting with a colleague at the annual dinner of his local psychoanalytic society, he remarked that thanks to the contemplative, hermetic life of an academic, he was able to avoid reality in almost every sphere of life. "How else could one become a student of the dynamics of perversion and be spared its realities? (Stoller 1991, p. v)." His colleague responded by asking him when he was going to join the real world, to which he replied that he really should, that he'd been thinking about it. And so he ventured from his office to the S & M subculture in West Hollywood, like an anthropologist observing the tribe.

It was only a short distance away geographically but light years away in terms of Stoller's mind-set. Initially he regarded the people he met as specimens to be studied scientifically but after awhile, he came to see how very human they were, and from that point on, he was well on his way to understanding them. His book *Pain & Passion: A Psychoanalyst Explores the World of S & M* (Stoller 1991) is the result.

The more I have read of Stoller, the more I feel drawn to him for several reasons. He liked to write the way he spoke, a conversational style, which is not usual in psychoanalytic writing. I try to write in the same way, presenting complex ideas in straightforward language, avoiding psychoanalytic jargon when possible. Stoller was deeply interested in people. I learned that he had formed a deep friendship with the late Masud Khan, a paradoxical and controversial figure, whose theory that perversion is an aspect of false self pathology was a significant contribution to the literature. (Please bear with me. There is a good reason I am telling you so much about Khan.) Khan and Winnicott developed the idea that all people have a dissociated self that possesses qualities of the opposite sex (Hopkins 2006). Khan was a wealthy Anglo-Pakistani, a magnetic figure in London's psychoanalytic circles during the 1960s and 70s. Although he gained an international reputation as a psychoanalytic theorist, he died as a disgraced, lonely alcoholic, expelled by the British Psycho-Analytical Society for inappropriate social and sexual relationships with patients. He published three highly regarded books, but his last book, *The Long Wait* (Khan 1989), published at the end of his life, mingled profound insights with a vicious anti-Semitic tirade and accounts of his sexual involvement with patients. In her *New York Times* book review, Janet Malcolm called it outrageous and repellent, and assumed that something terrible had happened to Khan (Hopkins 2000). In her biography, Linda Hopkins (2006) suggested that Khan suffered from undiagnosed bipolar disorder, exacerbated by alcoholism.

Khan was a paradox, a brilliant clinician and theorist who helped some patients and tortured others; who inspired love and admiration from some analysts and fear and loathing in others (Hopkins 2006). "Philosophically-inclined analysts talk about 'paradox' all the time, but when they're confronted with someone like Khan who *is* a genuine paradox, they don't know what to do with him" (Hopkins 2006, p. 363). But Stoller did. He and his wife Sybil regularly brought out the best in Khan. Although Stoller agreed with his colleagues that Khan had gone out of his mind, and despite his rage at him, he was still able to love him, in much the same way he came to feel affection for some of the sadomasochists he had met in West Hollywood. Stoller said that "it takes me upward of ten years of gathering observations, thinking about them, and soaking up the literature before an area of behavior becomes familiar to me, and even then, the full texture only begins to appear. So I have a long way to go in regard to perverse sadomasochism" (Stoller 1991, p. 5).

I too have a long way to go—in regard to understanding ecstasy. This book is only a beginning. Ecstasy may seem like a strange subject for a psychotherapist to write about. I will tell you how I became so absorbed in thinking about it, because this book is the result of that meandering process of free association and clinical practice combined with research. Scholarship is a joy for me. When I became interested in a subject, I begin noticing references that would otherwise have passed me by, and begin reading whatever I can find about it. Or while reading something that seems not at all related to it, I discover something in it that is related. It is a pretty messy process, but then again, ecstasy seems to be a subject that is pretty messy to write about. Part of this process is like that of a child, enjoying putting his paintbrush into a cup of thick paint and smearing it around on paper, happily unconcerned about the mess he is making. But writing something that will be published can't stop there at the pleasure part. You have to clean up the mess, so then comes the revising and editing, not at all a pleasure, although it does have some satisfactions.

ECSTASY AS A UNIQUE ALTERED STATE OF CONSCIOUSNESS

Ecstasy, I think, is a unique form of dissociation that we have heard little about. Mental health professionals have been late to learn and think about dissociation in general, for several reasons, one of which is that they tend to associate the term *dissociation* with the very flamboyant portrayals of Multiple Personality Disorder that we saw on television in the 1980s.That diagnosis, currently known as Dissociative Identity Disorder, remains controversial (Lilienfeld and Lynn 2004). Another reason is that although Freud (1910) was aware of dissociative processes in his patients suffering from conversion hysteria and recognized that their dramatic somatic symptoms were induced by psychological trauma, he subsequently dismissed the phenomenon of dissociation that his associate Josef Breuer believed was at the root of hysteria (Breuer and Freud 1895). The result in psychoanalysis is an emphasis on repression at the expense of dissociation.

To understand how and why someone might seek ecstatic experiences, we must understand more about different states of consciousness, different forms of dissociation, and multiple self-states. As Philip Bromberg said, "Part of our work as analysts facilitates the restoration of links between dissociated aspects of self so that the conditions for intrapsychic conflict and its resolution can develop" (Bromberg 1998, p. 13).

Like Stoller, Oliver Sacks too treasures paradox. In his wonderful neurological case studies, he sees in these *fascinomas*[1] a version of himself, and uses this identification to make what might otherwise be bizarre and freakish into something human and understandable to the rest of us. They stop being cases and become human beings who happen to be afflicted with autism or Tourette's or amnesia. In her review of Sacks' (1996) book *An Anthropologist on Mars: Seven Paradoxical Tales,* Wendy Lesser (1995) said "Everybody is peculiar. Oliver Sacks wants us to know that we are all links in the great chain of weirdness." This book is written in that spirit.

Something I noted in the first book but did not explore further was the finding from my dissertation study that although self-mutilating and eating-disordered behavior seemed to serve as a form of self-medication and helped many people feel better, at least momentarily, some described experiences with this behavior that might be called ecstatic. One bulimic woman described orgiastic, ecstatic states resulting from her vomiting. I remembered Stoller's three cases of what he called erotic vomiting and what he said about it. "Having found no literature on erotic vomiting, I want to report the following cases. We never know what clues may help solve puzzles of behavior, a truism that fits erotic life, so much of which is still unexplored" (Stoller 1985, p. 157). I wished I could have contacted Stoller to tell him that I knew something about erotic vomiting, from a bulimic woman I had never met.

I present here those who have a sadomasochistic relationship with themselves, and have a need to inflict pain on themselves, as well as those who practice sexual sadomasochism, finding an ecstatic release in these behaviors. And then there are those who not only find ecstatic release in inflicting pain on others but in killing them. So I wrote about ecstasies of killing, especially during war. And I wrote about the Nazis' Jew-killing ecstasies and the ecstasies of the suicide bombers. And then, a compelling film I saw got me thinking and writing about ecstasies of cannibalism. I began to think more about the phenomenon of people searching for meaning and enlightenment by joining esoteric cults and Pentecostal churches, and the ecstatic experience of being *born again.* I read about the ecstasies of the snake-handling sects in southern Appalachia, in a book written by a *New York Times* reporter who visited these churches. Not only did he witness it, but he allowed himself to be seduced into the ecstasy of this experience and he picked up poisonous snakes and danced around with them. He too is in this book. The born-again and snake-handling ecstasies reminded me of Saint Teresa of Avila's very erotic religious ecstasies, and the ecstasies of those who develop the stigmata. Many people reached a *peak experience* (Maslow 1964) in the encounter groups that grew out of the human potential movement, and in the human potential training seminars such as est, Scientology, and others. Were these peak experiences at times ecstatic experiences? Yes, it seems that sometimes they were. Large numbers of people spoke of experiencing profound changes in their lives that produced big breakthroughs, spiritual rebirth or being born-again, getting it, finding it, or suddenly becoming "clear." For some, it was a good thing. For others, however, their minds snapped, catapulting them into the land of ongoing dissociated ecstasies and psychosis.

Having long been intrigued by the subject of creativity and how it works, I explored creative ecstasies and their very complex relation to mental illness. I had come across a book, *The Midnight Disease: The Drive to Write, Writer's Block, and the Creative Brain* written by Alice Flaherty, a neurologist, which introduced me to *hypergraphia*, the neurological term for an overpowering desire to write, and I realized that I had a touch of it myself. Flaherty's interest in the connection between mental illness and creativity was both scientific and personal. After giving birth to stillborn twin boys, she developed a post-partum manic depression in which her mania was expressed in unstoppable round-the-clock ecstasies of writing. She had to be hospitalized. Once hospitalized and having learned how to manage her illness, she became intrigued by what her experience had to do with the writing of more or less normal people with a drive to write.

As you will read, I explore some very diverse means by which people attain an ecstatic state. You will read about how and why we are seeing in the culture of alienated youths and the culture at large, in drug and alcohol rehab centers, in psychotherapists' offices and psychiatric hospitals, people who are searching for ways to get out of their own skins by means of extreme high-risk behavior. I examine this historically, in the context of the influence of the cultural revolution of the sixties, when Allen Ginsberg told us that life should be ecstasy, a message that was taken to heart by millions of young people who came of age at that time. It continues to exert its influence.

MY OWN STRANGE EXPERIENCE OF SPIRALING UP TOWARD ECSTASY

I was not planning on writing about anything so personal but when I began thinking about ecstasy, I revisited a very strange experience I had had years before, in which I began to spiral up into a state of ecstasy in a way that was potentially life-threatening. Although it felt wonderful at the time, in retrospect it was eerie and uncanny. I felt like someone possessed by demons. It just seemed to happen, as if out of the blue. The more I thought about it, I came to understand it as a valuable gift I had received at a very painful time in my life. It was a form of dissociation that served to disconnect me from my overwhelming but quite realistic anxiety that my husband would die. A colleague, Judith Levy, PhD, used the term *manic defense*, which was new to me, and explained what it was, and I began to wonder whether the search for ecstasy serves as a manic defense in those who seek it, a concept which resonates throughout the book.

During the years of writing of this book, I continued to look for definitions of ecstasy. The word is typically used to connote joy. Look up images of ecstasy online and you'll find lots of grinning people jumping for joy. Sometimes it means a trance-like mystical state, but I could find no consistent definition. Although there have been neuroscientific studies of mystical states, there has been little neuroscientific study of frenzied ecstatic states. Fortunately there is so much recent literature designed to make neuroscience understandable to those of us who are not neuroscientists, which has been invaluable in formulating my own speculation about what happens in the brain to cause ecstasy and how we can intervene with patients who are hungry for ecstasy. I gathered new observations and looked at some old ones in a different way.

UNCONSCIOUS COMMUNICATION AND TELEPATHY

Stoller had written a paper in 1973 on a series of dreams, his own and his patients', that he reluctantly found himself calling *telepathic* However, fearing he would be considered a quack, he never submitted it for publication. When psychiatrist Brian Weiss' book *Many Lives, Many Masters* was published (Weiss 1988), and I discovered that it was about his experience with a patient who had a past-life regression, I wrote him off as a quack and would not even consider reading it.

Recently, after reading more about scientific study of paranormal phenomena, I decided to read Weiss's book. I found his account to be quite credible. I discovered that he had a medical degree from Yale, and more than forty published papers, very un-quack-like credentials. He was recognized nationally in biological psychiatry and substance abuse, and also specialized in depression and anxiety states, sleep disorders, Alzheimer's and brain chemistry. He distrusted anything that could not be proved by traditional scientific methods. Although he knew that studies in parapsychology were being conducted at major universities, this did not capture his interest; it all seemed too far-fetched. He was quite skeptical about life after death, reincarnation, out-of-body experiences, and related phenomena. Then his experience in treating a new patient changed his outlook not only on treatment but on life itself. While using hypnosis on Catherine, a phobic patient with depression and panic attacks, he told her to go back to the time and events that caused her phobias. To his amazement, she went back approximately 4,000 years to Egypt. After that session she began to improve, and her symptoms eventually vanished as she recalled more past lives during hypnosis. Soon, she was quite well, without the use of any medications. In the course of treatment, she began to channel messages from "the space between lives." Some of these messages contained some stunning surprises about Dr. Weiss's family and his son, who had died. Weiss's skepticism was shaken, and he began searching for any scientific papers that had been published on reincarnation, He studied the works of Ian Stevenson, a well-respected professor of psychiatry at the University of Virginia, who had published extensively in the psychiatric literature on the paranormal (Weiss 1988) and had collected over two thousand examples of children with reincarnation-type memories and experiences. Many of Stevenson's subjects demonstrated *xenoglossy,* the ability to speak a foreign language to which they were never exposed. His case reports are carefully complete, well-researched, and truly remarkable. As Weiss read further, he examined the extrasensory perception data from Duke University, the writings of Professor C. J. Ducasse of Brown University, and analyzed the studies of several others. He began to realize that even though he considered himself well educated about every dimension of the mind, his education had been very limited because he had not explored the libraries filled with research on the paranormal, research conducted, verified, and replicated by reputable clinicians and scientists. It took Weiss five years to write about his experience with Catherine, because like so many before him, he was fearful of damaging his professional reputation.

I had been acquainted and impressed with the work of John Mack, a Harvard-trained psychiatrist, through some journal articles and a book he had written on suicide. He was awarded a Pulitzer Prize for his life of T. E. Lawrence. I discovered that he had been treating some patients who, under hypnosis, recalled being abducted by aliens, and dared to publish a book on the subject, *Abduction* (Mack 1994). When I heard about this I was shocked. Had he turned into some new-age quack? Many in high places at Harvard seemed to think so. Shortly after *Abduction* was published, the Dean of Harvard Medical School selected a committee of peers to review Mack's treatment and examination of the people who had shared their alien encounters with him, and Mack came close to losing his faculty position (Tribute to Mack by M. Cohen in Mack 2008). The investigation lasted fourteen months, while many academics questioned the validity of the investigations of this tenured professor. In the end, Harvard finally issued a statement that the dean had confirmed Mack's academic freedom to study what he wished and to state his opinions without obstruction.

It is clear that writing seriously about the uncanny comes with risks. When it takes the form of fiction or science fiction, however, it is quite acceptable, such as in Marghanita Laski's (1954) *The Victorian Chaise-Longue,* in which her heroine had an terrifying but ecstatic out-of-body experience. The book was so well received that it was made into a program for CBS radio's General Electric Theater. Later, Laski began to wonder why such an extraordinary experience should be believed so readily, and she began to speculate about ecstatic experiences. With no research or scientific training, she ended up conducting research on ecstasy, and producing a very long book, *Ecstasy; a Study of Some Secular and Religious Experiences* (Laski 1961).

The subject of the uncanny was quite acceptable in Clint Eastwood's recent film, *Hereafter,* an intriguing meditation on the afterlife, and in Aimee Bender's award-winning novel, *The Particular Sadness of Lemon Cake* (Bender 2010). Nine-year-old Rose's mother knew that Rose had developed a taste for sour food, and so she lovingly made a special lemon birthday cake for her. When Rose began to eat it, at first it was delicious, but then something strange happened. The cake began to taste hollow, and her mouth began to fill with the taste of smallness and shrinking, and she began to know that her usually cheerful, capable mother tasted of despair and desperation.

Bender's fictional account of telepathy was a very different form of writing than Stoller's, far more acceptable. Despite his fears, Stoller was enthralled in the years before his death with the subject of unconscious communication and telepathy, which he continued to revisit (Mayer 2001). He believed passionately that the next major frontier for psychoanalysis would be additional investigation of telepathic communication.

History has shown that Stoller was correct about this. Clinicians who work with schizophrenic patients have found that they seem to have an uncanny ability to "read" the underlying emotions of better integrated patients and mental health professionals. Philip Bromberg suggests that dissociative processes operate between patient and therapist to produce a kind of nonverbal communication. The word *telepathic* can be aptly used to describe these forms of communication. Bromberg has proposed that when dissociation is a major component of the patient's defensive organization, this can actually induce a parallel dissociative process in the therapist (Bromberg 1998, 2001, 2006). This serves as a form of communication in which the patient disavows some unwelcome aspect of his experience and by means of an unconscious process, projects that same experience into the analyst, thus getting him to feel what the patient feels. Today, many analysts feel more comfortable in disclosing certain features of their own private reactions to patients and find that it often helps the therapeutic process. Bromberg's thinking about the interpersonal nature of empathic communication is compatible with current research in telepathy, the psychology of emotion and neuroscientific research in mirror neurons.

To return to Stoller and telepathy, several months after his death, his paper on telepathic dreams fell into the hands of Elizabeth Lloyd Mayer (2007), a psychoanalyst. After having a very strange personal experience, she had become intrigued by parapsychological phenomena. What had happened was that her daughter's beloved hand-carved harp was stolen in 1991. When no leads were found by the police, a friend suggested she call a dowser— a person who specializes in finding lost objects. Dowsing, a form of parapsychology, is done with the use of a Y- or L-shaped twig called a dowsing or divining rod. Dowsing had become firmly planted in new age practices, something psychoanalysts tend to have little use for. But Mayer's daughter had fallen in love with the harp, and was miserable; Dr. Mayer had nothing to lose and was desperate to find the harp, so she agreed. She sought out the name and phone number of the dowser with the best reputation she could find and called him. It took two days for the dowser to find on a map the precise California street coordinates where the harp was located.

Mayer was deeply surprised and yet determined to understand what had occurred. Mayer came to discover that many of her colleagues had had similar experiences but kept them secret for years for fear of being labeled crazy. Along with Carol Gilligan, she started an ongoing discussion at the American Psychoanalytic Association's midwinter meetings, called *Intuition, Unconscious Communication, and "Thought Transference,"* which led to some very interesting and surprising incidents. A colleague called her to tell her that she even had a paper of Robert Stoller's on telepathic dreams, written in 1973, a subject she had often discussed with him. He had showed a draft to Ralph Greenson, his mentor. Greenson found it utterly convincing, was shaken by reading it, and found his own thinking about the mind had been permanently affected by it, but allegedly told advised Stoller that if his professional future was important to him, he'd put the paper away and forget about it. Delivering an appeal for open-minded investigation of data, even data that have no reputable explanation, Mayer published his paper in 2001 and in 2007, published her book *Extraordinary Knowing: Science, Skepticism, and the Inexplicable Powers of the Human Mind.*

Even Freud had a profound interest in the uncanny, the occult, and "thought transference" (Freud 1919, 1922a, 1925, 1933, 1941a, 1941b). His least cautious paper was "Psycho-analysis and Telepathy." If Ernest Jones had not persuaded him to consider the damaging consequences his outspoken position might have on the whole fledgling psychoanalytic movement, he undoubtedly would have read it to the International Psychoanalytic Congress of 1922. As a consequence, the article was not published until 1941, after Freud's death.

Today, cognitive neuroscientist Daniel Bor tells us that "mind reading'" in various guises is beginning to dominate the field of neuroscience, and that recent advances in functional magnetic resonance imaging allow unparalleled contact with our thoughts and mental states. "And the method is still in its infancy—, the most exciting breakthroughs are no doubt still to come" (Bor 2010, p. 54). Recently one of the most respected journals in psychology (not parapsychology) assented to publish a paper submitting what was described as strong confirmation for extrasensory perception (Carey 2011b).This news was so remarkable that it was published on the first page of the *New York Times.* The stories about out-of-body experiences and near-death experiences, with universal reports of bright lights, dark tunnels, and feelings of rapture have become quite well known, with celebrities like Elizabeth Taylor and Sharon Stone disclosing them. It was Kevin Nelson, a neurologist, who studied and made the connection between these experiences, lucid dreaming, and the intrusion of rapid eye movement (REM) sleep into subjects' everyday lives. Even more startling is what is being reported about what constitutes reality and the mysterious nature of consciousness from the researchers exploring the current psychedelic research. They are producing confirmation that other worlds experienced through mind-altering tools may be quite as real as those that we recognize using our five senses (Strassman, Luna, and Frecska 2008).

Not long after Stoller's death, his contributions were summed up by Otto Kernberg, who described his extraordinary career and the many ways he advanced our field (Kernberg 1992a; Mayer 2001). After listing his many scholarly accomplishments and significant clinical ideas, Kernberg described how Stoller was startled to note at one point in his research certain divergence between usual psychoanalytic assumptions and that which he had observed. This shook him from a stance of reflexive acceptance of those assumptions to curiosity, which in turn led to his findings regarding gender identity, variations between male and female sexual development, and the interaction between biological determinism and psychological conflict. Stoller went on to write a book, *Presentation of Gender*, a major contribution to the understanding of gender identity disorders, and with tongue only slightly in cheek, included in the book an idiosyncratic list of proposals for a program of psychoanalytic exploration. Stoller suggested the following:

1. Do what you enjoy.
2. Be very curious (an essential feature of skepticism, which in turn is an essential feature of scientific behavior).
3. Do not have a clear-cut plan.
4. Do not know what your conclusions will be or even where you are heading; do not head.
5. Have patience; then always be impatient.
6. Think it over; let it soak; listen closely to the repetitions; let the discoveries find you.
7. Use whatever techniques for data collecting appeal to you, but never stop psychoanalyzing.
8. Find people more honorably committed to scientific method than yourself and stick them with the grubby work of properly confirming hypotheses.
9. Do not try for a grant if acceptance means you must accomplish what you promised.
10. Since no research anywhere comes to final conclusions, you need not rush. Act as if you will live forever; it will not make any difference to you if that estimate is wrong (Stoller 1992, p. 9).

Stoller's suggestions remind me of a whimsical poster I have called *How To Be An Artist*, by SARK (Susan Ariel Rainbow Kennedy). It begins with "Stay loose. Learn to watch snails. Plant impossible gardens. Invite someone dangerous to tea. Make little signs that say yes! and post them all over your house. Make friends with freedom and uncertainty. . . ." Stoller is, for me, a psychoanalytic ego ideal. This book does not pretend to be a scientific treatise presenting findings created by acceptable scientific method. I have no final conclusions about ecstasy, only hypotheses and questions. Writing this book was a terrific adventure that took me to unexpected places I never imagined I would go.

INTERVENING WITH THOSE ON THE ROAD TO ECSTASY

The manic defense that ecstasy can be is only one of the extraordinary powers of the human mind. To intervene with patients heading in the direction of ecstatic experience, that is, those involved in addictive, high-risk behaviors, is no easy task. The last two chapters address the question of how one might intervene effectively with such individuals. Although psychoanalytic concepts are presented, those who are not analytically trained clinicians can readily understand what is written, and use it creatively.

We need to reconsider traditional concepts of a psychoanalytic neutrality, abstinence, and anonymity. When these principles are followed slavishly, the result resembles a caricature version of psychoanalysis, an impractical therapy that does not serve the needs of the vast majority of patients. When followed creatively, the therapist can work intuitively and pragmatically, allowing the analytic relationship, with its powerful, reciprocal affective currents, to heat up the therapeutic action. Therapists need not fear taking a passionate stance, and should be open to understanding dissociated communications from patients.

Writing about messy extraordinary experiences has attracted people like Sigmund Freud, Sándor Ferenczi, Robert Stoller, Oliver Sacks, Kevin Nelson, Philip Bromberg, Elizabeth Lloyd Mayer, and John Mack. It has also attracted me. I think of these experiences as "strange attractors," a term that comes from chaos theory (Chamberlain 1998), meaning something like a turbulence that breaks up orderly systems and causes disorder to erupt. Strange attractor patterns in human dynamics tend to be created by the balance of opposing pulls or attractors that we experience in our communications with others. It is not limited to spoken or written language and includes the internal dialogues we have with others, unexpressed thoughts and feelings.

And so it is in the spirit of Sigmund Freud, Robert Stoller, Oliver Sacks, Philip Bromberg, Elizabeth Lloyd Mayer, Marghanita Laski, Kevin Nelson, and SARK that this book has been written. I hope it serves to connect me to others who have had thoughts about or experiences of ecstasy, and to stimulate others to further explore this strange and fascinating terrain.

ORGANIZATION OF THE BOOK

The first chapter is meant to convey something of the subjective experience of the ineffable state of ecstasy, what is known about what triggers it, and the difference between ecstasy that comes to one unbidden and that which is desperately sought, and the dangers of the latter. The second and third chapters are about ecstasy as a dissociated state and what occurs in the brain before and during ecstasy. The fourth is about how the cultural and psychedelic revolution of the sixties has influenced generations to seek ecstasy. The fifth is about how ecstasy is being marketed and produced by agents as diverse as clergy, producers of rock concerts, and those who produce drugs legally and illegally. Chapters 6 through 10 present ecstatic experiences coming from different sources. Chapter 6 is about cult-induced ecstasies and psychoses; 7 is about the ecstasies induced by pain and near-death experiences; 8 is about religious ecstasies; 9 is about killing, cannibalism, and other hellish ecstasies. The tenth is about creative ecstasies. These chapters will demonstrate how ecstasy functions as a manic defense. Chapters 11 and 12 are meant to address the concerns of mental health professionals, school personnel, and anyone who knows someone involved in the high-risk addictive behavior that can escalate into a search for ecstasy. They provide suggestions for how protective, preventive interventions can and should be made, and provide examples of such interventions from my practice. The twelfth chapter discusses the need for creative, innovative interventions in working with such individuals, and discusses the theory behind these interventions.

NOTE

1. Fascinoma: Medical slang for a fascinating case, usually involving a rare disease

Chapter One

Ecstasy: The Falling, the Dying, and Being Born Again

> Levered by ecstasy, one springs out of one's mind. Thrown free of one's normal self, one stands in another place, at the limits of body, society, and reason, watching the known world dwindle in the distance.
> —Diane Ackerman, *An Alchemy of Mind: The Marvel and Mystery of the Brain*

> Life should be ecstasy.
> —Allen Ginsberg

On Wednesday, November 20, 1991, the morning my husband was scheduled for the surgery we hoped would cure him of cancer, I awakened alone and began to cry. How had I slept at all? After five months of endless diagnostic procedures and second and third opinions, Stuart had been admitted to the hospital the day before. Now finally, it was happening. I needed to brace myself for a very long, grueling day. But how? I drove to Mount Sinai, down the West Side Highway on a balmy Indian summer day. The air smelled like morning. I had never seen the Hudson River so exquisitely blue, shimmering in the sunshine quite like this. I was stunned by its beauty. As I drove, I found myself joyful and excited, yet calm at the same time. "What an absolutely glorious day to get this cancer out of him!" I thought, noticing just for a brief moment how odd my exuberance was. But I did not think further about it; I did not want to ruin it. There was no question in my mind that the cancer *would be entirely removed* and that he and I and our son, a high school senior at the time, *would be alright*. (He is. I am. We are.) Somehow, the college applications would be completed and submitted and somehow or other, we'd take the trips to visit different colleges. That peculiar state of mind then shifted to a lower-key sense of calm and well-being which sustained me when I so desperately needed something to sustain me.

Three years after the surgery and the chemotherapy that followed, there was no recurrence and he was told he was cured. What no one told us was that sometimes a cure comes with a heavy price to pay. Just a year after the surgery, Stuart began having potentially life-threatening infections that were becoming increasingly resistant to antibiotics. Even though the cancer wouldn't kill him, a bacterial infection could. We lived with this ongoing anxiety for years.

Fast forward to eleven years post-surgery. I woke up alone unusually early and very anxious on a hot sticky August morning. Stuart was scheduled for another surgery that morning, a radical procedure that was hoped to resolve the unremitting infections. I drove to the hospital, trying to become strong for him, myself, our son. I *needed* something so badly. Now, looking back, what happened was eerie, uncanny. Zydeco music began playing in my head, and I was transported back to the French Quarter festival (pre-Katrina), where Stu and I were part of a crowd listening to Zydeco on the banks of the Mississippi. I popped a CD into the CD player, and as I listened to the pulsating sound of Aaron Neville singing "I put the voodoo on you", I found myself catapulted out of myself, flying higher and higher. The Hudson could just as well have been the Mississippi. The music flowed into my blood. I slapped out the beat on the steering wheel, bouncing on the seat, flexing my leg and gluteal muscles, and singing. (I rarely sing or listen to music alone in the car. I like it quiet.) I was in a groove, going higher and higher. My feet wanted to tap, to abandon myself to the experience.

Albert Einstein said that "all knowledge of reality starts from experience and ends in it"" (Mack 2008, p.24). In what realm of experience does ecstasy exist? The word "ecstasy" comes from the Greek *ekstasis*, meaning literally, a state of displacement, of being driven out of one's senses, mentally transported, to stand outside oneself. This suggests that it is an out-of-body experience. (More about this later.) Ecstasy had begun to take me by surprise, my mind and body disconnected. But I am a cautious person. No bungee jumping or hang-gliding for me. There was an inner signal that warned me that I could get myself killed. I knew I had to rein myself in immediately, and I did. It's not called *signal anxiety* for nothing. As quickly as it had begun, it was over. It never happened again.

THE MANIC DEFENSE

Years later I wondered what had happened as I had escalated up and become increasingly more manic. I came to understand that I had experienced a *manic defense*, a term I had not heard before. In the course of conversation with a colleague, she used the term. Understanding it in the context she used it, I came to think about it and one day, I had one of those AHA! moments. That's what it was, a manic defense!

To explain to readers what a manic defense is, I must first explain what a defense, sometimes called an *ego defense* or *defense mechanism*, is for those who are not familiar with this terminology. And in order to do that, I want to acquaint these readers with a few other concepts.

The word *ego* is used quite differently from the way it is used colloquially, to refer to self-centered self-involvement. Freud (1923b) uses the word *ego* to refer to one of three parts of the mind's structure, the organized, realistic part, differentiating it from the *id*, the set of uncoordinated instinctual trends, and the *superego,* which plays the role of conscience and criticism. Mental life is described in terms of the activity and interaction of these theoretical constructs, which are not structural brain regions of the kind dealt with by neuroscience. They are functions of the mind, and have no material form or location. The job of the ego is to mediate between the demands of the id and superego. If you think of the id as the "devil on your shoulder" that wants to do what it wants to do, and the superego as the "angel on your shoulder," cautioning and criticizing, the ego mediates between the two, considering their differing perspectives and then making a decision that creates a compromise. This is not at all a conscious process and is no easy task.

The term *defense* or *defense mechanism* refers to unconscious psychological strategies that help us cope with reality but at the same time, protect us against painful affects or emotions. Healthy individuals normally use different defenses throughout life. An ego defense mechanism becomes pathological only when its persistent use leads to maladaptive behavior, adversely affecting the individual's physical and/or mental health The purpose of an ego defense mechanism is to protect the self from anxiety, or provide a refuge from a situation with which one cannot currently cope. Some common defenses are repression, rationalization, intellectualization, and denial.

Because depressive anxiety is inherent in emotional development, the manic defense is very commonly used by people as part of their defensive repertoire. It plays a prominent role, however, in the lives of those who are terrified of grief and sadness and are unable to mourn (Akhtar 2001; Kavaker-Adler 1993). Because the manic defense is just another illusion, like all the other illusions, it is bound to fail. The clock strikes midnight and Cinderella's coach turns back into a pumpkin. Reality must be confronted.

The manic defense seemed to have been prominent in the case of comedian Richard Jeni's suicide. A brilliant comedian, he shot himself in the face several years ago. His family confirmed that the he had recently been diagnosed with both severe depression and paranoid schizophrenia. According to the police report, his girlfriend had overheard him talking to himself about a week earlier, mumbling "just squeeze the trigger" (Associated Press 2007). It seems that depression is a prominent condition with comedians, whose major energy goes into honing their sense of comedy to the ultimate to ward off the darkness that lurks inside. After Jeni's suicide a group called Comedians for Suicide Prevention held comedy benefits for suicide prevention in various American cities.

So if we consider my strange state of mind on the days of my husband's surgeries, we can understand my spiraling up into such a manic state as a defense against thoughts and feelings too painful to bear. After that day I had far too many days to anticipate becoming a widow and making funeral arrangements but on that day, I could not afford to feel or think about those things. My manic defense was quite adaptive, boosting my state of mind and energizing me for the long, difficult day ahead. Had it gone further, the result might have been disastrous. It was my signal anxiety, a very different kind of defense that arises in anticipation of danger, that protected me.

On that terrible day, I needed *something* very badly. It is said that necessity is the mother of invention and so I managed to spiral up into this strange manic state that for part of the day, served as that *something*[1] (Akhtar 2001; Klein 1935; Winnicott 1975a). The term *manic defense,* originated by Melanie Klein (1935), refers to a set of mental operations aimed at protection from depressive as well as paranoid anxieties. Basically, the manic defense is primarily directed against the experience of psychic reality, when that reality feels overwhelming. There is an element of magic in the manic defense, as it creates the illusion that the individual stands omnipotent, above his needy, vulnerable self.

Winnicott (1975a) outlined four components of manic defense: the denial of inner reality by denial of the sensations of depression; a flight to external reality from internal reality, often involving much daydreaming; suspended animation, in which omnipotent control of the bad internal objects stops all truly good relationships, and reversal of depressive feelings by opposite sensations, such as lightness and humor. "It is just when we are depressed that we *feel* depressed. It is just when we are manic-defensive that we are *least likely to feel* as if we are defending against depression. At such times we are more likely to feel elated, happy, busy, excited, humorous, omniscient, full of life . . . The manic defense comes in to the extent that dangers are forgotten . . ." (Winnicott 1975a, pp. 132-138).

But my manic defense was so bizarre, so over-the-top! I had never experienced anything like it. This peculiar euphoria defended me from feeling my anxiety and depression and was a most welcome flight away from the terrifying reality that my husband might die and I would become a widow. After his first surgery, when we had to go through the ordeal of chemotherapy, then the ongoing anxious visits to the oncologist every three months, a different kind of manic defense came to the fore for both of us. Although anxiety was our constant companion, so was our hilarious black humor. Cracking morbid jokes that no one else would find funny and laughing our heads off became a wonderful manic defense. But none of this could hold a candle to spiraling up towards ecstasy.

All defense mechanisms are potentially unhealthy when they are overused in order to avoid dealing with problems (Freud 1966). They can also be adaptive and allow us to function normally, and they are valuable because they protect us from psychic pain. Psychoanalysts are carefully trained to have great respect for a patient's defenses. When a defense mechanism gets too much in the way of a patient's relationship to reality, it may need to be analyzed, a process in which the therapist pays acute attention to the patient's ability to tolerate the process, and adjusts his interpretations accordingly.

My manic defense was a blessing for which I will always be grateful. At the same time, I will always be grateful for my signal anxiety (Freud 1926) that pulsed its way through my manic defense to warn me to rein myself in *right now*. As you read the many anecdotes in this book illustrating various paths to ecstasy, think of manic defense. And think about just what it is when we speak of reality.

I so much wanted to know how this strange experience happened and just what had happened to my brain. I did not know then how much our brains are wired for mystical, ecstatic experiences, out-of-body and even near-death experiences, such as those had by Jim Wickwire, one of America's most extraordinary high-altitude mountain climbers. His incredible exploits inspired a feature on *60 Minutes* and a full-length film. He was the first American to reach the top of K2, the world's second-highest mountain after Mt. Everest. In his book, *Addicted to Danger: A Memoir about Affirming Life in the Face of Death,* he told how several of his climbing companions died in his company, how his wife and children lived in constant fear, and still he could not stop flirting with death. Ultimately and fortunately, his manic defense failed, causing him to reassess his priorities (Wickwire and Bullitt 1998).

THE INEFFABLE NATURE OF ECSTASY

In the sixties, Bob Dylan sang that something was happening but we don't know just what it is. And something is happening today, right under our radar—a hunger for ecstatic experience—but little attention has been paid to understanding that strange state known as ecstasy. The implication for mental health professionals and concerned others is profound. If they are not able to identify and understand this phenomenon, they will be unable to intervene optimally with many of their patients and loved ones, and lives may be lost.

Most books on the subject of ecstasy are about religious mysticism, written by religious believers and assuming a supernatural origin for these experiences, while others are self-help books on how to achieve sexual ecstasy. These were really about how to achieve orgasm, the words *ecstasy* and *orgasm* being used synonymously. There is some fascinating writing on the subject in which the words *ecstasy* and *joy* are used synonymously, including Robert Johnson's (1989) *Ecstasy: Understanding the Psychology of Joy* and Barbara Ehrenreich's (2007) *Dancing in the Streets: A History of Collective Joy*. Although a very joyous state or any other emotional state, for that matter, can serve to trigger an ecstatic state, I do not think they are one and the same. The state of ecstasy seems to be void of emotion.

Psychoanalyst Michael Eigen's (2001) book *Ecstasy* is a wonderful prose-poem about the ecstasy that can be experienced in psychoanalytic treatment by both patient and analyst. These are the positive ecstasies. He also refers to the destructive ones, the blood ecstasies of murder and extermination, the "black hole ecstasies, mutilated ecstasies" (Eigen 2001, p. 17). Eigen, however, does not shed any light on what ecstasy is, at times equating it with joy, at other times with mystical states.

SOME THOUGHTS ABOUT ECSTASY

] To begin to think about what ecstasy is, the work of the late Marghanita Laski (1961, 1980) is a good place to start. Laski was not a scientist but a British journalist and novelist. She wrote a novel, *The Victorian Chaise-Longue*, in which her heroine had an ecstatic but terrifying out-of-body experience that was quite believable to her readers. The book was so well received that it was made into a program for CBS radio's *General Electric Theater*. Afterward, Laski began to wonder why such an extraordinary experience created by her imagination should be so readily believed, and she began to speculate about ecstatic experiences. She had read nothing about them and did not know how common they were but she had creativity, great intelligence, and perseverance. She had even made an extraordinary contribution to the 1972-86 supplement to the Oxford English Dictionary by adding around 250,000 quotations (Brewer 2010).

> An ecstatic experience gave a feeling of being outside time; did this mean that time was illusory and timelessness, perhaps, the reality? An ecstatic experience sometimes felt like translation to a simpler, purer state; was it? Sometimes it felt like a state in which one received new knowledge, wonderful beyond possible rendering into words; was ecstasy perhaps a foretaste of a next development of man when knowledge would be wordless and greater? And sometimes ecstasy felt like contact with a transcendent spirit.

> One can only accept the answers one needs. At this point I reached the conclusion that my speculations were nonsense, and that it would be interesting to know what ecstasy felt like to other people.
> A very few inquiries were enough to establish that other people knew these experiences, and their descriptions of them were similar in so many ways that it seemed they might be capable of systematization. So I drew up a list of standardized questions and proceeded to put them to people with a view to systematizing the answers (Laski 1961, p. 1) .

Although she had no research background and no intention of writing a book about ecstatic experiences, she conducted a study of what she called transcendent ecstasy and wrote a book about it. It was a big book, 544 pages, *Ecstasy: A Study of Some Secular and Religious Experiences.* Just thinking about what she did brought to mind something neurologist Kevin Nelson said "An old adage in medicine declares that you can gauge how much we know about a topic by how much is written about it—the more pages produced, the less we understand" (Nelson 2011, p. 59). There had been virtually nothing written about the state of ecstasy until Marghanita Laski produced her invaluable book.

Using classic literary and religious texts and administering a questionnaire, Laski examined these experiences, looking for the circumstances that tend to induce them, the language in which they were described, the general information they could provide, and most significantly, the effects they might have on our lives. Her research is based on interviews of 63 friends and acquaintances, 27 descriptions of ecstasy found in literature, 22 examples of religious texts about ecstasy and 52 cases of schoolchildren reporting their extraordinary experiences. She found that minor degrees of ecstasy, sometimes called mystical experiences or spontaneous "everyday ecstasies" were fairly common and can be triggered by such diverse events as watching a sunset, the moment when the infant emerges from the mother's womb, during sex, while being in love, during exercise, religious conversion, when listening to music, when feeling a sense of oneness with others, and when doing creative work. She also recognized that ecstatic states can be induced by drugs and morbid health conditions. She found that a far less common trigger for ecstasy can be a sense of desolation, which can be transformed into a state of ecstasy. (That helped me understand what I had experienced.)

Laski found that ecstasy seems to exist on a continuum, with the more frenzied, dramatic ecstasies being unusual, with only a few people having more than one or two in a lifetime. Laski lists five principal manifestations of the ecstatic experience. There are feelings of loss: i.e., loss of time, of place, of worldliness, of self, of sin, as well as feelings of gain: i.e., gain of a new life, of joy, of salvation, of glory, of new knowledge, and so on. The experience is ineffable, difficult to put into words. There are sensations suggesting physical feelings, such as floating sensations, a feeling of swelling up, an impression of a shining light. And last, there are feelings of intensity or withdrawal.

Laski found that for most people, ecstasy seemed to be an intense experience of tumescence and release. A force builds up, gradually accumulating and increasing, then ending in a powerful release lasting but a moment. Laski distinguished between gradations of ecstasy. One she calls *adamic*, referring to Adam's state of innocence, purification and renewal before the fall, an incommunicable form of knowledge. Another is what she called *knowledge ecstasies*, in which are found feelings of creativity or knowledge gained. "The more complete the knowledge is felt to be and the more incommunicable, the better the ecstasy. At the stage regarded as the best, ecstasies may involve complete or almost complete loss of sensibility, coupled with a feeling afterwards that any contact made has been complete. Ecstasies with these characteristics I shall call *union ecstasies*" (Laski, 1961, p. 92).

Although romance novels seem to equate orgasm with ecstasy, Laski's research indicates that this is a literary cliché. While sexual arousal can certainly trigger an orgasm and much less commonly, ecstasy, ecstasy and orgasm appear to be different. Laski found that the people who claimed to have had an ecstatic experience from a sexual encounter did not confuse ecstatic experience with orgasm. They could differentiate the two but unfortunately, did not elaborate further. Laski used the word *ecstasy* to apply to experiences that are quite different from those we would expect in the normal course of events. Orgasms lie within the normal course of sexual arousal; ecstasy does not. The subjects who reported having experienced sexually triggered ecstasy were clear that this was certainly not the norm for them.

Not only did Laski find ecstasy found to be a state of mind different from one's usual state, she also found that it had qualities of transcendence and trance. Some women had even experienced it in childbirth. Whatever the trigger that induced it, ecstasy, usually resulted from force building, increasing and accumulating, then producing a powerful release and sense of transcendence usually lasting but a moment. As in orgasm, ecstasy may be followed by a period of afterglow during which the experience is savored.

To sum up, Laski concluded that ecstasy is an altered state of consciousness with greatly reduced external awareness and expanded interior mental and spiritual awareness which is often accompanied by hallucinations. Although the experience is usually short-lasting, there are records of such experiences lasting several days or even more, primarily in the religious mystics, and of recurring experiences of ecstasy during one's lifetime. Subjective perception of time, space and/or self may strongly change or disappear during ecstasy. She demonstrated that religious experiences are essentially identical with other experiences had by people who would not interpret them in a religious context (Laski 1980).

In *Primitive Passions: Men, Women, and the Quest for Ecstasy* (Torgovnick, 1996), Marianna Torgovnick's theme is the potential for ecstasy to be beneficial but also dangerous. An English professor at Duke University, Torgovnick explored the West's fascination with primitive cultures, finding in them a heightened spirituality, stronger sense of community, and greater reverence for nature that motivates a quest for ecstasy. Although she never defined ecstasy, she seemed to understand intuitively what ecstasy, at its worst and at its best, can be.

She described how anthropologist Bronislaw Malinowski, in the Trobriand islands, was disturbed by a feeling of letting himself dissolve in the landscape. He sensed the danger in the pull to merge with the universe, an impulse as forbidden to him as that which the naked Trobriand women aroused in him. And so "when these sensations overcame him, he gave himself a good shake, checked to make sure he was not developing fever, and plunged back with determination into his data and abstract theory." Ecstasy, said Torgovnick, "has a spiritual register, of harmony and tranquility, which involves stepping outside the self and experiencing the eternal cosmos; but it also has a commonly perceived sexual register, which can be positive (a sign of eros or the life force) or can be imagined as a state of excess, frenzy, and potential violence" (Torgovnick, 1996, pp. 14-15).

Sudhir Kakar, thought to be the father of Indian psychoanalysis, was also an accomplished novelist, scholar, and translator with a special interest in ecstatic states. His interest was captured, as was mine, by the frenzied ecstasies. Kakar was educated in India, the United States, West Germany, and Austria. Although Kakar lives in Goa, India, on the margins of both Indian and Western culture, he divides his time teaching in India, Germany, and the United States. He studied ecstatic mysticism, finding, like Laski, that a mystical experience can be mild, such as contact with a sense of the beyond, or may be more extreme, with frenzied ecstasies or visions (Kakar 1991). He used Sri Ramakrishna's life as a case study of extreme ecstasies (Kakar 1991) and published a fiction study of Ramakrishna, called *Ecstasy* (Kakar 2003). So many of Ramakrishna's visions and fantasies seem quite bizarre and pathological when taken out of context but become much less so when one relates them to Bengal as it was in the nineteenth century. Kakar indicated that although certainly, from a psychoanalytic point of view, Ramakrishna could be diagnosed as a secondary transexual and psychotic, he was more interested in a meta-psychological non-pathological explanation that connects Ramakrishna's mystical realization with creativity. Kakar argues that concepts around eroticism and gender are relative to their culture, a factor contributing to the Western difficulty in comprehending Ramakrishna.

Kakar (1991) links religion to transitional phenomena in mental life. Transitional objects and other transitional phenomena are the stuff of illusion, the kind of illusion the infant creates when he picks up something that somehow reminds him of his mother. It can be a fuzzy blanket that has her scent, or a cuddly stuffed animal. When he holds it when he is alone, he can create the illusion that he is being held in his mother's loving arms, and then he can readily fall asleep (Winnicott 1953). As the child grows and develops, there may be a series of transitional phenomena that develop with increasing organization and complexity. So for example, the older child may sing himself to sleep, just as his mother used to sing to him at bedtime. Kakar calls transitional phenomena the realm which is allowed to the infant and in adult life is inherent in art and religion (Winnicott 1971). When observing religious phenomena, said Kakar, we must have a particular quality in our attitude. Just as we never challenge the baby by asking if he created his fuzzy blanket or stuffed animal or just found it conveniently lying around, we must have a particular quality in our attitude to religious phenomena, and not the hard edge attributed to Freud. "The intermediate area of experience unchallenged in respect of its belonging to inner or external (shared) reality, constitutes the greater part of the infant's experience and throughout life is retained in the intense experiencing that belongs to the arts, and to religion and to imaginative living, and to creative scientific work" (Winnicott 1971, p. 14).

When we look at ecstatic experiences in terms of ego functioning, we might differentiate them as being of two types, the pathological regression states such as are seen in borderline personality disorder and the psychoses and the healthier states of regression which serve personality integration and adaption (Allison 1967). In the latter category we might place creative activity and intense religious experience. Adaptive regression experiences are circumscribed, reversible, and have the potential to increase the individual's self-esteem. They are, to use the phrase coined by psychoanalyst Ernst Kris (1952), regressions in the service of the ego.

When ecstasy is not actively sought but occurs effortlessly, this seems to be a healthier kind of experience. According to psychoanalyst Daniel Merkur, religious experiences of ecstasy occur in a trance or dissociated state that is closely related to shock (Merkur 1989, 2006). Trance has the potential to be very beneficial but it can also be dangerous. Shock, in contrast, always has traumatic implications. In trance, as in shock, many of the normal functions of consciousness are repressed. As trance deepens, the normal functions of apperception, memory, sense perception of the external environment and the body are withdrawn, and in deepest trance, even verbal thought itself is withdrawn. Essentially, trance is contentless. If such states were allowed to proceed without interruption, they would continue indefinitely until the body failed for lack of nourishment, which actually occurred with a number of the medieval Christian mystics (Bell 1985; Bynum 1999; Farber 2003). As a defense against this danger, unconscious thoughts intrude to break the trance's hold. Mystical experiences are the most intensely pleasurable experiences that are possible. When used hedonistically as a drug, they become an end in themselves (Merkur 1989).

W. T. Stace (1960) wrote *Mysticism and Philosophy* in response to Bertrand Russell's assertion that mysticism was nothing more than an intense illusion that imparted no true insight about the universe (Nelson 2011). Stace described the core sense of mystical oneness as existing in two forms. There is the *extrovertive mystical experience* which looks outward to the world through the senses and finds unity, as everything that can be heard, seen, smelled, tasted, or touched is melded into one. In contrast, the *introvertive mystical experience* turns inward, often shutting out the senses, transcending them into a "pure" consciousness.

"AFTER THE ECSTASY COMES THE LAUNDRY"

Jack Kornfield is a clinical psychologist who also trained as a Buddhist monk. He wrote that mystical and ecstatic experiences are transient and do not last; what is most important is not attaining these experiences for their own sake, but how one lives one's life. This is Buddhism's middle path, not the extreme path, which Gautama Buddha came to advocate.

The story is that Gautama Buddha left his home, leaving behind his considerable material possessions, his dominion and power, his father, wife and his only child. Donning yellow robes, he shaved his head and marched towards Rajgriha, where many hermits lived in the caves in the neighboring hills. Gautama Buddha took Alamo Kalamo, a hermit, as his first teacher, but was not satisfied and so he left him and sought the help of another hermit named Uddako Ramputto, and finally learned to practice yoga, ultimately practicing severe Tapas (austerities) and Pranayama (breath control) for six years. Because he was determined to attain supreme peace through the practice of self-mortification, he ate almost nothing. Soon he became very weak and emaciated. Then some dancing girls passed by playing the sitar and singing joyfully. Their songs had no real deep meaning for them, but for Gautama Buddha they were filled with profound spiritual significance. They raised him up out of his despair, filling him with a sense of authentic authority, might, and courage. Gautama Buddha realized then that he needed to adopt the middle path by avoiding extremes and so he began to eat in moderation and gave up the earlier extreme practices. And so, Kornfield continues:

> Enlightenment does exist. It is possible to awaken unbounded freedom and joy, oneness with the Divine, awakening into a state of timeless grace—these experiences are more common than you know, and not far away. There is one further truth, however. They don't last. Our realizations and awakenings show us the reality of the world, and they bring transformation, but they pass. . . .Of course, you may have read traditional accounts of fully enlightened sages in

Asia or of wholly unblemished saints and mystics in the West. But these ideal narratives can be misleading . . . We all know that after the honeymoon comes the marriage, after the election comes the hard task of governance. After the ecstasy comes the laundry. Most spiritual accounts end with illumination or enlightenment. But what if we ask what happens after that? What happens when the Zen master returns home to spouse and children? What happens when the Christian mystic goes shopping? What is life like after the ecstasy? How do we live our understanding with a full heart? (Kornfield 2000, pp. xiii-xiv)

ECSTASY AS AN ALTERED STATE

The soul should always stand ajar
Ready to welcome the ecstatic experience.
—Emily Dickinson

As I looked back years later on my strange experience, I am convinced that my terrible need to escape from my own skin was what allowed me to welcome ecstasy. There also seemed to be something about the music I was listening to that did something to my brain. In his book *Music, the Brain, And Ecstasy: How Music Captures Our Imagination,* Robert Jourdain (1997) tells us that not only does music move us, it makes us move, and it is hard to resist its power. Oliver Sacks said "We listen to music with our muscles" (Sacks 2007, p. xi). Sometimes music's power is sexual, as concert pianist Linda Cutting (1997) described.

It's not something I've talked to other pianists about, but there's a definite sensuality to touch at the piano. When my fingertips caress the keys, or brush them slightly, or even when they are dancing very quickly over arpeggios or scale passages, I have sensations I don't want to admit.

Sometimes at night when Dan and I are falling asleep, I will flutter a trill on his leg, or grab a chord on his chest without realizing I'm touching him at all. It drives him crazy, but not in a good way. He's jealous of my music, almost as if I had another lover. Maybe I do. (Cutting 1997, pp. 55-56)

Cutting also said music can be like a mother rocking a child. "Five flats. my hands reach for G-flat and D-flat, and I'm playing 'Evening' the first of Schumann's *Fantasy Pieces.* The right hand melody is like a balm, and the left hand triplets soothe me like a mother rocking a child to sleep" (Cutting 1997, p. 68). Jourdain said "When music dissolves into ecstasy, it transports us to an abstract place far from the physical world that normally occupies our minds" (Jourdain 1997, p. 5). This abstract place was one that Freud seemed to fear, which may explain something of his well-known disinclination for music (Mayer 2007).

THE SOUL DWELLS IN THE BRAIN AND BODY

> And His Pure Brain, which Some Suppose the Soul's Frail Dwelling-House
> William Shakespeare (*King John*, Act VI Scene VII)

Neuroscientists have found that the mind is located not only in the brain, but also in certain hormones and enzymes that travel throughout the body, affecting our sense of touch, taste, smell, hearing, vision. "The 'soul's frail dwelling place' is not only an enormous switchboard housing trillions of interconnected pathways; it is a giant pharmaceutical factory that manufactures powerful, mind-altering chemicals" (Milkman and Sunderwirth 1987, p. xiii). We can release these chemicals by immersing ourselves deeply in mood-altering activities or by ingesting mood-altering substances and can literally change our brain structure over time (Doidge 2007).

The medieval Christian mystics who starved and flagellated themselves knew this well. So do Turkey's Whirling Dervishes, who once a year put on long white robes with full skirts, black cloaks, and tall conical red hats and twirl in unison to the sound of drums and flutes, faster and faster, whirling their way toward God and ecstasy. So do bearded Hasidic Jews, dancing and twirling in black coats and hats, spiraling up toward ecstasy and God. Music possesses us, takes us over, makes us move, and once we are engulfed by it, we give ourselves up to it, hurled into another state of consciousness, jolted out of our usual way of feeling connected to our bodies, our perceptions, the world, and others. We can emerge from it feeling as if we had been reborn.

Bob Dylan wrote the song "I Shall Be Released". Perhaps he was referring to ecstasy. Ecstasy is about experience at the highest pitch. Sometimes it can take us by surprise, and once we have a taste of it, we will want it again and again. We all need to be jolted out of ourselves from time to time, especially at those times when we need so much to be released. Young children know it too. They love it when their parents swing them around in the air or when they spin around in circles until they fall down. There's a good reason that Sit 'n Spin was such a popular toy in the seventies and eighties. Dr. Phillip Spackman, a neurological research expert, described the effects of spinning in circles: "They're literally scrambling their brains. The inner ear, which processes a complex series of stimuli in order to maintain balance, gets overloaded and the body simply collapses in confusion" (Ambrose 1976).

THE AUTHOR'S INTEREST IN ECSTASY

Ecstasy may seem like an odd subject for a psychotherapist to write about. My interest grew quite naturally out of my clinical practice, original research, and of course, my personal experience. Drawn to understand the mysteries of the mind, I have always been able to find something of myself in the most disturbed of patients and something of them in me. But I could not relate to people who starved themselves or binged and purged. I could not possibly imagine myself starving myself and becoming emaciated or making myself vomit. Wanting to understand these problems, I obtained specialized training in eating disorders and began treating such patients. Understanding eating disorders as potentially life-threatening illnesses, I wanted to know just what would make people take such risks with their lives. I discovered that these behaviors helped people suffering mental pain to feel better, at least momentarily. When feeling deadened inside, inflicting the pain of vomiting made them feel alive. And so did self-injury such as cutting or burning or otherwise inflicting pain and injury on themselves, which many people with eating disorders do as well. When I did my doctoral dissertation study on exploring the relationship between eating disordered and self-mutilating behaviors, I found that not only did doing these things help people to feel better, a small number of people described experiencing something sounding like ecstasy.

Freud (1930) thought that civilization is far more savage than it seems, a concept related to his theory of the death drive, which has gone out of favor in the United States. I have found it to make compelling sense, as it does to those in the Kleinian and Lacanian traditions (Farber 2000). This theory essentially has to do with an instinct that silently influences one to withdraw from human connections and retreat into a narcissistic position, silently driving one toward death. Freud assumed that the life and death instincts, or the constructive and destructive aspects of the personality, are in constant conflict and interaction, in much the same way that similar opposing forces are in physics, biology, and chemistry. As Karl Menninger put it, "To create and to destroy, to build up and to tear down, these are the anabolism and catabolism of the personality, no less than of the cells and the corpuscles—the two directions in which the same energies exert themselves" (Schneidman, Farberow, and Litman 1994, p. 18). And so I believe that those who are attracted to death like a moth to a flame are expressing an instinct that influences a person to withdraw from human connections and retreat into a narcissistic position that drives him toward death.

I have found that different kinds of self-harm such as eating disorders, self-mutilation, and compulsively getting one's body pierced, tattooed, or otherwise modified were dominated by a strange state of mind, an altered state of consciousness known as dissociation. The most common form of dissociation is depersonalization, commonly known as "spacing out" or going numb. The more I explored, I came to understand dissociation as the common denominator that linked eating disorders and self-injury with such bizarre occurrences as recovered memory syndrome, multiple personality disorder, Satanic ritual abuse, exorcisms, talking to the dead, even reports of alien abduction, past-life regressions, future-life progressions, and near-death and out-of-body experiences

Ecstasy is one of several kinds of out of body experiences. In an out-of-body experience, the individual seems to be awake and feels that his self, or center of experience, is located outside the physical body. He sees his body and the world from an elevated, disembodied location (Blanke 2004; Blanke and Thut 2007). "I was in bed and about to fall asleep when I had the distinct impression that 'I' was at the ceiling level looking down at my body in the bed. I was very startled and frightened; immediately (afterwards) I felt that, I was consciously back in the bed again" (Blanke and Thut 2007, p. 425).

Both Elizabeth Kubler-Ross (1997) and Raymond Moody (2001) have recorded near-death and out-of-body and experiences thousands of times. These experiences can be explained neurobiologically (Blanke 2004). Brian Weiss (2004) said that shortly before we actually die, our soul, which is aware when it leaves the body, pauses briefly in a floating state that can differentiate color, hear voices, identify objects, and review the life that has been lived.

THE SIXTIES AND ECSTASY

Allen Ginsberg's quest for ecstasy changed his life and he became an iconic figure of the sixties. When he said that life should be ecstasy, the culture responded with sex, drugs, and rock and roll. It was a time that turned the culture upside down, and our culture today is still reverberating with its aftermath.

When we think of ecstasy we tend to think of x-rated movies and Dionysian cults known for uninhibited orgies of drinking, eating and sex. Like the god Janus, Dionysus had two faces, a creative as well as destructive one. He was half mortal and half god, and represents the continual cycle of life and death. He has been called the god of wine, the god of abandon, the great liberator, and the god of ecstasy. As the god of wine, he could bring spiritual transcendence or addiction. As the god of ecstasy, he could bring transcendent joy or madness.

The sixties were like that—transcendent joy or madness. The inspiration for Ginsberg's poem *Howl* was Carl Solomon, whom Ginsberg met when both were hospitalized at New York State Psychiatric Institute. They felt an instantaneous connection. Ginsberg said, "He accepted me as if I were another nutty guru, saying at the same time . . . Oh well, you're new here. Just wait awhile and you'll meet some of the other mystics" (Watson 1995, p. 113). The institution was called "Rockland" in the poem, referring to Rockland State Hospital, where Ginsberg's mother, who suffered from schizophrenia and had been through a revolving door of mental institutions, had been a patient. At Psychiatric Institute, Ginsberg was considered to be very bright and extremely neurotic. He was urged to conform to the traditional legal and sexual mores. His doctors refused to discuss his visions, discouraged all homosexual expression, and labeled him as eccentric. Solomon thought that the doctors cared nothing about a patient's madness as long as it remained socially acceptable; he himself served as an antidote to the psychiatrists' prescriptions for sanity (Watson 1995). The opening lines of *Howl,* dedicated to Carl Solomon, set the theme and rhythm for the poem, questioning just what sanity was and what spirituality was.

For some, like Ginsberg, ecstasy is experienced spiritually, a manic defense allowing them to transcend briefly the terrible knowledge that ultimately we all will die. Ecstatic experience can be about the life force, as it had been for me, or it can be about excess, frenzy, and violence, especially when ecstasy is actively sought.

In her poetry Emily Dickinson referred numerous times to ecstasy's double-edged sword, warning us that death is often the price paid for a moment of ecstatic release.

> A wounded deer leaps highest,
> I've heard the hunter tell;
> 'Tis but the ecstasy of death,
> And then the brake is still (Dickinson 1892, p. 20).

For some, the way to ecstasy is through religion, nature, music, or sex. For others, it is through drugs or other high-risk behaviors. What is different are the ways of getting there but the resulting experience is the same. Today's cult of ecstasy pushes beyond hedonism to the darkest side of human experience.

NEEDING TO GET OUT OF OUR OWN SKIN

Some people, more than others, feel the intense need to escape the confines of their own skin, the deadness and desperation they feel inside. We can begin to understand this if we consider that our skin is our first means of communication, and literally our protector, insulating the soft tissues within our body (Farber 2000). According to Anzieu (1980, 1990), skin serves as a *psychic envelope*, a plane of demarcation between the internal and external worlds, between the internal psychic world and the psychic world of other people (Farber 2000). It also serves three psychic functions (Anzieu 1980).

> In its first function, the skin is the sack that holds in the goodness and fullness that accumulates from being suckled, cared for, and bathed with words. In its second function, the skin is the surface that marks the boundary with the outside and keeps it on the outside; it is the barrier that protects against the greed and aggression of others, persons, or things. Lastly, in its third function,

> the skin—along with the mouth and at least as much as it—is a place and principal means of exchange with others (Anzieu 1980, pp. 29-30).

Skin is regarded as a window on the soul, with clear skin seen as a sign of physical and mental health, while blemishes and scars mark a life out of balance (Brumberg 1997; Farber 2000, 2002). For Thomas Ogden (1996), skin's overriding importance is that it is the boundary between inside and outside and life and death.

Some people get under our skin. Sometimes we want to jump out of our skin. Ecstasy can be a means of getting out of our own skin. When it feels as if we can no longer live in our own skin, we want out. If being moved to tears by a piece of music registers as a temperature of 100 degrees Fahrenheit, if my experience listening to zydeco on the day of Stuart's surgery registers as 104, the experience of ecstasy registers somewhere around 105 or 106 degrees, a potentially dangerous range.

You can call it ecstasy or you can call it call it rapture, as religious Christians do, which literally means being seized by force or carried away. Doctors might call it *syncope,* the medical term for fainting, but that hardly tells you what the experience is like. Syncope was what Tony Soprano, the Mafia don of HBO's The *Sopranos*, suffered from, fainting and losing consciousness in the first episode, causing him to begin psychotherapy with the famous Dr. Melfi. The same word in French is much more nuanced, meaning an absence of the self, a cerebral eclipse so similar to death that there is the risk of never recovering (Clement 1994). It can refer to fainting, swooning, or vertigo, a kind of dizziness unrelated to a neurological disorder.

From early on, Freud (1917) treated vertigo as a manifestation of anxiety, and even wrote about the fun of playing with vertigo as a means of mastering the anxiety (1900). "There cannot be a single uncle who has not shown a child how to fly . . . by holding him up high and then suddenly pretending to drop him. Children are delighted by such experiences and never tire of asking to have them repeated, especially when there is something about them that causes a little fright or giddiness" (Freud 1900, p. 393).

Philosopher Catherine Clement wrote "First the head spins, overcome with a slight vertigo. It is nothing; but then the spinning goes wild, the ears start to ring, the earth gives way and disappears, one sinks back, goes away . . . *Where* does one go?" (Clement 1994, p. 1). It can refer to an irregularity in the heartbeat caused by a brief loss of consciousness or it can be a musical syncopation. Syncope is an element of rhythm and accentuation, beginning on a weak beat, a beat of hesitation, and carrying over onto a strong beat. "In the movement of syncope there is indeed a delay; but immediately, like the note in musical syncopation, the delay rushes into anticipation. . . . And yet how it burns, this desire for ecstasy! The flame of animal spirits runs between the lines and so does the passion for succumbing to passion" (Clement 1994, p. 31).

Ecstasy pivots from the doctor's office to the dance floor, to poetry, music, and the bedroom. Think rhapsody. Think orgasm, what the French call *la petite morte,* the little death. Think tango, that arousing combination of desire and restraint, two bodies entwined, moving as one, surrendering, without anticipation—to the music, to the other. Syncopation is there in the backward dip, inherent in the step itself—three steady steps at a trot, then nothing. Suspense, then release, two becoming one.[2]

The tango is a very sexy dance. No wonder that at one time the Catholic Church deemed it indecent and prohibited it. Time stands still and the self disappears in a cerebral eclipse that is similar to death. And just as suddenly, there is the awakening, the rebirth. *That* is the miracle, that one returns from it. It is a death and then a resurrection. But where does the person in a state of ecstasy *go* when he succumbs? *And what if he doesn't come back?*

TO HEAVEN OR HELL FOR ECSTASY

> Throw moderation to the winds, and the greatest pleasures bring the greatest pains.—Democritus

Western medicine has promoted a Cartesian dichotomy between mind and body, a dualistic theory that mental phenomena are not physical. But without the body, there is no brain, and without the brain, there is no mind. Some people may have a very active dopamine system in the brain, and with it, a sensation-seeking disposition, leading them to be impulsive and uninhibited (Fisher 2009), thus paving the way toward ecstatic states. Or the quest for ecstasy may arise from a state of desperation. When a sensation-seeking disposition is combined with a sense of desperation, that puts a person at very high risk mentally and physically.

The search for ecstasy is about the flirtation with death and near-death experiences. It has as much to do with pain as with pleasure, with life as with death. In the West, which fears death, the ideal death is unexpected and sudden. We want to die in our sleep, feeling nothing. Because we fear death, there can be an exquisite counterphobic ecstasy in flirting with it and living to tell the tale through near-death experiences (Joseph 1982). Those who have had a near-death experience typically describe it as traveling through a tunnel to a source of white light, where deceased loved ones lovingly hold out their hands to welcome their crossing over to death (Carroll 2002; Moody 2001; Newburg and d'Aquili 1994, 2001; Nuland 1995; Strassman 2000; Weiss 2004).

Philosopher Georges Bataille knew quite well the pleasures of excess (Bataille 1985). His preparation for it seemed to have been ideal: "from

Jesuit seminarian to pornographer to scholar of both Nietzsche and . . . Hegel. Bataille understood both the craving for systematic order and the drive to explode that order" (MacKendrick 1999, p. 4). After Bataille, philosopher Michel Foucault's love of transgression is paramount.

> I think I have real difficulty in experiencing pleasure. . . it's not as simple as that to enjoy oneself . . . Because I think that the kind of pleasure I would consider as the real pleasure would be so deep, so intense, so overwhelming I couldn't survive it. . . . A pleasure must be incredibly intense. But I think I am not the only one like that. I am not able to give myself and others those middle range pleasures that make up everyday life. Such pleasures are nothing for me (Foucault 1996, p. 378).

Foucault had always been fascinated by death and its link to sex. Influenced by Foucault, many today are experimenting with the *limit experience*, a particularly pleasurable kind of pain in which mind and body are pushed to the breaking point, and the state of consciousness shifts to a trance. Foucault (1977) advocates the individual's right of power over his own body in *The History of Sexuality,* which has become popular course reading in academia, giving sadomasochism a certain cachet as the intellectual's sexuality. Experiences of pain activate certain areas of the brain, setting off a chemical reaction that results in euphoria and an ability to break through pain barriers, at least temporarily. So do other limit experiences, such as all-night drug-enhanced raves, mosh dancing, and Pentecostal born-again ecstasies.

Some search for ecstasy to escape pain, while others embrace pain to induce the heights of ecstasy. Some people go to the most extreme lengths to induce ecstatic visions and trances, starving or mutilating themselves or through the most violent bulimic purging. They may search for ecstasy through sex, through the most extreme risk-taking and flirtation with death, through cutting, burning, and purging themselves of food, through hang gliding, bungee jumping and drug highs, through cultivating out-of-body and near-death experiences, and through the most extreme sadomasochism and body modification practices, far beyond body piercing and tattooing. And we have learned the hard way that some, like suicide bombers, find ecstasy in killing and in being killed.

It was an auditory hallucination, or vision, if you will, that sent Allen Ginsberg to India in a quest for ecstasy. In India, the Far East, and Asia, ecstasy is promoted and prolonged through practices which suppress consciousness and promote dissociation, such as yogic breathing and the Tantric practice of prolonging, sometimes for hours, the moment before orgasm. The search for ecstasy has taken many to India where death is revered and techniques for achieving ecstasy have been honed to perfection. In India, the ideal death prolongs the highest ecstasy. And so in the late sixties, hordes of Westerners descended upon India, seeking what was missing from their lives.

What was missing was ecstatic practices, but these practices, when removed from their indigenous cultural context, can take on meanings significantly different from those they originally held. These practices have long been marketed to us in the West by guru- entrepreneurs, some without scruples. We now seek good karma and cosmic consciousness, as Gita Mehta, a westernized Indian, wrote.

> The king of rock and roll abdicated. To Ravi Shankar and the Maharishi. . . As the sitar wiped out the split-reed sax, and mantras began fouling the crystal clarity of rock and roll lyrics, millions of wild-eyed American turned their backs on all that amazing equipment and pointed at us screaming, "You guys, You've got it!" . . . Into the vacuum of our unsatis- fied desires the great Western marketing machine disgorged peasant skirts with hand-printed mantras, vegetable dyes, and lentil soup. Eventually we succumbed to the fantasy that Indian goods routed through America were no longer boringly ethnic, but new and exciting accessories for the Aquarian Age. From accepting the fantasies it was a very short haul to buying them and, later and more successfully to manufacturing them. As our home industry expands on every front, at last it is our turn to mass market (Mehta 1979, pp. 6-7).

And so the net result of all that marketing is that when the traditions of an ancient culture become commodities to be sold to those who do not understand them, the consequences can be disastrous.

Like *syncope*, the word *jouissance* does not translate well from French, but what comes close is this: a dangerous but exquisitely perverse pleasure that flies in the face of all that our culture holds sacred. It conveys an excess in desire itself. It requires that one lose one's mind, at least temporarily. It transgresses the boundaries of mind, body, and states of consciousness. *Jouissance* has to do with pleasure, but only the sort of pleasure for which we would suffer endless pain (Apollon, Bergeron, and Cantin 2002). It has to do with a cult of ecstasy, a tradition of breaking all the rules and transcending every barrier—social, theological, sexual, and even temporal—in order to reach beyond one's own limits.

THE SPECTRUM OF NORMAL AND ECSTASY

It is a strange kind of travel, this ecstatic trip. After experiencing ecstasy, we may crave it again and again and cultivate it, regardless of its destructive potential.

Freud said that every normal person is only normal on the average. His ego compares to that of the psychotic in some part or another and to a greater or lesser extent (Freud 1937). Oliver Sacks (1995) suggests in *An Anthropologist on Mars* that there is a continuum running from the supposedly normal to the bizarrely ill. What I learned from my own brief experience of ecstasy is that I could find something of myself in the people I have written about in this book. They did not have to know what a manic defense is, but deep in their bones and in their gut they too knew its power. The headline of Wendy Lesser's (1995) review of *An Anthropologist on Mars* tells us: "Everybody is peculiar. Oliver Sacks wants us to know that we are all links in the great chain of weirdness" (Lesser 1995).

When one hungers for ecstasy, it can take control of one's life. "Hunger is a terrible pain and suffering deep in the self" (Farber 2000, 2002, p. 323). When that hunger is not satisfied, it can fill a person with a hole so deep, with a longing so deep and powerful to fill it that it can drive one to cut his own flesh, devour whatever can be devoured, or kill himself. When the body feels uninhabitable and we want out so desperately, we can faint, swoon, or have a seizure, and emerge feeling resurrected, as if we were born again, One may trip so far out that returning is impossible and only death or psychosis remains. And there lies ecstasy's dangerously seductive appeal.

NOTES

1. My appreciation goes to my colleague Judith Schweiger Levy, PhD for introducing me to the concept of the manic defense.

2. I am grateful to the work of Dr. Susan Kavaler-Adler. She is a psychoanalyst who combines lectures with actual tango sessions to demonstrate the similarities between psychoanalysis and tango. She says that "Argentine tango is perhaps the most subjective of all social dances, requiring each partner to surrender, without anticipation—to the music, to the other—in pursuit of the ultimate, the flow that is created when two individuals become one, the "partnership," moving as one body with four legs. (Kavaler-Adler and Sowchek 2003).

Chapter Two

Altered States of Consciousness

One morning Chuang Tzu awoke from his sleep. He told his students, "Last night I dreamt that I was a beautiful butterfly fluttering through the fields. Now I awaken. My question is this; how do I know if I am Chuang Tzu, who dreamt himself a butterfly, or if I am a butterfly, now dreaming itself Chuang Tzu?"
—Chuang Tzu

Our normal waking consciousness . . . is but one special type of consciousness, whilst all about it, parted from it by the filmiest of screens, there lie potential forms of consciousness entirely different. We may go through life without suspecting their existence; but apply the requisite stimulus, and at a touch they are there in all their completeness . . . No account of the universe in its totality can be final which leaves these other forms of consciousness quite disregarded. How to regard them is the question—for they are so discontinuous with ordinary consciousness. Yet they may determine attitudes though they cannot furnish formulas, and open a region though they fail to give a map. At any rate, they forbid a premature closing of our accounts with reality.
—William James, *The Varieties of Religious Experience*

The state of ecstasy is, I believe, an altered state of consciousness. Before considering ecstasy as such a state, we need to understand what is meant by the terms *consciousness* and *altered state of consciousness*. We hear about odd experiences such as out-of-body and near-death experiences, reports of past lives and alien abduction, all of which have to do with altered states of consciousness.

CONSCIOUSNESS AND THE SELF

In *The Principles of Psychology*, William James (2007) said that ever since Hume's time, the self has been regarded as the most puzzling puzzle with which psychology has had to deal. Neurologist Kevin Nelson addressed this puzzle.

> In our day to day lives, we have an overwhelming sense that we exist as individuals, separate from the things around us. It is the sense that it is "me" having experiences, such as the experience of reading this book. It is "me" that owns what I experience and is the agent of my actions. The "me" is overwhelming, except, that is, in rare moments of mystical union or deep meditation or certain forms of psychosis. I cannot make it go away and remain conscious. Consciousness and self are almost always intertwined and indistinguishable. (Nelson 2011, p. 60)

Dr. Francis Crick, who with James Watson discovered DNA, said that consciousness still is a major unsolved scientific problem of the twenty-first century, and solving it may alter our whole view of ourselves (Crick and Koch 2004). The scientific study of consciousness has emerged only relatively recently as an interdisciplinary effort that poses significant challenges to traditional psychoanalytic theory of the mind (Firlik 2007; Hopenwasser 2008).

Neurologists have shown that who we think we are is a complex and quite fragile synthetic process orchestrated by our brains, and that when something interferes with that process, our reality and sense of self fragment quickly and dramatically (Nelson 2011). Although in clinical neurology the term consciousness has a clear and concise meaning—an awareness of oneself and one's surroundings—and it engages certain brain systems in a certain order, there is much about how consciousness functions in the brain that is mysterious, according to Nelson, who explains it like this.

> While most of us view our "self" as concrete and coherent, akin to, say, Leonardo da Vinci's portrait of the Mona Lisa, to a neurologist the self is more like Picasso's cubist portrait of Dora Maar, his lover and muse: a fragmented amalgam of fractured planes. Or, if you prefer Impressionism, our view of the self is a little like a water lily by Monet: at a glance it appears coherent, but up close you realize its harmonious appearance is an illusion, that the object you saw at a distance is actually a bundle of discrete and unconnected parts. (Nelson 2011, p. 2).

Nelson became intrigued with the three states within consciousness, wakefulness, REM (rapid eye movement) sleep, and non-REM sleep, reminding us that the opposite of consciousness is coma. The brain is especially active during REM sleep. His research has focused on the switch in the brain stem that regulates the three states of consciousness, and has found that at least some of the spiritual characteristics of near-death experiences may be due to the switch in the brain getting stuck between the REM and wakeful conscious states (Nelson, Mattingly, Lee, and Schmitt 2006; Nelson, Mattingly, and Schmitt 2007; Nelson 2011).

WHAT IS AN ALTERED STATE?

We speak of an individual as being in an altered state in comparison to his usual state of consciousness, but we cannot assume that our own state of consciousness is very much the same as any other person's (Tart 1972). Charles Tart said that for any given person, his normal state of consciousness is the one in which he spends the major part of his waking hours. In an altered state, the individual clearly feels both a quantitative and qualitative shift in his pattern of mental functioning. Quantitatively, he may feel more or less alert, may experience more or less visual imagery, sharper or duller images. The qualitative shift is such that mental functions operate in an altered state that does not operate ordinarily, and perceptual features may occur that do not correspond to anything in the normal state.

When we first began to hear about dissociation in the 1980s, it was through sensationalized films such as *Sybil* and *The Three Faces of Eve* as well as TV news programs about Multiple Personality Disorder. We saw dramatic switching of personalities that seemed frankly unbelievable and a widespread disbelief about Multiple Personality Disorder developed in the public. But subtlety does not sell books and films; in real cases, the symptoms tend to be much less flamboyant. In the movie Sybil, at one point, Sybil says, "There are sixteen of us." It is not until they have been in treatment quite awhile that patients become aware of alter personalities. When they first present themselves to therapists, they are generally not aware of the existence of different personalities. They're aware of having mood changes that are not in their control. They're aware that they go from feeling very depressed to being very up, or they're aware of being capable of getting many jobs but not being able to hold a job. They're aware of not being able to maintain an intimate relationship. They may drink too much or use drugs. Even the recent television series, *The United States of Tara*, which used dissociative disorders experts as consultants, made the switching quite flashy because it is such drama that attracts viewers. Today the disorder is known as Dissociative Identity Disorder and remains quite controversial (Lilienfeld,and Arkowitz 2011; Lambert,and Lilienfeld 2007; Piper 2008).

When Marlene Steinberg (2001) titled her book on dissociative disorders *The Stranger in the Mirror* it was because she consistently heard from dissociative patients that they look in the mirror and don't know whom they're seeing. Sometimes they don't see themselves; they don't see anything. And if they see a face, they don't connect to it. In the film *Black Swan*, Natalie Portman's character has signs of dissociative identity disorder, but another personality doesn't emerge until she's in her twenties, demonstrating the struggle between the dissociated *good compliant part of the self* and the bad enraged part that is common in Dissociative Identity Disorder (DID).

One of the most common DID symptoms is depersonalization, the feeling of being disconnected from oneself, robotic. But many people suffer from depersonalization symptoms or depersonalization disorder and do not have DID. There is a spectrum of dissociative disorders, with DID at the most extreme end. The core dissociative symptoms are amnesia, depersonalization, derealization, identity confusion, and identity alteration (Steinberg 2001).

Dissociative amnesia is the failure to remember a specific significant block of past time, often referred to as *losing time*. *Depersonalization* is the experience of not feeling oneself to be a person. There is an alteration in the perception or experience of the self so that one feels disconnected from one's mental processes and/or body. In *derealization*, there is a feeling of detachment from one's environment, which feels unreal or foreign. Depersonalization and derealization often occur together. *Identity confusion* is the feeling of uncertainty, or conflict about one's identity, involving great effort to define oneself, including one's sexual identity, in a distinct way. *Identity alteration* is marked by shifts in role or identity, with changes in observable behavior, such as speaking in a different voice or using a different name.

There are a number of experiences which can trigger an altered state, ranging from illness, trauma, hypnosis, dreaming, alterations in rapid eye movement (REM) sleep, prayer, and of course drugs and alcohol. Dramatic shifts in light or sound can do it too, such as the pulsing strobe lights and trance music in dance clubs.

DISSOCIATIVE STATES

An altered state of consciousness could be of the kind known as a trance, a dissociated, or hypnotic state, or it can be altered in the direction of a hyperarousal response. Usually, however, when the term *altered state* is used, it refers to dissociation. The capacity for dissociation can manifest quite differently in different cultures and religions. Dissociative trances have been part of many community religious ceremonies, contributing to mystical experiences of rapture, ecstasy, and transformation. In some cultures, the switching of mental states, possession states, and trance states are considered desirable, such as the self-hypnotic trances induced by shamans, or the dissociative abilities of mediums (Howell 2005; Rhoades and Sar 2006). Dissociative altered states can provide a culturally acceptable means of expression of very intense feelings, such as are experienced in *ataques de nervios* and possession states (Gherovici 2003; Fernandez-Marina 1961; Lewis-Fernández, Garrido-Castillo, Bennasar, Parrilla, Laria, Ma, and Petkova 2002).

Within Western culture there are several commonly used words for naming dissociative states, such as trance, hypnosis, dream, and ecstasy, but strangely enough, however, none of them are very clearly defined. One might expect that within the psychological sciences, there might be more precise terms for describing various altered states and their components, but other than the terms for dealing with certain psychopathological states, this is not true. For example, when Charles Tart was compiling the first edition of his book *Altered States of Consciousness,* in 1967, he wanted to find a clear definition of the word *trance,* a very common psychological term, used in an explanatory as well as a descriptive sense. To his surprise, he found that for every defining characteristic of a trance mentioned by one authority, another authority would use the opposite characteristic (Tart 1972).

THE HISTORY OF ALTERED STATES IN PSYCHOANALYSIS

A major reason for the neglect of the subject of altered states is related to the history of psychoanalysis. The concept of dissociated states was basic to nineteenth-century views on hysteria, particularly by Jean-Martin Charcot, the founder of modern neurology, and Pierre Janet (1907), neurologist and psychiatrist (Farber 2006). Janet was the most important clinical investigator of dissociative states who studied what Felix Deutsch (1959) called the "mysterious leap from the mind to the body," known then as conversion hysteria, the process by which repudiated mental content is transformed into physical symptoms (Farber 2006). Freud worked collaboratively with Josef Breuer in studying hysteria. Breuer believed that a dissociative process was at the root of hysteria (Breuer and Freud 1895). Initially Freud recognized that the dramatic somatic symptoms of hysteria were induced in patients such as Anna O., Emmy von N., Dora, Lucy R., Elisabeth von R., and Katharina (Freud 1910) by psychological trauma, and acknowledged the state of mind that we know today as dissociation (Farber 2006). Freud cited Lucy R.'s response to an interpretation. "I didn't know—or rather didn't want to know. I wanted to drive it out of my mind and not think about it again . . ." (Mollon 2000). Freud wrote in a footnote "I have never managed to give a better description than this of the strange state of mind in which one knows and does not know a thing at the same time" (Breuer and Freud, 1895, p. 117).

However, Freud subsequently dismissed the phenomenon of dissociation that Breuer believed was at the root of hysteria (Breuer 1893; Farber 2006). The result in psychoanalytic thinking was profound and, influenced all schools of psychotherapy to emphasize repression overwhelmingly at the expense of dissociation (Farber 2006).

This neglect of altered states is oddly incongruent with what happened in the decade of the psychedelic revolution and the decades following. During the hippie movement, conservative writers in the mass media estimated that tens of thousands who lead an obviously hippie lifestyle, and many thousands, perhaps millions, of middle-class people who did not appear to be part of the counter culture, were having new experiences such as tripping on drugs, meditation, encounter groups, dream interpretation, sensory awareness, and communes. Two of Tart's graduate students at the University of California at Davis spoke to him about their experiences of their souls leaving their bodies, while a sociology graduate student told him of a group of students he met with regularly to discuss what to do with their state of consciousness and lifestyle after exhausting the LSD-25 experience (Tart 1972). A mathematics graduate student asked for a guide to the scientific literature on marijuana so that he might compare these findings to his own experiences (Tart 1972). They were representative of a whole new generation entering the established social structure who spent much time and effort in exploring their own consciousness, and today, approaching old age, continue to do so.

Until the recent interest in Western culture in Eastern meditative and yogic practices, Western culture tended to regard these practices as pathological, partly because of the Cartesian dualism in Western medicine, which regards the mind and body as separate entities. And when psychoanalysis, at the beginning, recognized that a dissociative response was a consequence of trauma, the emphasis was on dissociation in relation to psychopathology.

RESEARCH IN ALTERED STATES

Arnold Ludwig has presented one of the most comprehensive overviews available on altered states and the positive functions they can serve (Ludwig 1972). Altered states can be produced by a number of different physiological, psychological, or pharmacological processes, which obstruct the usual inflow of sensory or proprioceptive stimuli, the usual outflow of motor impulses, the usual "emotional tone" or flow and organization of cognitive processes. There may be considerable overlap between the various methods, but for the sake of classification, albeit artificial, they fall into several categories. Some altered states are associated with the *reduction of external stimulation and/or motor activity,* such as in solitary confinement or prolonged social and stimulus deprivation in the desert or at sea, in cultic groups, "highway hypnosis," extreme boredom, sleep, dreaming, or somnambulism. There are also altered states which are *associated with increased external stimuli and/or motor activity*, and/or emotion. Heightened emotional stimulation and fatigue may also contribute. These states can occur through sensory bombardment, "third degree" questioning or mind-control techniques, trance states associated with group process, emotional contagion, religious conversion, or healing trance experiences, shamanistic trance states, orgiastic trances, ecstatic trance of the kind experienced by the Whirling Dervishes. Trance states are often experienced during prolonged masturbation. *Increased alertness and/or mental involvement* may produce altered states such as absorption in a task or creative activity, listening to a charismatic speaker, even paying attention to one's own breathing. *Decreased alertness or relaxation of one's critical faculties* such as in meditation, mystical states, and free-associative states during psychotherapy can also produce altered states. *Somatopsychological factors*, including the mental states that can be produced by alterations in body chemistry or neurophysiology, such as hypo- or hyperglycemia, dehydration, thyroid or adrenal gland dysfunctions, sleep deprivation or narcolepsy, hyperventilation, migraines, and temporal lobe seizures.

Ludwig (1972) has described many features which the different altered states share in common, and has elaborated on certain shaping influences that seem to account for their differences, such as cultural expectations, role playing, transference feelings, general mental set, as well as the specific procedure. There are similar features that tend to be characteristic of most altered states to some degree. There are *alterations in thinking,* in which primary process (the thinking in dreams and psychosis) may predominate and reality testing is impaired, cause and effect are blurred, opposites may coexist without any conflict, and there is a general dimunition in reflective awareness. *A greatly altered sense of time* prevails, with subjective feelings of time slowing down, standing still, or speeding up. There are *feelings of loss of control*, which may evoke great fear or may be quite welcomed. There is often a *marked change of emotional expression*, becoming more primitive and intense, while some become detached and uninvolved. A sense of humor may become greatly diminished. There are often *marked changes in one's experience of one's own body*, with profound depersonalization, derealization, a sense of the mind and body being starkly separate, and a dissolution of boundaries between self and others. Different body parts may appear or feel withered, bloated, heavy, weightless, distorted, detached, or strange, while there may occur spontaneous dizziness, blurred vision, weakness, numbing, tingling and pain. *Perceptual distortions* are very common, including hallucinations, increased visual imagery, while in the altered states that psychedelic drugs or mystical contemplation cause, synesthesias may appear, in which one type of sensory experience is translated into another, such as a certain emotion tasting like strawberries or Tuesday being green. *Changes in meaning* is one of the most intriguing features of altered states, with "Aha!" moments of profound insight or illumination of truth very common, often accompanied by a *sense of the ineffable*, an inability to communicate verbally what the experience was like. After emerging from an altered state, one may feel a sense of *rejuvenation*. While in an altered state, the individual may become *hypersuggestible*, unusually susceptible to respond to specific statements, commands, or cues.

The presence and prevalence of altered states is a marker of their importance in our everyday functioning. Throughout history, man has used a variety of altered states to gain new knowledge or experience, express or relieve psychological tension or conflict, and function more productively in society. All of this is to say that the ability to produce altered states of consciousness can play a crucial adaptive function in our lives. It has played a major role in the healing arts and practices, such as in shamanic healing, in which the native healer falls into a trance state in order to diagnose his patient's ailments (Kakar 1982, 1991). During the actual treatment, whether conducted by a shaman, priest, physician, medicine man, or psychotherapist, the production of an altered state in the patient may be a crucial ingredient in the recipe for healing. The way the physician touches the patient, the laying on of hands, may determine whether the patient will shift into the altered state that allows healing to occur. Many of the same processes in shamanic healing play a major role in the placebo response as well (Specter 2011).

Arthur Deikman (1972) looked at the types of altered states often reported by mystics, and attempted an analysis from a psychoanalytic perspective. What distinguished these states were experiences based in emotions, senses, ideas, and images that were not exceptional and those that were. The two basic techniques used to produce mystical experiences are meditative contemplation and renunciation. A new vision flushed by an inner rapture seems to occur and the world seems newly brilliant, implying a change in sensory perception (Deikman 1972).

To sum up, the primary characteristics of the mystic experience are an intense sense of realness, uncommon sensations, a sense of unity, a quality of ineffability, and of phenomena that go beyond and across the senses. Whether the experience has been triggered by meditation or a psychedelic drug, it is believed to be undoubtedly real and true. "Perceptions of encompassing light, infinite energy, ineffable visions, and incommunicable knowledge are remarkable in their seeming distinction from perceptions of the phenomena of the "natural world" (Deikman 1972, p. 39). Regardless of the cultural context, experiencing the boundaries between the self and the universe or God is the hallmark of the mystical experience. As William James put it, "This overcoming all the usual barriers between the individual and the Absolute is the great mystic achievement. In mystic states we both become one with the Absolute and we become aware of our oneness" (James 1985, p. 419).

One kind of mystical experience is ineffable, and cannot be expressed to another person, because it most likely is based on infantile memories and fantasies of sensory experience. Some mystical reports speak of being blissfully embraced and bathed in God's love, suggesting the prototype of the undifferentiated state, in which the infant and the mother's breast are one (Mahler, Pine,and Bergmann 1975). In drug-induced mystical experiences, there is an ineffable revelation of the meaning and complex relationships of many of life's dimensions. In this kind of revelation, the individual has a simultaneous awareness of many levels of meaning. A third type of ineffable experience is the "trained-transcendent" mystical experience, in which the person is trained, usually as part of a group, in which there is a movement to a lesser experience of strong affect and ideation and a greater ultimate experience. This kind of mystical experience seems to describe that of Transcendental Meditation (Conway and Siegelman 1995), and does not include feelings of warmth, sweetness, or visions.

During a period of almost a year, Milton Erickson, an American psychiatrist, and writer Aldous Huxley planned separately for a joint investigation of psychological awareness, and finally met at Huxley's house to spend a demanding and exhaustive day looking at the thoughts recorded in their individual notebooks in order to ensure that they were both in agreement or clear about their differences (Tart 1972). Huxley reviewed concepts and definitions of conscious awareness, primarily his own. Then he and Erickson discussed Erickson's concept of hypnotic states. Erickson was deeply interested in Huxley's unique use of his unconscious mind in solving psychological problems, which they agreed to call "Deep Reflection," while Huxley was especially interested in hypnosis. He had done some hypnotic work earlier with Erickson, was an excellent hypnotic subject, and wanted to know if hypnosis could be used to help him further explore his psychedelic experiences. Erickson induced a trance in him, but when aroused from it, Huxley insisted that it was quite different from his "Deep Reflection" state.

Unfortunately, Huxley's Los Angeles home was destroyed by a brush fire in which everything inside was destroyed including valuable items, record notes they'd kept except for the few pages Milton Erickson had taken earlier for his own personal use. As a result, the project was dropped because it was too painful to discuss. But after Huxley's death, Milton Erickson respectfully published his sketchy outline of sessions with Huxley.

DISSOCIATION AS BASIC TO HUMAN MENTAL FUNCTIONING

I was never trained in hypnosis, but I have noticed something in my practice that seems to be related to hypnotic states. When I greet a patient in the waiting room, I usually receive a greeting in response. But I have noticed that after making the transition from the waiting room to my consulting room, I usually receive a second, somewhat different greeting from the patient, one that I have come to understand as signifying that now we will be entering a different state of consciousness together. I began to state these observations to patients and found that often their response confirms that yes, the official hello is in the waiting room, but the real hello starts in the more personal space and state of consciousness in the consulting room.

Only recently has there been a growing psychoanalytic interest in dissociation as basic to human mental functioning, and a view of the mind as a configuration of shifting, nonlinear states of consciousness, shaped not only by repression and intrapsychic conflict but also by trauma (Bromberg 2008; Farber 2006). For this we owe a tremendous debt to Philip Bromberg. With the publication of *Standing in the Spaces: Essays on Clinical Process, Trauma, and Dissociation* (Bromberg 1998), Bromberg elaborated the mutual dissociative processes engaged in by patient and psychoanalyst, thus building a bridge linking the world of psychoanalysis and the very diverse community of clinicians treating patients with dissociative disorders (Hopenwasser 2008).

ALTERED STATES CAN ENRICH OUR LIVES

Altered states seem to enrich our experience in many areas of life, such as the experience of *flow* or optimal experience while absorbed in creative activity, exercise, or dance, or even the flow that can accompany the seemingly trivial everyday experiences of cooking a meal or folding laundry (Csikszentmihalyi 1991). The altered state that may occur in a group setting, such as a religious ceremony, serves affiliative needs, when we may feel a sense of oneness with others.

It is clear that in altered states, there is a psychological regression to a more primitive mode of experiencing. In some cases, this regression is a positive one, from which the individual emerges intact, but there are times when a dissociative state, which arose in the past and was adaptive at the time, becomes transformed into a dissociative disorder.

Chapter Three

The Brain and Altered States of Consciousness

> The mind is not a Cyclops; it has more than one I. It has three—identity, integration, and imagination—and they all work inextricably together.
> —Giles Fauconnier and Mark Turner, *The Way We Think*

They were glued to each other, like one big body with lots of heads and limbs jerking and kicking. They clutched at each other, shrieking, crying, trembling, falling to the floor, invoking God and who knows what else in Italian. A group of seven women, young and not so young, had been brought by the police to the emergency room of Fordham Hospital, a Bronx municipal hospital, accompanied by a male family member who had called the police for help. The hospital no longer exists. The property has been razed, paved over, and turned into a parking lot for Fordham University.

They lived in the Arthur Avenue section of the Bronx, former home of Dion and the Belmonts, where many Italian immigrants spoke no English, and goat carcasses, with eyes and teeth intact, hang in the butcher's window. Two of the older women were dressed all in black. Some scratched at their skin and clothing, others bit their hands, and one bit the figure of Jesus on her crucifix. "Do something!" the doctor in charge of the emergency room shouted at me. What should I do? I thought frantically. It was my job to evaluate the psychiatric emergencies that presented themselves in the emergency room and it meant I had to think quickly on my feet. I was twenty-seven, at the beginning of my career. Nothing in my training then had prepared me for this. And if I were to encounter it now, many years and a good deal more training later, I can still say that nothing in my training prepared me for this.

I was the only person from the psychiatry department there. The only thing I knew for sure was to keep my distance or else I would have been clawed or knocked down. Survival first. Think later. Somehow, I intuitively knew that the first task was to have them separated, one from the other, and I managed to get attendants to separate them and put each woman in a separate small holding room. It was madness! They fought tooth and nail. Many years later, I came to understand why. The madness was an ecstatic release! Why *would* anyone want ecstasy to stop? My intuition was correct; separating them was like magic. No longer able to see or hear each other, slowly, the wave of ecstasy subsided and the group hysteria machine was dismantled.

Several weeks later I witnessed a Puerto Rican visitor at the hospital having one of these attacks. By then, I had done some research. I had learned that it was considered a culture-bound syndrome, also known as an *ataque de nervios* (nervous attack), an acceptable expression of distress in Puerto Rican culture, not a sign of mental illness (Gherovici 2003; Fernandez-Marina 1961). It was thought to come from an enemy who had cast a bad spell, or from evil spirits that had invaded the body. The solution was to get an *esperitista*, a folk healer, to exorcise them. *Esperitistas* worked at botanicas, the stores in Hispanic neighborhoods that sell herbs and amulets. Substitute crystals for amulets and move it to a more upscale neighborhood and it might be considered an alternative medicine practice today.

How could such a bizarre thing happen to a group? Many years later I discovered a bit more about mass hysteria, which has been recorded in the medical literature for centuries. One can catch anxiety from another and it can spread like a virus. The typical characteristics include fainting and hyperventilation, rapid onset and remission of illness, females affected more than males, and spread of symptoms by observing them in others. Usually the illness relapses when the involved individuals are separated from one another. My intuition was right! When people become excited and frightened, the rhythm and pace of their breathing changes. They hyperventilate or breathe too quickly and exhale too much carbon dioxide. When the level of carbon dioxide gets too low, the muscles in the extremities start to spasm. Altogether this explains the physical symptoms—the numbness, tingling and muscle twitching—that many experience. The solution is a simple one. If the victim simply breathes into a paper bag, the carbon dioxide levels are restored and the symptoms disappear (Small, G. and Vorgan, G. 2010). Readers who saw the film *Starting Over* many years ago might remember when actors Burt Reynolds and Jill Clayburgh were looking at furniture in Bloomingdale's when he had an anxiety attack. Clayburgh asked if anyone had a Valium and almost every woman in the area reached into her purse. Reynold's character's brother, a psychiatrist, was with them and produced a paper bag and told him to breathe into it. He did and soon was feeling much better.

When feeling quite anxious, it is easy to misconstrue normal physical sensations or the physical manifestations of anxiety. Hyperventilation and a rapid heartbeat can be misinterpreted as signs of a heart attack and the gurgles of a hungry stomach can seem like food poisoning. If others clutch at their hearts and collapse on the floor, your anxiety may increase and you too might fall to the floor. It is easy to get swept up in the power of the group process and become part of what Freud (1921) called the primal horde. The first one to exhibit symptoms may be accorded high status, with those immediately following also accorded high status (Farber 2000, 2002; Small and Borus 1983; Small 1983; Loa Zavala 2010.).

You don't have to be Puerto Rican to have an "ataque de nervios," which is associated with panic disorder and dissociation (Lewis-Fernández, Garrido-Castillo, Bennasar, Parrilla, Laria, Ma, and Petkova, 2002). A group of Italian immigrant women, from a culture given to physical expression of emotions, could also have an "ataque de nervios." Many years later, I came to understand it as a form of dissociation that had reached a tipping point (Gladwell 2000) and had spread like a virus through the group.

ECSTASIES OF HYSTERIA

> Infectious diseases spread by ecological change, modern technology, urbanization, jet travel, and human interaction. Infectious epidemics of hysteria spread by stories circulated through self-help books, articles in newspapers and magazines, TV talk shows and series, films, the Internet, and even literary criticism. The cultural narratives of hysteria . . . multiply rapidly and uncontrollably in the era of mass media, telecommunications, and e-mail.
>
> —Elaine Showalter: *Hystories: Hysterical Epidemics and Modern Culture*

The form ecstasy will take appears to depend upon the historical and cultural context. It often appears in the guise of illness, especially when diagnoses go in and out of fashion depending upon which cluster of symptoms is considered to be indicative of a serious illness (Shorter 1992). The word *hysteria* designates a shifting set of behaviors and symptoms—seizures, limps, tremors, paralysis, coughs, headaches, allergies, nausea, bulimia, anorexia, self-injury, depression, fatigue—for which doctors cannot find a medical diagnosis. In Freud's day, such illness was called conversion hysteria, because the mental and spiritual anguish became converted into somatic symptoms. The symptoms mimic culturally sanctioned expressions of distress, whether it be chronic fatigue syndrome, eating disorders, self-mutilation, multiple allergies, fibromyalgia, Gulf War syndrome, repressed memory syndrome, multiple personality disorder or as we now call it, Dissociative Identity Disorder. When the mind and body are not experienced as a unity but are instead dissociated, one from the other, hysterical illness abounds. "Hysteria is always with us, a kind of collective coping mechanism for changing times." (Showalter 1997, p. 16). Like an amoeba, it seems to change its form. "Hysteria is a 4,000-year-old diagnosis that has been applied to no mean parade of witches, saints and, of course, Anna O." (Kinetz 2006, p. F1). In the Renaissance, it was embodied by witches, women thought to be possessed by demons. During the Enlightenment, women in Paris' salon culture suffered from something called the vapors, and then in Freud's day, they exhibited erotically charged somatic symptoms (Micale 1994).

The word *hysteria* comes from the Greek word for uterus, *hystera* (Kinetz 2006; Showalter 1997), because the ancient Greeks ascribed the illness to either an irritation of the female sexual organs or a misplaced womb. Victorian physicians treated it by putting pressure on the ovaries and packing them in ice, or by surgical attacks on the clitoris (Appignanasi and Zarate 2004). Sometimes hysteria was attributed to a wandering womb, which traveled around the body; sometimes it was in the throat, sometimes in the breast, sometimes the foot, but wherever it was, it produced countless symptoms. Hysteria became a dramatic medical metaphor for all that men found mysterious or threatening about women (Micale 1994; Bronfen 1998; Kinetz 2006; Showalter 1997).

Throughout the history of medicine in both civilized and third-world cultures (Shorter 1992), it has been common medical practice to treat women's illnesses with genital circumcision and hysterectomy. The idea was that removing the organs of female sexuality removed the hysteria, stopped female masturbation and nymphomania, and generally restrained women, assuming, of course, that women needed to be restrained. From 1869 until World War I, England, Europe, and the United States treated hysteria by surgical removal of the clitoris or hysterectomy (Shorter 1992), and *The American Journal of Obstetrics* published numerous papers praising and reporting clitoridectomy (Shorter 1992). Other medical specialists had a radically different view, believing that hysteria was imaginary, resulting in dramatic play-acting.

When it was proved that the uterus did not migrate and that men too could sufferer from hysteria, doctors relocated the basis of hysteria to the nervous system. Then, women were described as the more nervous of the sexes, while men with the illness were called neurasthenics and their illness was described in terms of less dramatic aches, pains, and anxieties (Showalter 1997).

Functional neuroimaging technologies now allow scientists to sketch a physical map of what might be going on in the minds of contemporary hysterics; the results suggest that emotional structures in the brain modulate the function of normal sensory and motor neural circuits (Kinetz 2006). The group hysteria that occurred in the Italian immigrant women in the Fordham Hospital Emergency Room can be understood as a dissociated state induced by mirror neuron activity (Newberg and Waldman 2010; Wild 2001; Erb, and Bartels 2001). (More about mirror neurons later).

FREUD'S VICTORIAN LADIES SUFFERING FROM HYSTERIA

In Victorian Vienna, Sigmund Freud (1905) recognized that hysteria's theatrical physical symptoms were induced by a process in which certain traumatic memories were repudiated and converted into physical symptoms. Along with his medical colleague Josef Breuer (Breuer 1895), he published *Studies in Hysteria,* a set of case histories introducing his use of free association, or the "talking cure." Freud's first patient suffering from hysteria was Frau Emmy von N., who was afflicted by stammering, tic-like facial and neck movements, and Tourette's-like shouting and clicking sounds. Lucy R., an English governess, had olfactory hallucinations in which she smelled burned pudding. When Lucy R. acknowledged that an interpretation was true, she added "I didn't know—or rather didn't want to know. I wanted to drive it out of my mind and not think about it again." (Freud, 1895, p. 117). In a footnote, Freud said that he had "never managed to give a better description than this of that strange state of mind in which one knows and does not know something at the same time" (Freud, 1895, p. 117). That state of mind is known today as dissociation. Elisabeth von R. came to Freud because of long-term agonizing leg pain. His eighteen-year-old patient, Dora, complained of breathing difficulties, nervous cough, loss of voice, migraines, and depression. Her analysis found that she was an unwilling participant in a complicated sexual and emotional tangle. Her father was having an affair with Frau K., whom Dora knew quite well, and Herr K, a family friend, began making sexual advances to Dora when she was sixteen, which was when her strange symptoms began to appear. Freud understood all of these patients' illnesses as hysteria and used the free association method to discover the traumatic events, usually alleged incidents of early sexual abuse by male relatives or teachers. "I therefore put forward the thesis that at the bottom of every case of hysteria there are one or more occurrences of premature sexual abuse, occurrences which belong to the earliest years of childhood but which can be reproduced through the work of psycho-analysis in spite of the intervening decades"(Freud 1896, p. 203).

Freud claimed such events occurred with much frequency among school teachers and child attendants because they have the opportunity, and said that what seem like fantasies of being seduced are not fantasies but real memories (Freud, 1905). His professional community was enraged and turned on him ferociously. (It didn't help that he was a Jew, a member of an outsider group often believed to be perverted.) To be accepted as a scientist by his peers, Freud did not renounce the seduction theory, as has been frequently reported, but he allowed for the possibility that the patients' accounts of incestuous sexual abuse might be fantasies rather than realities (Farber 2000).

Basic to nineteenth-century views on hysteria was a view of a split between psyche and soma, or mind and body, particularly by Pierre Janet, the French neurologist and psychiatrist, and Charcot, the director of the Salpetriere mental asylum. But this was not basic to Freud's view, although he had studied neurology under Charcot at the Salpêtrière. Although Freud recognized that the dramatic somatic symptoms of hysteria were induced by psychological trauma (Freud 1910), he later came to dismiss the phenomenon of dissociation that Breuer[1] believed was at the root of hysteria.

HYSTERIA AND DISSOCIATION

Breuer (1893) believed that a split off portion of consciousness, mediated by a process of autohypnosis, was at the center of hysteria. In other words, the patient unwittingly induces a trance state in himself that allows the physical expression of that which could not be expressed in words (Farber 2000). Breuer's patient, Bertha Pappenheim, better known as Anna O., was an intellectually gifted girl of twenty-one, whose illness, which included physical and psychological disturbances, lasted for over two years. Her right arm and leg were severely paralyzed on the right side, and at times on the left side. Her eye movements were peculiar and her vision was restricted. She also had trouble holding her head up, eating and drinking, and had a severe cough. It had became difficult for her to speak or understand her native language; she seemed confused and delirious, often muttering a few words to herself. Breuer, after hearing these words, would put her into a trance and utter the same words to her, inducing her to free associate to them. This is how she began to speak of that which had been occupying her mind. Speaking of her fantasies seemed to free her, and bring her back to normal mental life for a few hours. The next day she would have another attack, which was treated the same way.

Although Breuer's method came to be known as the cathartic method, Anna O. called it "the talking cure" and referred to it jokingly as mental chimney sweeping. Freud and Breuer (1895) agreed that hysterics suffer mainly from reminiscences, meaning painful memories of a traumatic nature, but when Freud put forward his early theory of real sexual trauma or seduction, Breuer found this idea very disturbing, which led to a split between them.

FAINTING, SWOONING, AND SEIZURES

In *Hysteria Complicated by Ecstasy: The Case of Nanette Leroux*, historian Jan Goldstein (2009) wrote a fascinating multilayered account of one young woman's mental afflictions and experience of erotic ecstasy in nineteenth century France. The most obvious ecstasies are those that come from sexual or spiritual experiences, or from drugs, but there are other more secret ecstasies, such as those described by Lauren Slater, a Harvard-trained psychologist and prolific writer. She suffered from severe mental illness, including depression, anorexia, self-injury, and seizures. Even someone who suffers from seizures can long for one in the same way that one can long for a lover. Wanting the rapture of a seizure can sometimes cause one to occur, even in someone who does not register any EEG abnormalities. Slater wrote that she loved the strange auras that preceded her seizures, the smell of jasmine wherever she went, in the bath, in her dreams, even scenting her blood (Slater 2001).

> I didn't know, then, that epilepsy often begins with strange smells, some of which are pleasant, some of which are not. . . .
> My world, though, was the jasmine world, and I told no one about it. As the summer went on, the jasmine world grew; other odors entered, sometimes a smell of burning, as though the whole house were coming down (Slater 2001, pp. 4-5).

She also loved the ecstatic feeling that occurred when the altitude changes, as when ascending in an airplane.

> And we left Boston on a snowy dawn . . . and I drank chocolate milk as the plane went up. And a wonderful, ecstatic feeling came over me, a feeling which I attributed to the plane, but which I now know happens to some epileptics when the altitude changes, like you are getting closer to God, and gold, and sweet and smells, and I saw the sun rising from a whole new vantage point . . . And then we landed, and just like that the world was different. The ecstasy passed (Slater 2001, p. 12).

She also loved the ecstasy of surrendering to the fall, an ecstasy that ultimately brought her closer to God. Even in the ancient world, epilepsy was believed to have a sacred nature, recognizable by the fall it induced (Clement 1994).

> I think you can hold out for only so long. I think secretly each and every one of us longs to fall, and knows in a deep wise place in our brains that surrender is the means by which we gain, not lose, our lives. . . . We want to go down, and it hurts to fight the force of gravity. . . . I leaned to buckle my knees and let myself loose, slipping southward . . . (Slater 2001, pp. 51-52).

Slater takes anticonvulsant medication daily, has had auras all her life, and symptoms that have been diagnosed as being consistent with temporal lobe epilepsy. Temporal lobe epilepsy is not the problem for many suffering pseudo seizures (Benbadis 2005, 2006; Duncan, Oto, Martin, and Pelosi 2006). Slater wondered if she *really* had epilepsy or wished she did. "From my mother I learned that truth is bendable, that what you wish is every bit as real as what you are. . . . I have epilepsy. Or I feel I have epilepsy. Or I wish I had epilepsy. . . My epilepsy started with the smell of jasmine, and that smell moved into my mouth. And when I opened my mouth after that, all my words seemed colored . . ." (Slater 2001, pp. 5-6).

Or perhaps Slater did have temporal lobe epilepsy, thought to have triggered the vivid religious visions, voices, rapture, and even the overpowering drive to write (hypergraphia) experienced by Dostoyevsky, Saint Paul, Saint Joan of Arc, Saint Teresa of Avila, Proust, and others. Dostoyevsky, who had temporal lobe epilepsy, described it as a holy experience. He is reported to have had sexual fantasies and even orgasms during his seizures (Morgan 1990).

Neurologists Stephen Waxman and Norman Geschwind (1974) described a number of patients with temporal lobe epilepsy who had in common a cluster of certain personality traits, a cluster subsequently known as the Geschwind syndrome. It consists of the irresistible urge to write, a hyperphilosophical or hyperreligious emotional life, emotional volatility, including aggressive outbursts and altered sexuality, an extreme talkativeness caused by excessive attention to detail. Many of those with temporal lobe epilepsy have out-of-body experiences and *déjà vu* (La Plante 1993).

Even the normal brain is susceptible to seizures. We all have neural networks and electrical activity in the brain, all the equipment needed for a seizure to occur. Our seizure threshold can be lowered through electrical stimulation of the brain, hyperventilation, sleep deprivation, drugs, alcohol withdrawal, chanting or prayer, flickering or flashing lights such as strobe lights. (La Plante 1993). I find myself sensitive to flickering lights, such as those found on many bank ATMs or that which occurs when venetian blinds are turned a certain way. I feel slightly nauseated and off-kilter, and I knew to avoid such lights before I knew that they could provoke seizure activity.

ATAQUES DE NERVIOS AND OTHER ECSTASIES

> Dona Concepcion was having an 'ataque.' The four-poster rocked with it. The whole house vibrated to it. A purple and gilt image of Mary hanging against the blue wall at the head of the bed was particularly agitated. It seemed likely to fall and smash at any moment.
>
> —Ramon Fernandez-Marina, *The Puerto Rican syndrome: Its Dynamics and Cultural Determinants*

Some Navajo men who have been insulted had violent outbursts of murderous behavior that they did not later remember (Gherovicci 2003). During the 1950s, a new and puzzling syndrome was noted by US Army medical officers. Many of the Puerto Rican soldiers were behaving very strangely. They seemed frightened and disoriented and had bizarre seizures, during which they screamed, bit, kicked foamed at the mouth, and fainted, yet physical examination found no sign of illness. This odd group of symptoms was called "The Puerto Rican Syndrome" (Fernandez-Marina 1961; Gherovici 2004). Years later, psychotherapists treating Puerto Rican patients found that women also had the syndrome. And as the group hysteria incident in the Fordham Hospital Emergency Room illustrated, it is not limited to Puerto Ricans.

Today, these hysterias are understood to be dissociated responses to stress; how they are expressed is dependent on the sufferer's culture (Gherovici 2004; Showalter 1997). The somatic symptoms are disguised memories of overwhelmingly distressing events which had been banished from memory. Expressing them through bodily symptoms provided a powerful emotional discharge that at times became ecstatic.

Hysteria is very powerful. When someone needs to enough, is suggestible enough, she can "fall out," trembling and twitching as she is seized by the Holy Spirit. I say *she* because psychogenic seizures tend to occur three times more frequently in women than men (Benbadis 2005, 2006). When more people fall down and twitch in a Pentecostal healing service, the preacher's status increases accordingly.

There are big dramatic ecstasies and little secret ones. Even a sneeze can be a little secret ecstasy, jerking us out of ourselves. In some Scandinavian countries, sneezing while driving a car is a violation, because one can lose control of the wheel (Clement 1994). There is the sneezing premonition, the nostrils twitching, the hesitation, sometimes accompanied by a gasp, before, finally, gratefully, the sneeze, the *aaaah choo*! Laughter too can be a little secret ecstasy, "a divine jolt, an acceptable spasm" (Clement 1994, pp. 7- 8).

THE REMARKABLE, IMPRESSIONABLE HUMAN BRAIN

> Imagine the brain, that shiny mound of being, that mouse-gray parliament of cells, that dream factory, that petit tyrant inside a ball of bone, that huddle of neurons calling all the plays, that little everywhere, that fickle pleasuredrome, that wrinkled wardrobe of selves stuffed into the skull like too many clothes into a gym bag. The neocortex has ridges, valleys, and folds because the brain kept remodeling itself though space was tight. We take for granted the ridiculous-sounding yet undeniable fact that each person carries around atop the body a complete universe in which trillions of sensations, thoughts, and desires stream. . . Shaped a little like a loaf of French country bread, our brain is a crowded chemistry lab, bustling with non-stop neural conversations. . . .The brain is not the mind, the mind inhabits the brain.. . . Mind is the comforting

> mirage of the physical brain. An experience, not an entity. . . . And of course the mind isn't located only in the brain. The mind reflects what the body senses and feels, it's influenced by a caravan of hormones and enzymes. . . . Sometimes it's hard to imagine the art and beauty of the brain, beause it seems too abstract and hidden an empire, a dense jungle of neurons. . . . The art of the brain is to liken and learn, never resist a mystery, and question everything, even itself.
>
> —Diane Ackerman, *An Alchemy of Mind: The Marvel and Mystery of the Brain*

Understanding the basics of how the brain works can help us to understand why having experienced adverse events in life, especially in childhood, can be the source of a tendency toward looking for the kind of escape that ecstatic experiences can provide. I am not a neuroscientist and so my thinking about the brain and ecstasy is heuristic and speculative. I am grateful for those experts in the neurosciences from whom I have learned. I have borrowed from the work of Bruce D. Perry, MD, PhD (1999, 2006), psychiatrist and internationally recognized authority on brain development and developmental trauma, Robert Scaer, MD (2005) neurologist and traumatologist, Andrew Newberg, nuclear medicine physician, and Eugene D'Aquili, research psychiatrist (Newberg and D'Aquili 1994, 2000), Kevin Nelson, MD (2011), neurologist; Norman Doidge (2007) psychiatrist and psychoanalyst, who translated the understanding of neuroplasticity into accessible language, and Oliver Sacks (1987, 1996, 2007), neurologist, who has made neurological oddities wonderfully engaging and understandable to the reader. I have also borrowed from writer Diane Ackerman (1990, 1995, 1999, 2004) whose beautifully written passages demonstrate the workings of the human brain.

In *Proust Was a Neuroscientist*, Jonah Lehrer (2007) demonstrated that artists and writers made discoveries about the brain many years before the scientists did. Shakespeare said that the brain is the soul's frail dwelling place (King John, Act 5) long before the neuroscientists discovered that "the soul's frail dwelling place is not only an enormous switchboard housing trillions of interconnected pathways; it is a giant pharmaceutical factory that manufactures powerful mind-altering chemicals" (Milkman and Sunderwirth 1987, p. xiii). In fact, it was discovered that there are morphine-like compounds in the human brain (encephalin) that can alter the mind (Hughes, Smith, Kosterlitz, Fothergill, Morgan and Morris 1975). The brain produces its own pain-killing molecules, enkephalins and endorphins, that are strikingly similar to opiates. The realization that the central nervous system can produce its own mind-altering drugs helps us develop a higher level of understanding of human compulsion.

The neuropeptides, or *molecules of emotion* (Pert 1999), are small protein-like molecules used by neurons (nerve cells) that communicate with each other through electrical and chemical processes. A neuron can receive signals that either excite or inhibit it. When it receives enough excitatory signals, it will fire off its own signal, and when it receives enough inhibatory signals, it becomes less likely to fire (Doidge 2007). Neuropeptides are involved in all different brain functions such as eating, tying our shoelaces, learning to play piano, feeling rewarded, not feeling pain, and memory. Writer Diane Ackerman put it this way: "Most people think of the mind as being located in the head, but the latest findings in physiology suggest that *the mind* doesn't really dwell in the brain but travels the whole body on caravans of hormone and enzyme, busily making sense of the compound wonders we catalogue as touch, taste, smell, hearing, vision . . ." (Ackerman 1990, pp. xvi–xix).

How are the brain and mind related? Simply put, "perhaps the easiest way to understand the relationship between the mind and the brain is to regard the brain as the structure that performs all of the functions and the mind as the product of these functions. . . . All the nerve cells and nerve connections change with every new experience" (Newberg and D' Aquili 2000, p. 54).

As Winnicott put it (1975), the mind does not exist alone; it is a special case of the functioning of the psyche-soma. In psychosomatic illness, a split occurs between psyche and soma, and an illness experienced as somatic forms in the dissociated space between body and mind (Winnicott 1966). The positive value of psychosomatic illness is to draw the psyche from the mind back to the original intimate association with the soma (Schachter 1997).

THE BODY IS THE HOME FOR THE BRAIN

To understand the brain, we must start with the body because it is the source of the brain's information from the external world. In this way, the brain's home is the body, which provides the brain with information from the sensory organs, including those for smell, taste, hearing, seeing, and touch. Therefore, we may consider the body to be an extension of the brain. The two are very intimately linked (Newberg and d'Aquili 2000).

This connection occurs because the brain has a means of communicating with the body, of which the autonomic nervous system is one of the most important (Newberg and d'Aquili 2000). The autonomic nervous system helps the brain regulate different aspects of body function. The human brain has evolved in an adaptive manner that helps us to interpret the external world. "Whatever we experience or feel, it is our mind and our brain that create this world for us" (Newberg and d'Aquili 2000, p. 67).

There are four major parts of the brain: the brain stem, diencephalon, the limbic system, and the cortex, and although they are interconnected, each one controls a separate set of functions (Newberg and d'Aquili 2000; Perry,and Szalavitz 2006). The simplest, having evolved first, are the lower and most central regions of the brain stem and diencephalon, sharing a similar organization with animals as primitive as lizards. (Perry and Szalavitz 2006). The diencephalon contains such important structures as the thalamus, hypothalamus, and the posterior portion of the pituitary gland, performing many vital functions, most of which relate to the regulation of visceral activities by way of other brain regions and the autonomic nervous system. It is a main convergence zone of information from the brain and body (Perry and Szalavitz 2006). The limbic system is more complex, similar to that found in mammals such as cats and dogs, and the cortex shares much of its organization with a chimpanzee. But nonetheless, the cortex is the most uniquely human part of the brain, involved in higher-order thinking and behavior, regulating speech and language, abstract thinking, planning, and deliberate decision making. It might help parents of teenagers to understand their moodiness, troubling impulsivity, and risk-taking if they knew that their frontal lobes of the cortex are not finished developing until late adolescence and continue to reorganize until their early twenties (Walsh and Bennett 2004).

The brain is divided into right and left hemispheres, which appear structurally quite similar but have different functions. The left hemisphere is responsible for word usage, while the right lets us hear the emotional aspect of language, or to put it simply, "the left hemisphere helps us with *what* is said, and the right helps us with *how* it is said" (Newberg and d'Aquili 2000, p. 58). A series of connecting fibers called the corpus callosum, the anterior commissure, and the posterior commissar allow the two hemispheres to communicate with each (Newberg and d'Aquili 2000). While in most people, the left hemisphere is dominant for many functions, some people have relatively symmetrical brains; this unusual symmetry might lead to notable differences in both special creative abilities and special areas of difficulty, such as learning disabilities (Geschwind and Galaburda 1988; West 1991).

The limbic system's primary function is the expression and regulation of emotions, providing an emotional valence to our thoughts, feelings, and experiences (Newberg and d'Aquili 2000). The amygdala helps to modulate the hypothalamus and tends to be more arousal-based (Newberg and d'Aquili 2000). Sitting close to the amygdala is the hippocampus, which is important in memory functions; the amygdala and hippocampus each modulates the activity of the other (Newberg and d'Aquili 2000). Also within the limbic system is the nucleus accumbens, the most prominent of the brain's pleasure centers.

Functional imaging studies which measure different aspects of brain function such as blood flow, metabolism, and neurotransmitter activity, have been used to study these experiences (Newberg and d'Aquili 2000). The most common neuroimaging techniques are single photon emission computed tomography (SPECT), positron emission tomography (PET), and functional magnetic resonance imaging (fMRI) (Newberg and d'Aquili 2000).

Neurons, or brain cells, are linked in innumerable interconnected and very specialized systems, transmitting messages from one cell to the next (Perry and Szalavitz 2006). Projecting out from the body of the neuron are axons, which transmit information from one cell to another by means of electrical signals of constant strength but varying frequencies, at miniscule junctions called synapses. Information is transmitted across the synapses by neurotransmitters, tiny squirts of brain chemicals that serve as a chemical handshake (Ackerman 1995). At the synapses, the neurotransmitters fit into certain correctly shaped receptors in on the next neuron, the way only the right key fits into a certain lock. These synaptic connections create chains of neuron-to-neuron networks that allow for the many functions of the brain, including thought, feeling, motion, sensation, and perception. This is what allows psychoactive drugs, both street drugs as well as drugs used in the treatment of affective and anxiety disorders and psychoses, to affect us.

The stress response systems are only some of the systems in the brain that, if poorly regulated or abnormal, can cause dysfunction in all four areas. Of course, not all stress is bad. For the child's brain to grow and develop, risks and challenges are needed, in the context of a safe and secure attachment relationship. This attachment, which comes from the consistent attention, approval, and affection of at least one adult, is central to healthy development (Bowlby 1969; Farber 2008b).

ATTACHMENT AND THE BRAIN

Psychosomatic theorists contend that the first and primary developmental challenge encountered by the child "is the formation of a stable, integrated, cohesive mental representation of one's body—a core body image: what is inside, what is outside, and clear, distinct boundaries between the two" (Krueger 1989, p. 101). When the child is held and touched in a loving manner, this experience stimulates two major neural networks in his brain. The first network is the complex set of perceptions associated with the caregiver's face, smile, touch, and scent. The second is the stimulation of the child's pleasure or reward system, which is activated by relieving the child's distress. And when two patterns of neural activity occur simultaneously and with sufficient repetition, an association is made between them. This is what is meant by the expression "Neurons that fire together wire together" (Doidge 2007, p. 65), a concept initially proposed by Freud (1895) but was articulated in more detail by Canadian psychologist Donald Hebb (1949). This is one of the key factors in the human brain's ability to change via neuroplasticity. This association serves as the glue that creates healthy relationships, while inconsistent, disrupted, neglectful, or abusive care creates the most powerful pain, profoundly impairing the ability to relate normally and affectionately to others. Thus, the nature of the attachment relationship forms a memory template for one's human relationships, a world view of relationships. The findings of the Adverse Childhood Experiences Study tell us that the developing brain's cumulative exposure to the stress response associated with adverse childhood experiences is associated with impairment in numerous brain structures and function (Anda, Felitti, Bremner, Walker, Whitfield, Perry, Felitti, Bremner, Walker, Whitfield, Perry, Dube, and Giles 2006).

A mirror neuron is a neuron that fires both when an animal or person acts and when he observes the same action performed by another (Gallese and Goldman 1998; Doidge 2007). In this way, the neuron "mirrors" the behavior of the other, as though the observer were himself acting. When mirror neurons respond in synchronized attunement with the behavior of others, it is a form of mutual regulation which provides another basis for attachment (Gallese and Goldman,1998; Rizzolatti, Fogassi and Gallese 2001; Lachmann and Beebe 1997). Oxytocin, a hormone that encourages labor and contractions in childbirth, also plays an important part in the mother's love for her infant, creating a bond of trust (Kosfeld, Heinrichs, Zak, Fischbacher, and Fehr 2005). Oxytocin is found in human breast milk, and contains a wide range of nutrients, hormones, proteins, and other components which provide antibodies to protect the infant from infection before his own immune system has developed. It also contains many other hormones that help in tissue growth, and natural opioids that may help form the baby's brain (Angier 1994). The sound of the infant's crying makes the mother's body secrete more oxytocin, which makes her nipples grow hard and helps the milk to flow, thus serving as a mutual attachment behavior (Nelson 2005). His cries are welcome to her because now her painfully engorged breasts can be relieved.

When the baby smiles, the mirror neurons in his mother's brain usually respond with a set of patterns that are almost identical to those that occur when the mother herself smiles. It is the earliest feeding experiences which regulate the psychophysiological responses of mother and infant. When her nipple touches his mouth, the infant's rooting reflex causes him to turn toward her breast, surround the nipple with his mouth and suck vigorously, thus releasing more oxytocin, resulting in uterine contractions that stop bleeding and detach the placenta. The baby feels warm and safe during nursing, which helps the digestive and respiratory systems run smoothly. He recognizes the familiar smell and taste of his mother's milk. As he sucks and the milk flows, she experiences the painful pleasure of the let down reflex and the relief from engorgement. Infants suck differently at the breast than at the bottle, sucking in a burst-pause pattern that suggests that breast-fed babies are programmed for more social interaction.

When the infant is bottle-fed by an attuned caregiver, "she feels the glow of maternal love and yearning as she caresses, embraces, talks and sings to him. His skin is stimulated by her touch, and he further relaxes into her embracing arms, continuing to suck until he is sated and asleep" (Farber 2000, p. 137). The infant comes to feel that the caregiver is there for him.

Such are the beginnings of attachment and the development of the child's brain. Children who have suffered severe early neglect or trauma may develop a reactive attachment disorder, while infants who are born healthy but, due to emotional neglect and lack of nurturing physical and emotional attention, have reduced levels of growth hormones, which can stunt their growth and produce failure-to-thrive syndrome (Chatoor 1989, 2009; Farber 2000).

THE BRAIN'S PLASTICITY

The development of our brain is use-dependent, meaning "you use it or you lose it." If we don't give a child the time to learn how to be with, relate to, and connect with others, to deal with conflict and negotiate complex social hierarchies, those areas of his brain will be undeveloped. We know that the old idea that the brain is "hard wired" and unchangeable is not true. The brain is plastic, impressionable, like a piece of Play-Doh (Plasticina is the Spanish word for Play-Doh), which captures the meaning better than the scientific term, neuroplasticity. The brain undergoes constant change as a result of our life experiences, which actually can rewire the brain, producing either more flexible or more rigid behavior (Doidge 2007; Schore 1997).

> The brain bends, learns, effloresces, adapts. When we learn something, we grow new synaptic connections. Neuron trees grow new twigs along their branches, while some of the branches themselves grow stronger. Our brain can rewire itself. We do it all the time when we master ice-skating or learn surgery or pick up knitting (Ackerman 2004, p. 44).

The concept of neuroplasticity helps to explain why it is so difficult to break ourselves of a bad habit or addiction, and it also accounts for some remarkable functional improvements as a result of physical and occupational therapy, biofeedback, and neurotherapy. The brain can be retrained to compensate for the most challenging neurological condition, as Oliver Sacks (2007) has told us so eloquently. Discovering neuroplasticity is also good news for psychotherapists of all orientations, whose clinical experience has long told them what neuroimaging studies have more recently confirmed, that successful psychotherapy, in which a safe and secure attachment to the therapist develops, can help in rewiring the brain (Farber 2008b; Holmes 1996; Kroll 1993; Roffman, Marci, Glick, Dougherty, and Rauch, 2005). There is no longer any doubt that psychotherapy can result in detectable brain changes (Doidge 2007; Etkin, Pittinger, Polan, and Kandel 2005; Peres, Newberg, Mercante, Simao, Albuquerque, Peres and Nasello 2007). From the neurobiological point of view, the aim of the "talking cure" is to extend the functional sphere of influence of the prefrontal lobes.

SENSITIZATION, KINDLING, AND ADDICTION

Having entered a state of ecstasy, one can crave it so much that it becomes an addiction. Whether someone is addicted to drugs, alcohol, marathon running, sex, gambling, shopping, pornography, or Perugina chocolate, it is all mediated by brain chemistry. Whatever is their "drug of choice," they are addicted if they cannot control when they start or stop an activity. There is evidence that such behaviors share an underlying biopsychological process (Milkman and Sunderwirth 1987; Goodman 2008).

When the pleasure centers are turned on, everything we experience gives us pleasure. Addictions kindle the release of the neurotransmitter dopamine, the reward brain chemical, and eventually in cravings for it when the addictive substance or activity is withdrawn. Nora Volkow, head of the National Institute on Drug Abuse, tells us that addiction of all kinds "is all about the dopamine. The pleasure, pain and devilish problem of control are simply the detritus left by waves of this little molecule surging and retreating deep in the brain" (Zuger 2011, p. D1). Mood-altering substances and emotionally laden activities (sex, religion, drugs, eating, etc.) trigger the activity of neurotransmitters, making it possible to become addicted to the experience of ecstasy.

Long before I had any professional training at all, I worked as a counselor in an inpatient drug detoxification program, and learned so much about the nature of addiction. I discovered that the addicts were addicted not only to the drugs but to the ritualistic behaviors preceding their shooting up (Farber 2000). Just talking about what they did put them into a dissociated state of consciousness that was contagious. They seemed to be as addicted to talking about drugs and all the "people, places, and things" that went with them as they were to the drug itself. Some were called "needle freaks" because they seemed to be addicted to the act of shooting up water (Levine 1974) and perhaps to the pain itself, which induced an altered state of consciousness, specifically a dissociated state (Farber 2000).

The opponent-process theory of motivation (Solomon and Corbit 1974; Milkman and Sunderwirth 1987) posits that every life event that has a potent effect on mood or feeling will also trigger an oppositional biochemical process. This means when people are initially drawn to a pleasurable experience induced through certain activities or drugs, they are motivated by feelings of pleasure, and will often sustain the mood-altering behavior to avoid the unpleasant, or painful effects triggered by the opponent-process. So, for example, in those who are "needle freaks," like some of the drug addicts I worked with, the initial painful experience is followed by a most pleasurable reaction, probably related to the release of pain-relieving endorphins. In fact, it has been found that there is a serotonergic mediating mechanism in the pathophysiology of self-mutilation, which helps explain some of its compulsive, addicting nature. (Simeon, Stanley, Mann, Winchel and Stanley 1992; Winchel and Stanley 1991; Hollander 1993, Yaryura-Tobias and Neziroglu 1978, Yaryura-Tobias, Neziroglu, and Kaplan 1995). The same appears to be true for those who are addicted to running, dancing, or exercise (Yates 1991). In running, the initial painful experience is followed by a reaction so pleasurable that marathon runners and dancers continue despite acquiring injuries. Part of what maintains the addiction is the development of a craving for the biochemical opposition to the primary activity. Shopping can become a mood-altering addiction, in which moods can swing from extreme arousal to pleasurable satiation, and may end with depression and remorse (Benson 2000; Faber 1992; Krueger 1988; Lawrence 1990). In some, there is a steady roller coaster of mood changes, while others remain emotionally flat. How this opponent process manifests seems to vary from one person to another in terms of frequency and intensity.

Although the term *addiction* is usually used to refer to substance dependency or to behavioral addictions, it is interesting that the term *addiction* is not used in any diagnostic manuals, including the DSM IV. So when we talk about addiction, we must ask just *what* is addiction. Alcoholics too go into a dissociated state of consciousness. And dissociation is a common denominator in the eating disorders—anorexia nervosa, bulimia, and compulsive eating. When addicted gamblers tried to stop gambling, they had the same symptoms as drug addicts had when they stopped using—excessive moodiness, irritability, nausea, stomach cramps, headaches, sweats, anxiety, depression, even hallucinations (Grüsser, Plontza, Albrecht and Morsen 2007). When groups of compulsive gamblers, alcoholics, and compulsive overeaters were tested, they seemed to share a common set of dissociative-like experiences that differentiated them from a control group (Jacobs, 1988). Further, there is also evidence that an underlying biopsychological process is shared by those with substance use disorders, bulimia nervosa, pathological gambling, and sexual addictions (Goodman 2008).

There is a growing movement which views a number of behaviors as potentially addictive, including many which do not involve the ingestion of a drug. Essentially, addiction specifies a process in which a behavior that can provide both pleasure and escape from psychic pain is used in a pattern distinguished by persistent failure to control the behavior and continuing the behavior despite significant negative consequences (Goodman 2008).

Having started out in the field of drug addiction, I have found that Edward Khantzian's (1985) self-medication hypothesis of addictive suffering is comprehensive and pragmatic for understanding a range of addictions. Khantzian proposed that people do not become addicted to drugs or alcohol *per se* but to the feelings of pleasure and well-being that they provide. They do not select a drug randomly; after experimenting with a number of substances, they prefer one drug, but choose a "drug of choice" (Wieder and Kaplan 1969) that corresponds to the psychological state that that they want to stimulate or sedate. So, for example, someone who is depressed or bipolar may choose cocaine or amphetamines to elevate his mood, and someone who is painfully shy may choose alcohol to serve as a social lubricant, while the person suffering from the effects of severe trauma may choose heroin to numb himself to the pain. Similarly Brisman and Siegel (1984) used the self-medication hypothesis to explain the similarities between bulimia and alcohol abuse, supporting the view that it is the psychic function served by the drug of choice that is more important than the specific qualities of the drug. Previously, I extended the self-medication concept to the eating disorders and self-mutilation (Farber 1997, 2000, 2003, 2008a, 2008b, 2010; Farber, Jackson, Tabin, and Bachar 2007).

Those with addictions suffer greatly from certain overpowering affects, either being overwhelmed with painful affects or seeming not to feel their emotions at all; they also suffer from their relationships and behavioral difficulties (Khantzian 1985). Self-medication is an attempt at self-regulation primarily for those with difficulties regulating affects, self-esteem, relationships, and self-care.

In all addictions, a tolerance for the substance or behavior develops, so that with time, increasingly greater and more frequent doses are needed for the desired effect (Jellinek 1994), which is a dissociated state of consciousness that serves as a manic defense against anxiety or depressive affect. Preoccupation with, and ritualistic preparation for the act induces a dissociated state, which leads to the compulsion to perform the act. Once the act is performed, a sense of shame and despair cause the cycle to start again.

The addict's brain becomes sensitized to the drug or experience and craves it even when it no longer provides pleasure (Doidge 2007). What had begun as a defense has become transformed into an addiction. An overwhelming preoccupation and compulsion takes over the person's life, with one of the most disturbing features being withdrawal when trying to kick the habit. Take gambling, for example (Griffiths 1995; Phillips 2006). When addicted gamblers tried to stop gambling, they had the same symptoms as drug addicts—excessive moodiness, irritability, nausea, stomach cramps, headaches, sweats, anxiety, depression, even hallucinations (Grüsser, et al. 2007). Because all addictions excite but do not satisfy, they kindle an insatiable hunger for ecstatic release.

It works something like this. Despite the fact that the pleasurable feeling induced by drug use does not last, addicts will continue to use the drug. The drug that had activated the brain's reward system and releases dopamine, the reward neurotransmitter, sends the brain a message; "This is an important experience worth repeating" (Friedman 2010, p. D6). Over time, the heightened pleasure weakens as the reward circuit's neurons get used to so much dopamine, and eventually, even greater and greater doses no longer provide pleasure as the user tries to no avail to recapture the initial high. But drugs do more than hijack the reward circuit; they trigger the urge to use again. That is what Alcoholics Anonymous and other twelve-step programs mean when they speak of "people, places, and things." Where the drug user is, what he is doing, and whom he is with when getting high becomes linked to the experience of the high, and these associations become stored not only in conscious memory but also in unconscious memory, a kind of pathologic learning that is at the heart of compulsive drug use (Friedman 2010). Not only is pleasure no longer experienced with drug use, but the ability to enjoy everyday pleasure fades too. So the pleasure in watching a lovely sunset or enjoying the company of a good friend will be dulled. This is because drug dependency results in a significant reduction, about 25 percent, in dopamine carriers in critical brain regions compared to the control group (Volkow, Chang, Wang, Fowler, Leonido-Yee, Franceschi, Sedler, Gatley, Hitzemann, Ding, Logan, Wong, and Miller 2001; Volkow, Fowler, Wang, Swanson, and Telang, 2007) Whether or not the loss of dopamine carriers is permanent or can in time be reversed is not yet known (Friedman 2010).

Both sensitization and kindling are thought to be the driving mechanism in a number of psychiatric illnesses characterized by spontaneous and progressive worsening over time. Prominent are anxiety disorders such as panic attacks, obsessive-compulsive disorder, and post-traumatic stress disorder, eating disorders, self-injury, and substance abuse (Kraus 2000, Marra 2005, Post and Weiss 1998, Russell and John 1999; Scaer 2005).

The kindling of brain cells is analogous to kindling a log fire (Read and Purse 2005). It is very difficult to set the log directly on fire, but if you start by surrounding it with smaller, drier pieces of wood that are easier to ignite (kindling wood) and set these pieces on fire, then the log will soon catch fire. The amygdala, the center within the limbic system that assesses and mobilizes emotions, is the easiest brain region in which to induce kindling. For example, a small electrical stimulus in the brain, if repeatedly applied, will eventually generate seizure activity that can lead to convulsions. Dr. Robert M. Post of the National Institute of Mental Health first applied the kindling model to bipolar disorder, which was described by Demitri and Janice Papolos as follows: ". . . initial periods of cycling may begin with an environmental stressor, but if the cycles continue or occur unchecked, the brain becomes kindled or sensitized—pathways inside the central nervous system are reinforced . . .and future episodes of depression, hypomania, or mania will occur by themselves (independently of an outside stimulus), with greater and greater frequency" (Papolos 1999, p. 53).

To put it differently, brain cells that have been involved once in an episode are more likely be involved again, with more and more cells becoming sensitized over time. Individuals who tend to be highly emotional have had their emotionality kindled, so that they respond with high emotionality to even minimally stressful situations (Marra 2005). There is some research that demonstrates that the more episodes a person has, the harder it is to treat each subsequent one (Read and Purse 2005), just as once a fire has started to spread, it becomes more and more difficult to extinguish. In addition, cocaine and alcohol have their own kindling effects which can contribute to bipolar kindling, a particularly hazardous effect. Kindling is thought to contribute to both rapid cycling and treatment-resistant bipolar disorder (Read and Purse 2005).

In fact, knowing that that cocaine causes seizures led Dr. Post to link kindling in epilepsy with mood disorders. This understanding was in turn used by Dr. Joseph Goldberg to study patients diagnosed with both bipolar disorder and substance abuse. These patients were quite likely to respond to treatment that included an anticonvulsant/mood stabilizer, more than treatment with the mood stabilizer Lithium alone (Read And Purse 2005).

Marya Hornbacher (2008) is an author who is bipolar (Ode 2009). Her memoir, *Madness: A Bipolar Life* was on the *New York Times* bestseller list. Emphasizing the importance of early diagnosis to minimize the kindling effect, she said that over time, you start to lose the chemical ability to fight off episodes, so the earlier a diagnosis can be made, the better the chances of avoiding future episodes.

TRAUMA AND ALTERED STATES OF CONSCIOUSNESS

> I felt a Cleaving in my Mind—
> As if my Brain had split—
> I tried to match it—
> Seam by Seam—
> But could not make it fit.
> —Emily Dickinson, *The Complete Poems*

Ecstasy is often erroneously equated with joy, perhaps because it shares with it a sense of well-being, expansiveness, upliftedness, and a conviction of significance. Such moments bring with them intense mental and bodily sensations and a feeling that one has entered a whole new world of meaning (Jamison 2004). Ecstasy is, I think, quite different from joy in that it is not an emotion; it is about radically altering one's consciousness. Merkur (1989) too believes that ecstasy is a dissociated state, closely related to shock or trauma.

Trauma is not an objective event, such as rape or September 11. It is an individual's subjective experience of those events. What might be traumatic for you may not be traumatic for someone else. A single event or experience can be traumatic; so can enduring or repetitive events. Trauma completely overwhelms the individual's ability to cope with or integrate the thoughts and feelings involved with the experience. The sense of being overwhelmed need not occur immediately; it can occur weeks, years, even decades later, as the person struggles to cope with the immediate circumstances. The person with PTSD

> suffers from the inability to turn off a stream of consciousness that has become its own enemy, comprised of actual memories of traumatic events, distorted and fragmented memories, intrusive imageries and flashbacks, dissociated memories, unwelcome somatic sensations, negative self-commentaries running like tickertape through the mind, fantasied and feared elaborations from childhood of the abuse experiences, and concomitant strongly dysphoric moods of anxiety and anger. Much that the . . . patient does, in and out of therapy, is a response to, or an attempt to terminate or modify, the intolerable presence of this stream of consciousness (Kroll 1993, p. xv)

The overall pattern of mental functioning is altered quantitatively and qualitatively in relation to the individual's usual waking state of mind. Altered states exist on a continuum, from certain normal transient experiences to severe forms that can seriously impair our functioning. We have all experienced those normal brief periods of anxiety in stressful situations as well as normal "spacing out" during boring lectures or conversations, daydreaming, or other naturally occurring trance states like "highway hypnosis," when you become so deeply absorbed in thought, drive right by your exit, and wonder how it happened. When you become so deeply absorbed in thought, you can become disconnected from your body's signals to eat, take a break, or go to the bathroom.

The brain's autonomic nervous system is controlled independently of our will. If the sympathetic branch, which controls the fight-or-flight response, is stimulated, the heart rate, blood pressure and breathing increase, stimulating the secretion of adrenaline to the muscles. The hypothalamic-pituitary-adrenal (HPA) axis comprise the parts of the brain and endocrine system responsible for the fight-or-flight response and for releasing the stress hormone cortisol. It is involved in conditions such as irritable bowel syndrome, chronic fatigue syndrome, anxiety, depression, PTSD, and fibromyalgia. When the parasympathetic branch is activated, it slows heart rate, breathing, regulating cell growth, digestion, relaxation, and sleep (Scaer 2005). We activate the sympathetic system when we practice deep breathing relaxation, yoga, or meditation.

Our response to a potentially traumatic experience is determined by whether we can control the event, no matter how severe or intense the experience is. If we can control it by an effective defense mechanism or by escape, the brain will process it in a way that adds to our accumulated life experiences, and we will not be traumatized. If, however, we face a threat to our life and feel helpless to control it, the brain will process the experience quite differently, leaving us traumatized. To heal from trauma, one must change the survival brain's perception from a state of enduring helplessness to a sense of stable and ongoing control, thus changing one's self identity from being the victim of trauma to a survivor of trauma, and then to a vital and loving person who happened to endure some of life's most adverse experiences.

The fight-or-flight response has been honed by evolution, helping us and the rest of the animal kingdom survive when confronted by a deadly predator (Marks and Nesse 1994; Ehrenreich 1997). It can produce anxiety that ranges from mild to an unbearable fear of being annihilated (Hurvich 2003), making our heart pump much faster or our bodies tense up, ready to take action. This is consciousness at its most primitive level, "red in tooth and claw." But when this heightened arousal lasts too long, it can make you feel like jumping out of your skin because your body cannot contain so much sheer terror.

Then there is the freeze response, or playing possum, pretending to be dead, also an adaptive response to an encounter with a predator for a creature who is not big enough, strong enough, or healthy enough to fight or flee (Farber 2008b). In humans it is experienced as dissociation, the sense of feeling numb, spaced out, deadened. Prolonged dissociated states can put the autonomic nervous system into overdrive, causing a host of chronic diseases which medicine has not been able to explain (Levine 1997, Scaer 2005).

Hyperarousal and dissociation are the altered states which comprise the response to trauma, and usually alternate rapidly in individuals with PTSD. In 70 percent of those studied with PTSD, the hyperarousal response prevails, but in around 30 percent, the dissociative response was more prominent (Lanius and Hopper 2008). In some with PTSD, the hyperarousal and dissociative responses may alternate so quickly that they seem to be occurring simultaneously. This finding is supported by Newberg and D'Aquili (1994; 2001), who have found there to be four autonomic states: hyperquiescence, hyperarousal, hyperquiescence with arousal breakthrough, hyperarousal with quiescent breakthrough.

Nietzsche said that which does not kill us makes us stronger. Exposure to adverse lifetime events can result in increased resilience in some (Carey 2011a; Higgins 1994; Seery, Holman, and Cohen Silver 2010). But more typically, exposure to adverse life events is considered predictive of negative effects on mental health and well-being. Bruce Perry and associates (Perry, Pollard, Blakeley, Baker, and Vigilante 1995; Perry and Szalavitz 2006) found some sex-differentiation in children's physiological responses to trauma. Pre-adolescent boys who had been exposed to violence exhibited a mild tachycardia (rapid heart beat) during interviews and a marked tachycardia during interviews about specific exposure to trauma, while pre-adolescent girls exposed to traumatic events had normal or mild tachycardia. Their mild tachycardia diminished during interviews about the traumatic event. It seemed that males showed symptoms that were more externalized and females more internalized. That is, males were more likely to express it outwardly in actions or words, females were more likely to feel depressed and express these feelings concretely and directly with their bodies. So it should not be surprising that more boys tend to have externalizing disorders such as ADHD, conduct disorder, and oppositional defiant disorder whereas more girls have more internalizing disorders such as depression, anxiety or dissociative disorders (Perry, Pollard, Blakeley, Baker, and Vigilante 1995). Comedian Elayne Boosler put it like this on HBO's Comedy Channel: "When women are depressed they either eat or go shopping. Men invade another country. It's a whole different way of thinking."

The word *trauma* means a wound, and trauma wounds the mind by fragmenting it, which rewires the brain, freezing it in past events that continue to shape one's entire perception of reality. Trauma can produce post-traumatic stress and dissociative disorders, in which intrusive memories and reactions are common, but what distinguishes Post-Traumatic Stress Disorder are flashbacks and dissociative amnesia (Bryant, O'Donnell, McFarlane, and Silove 2010).

The trauma can be what I like to call trauma with a big T (shock trauma), suffered by people who have experienced earthquakes, fires, floods, or physical or sexual abuse, as well as the trauma many experience during medical or surgical procedures, or combat. Or it can be trauma with a small t (strain or relational trauma), cumulative childhood experiences of parental neglect, indifference, or unattunement (Herman 1992; Kris 1956; Schore 2001). The traumatic past is always there, waiting for a cue to spring into our present life, making itself felt as if it were happening now, in the present. It functions like a demonic puppeteer, pulling the strings to make us dance, shaping our thoughts, choices, values, and behavior. Traumatized people tend to respond to minor stresses as if they were traumatic events, reacting with a disturbing intensity.

When we cannot remember a traumatic event and cannot use language to tell about it, we lack what is called *narrative memory*. Traumatic memories, however, can be stored in our bodies as *somatic memories* and can be expressed as changes in the biological stress response (Terr 1990; van der Kolk 1994). For example, many sexual abuse survivors have not been physically injured but may go through their lives suffering chronic pelvic pain, a psychophysiological reenactment of the past trauma. Sometimes the body will remember what the mind wants to forget.

The events of September 11, 2001, will remain forever engraved in the brains of most of us, some to a greater and some to a lesser degree. Probably most of us experienced a process by which we shifted into the fight-or-flight response, when the hairs on the back of the neck stood up and our heart raced, then we escaped from it through dissociating and numbing our emotions, an oscillating back-and-forth process of defense. We experienced traumatic stress, a normal time-limited response to events so horrific that our minds could not process them. More than three years later, neuroimaging studies showed that adults who were physically closer to the catastrophe showed certain differences in the grey matter in the amygdala, hippocampus, insula, anterior cingulate, and medial prefrontal cortex, when compared with those farther away (Ganzel, Kim, Glover, and Temple 2008). When the amygdalas in subgroups with higher versus lower levels of lifetime exposure to trauma were compared, there were systematic associations between the volume of gray matter, functional reactivity, and anxiety. This suggests that in healthy adults who have suffered the effects of accumulated trauma, a nonlinear path has become engraved in the brain. This means that some people were more resilient to the long-lasting effects of September 11 than others. Even young children who witnessed people jumping from the burning towers tended not to have lasting problems, probably because they could not understand the enormity of what they saw. But preschoolers who had already experienced a number of traumatic events were 16 times more likely to have attention problems and 21 times more likely to be unusually emotionally reactive and/or to have depression and anxiety symptoms than children who had not had such experiences (Chemtob, Nomura, and Abramovitz 2008).

Doublethink is what George Orwell (1949) called dissociation in his novel *1984*, a peculiar kind of self-hypnosis that allows us to deny or disavow reality, to break with reality without being psychotic (Farber 2000; Shengold 1979, 1989). It allowed us to know the horror of what happened on September 11 while at the same time we could work and be with friends and family while not letting ourselves fully know what we knew. This *doublethink* is what allowed me to comb the Internet efficiently for gas masks, comparing and pricing them. Israeli gas masks, although the most costly, were the best. I considered whether I should order four, for my husband and me, our son and his fiancée. Or should I order two more for the parents of my son's soon-to-be-in-laws? Or does wedding etiquette suggest I order yet two more for my soon-to-be daughter-in-law's sister and her boyfriend? Getting off to a good start with the in-laws-to-be and stocking up on bottled water and canned food and planning an escape route out of New York got equal weight in my fragmented state of mind. One of my patients reported that she became mesmerized while looking at expensive shoes at the Neiman Marcus website, a welcome diversion from the repeating television footage of the exploding towers and Osama bin Laden's face. This was not so unusual, I discovered. In the week after the terrorist attacks, Neiman Marcus sales of ridiculously expensive Manolo Blahnik shoes were up 7 percent over the previous year.

In order to understand the increase in spending after September 11, it helps to understand that women who are compulsive shoppers (or shoplifters) go into an altered state when shopping. (Read Kathryn Harrison's1994 *Exposure: A Novel*, for great descriptions.) The anticipation of finding, then buying or stealing the most perfect pair of shoes is exciting, transcending thoughts of their mortality and destructibility.[2] For compulsive shoppers, it is the most exquisite pleasure (Lawrence 1990). In the wake of the terrorist attacks, the need to escape the terror of being annihilated can lead many to use a manic defense, and so many women entered a dissociated state of excitement at the prospect of acquiring beautiful apparel, and some may even have gone into a ecstatic state in obtaining it. Despite today's difficult economic climate, many who escape through shopping just keep on spending anyway.

Pathological dissociation seems to be the thread tying together our current bizarre phenomena of Dissociative Identity Disorder (formerly known as Multiple Personality Disorder), anorexia nervosa, bulimia nervosa, compulsive eating, self-mutilating behavior, recovered memory syndrome, satanic ritual abuse, alien abduction, and *ataques de nervios* with equally strange past syndromes such as the demonically possessed witches of the Renaissance, the "vaporous" salon women of eighteenth-century Enlightenment Paris, and Freud's celebrated patients, with their dramatic, erotically tinged physical symptoms whose origins could not be explained medically.

THE THIRD EYE AND ALTERED STATES OF CONSCIOUSNESS

Imagine the possibility that your own brain can manufacture psychedelic experiences without the use of psychedelic drugs. Dimethyltryptamine (DMT), a chemical derived from plants, is also manufactured by the human brain (Strassman 2000). The plant derivative has been used by South American and Caribbean shamans for millennia as a main component of snuff and in *ayhuasca*, an indigenous plant infusion. Psychiatrist Rick Strassman, who has done cutting-edge research on DMT, believes that DMT is involved in a variety of altered states, including near-death and mystical experiences. He believes it also exists in the brain's pineal gland, a small endocrine gland, located between the two hemispheres, deep near the center of the brain (Strassman 2000; Strassman, Wojtowicz, Luna, and Frecska 2008).

Psilocybin, the active ingredient in magic mushrooms, is closely chemically related to DMT, but is much longer lasting (Strassman 2000). Strassman tells us that the pineal gland is unique in being the only brain site that is unpaired; all others have left and right counterparts. It was considered an anatomical oddity for nearly 2,000 years, with no one having any idea what its function was. This endogenous DMT is described as DMT illumination and is thought to be the source of the light accompanying visions in transpersonal experiences, a brightness that has no relation to any ordinary light. Eastern and Western visionaries may have experiences with symbolic or religious content, which may become transformed into this dazzling light. The pineal gland has been called the *third eye* or the spirit gland. Bataille (1985) used the concept of a *pineal-eye* in reference to a blind spot in Western rationality and called it an organ of excess and frenzy. Hindus regard it as the site of the sixth chakra, while Descartes (2003) devoted a good deal of time studying it, calling it the seat of the soul.

Oddly, the *third eye*, like the two seeing eyes, is sensitive to light and has a lens, cornea, and retina. It helps regulate the body's temperature and skin pigmentation. It produces melatonin, a derivative of serotonin, that affects how wake/sleep patterns and seasonal functions are modulated. How much melatonin your body produces is dependent on light. During the winter, when the days are shorter, your body may produce melatonin earlier or later in the day than is usual, a change that can produce symptoms of seasonal affective disorder, sometimes called winter depression. The pineal gland contains more serotonin than anywhere else in the body, and can convert serotonin to tryptophan, a crucial step in forming DMT. The pineal gland sits strategically close to the crucial emotional and sensory brain centers, because it is surrounded by the limbic or emotional brain. The pineal gland, therefore, has direct access to the brain's emotional centers (Strassman 2000).

Strassman has found that DMT is a key that unlocks parts of the mind, allowing entry into different realities. He claims that it makes possible the soul's movement in and out of the body and is a central part of birth and death experiences, the deepest states of meditation and even sexually transcendent experiences. He also believes that the accidental release of DMT provides an answer to the puzzle of alien abduction experiences (Strassman 2000; Strassman, Wojtowicz, Luna, and Frecska 2008). He also speculates that at extraordinary times in our lives the pineal gland produces DMT in amounts that function as psychedelics; currently there is no published reliable scientific evidence supporting this hypothesis.

To explore his theory, Strassman conducted extensive testing, injecting volunteers with synthetic DMT, which is powerful and physically immobilizing. It produced a flood of surprising and overpowering visual and emotional imagery. Volunteers who took it said that it was like an instantaneous LSD peak experience. Many of them reported convincing encounters with intelligent presences that were not human beings, some of them "aliens." Most felt that their DMT sessions were some of the most profound experiences they had ever had.

Inhibitions can prevent the pineal gland from producing DMT. When inhibitions are greatly eased, it may secrete DMT and might even produce other chemicals that amplify and protract its effects. According to Strassman, the extraordinary conditions of birth may stimulate. DMT production in the newborn. Orgasm, childbirth, extreme physical stress, near-death, psychosis, physical death, and meditation could also stimulate the production of DMT. Strassman found that for the unanesthetized mother, childbirth itself can be a highly psychedelic experience.

Christiane Northrup, obstetrician-gynecologist and author of *Women's Bodies, Women's Wisdom*, wrote about an unanesthetized mother's ecstatic childbirth experience after interviewing the mother. Having had her first child delivered by cesarean section by her obstetrician, Amanda wanted her second to have an unanesthetized vaginal delivery. She thought that the hospital environment was a source of the problem the first time and did not want to have the baby in the hospital, Although she wanted her obstetrician, Bethany Hayes, to do the delivery, and Hayes agreed with and supported her plan, she did not do home deliveries. They reached a compromise, with Hayes agreeing to be present as source of support during labor, and Amanda agreed to engage the best midwife she could find. Her labor turned out to be long and painful. When she finally called her obstetrician and midwife, they arrived at her home to find her in a rocking chair.

> As the birth neared, Amanda lay in her king-size bed on her side. "As we tried to keep up with her," Bethany told me, "she circled the bed. Her head remained in the center and she made a full circuit around the bed twice, a maneuver that I had not seen before in the hospital. It was very primitive. Though it was not clear to me what it represented, I trusted her need to move in this way as part of her unique birth process."
>
> There was little talk. Amanda said nothing and made little noise. She pushed her baby out on hands and knees and then kneeled over her. She was somewhere else. We were all commenting on the baby, but she was not looking at her infant. Her body was in a pose of ecstasy. When spoken to, she did not respond. For a moment I was frightened that she might not come back from wherever she was. Then she looked down at her infant and slowly came back into her body—or was it back out of her body? Bethany took a picture of Amanda in that ecstatic state, and she showed it at a recent medical meeting at which we both lectured on women's health. From this and reading Vicki Noble's *Shakti Woman* and Ina May's *Guide to Childbirth*, I learned that Amanda's experience of ecstasy is potentially available to all women at birth. Since then, I have talked at length with some of my patients who have had home births. One recently told me that during her home birth, she "left her body" and became an eagle flying high overhead. She experienced no pain. She had never told anybody about this. From that moment on, however, she trusted her body completely (Northrup 2010, pp. 497-498).

Northrup's account seems to support Strassman's caution that the setting and context in which DMT is released in an individual's body is as important, if not more so, than the DMT itself in determining how they deal with their experiences. Before reading about Strassman's theory about the pineal gland and DMT, I happened to be talking with a friend who is a midwife and nurse practioner in San Francisco, and was surprised to hear her say that so many of her patients strive for an ecstatic experience in childbirth. She had no objection to it but was concerned that having an ecstatic birth seemed to of be far more importance to some of them than ensuring the birth of a healthy baby. Some were ready to ignore the midwife's or obstetrician's recommendations if they interfered with an ecstatic experience. I could not help but think that the Haight-Asbury influence was alive and well.

The neuroscientific study of the self is still in its early years and so there are currently no established models, little data, and not even the vocabulary to describe notions of the self (Blanke and Thut 2007). William James first drew attention to the importance of self for understanding behavior and formulated the foundation for its modern study (James 1890; Nelson 2011).

And so a complete account of the neurobiology of dissociation remains somewhat elusive, and there has been little neuroscientific study of the more frenzied ecstatic states. The basic scientific information about underlying processes in dissociation derives mainly from research in hypnosis and PTSD, providing only a speculative account of the psychological and neurobiological factors involved in dissociative experiences. So the notion that there are several types of dissociative experiences mediated by a variety of, as yet, undiscovered mechanisms is about all we have at this point (Brunet, Holowka, and Laurence 2001). And so I have pieced together what I could about the state called ecstasy and can only speculate about how it occurs.

The brain's sensory system is comprised of the temporal, parietal, and occipital lobes, which lie behind the frontal lobe. The right frontal lobe, located behind the right eye, and the limbic system, to which it is linked, is the main system for recognizing and regulating emotions and relationships (Doidge 2007). The frontal region of the cerebral cortex is the thinking brain, governing logic, problem solving, decision making, and gratification. It is the part of the brain that helps you do the more difficult thing, whether it be concentrating on an unwanted task, or keeping anger under control. The limbic system is the emotional brain. Brain chemicals such as serotonin and dopamine, commonly known as neurotransmitters, are related to emotions and moods. Serotonin levels are related to our sense of well-being and so reduced levels impair our ability to cope with stress and to sleep well. That is why the SSRI antidepressants (selective serotonin reuptake inhibitors) may be used to alter serotonin levels. Exercise and psychotherapy can do this as well (Kramer 1993). When we are hurt, the brain releases these natural pain relievers, which act like heroin or morphine to keep us from feeling the pain initially. Dopamine is also a "feel good" neurotransmitter activating the pleasure center. When secreted into the bloodstream, it can quickly prepare the body for action in emergency situations.

Many runners and ballerinas experience a high during running or dancing, because extreme stress on the body causes dopamine levels to rise, thus increasing the threshold for pain. While in such a state, they may cause themselves extreme injury. Iannis Kouros, a legend in the world of extreme running, said that he gets to a point where his body is almost dead and his mind takes over, an out-of-body experience often described as ecstatic.

> Some may ask why I am running such long distances. There are reasons. During the ultras I come to a point where my body is almost dead. My mind has to take leadership. When it is very hard there is a war going on between the body and the mind. If my body wins, I will have to give up; if my mind wins, I will continue. At that time I feel that I stay outside of my body. It is as if I see my body in front of me; my mind commands and my body follows. This is a very special feeling, which I like very much. . . It is a very beautiful feeling and the only time I experience my personality separate from my body, as two different things (Cirves 2010).

THE ECSTATIC PATH IS THROUGH THE SENSES

> Rapture means, literally, being seized by force, as if one were a prey animal who is carried away. Caught in the talons of a transcendent rapture, one is gripped, elevated, and trapped at a fearsome height. To the ancient Greeks, this feeling often foretold malevolence and danger—other words that drink from the same rapturous source—rapacious, rabid, ravenous, ravage, rape, usurp, surreptitious. Birds of prey that plunge from the skies to gore their victims are known as raptors. Seized by a jagged and violent force, the enraptured are carried aloft to their ultimate doom. Ecstasy also means to be gripped by passion, but from a slightly different perspective: rapture is vertical, ecstasy horizontal. Rapture is high-flying, ecstasy occurs on the ground. . . . To the Greeks, ecstasy meant to stand outside oneself. How is that possible? Through existential engineering. "Give me a place to stand," Archimedes proclaimed in the third century B.C., "and I will move the earth. . . .The euphoria of flying in dreams, or the longing to fly through the ocean with dolphins , fills us with rapture. Can one feel ecstasy and rapture at the same time?"the heart of standing is you cannot fly," William Empson muses in a poem about the simultaneous limits and grandeur of a love affair. These are two escape routes from the mundane, two paths to deep play, equally quenching, equally mystical, and subtly different. All roads may indeed lead to Rome, but one might be hilly, the other marshy (Ackerman 1999, pp. 15-16).

The path to ecstasy is through the senses. Walt Whitman knew this well. So did Proust, who knew that smell and taste create distinctively intense memories and that memory depends upon the moment and mood of the person remembering (Proust 2007, Lehrer 2007). When Swann brought the tea-soaked madeleine to his lips, it brought him back in time to a forgotten memory that was as alive as if it were happening in the present. Ecstasy can happen through music, which possesses you and makes you move, propelling you outside yourself (Jourdain 1997). Walt Whitman's poem "I sing the body electric" was like a prayer. His poetry delighted in the senses. For him, the body *is* the soul. He knew that the emotions generated by music pulse throughout the body. As soon as the orchestra starts to play, the pupils dilate, pulse and blood pressure rise, the electrical conductance of the skin lowers. The cerebellum, a brain region associated with bodily movement, becomes unusually active. And blood is even redirected to our leg muscles, so we start to tap our feet to the beat (Lehrer 2007). Music elevates dopamine levels in the brain's mood and pleasure centers, acting in much the same way as narcotics and antidepressants. Listening to music activates a cascade of brain chemicals in the brain regions involved in processing musical structure. First, the auditory cortex, next, the frontal regions and finally, the mesolimbic system, which is responsible for arousal and pleasure (Levitin 2006). When the frontal- and temporal-lobe circuits disengage, the higher brain functions dissolve (Austin 1998). If the frontal lobes are the main control center for restraint, this helps us understand how ecstasy is about tumescence and then losing all restraint (Jourdain 1997).

Neuroscience helps to explain the "miraculous healings" experienced temporarily by the crippled and the sick at charismatic faith healing services. It explains the apparent power of the words, "In the name of Jesus" uttered by a charismatic leader as he lays his hand on the head of the afflicted person. It also helps us understand how repeated experiences of ecstasy become encoded in neural pathways, changing the structure of the brain to produce an addiction to the experience of ecstasy, thus making the individual highly prone to going into mystical or ecstatic trances.

OUT-OF-BODY EXPERIENCES ARE EXTRAORDINARILY COMMON

> It does not do harm to the mystery to know a little more about it.
> —Richard Feynman, footnote in *The Feynman Lectures on Physics*

Kevin Nelson (2011) tells us that important aspects of the neurological self are within the tempoparietal brain. When that area is inactive, it leads to out of body experiences. Because ecstasy is one of several kinds of out-of-body experiences (OBEs), if we had a better understanding of OBEs, this might advance our scientific notions about self and body, and their experienced spatial unity (Blanke 2004; Blanke and Thut 2007), thus giving us a better understanding of ecstasy. An out-of-body experience is defined as a disembodied sensation, seeing the world from a perspective different from the body's actual location. Usually they are viewed from above its location.

Out-of-body experiences are, in fact, extraordinarily common. "In a survey of more than thirteen thousand Europeans, 5.8 percent reported that they had this kind of experience. At least one out of every twenty people has had one, or conservatively, 15 million Americans. Susan Blackmore, an English psychologist who has studied the phenomenon, reviewed several smaller surveys and has concluded that they probably occur even more often" (Nelson 2011, p. 137).

Although the public has shown great interest in these experiences and there have been many case studies, systematic neurological studies of out-of-body experiences are extremely rare. This may be explained by the circumstances around their occurrence; they usually occur unexpectedly, last only briefly, and occur perhaps once or twice in a lifetime,

Olaf Blanke and his colleagues discovered that out-of-body experiences are created by disrupting how the brain puts sensations together to form the body's schema. All it takes is just a small trickle of electrical current in the right place, the temporoparietal region, to induce such an experience. These experiences are affected by arousal and rapid eye movement (REM) sleep (Blanke 2004; Blanke, Landis, Spinelli, and Seeck 2004; Blanke and Thut 2007; Nelson 2011). They are fleeting, reflecting an unstable brain state. When occurring spontaneously, such as during the transition from wakefulness to sleep, or in near-death experiences, they usually last only seconds. They often happen between wakefulness and sleep, and can be brought on by a lack of sleep or danger. They can occur while awake during surgery, during recovery from surgery, when fainting, during seizures, with migraine headaches, while flying jet aircraft, during high-altitude mountain climbing, and under hypnosis. They usually occur when the person is lying down (Nelson 2011).

Out of body experiences have been observed by some clinicians in connection with various neurological conditions, mainly epileptic seizures and migraine, finding that lesions largely affected the junction of the temporal and parietal lobes (Blanke 2004; Blanke and Thut 2007; Nelson 2010). Out-of-body experiences have a clearly discernible role in near-death experiences, which includes contributing to a vivid sense of a transcendent self, an encounter with a higher being or power, and merging with universal consciousness (Nelson 2007). Out-of-body experiences were as likely to occur during the transition between waking and sleep as during near-death experiences (Nelson 2011).

NEAR-DEATH EXPERIENCES ARE MORE COMMON THAN YOU MIGHT THINK

> The unconscious psyche believes in life after death.
> —Carl Jung

> To die,—to sleep—To sleep! Perchance to dream! Ay, there's the rub; For in that sleep of death what dreams may come.
> —William Shakespeare, *Hamlet*

The near-death experience (NDE) is a specific kind of out-of-body experience that has been investigated (Kubler-Ross 1969; Moody 2001; Nelson 2011; Nelson, Mattingly, Lee and Schmit 2006; .Newberg and d'Aquili 1994; Ring 1993). It is one of the most compelling experiences that human beings have encountered throughout history. In the Tibetan Books of the Dead, during the European middle ages, and to the present day, near-death experiences have been experienced, written and argued about. The near-death experience has been described as an unfolding according to a single pattern as though the prospect of death seems to release a stored common program of feelings, perceptions, and experiences (Ring 1993; Moody 2001). The basic aspects (Moody 2001) are a sense of ineffability; the experience of hearing the news of one's own death, and often hearing a physician pronounce one dead. There are feelings of peace and quiet, noise or unusual auditory sensations; the feeling of going through a dark tunnel; feeling oneself float out of one's physical body; meeting others, usually deceased relatives. Usually there is an encounter with a brilliant light; a panoramic review of one's life events; approaching a border, apparently between this and the next life; and then a coming back from death. With this, there is the wish to tell others about the experience but also the fear that it will mark them as mentally ill. The individual is usually left with new goals and moral principles and a determination to try to live in accordance with them. There is a profound change in one's views of death, often one of no longer fearing it. There is often some corroboration of the near-death experience in which someone at the bedside of the dying person participates empathically in the experience. For many who have not had an out-of-body or near-death experience, all these experiences have become laughable stereotypes.

Like out of body experiences, near-death experiences are fairly common and have become a staple of books, movies, and talk shows. Extrapolating from Gallup polls and U.S. News and World Report surveys, Nelson (2011) estimated that 45 millions of Americans may have had some kind of unusual experience associated with near-death. Many consider these experiences to be proof that an afterlife exists and that our consciousness or soul can separate from the body. Studies show that people who have been confronted with death and see no chance for their survival are not afraid. Most survivors will say that they have been there, know what it's about, and it's not so frightening (Dlin 1976).

Being *near death* is quite different from *returning* from death. During a near-death experience the brain is *alive* and *conscious*. The brain does not die during a near-death experience, as some authors have implied, confusing clinical death with syncope, the loss of consciousness due to insufficient blood flow to the brain and reversible brain injury (Nelson 2011). If a vegetative state persists for a year, the coma is considered to be permanent.

Until recently near-death experiences were treated as anomalies. There have been well-publicized celebrity accounts, including several by actress Elizabeth Taylor. In one she had an encounter with her dead husband Mike Todd: "I went to that tunnel, saw the white light, and Mike. I said, 'Oh Mike, you're where I want to be.' And he said, 'No, Baby. You have to turn around and go back because there is something very important for you to do" (Nelson 2011, p. 95). To be sent back to the land of the living with a new or renewed sense of purpose is a common feature of near-death experiences. Sharon Stone suffered a serious brain hemorrhage and described her near-death experience: "I went into the vortex of that white light that was very, very beautiful, and very comforting and very peaceful, and quiet and clean" (Nelson 2011, p. 96). These kinds of transcendental experiences have been described as well by Jung (1961) in descriptions of his own near-death experience. Having broken his foot, he had a heart attack, followed by visions and delirium. His vivid encounter with the light, plus the intensely meaningful insights led him to conclude that his experience came from something real and eternal. Jung's experience is unique in that he saw the Earth from a vantage point of about a thousand miles above it. His incredibly accurate view of the Earth from outer space was described about two decades before astronauts in space first described it.

> It seemed to me that I was high up in space. Far below I saw the globe of the Earth, bathed in a gloriously blue light. I saw the deep blue sea and the continents. Far below my feet lay Ceylon, and in the distance ahead of me the subcontinent of India. My field of vision did not include the whole Earth, but its global shape was plainly distinguishable and its outlines shone with a silvery gleam through that wonderful blue light. In many places the globe seemed colored, or spotted dark green like oxidized silver. Far away to the left lay a broad expanse - the reddish-yellow desert of Arabia; it was as though the silver of the Earth had there assumed a reddish-gold hue. Then came the Red Sea, and far, far back—as if in the upper left of a map—I could just make out a bit of the Mediterranean. My gaze was directed chiefly toward that. Everything else appeared indistinct. I could also see the snow-covered Himalayas, but in that direction it was foggy or cloudy. I did not look to the right at all. I knew that I was on the point of departing from the Earth.

> Later I discovered how high in space one would have to be to have so extensive a view—approximately a thousand miles! The sight of the Earth from this height was the most glorious thing I had ever seen. After contemplating it for a while, I turned around. I had been standing with my back to the Indian Ocean, as it were, and my face to the north. Then it seemed to me that I made a turn to the south. Something new entered my field of vision. A short distance away I saw in space a tremendous dark block of stone, like a meteorite. It was about the size of my house, or even bigger. It was floating in space, and I myself was floating in space . . .
>
> . . . .This experience gave me a feeling of extreme poverty, but at the same time of great fullness. There was no longer anything I wanted or desired. I existed in an objective form; I was what I had been and lived. At first the sense of annihilation predominated, of having been stripped or pillaged; but suddenly that became of no consequence.
>
> Everything seemed to be past; what remained was a "fait accompli," without any reference back to what had been. There was no longer any regret that something had dropped away or been taken away. On the contrary: I had everything that I was, and that was everything (Jung 1961, pp. 289-91).

It took three weeks before he could decide to live again. He could not eat. The world seemed artificial and life struck him as a prison. He felt great resistance to his doctor, who had brought him back to life, but was worried about him at the same time. He thought his doctor's life was endangered because he had appeared to him as an avatar, which Jung understood to mean that he was going to die. He had the terrifying thought that his doctor would have to die in his place. He tried, to no avail, to talk to him about it. In fact, Jung was his last patient. He remembered that on April 4, 1944, he was allowed to sit up on the edge of his bed for the first time since the beginning of his illness, and on this same day the doctor went to bed. He never got up again and died of septicemia (Jung 1961).

Studies show that, the near-death experience and other paranormal phenomena are connected to REM sleep (Nelson 2011; Persinger 2001), which might explain why those who have had a near-death experience speak of "going toward the light." Paranormal beliefs and experiences appear to be related (Persinger 2001).Those who support the existence of extraterrestrial intelligence as the source for unidentified flying objects (UFOs) and the reality of reincarnation are less likely to accept traditional religious beliefs (Persinger 2001).

Nelson tells us that that in neurology, the brain mechanism that flip-flops between REM sleep and wakefulness is in either the REM-on or REM-off position ninety-nine percent of the time. But in those who had a near-death experience, rather than passing from REM sleep to wakefulness, their brains tend to fragment and blend those two states. When this happens, they, find themselves both awake *and* in the REM sleep state. They experience light and out-of–body sensations; they are conscious yet unable to move, and participate in stunningly imaginative narratives, all features of the near-death experience that are traced to REM sleep. In his research, Nelson and colleagues discovered that out-of-body experiences were as likely to occur during the transition between waking and sleep as during near-death experiences. That is, the near-death experiences were not like our usual nightly dreams but were more like the lucid dreams of the REM-waking borderland. Lucid dreaming mixes the two conscious states of REM sleep and wakefulness, but this occurs only in 3 percent of dreams. We might think of lucid dreaming as being awake while we dream. The dream feels as real as the world we know when we are in a fully awake state. Lucid dreamers can feel a wide range of emotions. They can feel fear, sexual bliss, and spiritual ecstasy. Lucid dreams can even end in orgasm (Nelson 2011).

If we look at the experience of ecstasy in terms of the characteristics of REM states, ecstasy seems to be a state of being disembodied, cut off from our bodily senses, corresponding to the temporoparietal REM deactivation. In ecstatic states, there is stillness, similar to REM paralysis. There may be the experience of light, corresponding to ambient light and REM visual activation. These similarities suggest that the state of ecstasy occurs in a fragmented REM state of consciousness.

Neuroscience is still far from explaining the bliss that accompanies so many near-death experiences, how the brain moves from terror to bliss. Doyostevsky, however, explained it quite well (Nelson 2011). He was sentenced to death in 1849, charged with being part of a group of intellectuals who were writing and speaking out against the bondage of the serfs in czarist Russia. He and other prisoners, similarly charged, were brought to Semenovsky Square, where they saw the scaffold. They were led up to the scaffold by a priest, and given a funeral shroud to wear. Dostoyevsky heard the drums roll. Having been an army officer, he instantly knew that the drums were beating a retreat and that his life would be spared. He was returned to his cell and had a spiritual awakening. He wrote to his older brother that facing death had given him a new grasp of life. While standing on the scaffold, waiting to die, he felt the urge to forgive and be forgiven. Years afterward he told his wife that he was never as happy as he was on that day. He wrote that he had been reborn in a new form. In *The Idiot,* written twenty years later, he described his transforming ordeal in Semenovsky Square through the eyes of his Christ-like hero, Prince Myshkin.

Like Saint Paul, Joan of Arc, Saint Teresa of Avila, and Emanuel Swedenborg. Dostoyevsky had what were thought of as sacred seizures stemming from abnormal electrical activity in the limbic structures of the temporal and frontal lobes. Limbic ecstatic seizures are the most distinctively spiritual of seizure types, and neurologists have long been fascinated by Dostoyevsky's (Nelson 2011).

> I have really touched God. He came into my, myself, yes, God exists, I cried, and I don't remember anything else. You all, healthy people he said, can't imagine the happiness we epileptics feel during the second before our attack. I don't know if this felicity lasts for seconds, hours, or months, but believe me, for all the joys that life may bring, I would not change this one . . . . might well be worth the whole of life (Nelson 2011, p.252).

Dostoyevsky suspected that his ecstasy might be kindled by disease, and wondered,

> What if it is a disease? What does it matter that it is an abnormal intensity, if the result, if the minute of sensation, remembered and analyzed afterward in health, turns out to be the acme of harmony and beauty, and gives a feeling, unknown and undivined till then, of completeness, of proportion, of reconciliation, and of ecstatic devotional merging in the highest synthesis of life (Nelson 2011, p. 252).

Neuroscientists still do not know if his spiritual ecstasies were psychotic or mystical, and do not understand, as far as the brain goes, how they can be both (Nelson 2011). For a look at another near-death experience, read the first chapter of Oliver Sacks's recent book, *Musicophilia,* (2007).

> Tony Cicoria was forty-two, very fit and robust, a former college football player who had become a well-regarded orthopedic surgeon in a small city in upstate New York. He was at a lakeside pavilion for a family gathering one fall afternoon. It was pleasant and breezy, but he noticed a few storm clouds in the distance; it looked like rain.
>
> He went to a pay phone outside the pavilion to make a quick call to his mother (this was in 1994, before the age of cell phones). He still remembers every single second of what happened next: "I was talking to my mother on the phone. There was a little bit of rain, thunder in the distance. My mother hung up. The phone was a foot away from where I was standing when I got struck. I remember a flash of light coming out of the phone. It hit me in the face. Next thing I remember, I was flying backwards."
>
> Then—he seemed to hesitate before telling me this—"I was flying forwards. Bewildered. I looked around. I saw my own body on the ground. I said to myself, 'Oh shit, I'm dead.' I saw people converging on the body. I saw a woman—she had been standing waiting to use the phone right behind me—position herself over my body, give it CPR. . . . I floated up the stairs—my consciousness came with me. I saw my kids, had the realization that they would be okay. Then I was surrounded by a bluish-white light . . . an enormous feeling of well-being and peace. The highest and lowest points of my life raced by me. No emotion associated with these . . . pure thought, pure ecstasy. I had the perception of accelerating, being drawn up . . . there was speed and direction. Then, as I was saying to myself, 'This is the most glorious feeling I have ever had'—SLAM! I was back."

> Dr. Cicoria knew he was back in his own body because he had pain—pain from the burns on his face and his left foot, where the electrical charge had entered and exited his body—and, he realized, "only bodies have pain." He wanted to go back, he wanted to tell the woman to stop giving him CPR, to let him go; but it was too late—he was firmly back among the living. After a minute or two, when he could speak, he said, "It's okay—I'm a doctor!" The woman (she turned out to be an intensive-care-unit nurse) replied, "A few minutes ago, you weren't (Sacks 2007, pp. 3-4).

Newberg and D'Aquili (1994) raise the question of the apparent reality of the near-death experience, and how it compares to that of baseline reality. Near-death experience archetypes, "like all archetypes, possess a certain quality of exaggerated reality compared to baseline reality. It is for this reason that archetypes are often the basis of mythology, 'divine reality" or the mysterious 'hyperreal' underlying baseline experience" (Newberg and D'Aquili 1994, p. 12).

RELIGION, SPIRITUALITY, AND ECSTASY

The study of brain activity during religious or spiritual practice began with studies of meditation in the 1950s and 1960s (Newberg and D'Aquili, 2001). Then in the early 1980s, Dr. James Austin, a neurologist, had a strange experience. While waiting for his train in London, he looked away from the tracks toward the Thames River. Suddenly his awareness of time, fear and self-consciousness disappeared and he was convinced that he understood the nature of the universe (Begley 2001). Afterward, trying to understand this, Austin deduced that in order to feel time, fear and self-consciousness disappear, certain brain circuits must have been interrupted. The amygdala's activity, which observes the environment for threats and registers fear, must be allayed. Parietal-lobe circuits, which familiarize ourself in space and help us distinguish between ourselves and world, must also go quiet. The frontal- and temporal-lobe circuits, which keep tabs on time and produce self-awareness, must disengage. When that happens, he concluded, our higher brain functions that provide our sense of self seem briefly to dissolve (Austin 1998).

Neurophysiologist Michael Persinger and colleagues examined the assertions made by the Transcendental Meditation movement regarding the efficacy of TM (Persinger, Carrey, and Suess 1980). University students who learned Transcendental Meditation (TM) displayed a significantly greater range of complex partial epileptic-like signs such as feeling vibrations, auras, hearing their name called, and religious experience, compared with a control group of students who did not meditate (Persinger, Carrey and Suess 1980; 1993). Dostoyevsky, thought to have had temporal lobe epilepsy, described personal religious events—conversions, revelations, visions—and called his seizures holy experiences. Persinger argues that temporal lobe epilepsy is the extreme end of a continuum of temporal lobe activation, with lesser degrees of activity occurring during strong religious feeling, and still lesser degrees during viewing a sunset or when we find beholding a work of art deeply meaningful (Persinger 1983).

The word epilepsy, from the Greek *epilepsia*, means to take or seize, as if from outside, and refers to any disorder having recurrent seizure states. In the dramatic grand mal or less dramatic petit mal seizures, the higher brain functions shut down, causing the person to lose consciousness. In grand mal seizures, they may fall and convulse; in petit mal, a state that looks like staring may occur. In the far more common temporal lobe seizures seen in adults, the epileptic activity remains localized, resulting in no apparent physical change, except sometimes a dull stare or trembling of the arm or mouth. It is an alteration *in* consciousness, but not a loss *of* consciousness, and results in a dreamy state. Persinger suspects that religious experiences can be activated by mini electrical storms in the temporal lobes that can be caused by anxiety, emotional crisis, lack of oxygen, low blood sugar and fatigue—suggesting why some people find God in such moments. Neurologist Kevin Nelson (2011) tells us that Dostoyevsky's ecstatic seizures might produce the experience of mystical oneness, and we might be able to discern the brain areas responsible for the mystical by studying them, but for one caveat; because they are so rare, so far we are not sure where they come from in the brain or what causes this particular seizure type. In mystical experiences, the role of the REM state may be an indirect one. Once the limbic system is activated by the fight-or-flight response or the REM switch, the mystical feeling of unity may depend more on the limbic system itself and less on the brain stem activity that ignited it.

In their book, *Why God Won't Go Away: Brain Science and the Biology of Belief,* Andrew Newberg and Eugene d'Aquili (2001) proposed that the origin of spiritual experience is closely intertwined with human biology. They suggest that the amygdala, which translates sensory impressions into emotions, engenders a sense of religious awe to distinctive ritual gestures such as bows or signs of the cross. What intrigues Newberg and d'Aquili is how religious rituals and practices stimulate the two major subsystems of the autonomic systems. They propose that certain religious rituals can markedly activate the body's parasympathetic (calm) system or its sympathetic (flight system) while simultaneously shutting down more of the other system. Whether the fast spinning of the Sufi Whirling Dervishes activates the sympathetic system or Zen meditation activates the parasympathetic system, distinct brain regions are stimulated and perceived by the mind as a higher state of consciousness. In states of very high activity around one circuit, they say, there can be a "spillover" of activity from the overstimulated system into the other (Newberg and D'Aquili 2001). That is, spillover results from overstimulating one of the systems so that the other, rather than being suppressed, becomes more stimulated. While it is unusual, this dual state can produce the sensation of an incredible release of energy that can feel like bliss. And in extreme cases of both systems being activated, there can occur brain activities experienced as the "Absolute Unity of Being," God, or nirvana. More recently, Newberg and Waldman (2010) found that spiritual practices actually tend to lower stress levels, which increases neuroplasticity.

This is true of glossolalia, usually known as speaking in tongues, generally regarded as the mark of a true Christian, a sign that he has been filled with the Holy Spirit (Balmer 1993). Speaking in tongues is a kind of spontaneous verbal monologue, sometimes accompanied by body gyrations and shaking. Instead of focusing one's attention on a specific phrase, which increases frontal lobe activity, those who speak in tongues surrender voluntary control, and with it a loss of ordinary consciousness by deliberately slowing down frontal lobe activity. This results in the limbic area of the brain becoming more active, thus increasing the intensity of the experience (Newberg 2010).Speaking in tongues is not a true language but a pseudo- language, "strings of syllables, made up of sounds taken from among all those that the speaker knows, put together more or less haphazardly but which nevertheless emerge as word-like and sentence-like units because of realistic, language-like rhythm and melody (Samarin 1972, p. 227)."

There are apparently two different kinds of speaking in tongues, a private and public kind (Lowenthal and Grady 1997). We tend not to hear about private glossolalia, an ongoing, habitual, personal practice usually accompanying mundane activities. Practioners regard it as a special form of prayer that has become a habit that promotes feeling greater closeness to God, as well as a sense of calm. The more public kind, which occurs in many Pentecostal services, is usually an exceptionally excited, dramatic frenzied activity, involving singing, vocal sounds and ecstatic experiences (Lowenthal and Grady 1997). It seems that the more one aspires to speak in tongues, the more the brain responds by actually doing it, demonstrating that they have been possessed by the Holy Spirit. We usually see this kind of experience through television coverage of Pentecostal services. As you might imagine, it is not easy to get those who speak in tongues to volunteer to be studied by neuroscientists, but Andrew Newberg and colleagues succeeded in conducting the first functional neuroimaging study to demonstrate brain changes during glossolalia in five Pentecostal research subjects (Newberg, Wintering, Morgan, and Waldman 2006; Newberg and Waldman 2010). Newberg compared the cerebral activity during glossolalia to that found in singing gospel songs, since singing is similar to glossolalia except that it involves actual language. The state of "possession" experienced during glossolalia was different than that while singing gospel. During glossolalia, decreased activity in the prefrontal cortex was found (Carey 2006; Newberg, et al, 2006). Donna Morgan, a coauthor of the study and also a born-again Christian, was a research subject. "You're aware of your surroundings. You're not really out of control. But you have no control over what's happening. You're just flowing. You're in a realm of peace and comfort, and it's a fantastic feeling" (Carey 2006, p. F5).

These new findings contrasted dramatically with images taken of other spiritually inspired mental states that activate the frontal lobes. It may be a common view that people who speak in tongues are mentally ill, but the findings suggest that those who speak in tongues are seldom mentally impaired. All five women in the study described themselves as Charismatic Catholics or Pentecostal Christians, and were active, solid members of their communities. When interviewed, none reported visual or auditory hallucinations, mood disorders, or displayed any evidence of Axis I or II disorders as found in the Diagnostic and Statistical Manual of Mental Disorders (American Psychiatric Association 1994). A recent study of almost 1,000 male evangelical English clergymen found that those who practiced glossolalia were more stable than those who did not (Carey 2006; Francis and Robbins 2003).

In a study meant to clarify the appeal of the Eastern-influenced Divine Light Mission to American youth, it was found that ecstatic experiences similar to an acute circumscribed hallucinatory episode were a central factor in the experience (Buckley and Galanter 1979). The leader of the group, Guru Maharaji, is thought to be the incarnation of God. Members described an experience lasting from 1 to 3 hours in which an outer radiance or light was seen, which filled them with a sense of ecstasy. There was an alteration in the sense of time and a feeling of being in touch with the divine. About 16 percent had sexual sensations at the time, of orgasmic intensity for 9 percent, suggesting that the transient loss of ego boundaries in orgasm is analogous to the mystical fusion with the divine that was described. Once the *divine light* had been experienced and they had received *knowledge* of it, it became a central part of members' inner world, and could be reinvoked through meditation. Following conversion, members experienced a marked improvement in their moods, describing themselves as happy, content, and sometimes filled with happiness. The most powerful factors involved in this experience were found to be strong group cohesion, a charismatic leader, and the occurrence of dramatic conversion experiences. Despite different belief systems, the Divine Light Mission was found to be similar to Pentecostal religious groups.

This conversion experience has been described by Christensen (1963) as an acute hallucinatory episode which serves the defensive function of maintaining ego integration in the face of overwhelming psychological conflict. Its occurrence is commonly confined to adolescence, when the developing and more fluid ego is especially vulnerable to stress. That is, their religious conversion can be viewed as a regression in the service of the ego that resolved their immediate intrapsychic and social conflicts.

Stephen Dubner's (1998) autobiographical account shows how ecstatic worship can serve as a potent mood enhancer. In *Turbulent Souls: A Catholic Son's Return to His Jewish Family*, he wrote about his parents' conversion from Judaism to Catholicism. Even in early adolescence, his mother Florence found her life flat and she feared death, especially because Jews tended not to talk much about death. Living in a Catholic neighborhood, she heard her Catholic friends and their families speaking about what a wonderful place heaven was, and why death was not to be feared. It made her want to be Catholic.

Dubner's paternal grandmother, mother of his father Sol, died when Sol was fifteen, ripping a deep hole in the family, leaving him with his five siblings and his orthodox Jewish father, whose piety sickened him. By the time he was in his early twenties, everyone who knew him knew that he was terribly depressed. Sol Dubner had been very lonely stationed in the South Pacific in World War II. At a time when being Jewish in Europe could mean extermination, he converted to Catholicism and became very pious, more like his father than he realized. When his father found out about his conversion, he disowned him.

When Sol met Florence he found that she, like him and many converts, was "more Catholic than the pope." They married and had eight children, moving to upstate New York to escape their earlier life. Having so many babies made them silly with joy, a joy Sol had never thought he would feel. He thought that the dark blotches on his soul had been wiped clean by the powerful goodness of Jesus. Stephen, the youngest, described an existence defined by Mass and catechism. The kids he was allowed to play with were other churchgoing Catholics.

On summer evenings, the entire family knelt on the grass in front of the house to recite the evening rosary. Stephen shuddered whenever a car drove by, for fear that a friend or classmate would see them, only reinforcing the belief "that the Dubners lived in the district of Devotion that bordered on Fanatical. It was one thing to be known as a churchgoing family and quite another to pray right out there on your own property" (Dubner 1998, p. 88). More than this, Stephen dreaded the Wednesday-night prayer meetings that his parents ran, part of something called the Charismatic Christian Renewal, The songs they sang were different from the regular church songs, and so were the people."

> They gathered in a circle of folding metal chairs under glaring fluorescent lights. They would begin with a song from a pale blue booklet . . . songs with strange, curvy melodies. They clapped as they sang. . . When the song was

> over, they'd close their eyes tight and pray, quietly at first, or together like in church but each of them on his own, voices swarming like bees—*Praise you, Lord Jesus . . . Lift us up, Jesus, lift us up. . . We praise you and love you, Lord Jesus . . . Alleluia! Alleluia!* Louder and louder, and soon it would begin: one voice, then a second, jagged outbursts of the strangest syllables, their faces twisted into what looked like pain, their strange syllables then blossoming into shouts, some of them standing as they shouted, a dozen grown-ups, my mother and father among them, crying into the air—and me, petrified, peeking through half-shut eyelids. I prayed from the heart: *Please, God, make me invisible.* Why were they making up this ridiculous language? Was I supposed to know it too? Afterward they all behaved as if nothing had happened. That was the most upsetting part. In these prayer meetings, though, my parents went wild. They were the chief clappers and shriekers, and then, riding home through the dark, they were totally calm. I would stew in the back seat, angry at the inexplicable madness that had transpired. Up front, my mother would squeeze in close to my father, which she never, ever did, and rest her head on his shoulder. 'It just really grabs your heart, doesn't it?' she would say to him.
>
> The Charismatic Renewal meetings really had grabbed my father's heart, much more than I knew at the time. They were, in fact, a lifesaver. My father was fifty-four by now and had tried everything to fight his depression, most recently the electroshock treatments. He was desperate for a healing, and through the Charismatics he finally found it (Dubner 1998, pp. 120-23).

Sol and Florence had always agreed that a truly spiritual life should include any number of conversions because like a battery, the soul could always stand to be recharged, and they began to experience their faith at a deeper level. Although Sol was able to hide his depression from the outside world, his children were used to his mental fragility. When the dark moods that at times caused him to stay in bed all day finally stopped, the world opened up to him. He lit up the house or wherever he went. Although he kept taking his antidepressant, he hardly needed it. Each week, he could barely wait for the Sunday night prayer meeting.

ORGASM AND ECSTASY

Returning to Laski's finding that ecstasy seemed to be an intense experience of tumescence and release, we can see the similarity of ecstasy to orgasm. In both, a force builds up, gradually accumulating and increasing, and then producing a powerful release usually lasting but a moment. Because ecstasy and orgasm are similar but not the same, exploring what happens during orgasm might provide a key to understanding what happens in the state of ecstasy.

In her autobiography, Saint Teresa of Avila, who also may have had temporal lobe epilepsy, wrote about her ecstasies the way others might write about their orgasms. Some women have had spontaneous orgasms for years, without direct genital stimulation, often many a day. Just fantasizing or dreaming can be enough. Brain scans showed their orgasms to be temporal lobe epileptic auras (Flaherty 2004; Komisaruk, Beyer-Flores, and Whipple 2006), a rare form of temporal lobe epilepsy known as ecstatic epilepsy. These women were in no hurry to seek medical help, perhaps because they were too embarrassed or were enjoying themselves too much to interfere with it. One woman refused to take her antiepileptic medication (Komisaruk, et al. 2006).

But some non-epileptic women can shed their restraints and climax without any genital stimulation at all, suggesting that activation of the right temporal lobe is essential for orgasm in women, while the brain source for the male orgasm is harder to locate (Komisaruk, et al. 2006). But for men and women alike, dopamine is released in sexual excitement.

The male and female brain develop along different tracks, although there is controversy about why this is so. Developmental psychologist Jerome Kagan (1994) calls it one of the two real mysteries of human evolution. (The other, he says, is why women outlive men.) Sex differences, he says, are not constant; the gaps widen and close with age. Evolutionary theory makes a case for why men become aroused more quickly and easily than women. A successfully reproducing man must inseminate a lot of women, so he'd better be wired for speed and efficiency (Blum 1997). In addition, men need to be aroused in order to produce the sperm and fertilize the egg, and must reach an orgasm to ejaculate. Women, however, need neither excitement nor pleasure to produce an egg, a basic unfairness of nature. Some biologists are puzzled about why women experience orgasm at all. One theory, called the "upsuck theory," is that the muscular contractions help suck the sperm where it needs to go (Blum 1997). The theory is also promoted as a female counterstrategy to rape, meaning that if a man forces himself on a woman, her biological defense against pregnancy is to make it harder for the sperm to reach its target. Although many feminists would consider rape to be more of an aggressive act than a sexual one, evolutionary biologist Randy Thornhill insists that rape is foremost a sexual act (Blum 1997; Thornhill and Thornhill 1992). Producing a child requires a major commitment from a woman, beginning with a long pregnancy and continuing with the production of a helpless, dependent infant who will die unless she finds a surrogate to feed it. Producing a child requires no commitment from a man. After sex, many women harbor anxiety about whether they will ever hear from the man again. A man who can walk away from a sexual encounter unencumbered can produce many more children than the man who stays and is responsible (Blum 1997). This basic sexual asymmetry, says Thornhill, might have influenced how males and females behaved. Males would be most successful if they got many women pregnant, essentially choosing quantity over quality, while women would best be served by insisting on quality. The most critical part of this argument is that women want to choose their mates, leaning toward healthy men with the promise of being good partners and providers.

Around a hundred years ago, Freud posed a question to Marie Bonaparte, one of his students: "The great question that has never been answered, and which I have not yet been able to answer, despite my thirty years of research into the feminine soul, is "What does a woman want?" (Jones 1955, p. 421). Regardless of whether they considered themselves lesbian, straight, or bisexual, women became aroused strongly and quickly when viewing pornography of the male homosexual, lesbian, or heterosexual variety. Men who considered themselves straight were excited by heterosexual or lesbian porn, but were largely unmoved by male homosexual porn, demonstrating a pattern of attraction that was the polar opposite of women's (Bergner 2009; Diamond 2009). This gender difference raises some interesting questions. Why does such a broader range of stimuli arouse women but not men? Do the bounds of culture constrain men more than women or are they simply more repressed?

Researcher Lisa Diamond (2009) has found that women's sexuality is quite fluid and bendable. Although a woman may have an innate sexual orientation, she has found that despite this orientation, desire can be superseded by emotional closeness and erotic attraction can become redirected. Many of her subjects typically described being attracted "to the person, not their gender" (Diamond 2009, p. 172). Taking a rather different view, researcher Marta Meana underscored the importance of being desired and of the wish to be the object of sexual admiration and need (Bergner 2009). What women really want is a real quandary, said Meana. "Women want to be thrown up against a wall but not truly endangered. Women want a caveman and caring. If I had to pick an actor who embodies all the qualities, all the contradictions, it would be Denzel Washington. He communicates that kind of power and that he is a good man" (Bergner 2009a, p. ST51).

But whatever it is that women really want, an orgasm, in any case, is literally a mind-blowing experience for a woman. When a woman is attracted to someone, her body quivers with a gush of phenylethylamine, a brain hormone that speeds up the flow of information between neurons, turning on her pleasure centers and creating a frenzy of excitement because everything she experiences gives her pleasure (Liebowitz 1983). It is another of the body's own naturally occurring drugs, and when the body is deficient in phenylethylamine, it renders the person weak, tired, and depressed. But the body uses phenylethylamine for more than infatuation; it keeps one alert, confident, and ready to try something new and thrill-seeking. Chocolate contains a lot of it, which may be one of the reasons many women consider themselves to be chocoholics, insisting that it is addictive, producing an immediate feeling of well-being, with abstinence leading to withdrawal symptoms (Liebowitz 1983).

Feeling cared for by her partner seems to be important in heightening arousal. As arousal increases, much of the woman's brain shuts down, turning off fear, anxiety, and all emotion, thus freeing her from all restraint. In comparison, men seem to require little time or trust in their partner to climax, just direct physical stimulation. In fact, obtaining meaningful brain scan data from men was problematic because their orgasms typically are so short-lasting. In men, we must differentiate between orgasm and ejaculation, although they usually occur almost simultaneously. Orgasm is a peak experience, both emotionally and physically, whereas ejaculation is merely a reflex action happening at the lower part of the spinal cord and resulting in the discharge of semen. Some men can recognize the separation of the two processes, allowing them to experience multiple orgasms without the occurrence of ejaculation.

Looking more closely at Marghanita Laski's findings about the difference between sexual orgasm and ecstasy triggered by sexual activity, those who have experienced both were clear that they had experienced ecstasy only a limited number of times. Of the 63 people who participated in her study, 26 were male and 27 were female, including a boy of 10, and two girls, ages 14 and 16. Of these, 11 (six male and five female), referred to ecstasy resulting from sexual intercourse alone and no other trigger (Laski 1961). Laski examined Chaucer's *Troilus and Cressida*, finding that his Old English description is couched in the language of ecstasy. She said that in modern novels, what people experience during sex is *always* called ecstasy, and that the word is used as a literary cliché. She wrote that "Sexual pleasure without ecstasy tends to be described in terms of sexually local physical sensation, male or female, as the case may be, while in descriptions of ecstasy derived from love-making, as from other triggers, sexually local physical sensation is never described and descriptions of men's and women's experiences are indistinguishable from each other" (Laski 1961, p. 152).

Laski quoted an example from a collection of novelists' clichés: "Love-making is accompanied (figuratively) by rising to the crests of tremendous waves or soaring towards blinding light, followed by slow descents to ineffable peace or a gradual floating down from the mountain tops to plains of golden bliss (Laski 1961, p. 151, citing Now and Then, Cape, Spring 1958)." While understanding her point about literary clichés, I might disagree here with Laski, thinking that perhaps they are not really such clichés as she thought. Her example contains several of the characteristics of near-death and out-of- body experiences (Blanke 2004; Blanke & Thut 2007; Carroll 2002; Joseph 1982; Moody 2001; Newberg and d'Aquili 1994; Ring 1993; Strassman 2000; Weiss 2004). La petite mort, or "the little death" in French, is a metaphor for ecstasy, sometimes used to refer to losing consciousness after orgasm. The colloquialism, "I thought I'd died and gone to heaven" captures it. A recent study of brain activation patterns using PET scans lends some support to the experience of a small death during female orgasm (Georgiadis, Kortekaas , Kuipers, Nieuwenburg, Pruim, Reinders, and Holstege 2006).

A steady interplay between the sympathetic and parasympathetic nervous systems controls the sexual response cycle (Komisaruk, et al,. 2006). Activation of the sympathetic system is necessary for arousal in men and women, and activation of the parasympathetic system accompanies orgasm. There are individual differences in how people experience orgasm and individual orgasms may differ in the same person. Nonetheless, all orgasms feature rhythmic contractions of the body and pelvis, increase in the heart rate, systemic hypertension, hyperventilation (rapid overbreathing), and muscle tension, followed by the rapid release of tension.

But in one very odd way, both sexes were similar in that they found it easier to have an orgasm when they wore socks! (Komisaruk, et al 2006). Yes, socks! No explanation was given so my speculation is that literally having cold feet may give people cold feet about letting go of inhibitions, which makes some kind of sense if cold feet are a sign of cold, tight muscles. Muscles must be very relaxed in order to constrict and relax in orgasmic spasms.

As Dutch psychologist Nico Frijda put it, we're continuously shifting the balance between restraint and letting go (Frijda 1987). What it takes for men and women to achieve orgasm may be different, but once they get there, the experience may be much the same. When an individual is sufficiently aroused, at some point a neural switch flips and the parasympathetic branch of the autonomic nervous system kicks in, and he or she has an orgasm. When college students of both sexes wrote descriptions of their own orgasms, they wrote of experiencing tumescence and release as a physical experience. While reading the descriptions, the study's judges could not distinguish their gender.

> Feels like tension building up until you think it can't build up any more, then release. The orgasm is both the highest point of tension and the release almost all at the same time. Also feeling contractions in the genitals. Tingling all over. A heightened feeling of excitement with severe muscular tension especially through the back and legs, rigid straightening of the entire body for about 5 seconds, and a strong and general relaxation and very tired relieved feeling. (Komisaruk, et al. 2006, p. 5).

Just where in the brain ecstasy is produced remains an unanswered question. It is no easy task to induce people other than porn stars or other exhibitionists to stimulate themselves in the laboratory, where according to Komisiaruk and associates(Komisiaruk, et al. 2006), they must lie as still as possible inside a giant magnet during an MRI scan.

To my knowledge, there are not descriptions of sexually-triggered ecstasy in men found in the literature. In a meeting I can only describe as serendipitous, Joe, a male friend I had known for a long time but did not know very well, knew that I was writing a book about ecstasy. He began to think about an experience he had had many years before and wondered if it had been an ecstatic experience. Joe described himself as being happily married to his second wife. He also told me that being in control was extremely important to him. He told me about his involvement with a woman between his first and second marriages. One night, they were in bed together, having intercourse with Lydia sitting on top of him. He was stroking her clitoris when she hinged backward from the waist, hit the mattress and bounced right back up as if an electric current had gone through her. He recalled laughing an anxious laugh. Never before had he seen anyone so out of control. The next time he saw her, he said that she seemed determined to turn the tables on him, sucking his penis and stroking his thighs. At an earlier date at her house, he had watched her run after one of her dogs and thought "God, what a beautiful ass she has!" He loved the shape and feel of it and had enjoyed anal sex with her. But this evening, as he stood behind her in the kitchen and started kissing her neck, she began rubbing her buttocks against his crotch, getting him very worked up. "It blew my mind that she was doing so much to entice me." Suddenly he just lost control entirely. This was more than an orgasm; it was different. He described himself as being out of his mind; not crazy, but out of his mind. There was no separation between them; they were one. Time stopped but he did not know for how long. Then it was over. Joe drove her to the train station to catch her train home. As unusual as his ecstatic experience had been, what he felt afterward was even better. As he drove home alone, he marveled that he had never before felt so peaceful. "God was in His heaven, and all was right with the world." What had happened was sacred for Joe.

When I asked him what made this experience with Lydia so different for him than other times he had been with her or anyone else, he said that seeing her lose control so dramatically meant that she trusted him enough to do that, and he had been deeply moved. And then, the next time, her wanting so much to please him made him feel so special. He thought that these factors made it easier for him to lose all restraint and let himself go. (I could not help but think that driving her to the train station rather than just relaxing into a nice afterglow with her, then falling asleep together, is what a man who always has to feel in control might do. I also was amazed that Joe had told me something so personal and felt honored that he trusted me with it. Even more touching was his note of appreciation for helping him process what had occurred so many years ago.) This experience made me begin to wonder if there are more men than we think who, like women, need to feel very special and cared for in order for their orgasm to turn into ecstasy.

The vernacular for sexual arousal, "getting hot," refers to kindling, a metaphor in popular culture and literature. Eighteenth-century poet John Donne's poem "The Dissolution," refers to the kindling of the fire of passion, to the notion of kindling desire through various kinds of foreplay. So much writing about sex uses the kindling metaphor. Freud wrote in a letter to another physician ". . . I liken the relationship between clitoral and vaginal excitement to that between flammable soft wood or kindling, and hard wood that is difficult to ignite" (Zaretzsky 1999, p. 99). In a memoir of her twenty-year affair with disgraced financier Bernard Madoff, investor Sheryl Weinstein (2009) wrote that although he was not well-endowed, when they made love, she was on fire.

The ecstasy experienced in some sexual encounters is often described as being transported to another non-ordinary reality. The late John Mack, professor of psychiatry at Harvard and Pulitzer Prizewinning author, wrote two controversial books based on accounts by people who claim to have been abducted by aliens. He contends that our knowledge of reality is limited and needs to change; the rationalism of science alone cannot explain the alien abduction syndrome. In investigating traditional views of reality and their implications for humanity in view of the abduction phenomenon, he insists that the experience is "real" for them, in the same way that the spiritual journeys of shamans are real to them. In writing about the sexual encounters between human beings and aliens, he said "When they do participate directly in sexual acts with humans, the experience seems curiously odd or new to the alien creatures, and they may act awkwardly or like students needing to learn. At the same time, for the human beings involved, the experience can range from cold and bodiless to ecstatic, beyond what is known to them in earthly love" (Mack 2008, p. 20).

Andrea, one of the subjects interviewed by Mack, is a 45-year-old married woman and the mother of two daughters. She believes she is the parent of a beautiful boy, Kiran, who is the offspring of mating with a man in another dimension, a very sexually and emotionally powerful union. She recalled playing with her "extra-terrestrial" lover as a child, and thought he had been her partner in several lifetimes. Several months after starting to meet with Mack, she was able to speak in detail about one of her intimate encounters with the human/alien man.

> at first she could not see his face. This time he was naked and in human form, with a "very nice brown body" and skin that was somewhat darker than her. . . . as she moved closer to him, he moved closer to her. After the man relaxed, they held each other standing up, and some sort of "very subtle" vibration began all over their bodies. Then he had an erection, "and his body moved into mine," Andrea said. But it was not like regular intercourse, she explained. "It was better, and I'm remembering how much we cared for each other and that it lasted a lot longer." Although pleasurable sensations may have

> begun in the genital area, they spread throughout her body. No back-and-forth bodily movement, as in regular intercourse, occurred, as the vibration brought about a feeling of merging. It seemed to Andrea as if "you expand everything, and it goes into the universe, like enlightenment. . . His heart came into my heart, and I loved it," she said. The whole experience "opened up . . . my heart."
>
> Andrea told me that for the past two years her body had been vibrating every night, and that she had sometimes brought such intense energy to her lovemaking with her husband that it "blew us both away." It was, she thought, not a normal way of having sex or an orgasm.: "It was a total kaboom, like expansion" (Mack 2008, pp. 274-75).

As fascinating as the stories of alien abduction are, as thought-provoking the questions raised about the nature of reality, neurologist Kevin Nelson (2011) tells us that stories about alien abduction and extraterrestrial sexual encounters can be attributed to lucid dreaming REM intrusion. A London research team investigated a group of abductees and found that they had a high incidence of sleep paralysis and were psychologically prone to interpret their experiences as alien abduction (French, Santomauro, Hamilton, Fox, and Thalbourne 2008).

THE BRAIN DURING ECSTASY: A SPECULATION

In his novel *Middlesex*, Jeffrey Eugenides provides the words that capture what happens in the state of ecstasy. "Ecstasy. From the Greek *Ekstasis*. Meaning not what you think. Meaning not euphoria or sexual climax or even happiness. Meaning, literally: A state of displacement, of being driven out of one's senses" (Eugenides 2007, p. 374).

Because they have informed us so much about how the brain works, we expect so much of the neuroscientists but they will be the first to tell us that the brain does not easily yield its secrets. Whatever the realm of reality in which ecstasy occurs, as we learn more about what happens in the brain during arousal, orgasm, religious ecstasy, and out of body experiences, this may well open the door to understanding what happens in the brain in all states of ecstasy. whether attained through sex, pain, drugs, or speaking in tongues. Having learned about the borderlands of consciousness and how frequently they are linked with perceiving a bright light and feeling a sense of peace, I wonder if ecstatic states may be attributed in part to the mixing of REM and non-REM states (Nelson 2011) and/or to the spillover effect from the overactivation of the sympathetic or parasympathetic systems (Newberg and D'Aquili 2001). It seems likely that to attain a state of ecstasy, there occurs a kindling of tension, increasing and building, at the same time that the frontal and temporal lobe circuits governing fear and anxiety increasingly shut down. At the moment of ecstasy, probably no emotion is experienced, just sheer release from restraint.

"I CAN'T GET NO SATISFACTION"

The Rolling Stones song "I Can't Get No Satisfaction" was released in 1966, and in the same year they performed on *The Ed Sullivan Show*. The line about "trying to make some girl" was deleted by censors (Nuzum 2009). It is considered to be one of the great rock songs of all time and became a staple at their shows. Mick Jagger strutted around, belting out the sexually suggestive lyrics, saying he can't get any satisfaction no matter how hard he tries. In a 1995 interview Jagger said that this was the song that really made the Rolling Stones a legend, changing them from just another band into a hugely successful band. "It has a very catchy title. It has a very catchy guitar riff. It has a great guitar sound, which was original at that time. And it captures a spirit of the times, alienation, which is very important in those kinds of songs" (Shmoop 2004) Guitarist Keith Richards claimed that the song's riff could be heard in half of the songs that The Rolling Stones had produced.

It is a song about anger, alienation, and maddening frustration that speaks to the hearts of so many young people today as it did in the Sixties. When there is no satisfaction to be had, after trying and trying every which way to get it, what comes next is trying to find ways to obtain ecstatic release.

NOTES

1. Breuer believed that lying at the center of hysteria is a splitting off of a portion of psychic activity that is also a splitting of consciousness.
2. In other words, the elderly, who are acutely aware of their mortality, heed the expression, "Don't buy green bananas," the implication being that they may not live the few days it takes for them to ripen.

Chapter Four

The Sixties: Something Is Happening Here

> People today are still living off the table scraps of the sixties. They are still being passed around—the music and the ideas.
>
> —Bob Dylan, in *Dylan Now*, interview in the *Los Angeles Time Magazine* by R. Hilburn, 1992.

In his song "Ballad of a Thin Man," Bob Dylan asked the cryptic question about just *what* was happening in the sixties because it was all so unclear. Buffalo Springfield also sang about it. Writing about a different time, Charles Dickens put it differently in *A Tale of Two Cities,* but it could have been written about the sixties.

> It was the best of times, it was the worst of times, it was the age of wisdom, it was the age of foolishness, it was the epoch of belief, it was the epoch of incredulity, it was the season of Light, it was the season of Darkness, it was the spring of hope, it was the winter of despair, we had everything before us, we had nothing before us, we were all going direct to heaven, we were all going direct the other way. (Dickens 2010, p. 5)

The sixties were a confusing, exhilarating, depressing time and the after-shock resonates in our lives today. The year 1961 has been called the upside-down year; if you turn the number upside down, it still reads the same (Brokaw 2007). It was a time that turned our culture upside down. No one knew which end was up. In 1961 I was a freshman at Barnard, right across the street from Columbia, our "brother" school, living in a dormitory where there were few non-white students. We were allowed to entertain a man only in the first-floor parlor of the dorm; the door had to remain open and three of four feet had to be visible on the floor. Curfew was midnight. Coed dorms were unheard of. As far as sexual intercourse, nice girls didn't. Panty girdles could not be shed with abandon and so were pretty effective at preventing "going all the way." Never could I imagine that only a few years later I would hear Allen Ginsberg urge us "Throw away your underwear, you're free!" or that years later, a formerly gay bathhouse in New York would morph into Plato's Retreat, a club for swingers.

I graduated from high school on the fringe of the sixties and from college the year that the war in Vietnam broke out, before the riots at Columbia, before the sexual revolution. It was a basic assumption that just about everyone was heterosexual, and that drugs were something used by the poor and disadvantaged. Drinking was common but far more restrained than the drinking that goes on at colleges today. It felt more like the fifties than the sixties

THE LEGACY OF THE SIXTIES

The fifties was a decade marked by conformity, consumerism, political paranoia, and the recently discovered terror of global nuclear annihilation, The fifties saw the rise of the other-directed character—middle-class upwardly mobile businessmen and consumers for whom appearances were most important (Lattin 2010), captured so well in the HBO series *Mad Men*. The film *Howl*, structured around the obscenity trial brought against Lawrence Ferlinghetti in 1957 (Watson 1995), also captures it. This became a landmark case establishing a legal precedent guaranteeing First Amendment rights for other controversial literary works. It also brilliantly captures a pivotal moment—the birth of a counterculture.

The influence of the Beatles extended into the 1960s counterculture, in which flourished a new individualism and nonconformist mentality that would soon make itself felt in the psychedelic drug culture. There were stirrings of racial discontent. I became active in the Congress of Racial Equality (CORE), alarming my parents with my intentions of going on a Freedom Ride. President Kennedy was assassinated in 1963. Shortly before I graduated I heard Malcolm X give an electrifying speech at Barnard on "The Black Revolution and its Effects on the Negro of the Western Hemisphere." Just three days later, I was shocked to learn that he had been shot to death in the Audubon Ballroom in Washington Heights. Three of the men implicated had links to the very same mosque that Malcolm X had helped to establish. Fellow Muslims had turned on him for his willingness to work with whites in the civil rights movement. Mainstream religion declined as the Jesus Freaks spread the evangelical movement.

In the early sixties, Allen Ginsberg was intrinsic to the hippie scene; one of the few radical events that he was *not* a part of was the Stonewall gay uprising, and he showed up at the Stonewall Inn the following day to demonstrate his support. The U.S. involvement in Vietnam that escalated in the early 1960s became active combat in 1965, the year I graduated.

There was the Stone Age and then there was the Stoned Age, when illicit drugs, narcotics, amphetamines, cocaine, psychedelics, MDA (the love drug), MDMA (Ecstasy), and amyl nitrate (poppers) became as American as apple pie (Torgoff 2004). Martin Torgoff, author and documentary filmmaker, described it.

> Getting high wasn't just about having fun; it was about rebellion and bohemia and utopia and mysticism and so many other things that were being embroidered into the experience by the counterculture at that moment. It was about being young and strong and carefree and unafraid of anything, refusing to accept or even acknowledge limits of any kind. It was about ecstasy, rapture, the ethos of the party being exalted above all else—the kind of soaring, mind-bending, heart-breaking romanticism you can know only when you are eighteen and stoned and naked with a girl in a creek on a summer night, making love in the mud amidst the frogs and bulrushes under an umbrella of shooting stars. . . .
>
> On the beach, a seashell came alive in the very palm of my hand, containing within its ridged textures a diorama of aquatic life that included prehistoric fish and seahorses, images of Greek gods, and whole underwater civilizations. Thoughts reverberated in my head like feedback in a never-ending loop, pushing me toward questions whether I liked it or not: *Who Are You? Do You Like Who You Are? What Is God? What is Death? What Is Your Purpose Here On Earth?* And so it went for hours, a relentless Technicolor wraparound movie of existence generated by the brain, nervous system, and soul. When it was over, despite searing moments of the most inexpressible existential loneliness, I couldn't wait to trip again. I felt open, completely free, invincible, as if I would live forever. I was never more certain that all would be well in my pursuit of drug experience as long as I remained fearless, immune, and ready for all (Torgoff 2004, pp. 8-9).

After college graduation, I got a job as a counselor at an inpatient drug detoxification program at Manhattan General Hospital, in the same building where the Methadone Maintenance Research Program ran clinical trials and later became the Methadone Maintenance Treatment Program. I learned that pot was considered a "gateway drug", a stepping-stone to harder drugs such as heroin. The addicts filled all the beds in winter, when they could no longer sleep in alleys. They called it "three hots and a cot" (three meals a day and a bed). Despite this, they made heroin sound very seductive and were addicted not only to heroin and other drugs but to the trance state they would enter as they spoke of how they would "shoot up two nickel bags of horse, take a couple or so *bombitas,* then a bottle of Thunderbird" or advising, "No, man, *bombitas* aint worth shit; you take *cibas*, you are *gone*, out of *sight*. (Farber 2000, p. xvi)."[1] Some of my colleagues who spent their days, as I did, counseling the patients to help them complete the 28-day program, were getting high on their own time on pot and LSD. One of the female counselors became seduced by heroin and became addicted.[2]

When a new psychologist joined the staff, something about her seemed familiar; I asked if she was Anita Hoffman, wife of Abbie Hoffman. She was. I had recognized her from television footage I had seen of their wedding in Central Park, where they were married by the Boo Hoo of the Neo-American Church in 1967. It was the first marriage license issued to the church. Although both had master's degrees in psychology, Abbie had worked in a Massachusetts State Hospital before abandoning his career and starting the Youth International Party (Yippies) in 1967. He was one of the *Chicago Eight;* he had been arrested and stood trial for conspiracy and inciting to riot during the Democratic National Convention in 1968 (Jezer 1993). Only a few years later, Abbie became a fugitive. Having been arrested on a charge of selling cocaine to a police officer, and facing a mandatory sentence of 25 years to life imprisonment, he disappeared, leaving Anita broke, on welfare, and caring for their child. Their painfully honest correspondence, published as *Letters from the Underground* (Hoffman and Hoffman 2000), documents their struggle to keep a few steps ahead of FBI agents and bill collectors. Their relationship was doomed by circumstances. We see Anita's dissatisfaction with just being Abbie's wife, and at the same time wanting his approval for striking out on her own.

> I could believe in your love for me more if it was because I was such a great individual rather than a familiar glove. Don't try to hurt me in your letters and I won't try either. How can you be jealous of me when all the position I occupy in the world is because of you? I just want to do better than that so I can be proud of myself. Maybe then you will be too (Hoffman and Hoffman 2000, p. 10).
>
> Just being apart from you, I feel like I've filled in parts of myself that were missing. I can't lose them again, I don't think. The question is, do I want to live with you or without you? (Hoffman and Hoffman 2000, p. 82)

Her feelings echoed those of many women in the counterculture, whose role was the traditional one of supporting their man. One of them was Anne Roiphe, who was determined to become a writer, something which seemed so implausible to someone who graduated from college in the late fifties. The next best thing was to become the muse to male writers, sleeping with them and cooking for them even when they were sleeping with other women. In her twenties, her memoir *Art and Madness: A Memoir of Lust Without Reason* (Roiphe 2011), captures the strange mixture of Eisenhower values and her beatnik obsession with the artist. Roiphe wrote about the excess and the great irresponsibility toward children in that circle of artists and writers.

Anita Hoffman too wanted to be a writer but became a welfare activist, which excited her but left her with no time to write.

> It's right. It's right, what I'm doing. . . . The more I grow, the more I do, the better I become, the closer I feel to you. Sometimes I think I understand you in totally new ways. The ecstasy of writing well or playing out an idea and making it real, these are new for me, but you've always known them. I'll write more later. Just wanted to share my excitement with you. I feel like a baby who's taken her first step (Hoffman and Hoffman 2000, p. 106).
>
> The best thing I've ever read on the subject of women's liberation is Virginia Woolf's essay, "A Room of One's Own." She says "a woman must have money and a room of her own if she is to write fiction." Imagine what a ridiculous thing writing fiction is for a welfare mother! I think that's exactly what pushed me into organizing. I want to make it possible some day for women like me to become artists. (Hoffman and Hoffman 2000, p. 185)

Abbie wanted her to come and visit him but she was afraid that her activities were being monitored by the FBI and that she might unwittingly lead them to him. She was lonely, feeling often overwhelmed, and her feelings about sex were changing.

> O. K. Cheer-up Time. Rest Break. Fifteen minutes of sex discussion coming up. Been meaning to reply to you for days. You are hilarious. You are devastating. What can I say? We're at different places, that's all. See, most women plan their lives around men, usually the source of sex. Their self-image depends on ego-gratification from the affection of men. That is not a healthy state. Besides, I have responsibilities. I'm trying to learn about gratification from achievement. A new trip. So I compartmentalize my life and I push sex into a corner where it only means relief from the tension, a businessman's trip. It's actually a relief to be immune from the pangs of love, the exhausting illusions of Romance. I'm having friendships with men I've never had before because either of us are preoccupied with love or possession. We value the friendship and want to be liked for who we really are, so we're honest. Although I don't get out much, I did have a boyfriend about a month ago. We saw each other regularly for two months and then it just sort of dissolved with mutual boredom or because we weren't in love. I called him first, by the way, something I'm real proud of. We like each other and are still friends. Maybe the thing I enjoyed most about this relationship was that we weren't in love (Hoffman and Hoffman 2000, pp. 58-59).

Anita wrote about her ambivalent feelings about her son America, her deep love for him and her great desire to get away from him and live unencumbered. In 1980, Abbie surrendered, was given a one-year sentence, and was released after four months. He was diagnosed with bipolar disorder in the same year he and Anita divorced (Jezer 1993). Seven years later, he was one of fifteen arrested for trespassing at the University of Massachusetts Amherst campus. The charges were associated with a protest against the CIA's recruitment on the campus. Many defense witnesses described the CIA's role in over two decades of secret, illegal, and often violent activities. Hoffman acted as his own attorney, and in his closing argument said his actions were within the best tradition of American civil disobedience. He and the other defendants were found not guilty (Jezer 1993).

Abbie was in conflict with the psychiatrists who wanted him to take lithium, a mood stabilizer; like many others who refuse to take mood-stabilizing mediation, he loved his manic highs, and stopped taking it. After an unsuccessful suicide attempt, he died of suicide in 1989, surrounded by many pages of his handwritten notes, many about his own wildly changing moods. Anita died of breast cancer in 1998.

But back to the end of the sixties, when I met Anita. At this time, there was a much harder edge to the drug scene and to the whole counterculture. Young people from all over the country flocked to the Haight-Ashbury in San Francisco. Many were runaways, and many of the girls were ensnared by pimps. The Maharishi Mahesh Yogi, founder of Transcendental Meditation (TM), achieved fame as the guru to the Beatles, offering TM as a way to achieve “cosmic consciousness” without drugs. Martin Luther King was assassinated in April 1968; two months later Bobby Kennedy was assassinated. Charles Manson had established himself as a guru in the Haight, and in 1969, the same year as the Stonewall riots, we were stunned by the news of the Tate/LaBianca murders by the Manson Family (Bugliosi 1974). The word *family* was starting to take on an ominous tone. We would hear more about a different cult, The Family, also known as the Children of God, and about other cults that sexually abused members, adults and children alike. A week after the Manson murders, when I was working for the Travelers Aid Society at the Port Authority Bus Terminal in Manhattan, a couple arrived having hitched their way from the Woodstock festival. Their money had been stolen there and they needed money to get home. Their opinion of Woodstock: “Peace and love? Bullshit!” Many lives were lost during the sixties revolution. The era of peace and love was also an era of hatred, with the Weather Underground throwing bombs. For Timothy Leary, it was the beginning of a long downhill slide. He was in and out of prison and began using heroin.

When I worked in the drug detoxification program, it certainly seemed unfair to me that the female counselors were paid at a lesser rate than the male counselors but that’s just the way it was. It never occurred to me to question it. Female consciousness-raising had not yet begun full force. I was exposed to it a few years later, while studying for my Masters in Social Work degree. My field placement supervisor at University Settlement on New York’s lower east side, when it was a poor, largely Hispanic neighborhood, was Rosalyn Baxandall, a founding member of a radical feminist group known as Women’s International Terrorist Conspiracy from Hell, also known as W.I.T.C.H. There was a lot that Ros and I did not see eye to eye about but did not talk about. W.I.T.C.H. had broken away from New York Radical Women, which crowned a sheep as Miss America in 1968, to protest that women were paraded around in bikinis like pieces of meat at the pageant. W.I.T.C.H representatives spoke only to female reporters and created a "freedom trash can" where they burned their bras, girdles, pots and pans and other feminine paraphernalia. It was all over the news. The problem was that because I did not have my own office, I had to meet with my clients in Rosalyn's office, where the walls were plastered top to bottom with W.I.T.C.H. posters. I did not want to use it that way but there was no other room to use. My solution was far from ideal but it was all I could think of. I thumbtacked newspapers over the posters before meetings, then removed them when they were gone. It must have seemed quite strange to these poor neighborhood residents, more concerned about welfare checks, health care, and survival, who did not have the luxury for such concerns. But it was not nearly as strange as the culture-shock of the W.I.T.C.H. posters. I doubt that Ros ever knew what I had done. She went on to become coauthor of *Dear Sisters: Dispatches from The Women's Liberation Movement* (Baxandall and Gordon 2001).

Even after getting my master's degree in social work, when I worked at the Rusk Institute for Rehabilitation Medicine at New York University Medical Center, the physician in charge called the women by their first names but expected us to address him as Dr. He was accustomed to patting the female physical therapists on their rears and they tolerated it. At Fordham Hospital's Department of Psychiatry, the male head of the department made suggestive remarks to me and other female clinical staff members. The very concept of sexual harassment had not yet been born. That's just the way it was.

There were angry protests on university campuses, provoking violent confrontations between police and demonstrators at the Democratic convention in Chicago. Tom Hayden was part of the violence at Columbia University in 1968 when around 1,100 students, members of Students for a Democratic Society (SDS), took over buildings, and were beaten, pounded bloody with nightsticks, and were arrested (Kifner 2008). Not even a year later, SDS split up and some became part of the much more radical Weathermen organization. Forty years later, around 500 of the SDS gathered at Columbia for a reunion, and were welcomed by Lee Bollinger, then Columbia president. Those who showed up were professors, teachers, poets, writers, musicians, lawyers and a few judges.

In 1968, we launched Apollo II and watched astronauts walk on the moon. But before then, in the early sixties, three brilliant scholars—Timothy Leary, Richard Alpert (later known as Ram Dass), Huston Smith—and one ambitious freshman, Andrew Weil, crossed paths at a Harvard psychedelic drug research project, and became some of the most important influences not only on the counterculture but on today's culture as well (Lattin 2010).

> "Sometime in the 1990s, American culture caught up with the counterculture. The counterculture became the culture. Yoga became big business. Meditation is prescribed by the family doctor. Supermarkets stock organic produce and homeopathic cures. The Rolling Stones provide the soundtrack for computer advertisements, and Dennis Hopper promotes corporate retirement funds on network TV (Lattin 2010, p. 183). Leary and Ram Dass came to represent exploration of consciousness expansion, Leary through psychedelics while Ram Dass's explorations were through the message of mindfulness (1971). As he aged and became severely disabled, he spreads the message that the wisdom we have developed can help us accept change, aging, and dying (Dass 2000). Then and now, religion classes in many colleges require students to read Huston Smith's books on world religion. Andrew Weil has become one of today's gurus of alternative medicine and nutrition.

Many children of the sixties joined communes. Some went to India and returned with some central truth that helped them live better lives. But many had been crippled by the psychedelic culture. Some joined cults, allowing a narcissistic leader to take control of their lives. Many became baby-boomer parents, raising their children as equal partners in a democratic process, losing sight of boundaries and discipline in the process. Today, soldiers from the war in Iraq come home with post-traumatic stress disorder, like the Vietnam vets before them. And today a man who is the product of a black African father and a white American mother is president of the United States, something that could not have happened were it not for the sixties.

The sixties fostered an ethos of pleasure and individualism, often expressed through rebellious group-think slogans that fostered a lack of thoughtfulness, even an injunction against thinking. Open *The Psychedelic Experience: A Manual Based on the Tibetan Book of the Dead* (Leary, Metzner and Alpert 1964) and you'll read that whenever you are in doubt, just turn off your mind, relax, and float downstream. John Lennon wrote the lyrics to a song in the Beatles album *Revolver* while listening to a recording of himself reading from *The Tibetan Book of the Dead* while tripping on LSD. The lyrics told people to turn off their minds and surrender to the void. Turning off one's mind in order to relax or meditate is one thing, but turning it off altogether is another. Whether the message is the fifties message of conformity or the sixties message of individuality, following blindly without thinking for oneself makes for what Freud (1921) called a primal horde.

LIFE SHOULD BE ECSTASY

> Life should be ecstasy. —Allen Ginsberg

Allen Ginsberg grew up in Paterson, New Jersey, the child of parents who shared bohemian interests and leftist beliefs. His father Louis, a high school teacher and poet with a way with words wrote in a newspaper column "If at first you don't succeed, try a little ardor. Is life worth living? It depends on the liver" (cited by Watson1995, p. 27). His mother Naomi taught disadvantaged children and was a social activist until the mysterious symptoms of schizophrenia appeared seven years before she gave birth to Allen. She had a revolving door course of hospitalizations, more than forty treatments of insulin shock, electroshock, and convulsive treatment with Metrazol at the at Greystone and Pilgrim State hospitals. Ginsberg was desperate to get his mother's violent behavior under control in order to stop the shock treatments, and so he consented to having a lobotomy performed on her. She died in 1956. Ginsberg chronicled the experience of watching his mother's continued mental decline in his poem *Kaddish.*

As he grew up his motto became "Do what you want to when you want to (cited by Watson 1995, p. 23)." And he lived that way, writing what he wanted, loving whom he wanted, and living a homosexual life. At Columbia University, which had one of the country's leading English departments, he fell in with a wild crowd, which included fellow students Lucien Carr and Jack Kerouac and non-students William S. Burroughs and Neal Cassidy (Jezer 1993).

In 1948, in the shadow of the atomic bomb, Allen Ginsberg heard a ghostly voice reciting a poem by William Blake, then had a vision of the sky as "the living blue hand itself" (Baker 2008, p. 19). We might wonder whether this was a vision or hallucination? Some of the beats who were regarded as visionaries (Jack Kerouac, Neal Cassady, Carl Solomon) had serious mental conditions. And so began his quest for beatitude that sent him to India and Japan, changing his life and generating several generations of beatniks, hipsters, artists and writers, gurus, shamans, cult leaders, and the mentally ill (Baker 2008; Watson 1995). "The point of Beat," said Ginsburg, "is that you get beat down to a certain nakedness where you actually are able to see the world in a visionary way . . ." (Watson 1996, p.4).

When he was arrested in a stolen car filled with stolen goods, his apartment was filled with opium pipes and other drug paraphernalia. To avoid prison, Ginsberg's mentors at Columbia, Lionel Trilling and Mark van Doren, advised him to plead insanity. He did and while waiting to be admitted to Columbia Presbyterian's Psychiatric Institute, met Carl Solomon, who became the inspiration for *Howl* (Watson 1995). He had 2-3 times a week psychoanalytic psychotherapy at Psychiatric Institute, where his therapists insisted on his ordinariness, denied his gift as a poet, and prescribed that he conform to the legal and sexual rules of America. He was discharged in 1950, resolving that he would start a new life—he would get a job, would have no more homosexual affairs, and would have sexual relationships with women. (Watson 1995). He planned to write poetry that showed a more ordered vision of the real world. His resolve did not last long. He pursued his vision, trying to recapture the transfiguring moment when he heard the voice of William Blake. He tried this through drugs, conducting his major drug experiment with Timothy Leary at Harvard in 1960, taking psycilocybin mushrooms, ayahuasca and LSD.

Ginsberg's search for spirituality shifted to the public arena of counter-culture politics. Ginsberg foresaw the hippies, the sexual revolution, and the eastern meditative influence and became the most iconic figure of the sixties. The practice of yoga from India and Tibet has found its way into Western culture. Mindfulness, a practice in the Buddhist tradition, is being used increasingly in the treatment of a number of mental and physical conditions, including obsessive-compulsive disorder and other anxiety disorders and in relapse prevention in depression and drug addiction. A number of therapeutic applications based on mindfulness have developed, including Morita Therapy, gestalt therapy, adaptation practice, mindfulness-based cognitive therapy, acceptance and commitment therapy, dialectical behavior therapy, Hakim, and internal family systems therapy.

In 1968 when Ginsberg declared that life should be ecstasy, the culture responded with sex, drugs, and rock and roll. "If it feels good, do it" became the rallying cry that remains embedded in our culture. When Leary left Harvard, he began urging young people to "tune in, drop out, and turn on." Some tripped so far out on hallucinogenic drugs that they could not return. The Beatles, who were taught Transcendental Meditation by the Maharishi Mahesh Yogi, also sang the words "Hare Krishna" in several of their songs, making both cults simply part of the colorful popular scene. With the culture's tolerance of what was new and strange, the Jesus Freaks, The Way International, the Hasidic Chabad Lubavitchers, and new religious movements also found their place in the sun.

GENERATIONS X AND Y

> I start to get the feeling that something is really wrong. Like all the drugs put together—the lithium, the Prozac, the desipramine, and Desyrel that I take to sleep at night—can no longer combat whatever it is that is wrong with me in the first place. I feel like a defective model, like I came off the assembly-line flat-out fucked, and my parents should have taken me back for repairs before the warranty ran out.—Elizabeth Wurtzel, *Prozac Nation*

Many who came of age in the 1960s have raised a generation of children who expect that they should be "blissed out" all the time, and so for some, getting high has become a way of life. Youth culture has embraced hookah (water pipe) lounges, where patrons share flavored tobacco from a communal hookah in the same way that pot or hashish is shared. In 1994 the second Woodstock Festival was held in Saugerties, New York, a silver anniversary celebration (Torgoff 2005). The smell of pot was everywhere and LSD was passed around. The use of illicit drugs had been passed to a whole new generation as part of a cultural search for identity and rite of passage. Miley Cyrus, former child star of *Hannah Montana*, became the poster child for *Salvia divinorum*, a powerful hallucinogenic that had been used by shamans in Oaxaca, Mexico (Detrick 2010). Shortly after her eighteenth birthday, a video surfaced on the Internet showing her laughing uncontrollably, her speech jumbled, with salvia and a bong. In the past decade, salvia dinorum, meaning divining sage, has become quite popular and is causing much controversy, with several states banning the herb, and the Drug Enforcement Administration calling it a drug of concern. Nonetheless, some researchers think that studying the effects of salvia could be useful in understanding Alzheimer's disease, cocaine addiction, and chronic pain, providing therapeutic benefits.

Although Bob Dylan had never publicly acknowledged his drug experiences and denied that lyrics referring to taking trips on magic ships had anything to do with drugs (Torgoff 2004), he sang that everyone must get stoned. Many baby boomers who used psychedelics in the sixties and seventies still do, and some even smoke pot with their kids. Others may still do it but, like Dylan, do not talk about it publicly or acknowledge it to their curious adolescent children. When their kids ask if they ever used drugs when they were younger, they often don't know what to say.

Several such parents have consulted with me about this dilemma. I remind them that they were older than their kids are now when they began using psychedelics, which means that their brains had developed further than their kids' brains had. This means that the younger an adolescent is when starting to use pot, the more opportunity there is for the drug to interfere negatively with brain development (Strauch 2004; Schweinsburg, Brown, and Tapert, 2008). Parents can still be truthful and yet convey a thoughtful message that their children can think about.

Many baby boomers are disturbed to find that not only are their children drifting, but that some are looking for ecstasy—not only in the ways their parents did—but also in ways their parents never imagined.

For some, a hovering threat of annihilation pre-dated September 11, 2001, while for others it began after. And child neglect, abuse, and other trauma have created a generation of children who have developed with an impoverished sense of self-worth and chronic anxiety. Taking Prozac or similar antidepressants became common as the acid generation morphed into the Prozac generation. Lauren Slater said "My generation, of course, is the Prozac generation, and no generation can be complete without a record of the substances that have irrevocably altered it" (Slater 1998, p. 25). We are also seeing increasing numbers of children who cannot sustain attention, regulate their anger, and moderate their pain, giving rise to the term *Dysregulation Nation* (Warner 2010).

DYSREGULATION NATION AND THE CULTURE OF NARCISSISM

Self-esteem problems seem more prevalent now than fifty years ago. When food, drugs, or alcohol no longer do the trick, people look for other ways to find release. No wonder that at the end of the millennium, many were convinced that the End Times were near, and were preparing to be "raptured" up to heaven.

Jimmy Carter was in the first year of his presidency when *The Culture of Narcissism* (Lasch 1979) was published. Carter publicly endorsed the book in his well-known "national malaise" speech. Lasch contends that America has produced a society that is self-absorbed, but not self-aware, a society that depends on consumerism, opinion polls, demographic studies, and government to define itself. In a narcissistic culture, it is easy for material objects to bolster a defective sense of self, at least for awhile, but ultimately, many find themselves living in a culture where everything tastes good but nothing satisfies. At the end of the 1990s, PBS aired a one-hour television program called *Affluenza*, documenting the the American culture of materialism, defining *affluenza* as a contagious social affliction in which possessions take over our lives.

Today therapists are not seeing so many patients with neurotic difficulties but more people with self-esteem problems, who struggle to bolster their sense of self with drugs, alcohol, sex, food (or lack of), compulsive shopping and spending, whose relationship with things is far more intimate than their relationships with other human beings. They have what has been called a hunger disease (Battegay 1991), referring to "the emotional problems based on lack of self-esteem, in which people are driven to possess and consume people and/or things in an addictive manner" (Farber 2000, p. 324). Ironically, the term *hunger disease* is apt for what Dr. David A. Kessler, the former FDA commissioner, has charged the American food and advertising industries with creating (Kessler 2010). Kessler has charged the food and advertising industries with deliberately creating lifestyle changes that bypass the body's own self-regulating system, making people overeat the very foods that contribute to obesity and other illness—salt, fat, and sugar.

In *Affluenza: The All-Consuming Epidemic* (De Graff, Wann, and Naylor 2005), the authors point out that there are twice as many shopping centers as high schools in the United States (Frost and Steketee 2010). Increasing numbers of rental self-storage units, almost non-existent forty years ago, cater to an insatiable appetite for belongings.

Narcissism is at epidemic proportions in the United States, claim Drs. Jean M. Twenge and W. Keith Campbell (2009), with scores on narcissm rising faster in the 2000s than previously. By 2006, 25 percent of college students agreed with most of the items on a standard measure of narcissistic traits. The diagnosis of Narcissistic Personality Disorder, the more severe version of the trait, has become more common than ever. The narcissism epidemic, with its often unattainable standards of physical beauty, has hit young girls the hardest, but it seems to have affected our whole culture, notably the Wall Street greed that has sparked the Occupy Wall Sttreet movement as well as the mortgage crisis with its extravagant sense of materialism and entitlement.

At the same time that narcissism is rising, empathy seems to be declining, with an especially steep drop in the past ten years. With a decline in empathy, sociopathy increases, a story told by T. Byram Karasu (2011) in *Gotham Chronicles*, his moving exploration of the life of a traumatized, deeply troubled young woman suffering from a severely disturbed sense of self and difficult relations with others. Drawn into a harsh and corrupt culture, she too becomes harsh and corrupt.

LIKE A MOTHERLESS CHILD

Traditionally adolescents who came of age felt a sense of pride in becoming part of the community of adults, but for so many kids today, this is no longer the case. The main developmental tasks of adolescence are to say good-bye to childhood and begin forging an autonomous personal and sexual identity (Blos 1962, 1967). Young people need a measure of freedom along with certain boundaries from adults. Kids need adults to help them navigate these developmental tasks but today so many adolescents are more isolated from adults than ever before and far more unsupervised. It was Polly Adler, a famous madam, who said that a house is not a home.

Until the economic crisis hit, most parents held full-time jobs and often did not return home until seven or eight o'clock or later. Even now, whether they are still working or have been laid off, many parents are so anxious and distraught about what the future holds that they fail to supervise their children. Whether it is unsupervised Friday and Saturday night partying or week day afternoons and evenings, these kids can readily get drunk or high or engage in sexual activity in their homes with their parents having no inkling about what is going on.

Most parents did not know what the term *hooking up* meant. If they had ever heard of it, most thought it meant meeting someone. But in 2000, most

American kids over the age of nine knew it referred to a sexual experience, varying greatly in terms of the nature and extent of what they did. Before this, American girls used baseball terminology with *first base* meaning embracing and kissing; *second base* meaning groping, fondling, and deep or French kissing, what earlier generations knew as *heavy petting. Third base* meant fellatio, usually known by the vague term "oral sex" and *home plate* meant sexual intercourse, otherwise known as *going all the way.* But then in the era of hooking up, the definitions changed. *First base* meant deep kissing ("tonsil hockey"), groping, and fondling; *second base* meant oral sex; *third base* meant going all the way, and *home plate* meant learning each other's names.

> In the year 2000, girls used "score" as an active verb indicating sexual conquest. In the twentieth century, only boys used "score" in that fashion. The continuing vogue of feminism had made sexual life easier, even insouciant, for men. Women had been persuaded that they should be just as active as men when it came to sexual advances.
>
> With the onset of puberty, males were able to get sexual enjoyment so easily, so casually, that junior high schools as far apart geographically and socially as the slums of the South Bronx and Washington's posh suburbs . . . began reporting a new discipline problem. Thirteen-and fourteen-year old girls were getting down on their knees and fellating boys in corridors and stairwells during the two-minute break between classes. . . .
>
> The President of the United States at the time used to have a twenty-two-year-old girl . . come around to his office for fellatio. He later testified under oath that he never "had sex" with her. Older Americans tended to be shocked, but junior high school, high-school, and college students understood completely what he was saying and wondered what on earth all the fuss was about. The two of them had merely been on second base, hooking up (Wolfe 2000, pp. 7-8).

If anything, "sexual revolution" was rather a prim term for the lurid carnival actually taking place in the mightiest country on earth in the year 2000. Every magazine stand was a riot of bare flesh, rouged aurolae, moistened cervices, and stiffened giblets: boys with girls, girls with girls, boys with boys, bare-breasted female body builders, so-called boys with breasts, riding backseat behind steroid-gorged bodybuilding bikers, naked except for cache-sexes and Panzer helmets, on huge chromed Honda or Harley-Davidson motorcycles.

The word "pornography" had disappeared down the memory hole along with "proletariat." Instances of breaking up because of Web-sex addiction were rising in number. The husband . . . would sit in front of the computer for twenty-four or more hours at a stretch. Nothing that the wife could offer him in the way of sexual delights or food could compare with the one-handing he was doing day and night as he sat before the PC and logged on to such images as a girl with bare breasts and a black leather corset standing with one foot on the small of a naked boy's back, brandishing a whip.

In 1999, the year before, this particular sexual kink—sadomasochism—had achieved not merely respectability but high chic, and the word "perversion" had become as obsolete as "pornography" and "proletariat" (Wolfe 2000, p. 5).

Some girls feel so competitive about giving good "head" to boys that many will get their tongue pierced with a metal stud because it makes oral sex even more pleasurable for the boy. Despite using their sexuality to become "popular," they may be called sluts by their peers. Dressed in the shortest skirts and showing lots of cleavage, girls dress seductively, with many parents feeling that they cannot or should not do anything about it because "they all dress like that." In the area where I live, a Smut List was posted online, naming nearly 100 girls from eight high schools known for hooking up. By the time it had been taken down, a day after it was posted, more than 7000 people had read it and endorsed the site. This is part of the fallout of the sexual revolution. So is *sexting,* sending sexually explicit images or text messages by phone, which has become disturbingly common. The aftermath of the sixties was that girls could behave like boys sexually and yet were expected to offer themselves up for their sexual pleasure. Human sacrifice is alive and well in America.

A few years ago a fifteen-year-old girl was referred to me after she was discharged from a psychiatric hospital, following a suicide gesture. Feeling uncared for by her divorced parents, she wanted more than anything to become popular with boys. She filmed herself masturbating, and sent it to a boy in her school that she liked. He was only too glad to reciprocate in kind, sending her a film of himself masturbating. The films ended up circulating in cyberspace, and the group of girls she wanted to be part of turned on her and ostracized her. Finally her parents were informed by the school. They became enraged with her, prompting the suicide gesture.

In *Reviving Ophelia: Saving the Selves of Adolescent Girls,* Mary Pipher (1994) asked why so many girls are in therapy in the 1990s and why are there more self-mutilators? "With all the sexual freedom, girls today are much more oppressed, coming of age in a much more dangerous, sexualized, and media-saturated culture. As they navigate a more dangerous world, girls are less protected . . . America today limits girls' development, truncates their wholeness and leaves many of them traumatized" (Pipher 1994, p. 12).

It is not only girls' development that is impaired by casual sex. For both girls and boys, physical intimacy is just part of the adolescent terrain, but emotional intimacy is something unknown. Far too easily, love can become just another corny word. The capacity to develop satisfying love relationships and friendships is arrested at a level which many do not rise above. And parents remain in the dark while all this is happening. Resigned to the attitude that adolescents live in a tribe apart, too many adults are leaving kids on their own, neglected and unprotected (Hersch 1998).

> All over the country the pattern is the same, the gathering up of young people, the leaving of adults to separate worlds, not to be brought together again until evening. Briefcases, diaper bags and backpacks, the totems of modern society, are lined up ready to grab as family members dash outside with a fleeting hope that they are adequately prepared for the day. Front doors open and shut, families disperse, rush, rush, rushing to get going, to get there—wherever—on time. Nobody stands at the door and waves at anybody else—everybody is on the run. By 8:30 A.M., neighborhoods stand still and silent, hollow monuments to family life (Hersch 1998, p. 11).

NEGLECTED AND UNPROTECTED

> I'm nobody! Who are you?
> Are you nobody, too?
> —Emily Dickinson, *The Complete Poems*

Whether they are devout Christians or frank unbelievers, many young people today, seem to identify with a wounded, bleeding, and emaciated Jesus (Farber 2003). Even a mass murderer can identify with Jesus. Cho Seung-Hui, who murdered 32 people at Virginia Tech in 2007, compared himself to Christ, nailed to the cross. Like breathing air and drinking water, these gory images have been absorbed in the minds and hearts of those who have been mistreated, neglected, or abused by their parents. Some may be conscious of it, others not. Jesus is said to have cried out on the cross: "*Eli, Eli lama sabachtani,*" interpreted as "My God, my God, why hast thou forsaken me" (Mark 15: 34; Matthew 27: 46). Even in the rock opera *Jesus Christ Superstar,* Jesus feels betrayed by God, his father. He demands to know why God chose to sacrifice him, and accuses him of murder. It is no wonder, then, that many children who have been neglected or abused seem to identify with Jesus as an unwilling sacrifice.

If it takes a village to raise a child, as the old African proverb says, then too many of our adolescent and pre-adolescent children are coming home to deserted villages. Feeling neglected and unprotected, many teens experience their lives in fragmented episodes, without a sense of continuity or future., Some are poor, some are middle-class, and some are "poor little rich kids," who feel like waifs and are drawn to the styles and practices associated with marginal groups—hip-hop culture, homosexuality, and sadomasochism. Listen to the lyrics to many of their popular songs and you will hear that they are about abuse, violence, and traumatic loss—Tori Amos' experience of having been sexually abused, Madonna's abandonment by her father, to mention only a few. They cultivate an ability to space out so as not to feel the pain, sometimes assisted by alcohol and drugs. The more necessary it is to dissociate, the easier it becomes to do so, even to the point of it happening automatically. Dissociation has been aptly called "the escape when there is no escape (Putnam 1992, p. 104)."

GROUP INITIATION RITES AND ECSTASY

> For he today that sheds his blood with me shall be my brother.
> —William Shakespeare

Kids are creating their own villages, tribes, and families, a complex culture of unrivaled freedom having rules but no structure, standards but no clear morality, codes but none that are consistent (Hersch 1998). Huddling together, they take care of each other in the ways they know best—with pot, other drugs, alcohol, and sex. Mythologist Joseph Campbell (1972) said that if societies do not create difficult rites of passage for adolescents to go through, they will create them for themselves, inventing all sorts of dangerous tests. They have created their own rites of passage to initiate newcomers into the tribe. The "elders," hardly more than children themselves, initiate the youngest and least experienced. Increasingly, these rites may be cutting, burning or starving themselves, bingeing and purging, extensive body piercing and tattooing, all of which feel less lonely, even normal, when done with others. Not only do these practices connect them to the tribe, they also help troubled people feel better.

And sometimes they can create states of ecstasy. As adolescence increasingly has fewer rites of passage, these behaviors have come to fill the void. In a society in which relationships are transient, marked by divorce, abandonment, foster placement, and repeated moves and relocations, scars and permanent body markings can create a tough, thick skin to ward off the pain.

Ever since Pink Floyd's *Dark Side of the Moon* was released in 1973 it has been uniquely successful among rock recordings. Its theme was the narrator's slow relentless descent into madness, including episodes of self-mutilation, overdoses, and suicide attempts. At concerts, there are mosh pits—masses of mostly teenagers and twenty-somethings who flail their arms and slam into each other. Some mosh pits accommodate diving from the stage into the pit and "body surfing," riding the wave of bodies. Moshing is very exciting to many teens and quite dangerous, which seems to be part of its appeal. "I've been hurt, but it's cool. That's what it's about. It's about getting in there and bangin' some heads."

In *A Bright Red Scream*, Marilee Strong (1998) wrote about Melanie, who like many kids, wanted a big happy family and sense of community, She tried to bring her family together by planning dinners and family outings, trying to gather everybody in the living room on Thursday nights to spend time together. She even got them to try family therapy. Melanie is 16. Her attempts to create some family togetherness all failed. "I hardly ever see my father," says Melanie's sister Jennifer, who herself started cutting herself a year ago. "The most we ever usually say is hi. We rarely even eat together. I usually just stay in my room. But Melanie was always big on trying to get everybody together, planning dinners and family outings. For awhile she tried to get everybody to spend time together in the living room on Thursday nights. We even tried family counseling but the minute we got home things were back to the way they were" (Strong 1998, p. 4).

Melanie cuts her wrist with a razor, even carved pictures and words into her arms and legs, burned herself with cigarettes, and in a perverse kind of irony, even burned a happy face symbol on her arm. Lots of the kids Melanie collects like stray cats do the same. Surrounding herself with them provides Melanie with a sense of community and a path to discover who she is, what she wants to be, and what she does not want to be. She said that she doesn't want to be dead; she doesn't want to be a junkie, she doesn't want to be homeless. "I just want to get my shit together so I can do something with myself where I'm happy" (Strong 1998, p. 5). But despite this, her tribe of strays is not enough. She has made several suicide attempts.

When individuals come together in a group and witness a member in the throes of ecstasy, whether it be by means of cutting, religious fervor, or anything else, it makes it much easier for each to lose their inhibitions and act impulsively on very primitive, often destructive instincts (Freud 1921). When ecstasy is experienced as a group, it is a far more intense experience than when alone. The behavior, whatever it may be, serves as a primitive form of communication among people who have difficulty expressing their feelings verbally. The drama, intensity and "more real than life" quality of the experience cements the bond between members, making more ordinary group experiences pale in comparison. It also sets the group apart from others. What often develops is a perverse pleasure in violating taboos and reversing the status hierarchy by destroying traditional values to create a new anarchy, a new "normal" in which the member who is not caught up in this contagion seems deviant (Farber 2000).

WHEN LIFE BECOMES ECSTASY

Those who came of age in the 1960s remember that for Allen Ginsberg and Ram Dass, the sacred was to be found in Buddhist immersion in the moment. Today this practice is known as mindfulness—being present and aware, here and now. When meditation is practiced to the extreme, these states of mind may become ecstasies, and that is what Ginsberg espoused: "Life should be ecstasy," Ginsberg (2001) says and poetry, he implies, should be life. And so the mantras, "if it feels good, do it" and "sex, drugs, and rock and roll" inspired the happenings, be-ins, protests and hedonism which characterized the sexual and cultural revolution that has become embedded in our culture.

We live today in America at a time marked by a deep hunger for spirituality that is far more important than doctrine, rhetoric, or meaning. People want transcendent experiences, in which their boundaries dissolve, and they become one with others and experience an uplifting sense of oneness with something larger than themselves. It may be a calm, peaceful experience and can happen through just looking at a sunset or it can occur within a religious context. For those who do not feel comfortable in their own skins, these more ordinary transcendent moments are not enough, and they hunger for something more extreme that will jolt them out of themselves and heighten their senses—the rhythm of drumming, songs sung, tambourines played, bodies swaying, affirming a sense of community. Once ecstasy is experienced, the hunger for it can grow and grow. Like an addiction to drugs or alcohol, it can take on a life of its own, at the razor's edge. Teetering at the edge, one can fall into an abyss from which there may be no return.

NOTES

1. A nickel bag of horse is drug slang for a $5 bag of heroin. Bombitas are a mix of heroin and cocaine. Thunderbird is a brand of cheap wine. Ciba is the name for the prescription drugs Doriden and Dilaudid, manufactured by Ciba-Geigy.

2. (For a fascinating look at the key figures in the Chicago conspiracy trial and how their lives unfolded subsequently, go to this link: http://odysseytheatre.com/current_season/images/Chicago/Chicago%20Trial%20insert.pdf.)

Chapter Five

Marketing and Producing Ecstasy

When Allen Ginsburg said that life should be ecstasy, it seemed revolutionary but it was really nothing new. Since the beginning of time, people have used mind-altering substances and behaviors in search of altered states. Whether they are producing and selling illegal drugs, or producing and selling ecstatic worship, they have developed the means of marketing and producing ecstasy.

A SEPARATE REALITY

As Aldous Huxley lay dying, he took 100 micrograms of LSD to pave the way to a different experience of death. It has been proven that LSD and other hallucinogens have a serotonergic basis of action, reinforcing the idea that serotonin (5-HT), the feel-good brain chemical, was an important neurotransmitter (Nichols 2004). He'd had ample opportunity to experience how good he felt on psychedelics; perhaps he knew that feeling good while dying might help him welcome death, serving as his manic defense. That was in 1963.

More recently, clinical trials by researchers such as Charles Grob and others found that administering magic mushrooms (psilocybin) or other hallucinogens to patients who knew they were terminally ill could reduce their fear of death (Slater 2012). Huxley had led the way in exploring altered states, describing his experiences in *The Doors of Perception*, first published in 1954 (Huxley 2009). The rock band *The Doors* was named after the book. Timothy Leary's and Richard Alpert's experiences in a Harvard psychedelic drug research project radically changed not only their lives but the culture at large. Huxley happened to be lecturing at MIT, heard about Leary, and introduced him to his friend, Huston Smith, a philosophy professor and religion scholar at MIT, who also joined the psychedelic crusade. By this time, Alpert had become disillusioned with academia, and Leary had Already left the university some weeks earlier. They were formally dismissed from Harvard in 1963, Leary for leaving Cambridge and his classes without permission or notice, and Alpert for giving psilocybin to an undergraduate. Having conducted ongoing experiments with LSD, psilocybin, and DMT (dimethyltryptamine), Timothy Leary advocated for the healing and spiritual benefits of psychedelics,. He was certain that they would revolutionize the practice of psychology. Alpert went to India, returning as Baba Ram Dass to lead the counterculture. He coauthored the bestseller, *The Psychedelic Experience: A Manual Based on the Tibetan Book of the Dead*, (Leary, Metzger, and Albert 1964), which became known as the hippie Bible, extolling psychedelics and meditation. In the next few years, there was greater consumption and abuse of LSD. The drug that had once been touted as instant nirvana was then portrayed as a dire threat to the mental health of an entire generation. Probably, the truth lay somewhere in between. Then in the early 1970s, a whole generation became captivated by a series of best-selling books written by Peruvian-born Carlos Castaneda, a former UCLA anthropology student. In *The Teachings of Don Juan*, Castaneda (1972) told extraordinary stories about his apprenticeship with a Yaqui Indian shaman in Mexico, which taught him about a reality radically different from ordinary reality.

> I remember having chewed six peyote buttons when the conversation became very lively; although I could not distinguish what language was spoken, the topic of the conversation. . . was very interesting, and I attempted to listen carefully so that I could take part. But when I tried to speak I realized I couldn't; the words shifted aimlessly in my mind. I sat with my back propped against the wall and listened to what the men were saying. They were talking in Italian, and repeated over and over one phrase about the stupidity of sharks. I thought it was a logical, coherent topic. I had told don Juan earlier that the Colorado River in Arizona was called by the early Spaniards "el rio de los tizones (the river of charred wood)" and someone misspelled or misread "tizones" and the river was called "el rio de los tiburones (the river of the sharks)." I was sure they were discussing that story, yet it never occurred to me to think that none of them could speak Italian. I had a very strong desire to throw up, but I don't recall the actual act. I asked if somebody would get me some water. I was experiencing an unbearable thirst. Don Juan brought me large saucepan. He placed it on the ground next to the wall. He also brought me a little cup or can. He dipped it into the pan and handed it to me, and said I could not drink but should just freshen my mouth with it. The water looked strangely shiny, glossy, like a thick varnish. I wanted to ask don Juan about it and laboriously I realized he did not speak English. I experienced a very confusing moment, and became aware of the fact that although there was a clear thought in my mind. I could not speak. I wanted to comment on the strange quality of the water, but what followed next was not speech; it was the feeling of my unvoiced thoughts coming out of my mouth in a sort of liquid form. It was an effortless sensation of vomiting without the contractions of the

diaphragm. It was a pleasant flow of liquid words (Casteneda 1972, pp. 23-24).

When he titled his second book *A Separate Reality*, Castaneda's readers, many of whom had experimented with psychedelics, knew just what he was talking about, and like Castaneda, were convinced that psychedelic insights and experiences were quite real, even if they were based on hallucinations. Although for several year anthropologists considered his work authentic and important, a number of exposés questioned its veracity. Today many academic critics claim the books are simply fiction. In any case, his readers did not seem to care, as his twelve books have been best-sellers in seventeen languages.

Whether marijuana is a psychedelic capable of inducing a spiritual experience is a controversial question. The psychedelic research that began as a way of mimicking psychoses became known for its exploration of a reality different from the one to which we are accustomed. Four studies conducted in 2008 found that the use of marijuana and MDMA, also known as Ecstasy, tends to impair many cognitive functions, while another highly publicized study challenged this perspective (Newberg and Waldman 2010). The work of Timothy Leary, Richard Alpert, Huston Smith, and Andrew Weil inspired a generation of Americans to redefine the nature of reality (Lattin 2010). Recently Andy Clark and David Chalmers (2010) introduced the concept of *the extended mind,* raising the question: Where does the mind stop and the rest of the world begin? They tell us that the mind exists not only in our head but externally. It is the philosophers and quantum physicists who are exploring this terrain, often in relation to chaos theory and complexity theory.

What is the relationship of ordinary reality to the experience of ecstasy? How does ecstatic experience happen? Are there certain formulations or procedures that can be used to induce ecstatic states? Answers are coming from tribal shamans, the illegal drug trade, neuroscientists, clergy, and cults. Clergymen have found that producing ecstasy in church fills the pews and collection boxes, while the producers of rock concerts and raves know that moshing and drug use create ecstasy.

PHARMACEUTICAL PARADISE

Those who produce and sell illegal drugs know how recreational drug use can become an addiction. Individuals try to self-medicate with various classes of drugs, settling on a "drug of choice" that corresponds to the emotional state or mood which needs to be stimulated or sedated (Khantzian 1985). Before becoming addicted, Lee Stringer, a writer, who held positions in advertising and public relations, described how smoking crack cocaine felt "like love, sex, winning the lottery and Christmas morning all in one" (Ames 2002).

More than two hundred years ago British poet William Blake said that man must be free to ponder the wonders of the universe, to see a world in a grain of sand, and heaven in a wild flower. When LSD first appeared on the streets more than four decades ago, people found that on LSD they could do that. Ram Dass and Leary began to explore other planes of consciousness, especially chemically induced enlightenment. Having discovered the powers of acid to open the doors of perception, Leary became the LSD guru. While some people saw God on acid, others glimpsed madness, and yet others descended into a madness from which they could not return.

Although LSD promised a fast way to spiritual enlightenment, it was notoriously unpredictable, and some people could go on tripping for days, weeks, months. I remember it well. Before obtaining any professional training, I worked at a small private psychiatric hospital in New York. Two young men were admitted within days of each other, after their LSD induced psychoses did not subside. They played "cosmic" games of pool in the dayroom, filled with all sorts of personal meaning. For one of them, the pool cues glowed and changed colors; he saw the billiard balls rise slowly off the table, into the air, out the window, and into the trees, where they attached themselves to branches and hung glowing like Christmas lights. He saw me glowing too and wanted me to join him on his trip so that I too could know these ecstasies as he did. At the height of his trip, the visions were ecstatic, absolutely glorious. He ranted about his plan to put LSD in all the water coolers in the hospital, to free patients from their illnesses and bring joy to the lives of the staff. I had no doubt at all that he would do it if he could; friends had tried to smuggle drugs in to him. But his visions could suddenly turn dark and violent, requiring that he be physically restrained. When taking LSD, "magic mushrooms" (psilocybin, or *shrooms,* as they are called today), marijuana, far more potent today than in the 1960s, or Ecstasy, the right hemisphere of the brain's cerebral cortex is activated in unpredictable ways (Milkman and Sunderwirth 1987).

The drug Ecstasy, also known as methylenedioxymethamphetamine, methamphetamine, or MDMA, comes as a pill or powder, produced in many different colors and sizes in underground factories in the Netherlands and in Israel. Ecstasy today is a lot like LSD had been in the 1960s and 1970s, an occasional recreational party drug for some, an addictive escape for others, and the ruination of some lives (Klam 2001). There is even a current television series, *Breaking Bad*, in which a high school chemistry teacher discovers that he has advanced lung cancer. A real family man, but desperate to secure his family's financial future, he resorts to producing and selling methamphetamine with a former student.

Matthew Klam, a contributing writer for the *New York Times Magazine*, was a college student when he first tried Ecstasy (Klam 2001). He described how it is so different from all other drugs that it has become the fastest-growing illegal substance in America.

> Unlike classic psychedelics, MDMA—or, as it's known to scientists, Methylenedioxymethamphetamine—doesn't disrupt your basic sense of who you are. You barely even feel weird. Also, it doesn't scramble your external perceptions, except that soft things feel softer, music sounds better. It was in no way hallucinogenic. With Ecstasy, I had simply stepped outside the worn paths in my brain and, in the process, gained some perspective on my life.
> (It wasn't that harsh LSD feeling, where every thought seems like an absurd paradox—like the fact that we're all, deep down, just a bunch of monkeys.) I yawned once or twice, but it didn't presage sleepiness. I felt like some reptile quadrant of my brain had been soothed. My emotions, my memory, my sense of smell—they were all as accessible as a photo album on my lap. . . .
> And: all afternoon, all night, I didn't hate myself.
> People have turned to mind-altering substances since the beginning of time in search of enlightenment. But while many other drugs, from ayahuasca to nitrous oxide produce euphoria, Ecstasy creates not just a rush but a singular kind of emotional elevation-- you are launched on a hot-air balloon ride that rides over the pitfalls of typical humanity. The what ifs, the self-doubts, are knocked flat, and instead a hunger for human connection and a desire to empathize firmly take hold. No other drug produces this kind of feeling. That day I had a tingling awareness that something important was happening inside me: a bubbling birth of new wonder. The slate of lifelong guilt was being gently wiped clean. I'd discovered son thing new; something that worked, and I'd found it without adult supervision. All of my neck, back, shoulder, elbow and knee pain from weight lifting injuries vanished. Ecstasy's a powerful analgesic
> It's also a whopper of an antidepressant. Whereas Prozac-type SSRI antidepressants keep your brain from emptying reservoirs of serotol too quickly, Ecstasy floods your brain with the stuff. Proponents say it improves memory, which may explain why you feel so connected to the continuum of your life. A subtle, purifying *something* descends like a cool cotton blanket. You feel restored, energized. MDMA is chemical related to amphetamines, so it raises your heart rate, blood pressure and body temperature slightly; You're warm. You're not hungry. Your mouth turns as dry as the dust on a Las Vegas rooftop parking lot. Eventually you start grinding your jaw so tightly you'd need a jackhammer to open it, and your head is sore the next day from the grinding. But at the time you're not really aware of these odd side effects. You have everything you need. Just breathing is really good on this stuff.
> My friends and I walked outside and sat out on the grass in front of Sigma Beta fraternity and watched the sunset as the crowds from the football game that had just ended flooded across campus. I felt flawless love for my friends, down to their barracuda jackets and college perms and bad New England accents.

> I had nostalgia for the moment I was living. I experienced a kind of wordless glory. This was the best I'd ever felt in my life. . .
> Ecstasy . . . has become, variously, a kinder, gentler party lube, an explosive catalyst in the search for meaning of life, as well as just another druggie escape fantasy. It has ruined some people's lives (Klam 2001, p. 40-41).

Ecstasy can provide the stamina to dance all night long to "trance music," making it the preferred drug for dance club "raves." No wonder that Ecstasy is even considered a sacrament of sorts. While the Prozac-type antidepressants (SSRIs or selective serotonin reuptake inhibitors) keep your body from emptying reservoirs of the feel-good brain chemical serotonin too quickly, Ecstasy releases far too much serotonin, depleting your supply (Klam 2001). When Ecstasy's effects are enhanced by Viagra, the combination of Viagra and Ecstasy, known as Sextasy, makes it possible for people to engage in vigorous activity, sexual and otherwise, for hours on end, making it a party drug among. among gay men and teen "ravers," a contributing factor in infection rates for HIV and other sexually transmitted diseases (Breslau 2002).

Although Ecstasy-related deaths are relatively rare, the drug has ruined some people's lives. As the name *methamphetamine* indicates, it is a stimulant related to the amphetamines, so its effects are an elevation in heart rate, blood pressure, and body temperature. Klam (2001) described how after awhile the warmth turns your mouth dry, and you barely notice that you've begun to grind your jaw or that you've developed hypothermia and dehydration. Those who use it at raves become so swept away that they don't feel themselves overheating and dehydrating, which can lead to seizures. The high is soon followed by a depression that seems to set in progressively more rapidly and severely with long-term use. Sometimes it may become a sense of acute despair and hopelessness. Users describe their first experience with Ecstasy as one of the best experiences they have ever had but the chance of reproducing it is almost nil, and the impact attenuates over time.

According to the National Institute on Drug Abuse, the hallucinatory herb *Salvia divinorum* surpasses Ecstasy in popularity with high school seniors. A recent video of pop star Miley Cyrus smoking salvia boosted sales greatly. Initially sold in "head shops" and gas stations as a legal alternative to marijuana, it has been outlawed or regulated by twenty four states. It was reported that Jared Loughner was high on salvia when he shot Representative Gabrielle Giffords of Arizona in the head, gravely wounding her, killing six people, and wounding twelve others (Incalterra and Henderson 2011).

Many have blamed Timothy Leary's psychedelic crusade for the crackdown on serious psychedelic research, in which the earlier psychedelic investigations of the 1960s and 1970s had been largely abandoned. In addition, reports of both laymen and scientists whose altered states of consciousness were induced by drugs were regarded as subjective, ephemeral, and unreliable, and the research was considered unscientific and trivial (Tart 1972, 1998). Ecstasy was outlawed by the Drug Enforcement Agency in 1986.

Paradoxically, the same effects that have made LSD, Ecstasy, and psilocybin such popular illegal drugs have made them the subject of scientific interest today, in the second generation of psychedelic research. Human studies in psychedelics resumed in the early 1980s, with the study of DMT (dimethyltryptamine) and has branched out into experiments using psilocybin to treat obsessive-compulsive disorder, to investigate the nature of the mystical experience, and to help the pain and suffering of cancer. A small but developing international movement is pressing for the use of these drugs as part of psychotherapy. Significant backing comes from the Boston-based Multidisciplinary Association for Psychedelic Studies, a non-profit organization that promotes legalization of psychedelic drugs and marijuana used for treatment. In the 1970s, Richard Yensen, a Maryland therapist, provided a drug quite similar to Ecstasy to his patients, writing that MDMA is nearly equivalent to psychotherapy in a pill (Klam 2001). In 1994, the FDA formally approved the use of Ecstasy for research use in humans.

MDMA has several effects on brain chemistry which may accelerate the psychotherapeutic process. First, it boosts levels of oxytocin, the hormone in the brain that also acts as a neurotransmitter (Thompson, Callaghan, Hunt, Cornish, and McGregor 2007).

Oxytocin is found in human breast milk and is associated with the impulse to bond (Angier 1994). It stimulates labor contractions and the letdown reflex of nursing mothers, and current studies have begun to explore the role played by oxytocin in orgasm, social recognition, bonding, anxiety, trust, love, and maternal behaviors (Diamond 2009). Oxytocin also plays a part in controlling the release of other crucial neurochemicals such as noradrenaline, dopamine, prolactin, and opiates, all involved in attachment behavior (Diamond 2009).

> Researchers now believe that oxytocin plays a key role in the psychobiological process through which mammals form stable, intrinsically rewarding bonds to specific partners, most importantly the mother. . . .on the basis of these findings, researchers have suggested that as we develop a bond with another person, we pursue increasing closeness and contact . . . This triggers oxytocin release, and over time, we come to associate the other person with the soothing, rewarding effects of oxytocin. . . . In addition to its role in attachment, oxytocin also appears to influence sexual arousability and satisfaction (Diamond 2009, pp. 226-32).

Further, oxytocin is known to help in controlling emotional responses and it increases cortisol and norepinephrine levels, needed for emotional learning. Oxytocin has been called penicillin for the soul and a psychic pain reliever.

These unique effects led some therapists to call Ecstasy an *empathogen* (creating an empathic state) or an *entactogen* (creating a touching within) before it became illegal in the mid-eighties (Torgoff 2004). The question has been raised whether some people who are mildly depressed might do better to take Ecstasy occasionally rather than Prozac daily for years.

MARKETING RELIGIOUS ECSTASY

Clergy have discovered that sedate services, bake sales, and spaghetti dinners no longer fill the church pews and collection boxes, and that producing ecstatic experiences in church is far more effective. Reuben Archer Torrey, an American evangelist, was a marketing genius ahead of his time, publishing more than 40 books on salvation and winning souls to Jesus. One of them was *How to Promote and Conduct a Successful Revival,* published at the beginning of the twentieth century (Torrey 1901).

Today, religion is marketed like cars, deodorant, and liquor, using sophisticated Madison Avenue techniques. Black and Pentecostal churches, with their ecstatic gospel worship, have provided a marketing model for clergy with dwindling congregations who have found that they have to provide, along with baby-sitting and an elaborate sound system, an intense ecstatic experience.

To lure young people back to church, Matthew Fox, a former Dominican priest, reinvented the Anglican Mass. A crowd of five hundred entered a loft in an industrial section of Oakland, California for a Mass called "Gaia Our Mother." Ethereal music pulsed hypnotically as slides of mountains, clouds, and women flashed on the walls above makeshift altars to fire, water, earth, and air. Fox urged the crowd to cry out to the mother, and their voices joined in a collective wail of *Ma!* as they danced ecstatically under flashing strobe lights (Fox 1997)

When Marjoe Gortner was nine months old, he learned from his mother how to shout "Glory!" into a microphone. When he was four, he was ordained as a minister. By the time he was an adult, he knew better than anyone how ecstatic experiences *are* entertainment. In *Marjoe*, his Oscar-winning documentary made in the late 1960s, Gortner exposed some of the tricks of the trade (Conway and Siegelman 1995). The divine moment of religious ecstasy was simply a matter of whipping the crowd into a frenzy. Just as back-up singers at a rock-and-roll concert warm up the crowd before introducing the main star, lesser evangelists get the crowd worked up before the main attraction. Marjoe explained that the power is given to the preacher by the crowd expecting to receive the preacher's special gifts. The real show was not the preacher as much as the audience.

> You start with a guy who obviously has a problem. . . . Things haven't worked out for him or he's looking for something . . . So he goes to one of these revivals. . . He sees a lot of people glowing around him and they're all inviting him to come in and join . . . They say, "Hey, my life was changed!" or "Hey, I found a new job!" That's when he's ready to get saved or born again; and once he's saved, they all pat him on the back. It's like he's been admitted to this very special elite club. . . . As the preacher, I'm working with the crowd, watching the crowd, trying to bring them to that high point at a certain time in the evening. I let everything build up to that moment when they're all in ecstasy. The crowd builds up and you have to watch that you don't stop it. You start off saying you've heard that tonight's going to be a great night; then you begin the whole pitch and keep it rolling . . . . It's the same as a rock-and-roll concert. You have an opening number with a strong entrance; then you go through a lot of the old standards, building up to your hit song at the end . . . . And sooner or later he starts to speak it out and go *dut-dut-dut*. Then everyone goes 'That's it! You've got it! And the button is pushed . . . *dehandayeloomos-atayleesaso* . . and so on and on.." . .
> The first time maybe you'll just go *dut-dut-dut-dut* and that's about all that will get out. Then you'll hear other people and the next night you may go *dut-dut-dut-UM-dut-DEET-dut-dut* and it gets a little better. The next thing you know, it's a new language you've got down. (Conway and Siegelman 1995, pp. 42-44)

But as you have read earlier, it is not really a language at all (Samarin 1972). It has nothing to do with a passive spiritual possession. It is a skill that must be actively acquired and practiced. While acknowledging that the gift of tongues is of human, not supernatural origin, Marjoe clearly had much respect for the experience as an expression of spirituality and fellowship, making him different from many other evangelist entrepreneurs.

> I really don't put it down. I never have. It's just that I analyze it and look at it from a very rational point of view. I don't see it as coming from God and say that at a certain point the Holy Spirit zaps you with a super whammy on the head and you're "gone for tongues" and there it is. Tongues is a process that people build up to. Then, as you start to do something, just as when you practice the scales on the piano, you get better at it (Conway and Siegelman 1995, p 44).

During his time in the Bible-Belt circuit, he began to regard the evangelical experience as a kind of popular entertainment, using simple techniques to foment the crowd's contagious emotions. It was a kind of participatory divine theater that provided its audience with profound emotional rewards, somewhat like psychodrama. He regarded it as his duty to give them the best show possible. "The people who are out there don't see it as entertainment . . . These people don't go to movies, they don't go to bars and drink, they don't go to rock-and-roll concerts—but everyone has to have an emotional release. So they go to revivals and they dance around and talk in tongues" (Conway and Siegelman 1995, p. 44). What Marjoe did for his Pentecostal audiences was an act of kindness, albeit one with "super whammy" power.

Marjoe's techniques were so powerful that they worked even when an audience had been plainly cautioned about their use. He demonstrated in a college sociology class how words alone—no group rituals, no music—could evoke the emotional response of "being saved."

> I tell them that I don't believe in it, that I use a lot of tricks; and the title of the lecture is 'Rhetoric and Charisma.' So I've already told them how large masses are manipulated by a charismatic figure. I've given them the whole rap explaining how it's done, but they still want to see it. . . . I say, 'No, you don't really want to see it'. And they say, 'Oh, yes. We do!' And I say, 'But you don't believe in it anyway, so I can't do it.' And they say, 'We believe. We believe!' So after about twenty minutes of this I ask for a volunteer, and I have a girl come up and I say, 'So you want to feel better?' And I say, 'You're lying to me! You're just up here for a good time and you want to impress all these people and you want to make an ass out of me and an ass out of this whole thing, so why don't you go back and sit down?' I really get hard on her, and she says, No, no, I believe!' And I keep going back and forth until she's almost in tears. And then, even though this is in a college crowd and I'm only doing it as a joke, I just say my same old line, *In the name of Jesus!* and touch them on the head, and wham, they fall down flat every time (Conway and Siegelman 1995, p. 46).

If you have an imagination, there is no limit to the many different ways of producing ecstasy. You have read here of only a few.

Chapter Six

Cult-Induced Ecstasy and Psychosis

Lo! I tell you a mystery.
We shall not all sleep, but we shall all be changed,
In a moment, in the twinkling of an eye . . .
—1 Corinthians 15:51

In the TM world, it was okay to be a 'Space Cadet.' That was, in fact, what we called someone who was spaced out. Being 'blissed out,' mindlessly wandering, twitching, shaking, having unconscious vocalizations were all signs of spiritual growth.
—Patrick Ryan, *A Personal Account: Eastern Meditation Group*

When people are made to think, sense, and feel quite differently than is usual for them, they become very vulnerable to the social influence induced by charismatic groups (Galanter 1999). These groups are very cohesive, believing that the leader or group's mission has transcendent powers, and they control members' behavior by means of a shared belief system (Galanter 1999). Some of these groups are harmful cults, religious sects, self-improvement groups, while others are political action movements, motivational seminars, and terrorist groups. The group is molded by a combination of psychological forces that have a compelling, palpable quality. These include the group's cohesiveness, shared beliefs, and altered states of consciousness induced by the group.

The intense psychological forces operating in the more harmful cults operate in a modified form in several spiritually oriented groups directed at relieving the burdens of illness. These range from a constructive movement like Alcoholics Anonymous (A.A.) and other twelve step programs that focus on a wide range of substance abuse and dependency problems, to more questionable approaches at the fringe end of alternative medicine (Galanter 1999).

EXTREME ALTERED STATES

What usually makes the deepest impression to outsiders is the glazed, withdrawn look in the eyes of cult members, a spaced-out appearance that suggests a trance or dissociated state. Dissociated states are wonderful ways to escape temporarily. From time to time, we all need a respite from the workings of our minds, and we may turn to meditation or relaxation techniques, which can be very beneficial when used in moderation. However, these rituals and techniques are used excessively by cults, resulting in shutting down the mind and the process of thinking. This is accomplished by engineering intense experiences which the brain cannot metabolize and digest. Along with this comes the parallel strain of actively suppressing one's emotional responses, which can ultimately numb a person's capacity for human feeling, rendering him robotic.

Not everyone who joins such a group finds his mind shutting down because people respond idiosyncratically to these experiences. Many may not sustain long-term damage and manage to leave with little or no harm done to them, or they may have been harmed in a way that is not so readily apparent. Some may find that their experience has served adaptive and developmental needs, and they may be less vulnerable to the negative effects. For example, a colleague who had been a management consultant before beginning her career in the mental health field came to her professional training with entrepreneurial skills. Ambitious about the business aspects of her practice, she participated in The Landmark Forum, coming away from her experience with an increased sense of confidence in how she presented her program. She and certainly many others were fortunate that they did not sustain harmful effects. But nonetheless, the dangers are clearly there for others who are more vulnerable. And of course, it is not at all clear at the outset just who is vulnerable.

Certainly not everyone who joins a cult is longing for ecstatic experiences but nonetheless, the cult experience can induce radical personality change, ongoing states of dissociation, as well as ecstatic and psychotic states. Former members have reported numerous adverse experiences while in the cult, including having had sexual relations with the leader (5%, 60% in the Children of God), menstrual dysfunction (22%), and physical punishment (20%). Conway and associates found that 52% reported experiencing "floating," or dissociation, 40% reported, nightmares, 21% reported amnesia, 14% reported hallucinations and delusions, 35% reported an inability to break mental rhythms of chanting,14% reported, violent outbursts, and 21% reported suicidal or self-destructive tendencies (Conway, Siegelman, Carmichael, and Coggins 1986). I have heard of several anecdotal reports of developing an eating disorder while in the cult. Cultic studies experts have found that the techniques used to produce altered states may be a combination of meditation, biofeedback, hypnosis and self- hypnosis, chanting, relaxation techniques, visualization, neurolinguistic programming, indoctrination, and yoga (Singer and Lalich1996).

Individuals who have been accustomed to achieving altered states of consciousness through the use of illicit drugs may be attracted to Eastern religious groups that emphasize meditation, which induces an altered state. For many, the meditative state serves as a substitute for the drug-induced altered state (Galanter 1999). Perhaps that is why comedian Russell Brand attributed TM with helping him give up his drug addiction (Aleksander 2011) and why a family member of mine said that if it were not for TM, he might still be a drugged-out hippie.

This seemed to be the case with Ellen, a drug abuser, who was interviewed by Galanter. The court had remanded Ellen's five children to her mother's care because they had been neglected during her long bouts of psychiatric illness and drug abuse. She was attracted to The Divine Light Mission, one of many groups of Hindu orientation that originated in India. It was a time of personal crisis, and she wanted help for the problems that were ruining her life (Galanter 1999). The group's support and structure allowed her to gain control over these problems. Her drug history included ten to fifteen barbiturate capsules daily, then LSD and later, opiates, such as morphine, Demerol, heroin, and methadone. She supported her expensive habit through prostitution. She had several psychiatric hospitalizations and suicide attempts. When she met several members of The Divine Light Mission, their acceptance of her made her feel immediately comfortable with them. She came to appreciate their religious devotion and wanted to join them to save herself from her profound sense of desolation. She began meditating, and ten months later, only occasionally reported smoking half a joint of pot. The group had exerted a remarkable influence on her addiction in a way that the usual therapies and addiction treatments failed to do. When interviewed about how the group helped her, she described it in a way that suggested that it served the transitional functions of self-regulation and self-soothing (Winnicott 1953), and that the altered states induced by meditation became a substitute for those formerly induced by drugs (Galanter 1999).

> Once I got to know them, I realized they loved me. They took me up, and it was as if they were holding me in their arms. I was like a baby whose mother guides its moves and cares for it. When I wanted to take heroin or even to smoke (marijuana), I knew they were with me to help me stay away from it, even if I was alone. And their strength was there for me, even before I could

> hardly meditate at all. I could rely on their invisible hand, moved by Mahara Ji's wisdom, to help me gain control. Just feeling their love was all I needed (Galanter 1999, pp. 27-8).
>
> At first, all I had to hold onto were the other premies, but I still kept thinking about heroin. After a week or two, I was able to meditate, and after awhile the meditations came to stand in for the drugs I was craving. At times the sensations I got from meditating felt like the high I used to get from drugs, and soon I could put myself into a drug-free space just by meditating—for a few minutes at first, and later for most of the day. Eventually I could summon it up when I had to (Galanter 1999, p. 68).

Interestingly, Alcoholics Anonymous had its origins in the ecstatic experience of its founder, Bill W. As he continued to deteriorate from drinking, he met an old friend, also an alcoholic, who had become healthy through his involvement with a zealous religious sect. Bill W. was struck by how powerful the experience was of sharing his struggle and he had a revelation.

> All at once I found myself crying out, "If there is a God, let Him show Himself! I am ready to do anything, anything." Suddenly the room lit up with a great white light. I was caught up on an ecstasy for which there are no words to describe. It seemed to me in my mind's eye that I was on a mountain and that a wind not of air but of spirit was blowing. And then it burst upon me that I was a free man. Slowly the ecstasy subsided. I lay there on the bed, but now for a time I was in another world, a new world of consciousness . . . and I thought to myself, "So this is the God of the preachers!" A great peace stole over me. (cited by Galanter 1999, p. 212)

It is striking to me how often these ecstatic states are associated with a sense of peace and the perception of a bright light, a phenomenon also associated with the near-death experience (Newberg and d'Aquili 1994; Nelson 2011; Moody 2001; Ring 1993; Strassman 2000). It is a spiritual process that seems to be experienced as falling into darkness, dying, and then being born again.

In their study of the Divine Light Mission, Buckley and Galanter (1979) found that the greater length of time members spent in meditation was associated with diminished psychological distress. They seemed to use meditation at scheduled times and on an as-needed basis. Similarly in Transcendental Meditation, EEG studies showed an increase in alpha wave activity during meditation, a calming state that is characteristic of all the major tranquilizers and which can be compared to that induced by marijuana (Galanter 1999; Persinger, Carrey, and Suess 1980). It is alarming, however, that Persinger and associates found an increase in theta activity, one of the most frequent components of brain abnormalities, which are common correlates of abnormal behavior such as epilepsy, as well as sociopathic and aggressive behaviors (Persinger, Carrey, and Suess 1980; Persinger 1993).

It is not only Eastern meditation groups that promote altered states. So do other religious groups, such as Pentecostal and fundamentalist Protestant groups, Catholic Charismatics, and Hasidic Judaism. Mainstream Christianity and Judaism have begun to incorporate practices such as chanting services and walking the labyrinth which induce an altered state.

Many current secular groups manage to engage sophisticated, well-educated adults in a new, zealously espoused ideology in which the techniques employed include the development of a cohesive group setting and attitudinal change by means of altering states of consciousness (Galanter 1999). One of them began as est, or Erhard Seminars Training, the most successful and most controversial of the encounter groups of the seventies, and the progenitor of hundreds of others that have been marketed to the public and the business community. Common to these groups was the belief that you create your own reality.

"YOU CREATE YOUR OWN REALITY"

> . . . after I realized that I knew nothing—I realized that I knew everything... everything was just the way that it is, and that I was already all right . . . I realized I was not my motions or thoughts. I was not my ideas, my intellect, my perceptions, my beliefs . . . I became Self.
>
> —William Warren Bartley III, *Werner Erhard The Transformation of a Man: The Founding of EST*

Erhard's early involvement with Scientology profoundly influenced the development of est and years later, the Landmark Forum. Est found steadfast and influential followers in universities, medical schools, the business and psychotherapy communities, and Hollywood. Est, the prototypical self-help therapy, like its many imitators, attacked the thinking process directly. The acronym *est* originates from the Latin word *est* meaning "it is." Est questioned the nature of reality in a most dangerous way.

The first weekend of training was meant to destroy the participants' belief systems, and the second weekend aimed at replacing it with the est belief system. Although est does not acknowledge having a belief system, it seems to be essentially a solipsistic one, meaning that the self is the only thing that can be known and verified or that the external world and other minds cannot be known and might not exist. In the vernacular of the sixties, if someone manipulates your thoughts and emotions, it was called mind fucking. Est was a real mind fucker. Like its imitators, it relies on a dangerously seductive paradigm, known as "You Create Your Own Reality" (YCYOR).

The YCYOR paradigm was coined in 1963 by an acclaimed spiritual teacher known as Seth, who was "channeled," meaning he spoke through the late psychic Jane Roberts in the early sixties while she was in a trance (Klimo

1998). Seth's paradigm has been acclaimed by leaders and authors in the human potential movement such as Louise Hay (*You Can Heal Your Life),* Deepak Chopra (*Ageless Body, Timeless Mind*), Shakti Gawain, (*Creative Visualization),* Marianne Williamson (*A Return to Love),* Richard Bach (*Jonathan Livingston Seagull*) and others. According to Seth, his empowering message literally launched the New Age movement.

> Your beliefs form reality. Your individual beliefs and your joint beliefs. Now the intensity of a belief is extremely important. . .
> And, if you believe, in very simple terms, that people mean you well, and will treat you kindly, they will. And, if you believe that the world is against you, then so it will be in your experience. And, if you believe. . . IF YOU BELIEVE THAT YOU WILL BEGIN TO DETERIORATE AT 22, then so you shall.
> And, if you believe that you are poor, and always will be, then so your experience will so prove to you. Your beliefs meet you in the face when you look in the mirror. They form your image. You cannot escape your beliefs. They are, however, the method by which you create your experience.
> It is important that you here realize that you are not at the mercy of the unexplainable, that you are not at the mercy of events over which you have no control whether those events are psychological events or physical ones, in your terms.
> As I have told you, there is little difference if you believe that your present life is caused by incidents in your early infancy or by past lives over which equally you feel you have no control. Your events, your lives, your experiences, are caused by your present beliefs. Change the beliefs and your life changes. –Seth

The Seth website claims that his books (written through Jane Roberts in a trance) have sold over seven million copies and have been translated into over eleven languages, which demonstrates that being an acclaimed spiritual leader and a powerful entrepreneur are not mutually exclusive. If the YCYOR paradigm were true, each victim of war, rape, or the Holocaust would be responsible for the horrors which have befallen him. In fact, at an est training, Erhard actually tried to convince a participant who was a Holocaust survivor that she as well and her family members who died in a death camp had created their Holocaust experience and were responsible for it (Pressman 1993). The solution to all this, according to est, is to think positively and imagine yourself overriding all the negative tapes you have stored away in your mind.

The YCYOR belief is exemplified by the opening online image at the website of one of the large group awareness trainings, Personal Dynamics (www.PersonalDynamics.com). You will see two men, each successfully pushing away a big, heavy wall. The image conveys that you can find superhuman strength to push away the walls you have erected that keep you from realizing your true potential. This is nothing more than magical thinking

(Freud 1913a), the notion that one's ideas are omnipotent. (An example is feeling guilty because someone you disliked died, the magical thinking being the irrational belief that your hateful thoughts killed him.)

To fully understand the destructiveness of the YCYOR belief, one must understand that what we each perceive as reality is unique for each of us, and is our own subjective psychic reality. We are only able to construct our reality based on the sensory input that enters our brain (Newberg and d'Aquili 2000). When that sensory input overwhelms the brain, his ability to process it becomes so impaired that he can become convinced that up is down, and in is out, and two plus two equals five and that he has superhuman powers.

EST, ALSO KNOWN AS THE FORUM AND LANDMARK FORUM: "IT IS WHAT IT IS"

Jean, a recently divorced 52-year-old college educated mother of three, was interviewed by Flo Conway and Jim Siegelman for Snapping: America's Epidemic of Sudden Personality Change (1995). After years of marriage and raising children, she was middle-aged, lived alone, and had no skills.

> What do you do then? You have no money, no security, nothing. Who are you? I had raised my children through every kind of crisis imaginable. When they were grown and healthy, I felt pretty good about it, but it was as though the most important part of my life was over. I had to find meaning. That's when I started to search" (Conway and Siegelman 1995, pp. 12-13).

Her search led her to Transcendental Meditation, and its impact on her was a profound relief from stress. Then a friend invited her to participate in an encounter group. She joined, but when it became overwhelming to her, she ran out of the room. A young woman followed her and they talked for an hour. She had never known before what it was like to feel so close to another woman, and it led her to explore other encounter groups. In the next one she experienced a form of transcendence that surpassed anything she had ever experienced before. "I thought I must be getting in touch with my psychic energy. How else would you explain it? It was all mind, nobody was doing anything or saying anything, and I just got high. I got so high I didn't know what to do with it. It was a beautiful feeling of well-being, warmth, and loving" (Conway and Siegelman 1995, pp. 13-14).

Her encounter high opened her to new dimensions of experience through intimate encounters with others in later groups and in her daily life. And then she heard about est, founded by a man named Jack Rosenberg, a charismatic former car salesman who later took the name Werner Erhard. Stephen Appelbaum, a psychoanalyst, heard Erhard speak of how he, the son of a Philadelphia Main Line Protestant mother and a Jewish father, got his name (Appelbaum 1979).

> While he was on a plane that was taking him away from his old life with parents, wife, and children, he recognized that members of the life he was leaving might try to find him at a time when he did not feel like being found. Thus, a change of name was in order. In scanning a handy newspaper, he noticed the names of Werner von Braun, the ex-Nazi rocket scientist, and Luther Erhard, the then leader of Germany, and appropriated their names." Some armchair psychologists have made much of this man with a Jewish name appropriating German ones and then establishing an organization in which he is the deified leader (Appelbaum 1979, p.197).

The initial cost of the large group awareness trainings makes it easy to recruit new members; the introductory meetings are relatively inexpensive but become increasingly more costly as members become increasingly more seduced and indoctrinated. And with this comes increased prestige in the organizational hierarchy.

To understand the history of est, you need to know that Erhard changed est's name to The Forum in 1985, raised the price of the introductory groups to $525, and replaced est's tough rules and procedures with more accommodating "dialogues" and training "requests" (Pressman 1993). But according to many trainees, this was nothing more than old wine in new bottles. Forum participants were given sickness bags in case of vomiting, and some trainees served as "body-catchers" to catch those who fainted, occurrences which were to be expected. But there were more serious casualties, such as the 25-year-old man who dropped dead during a Forum session. His lawyer said that this otherwise healthy man died of fright. In 1992 Erhard was ordered by a federal judge to pay $380,000 to a Maryland woman who suffered bouts of euphoria, anxiety, mania, and a complete mental breakdown after her Forum training. Landmark Education LLC, a personal training and development company founded in 1991, bought Erhard's intellectual property and began offering educational programs worldwide in approximately 115 locations. (Pressman 1993). Its standard introductory course is known today as *The Landmark Forum* (Pressman 1993). By the mid 1990s Landmark was among 200 groups listed in France as having cult-like features and having been accused of brainwashing. In 2004 reporters hiding secret cameras infiltrated the Landmark, following a scathing expose on France's Channel 3 TV, after which the government put it on a list of dangerous sects (ABC NEWS 2008). Landmark Education apparently left France permanently.

The following paragraph, found on the group's website, is a waiver participants must read and sign before participating, indicating that they have been informed of the risks involved. It essentially is meant to absolve Landmark from responsibility if a member becomes psychotic, suicidal, or commits suicide.

> From time to time, during or shortly after participating in the Program, a very small number of people who have no personal or family history of mental illness or drug abuse have reported experiencing brief, temporary episodes of emotional upset ranging from heightened activity, irregular or diminished sleep, to mild psychotic-like behavior. An even smaller number of people have reported more serious symptoms ranging from mild psychotic behavior to psychosis occasionally requiring medical care and hospitalization. In less than 1/1000 of 1% of participants, there have been reports of unexplained suicide or other destructive behavior. While we know of no independent studies to suggest that people who are physically, emotionally and mentally healthy are at risk in the Program, certain persons have claimed that the Program has caused or triggered in them a psychosis or psychotic event.

The name *est* was thought to have come to Erhard from a science-fiction novel, *est: The Steersman Handbook* by an author named L. Clark Stevens. For Stevens, *est* stood for *electronic social transformation*. His book anticipated the rise of the est people, a generation of post-literate men who would bring about the transformation of society. Shortly after formulating est, Erhard was said to have had his own transformative experience while driving over the Golden Gate Bridge. At some point along the highway, he *got it*, a revelation which became the basis for the est workshops. In a flash, he understood that "What is, is" and "What isn't, isn't," which have become colloquialisms that are part of today's vernacular. This is only a clue to how deeply "cult speak" is embedded in our culture. This led Erhard to additional revelations. "What I recognized is that you can't put it together. It's already together, and what you have to do is experience being together" (Conway and Siegelman 1995, p.18). The language of est is "a jargon-filled string of words that could mean anything to anybody. It was, more than anything else, a language without any real meaning (Pressman 1993, p. 230)." When asked what "est training" was, Werner Erhard's standard answer was that it is what it is: an experience, which can't be put into words (Frederick 2007). And so the expression, *it is what it is* became so embedded in current language that we hear it all the time.

Typically, Erhard began a sixty-hour workshop with some version of calling trainees assholes. "You're all complete assholes or you wouldn't be here" (Bry 1976).[1] I suppose you could call it a perverse Zen master approach. The est training consisted of endless hours of lectures on the nature of reality, perception, and belief systems, mixed in with a series of est "processes," mental exercises meant to erase the trainees' "tapes," or patterns of thought and feeling that prevent one from fully experiencing life. Est viewed the thought process fundamentally as tape recording, with the mind a storage space of problematic tapes that obstruct the real meaning of pure experience. In addition to the verbal assaults to which trainees were subjected, they were drawn into personal encounters with the trainer. In the course of these early weekends, many trainees cried, fainted, vomited, or lost sphincter control. At the end of the training, they were supposed to "get it,"[2] a moment of sudden realization that they alone were responsible for creating everything in life that happened to them.

"Sixty hours that transform your life" was one of est's marketing tools. Unfortunately, the implication that the transformation will be a positive one is quite misleading, because for many people, the transformation was not at all positive. The original est training served 250 people at a time, in four marathon sessions totaling 60 hours, usually held over two consecutive weekends. The trainees gathered in a large meeting area, usually a hotel ballroom, and signed agreements not to leave their seats without permission or to speak unless called on. No eating, except at designated times, smoking, or drinking was allowed. Bathroom breaks, which came every twelve hours in the beginning, were later increased because of frequent urinary or bowel accidents. This boot camp approach to self-improvement became increasingly attractive not only among artists, writers, and Hollywood stars, but among more corporate types as well. Est training was even conducted in a number of prison systems (Babbie 1977; Bry 1976). Jean spoke about her est experience. "Let me say first that I feel est was one of the most positive things I've ever done. Est was extremely different from anything I had ever been in. . . . I say that because I was personally encountered by the trainer and taken through a lot of trauma. I'm still afraid to talk about it, because I haven't found people to be very understanding" (Conway and Siegelman 1995, p. 14). As she felt reassured by Conway and Siegelman that she was certainly not the first person they had talked with who expressed reservations about est, her story gradually emerged—in jumbled sentences, in rushes of words and emotionally charged pauses, and tears. It was all so fragmented in her memory. But that is what trauma does; it fragments the mind. She told how est had been for her a grueling physical ordeal.

> During the first body process—it was a meditation technique—I experienced a great deal of pain in my legs. . . . After that first full day of training, we left very late and I had this terrible pain from my knees down. The next day I was scared. If I hadn't paid two hundred and fifty dollars I wouldn't have gone back. I was tired. I was on the verge of tears The first thing I did was tell the trainer how I felt. . . I said "I'm scared. I have some idea of what this is all about, getting things up from my past, but do I have to experience my whole life here?" That was when the trainer came over to me and encountered me, taking me back to the first time I ever experienced pain in my legs. Of course, it went back to when I had rheumatic fever as a child. I've always had weak legs. There were days when I couldn't walk to the bus stop because of the pain

> in my legs. I had been treated for arthritis over the years and I was in pretty bad physical condition when I started the training. The doctors had said they couldn't do anything for it. They said I had to live with it (Conway and Siegelman 1995, p. 15).

She told them that her trainer pushed to excavate buried experiences and emotions from the past. And then she had what she called a healing. "When the trainer focused on all that, it was indescribable. It was too much. The pain in my legs was so intense. Then I felt waves of heat come over me and all the pain went away. I wouldn't choose to go through that pain again, but since that day I haven't had a single pain in my legs" (Conway and Siegelman 1995, p. 15)." The resulting cure was real and dramatic, perhaps because the intensity of that confrontation accessed a trauma that had plagued her for her whole life. It left her in a euphoric state spiraling up toward ecstasy. Near the end of her second est weekend, however, she had a second overwhelming but very different reaction.

> It came up in me like a ball. I thought I was going to be sick. At the same time I experienced a release from my body as though somebody had pulled a ripcord in me. It just shot up and unraveled out of my body. That whole day I hadn't known where I was. Then suddenly I found myself screaming at the trainer. I was calling him a son of a bitch. It came out at him. I don't know why except that the sound of his voice was getting to me. He was encountering someone else when it came up and I let go. When I sat down, my body was flooded with feeling. I think the fact that all this anger had come up in front of two hundred and fifty people must have had some effect. I was so humiliated. It just kept coming and coming in great waves. I felt all this heat in my wrists and I felt like I couldn't move my arms. But I sat there with it because I knew there was going to be a break soon, and I said to myself, I'm getting out of here. And I did. I managed to leave the training at that point (Conway and Siegelman 1995, pp. 15-16).

Although Jean left the training in an attempt to defend herself from the process that was destroying her mind, it was too late. She snapped.

> I walked out of est and I walked about a mile home and just went to bed. When I woke up the next morning, I was disoriented and scared to death. I didn't want any part of est. I called the city's mental health service and they sent out a crew. They stayed with me for about an hour. They seemed to understand what I was going through. One of them asked me if I had blown my mind and I said, "Yes, I don't know what that means but it sounds like what's happened." I was afraid. I felt very shaky. My son was coming in that night and I didn't think I could drive out to meet him. After the first weekend of the training, I had sent him this incredible note: *Get your ass over here! I have to clean up my shit!* He'd never heard any of this language. It was est jargon and I was full of it. (Conway and Siegelman 1995, p. 16)

Later that day she called the est office and told the manager what had happened to her. The manager explained that it had happened because she had not completed the training. She agreed to repeat and complete it in the next training, which was a month away. In the interim, she experienced the most wonderful feelings in her body. She had never felt so good, high all the time. Then finally, she felt she had to share her feelings and went to the est office and shouted at the secretary, "IF YOU DON"T GET IT, THEN YOU AIN'T GOT IT!" Then she walked into the manager's office and he hugged her. She continued to feel the high, and she began fantasizing. Then the fantasies became real. "It was poetical. I was speaking in biblical languages. At times I couldn't open my mouth, but when I did, it came out in verse. I was alone in my apartment for a week. I felt like I was getting a whole new body. A renewal. I was extremely active. I couldn't stop dancing. I didn't want to stop. My body just felt so powerful" (Conway and Siegelman 1995, pp. 16-17).

The high changed, and she spiraled downward, becoming very frightened. She knew something was wrong with her so she called the est manager once again. He asked her where she was. He responded "We can't help you but we can assist you"[3] and told her to come to a seminar that night. In a panic, she called a friend who arranged for her to be admitted voluntarily to a psychiatric hospital. After two weeks she was released at her own request, without further medication or professional care. Soon afterward, her delusions returned and she was readmitted, then released on thorazine, a powerful anti-psychotic tranquilizer. For the next ten months she had weekly psychiatric care and was maintained on medication.

We can understand Jean's psychotic break as a manic defense that occurred after her trainer got her to re-experience her childhood illness. It served to defend against the reality of her current physical disability and the psychic and physical pain caused by the reliving of her childhood illness. She erected instead the fantasy that she had a powerful and strong body that could dance and dance for hours. As her mind further unraveled, the fantasy became a delusion. But like all manic defenses, it could not last indefinitely.

Reports appeared about psychological injury to members of encounter groups, and then of people having psychotic breaks after est training (Glass, Kirsch, and Parris,1977). and of suicides among est participants. Many lawsuits were decided in favor of plaintiffs who were ex-members of est, as well as Hare Krishna, Scientology, TM, and others. Many other suits were settled out of court for undisclosed sums.

CULTS, MOTIVATIONAL SEMINARS, AND THE HUMAN POTENTIAL MOVEMENT

Ever since 1980, after breaking away from a two-year participation in a large New Age sect, Joe Szimhart has been an exit counselor and cult information consultant. He defined a cult as follows: "Cult: A group or movement exhibiting a great or excessive devotion or dedication to some person, idea, or thing and employing manipulative techniques of persuasion and control . . . designed to advance the goals of the group's leaders, to the actual or possible detriment of members, their families, or the community" (Szimhart 2009, pp. 233-34).

A cult methodically induces psychological dependency in members, uses the members to advance the leaderships' goals, without concern about how they are harming them (Singer and Ofshe 1990). After publication of *Snapping: America's Epidemic of Sudden Personality Change* (1978, 1995), Conway and Siegelman's raw data was the subject of study at the University of Oregon. Their respondents included former members of the largest worldwide religious cults of the seventies and eighties—the Unification Church, Church of Scientology, International Society for Krishna Consciousness, Divine Light Mission, and The Way International—as well as smaller cults such as the Children of God and followers of Eastern guru Bhagwan Shree Rajneesh, participants in self-help therapies such as est, Lifespring, and several dozen Christian bible cults and extreme fundamentalist sects.

Years ago recruitment for cultic groups was far more obvious than today because extreme religious groups were easy to identify. They lived isolated from the general population, and the public had become aware of their deceptive recruiting techniques. Today many are attracted to organizations that are less overtly cultic, not overtly religious, and are often linked with the human potential movement, while others operate as businesses, with their tactics focused around financial success. Landmark Forum, for example, is a human potential/business hybrid.

The positive thinking movement began in the 1950s with the publication of Norman Vincent Peale's *The Power of Positive Thinking.* An ad for the book read: "EXECUTIVES: Give this book to employees. It pays dividends" (Ehrenreich 2009, p.100). Salespeople usually lead a lonely existence, cut off from company headquarters, and live much of the time on highways, in motels, and airports. They face constant challenge, in which each day is a test that is likely to end in rejection and defeat. Nonetheless, the salesperson must start anew and create fresh enthusiasm for the next customer, the next city. As the American downsizing that began in the 1980s wore on, salespeople urgently needed a way to overcome self-doubts and generate optimism. The timing was perfect for clinical psychologist Martin Seligman and the Positive Psychology movement to come along, bearing the message that not only is happiness desirable in and of itself, but is in fact useful, producing health and greater success (Ehrenreich 2009). The message was bought by corporate America, which sought to control their employees' minds by instilling positive thinking.

Even a pyramid sales schemes such as Amway, based on the sale of products as varied as water purifiers, soap, cosmetics and vitamins, can be considered to be a cult at the same time that it is the world's largest multi-tiered marketing organization (Butterfield 1999; Conway and Siegelman 1995; Ehrenreich 2009). A successful pyramid scheme combines an apparently credible but actually fake business with a simple-to-understand yet sophisticated-sounding money-making profit-forming formula. Recruits undergo intense indoctrination, paid for out of their own pockets, in the form of tapes, seminars, and rallies. One salesman described an Amway sales rally as being like a rock concert, with waves of reciprocal chanting sweeping back and forth, one side shouting "Ain't it great!" and the other answering "Ain't it though!" A huge video screen flashes slogans and circles at the front of the amphitheater, like strobe lights, in time to the driving music (Ehrenreich 2009).

Motivational speakers know how hard it is the resist the excitement of a crowd, often demanding that the audience stand or dance in place. The transformed employees may occasionally break down in sobs, and after the performance, grab the speaker's hands, hugging and kissing him, telling him he's their savior. Some business leaders develop a fanatic conviction that they know the best way of doing things and believe that they have an almost supra-human insight into reality. These charismatic visionaries have injected quasi-spiritual thinking into corporate America, taking business executives on shamanic healing journeys and vision quests, forming prayer groups, fire walking rites, and native American healing circles.

James Arthur Ray read the 2006 megaseller *The Secret* which promised wealth, good health and happiness as long as followers strictly adhere to its tenets. Ray did and it helped launch his career as a self-help guru, putting James Ray International on a list of the 500 fastest-growing private companies in the U.S. in 2009. The secret was "Decide what you want. Visualize yourself with it. Be open to getting it." Ray did that, conducting sweat lodge ceremonies that lead to broken bones, lost consciousness, and other medical problems. He continued to ignore the medical problems of participants in his Arizona "Spiritual Warrior" event, resulting in the deaths of three people and an indictment for manslaughter (Shepelavy 2010).

People began to wonder how this could have possibly occurred. How could people remain so long in a sweat lodge that they died? Why didn't they simply get up and leave? It seems that they had learned the secret well—too well. They were indoctrinated to let go of fear, know what they want and go after it. They also learned that they create their own reality, that everything they get is a result of their own thoughts and actions. When they signed up for the sweat-lodge retreat, Ray told them before they entered the tent that they should expect a struggle, that they might even think they were going to die, but they would not. It is likely that these strong, successful, ambitious adults remained in the tent because they were used to pushing themselves to their limits. They had invested thousands of dollars and spent five intense days of bonding together, leading up to the event. They trusted one another. And unfortunately, they trusted Ray.

I had an interesting experience a few years ago, when I did a presentation on the subject of ecstasy at a professional conference. I did not mention cults at all. During the discussion, a woman spoke about a strange experience she recently had, so strange that she had never spoken with anyone about it, except her son. Hearing me speak openly about my own strange experience in spiraling up toward ecstasy gave her the courage to reveal her own. She hoped we did not think she was crazy, but listening brought her back to remembering this strange thing that had happened to her the year before. In the faltering economy, her private psychotherapy practice had slowed down drastically, which made her quite anxious. She knew a few colleagues who had a supplemental source of income on the side, and so she decided to attend a large group meeting of a pyramid sales organization that held out the promise of an easy way to make money. It lasted a morning and she left very excited and hopeful. From there, she took a short flight to visit her son in another city, her excitement building on the plane. Upon arrival, her son could not take time off right then to be with her, so they made arrangements to meet at his office at the end of his work day. She left her luggage with him and went off alone. The next thing she knew was that her cell phone was ringing. It was 7 p.m. and her son was calling, frantic. "Where the hell are you?" To her bewilderment, she had no idea where she was and really did not care. She was confused, and could not remember how she had spent the past several hours She was in the midst of an uninhabited area, filled with vegetation and could not remember getting there. Her son was very alarmed, but she was not. In fact, she was quite happy, manic actually. Her son notified the police, who surveyed the area by helicopter until they spotted and rescued her. All she knew was that she had had such an uplifting experience at the sales conference that she was filled to bursting with the possibilities of her own potential for achievement. She felt that she could do anything. It took several hours for her to come down from her high. I think that both the process that occurred during the meeting of the pyramid sales organization as well as her anxiety about her low income conspired to create a powerful manic defense of ecstasy.

I spoke to my workshop participants about how if they thought about that experience, repeated over and over again, about how our experiences change the structure and functioning of the brain, and how the mind can become unhinged by experiences induced in groups, they could begin to understand how more pervasive and long-lasting damage can occur. I then told them about how pyramid schemes can have their cultic aspects and a little about what happens in cults of different kinds. I was surprised when afterward, one woman spoke with me privately about her own experience in a psychotherapy cult. She told me that she could identify at least ten people at the conference who she knew had been involved in a psychotherapy cult of some kind. Those who have been so involved tend not to disclose this information for fear of being pejoratively labeled or of other therapists assuming.

Training programs in psychotherapy and psychoanalysis have the potential to become cultic and plagued by authoritarian practices, some subtle and many pronounced, instilling fear and fostering blind obedience to the favored proclivities of the leaders (Kirsner 2009; Raubolt 2007; Shaw 2005; Siskind 2003). British psychoanalyst Adam Phillips said

> The transference of psychoanalysts to Freud, to their theory, and to their training institutions, has been stultifying. . . From my point of view a psychoanalyst is anyone who uses what were originally Freud's concepts of transference, the unconscious, and the dream-work in paid conversations with people about how they want to live. . . But when psychoanalysts spend too much time with each other, they start believing in psychoanalysis. They begin to talk knowingly, like members of a religious cult. (Bollas 1997, pp. xiv-xvi)
> I love psychoanalysis and I'm very interested in it, but it's not a religion. . . . it's not something about which one should have unquestioning faith. . . .. Well, I feel ambivalent about psychoanalysis. There are lots of things I love and value about it, but I have doubts about it. And it seems to me that both things need to be kept in play for it to be valuable. Otherwise it becomes a cult, and it should be the opposite, the antidote to a cult (Guner 2010).

This blind submission seeps into the therapeutic relationship, preventing both training candidates and their patients from developing creative, authentic, and meaningful experiences. As Otto Kernberg said, "Psychoanalytic education today is all too often conducted in an atmosphere of indoctrination rather than of open scientific exploration" (Kernberg 1986, p. 799). In "Thirty methods to destroy the creativity of psychoanalytic candidates," Kernberg (1996) said that the methods include an unquestioning approach to key papers by Freud and to theoretical approaches, isolation of candidates from professional and scientific activities of the psychoanalytic society, accentuation of the hierarchical relations among the psychoanalytic faculty, discouragement of original contributions by candidates, intellectual isolation of institutes, and the effects of institutional conflicts around the appointment of training analysts. Douglas Kirsner described the socio-political histories of the four most important American institutes affiliated with the American Psychoanalytic Association—the New York, Boston, Chicago, and Los Angeles Psychoanalytic Institutes. "Most psychoanalytic institutes are unfree associations of psychoanalysts where the spirit of free inquiry has been replaced by the inculcation of received truth and the anointment of those who are supposed to possess knowledge" (Kirsner 2009, p. 10).

Richard Raubolt (2007), who experienced the pressure to submit to the views of the elite in his own training, edited a book on the subject, *Power Games: Influence, Persuasion, and Indoctrination in Psychotherapy Training.* The most egregious offenses can occur when a teacher or leader with a sense of narcissistic entitlement violates the usual patient-therapist boundaries. This is what happened in the Sullivanian Institute/Fourth Wall Community, which began as an extreme experiment in therapeutic practice, which included patients and therapists living together in a so-called therapeutic community on Manhattan's upper west side. Basic beliefs were that traditional family relationships caused mental illness; to counter that, they promoted a communal, sexually promiscuous lifestyle. It eventually became an autocratic society with leaders and therapists wielding tremendous control over the patients and group members (Siskind 2003; Shew 2005).

And of course, established religions can become cult like. Born-again Christianity promises an easy ticket to heaven without having to think deeply about doctrine; for people who live with a good deal of emotional pain, it offers an ecstatic emotional release. While its foremost representatives, televangelists Jerry Falwell and Pat Robertson, told sinners such as gays and feminists that they would burn in hell, a friendlier approach was gaining ground, thanks to the positive thinking approach of televangelists like Benny Hinn, Joel Osteen, Joyce Meyer, Kenneth and Gloria Copeland, Harlem's "Reverend Ike" (Frederick Eikerenkoetter), and Creflo Augustus Dollar. Positive thinking will make you rich, they say, flaunting their wealth, while holding themselves up as role models for success. They promote a sense of omnipotence through their version of the YCYOR paradigm, "Once you accept the law of attraction—that the mind acts like a magnet attracting whatever it visualizes—you have granted humans omnipotence" (Ehrenreich 2009, p. 133). The mystery and awe of God is gone, or as Barbara Ehrenreich dryly says, he has been reduced to a personal assistant. "He fixeth my speeding tickets, he secureth me a good table in the restaurant, he leadeth me to book contracts" (Ehrenreich 2009, pp. 132-33).

Certain ultraconservative Roman Catholic sects, such as Opus Dei and Legionaries of Christ, have been accused by Catholic liberals of leading a double life. The Legionaries of Christ may be dissolving because of exposure of scandals involving sexual molestation by its founder, the late Father Marcial Maciel. Opus Dei Awareness Network (ODAN) has described Opus Dei as a cult-like Catholic mafia, exposing extremes of self-flagellation and self-mutilation. Ultra-orthodox Hasidic Jews are known for their ecstatic praying and singing, but recently their insulated world was shaken by members in

New York bringing charges against religious leaders who had sexually molested them, mirroring the scandal within the Catholic Church.

A number of parent organizations formed when parents discovered that their college-age children had joined cults and took concerted action. The first groups formed in the U.S. during the late 1970s. There was American Family Foundation (AFF), Citizens Freedom Foundation (CFF), then the Cult Awareness Network (CAN). After CAN had been the object of nearly 50 lawsuits, most associated with the Church of Scientology, it went bankrupt. Today, this movement has become the International Cultic Studies Association (ICSA), a worldwide network of parents, mental health professionals, and former cult members concerned about psychological manipulation and abuse in cultic groups.

SNAPPING AND ECSTASY

> Humpty Dumpty sat on a wall
> Humpty Dumpty had a great fall
> All the King's horses
> And all the King's men
> Couldn't put Humpty together again!
> —nursery rhyme

Conway and Siegelman (1995) have used the word *snapping* to describe the moment when the individual's mind shuts down. They have concluded that acts of speech, ranging from sermons to hypnosis to casual chatter, as well as non-verbal communication, have the power to affect biological functions at their most basic levels and human awareness in its highest states of consciousness. Such communication may push a person to the breaking point, and his mind may snap like a piece of brittle plastic or a rubber band (Farber 2000). This can occur

> when an individual, for whatever reason, stops thinking and feeling for himself, when he breaks the bonds of awareness and social relationship that tie his personality to the world and literally loses his mind to some form of external or automatic control. . . . It takes place as some invisible switch is thrown in the infinitely flexible human brain, whether voluntarily and in good faith or unwittingly and in a state of confusion, as personality is surrendered to some religion, psychology, ideology, technology or other recipe for living that requires no real conscience and no consciousness, no effort or attention on the individual's part (Conway and Siegelman 1995, p. 325).

Snapping results from an assault to the brain and nervous system. It can result from food and sleep deprivation and sensory overstimulation but can also result from other intense experiences that abuse an individual's capacity for thought and feeling. Such experiences are as powerful as any physical force in their potential to impair the brain's information- processing activities. The most prevalent result of snapping is an ongoing altered state of consciousness, often perceived as an uncontrollable sensation of "floating." A more extreme result may be vivid delusions and hallucinations that may lead to violent or self-destructive behavior. It may result in not thinking, literally shutting off the mind. When not thinking becomes the norm for an individual, he may be literally incapable of coming out of this state on his own. In the TM movement, this is the state that is strived for, what Maharishi Mahesh Yogi called *bliss* or *cosmic consciousness*. The repeated chanting of the Hare Krishna mantra can produce the same result.

Hare Krishna Hare Krishna
Krishna Krishna Hare Hare
Hare Rama Hare Rama
Rama Rama Hare Hare

Any meditation experience, not only the TM variety, can produce relaxation-induced anxiety, panic, confusion, depression, agitation, floating, hallucinations, sweating, trembling, shivering, and in some cases schizophrenic breakdowns and suicidal tendencies. When 221 university students who had learned to meditate (up to 70 percent using the TM method) were compared to 860 nonmeditators, the meditators displayed a significantly wider range of complex partial epileptic-like signs, supporting the hypothesis that procedures which promote cognitive kindling enhance complex partial epileptic-like seizures (Persinger 1993).

Snapping may happen suddenly and abruptly, or it may be a slower, more gradual process of subtle changes. A person may report that "Something snapped inside me," or "I cannot describe it. I just snapped." To try to make sense of the experience, they might become convinced that they had gone crazy or had quite literally blown their minds. In fact, there is evidence that many kinds of experiences can cause fuses to be blown in the brain, a sudden snapping of synaptic connections and lasting neurochemical changes in the regions of the brain where thinking, feeling, awareness, imagination, and long-term memory are concentrated (Conway and Siegelman 1995).

Conway and Siegelman use chaos and catastrophe theories to explain how snapping occurs, telling us that chaos theory takes us back to the notion of chaos describing the dynamics inherent in energy transformation (Gleick 1987; Chamberlain and Butz 1998). Both Freud and Jung were deeply concerned with how energy is transformed. "It is the spirit of the chaotic waters of the beginning, before the second day of Creation, before the separation of opposites and hence before the advent of consciousness. That is why it leads those whom it overcomes neither upwards nor beyond, but back into chaos" (Jung 1970 p. 252). Catastrophe theory, the cousin of chaos theory, is concerned with events that happen abruptly in fits, jumps, and starts, with discontinuous, catastrophic change of the kind described as the straw that broke the camel's back. They use these theories as a lens for understanding different forms of snapping—the kind triggered by a single overwhelming trauma, a more gradual buildup of stresses, or a masterfully packaged mix of communication techniques (Farber 2000) that delivers "a systematically engineered snapping moment" (Conway and Siegelman 1995, p. 210). Catastrophe theory can help to explain the disorientation and delusions found in many cult members and the ongoing ecstasies of many born-again Christians.

Only the theory of snapping can explain the profound personality shifts and other odd effects they so often produce the disorientation and delusions that occur in many self-help therapy participants, the sensation of experiencing mystical realms of consciousness among practitioners of Eastern meditation methods, the ongoing ecstasies common to self-help buffs and born-again Christians alike, and the strange trance-like states characteristic of so many cult members (Conway and Siegelman 1995). Conway and Siegelman have found evidence that snapping may also be implicated in the Tate-LaBianca murders by the Manson family in 1969, the armed robbery committed by heiress Patty Hearst in 1974, and the Son of Sam (David Berkowitz) series of random street murders in New York in 1977.

WHAT PSYCHOTHERAPISTS TREATING CULT-INVOLVED PATIENTS NEED TO KNOW

Most people, psychotherapists included, incorrectly assume cults to be small, isolated, bizarre, religious groups which attract only the impressionable, the unsophisticated, and the deeply disturbed. Despite the fact that several studies have reported ex-cult members' eye-witness accounts of antisocial and sexually and physically abusive acts by cult leaders (Burke 2006; Shaw 2003), most therapists know little about the impact that cult life can have on a member, and are likely to assume that the patient's sudden personality changes and other symptoms, even psychotic delusions and hallucinations, are the result of serious failures in family life, underlying anxieties, guilt-ridden insecurities, ego conflicts, and early childhood trauma. Therapists are likely to be incredulous upon hearing patients' accounts, because they do sound frankly unbelievable, just as the story about the mass suicide at Jonestown seemed so unbelievable. Therapists must understand that the distress levels of former members are comparable to those of inpatients in psychiatric hospitals. Although approximately one third of cult members studied were sufficiently troubled before joining that they sought professional help, the majority seem to have been relatively normal before joining (Martin, Dole, Lang one and.Wiltrout 1992).

One of the first mental health professionals to study cults was Harvard psychiatrist John G. Clark, a co-founder of AFF, who testified before a special committee of the Vermont State Senate investigating the negative effects of some religious cults. "The fact of a personality shift in my opinion is established. The fact that this is a phenomenon basically unfamiliar to the mental health profession I am certain of. The fact that our ordinary methods of treatment don't work is also clear, as are the frightening hazards to the process of personal growth and mental health" (Conway and Siegelman 1995, p. 86).

Both clinical and research findings suggest that it is during periods of stress or transition that a person can succumb to the cult's promise to transform their lives. Former cult members who enter therapy are likely to encounter a therapist who may find their story about the cult experience so incredible that they cannot consider the possibility that it or much of it is true. The wide variety of presenting problems displayed by former cult members are likely to be ascribed to other causes, an assumption which can further traumatize the already traumatized patient.

The first generation of cult members were young people who left home and school looking for meaning, and were seduced into thinking they had found it in such groups as the Unification Church, Children of God, The International Society for Krishna Consciousness, Scientology and others. As their numbers increased, the different faiths and practices began to blur in the public eye. Although some told stories about how they found true happiness, seemingly overnight, many seemed to have lost their spontaneity, humor, and ability to think for themselves. Alarmed by these changes, parents took extreme measures to rescue their children, seeking help from deprogrammers and as they were later called, exit counselors, and from therapists who specialized in cult-related treatment (Goldberg 1993, 1997 Langone 1993; Shaw 2003; Szimhart 2009).

CULTS AND THE CONSCIOUSNESS EXPLOSION

Ted Patrick, a black man from Southern California known to grateful parents as *Black Lightning*, became the first parent to take action against the cults. He saw the beaches filled with vacationing students being recruited by the Hare Krishna and Children of God cults. Then one day the Children of God approached his son and nearly abducted him. Patrick investigated and infiltrated the group, was shocked by what he discovered, and took a direct course of action, an antidote he called "deprogramming," to help cult members regain their freedom of thought. Soon, desperate parents from all over the U.S. were hiring him to deprogram their children (Conway and Siegelman 1995). When questioned about how the cults affect the mind so adversely, Patrick replied:

> The cults completely destroy the mind. They destroy your ability to question things and in destroying your ability to think, they also destroy your ability to feel. You have no desires, no emotion. You feel no pain, no joy, no nothing. They have the ability to come up to you and talk about anything they think you're interested in, anything. Their technique is to get your attention, then your trust. The minute they get your trust, just like that they can put you in the cult (Conway and Siegelman 1995, p. 59).

"It was the classic sales pitch, done so smoothly that it amounted to what Patrick called 'on the spot hypnosis'"(Conway and Siegelman 1995, p. 59). Once the potential member is hooked, he said, they keep up a steady barrage of indoctrination until conversion is complete. When he infiltrated the cult that tried to recruit his son, although he was acutely aware of their tactics, he found nonetheless that he was not immune to their effects.

> There's just so much the human mind can take. . . You can hear the same thing over and over and then it breaks you down. I went into one of the cults with the intention of staying a week. I stayed four days and three nights, and if I'd stayed six more hours I would have been hooked. I'd have never left. You can feel it coming on. You start doubting yourself. You start to question everything you believe in. Then you find yourself saying and doing the same things they are. You feel like you're sinking in sand, drowning—sometimes you get dizzy (Conway and Siegelman 1995, p. 60).

This was the moment of "giving up and going under," feeling the overwhelming emotional release of snapping. From this point on, the new member is taught daily rituals of chanting and meditation which prevent him from regaining control of his mind or of wanting to. He is broken. Patrick speculated that we all can be vulnerable to the cult influence.

Years ago, having had someone in my family become deeply involved in a cult, I toyed with the idea of infiltrating one to understand first-hand what newcomers were subjected to. After reading *Snapping*, I became fearful of the effect and decided against it, but when I was considering it, the most likely candidate was the Unification Church. Their headquarters and Reverend Sun Myung Moon's family home was Belvedere, a 25-acre estate, just around four miles from my home, an historical area largely known for Washington Irving's legend of the Headless Horseman. Many of the conferences and trainings have been held there and the area is home to many Moonie families. Although the children attend the public schools, these families otherwise live lives apart from the community. Years later, while having my hair cut in Irvington, Kathy, the hairdresser, was annoyed that most of the Moonie childen in her daughter's class had not responded to the birthday party's invitation RSVP request. "They never do," she said. "I'll just have to call Messiah's mother and check." "*Messiah's mother*?" I asked incredulously. Hispanic boys may be named Jesus but never before had I heard of a boy named Messiah.

Some of the most bizarre accounts of snapping moments came from former Krishna members. One of them described the ancient Hindu ritual called *arotika*, in which a candle is offered to their deities, accompanied by very loud chanting of Hare Krishna and jumping up and down.

> I was with these devotees who were all the way they get in the arotika, and I got caught up in it just like everyone else. I was closing my eyes hard, trying to get that bliss and make it come; and it did, more or less. I felt like I saw a white light. I felt like I was going to explode. I guess you can relate it to a sexual thing, like a climax or something. . . . Right at the peak the person who was leading the ceremony blew the conch shell, then everyone fell to the floor and started reciting their little prayers. Afterwards, everyone was really high. Some people were in a trance state. Others became very quiet. Then we all sat and received a lecture,. When we were totally drained, they poured in all the indoctrination (Conway and Siegelman 1995, pp. 130-31).

The Hare Krishna's belonged to the first generation of cult involvement. The following generation grew out of humanistic psychology, which led the way in the exploration of mankind's uniquely human capacities. Shaped by figures such as Gordon Allport, Rollo May, Carl Rogers, and Abraham Maslow, the new humanistic therapies used a person's own experience as a tool to help him alter not only his behavior but his state of awareness, even his whole personality. This new psychology and its offspring, the human potential movement, changed popular attitudes toward mental health (Conway and Siegelman 1995). Psychoanalysis, psychotherapy, and traditional group therapy were losing patients to weekend encounter groups, extended marathons, and more radical therapies that used intense physical and emotional experiences, including arm wrestling, body massage, verbal attacks, and prolonged confinement to produce peak experiences and breakthrough moments.

This new experimental climate soon grew reckless, and many participants responded by snapping, becoming violent, self-destructive, or frankly psychotic. Others snapped more quietly, dropping into fantasy states and remaining there, disoriented. The burden of treating these casualties of the consciousness explosion fell to mental health professionals who were ill-equipped to understand it.

ECSTASIES OF COSMIC CONSCIOUSNESS

In the seventies Transcendental Meditation (TM) was in the air, on television, everywhere, a supposedly harmless technique and scientifically validated program considered the IBM of the human potential movement. TM became the largest and most widely known of the new mass-marketed self-help techniques. Neuroscientist Michael Persinger and colleagues who studied the effects of meditation, TM and other varieties, characterized the TM movement as a half-breed between a psychotherapy and evangelistic movement (Persinger1993; Persinger, Carrey, and Suess 1980).

Although there was a great deal of medical and scientific support for it, much of the research reported as fact and published by the TM organization was questionable, with TM making unsubstantiated claims from biology and quantum physics. The TM organization claimed that unless meditators took TM's course and purchased their "custom-tailored" mantra, based upon secret criteria of "neurophysiological specificity," they were likely to suffer severe effects. The research conducted by the TM Organization was published in the *Journal of the American Medical Association* by wellness guru Deepak Chopra and associates (Chopra, Sharma, and Triguna 1991). Chopra probably has done more than anyone else to popularize the Maharishi's ayurvedic medicine in America. However, there was a good deal of criticism from the journal's readers over the validity of the article's argument, and the associate editor wrote a rebuttal criticizing the authors' conflict of interest in validating and selling their products. It included allegations of suppression of negative evidence, fraud and "gross scientific incompetence," lack of double-blind controls, refusal to submit raw data, failure to control for set effects, failure to control for expectancy of relief, failure to control for placebo/suggestible-prone subjects, and others (Skolnick 1991).

In the enthusiasm for meditation of all kinds, it was overlooked that meditation is not beneficial for everyone. There are numerous studies confirming the potential negative effects of prolonged or even short-term meditation (Conway and Siegelman 1995). Intense forms of meditation can alter serotonin levels. Some studies show that it increases, others show that it decreases, and many question whether the effects are beneficial or harmful (Newberg 2010). Most casual TM meditators use their twice daily meditation for simple rest and relaxation, and never succeeded in actually *transcending*. Barry Robertson, a man who practiced TM for 4½ years, earning his livelihood for nearly half that time as a TM instructor, cautioned that of the many varieties of meditation, TM presents a particular hazard, one that would probably be shocking to most casual practioners of the technique.

> There are four basic types of meditation and there is a major difference between TM and the others. First, there's *contemplation*, in which you take a sentence or a parable and you think about it. You just go into your mind and close out the outside world and you think. . . . Contemplation is similar to another type of meditation that I would classify as *Christian meditation*. This consists of studying the scriptures and pondering God and thinking about how you can use that scripture to give meaning to your life. The third type of

> meditation is simply *concentration*, where you concentrate on one spot on the wall or your navel or a spot on the middle of your forehead. You concentrate on one thing and you try to get the ability to hold your thoughts there. If you find yourself wandering off into other things, you bring your mind right back to that one point. . . In TM, you *empty* your mind. TM is switching your mind into neutral. You have no control over it; you try not to have control over it. You try to just let your mind go flat, with no thoughts whatsoever. When you concentrate on anything, you have at least one thought. TM attempts to go beyond that.
>
> According to Robertson, to achieve this emptying of the mind, each student is given what is said to be his own custom-tailored mantra, a Sanskrit word which the Maharishi Mahesh Yogi defined as a meaningless sound with a "vibratory effect" that helps the mind reach a quiet state. . . . To do TM, Robertson told us, you repeated the mantra over and over again in your mind, and as with anything, if you hear a steady noise over and over again, eventually your ears won't hear that noise anymore. . . . As the mind becomes accustomed to a particular one, the meditator's awareness begins to change. . . the first effect of TM is a soothing, emotional high brought on by the brain's response to repetition (Conway and Siegelman 1995, pp.171-72).

As the brain adjusts to this repetition, the sound of the meditator's inner voice diminishes, producing the soothing, tranquilizing effect TM claims to offer. Despite its immediate benefits, the initial high wears off quickly and many people stop meditating because it then becomes boring. But those who stay with it for any length of time become vulnerable to its long-term impact. Robertson continued:

> Soon your mind gets to a place where it no longer associates meaning to anything. You just have this sound going on in your mind, and you get to a place where there's no longer concrete meaning. You're just abstractly experiencing nothing. You'd think a person would become afraid in this emptiness or vacuum, but this happens to your feelings too. You reach a state where you're not feeling anything either. By the way, this is the state that Maharishi calls bliss (Conway and Siegelman 1995, p. 172).

It may also be called Cosmic Consciousness, in which one experiences himself as totally detached from the world. Robertson said

> You can watch yourself do things, you can even watch yourself sleep. You actually—it's hard to explain—dissolve would be a good word. . . I was sensing all kinds of telepathic things. I would see energy surrounding people, little thin auras of different pastel colors, and bigger egg-shaped ones made out of huge spirals. It was weird, trying to associate the ordinary world when you're seeing all these things happening around people (Conway and Siegelman 1995, p. 173).

Enrollment in TM had always depended a great deal on endorsement by celebrities such as the Beatles, Mia Farrow, George Lucas, Merv Griffin, and Clint Eastwood. After 1975, celebrity endorsement and enrollment had dropped a good deal, but then enrollment tripled with the help of celebrities like Russell Brand, Mehmet Oz, the singer Moby, and film director David Lynch. Lynch established the David Lynch Foundation, an organization offering TM at no fee to troubled students, veterans, homeless people, prisoners and others. Lynch is seeking $7 billion and 8,000 additional meditation students in the expectation that doing so will establish world peace (Aleksander 2011).

THE TRANSCENDENTAL MEDITATION "VISION OF POSSIBILITIES"

In 1975, when Patrick Ryan was a high school senior, recruiters from Maharishi International University (MIU) in Fairfield, Iowa, came to his school. He was from a middle-class Irish-Catholic family and was at a crossroads in his life, when decisions about college and what path the rest of his life would take loomed large, and made him vulnerable. He was readily persuaded to attend an introductory lecture at MIU, where he was introduced to Transcendental Meditation and its "vision of possibilities." Although he was told that the university is accredited through the PhD level, offering scientifically-validated "consciousness-based education," he was not told that the content of the program was shrouded in secrecy because of Maharishi's fear of infiltration by U.S. and foreign government agencies.

Ryan was not seeking cosmic consciousness, ecstasy, or enlightenment. These were matters he seemed not to have thought about, but once recruited into TM, he was indoctrinated to believe that seeking cosmic consciousness was the key to enlightenment. And enlightenment, whatever that was, was a very good thing. He was told that if he concentrated hard enough he would be able to levitate, also known as yogic flying. Some TMers spent thousands of dollars for this higher level of training, but if you look at videos online at youtube.com, what you see is not people flying. You'll see people sitting in the lotus position within a dome-shaped structure known as a levitation dome, on what looks like a thick layer of foam rubber padding, and bouncing and hopping around on their behinds. As Andrew Newberg dryly put it, "It may be an ecstatic, enlightened hop, but it isn't levitation" (Newberg 2010, p. 166). *David Wants to Fly,* a recently released film about a young man's interest in flying, has scenes of TM levitation, some of which can be viewed on Youtube.com.

Among the extravagant "visions of possibilities," the movement claims that if a large group of people practice TM simultaneously, it will have a peaceful effect on the immediate area and reduce crime. Their aim is to establish international Transcendental Consciousness, and they had obtained contracts to develop TM programs in schools, businesses, and prisons. Other possibilities for Ryan were advanced lectures, weekly and monthly meditation check-ups, residence courses, the Science of Creative Intelligence course, MIU education, and an introduction to the worldwide scope of the movement. The Science of Creative Intelligence course was offered for credit at a number of colleges, including Yale and Stanford, and found its way into the New York public school system (Appelbaum 1979). Ryan found this compelling enough to enroll at MIU for the introductory course, which cost $175 at that time. (As of 2008, it cost $2,500.)

He was told that his mantra was chosen specially for him based on secret criteria, and was never to be uttered aloud, because "If other people know it and say it, then the power is lost" (Persinger, Carrey, and Suess 1980, p. 57). Despite the mystique surrounding the mantra, what Patrick was not told was that in fact his mantra was chosen randomly and efficiently from a list, based on age and gender. He dutifully followed the program that had been laid out for him. Soon the residence course replaced his twice a day meditation with "rounding," a process of more frequent meditations, breathing techniques, yogic postures, and repetitive videos of the Maharishi. He was given a "buddy" to ensure that he was never alone with his own thoughts. He accepted the doctrine that the enlightened man has no use for critical thinking, because he lives in tune with the "unbounded universal consciousness." He was told not to watch television, read newspapers, listen to the radio, or make phone calls. There was a dress code, special diet, curfews, and his behavior was carefully monitored. During his first rounding, he experienced states of euphoria, periods of depersonalization, confusion, irritability, and memory difficulties. A fundamental concept he learned was that of stress release. It was explained that as a meditator progresses, stress is released, a process called *unstressing*, which can cloud the thinking process and lead to doubts about TM. So any doubts they might have were simply the product of *unstressing*.

The movement preys upon the tendency of many to rely on magical thinking, which reinforces the tendency to endow the leader with omnipotent and magical powers, much like the child's early conceptual depiction of the parent who at that time, did control his universe. The member can readily come to believe that the leader can read his mind or hear conversations at a distance. Slowly, greater and greater irrational power is attributed to the leader. TM and philsophies like it confuse the person who has difficulty discriminating fine semantic issues or difficult concepts, especially those that are emotionally laden, such as death, self identity, and the future.

If an individual is at all susceptible to psychotic breakdown, the practice of TM can readily precipitate it. Such philosophies offer the kind of metaphors and delusional systems to which the psychotic individual is prone—

control of matter by thinking, floating in the air, invisibility, projection through space and time, mind migration, being God. The promises of invisibility, translocation, telepathy, and levitation—all these are the incentives of TM (Persinger, Carrey, and Suess 1980).

Ryan went on to enroll in the advanced TM-Sidhi program, which promised to develop supernormal powers, such as levitation, omniscience, and invisibility, walking through walls, mind reading, extra-sensory perception, empathy, compassion, perfect health, immortality, and the creation of peace. Pat Ryan paid the $1,400.00 tuition with a federally insured student loan.

The beginning instructions were given by the Maharishi on tape. "'So you want to learn to fly?' He whispered the phrase 'relationship of body and akasha—lightness of cotton fiber' and told us to repeat it in 15 second intervals. This, he said, would make us fly. We were sent to the flying hall, a room covered with foam rubber mattresses. A few in our group began to hop like rabbits. . . . the group pressure to fly increased" (Ryan 1993, pp. 132-33). People hyperventilated, screamed, made jerky movements, laughed, and had out-of-body experiences, for which they earned academic credit. My family member who had been a TM instructor for many years and lived in Radiance, the first Ideal Village, said he slammed into the wall while levitating and broke his good watch, so he switched to a cheap Timex.

Ryan and others in the Sidhi program were required to assemble twice a day to levitate. The chairman of the physics department explained that the Maharishi had discovered that flying together in groups could create world peace, and to this end, teams of "flyers" were sent to war-torn areas of the world like Nicaragua, Iran, and El Salvador. The Maharishi then pronounced that world peace had been achieved. This was known as the *Maharishi Effect,* otherwise called *super-radiance* (Conway and Seigelman 1995). (If this sounds at all like God speaking the world into existence by saying let there be light, and there was light (Genesis 1: 3), it is no small coincidence.)

Radiance, the first TM Ideal Village, was formed in 1984 in an Austin, Texas suburb. In addition to a community swimming pool, Radiance had a 70-foot-wide meditation/levitation dome. Other Ideal Villages were formed in Fairfield, Iowa, in Philadelphia, and in the Netherlands, Scotland, Pakistan and Canada. Upon graduating from MIU in 1980, Ryan moved to Philadelphia to live and work with other "flyers," and with them formed an Ideal Village. By living together and flying together, they believed the world would be changed for the better more quickly. Many of those at the Sidhi level induced altered states of consciousness in themselves to the point that they occurred with little or no effort. Being a "space cadet" or being "blissed out" in ecstasy, along with mindlessly wandering, twitching, shaking, and Tourette's type utterances and tics were all considered signs of spiritual growth. As Ryan's commitment to the movement strengthened, he broke away from his family and old sense of identity, and became depressed and chronically ill.

His sister had joined another cult, The Way International, and his family arranged for an exit counseling, and asked Ryan to contact the Cult Awareness Network (CAN) for information about The Way. In speaking with two CAN representatives, he found himself feeling unsettled. When he told them that he was a member of TM, they told him that TM was controversial, to which he responded automatically, "TM is not a cult. It is a scientifically validated program" (Ryan 1993, p. 134). As he listened to the exit counselor explaining the nature of group involvement, he began to discover that he had a mind and could use it to think independently. He began to develop a new view about hypnosis and trance states. What had begun as exit counseling for his sister turned out to help him leave TM.

It took a year before he physically left the movement. During this time, he secretly began contacting former members and former MIU faculty, who provided shocking information about bogus scientific research, systematic cover ups of the adverse effects of TM programs—the tic disorders, mental breakdowns, and suicides, the money transfers, and shocking details of Maharishi's personal life. He discovered how brilliantly the Maharishi marketed ecstasy. Pat Ryan knew he would lose his friends if they discovered he had stopped meditating, and feared how they would respond to his questions. As he began to voice his concerns, he quickly became *persona non grata* and was not allowed in the local TM center. He feared how he would survive in the outside word. It took nine more years to recover. During this period he attended a session for former cult members at a CAN conference, and discovered that although the people he met had belonged to different groups, they were all talking about having had essentially the same experience as he had. The key process was the same; only the details were different. Despite having made the break from the movement, he had difficulties with reading, memory, concentration, focus, involuntary body shaking, and dissociation. When he broke the movement's code of silence by speaking to a reporter, he began to shake violently, and was confused and scared. At times he found himself defending the movement and wondering aloud if he was a spiritual failure.

Despite the movement's teaching that mental health professionals never solve problems, just "stir the mud," he began treatment with the late Dr, Margaret Singer, a noted cult expert, and discovered that his problems with recovery were similar to those of other long-term members. In the TM world, it was not only all right to be a "space cadet,' it was a sign of cosmic consciousness. He had been taught that we create our own reality, that our thoughts can magically materialize into matter. Having lived outside popular culture for ten years, he had no knowledge of popular music, films, literature, and world events. He had to learn how to carry on a casual conversation without turning it into a recruiting session. He found that he needed to work on his chronic depersonalization, on his orientation to reality, and his social skills.

Patrick Ryan has been a mind control consultant since 1981, and an exit counselor since 1986. He settled a law suit against TM for fraud and negligence in 1991, and is the founder and former head of TM-EX, an organization of ex-members of TM. He speaks openly about the movement's darker side, including psychiatric hospitalizations and suicides. He designs and implements the International Cultic Studies Association web site, www.icsahome.com..

SOUL MURDER

Soul murder is the term coined by psychoanalyst Leonard Shengold (1979, 1989, 2000) to describe "the deliberate attempt to eradicate or compromise the separate identity of another person. The victims of soul murder remain in large part possessed by another, their souls in bondage to someone else (1989, p.2)." Shengold cites George Orwell 's *1984*, in which O'Brien says to Winston Smith: "You will be hollow. We will squeeze you empty, and then we shall fill you with ourselves (Orwell 1949, p.260)." Cult leaders seem to know all too well something else that Orwell said: "Power is in tearing human minds to pieces and putting them together again in new shapes of your own choosing (Orwell 1949, p.211)." Sometimes, that process is an ecstatic one.

Even if they have left the cult but have not come to understand their cult experience, they may well be plagued by after effects long after (Goldberg 1993, 1997). They may feel flooded with emotions almost constantly, alternating with *floating* in altered states of consciousness. There is a deep sense of loneliness after leaving the cult; cult friendships are usually conditional, based on loyalty to the cult. There are also feelings of grief, the loss of a life that promised total fulfillment and disappointed so badly. There may be grief too for the years of missed possibilities while in the cult, perhaps not having had the opportunity to enter into a satisfying intimate relationship, to have children, or to acquire career skills.

SHE SAW ME GLOWING, JUST LIKE FREEDOM, HER GURU

Meryl was the first patient with cult-related psychopathology that I Ever treated (Farber 2000). When she came to see me, in the late seventies, all I knew about cults was that the leader had potentially dangerous charismatic powers. It was clear that she had been severely mentally ill long before joining the cult, and that her cult experience had greatly exacerbated her illness. .

Being a follower of Sai Baba Muktananda, a vegetarian, and a feminist defined Meryl's sense of identity. As a feminist, she used her maiden name. In the first session, she seemed troubled that I did not use mine. She insisted on knowing if I were a "meat eater"; my answer to that disturbed her too. Our differences were such that she doubted she could be in treatment with me. However, by the end of the first session she said that perhaps one day she would be able to ask me why I use my married name, not my maiden name. Her beginning interest in our differences demonstrated an openness to developing a capacity for ambiguity and to think for herself. She had quickly dropped her hard intellectualized manner and seemed almost shy and eager to be liked.

Even before beginning treatment, there was a positive transference-like wish for her new therapist to be omnipotent and to cure her. Meryl sought treatment at age 27, presenting herself in a very intellectualized fashion. About to receive her B.A. in gerontology and counseling the dying, and preparing to study on the graduate level, she was referred to me because she wanted to be sure that she was not going into this field to satisfy neurotic needs of her own. She also said that she wanted to explore the didactics of her personality, although she could not explain what she meant by that. She was also bothered by her husband's impotence, going on for several months. She wanted intercourse at least daily, preferably more.

She sought treatment at a time of crisis; her usual defenses of splitting, dissociation, intellectualization and obsessional thinking could no longer defend against the anxiety evoked by unacceptable drive and affect coming into consciousness. Her lifestyle had been geared to dampening down these feelings through yoga, fasting, chanting, and vegetarianism.

Terrified at the crumbling of her defenses, Meryl was actively and consciously involved in building a new defense which she called her filing cabinet. The filing cabinet was psychically built the same night her husband expressed sexual interest in her friend. It seemed that before arranging an appointment with me, a female friend was visiting, staying with her and her husband. He expressed to Meryl his sexual interest in her friend. She became enraged and was upset at how angry she felt because this emotion was not at all acceptable, believing as she did that people do not own each other and should be free to explore intimacy with others. Her anger was at odds with the teaching of Sai Baba Muktananda, who taught love and transcendence of such negative emotions. She experienced an overwhelming ego regression with loss of ego boundaries, cold sweats and shivering, heart palpitations, visual distortions in which objects changed shape and glowed. It was her desire to defend herself from psychosis that enabled her to construct her filing cabinet. Affects and memories were filed into psychic folders labeled

"Do not open *ever*," "Open only at own risk" and "Do not open until you see therapist." This was her "holding operation" until beginning treatment, or more accurately, until the establishment of safe and secure attachment, when she could experience herself as basking in the glow of the omnipotence and grandiosity which she had projected onto me.

At the same time that she fought against the symbiotic merger of psychosis, she was equally drawn to it consciously, as expressed by her wish to throw out the filing cabinet and "just go with the flow of the feelings." This was the most alarming problem, that the conscious desire for fusion was almost as great as the wish to defend against it, symbolized by the filing cabinet, with its drawers locked shut or opened wide, revealing a chaotic Pandora's box of horrors. She regarded the filing cabinet as bad, a crutch; it was bad because it meant that she had a need for it, and since she, like Buddha, should be without self and without needs, she wanted to dismantle it. She could not consider my suggestion to keep the filing cabinet available in case of future need, to repair and modify it rather than destroy it altogether, because that presumed an ability to tolerate ambiguity which she did not have. Everything was black or white, bad or good, false or true.

In the second session she complained about her husband's impotence. Although he stimulated her to orgasm manually, this is not what she wanted. She wanted vaginal penetration; if he could not do this with his penis, she wanted him to use his fingers instead. When I asked if she had told him that, she said that he should *know* that is what she wants and should be more sensitive to her feelings. When I told her that a man cannot know specifically what a woman wants sexually unless she lets him know, explaining that they are two different and separate people and that he cannot know what it feels like when she wants her vagina penetrated because neither his mind nor his sexual organs are the same as hers. He cannot possibly know what it feels like to be penetrated, just as she cannot know what it feels like for him to penetrate a vagina with his penis. This amazed her; what I said was so simple, but she had never thought of it.

As we continued in treatment, as the session was ending, she would linger, trying to prolong it. When I indicated that our time is over for the day, she has said enough times for it to have become a private joke, "Boy, time really flies when you're having fun." (Humor requires a capacity for ambiguity.)

Weeks later when once again her husband did not respond to her demand for sexual intercourse, Meryl physically attacked him, interspersed with her sitting naked on the floor, drooling, rocking back and forth, chanting in rhyme. Although she observed herself "acting like a real crazy," she was enjoying it too much to stop. She disclosed that she thought she may not have come to grips with her feelings about two abortions she had had in the past five years and thought that in some way she felt she had committed murder.

She rarely thinks about it but finds herself crying at diaper commercials on television.

Meryl's father had a history of mental illness, with many hospitalizations, suicide attempts, and violence toward his children. Meryl was born in the midst of her mother's psychotic depression. She had told Meryl how disappointed she and her father were that she was not born a boy, but simply decided to treat her as if she were. Meryl did not speak until age five, and had been diagnosed at various clinics as being severely retarded or brain damaged. At age eleven, she tried to strangle her sister, who had taunted her.

During adolescence she masturbated a great deal, read S&M pornography, and was often in a sexually aroused state. At 15, she had intercourse with her first boyfriend, Barry, often several times a night after he had tied her to the bed and abused her verbally. Once she tried to kill him after one insult too many. When she discovered he was involved with another girl, she set out on a campaign of promiscuity, picking up men in bars. She called it her 4 Fs: Find Them, Feel Them, Fuck Them, Forget Them. At the same time she was taking a lot of LSD, drinking, and taking tranquilizers, and had thoughts of suicide which one of her intended sexual conquests talked her out of. She saw a series of psychiatrists and psychotherapists, not finding them helpful.

Despite how ill she was, she had a certain resilience[4] Resourceful in seeking out treatment in adolescence and again in adulthood, and in getting the court to find her a foster family. From the beginning, a positive transference developed as I became a mother surrogate; she quickly began internalizing some of my ideas, specific phrases and expressions, and even part of my observing and synthesizing ego functions. However, a disturbing transference psychosis developed early on when I expressed interest in knowing more about her religious beliefs. She described an experience at Sai Baba's ashram. One of his avatars was a man named Freedom, who could read her mind, through one intense look was able to unite his soul with hers, and could extract from her all her evil thoughts so that they became reflected in his face. Although she did not say so, it seemed that she wanted that kind of relationship with me. She wanted to bring me some literature to read. To clarify, I told her that I was interested in her religion because she seemed to find so much in it that she needed, and I wanted to understand that better. She seemed not to hear me, smiled and said that I had started to glow, a golden glow. Then I saw her starting to glow too, and it frightened me. Was it contagious? Many years later I learned that this is what is known as the Isakower phenomena (Isakower 1992a, 1992b), the joint participation of patient and analyst that makes that relationship a unique analyzing instrument. It was a precursor to Bromberg's (1998) concept of how a patient can induce in the therapist the same feelings by means of a dissociated process of projective identification. She said that I looked very soft and golden around the edges, that I had a beautiful aura. Intuitively I knew to curtail this experience and said that she seemed to see me as she had seen Freedom but I did not have the special powers she thought he had. This brought her back to reality a bit, and feeling assured that I was on the right track, I asked if she had forgotten to pay me last month's bill, a question which seemed to bring her back to reality. Yes, she said, she had forgotten and would bring it next time. I suggested that perhaps she forgot because she did not want to pay for her therapy. She laughed, said she really did forget, but by now I know her belief that all health care should be free. I replied that perhaps that might happen in some perfect world but in this imperfect world we both lived in it was not possible; she had to pay for her treatment.

The transference psychosis reappeared from time to time. I had to interpret consistently how each time it was another somewhat different configuration of condensed experiences. My interpretations made it clear that I would not become a real part of her transference, and this seemed to help resolve the transference psychosis. She began to feel anxious about her sessions, wanting to cancel because it was so painful. I responded that bringing her back to reality was so painful for her; if I had the power to make it less painful I would. She voiced the wish to hurt me by throwing me against the wall, something her father threatened to do to her. She spoke of how scary he was, and said that she wanted to throw him against the wall so that she would not feel so frightened and immobilized. I reminded her of how she could want to throw me against the wall, and even tell me about it and yet could restrain herself from doing it.

She began cancelling sessions and when she finally came in, said how great she felt when she did not see me, and had been tempted to cancel this session. I said that I thought she was afraid of her angry, violent feelings toward me, that maybe she was afraid that she really would slam me against the wall. She could not understand why she might want to do that to me and so I interpreted that she seemed to be feeling the violent wish to throw her father against the wall while she was here with me, and somehow the intensity of her wish caused he to confuse me momentarily with her father, so that she felt for the moment that I *was* her father. She was stunned, remained silent a long time, then said it was amazing that as I spoke to her, she saw me fade and my facial features changed into her father's, so that for a moment she literally saw me as her father. She said she had no way to understand intellectually what had happened but it rang so true emotionally for her. Never could she have put it into words herself.

She cancelled the next session but called me four nights later, the second time that she had called me. She was happy to tell me that although she had physically attacked her husband a few nights before, she was able to observe herself, think a bit, and stop the attack quickly. Later she asked him to help her when she gets so crazy—either leave the room or physically restrain her.

She was able to ask for his help, and was beginning to use both her therapist and husband in transitional ways, to help calm her down. In her next session, she said that she had attacked him twice during the week, and the second time, he was able to help her to stop, and she cried in his arms and felt comforted.

I explained that I understood how intense and frightening these feelings were but that the only way to become less frightened of acting on them is to put them into words and to think about them, and for that she must keep her appointments. "Even if I have a terrible headache, even if I've been in an accident or broken a leg?" she asked. I asked wryly if she were making such plans, at which she laughed and said sometimes she'd rather be sick as a dog than see me. I had to remind her how much control she really has, that even in the sessions when she loses herself and feels completely adrift, she still can pull herself together again. She was afraid she'd hurt me and insisted I tell her *how* I could help her regain control. I said that when we could pinpoint these moments of loss of reality, at the precise moment they happen, then I could clarify for her what is real and what is not. She doubted that just my words were enough, to which I told her that just because she wants to slam me into the wall does not mean she *has* to do it. Wishes and actions are two different things. I said "Another very important thing is that I won't *let* you hurt me. You may not do anything to harm me or damage this office. Is that clear?" She sighed with relief and said "Now *that* makes me feel much better." She kept her next appointment but voiced her fear because after all, she tried to kill her boyfriend Barry, she'd tried to kill her sister, she'd attacked her husband. I reminded her that in those situations she and the other party were mutually embroiled in escalating violence; in our relationship, it was not at all mutual. Only she wanted a violent tangle with me. I had no such interest and would not allow it to reach the point of violence. If absolutely necessary, I would call the police but I doubted that would be necessary. I would be in control and she would too. (I did not realize it at the time but that was an order. She listened.)

She continued to use her treatment very well, and began talking with her husband more about her feelings. That relationship has improved. What she had wanted most of all was to find someone to be attuned to her, to understand her empathically, and to create boundaries in the way that her cult experience failed to do.

NOTES

1. To understand what is meant by *asshole,* the glossary in Adelaide Bry's (1976) *est: 60 Hours that Transform Your Life* provides some clues. Asshole is defined as "what everyone is before he or she knows what is real and what is not (p. 226)."

2. To understand what is meant by *get it,* Adelaide Bry's glossary provides some clues. *Get* means that someone realizes the importance of a communication, a revelation.

3. To understand what is meant by "We can't help you but we can assist you," *assist* is defined as "aid to another person, coming from the assumption that the other person is responsible and at cause" (Bry 1976, p. 226).This is in contrast to *help*, "To aid someone coming from the assumption that he or she is at effect, i.e., that he or she *needs* your aid (Bry 1976, p. 231).

4. The concept of resilience will be further explored in Chapter 11.

Chapter Seven

Ecstasies of Pain and Near-Death Experiences

> The Stoic split between body and mind, like the Christian split between body and soul, indicates how ancient the desire is to assign pain wholly to the flesh.
> —David B. Morris, *The Culture of Pain*

Bob Flanagan was nude when he mounted a scaffold at a performance at the Southern Exposure Gallery in San Francisco. The audience watched as he attached fifty clothespins to his body; then watched them slowly snap off. He then sewed up his scrotum with needle and thread, and nailed the remaining skin to a block of wood. He was speaking to the audience the whole time, and amazingly, was really quite funny (Juno and Vale 1993).

Pain is a very subjective thing. Diverting ourselves from our pain can be very welcome in providing a sense of control over it. For the woman in labor, for example, a deliberate focus on patterned breathing may divert her from her pain and relax her body enough to alter her subjective experience of the pain. It is really a form of self-hypnosis. I have noticed that when I am in the dentist's office, as I am being injected with the local anesthetic lidocaine, I find myself clenching my fists so hard that my nails dig into my skin. Feeling the self-inflicted pain is a welcome diversion from pain that is being inflicted on me.

For those who have been traumatized at the hands of others by physical abuse or by medical procedures, inflicting pain on themselves can feel empowering as they take control of the pain. For those who may have been neglected as children, inflicting pain on themselves can serve the same function. Some may cut themselves to relieve their pain, starve themselves, gorge on food and then vomit, painfully and violently. Some may be *needle freaks* (Levine 1974), addicted to the pain of the tattoo needle piercing their skin.

Some may have their bodies pierced extensively and repeatedly, even their nipples, penis, labia. Some people find ecstasy in the most extreme experiences of pain and flirtation with death.

BOB FLANAGAN: SUPER-MASOCHIST

Bob Flanagan: Super-Masochist is the title of both a book (Juno and Vale 1993) and documentary film about how Bob Flanagan's childhood discovery of painful and bizarre masturbatory practices enabled him to adapt to and survive a life of pain. He was born with cystic fibrosis, a hereditary disease that is almost always fatal. It causes the lungs, pancreas and intestines to become plugged with thick mucous. Although Bob was not expected to live to adulthood, he lived to the age of 43, crediting his bizarre practices for extending his life. He was born with a genetic illness that he was supposed to succumb to at two, then ten, then twenty, and so on, but he did not. In a never-ending battle not just to survive but to subdue his stubborn disease, he learned to fight illness with illness, the most extreme masochism.

One of Bob's sisters died in infancy of cystic fibrosis, another at age 21. He lived with a constant sense of his impending death and with a sense of no control over his body. As an infant he was strapped down while doctors inserted needles into his lungs and physical therapists pounded on his chest to release the mucus that was choking him. Severe stomach aches and painful bowel movements were part of the illness, and he soon discovered that when he rubbed against the sheets and pillows to soothe his stomach, he became sexually aroused. This was the beginning of masturbating that way. "One way of taking control of the stomachache was to turn it into an orgasm" (Juno and Vale 1993, p. 12). Being tied up flat to a bed became one of his favorite positions. He linked his fascination with bondage to his life of illness and constant thoughts of his death: "In order not to be terrified of it, I sexualized it" (Juno and Vale 1993, p. 36). Aware that he had no real control over his life, he craved surrender, but a controlled surrender. "I determine the surrender and who I surrender to" (Juno and Vale 1993, p. 56).

Flanagan tortured himself in private, tying himself into crucifix-like positions and whipping himself until he met the woman who became his personal dominatrix and life partner. She spanked and whipped him, ordered him to cut and brand her initials into his skin, to submerge himself in ice water, to hang ten-pound weights from his penis, to sew his lips closed, to put needles through his penis. He gladly submitted. He sewed up his scrotum, nailing it to a board with a hammer. They began performing these private rituals publicly, first at sex clubs and then at prestigious art galleries and museums. Museum installations included videos of medical procedures he was forced to endure and how they have become incorporated into his "masochistic cystic fibrosis lifestyle." One of his museum installations was called "Bob Flanagan's Sick." Playing in the background was a recording of his poem "Why." He does it, he says, because it feels good. It gives him an erection, making him feel invincible and triumphant over death. He likes the attention he gets because he was alone a lot and got little attention. He does it because his parents loved him even more when he suffered, like Jesus. He finds it so sweet to surrender to the pain. It's an addiction (Juno and Vale 1993).

In an installation at the Santa Monica Museum of Art, Bob sat in a hospital bed amidst a display of his sexual and medical art works and videos. Many people, most of them strangers, began to talk to him with an unusual intimacy, confiding their deepest problems and fears. Although he was part of the S & M community, he did not present the dark outrageous persona affected by many sadomasochists contemptuous of "vanilla" sex. He had a good sense of humor, was good-natured and kind-hearted. Since he was 18 he worked at a summer camp for kids with cystic fibrosis, initially playing the guitar for them, then becoming camp director. He outlived most of them and attended the funerals of many. As abhorrent as Bob Flanagan's behavior was, when we understand it as a manic defense against the terrible anxiety of being snuffed out by his illness and a lifetime of unbearable pain, we can understand that the normal and perverse exist on a continuum.

THE NATURE OF PAIN

> In writing this chapter, I sense a vocabulary weakness: there are not enough words for the colors of pain.
> —Robert Stoller, *Pain & Passion: A Psychoanalyst Explores the World of S & M.*

We tend to distinguish between physical and mental pain, yet the heartache of being rejected activates the same part of the brain, the anterior cingulated cortex, in the same way that physical pain does (Eisenberger, Liebman, and Williams 2003; Kross, Berman, Mischel, Smith, and Wager 2011). The poets knew this long before the neuroscientists did. Throughout history poets have written about the pain of a broken heart. It has been found that emotional distress dramatically increases a person's risk of suffering a heart attack, even among those with no prior cardiac history (Mostofsky; Maclure, Sherwood, Tofler, Muller, and Mittleman 2012).

Pain is a very subjective experience which occurs only in consciousness (Bond 1976). So is pleasure. Our experience of pain is formed by both our mind and the context in which it is experienced.

> Pain . . . is not simply an automatic and unchanging response somehow hard wired in the body. The impressions communicated by the sensory pathways

> and spinal cord must be construed or interpreted in the brain that receives them. Brains, of course, do not operate alone in vats . . . They belong to individuals who in turn exist only within human history and within specific cultures. Gertrude Stein could not say truthfully of pain what she said of roses. It is not true that a pain is a pain is a pain: everywhere and eternally the same. Pain can be described as always a cerebral phenomenon in the sense that it is never simply a sensation but rather something that the time-bound brain interprets and that the time-bound mind constructs: a specific human artifact bearing the marks of its specific human history. . . We experience pain only and entirely as we experience it. . . . "In perceiving our pain, we transform it from a simple sensation into a complex mental and emotional event that psychologists and philosophers call perception (Morris 1991, pp. 28-29).

Loss and isolation can cut like a knife. Grief or anger can be stored in the muscles of the neck, head, back, or gastrointestinal tract, and can cause allergies to flare. The waiting rooms of primary care physicians are filled with people in very real physical distress for which no medical cause may be found. Often the physician will tell them that it is all in the mind and may refer them to a psychiatrist or psychotherapist, which leads these patients to feel that their doctor has not been really listening to them. Their pain may well *originate* in the mind or psychic pain might greatly exacerbate the pain of a physical disorder. But in any case, it is *not* all in the mind. It is in the mindbrainbody. It is psychosomatic.

Georg Groddeck (1923), considered by some the father of psychosomatic medicine, linked free association with the mystery of the mind-body relationship in *The Book of the It*. Groddeck never clearly defined the *It*, but it was virtually synonymous with the forces of the id. In fact Freud derived the word "id" (*Es* in German) from Groddeck (Freud 1923). Groddeck spoke of the mind and the body not as separate entities but as facets of the whole, and said in a letter to Freud that "the distinction between mind and body is only a word, not an essential distinction . . . that the body and mind are a joint thing which harbors an *It*, a power by which we are lived" (Grossman and Grossman 1965, p. 69). Once we can face our deepest and darkest urgings, our *It*, said Groddeck, we will be free to live in harmony within ourselves.

Long before Descartes (1637) said that the mind and body were separate, even as far back as Plato, in Western medicine there existed a philosophical dichotomy between mind and body, while Eastern traditions saw the mind and body as coming from the same energy or source. In the West, this mind/body disconnect has directed the clinical evolution of Western medicine. It has had a powerfully negative effect on how patients are perceived and treated, based on the assumption that there is mental pain and there is physical pain and never the twain shall meet. "These two types of pain, so the myth goes, are as different as land and sea. You feel physical pain if your arm breaks, and you feel mental pain if your heart breaks. Between these two different events we seem to imagine a gulf so wide and deep that it might as well be filled by a sea that is impossible to navigate" (Morris 1991, p. 9).

Psychosomatic disorders may appear to be purely physical but they originate in emotions that are unconscious or dissociated from consciousness. There are hundreds of illnesses and disorders that are purely psychosomatic or have a psychosomatic component, yet it is quite astonishing that despite the prevalence of these disorders, the medical community remains in the dark about this, as they have done about the role of nutrition until 2002, when the *Journal of the American Medical Association* published scientific review articles recommending multivitamin supplements for all adults. (Fairfield and Fletcher 2002). When physicians are confronted with a psychosomatic disorder they do not recognize it, or if they do, they tell the patient that it is all in the mind.

John Sarno, MD, is a medical pioneer in psychosomatic medicine and the author of the *New York Times* best-selling *Healing Back Pain: The Mind-Body Connection* (Sarno 1991), *The Mindbody Prescription: Healing the Body, Healing the Pain* (Sarno 1999), and *The Divided Mind: The Epidemic of Mindbody Disorders* (Sarno 2006). He has said

> The enormity of this miscarriage of medical practice may be compared to what would exist if medicine refused to acknowledge the existence of bacteria and viruses. Perhaps the most heinous manifestation of this scientific medievalism has been the elimination of the term psychosomatic from recent editions of the Diagnostic and Statistical Manual of Mental Disorders (DSM), the official publication of the American Psychiatric Association. One might as well eliminate the word infection from medical dictionaries (Sarno 2006, p. 3),

Sarno is a professor of clinical rehabilitation at New York University School of Medicine and attending physician at the Rusk Institute of Rehabilitation Medicine at New York University Medical Center. When I worked at Rusk early on in my career, one of the patients baffled the staff. This man suffered from chronic pain in his lower back, neck, trunk, and limbs, which prevented him from walking completely upright. No real medical reason could be found and physical therapy provided minimal relief. As I met with him and he talked more and more about his life and family, and I helped him to express his feelings verbally, his symptoms lessened. I became convinced that his disability was largely psychosomatic. Yet when I voiced this opinion, the rest of the staff looked at me with disbelief. At that time, I did not know of Dr. Sarno's work but wished I had. I would not have felt so alone.

Many years later, when a friend who suffered excruciating back pain consulted several orthopedic physicians, surgery was recommended. She was put on bed rest, and hired a woman to come to her home a few times a day to empty her bedpan and bring her food. At the time I was a member of the Psychosomatic Study Group of the Psychoanalytic Association of New York and heard about Sarno's work there. I spoke with my friend about his success in treating people with chronic pain syndrome and urged her to see him for another opinion. She made the appointment and to get her there, her husband had to put down the back seat of their station wagon so that she could lie down for the ride. I got a phone call from her later in the day. She was home and was amazed to tell me of her experience. It felt like a miracle. She attended a psychoeducational lecture on the nature of chronic pain syndrome and learned that the brain actually induces physical changes in the body for the purpose of preventing the conscious brain from becoming aware of unconscious feelings like rage or emotional pain. She heard that chronic pain should always be approached as a symptom closely associated with emotional disturbances, either secondarily to persistent pain or as primary precipitants of pain (Bond 1976).

Sarno had her attend an exercise class that afternoon and she actually stood up and moved. She rode home sitting upright. It seemed that she suffered from what Sarno called tension myositis syndrome (Sarno 2006), a condition he described as characterized by psychosomatic musculoskeletal and nerve symptoms, especially back pain. It seemed that for her, the psychoeducation and continuing in the exercise class were enough for her to make what seemed to be a full recovery. Other patients might need, in addition, psychotherapy with a psychoanalytically oriented therapist who understands the nature of psychosomatic disorders.

Psychic pain can make one feel helpless and hopeless. If we understand how physical pain can be a wonderful diversion from the pain that plagues the heart, mind, and soul, then it makes sense that inflicting pain on the self or allowing others to do that can not only be a powerful diversion from psychic pain, providing a most welcome sense of control over it.

RITUALISTIC VIOLENCE IN MUSIC AND DANCE

Adolescents and many young adults are drawn to ritualistic violence in music and dance. In moshing or slam dancing people aggressively push or slam into each other. It is often associated with concerts featuring angry hardcore, punk, and heavy metal music. Moshing, like other painful tribal rites, is about creating an intense experience and sense of community.

We all need to touch and be touched by others. Touch is the first means of communication between the newborn and the mother (Montagu 1971). How the parents hold the infant sends the baby a message that shapes his growth and development. Infants need gentle, stimulating, and loving touch in order to thrive (Spitz 1945). In touch-deprived American and British culture, kids are finding ways to touch each other, violently and dangerously. Moshing is quite dangerous, which seems to be its manic defensive appeal.

Despite an unwritten etiquette to promote safety at these events, nonetheless, people have been injured and killed at them. Kids dive from the stage into the mosh pit to "body surf," or ride the wave of bodies. There have been deaths from moshing in Cincinnati, New York, Dublin, Vancouver, Sydney, and London. Despite the growing number of lawsuits over moshing injuries, many wear their injuries as badges of honor, signs that they've had "the experience." "I've been hurt, but it's cool. That's what it's about . . . It's about getting in there and bangin' some heads." A boy compared it to jogging as a means of releasing anger and calming anxiety (Hersch 1998). Despite a broken nose, wrist, and ankles, a twenty-seven-year-old speaks of moshing with something approaching reverence: "It's a thrill—a rush," he yelled over the blaring music. "It's like one big, happy family out there." And that seems to be quite the point. One girl spoke of how banging violently into others gives her a wonderful feeling of connection with them, a sense of their being merged together into something larger than themselves.

For their roles in the film *Black Swan*, Natalie Portman and Mila Kunis each reduced their body weights by about 20 pounds even though both were very thin to begin with. As ballerina Nina, played by Natalie Portman, descends into madness, she inflicts pain and violence on herself. She claws red lines in her skin, peels away pieces of skin from her fingers, pulls off scabs, starves herself, and makes herself vomit. The film has been called *eating disorder porn* and has already inspired a "Black Swan Diet." Many ballerinas who saw the film found that much of it rang true for them (Nir 2011).

SADOMASOCHISM

> Human life is an experience to be carried as far as possible.
> —George Bataille, *Theory of Religion*

American and British cultures are touch-deprived, and increasingly, people are seeking out their own "professional touchers"—physicians, chiropractors, massage therapists, Rolfers, shiatsu and other bodywork practitioners (Farber 2000). Someone deprived of loving, intimate touch may crave the intense skin stimulation that comes from being slapped, bitten, scratched or burned. The need for human touch is so important that even painful touch can be better than none at all. This seemed to be the case with Hedda Nussbaum, who watched while her husband Joel Steinberg beat their six-year-old adopted daughter Lisa with a stick, just as he beat her. Writer Daphne Merkin said

> Perhaps it is best . . . to regard this couple as popular sentiment would have it: a fiendish man, a victimized woman, a degeneration abetted by massive drug use, and the tragedy of a dead child (Merkin 1997, p. 40). . . . Our interpreta-

> tions of what we call love vary so much as to be mutually exclusive a good deal of the time. Undoubtedly, Joel and Hedda's idea of love had much to do with their cravings and frustrations. Almost certainly the hostile symbiotic connection that their involvement hinged on provided an emotional trade-off: Whether he was making love to her or beating her, Hedda remained at the center of Joel's attention (Merkin 1997, p. 39).

A relationship that is both intimate and violent can form a remarkably strong attachment bond. Although Hedda wanted to call for an ambulance, she could not defy Joel's order not to and so she stood by and watched Lisa die. She reportedly said, "Once you taste the stick, you don't want to give it up" (Merkin 1997, p. 38). Although her relationship with Joel did not involve the theatrical black leather gear associated with sadomasochism, it was nonetheless a consensual enactment of a master-slave relationship in which pain is ritually inflicted and consciousness is transformed.

Those in the sadomasochist scene spend much time and effort setting the stage for spending hours at their "games," catering to each other's desires and the need not to exceed the other's bounds, before arriving at the orgasmic culmination. For some, the degree of attention paid to them may be more than they have ever known, making this perverse attachment part of its seductive allure. Those who practice S & M know how pain can become sexual pleasure. The skin can be stimulated in ways ranging from light and gentle to hard and intense. For some, light spanking can warm and stimulate the skin like the invigorating needle-spray of a good shower, adding spice to a healthy sex life (McDougall 1992; Montagu 1971). But when the sadomasochistic component dominates a person's sexuality, it can become dangerous, even life-threatening (Kernberg 1992b).

Relationships require a dialogue, a sense of two souls meeting and touching. When physical aggression dominates sexual activity, people no longer "make love," they "make hate," (Kaplan 1991) doing it violently, sometimes ecstatically, treating their partner not as a human being but as a thing to be used. Both partners go into dissociated states that wall off the memories of experiences that cannot be transformed into fantasy or other mental activity (Grossman 1991).

When one person is behaving sadistically and the other masochistically, it often feels in the moment that the activity has a life of its own, like a runaway train. The person(s) involved may describe it as something he or she could have stopped if they chose to, but it was experienced as something in which they had no choice. When the "top" (dominant) treats the "bottom" (submissive) as less than human, it opens the door to do anything. Daphne Merkin (1997) intuitively knew this. She could not remember a time when she did not dream or fantasize about being spanked. Her normally wary self felt herself held in the grip of a wordless compliance that was at odds with her intellectually weighty, morally upright part of herself. "What is still more curious is that allowing myself to be treated as a naughty girl . . . . who must be punished not only arouses me but actually soothes me—enables me to jump over my own shadow, across the inhibitions that impede me, and to land on the other side of sexual pleasure, at a place where the body takes over and the mind leaves off" (Merkin 1997, p. 51).

In her late twenties, she told a man she had been dating of her fantasies, and he was delighted at the thought of enacting them with her. They married but the intensity of their relationship weakened over time with the sameness of domestic life, and they separated. Several years later she was on a date with a man when he casually remarked that what she needed was a good spanking.

> but inside I was lurching, drunk with excitement at being recognized. . . . The remark passed into the air, electrifying it. I was afraid to break the spell, to respond to the comment, afraid to ignore it. A day or two later, the man called me, and I referred to the comment by coy indirection. We played a guessing game—I said that something he said . . . intrigued me, involving a word beginning with *s*—and I couldn't decide if he had genuinely forgotten or was feigning ignorance. (My embarrassment about the subject of spanking has never faded even slightly.) In the days that followed, I could think of nothing else. . . . In any case, I confided in him, and we quickly became involved in a fairly conventional romance that included some light S & M. What we were doing may have been moderate by hard-core standards, but there was some danger in it: Our forays left me hungry for more radical sensations, and their tone began to permeate our relationship in disturbing ways (Merkin 1997, pp. 62-63).

When he began telling her stories about his forays into more hard-core S & M, involving pulling on a woman's nipples, belts, riding crops, and immobilization, the disaffected manner in which he told the story made her feel threatened and anxious, and so to protect herself, she did not see him again. What had always worried her was that fantasies were safe, whereas enactment of these fantasies was potentially risky, because the question of when to stop would always arise. "Did one proceed, inevitably, from hands to paddles to whips to chains to being strung up on pulleys? . . . Where did you draw the line between mutually agreed upon love play, however aggressive, and domestic abuse?" (Merkin 1997, p. 58). That is the critical question. Whenever there is an enactment of a master-slave relationship, there is always the potential for what was initially consensual activity to become nonconsensual brutality that can result in death.

Robert Stoller (1985) has defined perversion as the erotic form of hatred, describing it as originating in a childhood trauma in which pain took on overtones of pleasure and became eroticized, and became intertwined in the fabric of the developing personality (Bach 1994; Stoller 1985). In an attempt to master the trauma, he may compulsively reenact sadomasochistic scenarios in adulthood, playing the role of sadist (top) or masochist (bottom) or both. In the reenactment, the bottom has the illusion that he has control over how far things will go.

It is not so easy to distinguish between those who can "play" safely at inflicting harm on another from those whose play can escalate over time into danger (Farber 2000). Dossie Easton, a licensed marriage and family counselor in San Francisco, wrote how empowering and therapeutic she has found S & M to be in her healing from her childhood abuse. She even co-authored self-help books for sadomasochists. *The Bottoming Book: How to Get Terrible Things Done to You by Wonderful People* (Easton and Liszt 1996), while the companion book, *The Topping Book: Getting Good at Being Bad* (Easton and Liszt 1995), advises on how to dominate or inflict pain on others. In a sex column written in the *Village Voice*, Dan Savage posted his response to a question asked by a young Chicago woman inclined toward being treated roughly sexually, and referred to Dossie Easton.

> Easton . . . has been into S&M for almost 25 years. Before she "came out" about her desires she found herself in a similar situation to the one you describe. "I spent my idle youth hunting down rough trade in the streets of New York, and I finally wound up with a first-class batterer. So I'm not surprised she found somebody who was really exciting who turned out to be a 'head case'... There are many people into SM who experienced abuse, and many who have not. I am an abuse survivor myself, and SM has not made me sicker than my parents did. If anything, it's made me healthier. I've been bottoming since 1974, and I just get stronger all the time, and more assertive." If the abuse and neglect you suffered as a child trouble you, Easton strongly suggests you find a therapist, one who is "trained in working with child abuse but is not prejudiced against SM. Your local SM group will know who those people are. Too many therapists will say your desires are sick and you should just get rid of them. Not only is that not possible, but what I found in my 25 years of SM is that the experience is very empowering for me. I'm in control of it, making conscious decisions. My friend who plays the dominant has my safety as her chief concern. I can ride this rollercoaster knowing it has been safety-tested. SM has made a major contribution to my healing from child abuse, and I have seen it in other clients I've worked with" (Savage 1996, p. 121).

Although the experience of S & M may feel empowering for Easton, this does not mean that it is therapeutic. It serves as a reenactment of past traumatic experience in which she, and not her abuser, feels in control, thus providing a sense of empowerment. She remains fixated, or arrested developmentally (Freud 1917) in the need to reenact the past. The ecstasy she experiences seems to be a form of manic defense that prevents her from mourning the loss of the childhood she never had. If she were able to relinquish the reenactments, which serve as defenses against danger, and came to mourn this loss, this would be a much healthier level of development.

The eroticized pain and illusory sense of control in S & M combine to develop into an addictive relationship that can spiral up into ever more painful ecstasies. Many people who are clinically depressed and chronically suicidal have a pattern of sadomasochistic sexual activity, with partners or alone (Litman and Swearingen 1996). While the pain and flirtation with death may jolt them out of their depression, at least for awhile, many people have died or have been murdered while engaged in such activity. In 2000 there were more than 1,000 reported cases, primarily in men (Gosink and Jumbelic 2000). Some men cannot get an erection without choking themselves, and will masturbate after tightening the noose they have around their neck

When someone applies pressure to the noose by crouching and letting the rope slowly take his body weight, or by masturbating to orgasm, pressure on the carotid arteries in the neck may interrupt the blood supply to the brain, causing unconsciousness, slumping, then death by strangulation. Ironically, the behavior meant to shake them out of their depression may kill them instead (Johnson 2007), too hefty a price to pay for a moment of ecstasy.

Children and adolescents refer to the *choking game,* a practice suggesting something benign or playful. In studying child and adolescent deaths between 1995 and 2007, the U.S. Centers for Disease Control and Prevention (2008) reported 82 child and adolescent deaths between 1995 and 2007 linked to the *choking game*.

In 1997 suffocation was the number one way that kids aged 10-19 years took their own lives (Johnson 2007). How many of these were accidental is not known. More than 75% of adolescents know about it, also known as the *pass out game* or the *blackout game*, usually played when alone. In the adolescent way of thinking that they are invulnerable and only *other* people die, they say. "It's just passing out. No one ever dies from passing out." One adult man wrote in an Internet forum, "Sometimes I need to 'choke myself down.' When it's too much (I've only needed to do it twice in the past year), I slide my belt around my neck, stand on the end, and stand up against it. I choke, gasp, gag. I fall to my knees weeping and wailing. I don't want to die, although I tell myself to hang myself often."

PLAYING WITH DEATH AND RESURRECTION

Probably all of us would like to know what death feels like, but not all of us will try to come close to death. It is those who lacked warm contact early in life who can become masochistically addicted to the near-death experience (Joseph 1982).

> The Passion of Christ has provided Western culture with its most enduring images of human suffering: the bleeding and emaciated Jesus nailed to the cross, a crown of thorns piercing his scalp, his mouth open in agony. In some paintings a spear pierces his side, releasing a startling gush of blood. The Passion of Christ has also provided the West with our most enduring images of death and rebirth.
>
> Despite our anxieties about death, the wish to know what death feels like is universal. People want to know what death is like, and they also want to live to tell the tale. The closest they will get to experiencing death is in the painful ecstasies of near-death experiences, in which they come close to dying and then miraculously seem to be resurrected from the dead and reborn, like Jesus. . . . People desperately want to know what it is like to "cross over" to death, as television hits such as HBO's *Six Feet Under* and *Crossing Over with John Edward* (known as "the guy who talks to dead people") has demonstrated. Books about reincarnation, past life and near-death experiences are big sellers (Farber 2003, pp.182-83).

They might experiment with erotic strangulation, the most violent sadomasochism, or the pain of purging so violently that they become dehydrated so severely that only life-support systems maintain the tenuous connection to life (Farber 2000). They might experiment with the drug ketamine, a short-acting, hallucinogenic, dissociative anesthetic to induce a near-death experience (Jansen 1996). Because the psyche is so dissociated from the soma, it is possible to carry out surgical procedures painlessly, which is quite different from the unconsciousness produced by conventional anesthetics.

TO HUMILIATE AND TO BE HUMILIATED

> Those children who are beaten will in turn give beatings, those who are intimidated will be intimidating, those who are humiliated will impose humiliation, and those whose souls are murdered will murder.
>
> —Alice Miller, *For Your Own Good: Hidden Cruelty in Child Rearing and the Roots of Violence*

Sadomasochism is an aspect of all perversions including those that do not entail physical pain. The excitement of a perversion comes from the awareness, conscious or not so conscious, that one is *harming, needs to harm, or wants to harm* another human being (Stoller 1991). The harm done is an act of either physically hurting or humiliating another, an enactment of revenge for having been hurt or humiliated oneself.

Several years ago, I attended a meeting of an artists' and writers' group that met in my picturesque suburban town. We had fiction and non-fiction writers, poets, a photographer, a folk musician, a children's book writer, a graphics artist, several painters, a jewelry maker, and so on. At each meeting a member spoke of a current project. On this particular morning, a new member was introduced, a writer named Katherine Gates. She seemed to be mid-thirtyish, and was the mother of two young children. Coincidentally, she had published her first book in the same year I had published mine. And in another strange coincidence, she lived with her family in the same house that my husband and I almost bought years before. Although Hastings is known as a sophisticated artsy-craftsy suburb of New York City, even so, I was surprised that no one visibly batted an eye when she began to speak about her writing genre—fetish porn. She had published a book, *Deviant Desires: Incredibly Strange Sex* (Juno 2000), described on Amazon.com as

> a lavishly illustrated guide to the most fascinating and obscure outposts of the erotic frontier. Self-described pervert Katharine Gates takes us on an expedition into the latest sexual communities bursting forth at the beginning of the new millennium. Gone are the pretentious black-clad S/M posers and humorless fetish fashion victims. You'll meet the refreshingly funny and irreverent heroes and heroines of a do-it-yourself porn revolution.

Katherine had also published a piece in the *Village Voice* called "Eat Me! A Weekend among Suburban Cannibals.

> It's just before Thanksgiving and instead of roasting turkey with my family I'm in a whitebread suburb of Los Angeles, watching a woman being prepared as the main course of a feast. First, two female chefs strip the woman naked. They pull her arms back tightly and place her face-down on an oversize platter. They spread her legs wide, exposing her bald pussy, and use thick ropes to bind her ankles and wrists together at her thighs. They pour oil and honey over the woman until she glistens. They thrust a corncob into her vagina, shove a red apple into her mouth, and maneuver the platter into a large fake oven. After a while, the chefs remove the roast from the heat and poke a gigantic meat thermometer into her ass. The needle on the dial points to well-done pork. Dinner is served! (Gates 2005).

What may be hell for one person may be ecstasy for another. There is no comparison between ordinary orgasms, even extended multiple orgasms, and the ecstasies induced by the perversions. As Daniel Bergner wrote about the perversion of a man named Jacob, for intensity, there is no comparison between his experience at that of someone relatively normal sexually.

> For sheer driven need, for keen and exalted erotic hunger, for the loss of consciousness that typical desire and typical sex may never provide or may offer only at the instant of orgasm and even then not quite completely despite the brain's dimness and the involuntary cries, for true negation of control and obliteration of self, Jacob had been granted something superior. He owned the chance for ecstasy (Bergner 2009, p. 7).

PLAYING WITH DEATH THROUGH STARVING, PURGING, AND MUTILATING THE SELF

The world was stunned by the gruesome murders of actress Sharon Tate, her houseguests, and Leno and Rosemary La Bianca, commited by the Manson Family. Ever since "Charlie's girls," Leslie Van Houten, Susan Atkins, and Patricia Krenwinkle appeared in court with crosses carved into their shaved heads, cutting one's own flesh has been associated in the mind of the public with the demonic and freakish.

We tend to think of sadomasochism as a relationship between two people in which one plays the role of sadist and the other the role of masochist. There are however people like Bob Flanagan who have a sadomasochistic relationship with themselves. Both eating disorders and self-injury are masochistic practices in which one is the sadist and masochist all at the same time. That is, in a dissociated state, one can be the sadist, inflicting pain on the self at the same time that she is the masochist, craving the pain (Farber 2000, 2003, 2008a, 2008b; Farber, Jackson, et al. 2007).

These practices have gotten so much media attention that one might think that they are new modern afflictions. Not at all. Fasting, purging, and self-injurious rituals were part of religious practices in ancient Western cultures and in Islam (Farber 2000). Self-starvation and other mortifications of the flesh became prominent for religious reasons in medieval Christian Europe. These practices all stem from a long-established Western tradition of health and healing, in which illness was treated by getting rid of something evil that was foreign to the individual—a spirit, demon, or toxic substance—that was thought to have invaded the body (Rizzuto 1985). Or it was thought that an imbalance in the four basic humors or temperaments—the sanguine, phlegmatic, melancholic, and choleric—could become properly balanced by means of blood-letting, blistering, purging (Farber 2000).

Colon cleansing, also called colonic irrigation, has been around a long time and became especially popular in the 1990s. Advocates believe that a variety of health problems can be caused by toxins in the gastrointestinal tract; cleansing the colon of toxins can prevent these problems by promoting healthy intestinal bacteria to boost your energy and enhance your immune system. There is scant scientific verification to support this claim. Not only is colon cleansing unnecessary, because the bowel is a naturally self-cleaning organ (Brody 2008), it can be harmful because it can increase the risk for dehydration and can create a medically dangerous electrolyte imbalance.

Colon cleansing may take the form of enemas, forcing water into the colon via the rectum, laxatives, or oral cleansing regimens with dietary supplements, sales of which have increased greatly in the last decade. Healthy eating has become a national obsession; for some, it has taken the form of an eating disorder colloquially called *orthorexi*a (Bratman 2004), when so-called healthy eating becomes a harmful obsession. In the name of healthful eating, individuals adopt increasingly rigid diets that eradicate critical nutrients and food groups, ultimately costing them their overall health and personal relationships. This faulty logic is the basis of The Zone diet, macrobiotics, the raw-food movement, and colon cleansing regimes (Bratman 2004). As the Food and Drug Administration continues to reject various prescription diet pills because of safety concerns (Pollack 2010), people are flocking to buy unregulated diet remedies in so-called health food stores. Although Fen-Phen was first withdrawn from the market in 2004 due to its association with heart valve problems and brain neurotoxicity, pills containing ephedra, a stimulant known to constrict blood vessels and increase blood pressure and heart rate, are still sold in health food stores and online.

Orthorexia is not a DSM diagnostic category, but like the majority of eating disorders, it does not fit the criteria for anorexia nervosa or bulimia nervosa but falls instead in the huge category called Eating Disorder Not Otherwise Specified. Newer versions of colonic cleansing come in the form of juice diets, touted by celebrities. After Judith Newman, a reporter, went on a juice cleanse, she wrote

> A month ago I went on a juice cleanse. You know what it cleans out of you best? The will to live . . .
> Peter Glickman, Scientologist and entrepreneur, repackaged a 1940s diet called the Master Cleanse. . . The Master Cleanse involves lemon juice, cayenne pepper, maple syrup, and 10 days of your life. Celebrities as varied as Beyonce, Jared Leto, and the Moore/Kutchers (Demi and Ashton were tweeting about it this week) swear by its energizing and weight loss effects, weight loss being not all that surprising, when you consider that you are essentially sucking lemons and a few teaspoons of sugar for 10 days. And the diet has a glorious circular logic to it. As Mr. Glickman explains on his Web site, if you experience symptoms like cravings, fatigue, irritability, headaches, pains, nausea, vomiting, hot bowel movements (!) . . . congratulations! That means you were supertoxic, and the cleanse is working. . . .
> At the end of three days, I felt rather lithe and long-limbed, like a gibbon. I also felt a kind of shimmering on the surface of my skin as excess weight worked its way out of my pores and escaped my body. No one would have known I was hallucinating. Or so I thought, until the night of my second food-free day. As I was putting my sons to bed, my son Henry whispered: "Mom, listen, when we're all asleep, just eat something. *No one will know*."

This wish to be free of hunger and be master of one's appetites is the overriding appeal of anorexia nervosa. A recent tabloid captured the common thinking about the illness. In an interview, actor Christina Ricci placed the blame for her struggle with anorexia on the pressures of success. The headline read, "Ricci: Hollywood made me anorexic." This is not really true. Although Hollywood's pursuit of thinness has become a pursuit in contemporary culture, it did not make Christina Ricci anorexic. Not everyone in Hollywood is anorexic.

Crossing the line between thin and emaciated is to lose a basic survival instinct, eating in response to hunger. Although real hunger, not cravings, is felt as a sensation in the stomach, this is not so for anorexics, whose self-starvation and other extreme asceticism give rise to a perverse sense of hedonistic pleasure (Gura 2008). Self-starvation promotes the dissociation of psyche (mind) from soma (body), which helps us understand why so many anorexics feel more energized and alert when starving. Starving themselves boosts their metabolic rate, in contrast to the slowing of metabolism in most people during a controlled fast. Brain scans show that anorexia nervosa is associated with disturbances in the brain's reward system, which suggests an inability to enjoy life's pleasures, whether they are food, sex, the company of others, or winning the lottery. For the anorexic, the *drug of choice* to which she becomes addicted is deprivation itself (Gura 2008). This helps to explain how the anorexic, the queen bee of the eating disorders, gloats over others as she cooks for and feeds them, enjoying her own deprivation. Over time, however the anorexic's brain becomes sensitized to the starvation, and craves it even when it no longer provides pleasure. When this occurs, this loss of the pleasure of starvation can lead to an overwhelming depression, and with it comes the risk for suicide. It is thought that of the 20% of anorexics who die from their illness, more die of a successful suicide attempt than die of self-starvation (Bachar, Latzer, Canetti, Gur, Berry and Bonne; 20002; Coren and Hewitt 1998).

The medieval Christian mystics starved and mutilated their bodies to perfect their spiritual lives, while many nonreligious people do the same thing today to become extremely thin (Bell 1985). These practices go deeper than that. Today self-starvation, self-mutilation, and severe dissociative disorders and other mental illness are associated with histories of severe trauma (Farber 2000). It can be the trauma of being preyed upon by one's parents, whose duty is to protect the child from predators, or the trauma of being neglected or having parents unattuned to their needs.

Trauma fragments the mind, separating thought from emotion and mind from body. When this occurs, that which should be processed mentally is dissociated and experienced instead somatically. Thus, those who harm themselves often feel as if they were possessed by demons, an expression of the dissociation of feelings from thoughts, of mind from body. "It's like there is a monster or a devil in me urging me to stuff myself and make myself throw up." Or, there is an external seductively caring voice urging, "Go on, sweetheart. Do it. Just a little cut will make you feel so much better. You know it will." Today we are seeing increasingly larger numbers of people who are trying their best to heal their broken selves with the help of vomiting, laxatives, blood-letting, tattoos, body piercings and other contemporary exorcisms. Here is what several subjects who participated in my study said:

> I feel stress and panic inside. I eat to vomit. My decision to vomit is made before I eat. The vomiting helps the panic & constant running feeling inside. I feel not in balance.
> I starve myself and then eat a regular meal and throw up. I take lots of laxatives, diuretics and enemas all the time, so nothing stays in me. sometimes I freak out and think I didn't throw everything up and then I take ipecac and get deathly sick. then sometimes I start all over again and eat more but usually it's just once—then I get a tranquil feeling and relax.
> (Cutting) It's someplace you go when you're about to get too angry or too sad—Nowhere land.
> I eat to numb when feelings are overwhelming. Sometimes binging is a lesser alternative to self-mutilation.
> I pick at scabs on my head. I've done this since adolescence. I find the activity soothing—and am trance-like while doing it. (Farber 2000, p. 265)

One woman who identified herself as having Dissociative Identity Disorder wrote, "I do not eat a lot at one sitting—but rather eat a little all day—then at night I wake up and vomit. Sometimes I feel very sick and need to vomit but just can't, this is when I will make myself. We eat when memories are coming—when we feel scared of sexual feelings—anger, strong feelings" (Farber 2000, p. 265).

Vicky, who had been in psychotherapy awhile, had become more aware of how inflicting pain on herself both expressed and regulated her feelings, helping her to soothe herself:

> When I binge and purge, it is always to relieve feelings that seem intolerable, whether it be anxiety, fear, loneliness, and—sometimes feeling really good. When I first started I had no idea why I was engaging in this behavior, but as I progressed in therapy I came to connect my behaviors with other experiences. By bingeing and purging many things happen. 1) Focus is on something other than feelings (distraction), 2) Feelings repressed seem to be "let out" 3) I become numb and dissociated in the process. 4) I felt calmer afterwards, at least for a short period of time, 5) I felt "clean" afterwards. . . .I felt like I couldn't feel, like maybe I wasn't really alive—by burning myself, I felt something! A validation I was alive. . . . I feel like I am in a trance, like it's not really me who is harming myself. I know I wasn't the person that I usually am. I feel very dissociated and distant from myself. . . . I had repetitive thoughts about burning myself. Afterwards, I was proud of myself & and felt I had done something that was special. It felt good to feel bad. It's strange but I felt strong for being able to burn myself—also I had a secret that no one else knew about. . . . I felt like I deserved to feel pain. The laxative abuse was the most harmful because of the severity of my abuse. I couldn't see the laxatives as being self-abusive until I was in therapy a long time, but the physical pain of

> laxatives was worse than anything else, including burning, that I did to myself. It felt better to be in pain than to feel good. (Farber 2000, pp. 270-71)

Vicki was different from the majority of bulimics who long for the feeling of fullness they get from the binge, whose purging is a necessary evil needed to "undo" the effects of the binge. Vicki and others like her crave the violent cramping they get from the most severe purging (Farber 2000). Some will binge so that they have something to purge and some will purge after eating even the smallest amount of food. They may induce severe purging to a degree that can be life-threatening, purging very severely, using multiple methods, such as self-induced vomiting, laxative abuse, enemas, syrup of ipecac (a poison antidote that induces a most violent purge), and diuretics. Some may sit in a sauna far too long to dehydrate themselves even further. They may consume food, even inedible, caustic substances, such as food from the garbage can that has spoiled, or nutshells, household cleansers, bits of broken glass, all meant to cause the most violent convulsive purge, whether it is oral or anal. Their purging may include several or many purges for each binge, even to the point of dry heaving and vomiting up blood. Some may purge for as long as two or three hours and as many as 40-100 times after eating (Hall and Beresford 1989). Their purging is literally a form of self-mutilation from the inside out; their purging lacerates inner organs and causes internal injuries and bleeding. It can result in depletion of certain trace minerals needed to maintain the health of many body systems, resulting in cardiac irregularities, cardiac failure, even cardiac arrest, as well as muscle weakness, dehydration, and eventual loss of kidney function. Severe purging is the primary cause of death in eating disordered patients (Sharp and Freeman 1993). When the body is in a serious deficiency state due to self-starvation as well, the cumulative effect is even more life-threatening (Farber, Jackson, et al. 2007).

Writer Marya Hornbacher found the possibility of dying very exciting (Hornbaacher 1998; Farber, Jackson, et al. 2007). She is bipolar (Hornbacher 2008), and the arousal provided by the very real possibility of dying served as a manic defense.

> Death is a fascinating thing. The human mind continually returns and returns to death, to mortality, immortality, damnation, and salvation. Some fear death, some seek it, but it is in our nature to wonder at the limits of human life, at least. When you are sick like this you begin to wonder too much. Death is at your shoulder, death is your shadow, your scent, your waking and and dreaming companion. You cannot help, when sleep begins to touch your eyes, but think of: What if? What if? And in that question, there is a longing, too much like the longing of a young girl in love. The sickness occupies your every thought, breathes like a lover at your ear; the sickness stands at your shoulder

> in the mirror, absorbed with your body, each inch of skin and flesh, and you let it work you over, touch you with rough hands that thrill.
> Nothing will ever be so close to you again. You will never find a lover so careful, so attentive, so unconditionally present and concerned only with you. Some of us use the body to convey the things for which we cannot find words. Some of us decide to take a shortcut, decide the world is too much or too little, death is so easy, so smiling, so simple; and death is dramatic, a final fuck-you to the world (Hornbacher 1998, p. 125).
> . . . . I was trying to die, in a curious, casual sort of way. Some women I've talked to say they were just testing the limits of the human body—eating-disordered athletes in particular seem to have this idea—but they speak in a bizarre, almost proactive tone, as if they had always intended to stop. The eating disorder just got out of hand.
> I did not intend to stop. I was not testing the limits of the human body—which implies a certain respect for those limits—so much as I was wondering what it would take to break through them. I wanted to see what was on the other side.
> In retrospect, I can see that my manic run toward success may have been based on the belief? knowledge? that I had only a small window of opportunity in which to succeed. One night, earlier in the school year, Lora had asked me how long I thought I would live. I lay there in bed and considered the question for a minute. I said, Maybe twenty. I figured it would take me about that long to starve to death. I came very close. Three years later, two months shy of my nineteenth birthday, the doctors gave me a week to live (Horbacher 1998, p. 135)
> Washington was very exciting. I remember it vaguely, for the most part, because I was dying. Dying is also very exciting. It's a pity I didn't' notice it sooner. . . . But I did not notice.. . . It did not occur to me that I was too thin. After all, what is *too* thin. After all, you can never be too rich or too thin. But I stood in front of the mirror, saying, Maybe. Maybe thin *enough.*
> This was a miracle. The absolute truism of eating disorders is that you never believe you are thin enough. Whereas most people set out to lose a few pounds,—say five, ten, fifteen—and stop when they get there, the anorectic sets out to lose ten pounds and then says, well, maybe fifteen. She loses fifteen and says twenty, loses the twenty, says thirty, loses thirty, says forty, loses the forty and dies. Oops. She really hadn't meant to die. She just wanted to see how far she could go. And then couldn't quite bring herself to break the fall. (Hornbacher 1998, pp. 244-45)

As controversial as the Terry Schiavo case has been, little attention has been paid to the apparent fact that she suffered cardiac arrest at age 26 because of an electrolyte imbalance, seemingly caused by a chronic eating disorder. She spent more than a decade fighting an eating disorder, starving herself, and binging and purging severely, at times with syrup of ipecac. When her heart stopped, it deprived her brain of oxygen, causing severe brain injury, putting her into a coma, and ultimately causing her death (Cline 2003).

The terrible paradox is that when someone walks through life feeling deadened inside, the self-inflicted pain that can ultimately cause her death can momentarily jolt her out of a depression or dissociated state and make her feel alive again. To see the shockingly red blood, to feel the stomach cramping, is to know that one is real and alive, like being resurrected from the dead. And as strange as it seems, self-inflicted pain can even be very arousing for some and can produce a state of ecstasy (Farber 2000; Stoller 1991). Delia, a subject in my study (Farber 1995) was uncertain if she had been sexually abused as a child but knew she had been physically abused. She described how tension builds up before she binges, much like sexual arousal, and the vomiting is an orgasmic release. "I'll feel real nervous and tense and then it'll build until I can't take it and in a sense, it's sort of like sex (build-up). I start to settle down when I eat and the throwing up is kind of like an orgasm. I usually feel extremely relaxed after I vomit" (Farber 2000, 2002, p. 284). It is to be noted that she uses the words "build up" again, here to describe the self-hatred she feels when cutting, burning, and sticking herself. Perhaps the self-mutilation serves as punishment for sexual pleasure and gratification of sexual wishes at the same time: "I just build up such an incredible amount of self-hatred that I can't keep it in anymore. I'll just cut myself real hard and deep and watch it bleed. I almost always feel better the next morning" (Farber 2000, p. 284).

A Phi Beta Kappa college student said "When I stick open scissors up my vagina, the cold hard steel gives me an explosive orgasm. (Favazza 1996, p. 245)." When one cannot speak of one's rage and hatred, expressing these feelings through the body can provide an ecstatic release. A patient of the late Robert Stoller (1985) wrote

> It is extremely difficult to verbalize the sensations derived from vomiting except in slang expressions used by people who use drugs. For instance, to "dump" means to vomit, but it's a different kind of vomiting than what you do, say, if you had the flu. When I begin to vomit I get a "rush." My thought about a rush is a flood of good feelings throughout my entire body. Usually when you inject a narcotic in the vein you experience a rush and then you dump, which is often pleasurable. . . Vomiting for me is like sex or an orgasm in that I'm tensed, I feel the rush . . . almost continually throughout the vomiting, and experience relief and quiet warmth in my body when I'm finished. It is not identical to an orgasm. I do not feel it intensely in my genitals alone, but I do feel it there as well as the rest of my body and feel pleasure in my mouth (Stoller 1985, p. 159).

The same woman also wrote about someone she knew who did the same thing.

She says she began to actively masturbate at about age 11 years. She was caught by her stepfather, who placed her across his lap and spanked her very hard. She said she could feel his penis against her stomach (erect?). She began to vomit and came to orgasm, the best and most intense sensation has ever had . . . She says that she doesn't get any pleasure from regular sex . . . rarely has an orgasm—with the exception of manual masturbation or a vomiting episode (Stoller 1985, pp. 159-60).

Many people are compulsive about exercise and can't get enough. In an upwardly escalating spiral, many athletes and dancers, male and female, exercise to compensate for food consumption, a pattern called *exercise bulimia* (Yates 1991). They may also binge and/or purge as well. They become addicted to the endorphin rush that exercise and purging produce. In the film *Black Swan,* ballerina Nina continues to dance even though she is injured. In one scene, her toenails crack off in her toe shoes; she continues dancing, oblivious (Nir 2011).

Despite the potential for death, those who practice these behaviors often present a remarkably disturbing lack of anxiety about their own life-threatening behavior (Farber, 1995, 1997, 2000, 2003, 2005a, 2005b, 2008a, 2008b; Farber, Jackson, et al. 2007). Because dissociation compartmentalizes and separates psychological and somatic aspects of traumatic experience, it enables these patients to disavow the life-threatening nature of their behavior, which makes the dissociative processes the most destructive factor in this psychopathology.

TO BE INITIATED INTO THE TRIBE IS TO DIE AND BE BORN AGAIN

> Ritual knowledge is nothing if not sensual. A rite is an activity that engages the hand and pricks the ear; it catches the eye and lifts the heart."
> —Ronald Grimes, *Readings in Ritual Studies*

In non-tribal cultures body decoration, along with clothing, gesture, and posture, is a semaphore system allowing even complete strangers a means of relating to one another. Adornment and body marks serve as advertisements for the self, to let someone know "where we are coming from." We use props, such as clothing, makeup, hairstyles, and other adornments, to communicate what we want to communicate about ourselves to others in public. These props let others know who we are, who we would like to be, or who we would like others to think we are (Polhemus 1998).

The human body stands as a symbol of society and its values and so we tend to describe behavior in ways that are corporeal and social. For example, someone may be upright, uptight, hard-assed, straight, bent, twisted, loose, upfront, hard-headed, soft, hard, forward, backward, balanced. At the same time, inside and outside describe both physical and social boundaries (Farber 2000, Polhemus 1998). In analyzing the symbolic interface of the physical body and the social body, anthropologist Mary Douglas has said, "The physical experience of the body, always modified by the social categories through which it is known, sustains a particular view of society. There is a continual exchange of meanings between the two kinds of bodily experience so that each reinforces the categories of the other" (Douglas 2002, p.12).

No culture accepts the body in its natural state. It may be modified by permanent or non-permanent markings, such as makeup or body paint, which have existed throughout time in cultures everywhere (Farber 2002). The unique way each group decorates itself is a function of cultural and ethnic factors, with tattoos more prevalent among people whose skin is light enough to display them and scarification more popular among darker skinned people whose skin forms more prominent keloid scars. The universal practice of tattooing reached its height in the Pacific Islands, where they have religious significance, while in Japan the tattoo folk art *irezumi* is a product of lower social classes, geishas, and criminals. *Irezumi* is still practiced in Japan, a nation fascinated with the perverse, erotic, and sadomasochistic aspect of tattoos. A Japanese wearing the art of a grand tattoo master might donate his skin to a museum or university upon his death. Tokyo University owns several hundred of these bizarre masterpieces (Farber 2000).

Western culture has been influenced more than you might think by the initiation rites of tribal cultures. Many children's games involve a ritual of pain for the loser, such as the pain of *knucks*, in which the child who has lost must tolerate being rapped hard on the knuckles with a deck of playing cards, or the more muted musical chairs, in which he who does not scramble fast enough for a chair is left to suffer being left out in the cold, an isolate, without a protective community. Until recently, the phenomenon of initiation rites, or rites of passage was the central cultural form for marking a person's progress from one stage in life to another, in a process that clarified and affirmed new roles and status in the adult community (Grimes 1995; Scott 1998; van Gennep 2004). In tribal cultures, adolescent initiation rites are usually much more elaborate and can be truly terrifying, involving physical pain and blood, and leaving a permanent mark on the body (Morinis 1985). Ritually inflicted pain serves as a cultural means for causing and signaling a transformation of consciousness (Morinis 1985).

The initiation process is often understood as a simultaneous death and rebirth; in addition to being a beginning, it also involves an ending, as existence on one level drops away as the individual ascends to the next. In all initiation myths and stories, there is an archaic pattern of retreating into chaos and annihilating all things before the new order can be created again. It marks a transition, either an adolescent coming of age or the start of a personal or spiritual quest, or even the transition from dying into death. Through these reenactments the initiate had a second "birth" and thus was transformed into a man (Morinis 1985).

In the 1970s after the Australian territory of New Guinea attained self-government and became Papua New Guinea, the Prime Minister returned to his home village in the Sepik area to be installed as traditional chief of his clan. It marked a time of transition, the tribesmen moving in a lifetime from the Neolithic period into the globalized Western economy (Flannery 1999). Recalling his own boyhood initiation, the Prime Minister sang an initiation song about how when, as a child, you live under your mother's care, you do what you want and have what you want. You ask for food and get it. You ask for water and get it. You cry that you want a big fish to eat and your mother cooks it for you. But now, when you become older and live under your father's domain, it is time to pay for these indulgances, and a new time begins (Jilek and Jilek-Aall 1978). "Plutarch's dictum, 'To become initiated is to die' is true for initiation ceremonies in New Guinea as well as for the mystery cults of classical antiquity (Jilek and Jilek-Aall 1978, p. 258).

To understand the initiation rite in Papua New Guinea, it is best regarded as a social learning process in which the revelation of ancestral secrets and ritual testing by excruciating ordeals establishes group consciousness and loyalty. In the gauntlet run of the Sepik and Highland groups, an all-male ceremony, the young men are led by their uncles to the ceremonial house as they are hit with sticks by villagers. In the ceremonial house they are led through a gauntlet, crawling between the legs of a long line of elders, symbolizing the birth canal. During this passage they are beaten with sticks and burning embers and are cut all over their bodies in traditional patterns replicating the patterns on a crocodile's hide. During and after the cutting the young men are given plant leaves to chew for their narcotic effect. Their young, intact skin is transformed into toughened, raised keloid scars, which are produced using sharpened bamboo and crocodile teeth, and more recently, razor blades. The open incisions are washed, then treated with oil (for lubrication) and mud (to darken the raised scars). Then one by one, the dogs which are present are clubbed to death, a portent of what could happen to the boys if they did not survive the ordeal. The boys are carried away to recuperate and are attended to by their initiators. After weeks of confinement there is a ceremony in which the villagers rejoice that the young men have survived. Each one steps forward to receive his crocodile name, which connects him with his crocodile kin in the land of dreams, where crocodiles and men still remain brothers. Behind their crocodile masks, they march through the village to be welcomed by the villagers as men. The young men plunge into the water to join their crocodile brothers, completing their transformation. Coinciding with the young men's ordeal, baby crocodiles are born, to be guarded by their mothers as best they can, but only a few will survive. These few will be connected to the newly marked crocodile men, as brothers. In this most elaborate ritual, man, like the crocodile, becomes transformed from being vulnerable prey into the powerful predator.

Rites of passage in adolescence have existed throughout human history. In Western culture, there are Sweet Sixteen parties, Roman Catholic confirmation, Jewish Bar and Bat Mitzvah, and Hispanic Quinceañera. Mythologist Joseph Campbell (1972) said that if societies do not create difficult rites of passage for adolescents to go through, they will create them for themselves, inventing all sorts of dangerous tests.

Body art in civilized culture can also signify membership in a tribe. Today we are seeing a new kind of tribalism—postmodern "tribes" whose initiation rites mimic tribal tattoos and piercings but also include cutting, branding, starving, tattooing, drugging, bingeing, and purging. These bodily signifiers have come to identify a generational consciousness "composed of "brothers or sisters" who are linked together in their time. (Bollas 1992, p. 270). These tribal rites serve as marks of disaffiliation from the mainstream society or a "declaration of independence" from their families, at the same time that they serve as marks of affiliation with marginalized social groups and deviance.

BODY MODIFICATIONS

When I was eighteen, I had my ears pierced, nothing radical by today's standards, but back then, it was more acceptable for a female to wear clip-on earrings. To "respectable" people, pierced ears were the sign of a foreigner, a gypsy, a prostitute, or almost as bad, a dancer. Quite predictably, my father, an Orthodox Jew, became furious because any mutilation of the body, other than circumcision, is prohibited in the book of Leviticus. "Ye shall not make any cuttings in your flesh for the dead, nor print any marks upon you: I am the LORD" (Leviticus 19: 28). For me, wearing these little pearl studs was my personal "declaration of independence," stating that this is my body and I'll do with it what I want. Years later, my son, a cautious type, came home one day when he was 15. "Notice anything different, Mom?" He had a little hoop earring piercing one ear. He was the first boy in his grade to do this, instantly starting a trend and boosting his social status.

Fraternity and sorority hazing are common rites of passage at college, but it seems that acquiring at least one tattoo or body piercing has become a more recent rite of passage. In a large Internet study of 766 students in 20 universities (19 American and one Australian), it was found that almost every student with a tattoo or body piercing had arrived at college without it but had acquired one or more while in college. Those with body piercing reported more frequent health problems and impulsivity compared to those with tattoos. Three cases of hepatitis were reported, one from tattooing, two from piercing (Greif and Hewitt,1996; Greif, Hewitt, and Armstrong 1999).

Body modifications are expressions of both individuality and conformity, as the words of people who acquired a tattoo tell us.

> Having a tattoo changes the way you see yourself. It is a way of choosing to change your body. I enjoy that. I enjoy having a tattoo because it makes me different from other people. There is no one in the whole world who has a right arm that looks anything like mine. I've always valued being different from other people. Tattooing is a way of expressing that difference. It is a way of saying, "I am unique" (Sanders 1989, p. 51).
>
> I get more positive reactions than I do negative reactions. The negative reactions come from people who aren't like me—who have never done anything astray. It is the straight-laced, conservative person who really doesn't believe that this is acceptable in their set of norms. It seems as though I can actually tell how I'm going to get along with people, and vice-versa, by the way they react to my tattoo. It's more or less expressive of the unconventional side of my character right up front. Most of the people who seemed to like me really dig the tattoo too (Hill 1972, p. 249).

Each story inscribed upon the body—by tattoos, starving, cutting, and purging—is unique and yet the paradox is that they are so very uniform in serving as marks of group affiliation. The marks that are stigmatizing in more conventional circles can not only serve as keys of entry into marginalized groups but can serve as signs of personal transformation. For example, although body modifications have been traditionally prohibited to Jews, Amy Krakow, author of *The Total Tattoo Book* (1994), calls herself "A Tattooed Jew." A woman acquiring a tattoo became a symbol of subversion. Take, for example, a number of women who following mastectomies had their chests covered with tattoos.

> In a culture where surfaces matter, skin, the largest organ, is the scrim on which we project our greatest fantasies and deepest fears about our bodies. Expose too much of it and Christian fundamentalists or anti-porn feminists will come after you. Puncture it with holes and fill them with rings, and you assume the camp uniform of the counterculture. Nip and tuck it through surgery, and you drink from the fountain of youth or buy into the beauty myth (Mifflin 1997, p. 6).

A lone self-cutter or bulimic, with a low sense of self-esteem and sense of emotional isolation, may note another person who performs similar acts of self-harm, reveal herself to that person, and immediately, a little group of two is formed that enhances the esteem of both. Self-esteem is dependent upon the continuation of the group (Walsh and Rosen 1988), and so it is important that new members be added. If a member leaves or the group disbands, the members suffer a profound loss of self-esteem. Television documentaries feature quiet, shy people who, once getting themselves tattooed, acquired a newfound acceptance—people stopped them on the street to admire them and talk, they won body art competitions, and made new friends.

> Having a tattoo is like belonging to a club. I love seeing tattoos on other people. I go up and talk with other people with tattoos. It gives me an excuse because I'm not just going up to talk with them. I can say, "I have one, too." I think maybe subconsciously I got (the tattoo) to be part of that special club (Sanders 1989, p.53).
>
> Being tattooed has opened up a whole new way of life for me. I now have a whole circle of interesting friends (Miss Cindy Ray, *The Story of a Tattooed Girl*, quoted in *Modern Primitives*, Vale and Juno 1989, p. 203).

One could say that these visible changes in the body are marks of a duality, distinguishing a public from a private persona. "My husband is a chef and our friends tend to be bikers, so it gets me accepted more into that community. They all think of me as the 'college girl' and I'm really not. So this (tattoo) kind of brings the door open more. . . The typical biker would tell you that you almost have to have tattoos to be part of the group" (Sanders 1989, p. 52).

What is more predictable as a mark of the S&M subculture than nipple and genital piercings? Yet body modifications can be hidden under long sleeves or a corporate suit, seen only by those chosen to see them.

> Usually I'm fairly careful about who I show my tattoos to. I don't show them to people at work unless they are really close friends of mine and I know I won't get any kind of hassle because of them. I routinely hide my tattoos. . . I generally hide them from people who wouldn't understand or people who could potentially cause me trouble. I hide them from my boss and from a lot of the people I work with because there is no reason for them to know (Sanders 1989, p. 54).

Self-made tattoos or other self-inflicted scars seem to be the marks of those who have done time in prison, gangs, psychiatric hospitals, and residential treatment facilities.

NEEDLE FREAKS, PIERCING JUNKIES, AND SELF-AMPUTEES

Body modification may be defined as the voluntary modification of the body. It includes tattooing, piercing, branding, scarification, transdermal implants (implants that pass through the skin), subdermal implants (implantation of three-dimensional objects under the skin), tongue splitting, ear reshaping, silicone injections, and amputations (Hicinbothem, Gonsalves, and Lester 2006). Body modifications have been sanctioned in many cultures, for centuries, from male ritual nose bleeding in New Guinea that is believed to be a protection against illness and a form of male menstruation, to the finger amputations common to some Polynesian, African, North American Indian and New Guinea tribes, to the head-slashing of a Moroccan cult, to the self-flagellation and other self-mutilation endemic in Christianity (Farber 2000).

> From Africa to Asia, the Arctic to the South Pacific, tribal peoples cut, shave, dye or decorate their hair; paint, tattoo, scar or pierce their flesh. . . . Some bind the heads of their infants, stretch their necks or compress their waists. Most groups attach feathers, shells, bones, flowers, leaves or ornaments made of metals or some material to their bodies. No group of which I am aware does all these things but—what is more important—*no group does none of them* (Polhemus 1988, p. 31).

Until recently, we have regarded permanent body modifications as belonging to primitive people, not to civilized Western culture. Before the 1990s, body piercing and other body modifications existed in Western culture in marginal groups, largely motorcyclists, skinheads, English punks and Teddy boys, prisoners, gang members, prostitutes, homosexuals, and the S & M culture.

Until recently, there was little about body modifications in books, other than *The Story of O*, in which a woman wears rings and chains through her labia to signify her status as a sexual slave (Reage 1981). Then Madonna's book *Sex* (1992) introduced nipple piercing to a wide audience, and by 1993 pierced lips, brows, and navels were more common. Rock festivals began to include booths for tattooing and piercing (Torgovnick 1996).

What is a culturally acceptable form of body modification in one era shifts in another. In the sixties a man with a pierced ear was conveying his homosexuality to other homosexuals, while the particular ear pierced signified his sexual availability or commitment to a partner. In the first half of the century in the United States, females wearing earrings in their pierced ears were identified as immigrants, gypsies, or other "undesirables," while "real Americans" wore clip-ons. Whereas fifty years ago, middle class parents might be horrified if their eighteen-year-old daughter came home with her ears pierced, today it is not unusual for parents and children to have piercings in various parts of their faces and bodies and at times, parents may even accompany their adolescent child to the tattoo or body piercing studio (Farber 2000).

But more recently, these body modifications as well as cosmetic surgery, liposuction, and bariatric surgery have become common, and about half of tattoos are done on women, including career and professional women (Armstrong 1991). Many who get themselves pierced or tattooed simply tolerate the pain in the way that one tolerates a painful medical procedure, while for others who want the look of extensive tattooing but not enough to tolerate the pain, they can purchase online the Suicide Kings Tattoo Long Sleeve Shirt or Tattoo Body Suit.

In the process of acquiring a tattoo or piercing, some discover that the sensations produced, although painful, can produce a sense of well-being.

They may become addicted to the experience of being tattooed, pierced, or branded, much like some of the drug addicts I worked with in an inpatient drug detox center, known as needle freaks (Levine 1974; Farber 2000) because they seemed to be as addicted to the experience of sticking themselves with the needle as they were to the heroin itself, and could even get high shooting up water (Farber 2000).

Bree was a needle freak..

> I know if I go back to drugs they will kill me. So sometimes I feel like cutting is the only thing I have left, the only really satisfying release in these situations where the pain is too great. Fortunately, because I'm not doing drugs, I'm not coming across situations that are too painful too often anymore. (Strong 1998, p. 186)

She has, admittedly, transformed some of her cutting impulses into getting herself pierced and tattooed.

I can at least pretend that's healthy, she says with a laugh. .But the fact of the matter is when you get pierced or tattooed, you do have a big needle going through your skin. I definitely have a fascination with the sadistic, masochistic, darker kind of stuff. I guess this is the most positive expression I've found so far for that side of me. About an hour into it, you feel like you've got the heroin nods. I remember looking forward to that feeling the last time I got a tattoo. It feels like you're on drugs without the negative effects (Strong 1998, p.186).

Some people cannot get enough of it. These are the people you see covered with tattoos or piercings, who feel an erotic rush as the needle penetrates their skin. In White Plains, a few miles from my office, a tattoo and piercing studio is called "Addicted to Ink" and a storefront studio in Downingtown, Pennsylvania, has a sign that reads "Welcome to Your New Addiction." Some people have their nipples or genitals pierced to enhance sexual pleasure, while some have their tongues pierced and a "barbell" stud inserted to provide greater stimulation to their partner during oral sex. Others have their tongues split or may even have three-dimensional metal objects implanted under their skin. The scalp is a popular site for transdermal implants, and the *metal Mohawk* and *stegosaurus*, a series of spikes sticking out of the scalp, are popular designs. Dr. Norman Goldstein, a dermatologist and expert on body modifications in Hawaii said, "People want to do the ultimate so they start off getting tattoos. . . But everybody and their mother has a tattoo. Then they'll go into piercing. But everyone's doing that. So the people who get branded seem to want to go to the max. Short of total body mutilation, where digits are amputated, branding is the next step" (Farber 2000 p. 58).

In fact, enough information has been acquired about self-amputation of body parts that Dr. Michael B. First, one of the authors of the upcoming

DSM-V, has defined a new diagnostic category, Body Integrity Identity Disorder and proposed that it be included in the new DSM (First 2005). The word is spread about it largely in cyberspace on listservs, in what science historian Ian Hacking called a *semantic contagion*, creating the means by which the condition spreads and becomes a possible DSM disorder (Elliott 2003). One such listserv has 3,200 subscribers. The idea of having a limb amputated may never have occurred to them, until the idea took root by means of suggestion online. But once it is suggested and associated with imagery that the person's past may have groomed him to appreciate, that act becomes possible (Elliott 2003). Elliott goes on to say that if you give it a scientific sounding name and treatment, associate it with other related disorders, explain it as scientifically based in childhood memory, set up a conceptual category, all that turns it into a treatable psychiatric disorder. The act has been redescribed to make it thinkable in a way that had not been known before. What might have been regarded as the most destructive self-mutilation becomes transformed into a treatment for a psychiatric disorder. Without any doubt, these people need professional help, but when the treatment in question is permanent and causes a disability, it is not so clear what that treatment should be.

"Yet surgery continues to avoid the kind of ethical and regulatory oversight that has become routine for most areas of medicine" (Elliott 2000, p. 235). Somehow, the usual medical injunction "First, do no harm" seems not to apply to surgeons, who enjoy the privilege of high status in medicine. Years ago it was lobotomies. Today they can suck fat from your thighs, lengthen your penis, beautify your labia, augment or reduce the size of your breasts, even staple your stomach to make its capacity only a fraction of its original size. So given the acceptability of these surgeries, asks Elliott, why not amputate a limb?

This line of thought as well as the wish to relieve human suffering seemed to have factored into Dr. Robert Smith's decision to amputate the legs of two men. Self-amputees may start off with amputating a few fingers or toes, then, in the manner in which addictions can be kindled, they develop an intense desire to have a specific limb amputated. The wish is usually quite specific, such as "I want a three inch below the left knee amputation." People have gone to great lengths to convince a surgeon to perform the amputation, and Robert Smith, a surgeon in Scotland, became convinced (Elliott 2003). Smith was planning on a third amputation when his hospital stopped him. The people involved were physically healthy people and according to the psychiatrist who examined them, were not incompetent. Both men declared publicly how much happier they were now that their legs had been amputated. There are those so desperate for an amputation that they will do it themselves, which can be potentially fatal. A female legal investigator for the California state bar was refused a hospital amputation, and so she tied tourniquets around her legs, then packed them in ice, hoping gangrene would set in, so that she could have her hospital amputation. She fainted and eventually gave up, saying that now she thought she probably had to lie under a train or shoot off her legs with a gun.

The question of what drives this desperate, bizarre desire baffled Dr, Smith initially, but he had been so struck by the language of identity and selfhood used by each of the two men, that he became convinced that he had to perform the surgery. He heard of the suffering they endured. He heard that they had nowhere else to turn. They did not want to have to perform the amputation on themselves. He agreed to perform the surgery, and afterward, said of all the operations he has performed, these were the most satisfying (Elliott 2003).

> Yet what exactly does it mean to be stuck in the wrong body? Even people who use more conventional enhancement technologies often use the language of self and identity to explain why they want these interventions. They include a woman who says she is "not herself" unless she is on Prozac, a bodybuilder who says he took anabolic steroids because he wants to look on the outside the way he feels on the inside, a transsexual who describes her experience as being "trapped in the wrong body." The image is striking, and more than a little odd. In each case the true self is the one produced by medical science (Elliott 2003, p. 211).

Might there be unusual sexual gratification involved in being an amputee? Might it be a perversion? Or is it as Michael First thinks, a new kind of identity disorder? *Apotemnophilia* is the wish to be an amputee, different from *acrotomophilia* , which describes a person who is sexually attracted to *amputees* (Elliott 2003). However most people with Body Integrity Identity Disorder do express a sexual motivation. Both First and Elliott believe there is some relationship between the disorders; some individuals manifest more than one condition. And many with self-amputations also seek other extreme body modifications such as body piercing, scarring, branding, and transsexual surgery.

Geek Love (Dunn 1989), a darkly comic novel that occasionally appears on self-amputation websites, explores the link between identity, deformity, and erotic desire (Elliott 2003). It takes a close look at a darker side of life that tends to be ignored in the mainstream, and makes some sense of it. It is all about freaks, geeks and other human aberrations who travel together as a whole carnival family. The world that comes closest to the *Geek Love* aesthetic is that of the most extreme body modifications.

The heroes of *Geek Love* are not *norms*, as ordinary Americans are called in the book. The heroes are the freaks of the Binewski Carnival Fabulon. This carnival family was conceived by the perverse originality of Al and Lil Binewski. Lil had ingested pesticides, radioactive materials, and various drugs in order to create children who are *special:* Iphigenia and Electra, piano-playing conjoined twins, Olympia, a bald albino hunchback dwarf, Chick, who has telekinetic powers, and Arturo the Aqua Boy, who was born with flippers instead of arms and legs. "We are masterpieces," said Olympia when asked if she would like to be a *norm*. "Why would I want to change us into assembly-line items? The only way you people can tell each other apart is by your clothes" (Dunn 1989, p. 282).

Some of the people in the extreme body modification movement have had toes or fingers amputated, castrations, or had their penis surgically removed, all of which had been associated for many years with pornography and sadomasochism. It has since blossomed into a thriving subculture. In someone who feels alienated, getting some kind of a body modification is a way of choosing to stigmatize oneself, a way of proclaiming. "Look at me and watch out! I'm someone to be reckoned with." On *The L Word*, a television show about the lesbian lifestyle, many of the women seem to have the real thing, arms covered with *full sleeve* tattoos. But the sight of someone with a full body suit, tattoos covering the torso down to the ankle, is still rather startling. It brings to mind those politically incorrect Coney Island circus freak shows.

When you come upon a person with extensive tattooing or a full-body suit, bear in mind the considerable pain and cost involved. Not only will parts of the body that are more sensitive hurt more when tattooed, completing these areas may take longer than other parts of the body. The most painful area to be tattooed is the genitals; not everyone with a full-body suit will do this. The rib cage, kidney area, and anywhere the skin is thinner and has less fat and/or muscle are also very painful because there is little to cushion the impact between skin and bone.

For many, acquiring a body modification can serve to gratify conscious, unconscious or dissociated wishes. *The Piercing Fans International Quarterly* is an expensive glossy magazine catering to those with a special interest in body modifications and sadomasochism. In some states, it is considered pornographic and it is illegal to send it through the mail. Penetrating the skin with a blade or needle can provide some gratification of the wish to be penetrated. In a man, it can express homosexual wishes. When we see someone who seems to be addicted to having his body pierced, tattooed, carved and branded, having 3D art implants, having his tongue split like that of a serpent, we need to wonder what psychological functions these behaviors serve, what early experiences of being held, cared for, and touched they have been deprived of, what unconscious fantasies underlie the need for body modifications. Male piercer and performance artist Genesis P'Orridge said, "My nipples were a dead zone before they got pierced. Then they became a whole new discovery. It was nice—like being female as well. I used to like Paula to suck on them and play with them. So I discovered nipples, which was good—two more erogenous zones added" (Vale and Juno 1989, p. 177).

A man with a penchant for body piercings said, "I like the jewelry very much, but the real turn on comes from having my body penetrated. Every time I see that sharp, shiny needle heading towards my flesh I know I'm going to get either a dick orgasm or a head orgasm or maybe both" (Myers 1995, p. 163).

The Piercing Fans International Quarterly featured a letter from a 66-year-old man who wrote that when he first pushed the needle through his wife's ear, they each felt more arousal than they had in years. They immediately agreed that he would have to pierce her nipples as well. He described the exciting ritual of laying out the materials used: stainless steel fish hooks, a file, emery cloth, pliers. He stated enthusiastically that they could not keep away from each other, that he had became so aroused that he would have pierced her big toes if she had wanted (J.B. 1993).

I received an e-mail from a man saying that after years of cutting and burning himself, he started getting himself pierced and tattooed, a more acceptable way of experiencing the pain he craved.

> I started getting pierced at age 16, after years of self-mutilation, cutting, burning, etc. I thought that tattoos and piercings would be a more acceptable way to experience the physical pain I was craving and it also gave me something of beauty to turn my pain into. I have been diagnosed BPD (Borderline Personality Disorder) and bipolar. What I experience while getting these things done is a complete release of negativity. It feels as though a weight has been lifted off my chest, an emotional release. . . .

He took a job working in a piercing/tattoo studio. His girlfriend came in to get her nipple pierced and she too felt an ecstatic release from pain. He found, as did others who did this kind of work, that many of their clients get "something emotional" out of it, and concluded that many troubled people go in for these body modifications for this reason. "When nothing else seems to help them, they turn to this form of therapy. . . ."

Some are members of the *hate tribe*, said Wendy, who worked as a body piercer at *Notorious Ed's Underground Tattoo* on 6th Street in Austin, a college town and state capital of Texas. A typical Friday night in Austin is somewhat like New Orleans' Bourbon Street, but with a difference. Instead of drunken tourists holding $10 Hurricanes and Mardi Gras beads, the streets are filled instead with dreadlocked, tattooed, pierced and otherwise tribally marked kids. They were sent off to college in pressed chinos and cable knit sweaters and came home for spring break with pierced tongues and who knows what else. Wendy, from California, has many piercings herself and says the scene in Austin is a little primal compared to California, which is "cool, because people here aren't doing it just because it's popular, they're getting pierced because they are into it, because they are members of the hate tribe. . . The *hate tribe* is a name for people throughout the world who hate all aspects of this fucked up society, and express their frustration by hurting themselves, apparently adopting Nietzsche's adage, 'That which does not kill me, makes me stronger'" (Gans 2000, p. 171). Wendy refers to scarification as "battle scars" of the tribe She plans to get her clitoris pierced, which not only creates extreme arousal but also symbolizes extra strength.

Living in a world of disconnected connection through faxes and computers, some Westerners find themselves moving away from organized religion but nonetheless yearning for something spiritual. A romanticized, idealized view of tribalism can lead them to yearn for tribal life. Even cosmetics are marketed through a spiritual lens: *Bliss* moisturizer, under the Chakra VII line by Aveda, *Rebirth* powder, and *Spiritual* nail polish. And Madonna has changed her tough-as-nails S & M persona in favor of a spiritual look while she studies Kaballah.

Today for many, appropriating the rites of passage of tribal people evokes a sense of completeness and simplicity in a fragmented and complex world, and a sense of gender, personal, and group identity. We are seeing several seemingly different but overlapping contemporary tribes, comprised of individuals whose experiences in life and relationships have made them feel drawn to the primitive. They often feel inadequate and incapable of functioning or competing in more conventional groups and may have been rejected by the usual peer groups. To be initiated into a counter-cultural tribe is to be initiated into a group that is very tolerant of physical or personality flaws. To become fully accepted by such a group can be a very profound experience for people who have felt like outcasts.

So tribal initiations have something of the magical about them, evoking the promise of *communitas*, the feeling of radical collective identity and connectedness that characterizes the primal horde (Freud 1913a; Torgovnick 1997). There is a sense of finally coming home, to an idealized new family that offers a sense of acceptance they have never before experienced. Above all is the experience of having one's old self die and be born again into a new self, respected by the new community.

Despite the Old Testament prohibition against bodily mutilation, male circumcision is obligatory for Jews as a sign of the covenant made between God and Abraham. "And God said to Abraham, Thou shalt keep my covenant, therefore, thou and thy seed after thee in their generations. This is my covenant, which ye shall keep, between me and thy seed after thee. Every man child among you shall be circumcised. And ye shall circumcise the flesh of your foreskin and it shall be a token of the covenant betwixt me and you" (Genesis 15:9-11). Male infants are to be circumcised on the eighth day after birth, and converts who are already circumcised must have a *mohel,* a ritual circumciser, draw a token drop of blood. However when David Klinghoffer (1998), a *National Review* editor, converted from Reform to Orthodox Judaism, he was troubled by the thought that his circumcision was not ritually correct. He took matters literally into his own hands by immersing himself in the bathtub and drawing a drop of blood from the tip of his penis with a straight razor. Then he had two more circumcisions— first by a Conservative, then by an Orthodox *mohel* before he was satisfied that he was truly a Jew. In a hilarious off-Broadway show called "Circumcise Me," Orthodox-convert comedian Yisrael Campbell tells how he came to have three circumcisions, one Reform, one Conservative, and one Orthodox. You can see and hear him on YouTube.

For those who feel alienated and vulnerable, having a predatory appearance can defend against the fear of being preyed on. Although not that long ago, the Mohawk haircut or hair that is gelled into stegosaurus spikes gave the message of a predator, there are those who actually have their bodies mutated to serve predatory functions, and have cyber-weapons implanted. Pre-dated by James Bond movies, some of these implants are the most vicious cyber-weapons imaginable, meant to harm the source of any real or perceived danger. Belonging to a tribe of similar others can provide an even greater sense of strength. "Cyberweapons are great, they can be hidden inside you or under your skin right until you close in for the kill, or better still, wait until your opponent is closing in and give them a real surprise!" (Cyberweapons 2012). Those with these implants need not carry knives or guns; they transform their bodies into lethal weapons that can claw, bite, or spray toxic substances. Implanted body-blades, bone spikes, small machetes, elbow spikes, extended canine teeth and fangs, needle skin quills, pop-up hand blades, and other "rippers" and "scratchers" all mimic the ferocious puffer fish, porcupine and poison-spitting cobra.

OUR CULTURAL OBSESSION WITH SKIN

American culture has become obsessed with skin, which tends to be regarded as the window to the soul (Brumberg 1997; Farber 2000, 2002). Unlike ancient cultures that prize the wrinkled faces of the elderly, we spend a fortune to achieve a youthful look. To rid our skin of all perceived imperfections, there is an enormous variety of cosmetic surgeries from which to choose. We have Botox injected to rid ourselves of wrinkles, collagen injected to plump up our lips, silicone injected to enlarge the breasts or penis. We can even have excess skin removed after losing a large amount of weight. We invest time and money to make our skin lighter or darker through tanning and makeup. And all too often this is done without concern for the possible hazards.

In 1929, Charles Atlas developed a landmark bodybuilding and exercise program featuring his name and image (Gaines and Butler 1982). He proclaimed that once he too was a ninety-seven-pound chicken-chested scrawny weakling but he was able to develop his body, and became musclebound and strong. His company was founded in 1929 and still markets a fitness program. Today, men and women spend many hours trying to develop "buns of steel" and equally hard pecs and abs.

We rarely think of what functions skin serves but several theorists have elaborated on its psychic functions (Anzieu 1980, 1990; Ogden 1996; Lappe 1996; Farber 2000, 2002). Anzieu tells us that skin serves transitional functions, serving as a psychic envelope, a plane of demarcation between the internal and external worlds, between the internal psychic world and the psychic world of other people

> In its first function, the skin is the sack that holds in the goodness and fullness that accumulates from being suckled, cared for, and bathed with words. In its second function, the skin is the surface that marks the boundary with the outside and keeps it on the outside; it is the barrier that protects against the greed and aggression of others, persons, or things. Lastly, in its third function, the skin— along with the mouth and at least as much as it—is a place and principal means of exchange with others (Anzieu 1980, pp. 29-30).

For Ogden too, skin is of overriding importance as the boundary between inside and outside and life and death. And for Lappe, author of *The Body's Edge: Our Cultural Obsession with Skin* (1996), skin is a barrier and a sieve, denying access to the body of some things and actively encouraging the passage of others. . . Under some conditions it lets water out, permits toxic chemicals in, and allows bacteria to reside within its own confines.. . .we have tended to think of the skin as our boundary, a watertight covering that enfolds ourselves and our organs and keeps them separate from the world out there. We visualize the skin in purely Euclidean terms, as a two-dimensional sheet that envelops us in a kind of perpetual Saran Wrap (Lappe 1996, pp.70-1).

THE TRIBE OF LAMBS WHO LAY DOWN FOR THE SLAUGHTER

Having cosmetic surgery has become a rite of passage for many women as they age. Women have subjected themselves for centuries to masochistic practices for the sake of beauty, and today making the body a docile body that can be controlled has become a hallmark of contemporary culture (Foucault 1977; Bordo 1977). When a woman speaks of *getting some work done*, she may not be talking about re-doing her kitchen. To have work done or not is the question many women wrestle with. At a clinical conference I attended, there was a panel on the subject from the personal point of view of psychoanalytic clinicians who had had cosmetic and weight loss surgery. Having considered having my droopy eyelids done, I was eager to hear from a female psychoanalyst who had her eyelids lifted. She had done it, she said, because it was interfering with her vision, a more dignified motivation than mine. Mine were not interfering with my vision, only my vanity. When I was younger, I liked being taken for someone several years older. Now it is reversed, and I want to look younger. I have not had the surgery done and as I age, I think about it less and less but every once in awhile, especially after running into a woman I know who has had it, I think perhaps I might.

Cosmetic surgery can promise but it cannot guarantee transformation of the self and body. The medical risks are publicly recognized, but the emotional sacrifices and the impact on identity and relationships are less readily known (Baker-Pitts 2009). To have or not to have the surgery was a question that writer Erica Jong struggled with.

> At fifty, we are more ready to forgive. And this is when the flesh becomes most unforgiving. . . I look in the mirror and see my grandfather's jowls starting to form where my apple cheeks once were. I hurriedly pass a reflection of myself in a store window and see my grandmother. And what an insult this metamorphosis is, coming just when I feel freer than I have ever felt in my life. Just when I'm feeling younger every year, why do I *look* older? . . .
>
> I don't want to know what the knife can do. There is something eerie and strange about recutting my face like an old suit. I even like my furrows and wrinkles. I earned them. Why give up these badges of a life deeply lived?
>
> I don't believe that women should be defined by their looks, that age equals ugliness, or that youth and beauty are synonymous—so why should I change my face? It goes on aging as I go on trying to come to terms with it.
>
> But then a friend comes home from California with a new face. No lowering forehead creases, no downturned mouth, and an attitude lifted as well. I make an appointment with the wizard of San Francisco.
>
> It is still hard for me to believe that I flew three thousand miles, lay down in a stranger's office, and allowed myself to be cut up like a Christmas lamb.
>
> All my life I have defined myself by ceaseless activity—and now I was forced to keep still. I felt like I was dead. I felt like I had entered a bardo between one existence and another. . . .
>
> So I too must surrender to my new face. . . Now that it's over, I torture myself by imagining the procedure. A gash was made into the top of my head. My scalp was peeled back from the skull. My eyes were tucked up with black thread. I savor all the gory details (Jong 1998, pp. 61-63).

Joan Rivers, age 77, is known as much for her many cosmetic surgeries as for her brash, raunchy humor. She has been called the poster child for Extreme Celebrity Plastic Surgery and becomes weirder looking by the year. A documentary, *Joan Rivers: A Piece of Work*, premiered in 2010. Rivers is the author of *Men Are Stupid. . . And They Like Big Boobs—A Woman's Guide to Beauty Through Plastic Surgery.* (Rivers and Frankel, 2008). She seems to have become as addicted to cosmetic surgery as to being onstage, and says that being onstage is the only time she is truly happy. The night her husband committed suicide, she was having liposuction. Having left him three days earlier, she felt responsible and thought about killing herself. She became bulimic, an apparent compromise formation, and incorporated his suicide into her comedy act; "Thank God my husband said in his will that I should cremate him and then scatter his ashes in Neiman Marcus. That way he knew he would see me five times a week." Her humor and cosmetic surgeries serve as manic defenses for her, bringing her husband back to life and keeping her young and alive forever.

BODILY SELF-HARM, BODY MODIFICATIONS, AND SUICIDALITY

Just as building up a thick layer of muscles can serve as a form of psychic armor for some, others are having extensive body modifications with the same motivation. A number of books have been written about the contemporary trend for tattoos. In Amy Krakow's *The Total Tattoo Book* (1994), someone who was interviewed said, "You wonder if all those tattoos make your skin so thick and tough that you don't feel anything anymore" (Krakow 1994, p. 40). When seeing a person with extensive body modifications and wondering why someone might have had so much of it done, one must consider what may have occurred in his life to compel the acquisition of such a thick coat of armor.

The findings of my dissertation study, designed to explore the relationship between the high co-morbidity between eating disorders and self mutilation, suggest that when the self-harm behavior (eating disorders, self-mutilation, body modifications) that had enlivened a deadened self comes to lose its self-medicating strength, this is when the risk for suicide is greatest (Farber 1995, 2000, 2002, Farber, Jackson, et al. 2007). This is because, as in other addictive behaviors, a tolerance for the "drug of choice" seems to develop over time, going from piercing and tattooing non-erogenous parts of the body to erotic piercings and tattoos. This is the kindling effect in body modifications, a passive form of self-mutilation (Russell and John 1999). Despite the self-medicating power and extreme stimulation provided by being tattooed and pierced, as well as the ongoing stimulation produced by erotic piercings, the Body Modification subgroup scored even higher than the Severe Self-Harm subgroup on suicidality. When the tattooing and piercing that had enlivened a deadened self comes to lose its self-medicating strength, the risk for suicide is greatest.

My findings and conclusions are supported by the findings of suicidologist David Lester, whose online survey of those who belong to a website for body modifications found that only 34% of some 4,700 participants admitted to *not* considering suicide. Lester said that he had anticipated a lesser association with suicidality, because tattoos have become so much more popular since several decades ago, when they were considered deviant (Jancin 2005; Hicinbothim, Gonsalves and Lester, 2006). No matter how much more mainstream they have become, there is still a strong association with suicidality. Two-thirds reported suicidal thoughts at some time or had attempted suicide, and 39 percent disclosed that they only contemplated suicide. Twenty-seven percent stated that they made one or more attempts.

Both the type of body modification the person had as well as the anatomic site they selected seemed to be related to their history of suicidality (Jancin. 2005; Hicinbothim, Gonsalves, and Lester, 2006). For instance, a pierced eyebrow is a relatively common form of body modification, yet 27 percent of men and 46 percent of women with a pierced eyebrow reported that they had attempted suicide. Twenty-four percent of men with a tongue piercing reported previously attempting suicide, compared with 18 percent of those without a tongue piercing. Similarly, 37 percent of women with a pierced tongue reported prior deliberate self-harm, compared with 30% without one. Some of the highest suicidality rates were found among those engaged in scarification. Some 39 percent of men and 48 percent of women whose upper arm or shoulder had a scarification reported at least one suicide attempt, compared with 18 percent and 32 percent respectively, without this specific body modification. Considering that the sample size is so large, these differences are even more significant.

There is considerable overlap between the body modification and Goth subcultures. What characterizes Goth subculture is adopting unusual fashions and styles to distinguish themselves from other youth. Some may just dress in black and paint their fingernails and lips black, while others, like a fifteen-year-old girl I treated, become deeply involved in a pseudo medieval world of dark images, Renaissance Fairs, and becoming fascinated with S&M fashion. When 19-year-olds in this subculture were studied in Scotland (N=1258), it was found that identification with the Goth subculture was the best predictor of self harm and suicide attempts (Young, Sweeting, and West 2006).

BEWARE THE GURUS AND SHAMANS OF PAIN

> Youth subculture forms in the space between surveillance and the evasion of surveillance—it translates the fact of being under scrutiny into the pleasure of being watched. . . . If teenagers possess little else, they at least own their own bodies. If power can be exercised nowhere else, it can at least be exercised here. The body can be decorated and enhanced like a cherished object. It can be cut up and "cooked" like a piece of meat. Self-mutilation is just the darker side of narcissism. The body becomes the base-line, the place where the buck

> stops. To wear a mohican or have your face tattooed is to burn most of your bridges."
> —Dick Hebdige, *Hiding in the* Light

> That is always the thing with depravity; just when you think you've plumbed the very depths, there's always someplace lower to fall."
> —Kevin Baker, *Dreamland*

In the 1960s Eastern religions, with their emphasis on cultivating trance states, became appealing, and the shaman, who could self-induce trance states in order to heal people of "spirit illness," acquired a romanticized image as a very wise man with knowledge of another *separate reality* (Kakar 1982). Allen Ginsberg emphasized the ability to see the world in a visionary way (Watson 1995), paving the way for generations of self-styled shamans to spring up in Western culture. Ever since the publication of Carlos Castene-da's (1972) *The Teachings of Don Juan: A Yaqui Way of Knowledge,* Western culture has grown to idealize the shaman.

The term shaman comes from Northeast Asian origin and means "one who is excited, moved, raised." A shaman is thought to be someone whose great suffering has made him ill. Out of his suffering has come the special wisdom to become a native healer. Shamans treat those with *spirit illness* through courting extreme pain and risk in order to go into a trance and make contact with the spirit world (Kakar 1982). In tribal cultures, where healing and the sacred are part and parcel of each other, the shaman is simply part of everyday life. Today, many in Western cultures have come to understand their mental suffering as a sign to explore a shamanic path.

Just as the talented psychoanalyst comes to his or her clinical wisdom through an understanding of his own suffering, the shaman's wisdom is believed to come to him through his suffering, specifically the voluntary mutilation and starvation of his body (Kakar 1982). The illness really is an initiation rite to be survived so that he can emerge from it reborn, with the wisdom to heal.

According to anthropologist Claude Levi-Strauss (1976), the shaman provides the sick member of society with the verbal means for expressing unexpressed and otherwise inexpressible psychic states. Levi-Strauss delineated the parallels between the roles of the shaman and the psychoanalyst, considering the shaman to be the precursor of the psychoanalyst (Kakar 1982). Like the psychoanalyst, the shaman establishes a direct relationship with the patient's conscious mind and an indirect relationship with his unconscious. The analyst does this through listening, bending his unconscious to the unconscious of the patient, and the shaman does this through discourse. The patient puts words into the mouth of the analyst by projecting onto him his own feelings and wishes, whereas the shaman speaks for the patient, putting into his mouth the answers to questions that correspond to his interpretation of the patient's condition, imbuing himself with the patient's subjective state.

The Western image of the shaman, however, is full of contradictions. He may be seen as a mentally ill person or may be regarded as a religious specialist who connects his community with everything that is sacred and gives meaning to life. The more positive image of the shaman is related to the Western idealization of tribal cultures and the adoption of their practices.

The shaman (or spirit doctor, sorcerer, witch doctor, native healer) continues to be invented and reinvented according to the changing needs of Western culture. Kakar tells us that the shamanic reality that he is familiar with bears little resemblance to its portrayal in much of Western literature and its restless Zeitgeist. The kind of introspection that psychoanalysis requires of both patient and psychoanalyst is a peculiarly Western trait, deeply rooted in Western culture. Western definitions of self and identity are contingent upon an active process of self-examination, a kind of introspection which simply is not a feature of Indian culture (Kakar 1982).

In the West, there is no shortage of cults and gurus to be worshipped and obeyed, some imported from India, a leading producer and exporter of spiritual wares. Others may be home-grown, influenced to follow a shamanic path. Several years ago I was treating a young woman, a mental health professional, who told me that she was dating a man who was studying to become a shaman. That is how I discovered that there are courses at New Age centers and how-to books such as *So You Want to Be a Shaman* (Lawson 1996) and *The Complete Idiot's Guide to Shamanism* (Scott 2002) to chart the way.

Given that my bias is that of Western trained psychoanalyst, I think that because psychotherapists, shamans, medicine men, and physicians wield great power in their relationships with patients, they are morally and ethically obligated to respect that power and not abuse it to meet their own needs. There are, nonetheless, psychotherapists and psychoanalysts, just as there are shamans, who can be harmful to patients. Jung might have described them as fitting the archetype of the *wounded healer* (Jung 1951) whose scars are both a burden and a driving force in his need to fix the problems of others while destroying himself. Jung believed that illness of the soul might be the best means of training for a healer, and thought only a wounded healer could heal effectively.

The healer's wounds may be activated in certain situations, especially if his patient's wounds are similar to his own, infecting the countertransference, the core issue in depth psychology and psychoanalysis. When the wounded healer cannot use introspection and self-examination to heal himself, he can be a danger to others. Whether one is seeking a shaman, spirit guide, psychotherapist, psychoanalyst, clinical supervisor, or physician, this is a major decision. We must be careful and take our time. No matter how impressive the credentials are, they do not offer protection from being harmed by a wounded healer.

Today so many of the veteran psychiatric patients, the sadomasochists, the competitive cutters, burners, and piercers seem to have become the new shamans, influencing suggestible and troubled young people to hurt themselves in ecstasies of pain. Some of them are *Modern Primitives* (Vale and Juno 1989), who have appropriated the extreme body modification practices of tribal cultures, in which pain and ecstasy all go hand in hand. Some may even be members of the Church of Body Modification, which believes that more extensive body modifications are a path to spiritual modification (Elliott 2003).

Fakir Musafar, self-styled guru of the Modern Primitive movement, and Raellyn Gallina are two of those shamans. Unlike tribes who shun the camera, Modern Primitives love it (Torgovnik 1996). Like models in a photo shoot, they gladly face the camera to exhibit themselves, and flaunt their new transgressive identity and community. To look at *The Piercing Fans International Quarterly* (I really am not making that up) is to look at a glossy expensive magazine filled with page after page of photographs of pierced nipples and genitals, surgically forked tongues and penises, scarifications, and other "in your face" body mutilations. Extreme sadomasochism is a flirtation with death, and for the Modern Primitives, awakening the deadened body through their extreme practices is a way of getting as close to death as they can, having near-death experiences from which they may or may not return.

RAELLYN GALLINA, QUEEN OF BLOOD SPORTS

Raellyn Gallina is an artist who makes custom jewelry to be worn in the body piercings she creates. She asks her clients to bring in meaningful objects or writings to create a "sacred space" (Myers 1995). She believes that being pierced or cut can be empowering, even therapeutic, for someone who has been abused. She loves to cut people, admitting that both she and her clients get a high from cutting and burning, adding with a sly smile that she likes blood. She initially indulged this exotic taste by cutting and piercing herself, then began to cut and pierce others privately and in group workshops attended primarily by lesbians (Vale and Juno 1989). Raellyn greeted them "Hello, fellow blood sluts." Attached to her equipment case is a button that reads "I'm hungry for your blood."

Her specialty is her "slash and burn" technique. Rosie, a fortyish woman, stripped down to the waist to obtain her cutting, which Raellyn then blotted. Anticipating the alcohol rinsings by Raellyn, Rosie braced herself, then Raellyn ignited the final rinse with her cigarette lighter. It sounded just like a hibachi restaurant. "A loud poof was heard, and a bluish flame danced across the entire left side of Rosie's back. . . . This flame show was repeated two more times as the audience oohed and aahed" (Myers 1995, pp.169-71).

FAKIR MUSAFAR

A man named Roland Loomis at birth came to readily embrace an identity as a shaman; in order to conduct young people through rites of passage, he changed his name to Fakir Musafar. He believed that starting at puberty, certain "magical events" or rites of passage must happen periodically if human beings are to progress,

By his own account (Favazza 1996; Vale and Juno 1989) Musafar felt the urge from a very early age to make marks on and put holes in his body, and did this secretly for thirty years, driven into isolation and a sense of shame. He knew that if what he was doing became known, he might have been institutionalized. Why he felt these impulses is anyone's guess but whatever it was, he could not live comfortably in his own skin.

His public persona included getting degrees in electrical engineering and creative writing, and for many years holding executive positions in San Francisco advertising agencies and operating his own ad agency in Silicon Valley. Over the years, he has had a checkered career path that included being an army instructor in demolitions and explosives and a dance instructor at Arthur Murray's Dance Studio. All this time, he was practicing in private what had been revealed to him as a compelling but unsanctioned way in this culture to reach spiritual heights through the body.

He haunted libraries for years, searched archives, and listened to the tales of Native American elders in South Dakota, looking for any cultural or social sanction for his secret pactices. He was glad to discover reasons and traditions for the urge to mutilate himself in other cultures, in which various forms of self-mutilation had spiritual underpinnings. He was pleased to discover that the states of mind associated with the act in these cultures were often considered states of grace, not illness. He found role models in religious people who put needles through their skin and went into trances or walked barefoot through hot coals. He ended his isolation when a mentor encouraged him to go public, arranging a "showing" at the First International Tattoo Convention in Reno, Nevada in 1978, where he pierced his body, displayed his extensive body tattoos, demonstrated his contortions and corseted waist, and lay on beds of sharp blades and spikes, all the while in a trance state. The audience loved it, seeing in him the impulses they had themselves. Not only did his acts serve as his rite of passage into this new tribe but their extreme nature quickly distinguished him as an honored elder.

His next step was to become a shaman who guided others on trips to unseen spaces.

Fakir Musafar was an unlikely name for a child born into a Lutheran family in South Dakota, but it has a certain cachet if you want to be a shaman. And being a shaman was a lot better than being a weird kid who went into trances, saw faces melt and change, and pierced the foreskin of his penis. Better to be a shaman, like the nineteenth-century Sufi who wandered around for eighteen years with daggers and other objects stuck in his body, trying to educate others in the mysteries he had discovered. The Hindus in Kuala Lumpur claim that when fishhooks pierce their bodies and skewers pierce their mouths, the god has come into them and frees them from the pain (Thernstrom 2010). Musafar puts it this way:

> If you get into any practices of other cultures you're bound to be involved with a lot of sexuality in other states and guises that aren't even acknowledged as being in existence in this culture. And a good shamanistic answer to "Why do these things?" is BECAUSE IT'S FUN! . . . Experiencing ecstatic states: why would one want to experience an ecstatic state? Well, you might learn something out of it. You might be able to help others. You might see other worlds. There may be all kinds of reasons, but basically you do it because it's fun. Why not? (Vale and Juno 1989, p. 15).

To say he does it because it is fun seems inadequate. More to the point is that it provides him from ecstatic escape from himself. To do this,he has turned his whole body into a deformed erotic so-called *objet d'art* with weights stretching his penis, his body gilded in gold paint. In one photograph he is masked, and looks like a grotesque human Christmas tree with twenty-four shiny one-pound balls hanging from fishhooks embedded in his chest. Musafar's lifelong quest for ecstasy has led him to the most extreme feats of mortification of the flesh that include stretching his neck; hanging three-pound weights from his penis; elongating his scrotum with metal rings; sealing his genitals in plaster; having his chest and back pierced with ninety steel rods, and corseting himself until his waist was reduced to a permanent nineteen inchesA all these are described and pictured in *Modern Primitives* and, his periodical, *Body Play and Modern Primitives Quarterly,* which has become something of a commercial success.[1]

Musafar will go to any length to heighten erotic experience, but orgasm itself is to be avoided. "If you're seeking an altered state, the last thing in the world you want is to have it turn into a sexual release" (Vale and Juno 1989, p.17). He will hang weights from his penis to stretch it, in imitation of the Indian Sadhus who believe that God is located in the penis, and will use numerous other Tantric techniques to inflict pain genitally so that he can maintain an erection for hours on end. "SM, in this culture, is one of the few places people can get started on the road back to their god. . . . Orgasm builds, it gets delicious, you get anesthetized, people can claw and scratch you and you don't feel any pain—*boom*, the great moment comes—*Uhhh*! And then it's all over" (Vale and Juno 1989, p.20). Penile "weight training" without orgasm, he states, is far superior, and if the penis is stretched long enough "you get to the point where you can't have a physical orgasm at all. And that's ultra-sexual life. That's what the Sadhus do: they lead an ultra-sexual life, going around in a perpetual orgastic state" (Vale and Juno 1989, p.20).

Despite his extensive knowledge of the rites of passage of various tribes—Native American, Burmese, New Guinean, Balinese, and Indian—he is a thoroughly entrepreneurial shaman with his own website. He speaks, performs and presents his body modification rituals to any receptive audience. Musafar is an evangelist, eager to recruit new members and spread the "good news " about the alterations in consciousness that come from returning from a near-death experience.

> In another body-oriented adventure, I invited trusted friends to pierce my chest with two large hooks and suspend me by these two piercings in the style of the Native American Oglalas Sioux Sun Dance and Mandan O-Kee-Pa ceremony. That experience proved to be truly transformative. I lifted out of my body, drifted up to a white light that radiated incredible love and understanding. The light said, "Hello, I'm you!" I was never the same after that remarkable trip. Years later I discovered many others had had a similar transformative experience during what is now called the "near-death experience." I repeated the hanging many times after the first one; each had its own lesson and special place to visit. My fifth hanging was beautifully filmed for a documentary titled *Dances Sacred and Profane* (Favazza 1996, p. 328).

His bizarre ecstasies serve the function of a manic defense, allowing him to believe that he is following a tribal spiritual path rather than suffering from some neuropsychiatric disorder and that through his near-death experience, he can elude death.

Body suspensions often serve as performance art, which are often videotaped, while audiences sit drinking and enjoying a picnic as they watch. They may be done at international fetish events which draw an audience of thousands. In her memoir about her life as a professional dominatrix, Melissa Febos (2010) described the suspension she witnessed at the Black & Blue Ball, one of the biggest fetish events of the year in New York.

> Skye, our colleague, was up on the balcony that overlooked the main floor of the club. I knew that Skye was into suspension but had never seen it before. We found Skye at the center. She had sculpted her hair a foot high, weaving razor wire and Kewpie dolls into it . . . She smiled down at us as we pushed our way to the front . . . Dangling off the ground by a few feet, she wore a spangled bra and hot pants. Strung from the ceiling by rope were two large

> silver hooks. They pierced through the flesh of her back, and from these she hung, a head above the crowd (Febos 2010, pp. 199-200).

Musafar's film essentially provided visual instructions for having oneself suspended from flesh-hooks. They must pierce through enough flesh to support the person's entire body weight, to avoid ripping through him. The Internet now provides instructions for doing a suspension as well as schedules for upcoming suspensions that can be witnessed, photos of suspensions, and comments from people who have had them. Here are some of them.

> Most people that I spoke to tried their best to discourage me from doing the suspension but in the end, I was surprised by the support and understanding that I received from my friends, and to those that gave their support, Thank You!
>
> It was only the day before the Suspension, and after I had seen the completed rig and all the gear, that I was able to relax . . . I was perfectly calm. . . . I went and sat on the stage and tried to develop communication with the waiting crowd which had gathered around the rig, waiting for the spectacle to begin. While the music really pumped and the people crowded in to get a better view, the excitement was electric. I noticed many familiar faces which was really encouraging.
>
> Then we started. We lay down on the stage and before I realized what was happening, the hooks were being inserted. The clamps were a little irritating but I managed to shut from my mind all sensations of pain. Cade relaxed me with a massage while the ropes were being inserted into the hooks. I noticed the audience around me and plenty of movement and can remember wondering whether my brain was still part of my body at that stage. As the rig was lifted and the ropes became tighter, I thought that I would not be able to go through with it. I saw the skin begin to lift and stretch. One girl put a bracelet in my hand just before we lifted. I remember holding it tightly and eventually as we lifted, I could no longer feel it in my hand. The noise of the chain through the chain block I heard above the sound of the music. Eventually as the chain stopped clattering, I realized that I could no longer hear the music . . .
>
> Thank you to everyone that made this memorable experience possible and thank you in anticipation to those who will make it possible in the future.

The suspension experience was written about on a listserv in a very different context by a colleague who treats severely traumatized, dissociated patients. A patient she was treating had been raised in a cult and experienced body suspension as a child as part of ritual abuse. Once again, what is torture to one person is ecstasy to another.

The answers to some of the frequently asked questions (FAQs) convey the experience some have while being suspended. Some of them would be ludicrously funny if they were not so horrifying (Suspension.org 2002).

Q. What is the experience of suspension like?

A. On a simplistic level, physically the experience is a feeling of pulling, burning, and pain all jumbled up, but for most people this physical aspect is "tuned out" very quickly. Although individual experiences differ greatly, ultimately the act of suspension can be a euphoric floating sensation. On one end of the spectrum you find people that enter a trance like state, feeling no pain whatsoever, and on the other end you find people that experience extreme pain, nausea and panic attacks. In general, most people enter a shock-induced state of disorientation spiked with moments of pain and euphoria. In laymen's terms, the act of suspension causes the body/mind to enter a state of shock while being physically positioned and restrained in a "floating" state. There are some general commonalties expressed by most suspendees, such as the feeling of intense tugging which gives way to a more relaxed sensation as the body leaves the ground. However, the varied motivations for suspending make it such that different people have different experiences. As with much of life, you get out of it what you put into and your expectations will often become self-fulfilling prophecies. Some people find it boring, others are changed forever, and some don't ever even think about it beyond simply performing the act. Many find that, good or bad, it is not what they expected. Many people feel intensely at peace while suspended; an experience of complete surrender. They enter a state of hyperawareness and deep trust in themselves and the universe. Almost everyone agrees that the hooks are painful, but some people find the sensation of tension on the skin moving and inspiring. For some people the experience is much lighter; they just want to try it, and when they do they get no emotional release and find themselves giggling and smiling and instead just enjoying the feeling of "flying."

Q. Can I "meet God" if I suspend?

A. For some, the suspension creates an ecstatic state that is not unlike deep meditation. That combined with an extreme influx of hormones and rapid changes in heart rate and blood pressure, and anything is possible. All of this is of course completely dependent upon your god, you, and how you communicate. There is nothing necessarily spiritual about suspending but, like fasting, psychedelic drug use, and many other activities, it can be used and play a major role in a person's spiritual and religious life.

Q. Will I "be cool" if I suspend?

A. "Coolness" is simply an individual's perception of what peers will find to be a positive attribute. It is entirely possible that some people will think you cool if you suspend, and there are certainly some who will think you are nuts and a freak. As the after school special says, being you is what's really cool. A suspension is a serious undertaking and your motivation should come from within, not concern about what anyone else might think. Ultimately you will only be "cool" to those who are ignorant of themselves and have no idea what getting present to being and being present means.

Q. What has suspension generally been used for?

A. Historically, suspensions have been performed as rites of passage, vision quests, healing rituals, penance, rituals of deity devotion or as means to gain visions by leaving the body and/or communication with the spiritual realm. They have been used for testing the endurance of the mind and body, or even just to freak people out. . . . suspensions are being increasingly used as performance art and even for entertainment.

Q. What other cultures used suspension-like rituals?

A. Most notable are some Native American tribes and different sects of the Hindu religion. Although other cultures may have used suspensions ritually, these two are the best documented in that they are still in practice today.

Q. What are the possible negative side-effects of suspension?

A. The potential risks are significant, and include but are not limited to death, extreme shock, convulsions, dizziness, pain, bleeding, loss of consciousness, nausea, vomiting, scarring, and numbness.

Q. What medical conditions could make hooking dangerous?

A. People suffering from high (or low) blood pressure, heart conditions, epilepsy, diabetes, immune deficiency, hepatitis, blood clotting problems, and individuals that have experienced multiple states of extreme shock should seek the advice of their physician before suspending. If you suffer from any medical conditions it is essential that the people helping you are entirely aware of them.

Other FAQs are: What should be done if a suspended person faints? While in the air? After coming down? What should be done if someone goes into shock? Remarkably, they do not ask what should be done if someone dies. That possibility seems not to be taken at all seriously. Such is the nature of a manic defense.

It is not surprising that Fakir Musafar, along with self-proclaimed sex pioneer Annie Sprinkle, wrote rave reviews for Katherine Gates's *Deviant Desires*. Despite his embrace of Hindu practices and repudiation of Christian beliefs, Fakir Musafar brings to mind the Christian martyrs who sought holiness through the mortification of the flesh. He has rejected his Lutheran upbringing but is evangelical about his new "religion," the Church of Body Modification. He has gone to the other side of consciousness, gambled on returning, and so far, he has won. Musafar plays Russian roulette. Which of his followers will gamble and lose? He is conspicuously silent about that possibility. Without the *Modern Primitives* movement to glorify his pathology, Fakir Musafar would just be a very disturbed man who loves to gamble with death. Beware the gurus and shamans.

NOTE

1. You can also see them online at https://www.google.com/search?q=Fakir+Musafar+images&ie=utf-8&oe=utf-8&aq=t&rls=org.mozilla:en-US:official&client=firefox-a.

Chapter Eight

Religious Ecstasies

We come into this world with only the slender word 'I,' and giving it up in a sacred delirium is the painful ecstasy religions demand."
—Diane Ackerman, *A Natural History of the Senses*

None of my sufferings has been equal to that of not having suffered enough."
—Blessed Margaret Mary Alacoque, cited in E. M. Cioran, *Tears and Saints*

French neurologist and psychiatrist Pierre Janet (1859-1947) was the most important scientific and clinical investigator of dissociative states. He studied conversion hysteria, the process by which repudiated mental content is transformed into physical symptoms. More than a century ago, Janet studied several women with religious inclinations at the Salpêtrière mental asylum in Paris. He looked through magnifying glasses at his patient Madeleine's feet to observe the formation of stigmata and watched her delirium ebb and flow (Clement 1994). She called herself *le bouc* (scapegoat) because she had to take on the sins of the world. Her ecstasies were preceded by long periods of fasting, and lasted two or three days, rendering her immobile. Madeleine described her union with God in erotic terms.

> I have large sweet patches on my lips and on my stomach that throb with truly divine tremors . . . My whole body trembles when God softly places his burning hands on my body and caresses me all over, it is indescribable, and it seems like the *jouissance* that I feel makes me faint. I feel as if I am being lifted into the air, . . . as if my body is being carried by a thick rope between my legs. . . pressing on my genitals. . . It begins to affect my bladder; a seal is placed on the opening but this difficulty in urinating is not an agony but a rather a sensual delight . . . I very often feel the sweetest tremors both on the inside as well as the outside of my body which are so unusual that I cannot describe them (Clement 1994, p. 204).

Janet insisted that there really was no difference between the ecstasies of his patients and those of the medieval mystics. Madeleine would remain a psychiatric patient, when in an earlier era and context, she might have been regarded as a holy woman (Clement 1994).

> What does it mean to be holy? To Emile Durkheim, it smacked of psychopathology. It is certainly true that religious life cannot attain a certain degree of intensity without implying a psychical exaltation not far removed from delirium. That is why the prophets, the founders of religion, the great saints, in a word, the men whose religious consciousness is exceptionally sensitive, very frequently give signs of an excessive nervousness that is even pathological: these physiological defects predestined them to great religious roles (Durkheim 1965, p. 258).

Madeleine's description of her ecstasy suggests that religious and sexual ecstasies are often quite similar. Candles, music, flowers, wine, the taking of vows, the plighting of troths, the all-consuming fire in the flesh are all the props of romance, sex, and love. But they are also the props of religious ritual, the most sacred rites (Eisler 1996; MacKendrick 1999).

> Why is there this striking, though seldom noted, commonality? Is it just accidental that passion is the word we use for both sexual and mystical experiences? Or is there some long-forgotten but still powerful connection? Could it be that the yearning of so many women and men for sex as something beautiful and magical is our long repressed impulse toward a more spiritual, and at the same time more intensely passionate, way of expressing sex and love? (Eisler 1999, p. 15).

When erotic feelings are feared or forbidden, they may take the form of religious feelings.

> Religious asceticism sacrifices and sanctifies, scars and sacralizes the body, whether or not it is 'spiritual'—and so too do the erotic pleasures of pain and restraint, spiritual or not. The search for the ecstatic and the sacred takes place in the body . . . To make sacred is to render, not necessarily godlike, but divine" (MacKendrick 1999, p. 157).

It is in this way that the saints and sadomasochists become strange bedfellows, brothers and sisters under the skin.

RAMAKRISHNA'S ECSTASIES

Sudhir Kakar and Wendy Doniger translated a new translation of the Kamasutra (Vatsyayana 2000), the ancient Hindu text, considered to be the standard work on human sexuality. Kakar focused on the ecstasies of Sri Ramakrishna (Kakar 1991, 2003), an heir to the Hindu mystical tradition, which despite similarities to the mysticism of other faiths, has its own unique context. Specifically, Hindu religiosity is not monotheistic, and a large number of personal gods, aspects of the Supreme Being, are worshipped. Because Hindu mystics generally do not have the constraints of monotheistic mystics, they are far more uninhibited in expression of ecstasy.

Had Ramakrishna been born into Western culture, surely he would have been treated as a madman. Because so many in Western culture are appropriating practices from Eastern cultures without appreciating the context from which they originated, it is worth elaborating on Ramakrishna's story. In the two schools of Hindu mysticism, there is no yearning for communion with God. Mystical liberation is attained entirely through the mystic's own efforts, without the intervention of any divine grace.

Ramakrishna's preferred form of mysticism was *Bhakti,* devotional mysticism, the only form involving love for the Deity. It is only when the mystic's soul or self is finally united with God (or Goddess) in an ecstatic surrender, that Hindu mysticism resembles the mysticism of the monotheistic faiths. Kakar uses the life of Ramakrishna as a case study, discussing three interrelated features that are necessary in creating an ecstatic mystic: particular historical life experiences, a certain artistic or creative gift, and a facilitating socio-cultural environment. He compares the mystical journey to the psychoanalytic process, seeing in both a creative immersion, with its potential risk of phases of chaos and disintegration.

Ramakrishna was born in 1836 in Bengal, the youngest son to poor, pious, and relatively old parents. His devoted mother was quite over-protective when he began exploring the world, fearful that he would be harmed. He once hid behind a tree to peep out at women as they washed clothes and bathed at the village tank. One of them saw him and complained to his mother; she scolded and shamed him, saying that all women were the same as she; and that insulting their honor was insulting hers. Mortified, Ramakrishna never did this again, apparently having his natural sexual curiosity squelched by the association with incestuous anxiety. This influenced his developing sexuality and was a great factor in his decision to remain celibate forever. It also seemed to be transformed into his ecstatic experiences.

He loved painting in school, and spending time with the village potters making clay images of the gods and goddesses. It was his first aesthetic emotion that evoked his first ecstasy. He looked up to the sky and saw a great black cloud spreading quickly until it covered the sky. Suddenly at the edge of a cloud a flight of snow-white cranes flew overhead. The contrast was so beautiful that his spirit wandered far away, causing him to lose consciousness and fall to the ground. Someone picked him up and carried him home. He became overcome with joy and emotion and for the first time in his life, was seized with ecstasy.

At eight, his father died, and Ramakrishna became withdrawn and isolated from others. School attendance fell. He spent much time listening to village ascetics talking about spiritual matters. There were other fainting episodes which he attributed to spiritual stirrings. Family life became tumultuous, pushing him further away from everyday reality, toward transcendental matters and religious life, an easy transition in rural India, where spirituality courses through life. He participated in many daily rituals, frequent religious plays and festivals, singing and dancing with abandon. Often he found himself seized by sudden inward abstracted states. At other times, he was at home with his mother, helping with household chores. The village women who dropped by seem to have adopted him. They would ask him to sing or tell stories from the sacred texts which he enjoyed doing. He loved their company and soon began dressing as a woman, going out and passing in front of men who never suspected that he was not really a woman. He mimicked feminine gestures and movements perfectly. A recurrent fantasy was that if he were to be born again, it would be as a beautiful child widow who would not know anyone other than Lord Krishna as a husband. As the day was ending, he would sing songs about Lord Krishna, and after dark, would cry for him. Krishna would come secretly and Ramakrishna would feed him sweets made especially for him. A new opportunity opened up when his eldest brother Ramkumar, the priest of a temple, became sick and handed over his duties to Ramakrishna. When Ramkumar died, his death had a profound effect on Ramakrishna, kindling a wish to renounce all things of the real world, and a conviction of how transitory it was. He became more and more engrossed in worship of the Mother Goddess. When the temple closed at midday and midnight, he roamed around in the jungle, yearning to behold and revere her, and for her to behold and revere him, conferring a blessing. In his spiritual thirst, he became restless, slept poorly, and barely ate. His nephew thought he had gone mad when he found him naked, sitting under a tree. He wanted to kill himself when he suddenly had a vision of the Mother Goddess and passed out. He felt intense bliss flowing into his heart and saw a boundless sea of light, then waves coming forward toward him, falling on him, and making him sink to the abysmal depths of infinity. This vision left an aftertaste that whetted his appetite for repeated ecstasies. Ramakrishna's behavior appeared bizarre even to the visitors to the temple, accustomed to a wide range of religious fervor. He decorated himself with the flowers and sandalwood paste meant for worship of the goddess. He would feel the statue of the goddess breathing, try to feed her stony mouth, and would carry on playful conversations with her. Any lessening of the sense of her presence made him throw himself on the ground and roll violently, wailing, struggling to breathe. When he again received an ecstatic vision of the goddess, he would beam with joy and become a different person altogether. He worshipped his own penis and was seized by ecstatic visions while he defecated. He was thought to have become insane and was treated for it, to no avail. Finally, through treatment by an exorcist and an Ayurvedic doctor, he slowly recovered. To safeguard these gains, the family arranged his marriage, a step that even today is considered to be the best antidote to psychic breakdown. Of course, there was no question about the marriage being consummated. He saw himself from the beginning, in relation to his child bride, as either a woman or, in his ecstatic state, as a child.

He returned to his priestly duties at the temple, and had a relapse. For the next eight years he systematically followed the prescribed practices laid down by different schools of Hindu mysticism. During these visions, at times he shuddered while tears of joy ran down his cheeks. At other times, his eyes would become half-closed and out of focus, with a faint smile playing around his mouth, while his body became completely rigid and had to be supported by a disciple lest he fall and hurt himself. While in other trance states his chest flushed or he had a burning sensation all over his body. He became so hot that when he lay on the ground, the earth that stuck to his body became baked. At times he felt famished and stuffed himself with food.

The gurus who guided him were amazed at his natural facility and speed in reaching his goals. His mystical genius soon became trumpeted by layman and experts alike. Disciples gathered around him and the theologically learned visited to share in his clear insight but most of all, they were attracted by his riveting presence, even when he was absent for days in ecstatic trances. He had become a great teacher and mystic, having finally merged with God or Goddess in an ecstatic surrender.

Kakar (1991) said that for Ramakrishna, the mystical path was a way of lessening the agony of separation, mitigating the grief at loss, reducing the sadness of bereavement. He attributed his acute sensitivity to the mystical gift of a specific kind of creative experiencing. Ramakrishna insisted that his male sexuality was the greatest obstacle to mystical experiencing. The renunciation of adult masculinity is not only a feature of Hindu devotional mysticism but is also a feature of medieval and early modern Christianity. Both are pervaded by femininity. In medieval Europe, most of the mystics were women, and even the outstanding male mystics show strong feminine identifications. The stance of the Christian ecstatic toward God is either that of the infant toward a loving maternal parent or of a woman toward her lover. Most of the widely known mystics in the Hindu and Christian traditions were celibate, leading one to wonder whether celibacy is an important physiological component for ecstasy.

Kakar was asked if mystical and sexual ecstasy are two sides to the same coin, and how the tradition of *bhakti* (devotional mysticism) addresses both types. He replied

> Here I can only say that I believe they are two sides of the same coin although, like a man being asked about women's experience of sex, I do not know for sure since I have never experienced mystical ecstasy myself. Bhakti addresses mystical ecstasy but the whole mode of its address, its charge, comes from the memory of sexual ecstasy. And in some of the best bhakti poems the sexual and mystical are so intertwined that it is difficult to separate the two (Asia Society 2002).

SACRED EROTICA AND ECSTATIC SEIZURES

Religion, Catholicism especially, often adopts an anti-sexual attitude toward love, advising believers to seek the spiritual while distrusting the body (Ackerman 1995). Celebrating passion and defining love in natural terms were equally sacrilegious in the Catholic Church, which taught that erotic love was dangerous, a trapdoor leading to hell, not even to be condoned between husband and wife. He could kiss, fondle, and caress her, just so long as he did not really enjoy it. It was normal and acceptable to have a sexual appetite, but not to feel passion. A man feeling too much passion for his wife was committing an act of adultery. They were supposed to live together, like affectionate partners who got along well, and just happened to have children. Although the Stoics believed that the human body was inferior to the mind and spirit, it was later, with Saint Paul and Saint Augustine, that the idea that the human body, especially the woman's body, was corrupt, even demonic (Eisler 1996). Nonetheless, in writing about the crucifixion Saint Augustine described the cross as a marriage bed and Christ as a bridegroom consummating his nuptials.

> He came to the marriage-bed of the cross, and there in mounting it, he consummated his marriage. And when he perceived the sighs of the creature, he lovingly gave himself up to the torment in place of his bride, and joined himself to the woman forever (cited by Ackerman 1995, p. 317).

For Marcel Proust, waiting for what one yearned for had a passion of its own. The essence of waiting, said Ackerman, is that it makes us suffer.

> To wait. To feel her ribs pressing against the walls of the chest and a hollow ache, as of someone knocking, in the vault of the stomach. The minute hand of the watch seems frozen. All of life's processes stop. . . The world grows slack. Silence reigns. Yet her pulse is leaping like a frightened stag" (Ackerman 1995, pp. 112-13).

In *Sacred Pleasure: Sex, Myth, and the Politics of the Body*, Riane Eisler (1995) asks why sex, at one time regarded as a sacred gift from the Goddess, become synonymous with evil and shows us how history has consistently promoted the link between sex and violence. Just as Catholic nuns do today, medieval nuns took their vows as brides of Christ. Prohibited from enjoying sexual ecstasy, they enjoyed instead the ecstasies of pain (Eisler 1995).

Teresa of Avila, born into an aristocratic family in the sixteenth century, became a nun and mystic. Her grandfather was a *converso,* one of many Jews who, since the persecutions of the fourteenth century, tried to protect themselves by converting to Christianity but clung secretly to their Jewish identities and practices (Medwick 1999), which included heterosexual love as earthy, sensual, and material. Teresa wrote in her *Meditaciones* about her marriage to Christ using a style known as sacred erotica, influenced by the Song of Songs (also known as the Song of Solomon) in the Hebrew bible. Although it is understood in some circles to symbolize the relationship of God and Israel as husband and wife, in the fourteenth and fifteenth century Jewish mysticism and the Kabbalah took on a strong erotic element (Idel 1985). (I speculate that the Jewish acceptance of eroticism, in contrast to the Catholic prohibition of it, was a factor in developing the anti-Semitic stereotype of Jews as not only Christ-killers but perverted ones as well.) The main characters of the Song of Songs are a woman and a man, and the poem suggests development from courtship to sexual intercourse. The husband sings to his wife:

> How beautiful are thy feet with shoes, O prince's daughter! the joints of thy thighs are like jewels, the work of the hands of a cunning workman.
> Thy navel is like a round goblet, which wanteth not liquor: thy belly is like a heap of wheat set about with lilies.
> Thy two breasts are like two young roes that are twins.
> Thy neck is as a tower of ivory; thine eyes like the fishpools in Heshbon, by the gate of Bathrabbim: thy nose is as the tower of Lebanon which looketh toward Damascus.
> Thine head upon thee is like Carmel, and the hair of thine head like purple; the king is held in the galleries.
> How fair and how pleasant art thou, O love, for delights!
> This thy stature is like to a palm tree, and thy breasts to clusters of grapes.
> I said, I will go up to the palm tree, I will take hold of the boughs thereof: now also thy breasts shall be as clusters of the vine, and the smell of thy nose like apples;
> And the roof of thy mouth like the best wine for my beloved, that goeth down sweetly, causing the lips of those that are asleep to speak (Chapter 7, verses 1-9).

In return, the wife sings to her husband:

> I am come into my garden, my sister, my spouse: I have gathered my myrrh with my spice; I have eaten my honeycomb with my honey; I have drunk my wine with my milk: eat, O friends; drink, yea, drink abundantly, O beloved.
> I sleep, but my heart waketh: it is the voice of my beloved that knocketh, saying, Open to me, my sister, my love, my dove, my undefiled: for my head is filled with dew, and my locks with the drops of the night.
> I have put off my coat; how shall I put it on? I have washed my feet; how shall I defile them?

My beloved put in his hand by the hole of the door, and my bowels were moved for him.
I rose up to open to my beloved; and my hands dropped with myrrh, and my fingers with sweet smelling myrrh, upon the handles of the lock.
I opened to my beloved; but my beloved had withdrawn himself, and was gone: my soul failed when he spake: I sought him, but I could not find him; I called him, but he gave me no answer.
The watchmen that went about the city found me, they smote me, they wounded me; the keepers of the walls took away my veil from me.
I charge you, O daughters of Jerusalem, if ye find my beloved, that ye tell him, that I am sick of love (Song of Songs, 5: 1-8).

Teresa was known to have an expansive, earthy personality. She spoke of the mystics as quite human and said, "We are not angels but have bodies and bodies respond as they can (Medwick 1999, p. 58)." The mystics' response to their own eroticism was in the guise of religious ecstasy (Eisler 1995). As Teresa said in her autobiography, at the height of ecstasy "The soul neither hears nor sees, nor feels. While it lasts, none of the senses perceives or knows what is taking place (Teresa of Avila 1988, p. 142)." Teresa, who may have had temporal lobe epilepsy, which is often associated with religiosity and creativity (Flaherty 2004; Nelson 2011), described her best known ecstatic vision in terms of pain and penetration. Her ecstasies were remarkably frequent, and came swiftly and powerfully, without warning, leading Freud's colleague, Josef Breuer, to call her "the patron saint of hysteria." She often dropped to the floor, frozen in one position for hours. Bernini's marble sculpture, The Ecstasy of St. Teresa, depicts her ecstasy at the vision of an angel in a way that suggests she was having an orgasm. "The visual details all tell of mystical insight: the unseeing, heavily lidded eyes (absorbed in visions). The mouth half-open in painful rapture, and the almost postcoital loosening of the limbs (Morris1991, p.132)." Teresa wrote:

> It pleased our Lord that I should sometimes see this vision. Very close to me. . an angel appeared in human form . . . and his face was so aflame that he seemed to be one of those superior angels who look like they are completely on fire. . . In his hands I saw a large golden spear, and at its iron tip there seemed to be a point of fire. I felt as if he plunged this into my heart several times, so that it penetrated all the way to my entrails. When he drew it out, he seemed to draw them out with it, and left me totally inflamed with a great love for God. The pain was so severe; it made me moan several times. The sweetness of this intense pain is so extreme, there is no wanting it to end, and the soul isn't satisfied with anything less than God. This pain is not physical, but spiritual, even though the body has a share in it—in fact, a large share (Medwick 1999, pp. 56-57, citing Teresa's *Libro de la Vida*).

Another saint, St. Marina, was a second-century martyr, depicted wearing a belt covering her kidneys, and wielding a hammer and a cross. She reportedly had the power to cure urinary diseases and is considered to be the patron saint of kidney sufferers (Eftychiadis and Marketos 1999). Because bodily functions were considered uncivilized in the Victorian era, especially among women, attempts were made to keep normal urination to an extreme minimum. One enterprising entrepreneur even marketed a St. Marina corset, designed to allow for less frequent trips to the bathroom. After a day of withholding urine, a woman could experience a near state of "religious ecstasy with relief" (Largo 2010, p. 163).

ECSTATIC STIGMATICS AND HOLY ANOREXICS

> There are many seizure types and the one that has been most readily tied to spiritual expression stems from abnormal electrical activity in the limbic structures of the temporal and frontal lobes.. . . Limbic 'ecstatic' seizures are the most distinctively spiritual of seizure types. . . . We still don't know if they were psychotic or mystical—and we don't understand, as far as the brain goes, how someone can be both.
> —Kevin Nelson, *The Spiritual Doorway in the Brain: A Neurologist's Search for the God Experience*

Like many other European Christians who wanted to take on Jesus's suffering as their own, Teresa fasted, flogged herself, and wore a cilice, a device worn to inflict pain on oneself as a sign of repentance. She tied nettles, small plants with stinging hairs on them, to her wrists. Many of the medieval mystics also burned and cut themselves, some cutting religious symbols into their skin. Some set themselves on fire, bit themselves, and chained themselves with barbed wire. Some even put pins or other "stingers" in their underwear (Bell 1985; Bynum 1999; Farber 2003; Frenken 2000). They believed that the *body of desire*, with all its pleasurable cravings, must be mortified or obliterated. To accomplish this, they sought the pain of starvation and self-inflicted injuries, both means of contact with the divine. Those who practice S & M know how pain can become eroticized, producing sadomasochistic ecstasies.

Such ecstasies are well known to Opus Dei, an ultraconservative Roman Catholic sect made up of lay members and priests, founded in Spain in 1928 by Josemaria Escriva de Balaguer. Its stated aim is to spread a profound awareness of the universal call to holiness through one's professional work carried out with freedom and personal responsibility. Catholic liberals describe Opus Dei as a cunning, cultic Catholic mafia, with members leading a double life (Farber 2003). Among its most startling practices is the mortification of the flesh. Unmarried members wear a cilice, a chain of barbed wire worn around the groin for two hours daily, and whip themselves. Sharon Clasen (2008), a former member who is now a member of Opus Dei Awareness Network (ODAN) cited a clandestine internal document in which Father

Alvaro del Portillo told of an incident which happened while he and Escriva were hiding in the Honduran consulate in Madrid in 1937 during the Spanish Civil War. Escriva wanted to use the bedroom alone for his spiritual practices. Once, however, his chief aide, Father Alvaro del Portillo (who would later succeed Escriva as head of Opus Dei), was sick and could not leave, so Escriva told him to cover his head with his blanket. Portillo described what followed: "Soon I began to hear the forceful blows of his discipline. I will never forget the number: there were more than a thousand terrible blows, precisely timed, and always inflicted with the same force and the same rhythm. The floor was covered with blood, but he cleaned it up before the others came in" (http://www.odan.org/tw_making_modern_martyrs.htm).

The late Cardinal John O'Connor said at a special Mass for Opus Dei in 1998 that the "kind of life Opus Dei offers as an ideal is the life of holiness to which everyone is called" (Cohen and Stern 2001). In 1992, Pope John Paul II, who engaged in self-flagellation himself, beatified Monsignor Scribal, who then was canonized as a saint in October 2002. The first celebration of the feast day of St. Josemaría Escriva, was on June 26, 2003 with special Masses held by Cardinal Edward Egan at St. Patrick's Cathedral in New York and in other major cities.

One needs to know something about the history of religious art in order to understand how mortification of the flesh became a trend within Roman Catholicism. Prior to the thirteenth century, it had been symbolic, with churches decorated in the stiff and formal Byzantine style. Jesus was portrayed on the cross wearing a long garment that covered his body and with his eyes wide open, expressionless. A more emotionally evocative and realistic rendering would have been unthinkable. Then in the thirteenth century pious Christians began to focus on the nature of Jesus as a human being and on his suffering, especially his fasting for forty days in the wilderness and his agony on the cross. With this shift, religious art became startlingly realistic and gory. The Passion of Christ became a Christian icon, providing Western culture with its most enduring images of human suffering: the bleeding and emaciated Jesus nailed to the cross, a crown of thorns piercing his scalp, eyes closed and mouth open in agony (Farber 2003). Sometimes a river of blood was shown gushing from a wound that lanced his side. In this religious climate, the stigmata made its first known appearance in Francis of Assisi (Farber 2003; Harrison 1996; Wilson 1988).

The term *stigmata* originates from a line at the end of Saint Paul's letter to the Galatians (Galatians 6: 17) in which he says, "I bear on my body the marks of Jesus" (The Holy Bible 1991). The stigmata are marks, sores, or sensations of pain in locations on the body corresponding to Jesus' crucifixion wounds. Reported cases of stigmata exhibited all or some of the five wounds thought to have been inflicted on Jesus: puncture wounds from nails in the hands and feet and from a spear in his side. Yet many stigmatics have had wounds in different parts of their bodies, for example in their palms despite the many studies that suggest that suspending Jesus by his hands would have been impossible because they would not have been able to support his entire body weight, suggesting that Jesus' arms would have to have been nailed by his wrists to bear his weight. Scientists have studied contemporary stigmatics and found that their wounds matched the wounds that they saw regularly in their own personal religious images. of Jesus. So if the statue or picture owned by the stigmatic had nails in the palms, then the blood would flow from the stigmatic's palms. If the statue is nailed through the wrist, then blood would flow from the wrist. If blood dripped down Jesus' face under the wreath of thorns, then blood would drip down the stigmatic's face. These findings thus suggest that religious art served as a template for the expression of piety, thus inducing a psychosomatic phenomenon.

Some stigmatics feel the pain of wounds that have no external marks; these are referred to as *invisible stigmata* while in other cases *visible stigmata* are accompanied by extreme pain. Some stigmatics' wounds do not seem to clot, remaining fresh and uninfected. In some cases stigmata have appeared on the palms, on the wrists, and the larger spear wound on different sides of the body. The stigmata often exhibit some chronological precision in their appearance, seemingly at the command of the stigmatic's own inner clock. Sometimes it is a special day of the week, notably Thursday and Friday, the day of Jesus' Passion and crucifixion, or a special anniversary such as Easter. Might an "inner clock" determine the year a stigmatic would die? History suggests that it might. Before New Testament scholarship complicated the picture, it was believed that Jesus lived for 33 years. A small but significant proportion of stigmatics lived for 33 years, among them Lukardis of Oberweimar, St. Catherine of Sienna, Mother Agnes of Jesus, Madeline Morice, Domenica Lazzari, Louise Lateau, and Teresa Musco (Wilson 1988).

As in the history of other hysterias, once a case of stigmata emerged, whole communities, even a whole culture, became caught up in a contagious process. Although there were many who identified with Jesus's suffering and took it on as their own, not all manifested the stigmata. Most of those who did were unusually pious laywomen or nuns, but those who led the way were men, notably Saint Paul, Francis of Assisi, and more recently Padre Pio. Saint Paul was beaten very badly while trying to win converts to Christianity, and said in his Letter to the Galatians "I bear on my body the *stígmata* of Jesus" and called on other believers to share similarly in Christ's suffering. It was a man who was the first known stigmatic, Francis of Assisi, whose stigmata appeared in 1224 on the Feast of the Holy Cross. In the year before, he was reported to have been ill with several ailments (Harrison 1996). While ill, he fasted for 40 days while meditating on the Crucifixion, and then passed into a state of ecstasy during which he had visions of Christ's Crucifixion. Emerging from this state, he was startled to see the open wounds on his body, as if he too had been crucified. During St. Francis' time, reenactments of the crucifixion appeared both in passion plays and exhibitionistic acts of self-mutilation. Two years after his stigmata appeared, Francis died and two years later, he was canonized as a saint, and October 4 was declared the Feast of Saint Francis. Then eleven years after his death, on the anniversary of the Feast of Saint Francis, stigmata appeared on Helen of Veszprin, a Dominican nun.

Within a hundred years of Saint Francis' death, there occurred over twenty more cases, the great majority of them women. I suspect this is because women tend to be more masochistic than men, for complex reasons having to do with biology and gender expectations (Farber 2000). In the medieval era, good European women were expected to marry at age 12 or 13, and stay at home raising children. Contemplation of religious matters was in effect forced on them by lack of other opportunities, and many directed their ambitions into an ascetic mysticism (Bell 1985; Egan, 1999). In a paradoxical twist, their extreme suffering endowed them with a degree of influence and power that was unknown for women at that time (Farber 2003).

Those who developed the stigmata became local curiosities, evoking the devotion of many, who in turn took on Jesus' suffering as their own, bleeding for and with him. It was discovered that some reported stigmata resulted from self-inflicted wounds. This would not necessarily have been regarded as fraudulent in the medieval era but as evidence of genuine piety. That is, the person had so identified with Jesus' suffering that he would do what was necessary to obtain the "mystical marks" (Harrison 1996). At times the self-mutilation was done by someone who today might be diagnosed as having Dissociative Identity Disorder and the act of self-injury was so severely dissociated that there was no conscious awareness of it. Often the true stigmatics identified strongly with previous stigmatics and mystics bearing the same name (Wilson 1988). St. Maria Maddalena de Pazzi, born Catarina de Pazzi, seemed to emulate her predecessor and namesake, St. Catherine of Sienna. Therese Neumann seems to have modeled herself after Therese of Lemieux, Teresa Higginson, in nineteenth-century England, may have been influenced by her sixteenth-century namesake, Teresa of Avila.

Although the trend continued, the pattern had changed significantly by the twentieth century. By 1908, there were 321 recorded stigmatics in Roman Catholic countries, primarily Italy (Harrison 1996, Wilson 1988; Nickell 2000). Nearly all were cloistered nuns; about a fifth became beatified or canonized as saints. Then the geographic pattern changed, as cases were reported in Great Britain, Australia, and the United States and not all were Catholic. At least three Anglicans in England have exhibited stigmata (Harrison 1996), as well as a ten-year-old Baptist black girl in California who bled from her palm while in her classroom (Favazza 1996). She had just read a book about the Crucifixion during Lent, and wounds on her hands, feet, and forehead appeared

In 2002, the Vatican canonized Padre Pio, an Italian priest, the other best known male stigmatic. Padre Pio developed invisible stigmata on the anniversary of his namesake St. Francis' stigmatization and visible stigmata on the same anniversary three years later. Known to have manifested the stigmata for 50 years until his death in 1968, he was a most controversial figure. Considered by many to be a miracle worker, he was thought to have performed levitation, was capable of bilocation (the ability to appear in two different places simultaneously), and possessed the odor of sanctity, which reportedly smelled like flowers. Others simply thought he was mentally ill. Throughout his life he fasted rigorously. He was plagued by lung infections and high fevers. By the time he was canonized, he was considered a *victim-soul*, who, like Jesus, sacrificed himself as expiation for the sins committed in the world. Padre Pio is buried at San Giovanni Rotondo, a shrine. Annually more than six million people from all over the world make a pilgrimage there. When a 1959 Mercedes-Benz was given to him from a wealthy family grateful for a miracle, the newspaper *Il Gazzezettino* said that "The latest miracle of Padre Pio was to have elevated the price of a car worth about twenty thousand euros to more than ten times that amount" (Norris 2007, p. 43). Padre Pio is the rock star of saints, with a huge cult following, much like the Maharishi Mahesh Yogi. "By the time Padre Pio . . . died in 1968, he was receiving 5000 letters a month and thousands of visitors a year were converging on him from all parts of the earth" (Ruffin 1982, p.1). His followers have even named their children after him, thus cultivating a new crop of stigmatics-to-be. The theme of the stigmata has even found its way into popular fiction, in Jodi Picoult's (2010) *Keeping Faith* and Ron Hansen's (1991) *Mariette in Ecstasy.*

Louise Lateau of Belgium, along with Padre Pio and Therese Neumann, may be the most thoroughly examined stigmatics of all time. In 1869 at age 18 Louise Lateau was seriously ill with throat abscesses and was experiencing mystical visions. A year later she developed the stigmata, which bled every Friday until her death at age 33, possibly the age of Jesus' death. Studied by Dr. Warlomont under the auspices of the Belgian Royal Academy of Medicine, Lateau noted that every Thursday morning one-inch oval spots on her hands, feet, and chest turned pink and after a few hours, turned into blisters, which then ruptured in the middle of the night, and bled for a day. These lesions did not seem to be deliberately induced, at least, not consciously. When examined the blood seemed quite normal. These experiences worsened with time; she no longer responded to heat or cold, she stopped sleeping, and she refused anything to eat or drink other than daily communion. When she bled, she was in an ecstatic state, and had visions of Christ and all the aspects of his Passion (Favazza 1996). The stigmata of Theresa Neumann (1898-1962), a Bavarian nun, also bled every Friday for 36 years from her hands, feet, chest, scalp, and eyes. Some of the lesions bled continuously for awhile but then only on Fridays. She had episodes of blindness, deafness, and paralysis that suddenly remitted. Her conviction that she was medically ill was probably strengthened by her parish priest, who continually spoke of Christ's suffering and the virtue of emulating his martyrdom. When she bled, she too was in state of ecstasy, living through the scenes of Christ's Passion. She once said that she can live on the Holy Breath, and did from 1926 to-1962, when she only consumed the wine and wafer of communion. Dr. G. Ewald, the psychiatrist who examined her, concluded that her stigmata were genuine, and considered her a hysteric (Favazza 1996).

People tend to attribute to God that which cannot be otherwise explained, and many believe the stigmata is a miraculous gift from God. Since the sixteenth century the Roman Catholic Church has been cautious and skeptical about the stigmata, having found many such claims fraudulent. For more than a century, cases of religious stigmata were examined, photographed, and investigated by skeptical physicians, who have found that in dozens of these cases, the wounds are real; they bleed real blood and are painful. Only 62 of all stigmatics became saints, usually *despite* having the stigmata rather than because of it. Although the stigmata are considered to be psychosomatic phenomena, medicine had not been able to explain just how and why it occurs (Harrison 1996; Poulain 1912; Wilson 1988) until the recent discoveries of neurologist Robert Scaer (2008), whose understanding of the neurophysiology of the stigmata is, to my knowledge, the only known scientifically credible explanation..

Scaer tells us that it is important to understand that not all stigmata are religious. *Stigmata* is a medical term for marks on the skin for which there is no medical explanation. Emotions and states of mind can produce changes in the skin, as are seen in blushing or eczema. Derived from the word *stigma*, *stigmata* also refers to a mark of disgrace or shame. People who have been abused often feel a sense of shame about the abuse, feeling that they were responsible for it. In fact, physicians have found medical stigmata occurring in some patients who have suffered severe psychological trauma, such as physical or sexual abuse or an automobile accident (Harrison 1996; Moody 1946; Scaer 2005). The stigmata would occur for some time after the traumatic event, often many years after. The patient might experience a reddening of the area that was assaulted or injured and often chronic pain in the area. Many survivors of sexual abuse have urinary tract symptoms, chronic pelvic pain, or other gynecological symptoms with no known medical origins (Anderson and Nghiem 2009; De Bellis, Lefter, Trickett, and Putnam, 2004). Some have late onset psychogenic nonepileptic attacks (Duncan, Oto, Martin, and Pelosi, 2006; Harden 1997). These symptoms fluctuate in appearance or may even disappear at times, usually in relationship to the degree of emotional distress being experienced. For example, Scaer (2005) told of a woman who had been severely beaten by her husband for several years and was being treated for post-traumatic stress disorder. As she suddenly remembered and relived a particularly violent beating, she burst into tears, and a bright red blush appeared on the left side of her face, the clear imprint of a right hand, fingers extending toward her ear. Her face felt strange, as if it were not quite part of her, a description of somatic dissociation. Scaer understands this process in cases of religious stigmata as a dissociative process causing the autonomic nervous system to go into overdrive, resulting in the blood vessels expanding abnormally, bringing an unusually large volume of blood flow to the areas of the body believed to have been the sites of Jesus' wounds. The area may become reddened, and may release a fluid, which Church physicians have found to be blood.

In virtually every documented case of the stigmata, prolonged fasting preceded the state of ecstasy. Fasting, known to promote an altered state in which the religious feel at one with God, became the most prominent form of asceticism for the early Christians. By the medieval era, fast days were appointed for fully a third of the year, turning fasting into a very ordinary routine. The stigmatics, however, turned it into something most extraordinary—ecstatic raptures. The stigmatics suffered great physical pain and illness throughout their lives, with complex medical histories, seizures, and symptoms which have been described as "mystical" and "hysterical" (Fessler 2002; Harrison 1996;Whitlock and Hynes 1978). There is also evidence that many stigmatics had suffered traumatic events in their life, including gross neglect, deprivation, and physical and sexual abuse (Farber 2000; Frenken 2000; Harrison 1996; Wilson 1988). For the medieval mystics, starving themselves and inflicting pain on themselves may well have been their way of dissociating themselves from their psychic pain. If they were to be examined psychologically today, probably most would be diagnosed with complex post-traumatic stress disorder and a dissociative disorder.

For example, if we explore the life of Saint Catherine of Siena (Bell 1985), who manifested the stigmata in the fourteenth century, we know that she cultivated pain which, like extreme fasting, produced a trance-like state. In adolescence she wore a coarse hairshirt, then added an iron chain trussed tight against her hips, which she used to whip herself three times a day. At twenty, she had a vision of her sacred marriage to Jesus. Afterward, she always saw the ring on her finger, although it was invisible to others. While frozen for hours in an ecstatic state, she once toppled over, falling directly into a fire in the kitchen, and felt no pain. (A dissociated state can serve as a potent pain killer). While she meditated on the crucifix at twenty-six, she experienced stigmata so painful that she keeled over. She prayed for the marks to be inconspicuous, and so they became invisible. It is said that

Catherine went for eight years consuming nothing other than the host of the Blessed Sacrament. Her anorexia and self-injurious behavior, both of which caused and maintained her dissociative experiences, caused her death at thirty-three, the age at which it is believed that Jesus died on the cross (Bell 1985; Fessler 2002; Harrison 1996). Catherine's history suggests that her masochistic practices were the product of childhood trauma (Bell 1985; Egan 1999). Of twenty-five children, she was the second youngest. It is likely that at best she was severely deprived, neglected, and suffered traumatic losses. Some siblings, including her twin sister, died as infants, which probably induced terrible survivor guilt, which has been found to be a factor in self-punishment (Farber, Jackson, Tabin, and Bachar 2007). An older sister died during childbirth, which certainly made pregnancy and childbirth terrifying, and so she resolved not to marry. To repel prospective suitors, she cut off her long blond hair and treated her body brutally, producing scars and bruises. Hers was a life of suffering. It was undoubtedly easier to identify with Jesus's suffering than to think about her own, and through her identification with Jesus, she took on his suffering on as her own, bearing the visible sign of the stigmata.

The common denominators in the formation of stigmata, religious as well as nonreligious, seem to be a history of severe trauma, a tendency toward severe dissociation, and chronic pain. Just as the same masochistic practices that have become so common today in a secular context can help suffering people feel better, even achieve a state of ecstasy at times (Farber 2003), for the stigmatics and other mystics, inflicting pain on themselves and suffering like Jesus was far better than allowing themselves to know and remember the devastating, often shameful experiences they suffered.

BORN-AGAIN ECSTASIES

> Upon my arrival in the United States, the religious aspect of the country was the first thing that struck my attention.
> —Alexis De Tocqueville, 1835

> For our purposes, any discussion of the terms evangelical, fundamentalist, charismatic, and pentecostal should steer a middle course between an extended, technical treatment and the kind of dismissive description suggested by Potter Stewart's attempt to define pornography a few weeks back. "I can't define it." the Supreme Court justice acknowledged, "but I know it when I see it.
> —Randall Balmer, Mine Eyes Have Seen the Glory: A Journey into the Evangelical Subculture in America

During slavery, the practice of religion was the one arena where African Americans had some freedom, giving meaning to their noisy, dramatic form of worship. Ecstatic practices through music, song, dancing and shouting gave expression to the experience of being born again that punctuated almost every worship gathering. It continued in the Pentecostal movement, which began in 1906 in Azusa Street in Los Angeles. William Joseph Seymour, a half-blind preacher from Louisiana, led a series of revival meetings that grew into a worldwide movement. The name *Pentecostal* is from Acts 2, which describes the gathering of the apostles soon after Christ's ascension. "And when the day of Pentecost was fully come, they were all filled with the Holy Ghost, and began to speak with other tongues, as the Spirit gave them utterance."

The Catholic Charismatic Renewal is a movement characterized by ecstatic worship, quite similar to Pentecostal worship, with the addition of an animated Mass. Many Latinos, charismatic Catholics, and other immigrants identify themselves as *born again* and are drawn to a different religious experience, something that will shake their bodies as well as their souls. They come from countries with a Christian population—the former Soviet Bloc countries, China, Africa, Haiti, the West Indies, the Philippines, the Netherlands, Spain, Germany, Australia, New Zealand, Papua New Guinea, Italy, Norway, Sweden, Denmark, Finland, South Korea, Vietnam, India, Indonesia, Pakistan, South America, and Lebanon. Even Episcopalians, traditionally America's wealthiest and most staid denomination, known as "God's frozen people" (Balmer 1993) are turning away from language and thinking and are expressing themselves through ecstatic utterance and movement (Armstrong 2000). Christian fundamentalism is apocalyptic by virtue of the belief that the world will end in a great fire of destruction, and only those who have a spiritual rebirth will find salvation. The best-selling *Left Behind* fictional series describes these horrors. The fundamentalists believe that a spiritual rebirth is necessary for salvation. This experience is marked by singing, dancing, stomping, trembling, shrieking, crying, laughing, and sometimes falling to the floor in an ecstasy that bears more than a slight resemblance to epilepsy or orgasm. It is interpreted as the attainment of a higher spiritual realm. *Speaking in tongues* is generally regarded as the mark of a true Christian (Balmer 1993). Many report other intense physical sensations at the born again moment: a tingling feeling of energy, alternating feelings of heat and cold, an impression of a cleansing flow of water, accompanied by an uncontrollable surge of tears. Some may speak of seeing the light, meant sometimes metaphorically or sometimes literally. The immediate impact may be felt as awe, ecstasy, or a frightening state from which they may not emerge.

The Pentecostal movement is characterized by rituals involving a significant degree of altered consciousness. These include speaking in tongues, or *glossolalia,* strange utterances thought to represent the voice of God, *possession behavior*, during which a person may dance and gyrate or roll on the floor, and the testimonial, a fervent and spontaneous statement of faith (Galanter 1999). All three behaviors associated with altered states are also associated with relief of emotional distress (Ness and Wintrob 1980).

The born-again movement emerged from the Methodist Holiness movement and the revival meetings of the nineteenth and early twentieth century as a grassroots rebellion against the modern cult of reason. It shares many characteristics with the extreme religious and personal growth cults that can lead over time to sudden personality changes. The born-again movement is also related to exorcism, an official rite of the Roman Catholic Church that was popularized in the film *The Exorcist*. Exorcism grew out of the treatment of the physically or mentally ill, which until the beginning of the nineteenth century, involved getting rid of something foreign and evil—a spirit, demon, or toxic substance—that had invaded the body (Rizzuto 1985). It was believed quite literally that demons are external evil spirits that can intrude into a person's body and cause him to do all sorts of evil things. The solution is to expel these demons by means of an exorcism. Although exorcism is an official rite of the Roman Catholic Church, carried out by a priest who has been specially trained and authorized, with advances in medicine and more sophisticated understanding of neurological and psychological illness, it has become an embarrassment to many religious within the Church, who regard it as a superstitious vestige of an outmoded religion (Baglio 2009). But recently, with the fascination with occult practices such as Wicca, the 1973 release of the film version of William Blatty's *The Exorcist,* one of the most lucrative horror films of all time, and *The Rite*, a television series, all this tapped into Americans' deepest spiritual anxieties, spawning a huge business not only for Catholic exorcists but for Protestant and freelance exorcisms performed by New Age entrepreneurs (Cuneo 2001).

In the film, a mother is disturbed by dramatic and unsettling changes in 12-year-old daughter Regan's behavior. First there was a seizure, then strange, unnatural powers, including the ability to levitate, extraordinary strength, and cursing in a deep rasping male voice. After medical tests show nothing unusual, Regan is referred to a psychiatrist, whom she assaults. Finally, a physician recommends an exorcism, which was conducted by a physician who is also a Catholic priest. The sounds and images of Regan's head-spinning, her face contorted, guttural utterances, and projectile vomiting became seared into the popular consciousness (Cuneo 2001). Then many Americans, many of them ordinary middle-class people, people whom you might chat with while waiting on line in the post office, began having exorcisms of one kind or another, with many claiming to have emerged much the better for it. Charismatic Catholics, Pentecostals, and even mainstream Protestants began embracing exorcism in untold numbers (Cuneo 2001). New exorcism ministries emerged to deal with the sudden onslaught of demonism, and older ministries were reinvented and found themselves with more business than they could possibly handle. Cases of demonic possession were reported long before dissociation was understood (Freud 1923c), and the treatment often successful was an exorcism (Grotstein 1979; Krakauer 2001; Ferracuti and Sacco 1996; Taylor 1978), leading some clinicians who treat people with Dissociative Identity Disorder to use a version of exorcism in treatment (van der Hart, Lierens, and Goodwin 1996; Krakauer 2001). Many scientists believe that understanding what happens with patients who have Dissociative Identity Disorder offers the best explanation for demonic possession.

As discussed earlier in the chapter on cult-induced ecstasies, intense physical experiences such as singing, dancing, jumping, drumming, and enduring an exorcism and intense stresses like noise, isolation, and other forms of sensory overload or deprivation may trigger a moment when he may snap like a piece of brittle plastic (Conway and Siegelman 1995). The Jesus movement, a born-again movement of the sixties, spawned several destructive cults, the most notorious of which was the *Children of God*, also known as *The Family*, known for using sex "("flirty fishing") to recruit new members. The born-again movement seems to be taking over more of America's minds as the numbers of born-again Christians continue to increase, making all of America the Bible Belt.

Even the ever-popular Bruce Springsteen, one of the most popular rock musicians of the past several decades, has been belting out the Gospel of Bruce. He lives for the joyous rush he gets on stage. In his version of *Take Me to the River*, he was like a Pentecostal preacher at a revival meeting, bringing a gospel touch to his spontaneous, ecstatic riff. He danced alone and with members of the band; he strutted, climbed up on a piano, fell to his knees, and shrieked. And the audience stood, swaying, and holding their arms up, palms facing out, as if to receive the holy spirit. He wanted to take his audience to the river of sanctification and resurrection.

SPEAKING IN TONGUES AND SNAKE-HANDLING ECSTASIES

> And these signs shall follow them that believe; in my name they shall cast out devils; they shall speak with new tongues; They shall take up serpents; and if they drink any deadly thing, it shall not hurt them; They shall lay hands on the sick and they shall recover.
>
> —Mark 16. 18

By virtue of their inclusiveness and breaking down of racial and class barriers the boundaries between Christian fundamentalism, evangelism, Pentecostalism, and the charismatic movement have become increasingly fluid. This culture includes affiliating with a local church, sending children to Sunday school, youth meetings, Bible camps, and eventually a Bible school or college. And being a Christian meant *witnessing*, sharing their faith with non-Christians in the hopes of converting them. This movement appeals to people's wish to be special ("join us and you can be one of God's chosen"), and it appeals to people's fear ("you can't be saved without becoming one of us"). Its broadest appeal, however, is that it promises an easy ticket to heaven without having to think too deeply about doctrine, and offers an intense emotional release for people who live with a great deal of emotional pain.

Ever since the gospels were written, many Christians have interpreted biblical signs of the end of the world, the *End Times*, as applying to their generation and have been setting dates for the Second Coming. When I was a college student, a man who called himself Yahweh Yumke walked up and down Broadway wearing a sandwich board sign proclaiming that the world was coming to an end on a specific date. That date came and went and the world never came to an end. How did Yahweh Yumke reconcile this? He continued to pace up and down Broadway, but the old *End Times* date on his sandwich board had been painted over with a new date. It seems that when Jesus fails to appear, it is simply attributed to errors in mathematical calculation and a new date is set. A favorite evangelical bumper sticker is "Warning! In case of rapture this car will be unmanned." With the advent of the millennium, fundamentalists became even increasingly more convinced that the Second Coming is close at hand, and the September 11 attacks have further revived the doomsday theology. The best-selling *Left Behind* series, with over eleven million copies sold, was written by Pentecostal minister Dr. Tim LaHaye and Jerry B. Jenkins. It is a fictional account of people struggling amid the *End Times of the Second Coming* of Christ, coinciding with the Rapture and the Resurrection, believed to occur at the end of the Millennium.

The late Jerry Falwell was so certain that he would soon be "raptured" (yes, raptured is a verb), caught up in the heavens to meet the return of Jesus, that he said he has no need to plan for a burial plot (Gardner 2000). The rapture is believed to be the experience that will happen when Jesus calls His followers, born-again Christians and converted Jewish believers, with the blast of a trumpet and in the "twinkling of an eye" they will find themselves transported from earth to be with Jesus in the heavens. Those left behind must contend with unprecedented natural disasters, attacks by demons, and with the rule of Satan, a scenario found in *The Book of Revelations,* predictions which many mainstream Christians find embarrassing.

Maurice Bessinger is a politically influential South Carolina Bar-B-Q mogul who puts a folksy spin on the Rapture at his weekly Bible-study meetings at each of his nine Confederate flag-flying Piggy Parks. "I believe that after the rapture there will be a big barbecue, and I hope the Lord will let me cook" (Hitt 2001, p. 31). His recipe for his heavenly barbecue sauce has something to do with Jesus' parable of the mustard seed. Undoubtedly there will not be blacks or Jews at the Great Barbecue in the Sky because Bessinger's racist and anti-Semitic views are well known. In the 50s and 60s, he was head of the National Association for the Preservation of White People.

Pentecostals also emphasize the words of the bible as fundamental truths, the need for being born again to transform ones life with faith in Jesus, and how the Holy Ghost works within the individual. It was spread by hippies-turned-Jesus Freaks who identified with Jesus the dropout, outlaw, and revolutionary who disdained the religious establishment (Prothero 2003). The Brownsville Assembly of God in Pensacola, Florida, began as a temporary revival meeting in 1995 and has snowballed into what may be the largest and longest-running Pentecostal revival in America in almost a century, drawing 3,000 to 6,000 people almost every night. The music is Christian rock, and people come from all over the United States, from the Christian Europe, Japan, Korea, Russia, South America, and Australia, and dance in the aisles. Even gang members and Bikers for Jesus, tattooed and pierced to the hilt, come to be born again.

In St. Petersburg, Florida' Christine Rosen learned at Keswick Christian School to believe in creation science (Rosen 2006). Her school was deeply philosemitic, even putting on student productions of *Fiddler on the Roof.* Children with thick Southern accents stomped around the gymnasium shouting, "L'Chaim!" The boys were decked out in glued-on beards, and corkscrew-curl side locks, and *tzitzis* (knotted ritual fringes attached to the four corners of the prayer shawl), and the girls wearing headscarves to cover their hair. They also prayed that the Jews would come to their senses and realize that Jesus died for their sins, and convert to Christianity, thus ushering in the rapture. To her Jewish neighbors David and Josh, Christine would ask "How does it feel to be one of God's chosen people?" but would then ask "why they did not admit that Jesus was the Messiah. "Didn't they believe that Jesus walked the earth and died for their sins? Couldn't they see that He loved them and was all powerful? How could they not believe He was the Messiah? Didn't they realize He was watching them *right now*?" (Rosen 2006, p. 65). Christine heard how the atheist Russians were threatening nuclear annihilation, and she prayed even harder for rapture.

Believing that speaking in tongues is the sign of a true Christian, many such individuals surrender to be "seized by the spirit." The younger the worshipper, the easier it is for the Holy Ghost to descend and speak. Called *glossalalia* by linguists, it is a pseudo-language (Samarin 1972), a language in some ways but only because the speaker *wants* it to be a language. That is, the intense *desire* to speak in tongues becomes transformed into the *ability* to speak in tongues. It happens by means of a self-hypnotic process by more or less haphazardly stringing together syllables made up of sounds taken from those that the speaker knows, to emerge as something that sounds like language, with word-like and sentence-like units and language-like rhythm and melody. "*Hebamashundi welaka oma hebamashundi . . . welamaka oma hebamashund.*"

As a child, I learned to speak Pig Latin and Abi Dabi (which has nothing to do with the capital of the United Arab Emirates). My name at the time was Sharon Carol Klayman, which in Abi Dabi became *Shabarabon Caborabal Klabymaban.* That is all I remember of Abi Dabi but I suppose if I really wanted to speak it again, I could. I do not have a talent for learning languages but I suppose if I wanted to speak in tongues, wanted it enough, I could. There is nothing magical about this. You could learn to speak pig Latin or Abi Dabi or speak in tongues, if you wanted to enough. To speak in tongues, all you have to do is want to badly enough and be in an environment that expects and facilitates it. Sheri Reynolds, born and raised in rural South Carolina, knows this well. In her novel, *The Rapture of Canaan* (Reynolds 1995), fifteen-year-old Ninah worshipped at a church where just about everything was forbidden, especially the thoughts and feelings she was having toward her prayer partner James. To distract herself she concentrated on Jesus' pain as hard as she could. She put sandspurs in her bed and pecan shells in her shoes to remind herself with every step of Jesus's suffering. She cut out a picture of Jesus on the cross and taped it to the inside of her underwear for protection. Then one day in church another wonderful distraction came to her.

> One Sunday in church. . . I decided to speak in tongues. . . It wasn't something I'd been planning. And it wasn't something that God told me to do either. It just happened, all of a sudden, like a rooster that crows in the middle of the day for no apparent reason. I stood right up and spoke out. I said something like, "Lord, please open my heart and fill me up with your beauty and love. Lord, I'm asking you for your precious gift." In front of me, Mamma and Daddy, David and Laura, Everett and Wanda, Bethany and Olin all opened their mouths and started praying out loud, so loud that I felt like I needed to shout. "Lord, I'm here. Take me and fill me up," I said again. "Praise God," Grandpa Herman yelled. All around me I could feel a heat, and I wasn't sure if I was going to pass out or not. "Lord, I want to know you inside and out," I hollered. "I want to know your hebamashundi welaka oma hebamashundi." The only word I knew for sure that I'd heard people speak in tongues was hebamashundi; so I let that one move my lips again and again.
>
> Then I knew I was going to pass out. I was almost certain. I felt sick and weak and carried away. As far as I could tell, God wasn't leading me anywhere. I was making the words up as I went, and they seized up in my mouth and spilled like lies all over the hard wood floor. "Help me, Jesus," I tried. "Help me not get caught in your welamaka oma hebamashundi," and then I began to whisper or maybe to cry."
>
> . . . It was the longest day in church I'd ever known. I couldn't break the trance I'd induced myself. I walked around for days whispering under my breath, hebamashundi, hebamashundi (Reynolds 1995, pp. 152-54).

When there is the expectation to speak in tongues, people tend to do just that. When there is the expectation that you might grab a poisonous snake and dance with abandon at a Pentecostal snake-handling service, you just might do it. Although it is not common, snake-handling is more prevalent in the South than one might think. Sometimes it includes playing with flaming blow torches and drinking strychnine. A rural snake-handling sect named The Church of God with Signs Following was founded in 1909 by George Went Hensley as an offshoot of the Pentecostal movement, and spread from the backwoods of Tennessee to mid-Florida to West Virginia and even as far west as Columbus, Ohio (Ruthven 1989). The publicity given to an extraordinary inter-state convention of snake-handlers in Durham, North Carolina in 1948 aided the spread of the sect. In 2001 there were about 40 small churches that practiced snake handling. In 2004 the practice crossed the border and there were four snake handling congregations in the Canadian provinces of Alberta and British Columbia (Melton 1998). The sect has survived fines, jail sentences, and a number of deaths from snakebite, including that of Hensley, its founder, who claimed to have been bitten over 400 times (LaBarre 1969). His funeral service in 1955 was the occasion for over 300 people to gather for a marathon snake-handling service that lasted 36 hours. Also in the same year, 4,000 gathered for a memorial snake-handling service for Reverend Lee Valentine, who had died of snakebite.

Members originally were poor Scotch-Irish who worked long hours in tobacco plants, cotton mills, or factories. With the breaking down of racial barriers, some churches had become integrated. They were fundamentalists, conforming to literal interpretations of the Bible, leading extremely repressed lives and adhering to a strict moral code that included dressing very plainly, frowning on jewelry and makeup, abstaining from tobacco and alcohol, regarding homosexuality as a sin, and avoiding movies, bars, and rock concerts. Oddly enough, as members enter the church, they greet one another with a "holy kiss" on the mouth, men kissing men; women kissing women. The "saints," as the men with unusual faith are sometimes called, may greet each other with, "How are you, honey?" and sit apart from the women (La Barre 1969; Schwartz 1960). Some of the leading saints had in their past histories crimes of violence, bootlegging, and patronizing prostitutes. It is customary in many of these churches to attend church two nights a week, and some even attend every night. It is usually the saints who find ecstatic release in drinking strychnine, handling fire and poisonous snakes, the age-old symbol of sin and eternal life. But sometimes women join in. Religious ecstasy can become even more erotic when snakes, a symbol of phallic power, are added to the mix. In both religious and sexual ecstasy there is a surrender and a loss of self. At the same time, snake-handlers will tell you that when they are filled with the Holy Spirit, the Spirit protects them and they are not afraid of the snake. The snake also represents the devil, and those who become "filled with the Holy Spirit" demonstrate God's power over the devil by dominating the snakes while in a dissociated state (Schwarz 1960). The snakes are not hypnotized by the music because they cannot hear the way people do. What they respond to are vibrations so it may be more correct to say that they feel the music. They also respond to the sight of the flute and match the snake charmer's swaying movements and become lulled into a submissive trance. The snake-handler, feeling a tremendous sense of power over the snake, becomes lost in ecstasy. One snake-handler said that he'd been high on dope, and high on whiskey, but that they are nothing compared to being high on the Holy Spirit (Covington 1995).

There was a sensational trial in Scottsboro, Alabama in 1965 featuring snake-handling. Scottsboro was known for a sensational trial in 1931 when nine young black men were falsely convicted of rape and sentenced to death, so Scottsboro was once again on the map. Dennis Covington (1995), a feature reporter for The *New York Times*, covered the trial. The story was that Glen Summerford, pastor of the Church of Jesus with Signs Following, had been charged with attempting to murder his wife Darlene by forcing her hand into the wooden box in which he kept his poisonous snakes. Darlene was used to handling them but being forced was different. When she asked what it was like to take up serpents, she said "It makes you feel different. It's just knowing that you got power over them snakes" (Covington 1995). *Power over them snakes*. Covington wondered exactly what she meant. The moment Darlene told him what it felt like to take up serpents, he knew the real story would not be over until he had seen and experienced what she was talking about. And so began the journalist's strange journey. When Covington, also a creative writing teacher at the University of Alabama, an award winning novelist, and never a religious man, was invited to attend a service at Glen Summerford's church, he went, and returned, over and over again, enthralled.

> They were shouting praise or praying out loud. Some were speaking in tongues. Things were beginning to spiral out of control. . . young Jeffrey Hagerman, twenty-five, the son-in-law of the last member to die of snakebite, grasped a rattlesnake in either hand and hopped joyfully with them while his wide-eyed children. . . watched from a nearby pew. *"Everything's gonna be all right."* . . . At one point all six snakes wound up with Brother Charles . . . *"Everything's gonna be all right."* For twenty minutes, we continued to dance and sing, while the music ground on like some wacko, amphetamine dirge. . . *"Everything's gonna be all right."* At one point Dewey Chafin gathered all six rattlesnakes together and held them up with one hand. Then Brother Carl took the rattlesnakes and put them on top of his head before distributing them back to the other men. The action was so wild and fast, I lost track of where the snakes were or who had them. I didn't care. . . We felt invulnerable, forever alive.

> . . . seeing a handler in the ecstasy of an anointing is not like seeing religious ecstasy at all. The expressions seem to have more to do with Eros than with God, in the same way that sex often seems to have more to do with death than with pleasure. The similarity is more than coincidence, I thought. In both sexual and religious ecstasy the first thing that goes is self. The entrance into ecstasy is surrender (Covington 1995, pp. 98-102).
>
> There was so much racket that at first it was hard to hear what Aline was [8.96] doing over in the corner . . . Her back was to us. Her hands were in the air, and she was rocking slowly from side to side, her face upturned and her voice quavering, "Akiii, akiii, akiii. Akiii, akiii, akiii . . ." It was the strangest sound I had ever heard . . . like the voice of a rare night bird, or some tiny feral mammal. And then the voice got louder, mounting up on itself, until it started to sound like that of a child who was lost and in great pain. But even as the hairs on my arm started to stand on end, the voice turned into something else, a sound that had pleasure in it as well as torment. "Akiii, akiii, akiii . . ." The singing and praising elsewhere in the brush arbor had started to diminish . . . the air fell silent around Aline's voice. Everyone was listening to her now. I could not disentangle myself from the sound of her voice, the same syllables repeated with endless variation. At times, it seemed something barbed was being pulled from her throat; at other times, the sound was a clear stream flowing outward into thin air. Her voice seemed to be right in my ear. It was a sobbing. A panting after something she could not quite reach. And then it would be a coming to rest in some exquisite space, a place so tender it could not be touched without "Akiii, akiii, akiii . . ." (Covington 1995, pp. 78-9).

There was so much racket that at first it was hard to hear what Aline was doing over in the corner . . . Her back was to us. Her hands were in the air, and she was rocking slowly from side to side, her face upturned and her voice quavering, "Akiii, akiii, akiii. Akiii, akiii, akiii . . ." It was the strangest sound I had ever heard . . . like the voice of a rare night bird, or some tiny feral mammal. And then the voice got louder, mounting up on itself, until it started to sound like that of a child who was lost and in great pain. But even as the hairs on my arm started to stand on end, the voice turned into something else, a sound that had pleasure in it as well as torment. "Akiii, akiii, akiii . . ." The singing and praising elsewhere in the brush arbor had started to diminish . . the air fell silent around Aline's voice. Everyone was listening to her now. I could not disentangle myself from the sound of her voice, the same syllables repeated with endless variation. At times, it seemed something barbed was being pulled from her throat; at other times, the sound was a clear stream flowing outward into thin air. Her voice seemed to be right in my ear. It was a sobbing. A panting after something she could not quite reach. And then it would be a coming to rest in some exquisite space, a place so tender it could not be touched without "Akiii, akiii, akiii . . ." (Covington 1995, pp. 78–9).

Have your way, Lord, someone said as Aline trembled in ecstasy with the big black rattlesnake outstretched in her hands. I was only an observer but I felt I had been drawn into something so painfully intimate that I was morally obliged to look away even as I stared the harder (Covington 1995, p. 110).

Covington's hand reached out and picked up a snake, and in that ritual moment, he was transformed from being an observer of the tribe to an initiated member.

> The longer you witness it, the more you become a part of it. . . So I got up there in the middle of the handlers. . . Carl's eyes were saying, you. And yes, it was the big rattler, the one with my name on it, acrid-smelling, carnal, alive. . . This was the moment. I didn't stop to think. I stepped forward and took the snake with both hands. I . . . lifted the rattlesnake up toward the light. It was moving like it wanted to get up even higher, to climb out of that church and into the air. . . I felt no fear. The snake seemed to be an extension of myself. And suddenly there seemed to be nothing in the room but me and the snake. . . And I could not hear the earsplitting music. . . I too was fading into the white. I was losing myself by degrees. . . The snake would be the last to go, and all I could see was the way its scales shimmered one last time in the light . . . I knew then why the handlers take up serpents. There is power in the act of disappearing; there is victory in the loss of self. It must be close to our conception of paradise, what it's like before you're born or after you die.
> . . . I came back in stages, first with the recognition that the shouting I had begun to hear was coming from my own mouth. Then I realized I was holding a rattlesnake, and the church rushed back with all the clamor, heat, and smell. I remembered Carl and turned where I thought he might be. I lowered the snake to waist level. It was an enormous animal, heavy and firm. The scales on its side were as rough as calluses. I could feel its muscles rippling beneath the skin. I was aware it was not part of me now and that I couldn't predict what it might do. I extended it toward Carl. He took it from me (Covington 1955, pp. 169–170).

For Covington, the feeling of having power over the snakes had been a wonderful manic defense against the knowledge of his own mortality and that of his wife and children, whom he even brought to the prayer meetings.

Darlene Summerford was right; snake-handlers *do* have power over the snakes. If you consider that although there have been over seventy recorded deaths from snakebite, given the number of people involved in snake-handling and the risks they take, this is a surprisingly low number. During the service, when some members put their hand in a blowtorch's flame, there was no evidence of painful reaction or burns, which is also true of the Hindus and Native Americans who walk on hot coals. Although drinking strychnine was rare, when it occurred it did not produce convulsions or death in those who drank it. What can possibly explain that?

Under ordinary circumstances, snake-handlers may be frightened of harmless garter snakes. It is the state of ecstasy that confers their sense of omnipotence over the snakes. If a snake-handler is bitten by a venomous snake, no medical treatment is obtained, as the sect believes that their prayers and faith will save him. If he dies of snakebite, it is believed that he did not have enough faith. Snakes are most likely to release their venom when startled or provoked. Darlene Summerford did just that when her drunken husband held a gun to her head, dragged her by the hair to the shed where he kept his seventeen diamondback rattlers and gave her a no-win choice; she could stick either her hand or her face into the box. (Bitten twice, she was treated at the university hospital in Birmingham, while Glenn Summerford is doing ninety nine years in the state penitentiary.)

When members handled snakes when they were not in deep dissociated states, they often handled them roughly, and were bitten, which suggests that extreme dissociation can afford various degrees of immunity. A colleague who studied in Sydney told me that when in the Daintree Rainforest near Cairns, Australia, his tour guide told him that the aboriginals know how to put themselves into deep trances if they are bitten by a snake. By doing so, they reduce their metabolism long enough for the neurotoxins in the venom to break down (Martin Katchen, personal communication).

I was surprised to discover that a fearless snake-handler in the midst of an ecstatic state asserts his dominance and really can scare the hell out of a snake, which freezes into submission. This comes from the animal's survival instinct to feign death when threatened by a predator. And as the driving music induces a trance in the congregation, it induces a freeze state in the snakes (Scaer 2005, personal correspondence. Schwartz 1960) and these symbols of phallic power go limp.

In addition, not all venomous snakes release venom when they bite. Some may provide a "dry bite" instead of wasting their venom on a creature too big to eat. Gracie McAllister, an older member, said that the last time she got bitten, the only thing that happened was that her heart beat fast. The brothers laid hands on her, she went to sleep, got up the next morning, cooked, got dressed, and went back to church again. To understand this, it helps to know that when someone is bitten again and again, he builds up protective anti-venom antibodies. Because Gracie had been bitten the previous two Julys, she vowed she'd never handle snakes in July again and decided that to simply play it safe by just handing fire and drinking strychnine that night. "Good idea, I thought. It always pays to be on the safe side (Covington 1995, p. 182)."

THE SPIRITUAL ECSTASIES OF GENERATIONS X AND Y

Generation X, the approximately 80 million Americans born between 1961 and 1981, and Generation Y, born later but sharing the X culture, is largely middle class and covers a spectrum of racial, ethnic, and sexual identities. Generation X has been called the tuned-out generation, a generation adrift, the numb generation, and the whiny generation. Each generation has its signifiers—its music, fashion, books, and language—to define and differentiate it from the generations before and after (Bollas 1992). Generation X's signifiers are tattoos, body piercings, the grunge look, and MTV videos which unashamedly juxtapose religious and sexual imagery, emphasizing the sacred potential of human experience. Madonna has become a Generation X icon, outraging many with her MTV videos that merged images of the saints with eroticism. In her "Like a Prayer" video, Madonna links her sexuality with God and with erotic images of ecstasy. She picks up a knife, and as many alienated young people do today, cuts the stigmata on her open palms. Her videos, with images of sadomasochism and group sex, have become spiritual symbols for Generation X.

They may or may not accept Jesus as the Messiah, but are very interested in Jesus, the man. They look to Jesus' life, wanting to understand the meaning of how he lived (Beaudoin 1998). Did Jesus have a love life or a sex life? Was he a martyr, choosing to suffer or was he sacrificed by God? What kind of sadistic father sacrifices his own son? Many Generation X'ers have experienced some degree of emotional deprivation, abuse or neglect in their early years, and are deeply identified with Jesus's suffering. There is a fascination with Jesus in music videos. The video for R.E.M.'s "Losing My Religion" depicts two interrelated themes: Jesus falling from his position as an exalted icon, and a sense of the loss of religion as an organizing force in the lives of young people (Beaudoin 1998).

Tom Beaudoin, a former altar boy, said,

> My experiences playing rock were usually more religious than I had found in most churches. I discovered a sense of spirituality "in the pocket," playing tightly with a drummer. As a bass guitarist, when I am traversing the deep rhythm, riding the low notes, or stomping through a syncopated rumble, *something happens*. After the band's last concert, a woman approached me and said, "You play the bass like it is part of your body." Later I thought, that is the way good religious ritual, or liturgy, works. We move our bodies and souls in harmony with the music, which is in harmony with the Spirit, with God. The spectacular liturgies of rock are part of my continued affinity for arena or stadium rock bands. I treasure the irreverence of this rock religiosity, considering it just as important to my own sense of spirituality as any commitment to an institutional. church (Beaudoin 1998, p. 14).

In the 1960s, when rock music developed artistically, it became associated with the counterculture, which alienated many Christians. However, some musicians challenged the view that rock music was anti-Christian. By the

1990s there was an explosion of Christian, mainly Protestant, rock music, which has been most successful in recruiting members.

Unlike the Pentecostals, the Hasidim, with the exception of the Lubavitchers, are not evangelical. If anything they keep to themselves and are often considered clannish. All Hasidic groups were decimated after the Holocaust and many of the Eastern European Jews who still believed in God turned inward to Talmudic study. However, many felt that Jewish life had become too scholarly, no longer emphasizing spirituality or joy, leading to the development of Hasidic Judaism (Schochet, 1990).

The Hasidim are a mystical branch of ultra-orthodox Judaism, whose ecstatic *davening* (praying), singing, and dancing expresses a total surrender to God. Their *shuckeling*, meaning "shaking" in Yiddish, is the ritual bobbing up and down or from side to side while praying, a practice which can be traced back to at least the eighth century. It is seen as the body's demonstration of the soul's wish to abandon the body and rejoin with its source. I think of it as "rock and roll" Judaism, and its form bears a great similarity to Pentecostal worship.

Although Oliver Sacks had no religious faith or feeling, he recalled that when he was a boy in London, he loved Simchas Torah, the Rejoicing of the Law, which was celebrated in his family's normally staid Orthodox congregation with ecstatic chanting and dancing, passing the Torah from one member to the other. He told about a case of "Accidental Davening" (Sacks 2007).

> Solomon R. was an intelligent middle-aged man with dyskinesia, an unusual movement disorder which, in him, took the form of rhythmic pulsions of various sorts: Forcible expulsions of breath, accompanied by loud phonations ("eughh, eughhh . . ."), and asynchronous contraction of abdominal and trunk muscles, causing his body to bow or rock with each expiration.
>
> Over the weeks that I saw him, there was a strange elaboration of this picture. The expiratory, phonatory "beat" began to acquire a sort of melody, a repetitive singsong to accompany it and . . a half articulate murmuring quality . . . With this, and his now increasing bowing movement, Mr. R. seemed to be cantillating, praying—"davening," as such murmuring, rhythmically motoric prayer is called by religious Jews. Indeed, a couple of weeks later, I was able to catch a number of Hebrew words. . . But when I asked Mr. R., he told me that though they were indeed Hebrew words, they made no sense—they were "plucked out of the air," he said, as if to fill the prosodic and melodic demand of his dyskinesia. . . Not originally a man attracted to cantillation or prayer, he had now been drawn to this through the physiological accident of dyskinesia (Sacks 2007, pp. 224–5).

Chabad-Lubavitch is one of the world's largest Hasidic movements, with headquarters in Brooklyn's Crown Heights. Although Jews are not evangelistic, the Lubavitchers are evangelical toward other Jews, spawning a new generation of Lubavitchers who travel all over the world on their own mission, which is getting secular Jews to adopt Orthodox practices. This, they believe, will hasten the coming of the Messiah. Many believe that their late Grand Rebbe, Menachem Schneerson, a charismatic leader who believed he was the Messiah, is the Messiah. Jewish trekkers in Katmandu, business people in Shanghai, students at Harvard, and vacationers in the Virgin Islands can come to a Chabad House, a ready-made, welcoming family of Lubavitchers prepared to help them feel at home in an otherwise alienating world (Helman and Friedman 2010).

By 1968, as the hippies were urging people to drop out, the Lubavtichers launched the mitzvah campaign, urging secular Jews to drop in to Judaism. The Torah contains 613 mitzvahs and rabbis added many more in the Talmud and legal codes. They apply to daily personal and religious life, two realms which became almost indistinguishable.

> Mitzvahs shape the life. Upon waking, immediately wash your hands. Then thank God for "restoring my soul" after the night's sleep. After using the toilet, thank God "who with wisdom fashioned the human body, creating openings, arteries, glands and organs, marvelous in structure, intricate in design." Put your right shoe on first, then your left shoe; but tie the left one first, and then the right. Prayer, either individual or communal, comes before breakfast. Put on your prayer shawl and bind the tefillin—black leather straps and boxes containing verses of scripture—on your left arm and forehead. Breakfast is, of course, kosher. No ham and eggs here. If you are having bread, ritually wash your hands. After eating, say grace. And don't forget to wear your yarmulke
> And mitzvahs don't end there. Being honest in business, telling the truth, sharing with a friend, honoring one's parents, visiting the sick, giving charity to the poor, all these are mitzvahs too (Goldman 1992, pp. 28–9).

Rather than trying to get unobservant Jews to observe the 613 Torah mitzvahs, they aimed for ten concrete Jewish acts meant to redeem them. Starting to do just one is celebrated. These concrete acts are getting females over age three to light Sabbath candles, getting males over thirteen to don *tefillin*, attaching mezuzahs (cases filled with a piece of parchment inscribed with Hebrew verses from the Torah) on the doorways of Jewish homes, daily study of Torah, giving charity, owning holy Jewish books, observing the dietary laws, getting a Jewish education, getting women to use the ritual bath after menstruating, and loving one's fellow as oneself. There were *tefillin*-mobiles, vehicles into which a Jew could go to be instructed in putting on *tefillin* (the leather phylacteries or straps orthodox Jewish men wrap around their arms while praying) and reciting a prayer. "*Tefillin* on the spot for people on the go!" In Greenwich Village's Washington Square Park, I watched in the seventies as heavily bearded men wearing yarmulkes and *tzitzis*, the fringed four-cornered garments worn by observant Jewish men, stopped male passersby and asked, "Excuse me, are you Jewish?" The question was jarring because Jews were living at a time when standing out as a Jew, rather than blending in, was risky. Ever since the Holocaust, Jews have felt an anxiety about survival.

Fueling Jewish anxiety about survival are burning images: the beheading of American journalist Daniel Pearl in Pakistan, forced to confess that he was a Jew, and twenty-eight Israelis massacred by suicide bombers as they gathered in Netanya to celebrate a Passover seder. Passover celebrates the deliverance of a people from bondage into freedom, so this attack, probably more than any other, felt very intimate and personal for American Jews. Linking this with the ferocious anti-Semitism at the Durban conference, the attacks on synagogues in France and other anti-Semitic attacks and vandalism in Europe and Russia, and the Nobel committee's wanting to take away Shimon Peres' prize but not Arafat's, the net result is that Jews are feeling threatened not only in Israel but in Europe, where there has been an upsurge of anti-Semitism, and in the United States as well. "As said before, if a loudspeaker goes off and a voice orders all Jews to gather in Times Square, it would not be a surprise" said The *Village Voice*'s Nat Hentoff (Wilentz 2002, p. 101).

Despite American Jewry's anxiety about being clearly identified as Jews, the Lubavitchers are saying loudly and proudly that they are Jewish. They are deeply involved in *Tikkun Olam,* a term often used to refer to social action and social justice. And here Chabad is outstanding, opening drug rehabilitation centers, establishing programs for children with special needs, and catering to Jewish immigrants.

Like other religious fundamentalists, from Jerry Falwell to Osama bin Laden, Chabad uses the Internet and television to spread their mission, setting up Chabad Houses all over the globe. At its core, the Lubavitcher goal is to pass Rebbe Schneerson's message to the Jewish people and carry out his mission to prepare the world for the imminent coming of the Messiah. Many thought Schneerson was immortal. When he died in 1994, many believers could not believe it, while others thought he would be resurrected and return as the Redeemer. Many who believed this also thought it better to be discreet about the belief and not make it public.

A.J. Jacobs, author of *The Year of Living Biblically: One Man's Humble Quest to Follow the Bible as Literally as Possible* (Jacobs 2007) wrote about a Lubavitcher Simchas Torah party he attended:

> I'm at the loudest, rowdiest, most drunken party of my life. Me and several hundred Hasidic men. . . I came for the dancing. There's a part of the Bible where King David celebrates the arrival of the Ark of the Covenant to Jerusalem. This was an older David, years after he slew Goliath . . . . He has defeated his increasingly paranoid mentor Saul to become king of Israel. And he brings

> home the arc, a sacred box containing the Ten Commandments. He celebrates by dancing and, man, does he dance. He dances with such abandon, with such joy, that he doesn't notice that his robe is flying up, exposing his nakedness to the young handmaidens of the kingdom . . . I do love the image of the king doing a wild holy jig. . . . I wanted to feel what David felt, so I took a subway to Crown Heights. . . My guide, Gershon, is . . .a kind, bespectacled, newlywed Hasid . . . I get to see a side of ultra-Orthodox Jews that I'd never seen before. They always look so somber on the subway. . . But here they are, well, wasted. They're weaving down the sidewalks, some holding bottles of Crown Royal whiskey, some singing loudly in Hebrew. . . . On this holiday, it's not only OK to drink, it's pretty much mandatory. Gershon and I go to his parents' house and pound a few shots of vodka in their front-yard sukkah. . . . When Gershon says the prayers . . . before drinking, I sneak a peek at him. His eyes are half-closed, his eyelids fluttering, his eyeballs rolled toward the back of his head. . . After our vodka shots, we head over to the party's headquarters—the huge building known as 770 Eastern Parkway, the nerve center of this branch of Hasidism. The doors are glutted with dozens of revelers in their black coats—all men, no women (the Hasidism aren't much for gender mixing). We have to elbow our way through, and there, we found an ocean of undulating black hats—hundreds, maybe thousands of them in a hall the size of a large gymnasium. It's as loud as any concert I've ever been to. But instead of drums and guitars, it's a village of men singing *Ay yi yi* . . . the floor is exactly like a Seattle mosh pit circa 1992. Everyone's bumping, smacking, thumping onto one another. . . . We are making a slow, huge circle, sort of a Holy Roller derby. If you look up, you can see the occasional Hasid bouncing up in the air like a pogo stick. When there is a patch of free space on the floor—which isn't often—a reveler will do a somersault. . . I tell you, I've never seen such pure joy. It is thick, atmospheric, like someone had released a huge canister of nitrous oxide into the room. Here we are, hundreds of dancing King Davids. Even for a control freak like me, there's no choice but to go along with it. You are overwhelmed. You follow the sweating, bouncing, shouting *ay-yi-yi*-ing hordes, or you are trampled" (Jacobs 2007, p. 84–6).

Thirty years after the Woodstock Festival, a devoted fan base began turning to the band Phish for a sense of spiritual meaning, often traveling for several days just to see one more show. Bass player Mike Gordon, raised as an observant Jew but no longer observant, says that his Judaism is in the music. "I've always compared my movements on stage to *davening* [praying]," he added. "To me, music has always served as that type of religious release." Phish has incorporated Jewish and Hebrew songs into their repertoire. One could hear amphitheaters fulfilled with Jews and non-Jews belting out *Avenu Malkenu*, a traditional Jewish prayer, or *Yerushalayim Shel Zahav* (Jerusalem of Gold). Rabbi Shmuel Skaist was founder of *Gefiltefish*, a group of observant Jews, Phish groupies, who trailed Phish across America, an advertisement to people of all faiths that spirituality rather than drugs was pretty good for getting high (Penn 2000). Skaist thought of himself as fishing for Jewish souls at music venues, a practice going back more than 40 years to the work of the late Rabbi Shlomo Carlebach, the "Singing Rabbi," who spent years "returning" disaffected Jews to Jewish observance. He took his outreach and his music to cafés, bars and music clubs from the Haight-Ashbury to Greenwich Village, jamming with Bob Dylan.

Skaist, who plays guitar himself and had experimented with drugs as an adolescent said, "Phish's jams are like a metaphor for the search for truth. They're jamming and they can't take it any higher, and then it gets more intense. Just when you think it can't get any more intense, they go to the next level. And that's what the big questions in life are like" (Penn 2000). Phish played for the last time in 2004.

> This weekend, on the 35th anniversary of the Woodstock Festival, the band Phish, arguably the kingpin of alternative rock bands of the last three decades, played its last gig. A crowd of close to 70,000 trudged through wind, rain, mud and muck . . for a two-day concert that symbolized the proverbial end of the neo-hippie era. And with it ended one of the most unique Jewish identity movements in popular culture (Hahn and Tapper 2004).

THE OCEANIC EXPERIENCE: RIDING THE WAVES OR GOING UNDER?

Religion has always provided an honored place for oceanic emotions such as nirvana experiences and ecstatic experiences. Experiences of ecstasy, when the boundaries between the self and the rest of the world fall away, have the potential to be healing or destructive. The ocean as a symbol for boundless unity and oneness goes back to the Hindu tradition and is a preferred metaphor in Buddhist, Christian and Muslim traditions. Christian mystics believed they lived in God's ocean in the same way that fish live in the sea, and Jesus, of course, was called a fisher of men. The first letters of "Jesus Christ, Son of God, Savior" spell *icthus*, the Greek word for fish, (Balmer 1993, p. 203) so the fish has long been a symbol of Christianity.. The longing to return to and merge with our origins in the sea, the earth, and animal life is deeply spiritual.

Submitting to the power of nature can be a humbling experience, at times a mystical one. More and more parents are sending their out-of-control teenagers to Outward Bound wilderness programs. These kids, who have lived terrorizing their parents and manipulating and blaming authority, find that they cannot dominate the wild but if they want to survive, they must submit to its power and become just another cog in the greater wheel of the cosmos.

At fifty, Alix Kates Shulman (1995), author of the feminist novel *Memoirs of an Ex-Prom Queen*, left her New York City life of political activism, family, and literary community to live alone and write on an island off the coast of Maine. On a windswept beach, in a cabin with no plumbing, power, or telephone, she found to her astonishment that she was learning to live all over again, discovering capacities for thought, feeling, sensual delight, and meditative solitude. As she foraged for food, it took only a few weeks before her basic island diet consisted of wild vegetables, fruits, and shellfish. . . She began to pay attention to things in a new away, slowing down and focusing on what was right there in front of her—a leaf, a seed, a crab, a flower. As she circled around with her bucket, she felt a sense of joy in all that she had learned and all that nature had provided. A world that was as old as the sea had opened up to her and had become new.

> I, who had been such a stranger to prayer that my response to grace at table was always embarrassment, now find . . . spiking my tastebuds, stimulating my heartbeat, spicing each delicious mouthful that rich emotional stew of awe, gratitude, and delight that must have prompted the first blessing of food. Hardly by design or even desire, I soon discover I can no longer eat without grace on my lips (Shulman 1995, pp. 48–9).

Looking out at the sea, Shulman recalled a strange episode on a speeding subway train. She had been sitting alone on the downtown IRT on her way to pick up her children at their after-school music class. Having just pulled out of the Twenty-Third Street station, the train was accelerating to its cruising speed. All around her people sat all bundled up in mufflers, damp woolen coats, and wet slushy boots, reading their newspapers or magazines or staring off blankly as the train jerked along the track. The air was cold and close and smelled of stale tobacco. An elderly couple spoke in a Slavic tongue, while a mother read an advertising sign to her three bedraggled children. All of a sudden the dull light in the car began to shine until everything around her glowed with an indescribable aura. She saw in the row of motley passengers opposite her the miraculous connection of all living beings. It was not just a feeling. She saw the connection, which turned into a vision

> in which all the people in the car hurtling downtown together, including myself, like all the people on the planet hurtling together around the sun—our entire living cohort—formed one united family, indissolubly connected by the rare and mysterious accident of life. No matter what our countless superficial differences, we were equal, we were one, by virtue of simply being alive at this moment out of all the possible moments stretching endlessly back and ahead. The vision filled me with overwhelming love for the entire human race and a feeling that no matter how incomplete or damaged our lives, we were surprisingly lucky to be alive. Then the train pulled into the station and I got off (Shulman 1995, pp. 55–56).

She emerged from the subway stunned and thrilled. She looked around at the familiar world, which was the same, yet not the same. Her ordinary existence had been shattered, letting her glimpse something she had never before imagined, something she could not begin to describe. It had occurred unbidden, suddenly, as if by magic—and then, just as suddenly, it was over. She wished she could see it again but had no idea how to get it back. It had come and now was gone. It was as if she had suddenly fallen through a deep hole into another world only to emerge again as suddenly. If she didn't hurry she would be late for the children.

> In order to keep it alive, at least prevent the memory from fading too quickly, I needed to speak of my experience. But whom could I tell? Who would care to believe me? No one I knew. In my Manhattan, mysticism was scorned. Mystics, like Communists, and the few bookstores that catered to either, were underground. Still, I could not doubt that my vision had occurred, even though I had no way to verify it. And this inspired in me a new humility toward such knowledge and a secret gratitude that the vision had appeared to me, an atheistically tending agnostic (Shulman 1995, pp. 55-57).

Urban commuters know that there can be brief but magical moments in the subways. At rush hour a crowd gathers around a lone saxophone player at Grand Central Station. Near the Times Square shuttle, the haunting music of voices, pan pipes, and flutes blend with the sounds of the *charango*, made from an armadillo shell. In the midst of the hurry to get home, the breathtaking music of the Andes mountains wafts upward as strangers stop to share a special moment of community and the sacred.

When my granddaughter Ava was born, I sent emails to friends and local colleagues.

> I am so happy to tell you that my first granddaughter, Ava Morgan Farber, came into the world yesterday evening . . . I guess she wanted to meet her family before Tuesday, the date of Rebecca's scheduled caesarian section. When my husband and I walked into the room and saw her earlier today, my eyes filled with tears. Awhile later I held her and felt the urge to breastfeed her. The body really *does* remember. I had never seen my two grandsons, Sammy, 6 1/2 and Jake, almost 4, and their cousin Maya, also almost four, so interested in bellies before. They patted each others' belly, seeming to know that that's where babies come from. Yesterday, before Ava was born, Jake said that having a sister wouldn't be so bad when she started to talk. (He and Sam had wanted a brother but I heard that they came into the room this morning so excited to meet their sister.) Jake wore a big brother t-shirt and Sam wore a biggest brother t-shirt. Later when we were having lunch together, I was sitting next to Sam. He leaned over and nudged me asking, "Grandma, did you ever *have* a baby?" Although he knew that we were his father's mother and father, but he seemed to be making the connection in a different way. I told him yes, I had had a baby, his daddy David, sitting across the table from us. Knowing it was such a leap to understand that his 6'4" daddy was once a little baby in my belly, I explained that this was really true. Then Sam asked his other grandmother, Nana, if she ever *had* a baby, and she told him that his mommy and

> her sister Stacey were once her little babies. Then Sam asked me if Nana had ever *been* a little baby too. It was so wonderful to help him make the connection that he was part of the wonderful interconnectedness of us all.

Psychoanalyst Michael Eigen, who suffered from terrible feelings of aloneness, came to experience himself as a thread in the great human tapestry, allowing him the empathy to help depressed and anguished people to become threads in the same tapestry (Bollas 1997).

> Nowadays, more and more people come in and actually say that they don't feel alive. . . I remember certain people I've met in my life, like Winnicott, Allen Ginsberg, or the rebbe Menachem Schneerson. When I was with them, I felt it was okay to be the sort of person I am. With them it was okay for me to be somehow off the map, beyond the map; it was okay for there to be in life such a person as I was. In that passage, then, I was trying to encode, for whomever it might reach, something like a message in a bottle. Floating on the sea, it might then reach some people, who would hear the message that it's okay for them to be the sort of alone person they are. And by some miracle, by making room for such a message, some of these people, through the course of years, have tapestried out. They've found themselves situated in a larger tapestry that makes room for the sorts of being they were and are, whereas earlier there didn't seem to be any place for them (Bollas 1997, p. 101).

The experience of one's boundaries dissolving through the interpenetration of the self with the cosmos is a universal spiritual experience and the core religious emotion, according to Romain Rolland, a leading French theologian and novelist. His model was the life of Ramakrishna, who described himself as being like salt dissolved in the great ocean of the universe. Rolland (1929) called this the oceanic experience. The ocean as a symbol of boundless oneness and unity in which multiplicities dissolve and opposites fuse is one of the preferred metaphors for the melting of ego boundaries of mystics in the Buddhist, Muslim, and Christian traditions.

President John F. Kennedy said at a dinner for the America's Cup yacht crews in Newport Rhode Island, 1962

> I really don't know why it is that all of us are so committed to the sea. . . . I think it's because we all came from the sea. And it is an interesting biological fact that all of us have in our veins the exact same percentage of salt in our blood that exists in the ocean. And therefore we have salt in our blood, in our sweat, in our tears. We are tied to the ocean and when we go back to the sea . . . we are going back from whence we came (Kennedy 1962).

There is something dangerously seductive about the sea's power, as we hear in the first movement in Debussy's *La Mer.* The cloudy blustery day becomes more menacing as the storm brews, the winds whipping the sea into a frenzy of whitecaps, and the waves crashing louder and louder. We can get lost in the sea, lose our way and drown. That is what happened to John F. Kennedy Jr., who lost his sense of orientation, plunging the plane carrying his wife and sister-in-law into the sea. Some time ago on a weekend at Montauk, the easternmost tip of Long Island, while walking along the part of the beach where fishermen fish from shore, I came across a makeshift shrine to a man who had apparently drowned while fishing. The wooden monument was already quite weathered but I could make out the words "He loved the sea and he has been returned to it." Returning to the sea can be like returning to the womb, where it is safe, secure, and peaceful.

The yearning to be enveloped in the water's depths can take a dark turn, as it did for Kathy, whom I knew since she was seven or eight (Farber 2000). She lived several houses down the street with her parents and younger sister. At seventeen she was voted the Nicest Person in School by her classmates, and like many of her classmates, she used drugs. But she used drugs differently than the others, not just for fun or because everyone was doing it. She wanted nothing more than to get out of her life, taking any drug that came along, with anyone, anytime, in a frenzy to get out of her own skin (Name withheld, 1997). "Special K" (ketamine), a hallucinogenic veterinary tranquilizer and medical anesthetic, was a favorite, known to induce near-death experience. It was a brilliantly sunny, unusually warm winter day when Kathy jumped from the George Washington Bridge to her watery grave in the Hudson River. Before she jumped, she wrote in the dust and mud on her car's windshield, "I Love You All, Kathy." Two days later I joined her family, classmates, teachers and neighbors for a memorial service on a hilly shore of the river. These usually raucous kids came directly from school, somber and subdued, gripping their backpacks and each others' hands, some carrying flowers. One girl was overwhelmed when it dawned on her that there was no coffin to put the flowers on, no body to be viewed. What there was a little shrine to Kathy's memory, complete with her brutal suicide note, the photograph she had taken for graduation, and a poem.

The poem, written by Mary Elizabeth Frye, (1932) might be comforting in other circumstances, but given that this was a suicide, I was horrified when a classmate led the group in reading the poem aloud, sanctifying Kathy. The poem told the mourners that they are not to stand at her grave and weep, because she is not really dead; she is in the winds that blow, in the sparkling snow, sunlight, rain, the rush of birds flying high, the night stars. I was angry at Kathy for killing herself and said so at the service. This seemed to free her father to say how angry he was at her. How they could say that Kathy did not die? I wrote a passionate letter to the editor of our local paper (Farber 1997b). Perhaps ultimately she'd live on in their memories but in the immediate shocking aftermath, it was premature for that. I could not think of Kathy as the swift uplifting rush of birds in flight. There was nothing uplifting about the image of her slim body plunging to her death, an image which still pops into my mind from time to time when I pass her family's home or drive past the George Washington Bridge. There would be no more morning awakenings for her, just her body being swept along by the river's current. These dazed youngsters were glorifying a final act of violence and self-destruction, turning this poor, anguished girl into a saint—to be revered and imitated (Farber 2000).

Kathy's suicide occurred almost two years after the suicide of a fourteen-year-old boy in her school, a boy whom she did not know. Grief-stricken classmates had spontaneously erected a shrine to his memory at the Metro North railroad tracks that ran along the river's edge, the tracks where he had lay down and been killed moments later by the train. Kathy had been deeply disturbed by this episode and had set up her own shrine to his memory in her room. How many more would be swept up in the deadly contagion (Phillips 1996) that often follows a suicide attempt? Terrified parents and teachers wondered who would be next. In the weeks immediately following, four more students in this small high school made suicide attempts.

There are "suicide watches" in some local schools in my area in March, as suicides and suicide attempts have occurred around this time for a number of years (Farber 2000). Spring is the time after the cold hard winter when green shoots emerge from the ground and robin redbreasts appear, and spring is the time of Christ's crucifixion and resurrection. It is also the time when suicide attempts increase, when desperate people cling to the idea that they will die and be reborn into a new and better life. It is a time for some when the life that many believe exists after death shines like a beacon, beckoning those adrift to come home. It is the time extolled by rousing hymns and gospel music, the time of deliverance from pain and suffering. It is not by sheer coincidence that mass suicides in religious cults have also been found to occur at around this time, and the potential for mass suicides and suicide bombings is especially great at the time of the millennium, when the era of physical life may end to be replaced by "everlasting life" (Farber 2000).

It was in April 1993 that the mass suicide in David Koresh's Branch Davidian cult near Waco, Texas, occurred. Eighty followers were reported to have committed suicide by setting fire to the compound, believing that it was like Noah's ark, a place where the faithful were to gather to await the destruction of the world by fire. Some of the 74 murder-suicides by members of the Order of the Solar Temple occurred in March 1997. Also in March 1997 the world was stunned to hear of the mass suicide of 39 members of the Heaven's Gate millennium cult in San Diego. The bodies of men and women were found on their beds, dressed alike in black, wearing the same buzz cut haircuts, and with a purple shroud draped over their bodies. Some of the men had been castrated to ensure their celibacy. The Heaven's Gate cult still maintains an active website. In March 2000 235 or more members of a millennium cult died by their own hands in Uganda. In another millennium cult, followers of the "Movement for the Restoration of the Ten Commandments of God" barricaded themselves in the church, chanted and sang for hours before and setting the church on fire. The cataclysmic destruction of these cults, and the mass suicide and murder of 913 people in 1978 in Jonestown, Guyana all conformed to the dynamics of a cult death spiral (Conway and Siegelman 1995).

WITHOUT THE DARKNESS THERE IS NO LIGHT

> A sensible man will remember that the eyes may be confused in two ways - by a change from light to darkness or from darkness to light; and he will recognize that the same thing happens to the soul.
> —Plato

Just as we see in the ocean the potential for both the sublime heights and the destructive depths, we can also see in human beings the potential for both health and creativity as well as for madness and destruction. Experiences of nirvana, when the middle path advocated by Gautama Buddha is followed, can be healing but can be destructive when the extreme path is taken, When individuals immerse themselves in the deepest trance or meditative states possible, this can lead to a dangerous lack of regard for reality. Take this example from the Devi Mandir Internet newsletter, for devotees of Shree Maa and her American-born assistant, guru Swamiji. She is considered a saint by her followers, who treat her like a rock star, following her throughout India, Europe, and North America. Shree Maa tells this story:

> It was the monsoon season and we were in the Himalayas performing nine days of worship . . . I had been with Swamiji for a few years by that time. . . He would chant for the entire day, and stay up sitting by the fire for most of the night. Swamiji always slept very little. We were staying in a mud hut next to the Shiva temple. Swamiji had been performing *homa* all day long, sitting in front of the fire and chanting the Chandi forwards and backwards from morning until night. Because it was the rainy season, Swamiji had placed the green wood all around the fire pit so it would dry out and could be used for later *homas*. I was meditating on a cot to support his *sadhana*. I had been deep in *samadhi* for about five or six hours when suddenly my body felt like it was burning up. When I opened my eyes, I saw that all the wood around Swamiji's fire pit had caught on fire, yet Swamiji was sitting as still as a rock, with his eyes closed and a big smile on his face, while chanting loudly and throwing grains into the fire. He was completely unaware that everything around him was in flames. Then I saw that his clothing was on fire, yet he just sat there, completely absorbed in his worship of the Divine Mother. As brightly as the fire burned, so much louder did his chanting become. I jumped up and wrapped him in a blanket, smothering the flames that were starting to engulf his entire body. Then I poured water over the wood on the outside of the *havan*

> *kund*, the sacred fire pit that had caught on fire. Swamiji just kept on chanting, never worrying about his personal safety nor the danger he had faced, determined only to fulfill his vow and finish his worship. When he had finished his chanting, Swamiji stood up and discovered that only a small portion of his loin cloth was left intact on his body. The rest of his clothes had burned in the fire. Fortunately, there were no burns on his skin. That Swamiji was saved from harm did not surprise me. His one-pointed focus while worshipping the Divine Mother in the form of Chandi has always been exemplary. How could She not protect her child, who ceaselessly displayed such intense love and unwavering devotion? (Shree Ma 2001).

My pedestrian take on this is that Swamiji would be better off with less exemplary worship. He was simply lucky that Shree Maa was there to put out the fire.

Freud's concept of the death drive was a product of a pragmatic Jewish sensibility about the integral relationship between the life force and the destructive inclinations. The Jewish view is that we all have both a *yetzer tov* (proclivity for good) as well as a *yetzer ra* (proclivity for evil) within ourselves, and therefore harbor inclinations toward both. The major religions prohibit suicide. It follows from Freud's theory that we can only try to nurture the good in ourselves while being aware of the destructive so that the good can prevail. If we do not struggle with these opposing impulses, we can be seduced by our destructive impulses. Freud's view was basic to his idea that civilization is far more savage than it seems (Freud 1930), a concept which has gone out of favor in Western culture. But when we see so much destructiveness in our culture, Freud's theory makes compelling sense, as it does to those in the traditions of Klein and Lacan (Farber 2000). For Freud (1920), both self-destructive as well as life-affirming impulses exist in all of us, in different balances and at different times. The tension between these opposing parts of the personality is an unstable one, prone to eruptions of destructive impulses. Some of us manage to live lives in which we manage to balance the conflicting tension, acting only occasionally on the destructive wishes, while others live lives dominated by the destructive impulses, drawn to death like a moth to a flame (Farber 2000).

CROSSING THE BORDER

> El Paso is a border town in Texas, and one can see Juarez in Mexico, on the other side of the Rio Grande. At night beneath the canopy of stars, El Paso and Juarez came alive to the night. The white sober streetlights of El Paso gave way to the shimmering green lights of Juarez, a tropical and brazen green that seemed to throb and surge, that seemed to say, *Ni modo*—anything goes.
> —Abraham Verghese, *The Tennis Partner: A Doctor's Story of Friendship and Loss*

When does religious expression cross the border into mental illness? When does it serve as a healthy comfort for the losses and pain of living? Although the line between religion and mental illness can be an ambiguous one, a strong inclination toward mystical experience and the occult is common in those whose psychological structure lies in that broad borderland between the psychotic and the "normal neurotic" known as the borderline range of personality organization (Kernberg 1975). Borders are exciting and dangerous places. The murder rate in Juárez, on the Mexican side of the border, rivals the most dangerous cities in the world.

The dilemma of those who live in the borderland seems to be an intense yearning to merge with another. At the same time that they fear irrevocably losing themselves in the experience. At times they may seem quite normal, at other times quite disturbed. They may search for ecstatic experiences any way they can. When straddling the border fails, they may fall into the abyss of psychotic states.

So much of the thinking about religion among mental health clinicians has been influenced by Freud's (1927) idea that believing in God represented a neurotic longing for a father, a comforting illusion in view of the harsh realities of life. Ana-Maria Rizzuto (1998) thinks that Freud's initial mental representation of God developed through his relationship with his father, an initially exciting but ultimately disappointing Jewish man. Ernest Jones (1957) said that Freud's parents only paid lip service to a belief in God but in practice were really secular Jews. A careful reading of Freud brings to light that what is regarded as his anti-religious bias is really more a bias against religious fundamentalism or religion without thoughtfulness. Although still an atheist at the end of his life, Freud began to see Judaism's commitment to a belief in an invisible God as a source of introspection and a capacity for abstract thinking, a triumph of intellect over faith. In short, he found his psychoanalytic thinking to stem from Judaism (Edmundson 2007; Freud 1939). There was too much of enduring value in religion to abandon it completely.

Freud oscillated between skepticism about the occult and belief in it (Jones 1957). In a letter to Rolland, he thought mysticism and the occult were dangerous, a belief that reflected his personality, which he defined. by limits, moderation, and his Jewish sobriety (Freud 1960).

Kakar (1991) finds Ramakrishna to be an especially apt choice for a psychoanalytic study of ecstatic mysticism because Freud's observations on the mystical experience were indirectly evoked by Ramakrishna's ecstasies. Freud had developed a friendship with Romain Rolland (Freud 1960), and despite enormous differences, was magnetically drawn to Rolland and his ideas. Rolland was working on a biography of Ramakrishna at the time he wrote to Freud, saying that although he found Freud's analysis of religion (Freud 1927) to be correct, ideally, he would have liked Freud to do an analysis of spontaneous religious feelings, or religious sensations which are quite different from religion proper, and far more enduring (Kakar1991). Rolland went on to call this sensation *oceanic*, meaning without perceptible limits, probably having taken the term *oceanic feeling* from Ramakrishna's imagery to describe the ineffable. Rolland said that all his life he had found the oceanic feeling to be a source of vital revival. Freud's response to Ramakrishna, as to India in general, was quite uneasy. He found Ramakrishna's florid ecstasies not only distant from his sensibility but quite distasteful. In acknowledging Rolland's book about Ramakrishna, Freud wrote,

> I shall now try with your guidance to penetrate into the Indian jungle from which until now an uncertain blending of Hellenic love of proportion, Jewish sobriety and philistine timidity have kept me away. . I really ought to have tackled it earlier, or the plants of this soil shouldn't be alien to me; I have dug to certain depths for their roots. But it isn't easy to pass beyond the limits of one's own nature"(Freud 1960, p. 392).

Kakar (1991), Kris (1952) and other Freudians, although seeing mysticism as a form of regression, see its outcome as positive in terms of creativity and the development of the self. (Hay and Morisy 1978). Further, Freud himself said that "devout believers are safeguarded in a high degree against the risk of certain neurotic illnesses; their acceptance of the universal neurosis spares them the task of constructing a personal one" (Freud 1927, p. 44). Maslow (1964), the founder of humanistic psychology, regarded religious experience as a kind of peak experience, which is characteristic of mental health, so that people reporting such experience should have greater degree of psychological well-being than others. This, in fact, can be tested using the Bradburn Balanced Affect Scale (Bradburn 1969). Studies in the U.S. and the U.K. show that experiences that were ecstatic, telepathic, or religious is widespread in both, and that people reporting religious experience tended far more to report a high level of well-being (Hays and Morisy 1978).

Freud was so troubled by Rolland's concept of the oceanic experience being the core religious emotion because he equated the oceanic experience with infantile regressive states such as those which occur in psychosis (Freud 1930) and also because he thought it was dangerously connected to the death instinct (Freud 1923a). Despite his fear of mysticism, he was nonetheless fascinated by it and regretted that his study of religion did not include the religious experience of the mystics and saints (Jones1957). Trained in neurology, he undoubtedly would have been very interested in current studies of the neurological underpinnings of mystical experiences. When the late Elizabeth Lloyd Mayer (2007) was in London, visiting the widow of English composer Ralph Vaughan Williams, she met with some musician friends of Williams, one of whom reminisced about a salon held at the home of the Freud family. Several of the guests had attended these salons regularly, and recalled the way Freud seemed to slip away just as music was about to start. His lack of interest and insensitivity to music was well-known, an anomaly in late nineteenth-century Vienna (Diaz de Chumaceiro 1993). One woman commented, "He didn't like how music made him feel. We spoke about it once. He was free in his admiration but it transported him more than he enjoyed. I believe he preferred to be more controlled in his feeling" (Mayer 2007, p. 269).

Nonetheless, Freud was fascinated with the occult, and continually corresponded with colleagues, particularly Ferenczi and Jung, regarding his belief that "thought-transference" was a genuine and clinically important occurrence (Freud 1922a, 1925, 1933, 1941a, 1941b). Freud developed several hypotheses about telepathic communication, seeing it as an archaic mode of communication between individuals and perhaps even a physical process that had become mental. Freud was open in his attitude toward it because of its nearness to the unconscious, and, at the same time, had reservations, fearing that the science of psychoanalysis might find itself compared to occultism. When Ferenczi went to a séance conducted by a medium, it was with Freud's full endorsement and interest. He was eager to hear all about it but warned Ferenczi to be silent about it. His interest was largely a personal one, because he believed that he connected remotely with his fiancée Martha by thought itself when he was in Paris (Phillips 1995; Jones, 1957). Freud and Ferenczi even visited a medium in Berlin together in 1909 and Freud visited one alone in Munich (Jones 1957). In 1921 Freud was invited to be co-editor of three periodicals devoted to the study of occultism, and although he refused, he wrote "If I had my life to live over again I should devote myself to psychical research rather than to psychoanalysis" (Jones 1957, p. 392).

THE HUNGER FOR SPIRITUALITY

> To find your own way is to follow your bliss. This involves analysis, watching yourself and seeing where real deep bliss is—not the quick little excitement, but the real deep, life-filling bliss.—Joseph Campbell, *The Hero with a Thousand Faces*

We have been living in America at a time marked by a deep hunger for spirituality, a desire to connect with the mystery of life. And so there has been a vast change in the American spiritual landscape. It is like being at a huge spiritual supermarket and being able to put any spiritual experience you want to try in your shopping cart (Greenfield 1975). There is a lot of "God-Talk" (Tickle 1997) going on, only some of it traditional, and far more of it with a born-again or New Age flavor. There is a yearning to experience the divine that is far more important than doctrine, rhetoric, or even meaning. Prayer is not necessarily a conversation with a deity. It can include meditation, reflections, communal reading, and expressions of gratitude to nature. The way to go, according to New Age mythologist Joseph Campbell (1988), is to "follow your own bliss." We are not, said Campbell, seeking for the meaning of life; we are seeking the experience of being physically alive.

That is, people want an experience that appeals to their senses—the sounds of prayer chanted, tambourines played, the smells of incense, the rhythms of their repetitions and rituals. There is a yearning for an experiential religion within an affirming community, reflected in the tremendous growth of ecstatic worship within the charismatic renewal or neo-Pentecostal movement. This movement began in the late sixties (Balmer 1993; Cuneo 2001, Tickle 1997) and was focused from the beginning upon "baptism in the Holy Spirit," an experience from which "spiritual gifts"—speaking in tongues, prophecy, and miraculous healing—presumably arose. There are also experiential movements that may strike one as more iconoclastic and rebellious than spiritual: the growth of Yoruba (voodoo) and Santeria, the increase in organized goddess worship and the spread of Wicca (witchcraft). Even Madonna's "Like a Prayer" video, regarded as sacrilegious and offensive to many, may be her personal kind of prayer, one that appeals to many Generation X-ers (Beaudoin 1998). Even those who are formally religious in America are being influenced by their proximity to the passion and spirit of those who are not (Tickle 1997).

People are talking and writing about religious or spiritual experiences as never before. Inspirational books about spirituality are immensely popular. Writer Anne Lamott's (1999) account of her spiritual journey, *Traveling Mercies: Some Thoughts on Faith,* so endeared her to millions of believers and nonbelievers that it became a surprise *New York Times* bestseller. Like many baby boomers, she always felt an innate spirituality, but never knew what to do with it. She was the daughter of nonreligious California intellectuals who worshipped Allen Ginsberg and Miles Davis. While she was deeply moved by the rituals of Catholicism and there was much in Judaism and Buddhism to which she could relate, she had little tolerance for organized religion. She hungered for something to dull the ache of her self-hatred, turning to alcohol, drugs, and binge eating and purging. Feeling herself ugly so much of the time, and an outsider, she was drawn to the ecstatic gospel music of a small black Presbyterian congregation. For months she stood in the back of the church, staying only for the music. In time this congregation became her spiritual family, helping her to overcome her addictions and helping her raise her infant son. Friendship, she claimed, is the best salve for anyone's pain. As Lamott toured the country to talk about her books and about writing, she was instead approached by people who wanted to talk to her about God. She described her book as being about people like her, who surprised themselves by coming to believe in a loving God who is with us all the time—even when we are at our worst.

Anne Lamott is far from alone in her spiritual quest. In numerous surveys since the 1960s, 30 to 40 percent of those participating said they have at some time felt a powerful, sacred energy that seemed to lift them up and out of themselves. More recently Gallup polls found that the majority of American adults said they had had "a moment of sudden religious awakening or insight" (Begley, 2001). Some are actively seeking ecstatic experiences, while many are seeking a state of nirvana.

The hunger for something lacking in the soul brings many people to New Age practices, alternative medicine, and to churches, temples, and psychotherapists' offices, looking for something they cannot name. They want to get back to the land of vibrant living where life has meaning. By entering treatment they turn to another human being in the hope that their spirit can be rekindled. When we do not allow ourselves to be our true selves, when we become the false selves that we believe others want us to be, we suffer from depression and anxiety, an endless sense of aloneness and psychic numbness that leaves us feeling dead inside. We feel alienated from ourselves.

When consumerism becomes the new god, when we live to acquire the best, these objects of desire lose their desirability soon after they have been acquired, leading one to acquire yet the newest object of desire, which soon becomes meaningless. Despite almost instant communication through fax, e-mail, and cell phones, many feel isolated and alone, disconnected from community, the earth, and the sacred. The magazine *Real Simple* has become very popular, revealing the longing to bring ancient, simple values to our lives, to cash out, simplify, and become part of a tribe. Some find satisfaction in a deep relationship to nature and the environment, through hiking and camping, through involvement in ecological groups and a move toward living simpler low-tech lives. Some satisfy their souls through creative activity, feeling most alive and connected to others through their writing, painting, dancing, or music.

WHAT IS THE SACRED?

For German theologian Rudolph Otto (1923) the encounter with the sacred affects the person at a deep, emotional level which he called the numinous experience. Mircea Eliade (1958), a French religious historian, considered the sacred and the profane as two modes of being in the world. He found tribal cultures to be permeated by the sacred, not only in sacred places and times, but even in the daily functions of living, such as eating and sex. Modern societies, by contrast, live in the profane mode, having little sense of the sacred. For Eliade, the sacred is a manifestation of a deeper level of reality and our contact with this most intense level of being and power causes the powerful emotional experience of the sacred.

Martin Buber, a Jewish theologian, bids us to make the secular sacred. "God is present when I confront You. But if I look away from You, I ignore Him. As long as I merely experience or use you, I deny God. But when I encounter You I encounter Him" (Buber, 1970, p. 28). For Buber, the sacred is potentially present in any relationship, with people or with nature. When we experience that, we transform an ordinary I-It relationship into an *I-Thou* relationship, in which the encounter is one of intense poignancy. "I-Thou comes by grace, a shaft of sunlight that penetrates our normal world . . . the sacred suddenly manifesting in what was only moments before an ordinary relationship" (Elkins 199, p. 71).

William James (1902) was a physician, philosopher, and psychologist. His classic, *The Varieties of Religious Experience* (James 1985) was subtitled *A Study in Human Nature*, and for good reason. He regarded psychology as being at the very center of spirituality and he tied the two inextricably together. He defined the divine not in terms of a concrete deity but in terms of the basically sacred nature of the universe. James divided the religious field into institutional religion and personal religion, and believed that personal religion is the more important.

> Religion . . . shall mean for us the feelings, acts, and experiences of individual men in their solitude; so far as they apprehend themselves to stand in relation to whatever they may consider the divine. . . .it is evident that out of religion in the sense in which we take it, theologies, philosophies, and ecclesiastical organizations may secondarily grow (James1902, p. 53).

Put another way, James was an unabashed earthy moralist, suspicious of impressive-sounding theories and principles for their own sake. He was a pragmatist; religion interested him in terms of how it helps us live our lives.

Eighteenth-century poet William Blake (1973) regarded spiritual energy as the God in man which must be free to express itself in love and creative activity. Behind the quest for spirituality lies a growing need for passion and depth in our lives, for the sense of wonder and joy that innocent young children have easily and naturally. Man must be free

> To see a World in a Grain of Sand
> And a Heaven in a Wild Flower
> Hold Infinity in the palm of your hand
> And Eternity in an hour (Blake, 1973, p. 1475).

For Henry David Thoreau, nature was the way to the sacred. Walks through the woods and fields around Concord were for him what worship at church was for others. For Thoreau, nature was the temple of God and the perennial source of life. Thoreau warned us, "Simplify, simplify, simplify. Don't come to the end of your life and realize you never lived."

For psychologist Abraham Maslow (Maslow 1971), the sacred dimension is found in peak experiences that transport us out of ordinary consciousness and into the realm of Being, the highest dimension of human experience. For humanistic psychologist and former minister, David Elkins (1998), the sacred can be found within a church or temple but also in a therapist's office, a mountain park, an art studio, in relationships, in bodily experience, and in the bedroom. For surgeon Richard Selzer, the operating room becomes, at times, a sacred space (Selzer 1996, 2001a, 2001b). Psychoanalyst Donald Winnicott's work resonates with a sense of the sacred, as does Michael Eigen's (Eigen 1999) who at times experiences the encounter with his patients as a form of prayer.

For Allen Ginsberg, and for Richard Alpert (Ram Dass), the sacred was to be found in Buddhist immersion in the moment. Ginsberg's discovery of Buddhist meditation practice, with its concentration on breathing, led to his idea of poetry as breath, emanating as much from the body as the mind. Ram Dass' two million-copy bestseller *Be Here Now* became known as the hippie Bible, extolling psychedelics and meditation. Now that Ram Dass has gotten old and a stroke has confined him to a wheelchair, he is still sharing his wisdom with others who are struggling with illness and aging. In *Still Here: Embracing Aging, Changing, and Dying* (Dass 2000), he applies his Buddhist spirituality to aging and dying, telling us how age is teaching him about letting go of old attachments and dispelling fear of aging, change and death.

The form of Buddhism that has most influenced America is Zen, the essence of which is the practice of sitting concentration and deep breathing and exhalation. It is the practice of waking up to reality, of being present and aware, here and now. At their most extreme, these meditative states may become raptures or ecstasies and that is what Ginsberg espoused: "Life should be ecstasy." The ethic of immediacy inspired the happenings, be-ins, street theatre, and protests as well as the hedonism that characterized the sexual and cultural revolution. But for Jack Kornfield (2000), enlightenment exists, and so does unbounded freedom and joy, oneness with the Divine, and states of timeless grace. But, ever the pragmatist, he reminds us of one down-to-earth truth: these exhilarating experiences do not last. It is not ecstasy that is the hallmark of a spiritual life but how we live our day-to-day lives.

In *The Psychoanalytic Mystic*, Michael Eigen (1999) tells us that many psychotherapists and psychoanalysts, whether religious or not, are somewhat or deeply mystical and may be touched by intimations of something sacred in the work. For Eigen and for me too, there are moments when psychoanalysis is a form of prayer. When Eigen reads religious texts, he stays open to the experiences they induce in him.

> I need these experiences. They reset, deepen, redirect, renew me. . . . I read psychoanalytic texts the same way. I need texts that add to my life, that open

> experiencing, that speak to my condition. I am not in psychoanalysis merely as a business or intellectual exercise. It is a life and death matter. It is my life I am spending in it, my time. Either I get the most I can from it or it is worthless. I also want others to get the most they can or why bother? I can go back and forth between psychoanalytic and religious writings, moment to moment, each feeding, correcting, amplifying, opening the other. I say this because I think there are many of us who do, but are afraid to own this double tendency. Either we are put down for being psychoanalytic , or put down for being mystical. . . It is awful to think one must stay on one or the other side of a permeable membrane and try to stop the flow (Eigen 1999, p. 39.

Today more psychotherapists understand that the word *psychotherapy*, originating in the Greek word *psyche*, meaning soul, is the treatment of the soul. More and more psychotherapists understand that religion can play an important part in sustaining meaning and hope in the face of adversity, and believe that it is important to distinguish between unhealthy and healthy religious experience.

Many psychotic patients have what they consider to be ecstatic visions, but are called hallucinations by those in the mental health field. They may believe that they are God. For example, Neil, a man with schizo-affective disorder experienced ecstasies of prayer that would go on continuously. Like Franny, J.D. Salinger's adolescent girl who says the Jesus prayer incessantly and has a psychotic break (Salinger 1961), Neil's manic ecstasies were destroying his life. He thought he was talking to God, then thought he was God, and would stop taking the medication that stabilized his moods. His psychiatrist, Dr. Tony Stern, who had been treating him with medication and psychotherapy, prescribed prayer, three times a day. Neil followed the prescription and it has helped him to rein in his ecstasies and stay on his medication (Shorto 1999).

When patients come to give me their trust, I hold that trust as something sacred. My patient Jane, like many others who had given up alcohol, began to eat compulsively instead. In therapy she came to understand that what she had hungered and thirsted for was not the alcohol she drank or the large quantities of food she ate. She was hungry for something to nourish her body, mind and soul. I told her of Margaret Bullitt-Jonas (1998), an Episcopal priest, who wrote in her memoir *Holy Hunger* of her life-threatening binge eating as a thwarted spiritual desire; she could barely wait to read it. It spoke directly to her. Jane too was a practicing Episcopalian. She left her high-paying position because it did not meet her spiritual needs and decided to become an Episcopal priest. Even before enrolling in the seminary, at the height of the Atkins diet craze, when people were renouncing bread and other carbohydrates but were eating lots of red meat, Jane gave me a copy of a sermon she had written. It was about the sacrament of the Eucharist, the injunction to eat Jesus's flesh and drink his blood through consuming the wafer and wine. She understood this ritual not in its literal sense, as a fundamentalist might, but as having symbolic food for thought.

> Today Jesus tells us that if we eat his flesh . . . then we will be in an inseparable relationship with God the Father through Him. . . . This grisly image is intended to send our minds reeling! Is there anyone here on the Atkins diet? If so, I know you have been talking about bread. In fact, I have noticed recently exactly how much time I am devoting to thinking about what I am eating. . . I wonder—how many of us spend as much time worried about the content of our spiritual diet. . . . These past weeks I have thought more about the bread my soul feeds on. . . I find bread—real food—in the relationships I have with others.

There is thoughtful religion, of which Jane's sermon is an example, and there is mindless or thoughtless religion, in which emotional expressiveness is key. The latter is more likely to lead to ecstatic frenzy.

Chapter Nine

Killing, Cannibalism, and Other Ecstasies from Hell

> Violence is at the heart and secret soul of the sacred.
> —Rene Girard, *Violence and the Sacred*

A band of 87 American pioneers known as the Donner party departed for California in a wagon train in 1846. Some never made it there. The route to California was through the Donner Pass, a passage high in the Sierra Nevada Mountains, about nine miles above Donner Lake, created by the central Pacific Railroad. This was a new route for them along rugged terrain and they ran into a number of problems, resulting in losing cattle and wagons, divisiveness within the group, and becoming trapped by huge snowbanks at Donner Lake (Johnson 1996; Rarick 2008). As their food supply steadily diminished, some left by foot to get help. Many who remained were sick and starving. To eat, these ordinary people in extraordinary circumstances, had to resort to cannibalism before the first relief party arrived. Survival depended on it. And so they ate those who had succumbed to the early, heavy snowfall. Only 48 of the original group survived and reached California.

This episode in American history has been described by historians as one of the most spectacular tragedies in the record of western migration. Given that thousands immigrated to California, the Donner Party episode could even be considered a minor chapter in American history, but in the popular mind the cannibalism became the chief truth remembered about the Donner Party and became the basis for many works of history, fiction, drama, poetry, and film. The taboo against cannibalism is fascinating in this story, because the events focused on families and ordinary people who had to resort to cannibalism to survive, rather than those rare individuals who engage in cannibalism for other reasons. Hannibal Lecter's cannibalistic crimes in the film *The Silence of the Lambs* were repulsive, as were the crimes of serial killer Jeffrey Dahmer, who murdered many people, cut them up, and devoured them. The dark truth is that when survival is at stake, any one of us might eat the flesh of another human being.

AN ANCIENT TABOO IN MODERN TIMES

> "Do you people eat human bodies?" I said one day, upon entering a native village, and pointed to a quantity of meat, spitted upon long skewers, being smoke-dried over numerous smoldering fires. 'Io; yo te?' was the instant reply—'Yes; don't you?' And a few minutes later the chieftain of the village came forward with an offering, which consisted of large and generous portions of flesh, only too obviously of human origin. He seemed genuinely disappointed when I refused.
> —Herbert Ward, *A Voice From the Congo*

The notion that any one of us, under certain circumstances, might be capable of cannibalism is why there is an underlying anxiety for many about the communion ritual of the Eucharist. The Roman Catholic version is the closest to cannibalism, in that it is believed that *transubstantiation* occurs, the literal transformation of the wafer and the wine into "the living, risen and glorious body and blood of Christ, really, truly, and substantially present and offered in sacrifice." When consumed, the wine and wafer become transformed into the body and blood of Christ. The Protestant reformers did not accept this belief literally, with Martin Luther compromising, speaking of cosubstantiation instead of transubstantiation, and Calvin taking the compromise a step further when he declared that Christ is only spiritually, rather than actually, present in the Eucharist (Bergmann 1992).

Wanting to know what the Episcopal Church, the Protestant denomination closest to Catholicism, believed, I consulted two Episcopal priests and was told that the transformation of the bread and wine is more than symbolic; it is an *actual* transformation into the body and the blood of Christ that transforms those who partake of the Eucharist. At the same time, however, I was also told that it is *not* believed that those who take the sacrament are actually eating the body and blood of Christ. One priest, struggling to convey the meaning to me said, "It's not as if God is a baked potato," a metaphor which gave me some pause. I would think that it might have been more to the point although far more disturbing to say "It's not as if God is a juicy sirloin steak." There is a troubling paradox here. While the wine and wafer are believed to be a transformation into the body and blood of Christ, at the same time they are not. There is a disquieting duality, an acceptance of the cannibalistic wish and at the same time a need to disavow it.

In fact, Catholic children are warned that they must not bite or chew the wafer (Farber 2000). In his novel *Snow in August*, Pete Hamill wrote about this.

> Mumbling Latin, his left hand holding the gold chalice . . . Father Heaney deposited a host upon each outstretched tongue, while Michael held the paten under their chins. This was so that no fragment of the host, which had been transformed into the body of Jesus Christ . . . would fall upon the polished floor.
> The first woman's eyes were wide and glassy . . . The other closed her eyes tight, as if fearful of gazing too brazenly at the divine white wafer. . . They each took the host the same way: the lips closing over it, but the mouth stretched high and taut to form a closed fleshy little cave. To chew the host, after all, was to chew Jesus. Bowing in piety and gratitude, they rose and went back to the dark pews to pray until the host softened and they could swallow (Hamill 1997, pp. 24-25).

"I AM A CANNIBAL"

> I have been assured by a very knowing American of my acquaintance in London, that a young healthy child well nursed is at a year old a most delicious, nourishing, and wholesome food, whether stewed, roasted, baked, or boiled; and I make no doubt that it will equally serve in a fricassee or a ragout.—**Jonathan Swift**, *A Modest Proposal and Other Satirical Works*

Tobias Schneebaum was born on New York's Lower East Side in 1922 and was raised in a family of Polish-Jewish immigrants in Brooklyn, (Fox 2005). A frequent visitor to Coney Island with his mother, he loved a sideshow attraction, "The Wild Man of Borneo" and came to love the books in the *Bomba the Jungle Boy* series, reading how the headhunters invaded tribes to decapitate some of them. "The minute I read Bomba, I knew that someday I would go live like him (Zalewski 2001, p. 57)." This is just what happened to this man who became an artist, with an artist's sensibilities and sensitivities. A bright boy, he attended Stuyvesant High School, an elite public high school, studied at City College of New York and at the Brooklyn Museum School of Art with the distinguished Mexican painter Rufino Tamayo. And nonetheless, he became a cannibal. His memoir, *Keep the River on Your Right* was made into a documentary film released in 2000 (Schneebaum 1969).

Although his abstract paintings in New York galleries gained some recognition, he suffered discrimination as a Jew and a gay man and felt deeply his otherness and alienation from society. In 1955 while in Peru on a Fulbright fellowship, he impulsively left the world of art museums for the rainforest, with no suitable clothing, equipment, companions, not even a map, only with the advice Catholic missionaries gave him to "keep the river on your right."

Chafing at societal restraints and wanted to get away from Western culture, he hitchhiked to central Peru, found his way into the Amazon jungle, and joined up with the isolated but friendly Arakmbut tribe. Hungry for a place that had not been touched by Western culture, where he would be accepted as he was, he ended up living with them for seven months (Schneebaum 1969; Zalewski 2001). No one knew what had happened to him. The U.S embassy in Lima had reported him dead, although months later, he emerged from the jungle wearing only body paint.

What had happened to him during the time he was missing is profoundly disturbing. He had been walking alone in the forest when he first met the naked Arakmbut. He stripped naked in response and smiled. They laughed in wonder at his tan lines, took him home, and treated him with affection. Word by word, they taught him their language, decorated his body with paint and shared their food with him. And at night, they welcomed Schneebaum into their communal hut into a warm tangled pile of bodies, which often became what we might call an orgy. Schneebaum was delighted that there seemed to be no categories of straight, gay, and bisexual. Having sex with a partner of the same or opposite sex, or with a group was all quite acceptable. As Schneebaum and his companions trekked through the forest, they slept on the stone slabs that jutted above the Amazon River, looking up at the moon. Schneebaum was a terrible hunter, always slipping and sliding on the muddy floor of the forest; he was moved that his gentle companions were amused, not irritated, by his pratfalls. It seemed to Schneebaum that he had found heaven on earth.

After months of living with the tribe, they went deeper into the forest, Schneebaum thinking it was a hunting expedition. It was a day in July or August, 1956, after trekking from dawn to dusk, when they stopped. Schneebaum could see a hut through the trees and could hear the men's voices inside. The women were cooking outside. All of a sudden, the Arakmbut charged, shouting and brandishing their spears. A wave of panic rose in Schneebaum's throat. He wanted to run but knew he was too far into the forest. He knew what was happening but could not look, and waited for the ritual killing to be over. In a flash, heaven on earth had become hell.

When the numbed and traumatized Schneebaum saw the six dead bodies, he turned away by himself to vomit. Then he began to chant the *Shema Yisrael* in the Hebrew he had learned as a boy: "Hear O Israel, the Lord is Our God, the Lord is one." The Arakmbut dismembered their victims, wrapping their body parts in leaves, giving Schneebaum one of the packages to carry. They captured women and children and returned to the forest. Soon they stopped and lit a fire. Laughing and in a triumphant mood, they began singing and dancing ecstatically. Initially, Schneebaum refused to join them and watched as his friend took a heart and "bit into it as if it were an apple, taking a large bite, almost half the heart, and chewed down several times, spit it into his hand, separated the meat into six sections, and placed some into the mouths of each of us" (Schneebaum 1969, p. 107). He ate the partially cooked meat. Later they continued homeward, stopping to sleep on a cool cluster of rocks in the river. Lying there, his sated companions asleep, Schneebaum could not sleep. He knew that it was time for him to get out of the jungle.

Although he went into the jungle to escape the oppressive mores of Western culture, he has struggled ever since with the fact that he broke one of its biggest taboos (Zalewski 2001, p. 56). Although Schneebaum's discovery of a very dark side to the Arakmbut shook him to the core, what shook him even more was that he had discovered that same dark side in himself. He had to acknowledge "I am a cannibal. . . . No matter into what far corner of my mind I push those words, they flash along the surface of my brain like news along the track that runs around the building at Times Square" (Schneebaum 1969, p. 110).

HUMAN SACRIFICE AND THE DEMON GOD

> To behave like beast of prey . . . betokens that one has ceased to be a man . . . that one has in some sort become a god. . . On the level of elemental religious experience, the beast of prey represents a higher mode of existence.
> —Mircea Eliade, *Rites and Symbols of Initiation: The Mysteries of Birth and Rebirth*

At the heart of all the religious traditions are concepts and practices meant to acquaint man with both the animal and the divinity within him. Although the tradition of human sacrifice became the core religious rite, it was also understood to be murder, a terrible moral transgression. In the more primitive religions, the god is fed through human sacrifice, meaning that the victim is a meal for the carnivorous predatory god. In the Old Testament story of the binding of Isaac, God asks Abraham to sacrifice his son Isaac on Mount Moriah (Genesis 22) and Abraham starts out to obey without questioning God's command. Some think that God was testing Abraham, which suggests that he does not want Abraham to really sacrifice his son. After binding Isaac to an altar, Abraham is stopped by the angel of the Lord at the last possible moment. Abraham then spies a ram entangled in some nearby bushes and sacrifices the ram instead of Isaac. Animal sacrifice is a more moral act. As man evolved, so did his mind and moral sense. At its best, religion provides guidance for living an ethical and moral life, offering man not only the opportunity to get to know his opposing states and their essential unity, as well as the opportunity to allow his divine self to triumph over his animal self.

We tend to divide the world into *them* and *us* according to any quality that makes others different from us: race, ethnicity, religion, sexual orientation, and politics. We demonize them, making them not human. Humankind is different from the other species in that we have the capacity to torture and murder other members of our species in cold blood and to threaten our species' very existence (de Zulueta 1994). But when we commit savage acts without remorse, as happens in wartime, it seems as if we too are no longer are human. The so-called holy wars, the wars in the name of religion, are the worst.

It has been said that war is hell. When soldiers believe they have God on their side, they can do anything (Ehrenreich 1997). Take the Crusades, the Inquisition, the jihads. Not only are soldiers expected to set aside all that was taboo in ordinary life, they are rewarded for doing so. For many, the fervor of wartime, the sense of losing oneself in the greater whole, can become an ecstatic experience.

When people kill in the name of God, they are worshipping the dark side of the demon-god. To transform oneself from prey to the predatory beast is to become godlike—like Titan Cronus who required human victims to feed his voracious appetite; or like Artemis, a "lion among women" who killed at her pleasure. Sometimes the demon-god is depicted as having a human body but the head of a beast. Being a demon-god means that one can transgress sacred taboos, break all the rules, have sex with children, or enjoy killing others.

The shocking truth is not only that torture and killing can be fun; it can be arousing, exciting, joyous, and even ecstatic. As a nation we could not get enough of the HBO series *The Sopranos*, watching week after week as Mafiosi maimed and murdered, some with detachment, others with glee. Nothing can bind a group of people together like a killing spree. Gang leaders know this, and slashing or killing someone is an initiation rite in some urban gangs. The Bloods originated in Los Angeles in the 1970s and later spread to New York with names like Gangsta Killer Bloods and Blood Stone Villains, Their motto, "blood in, blood out" means that they have to draw blood to get in and the only way a member can leave the gang is by his own natural death or his death at the hands of the gang (Farber 2000). This is especially true of prison gangs.

The Academy-Award-winning film *The Hurt Locker* begins with a quotation from *War Is a Force That Gives Us Meaning,* a best-selling book by war correspondent Chris Hedges (2002): "The rush of battle is a potent and often lethal addiction, for war is a drug" (Hedges 2002, p. 3). A Vietnam vet put it like this: "There is incredible . . . sense of power in killing five people. The only way I can equate it is to ejaculation. Just an incredible sense of relief, you know, that I did this. I was very powerful" (Baumeister 1999, p. 224).

Another, who did not want to return home from Vietnam, said, "I've been having a blast, killing dinks . . ." William Broyles Jr. , past editor of *Newsweek* and Marine officer in Vietnam, wrote that he loved war "in strange and troubling ways" (Jamison 2004, p. 260). After one battle, after many enemy soldiers had been killed and their naked bodies piled up for removal, he saw a look of saintly bliss on his colonel's face, the same expression he had seen in charismatic churches, the look of someone in the throes of ecstasy. "And I—what did I do, confronted with this beastly scene? I smiled back, as filled with bliss as he was. That was another of the times I stood on the edge of my humanity, looked into the pit, and loved what I saw there" (Jamison 2004, p. 260).

Several serial killers apparently got their start in war (Norris 1988; Baumeister 1997). Arthur Shawcross, a notorious murderer, thought his tour of duty in Vietnam was one of the best times in his life. He had the freedom to kill men, women, and children. Not only did he kill them, he tortured and mutilated his victims, at times dismembering them and eating parts. Joe Fischer, another serial killer, got his start in World War II. The war whet their appetites for more. Killing tasted too good to stop (Baumeister 1997).

The demon god was alive and well during the lynchings of blacks in the South. Some of them drew crowds of ordinary people, who brought picnic baskets and children, just as in 1941 the Poles in Jedwabne made a sporting event of beating, humiliating, and killing all but seven of the town's 1,600 Jews (Gross 2006). The dialectic of the demon-god was a driving force in those American soldiers who broke all the rules in Abu Ghraib, subjecting prisoners of war to sadistic, shameless criminal abuse. It was the same force in the psyches of the Islamic terrorists. The brutality of the Christian Crusades in conquering the Muslims and taking the Holy Land has produced a Muslim bitterness as alive today as if it happened yesterday, and a wish for revenge that is equally alive. Experiencing violence as sacred is the story behind the Palestinian *intifada* and the Islamic suicide/homicide bombings in Israel, Iraq, and in the United States on September 11, 2001.

Among Army personnel rates of suicide have grown considerably since the current conflicts in Iraq and Afghanistan began. For many of those who killed with abandon, once they return home to the everyday life and moral expectations, they become tortured by the horror of what they have done. This is when all the drinking in the world will not banish those ugly flashback memories and suicide becomes the drug of choice.

THE ECSTASIES OF HITLER'S WILLING EXECUTIONERS

Daniel Goldhagen and other historians have refuted the prevalent idea that those who carried out the genocide of Jews were mainly S. S. men or Nazi party members (Starkman, Steinitz, and Stern 2010). Ordinary German citizens, including Catholic and Protestant clergy as well as physicians, were *Hitler's Willing Executioners* (Goldhagen 1997; Lifton 1986). They heard their victim's screaming, saw their agony, smelled the death stink that often saturated the killing sites, and very often became literally stained with their blood.

A concrete example is the action of Police Battalion 101, a unit of the German Order Police. When they were first introduced to mass murder, the unit was comprised of 11 officers, 4 administrators, and 486 men. Major Wilhelm Trapp, the commander, was pale, choked up and had tears in his eyes when he announced that the battalion had a terribly unpleasant task to perform, not at all to his liking, but the orders came from the highest authorities and he had to obey. He suggested that it would make their task easier if the men could remember that the bombs were falling on women and children in Germany. His men were to concentrate the Jews in the village square, then remove them in smaller groups to the village's outskirts to shoot them. Trapp made a remarkable offer to his men, telling them that those who were not up to the task would be given other duties instead and would not be penalized. Despite his offer, of the 486 men, only a dozen stepped forward to be reassigned.

Ordinary citizens carried out "Jew-Hunts" (*Judenjagdeinsätze*), torturing and killing Jews willingly, zealously, at times even ecstatically. A belief that Jews were the demonic enemy was deep-rooted and pervasive in German society before Hitler came to power. Even a popular children's book, *The Poisoned Mushroom*, was an illustrated vicious account of the treachery of the Jews who, like poisoned mushrooms, appear good but are fatal. The final chapter expressed the necessity of purging the world of Jews.

> The German's use of the term "Jew-hunt" was not casual. It expressed the killers' conception of the nature of their activity and the attendant emotion. Theirs was the exterminatory pursuit of the remnants of a particularly pernicious species that needed to be destroyed in its entirety. Moreover the word *Jagd* has a positive *Gefuhlswert*, a positive emotional valence. Hunting is a pleasurable pursuit, rich in adventure, involving no danger to the hunter, and its reward is a record of animals slain—in the case of men of this police battalion and other German "Jew-hunters," a record of Jews ferreted out and killed. . . . (Goldhagen 1997, p. 238).
>
> This "hunt," "the likes of which mankind had never seen," was entirely typical for German ghetto-clearings. It was reminiscent of the "Jew-hunts" conducted both within the ghettos and in the countryside by the ordinary Germans of many police battalions . . . The overwhelming impression of those who ever witnessed a German ghetto clearing was that they were observing not men who were brought to their tasks reluctantly, but men driven by the passion, determination, tirelessness, and enthusiasm of religious zealots on a holy, redemptive mission (Goldhagen 1997, p. 396).

The collusion of the German people with Hitler's plan to annihilate the Jews as well as others who did not conform to his ideal of racial purity had violent origins that were both conscious and unconscious. Although the Romans were largely responsible for the crucifixion of Jesus, and despite the notion that Christianity is based on love, Christians have been given license to hate Jews through the development of an historically weak but psychologically attractive view that Jews were responsible for Jesus' crucifixion (Baumeister 1997; Carmichael 1992). Two parallel views of Jewish evil developed over the years, one secular and mundane, the other cosmic and metaphysical. Jews were depicted as greedy money lenders, even though because of job discrimination and prohibitions against Jews owning property, along with Christian prohibitions against money-lending, Jews became money-lenders. Money was considered to be *filthy lucre*, and Christians were not to be sullied by it. Jews were also believed to have supernatural powers connected with exotic, secret evil forces, so it was fitting that they take up money-lending. So it was no wonder that Jews were thought to be the devil and have horns.

There is a link between the high levels of violence in a culture and the effects of traumatic childhood and adult abuse. It is the victims' compulsion to repeat the trauma coupled with an inherent degree of aggression that is at the core of the traumatic origins of violence (de Zulueta 1994). It is through the compulsion to repeat the trauma that violence begets more violence (Farber 2000). In Alice Miller's work on violence's unconscious origins, she explains the Germans' collusion with Hitler in the Holocaust as being a function of their authoritarian upbringing, which was often emotionally and physically abusive, having as its aim the production of extremely obedient individuals (Miller 1983). She wrote of the remarkably positive reception the German edition received: "All I needed to do was describe Hitler's childhood in such a way that it served as a mirror and suddenly many Germans caught their reflections in it" (p. ix). In a detailed case study of Hitler, Miller demonstrates how his traumatic upbringing at the hands of physically abusive parents became dissociated from his understanding of his history. The Fuhrer and his people recreated a victorious version, projecting onto their Jewish victims all that they hated about themselves and their parents.

Even Germany's diplomats played a far greater part in carrying out the Holocaust's mission than has been previously known, as a new report about the Foreign Ministry's Nazi past demonstrates (Grieshaber 2010). For example, Franz Rademacher, head of the ministry's so-called Jew Department, went to Serbia to help organize the killing of Jews in eastern Europe. His travel expenses were found. itemizing "liquidation of Jews in Belgrade." In October 2010 an exhibit, *Hitler and the Germans: Nation and Crime* opened at the German Historical Museum in Berlin, advertised as the first in Germany to focus entirely on the fascination Hitler held for the Volk, the ordinary German citizen (Axelrod 2010; Starkman, Steinitz and Stern 2010). It opened just a few days after Friedrich Ebert Foundation's new study was released, finding that around 10 percent of Germans still wish they had a Fuhrer to tell them what to do during these difficult economic times. Constanze Stelzenmuller, a senior trans-Atlantic fellow with the German Marshall Fund of the U.S. in Berlin, said

> This exhibition is about Hitler and the Germans—meaning the social and political and individual processes by which much of the German people became enablers, colluders, co-criminals in the Holocaust . . . That this was so is now a mainstream view, rejected only by a small minority of very elderly and deluded people or the German extreme right-wing fringe. But it took us awhile to get there (Starkman, et al. 2010,p. A7).

It also took writer Ursula Hegi awhile to get there. She came from Germany to the U.S. when she was 18. As she got older and raised her own family, she became disturbed by questions about her roots and her native land her until she was compelled to write about them, and about the secrets Germans kept about their role in the Holocaust (Hegi 1994, 1997).

> 1950: The lens through which I am allowed to see as a child is narrow. I live within a family, a church, a school, a country that preaches obedience. My questions—even at age four, are met with reminders that it is a sin to doubt. I wander into a room where my parents and their friends are talking about some trains. They sound upset. When they see me, they stop. I ask about those trains. No one answers (Hegi 1997, pp. 29-31).
>
> Some people had sins attached to them like second skins, even the sins of their parents. . . . That skin of sin—the town wouldn't let the people take it off entirely even though everyone pretended it was not there. The town knew (Hegi 1994, pp 86-87).
>
> April 1984: I'm driving in my car with a lover, who notices a Velcro holder for my cigarette case on the inside lid of the glove compartment. "How efficient," he says. I want to spill coffee on my sweater, create a mess in my car—anything not to be called efficient. To me efficiency means the German efficiency, the concentration-camp efficiency. . . . (Hegi 1997, pp. 29-30

Nazism was a mass religion of nationalism with Hitler its demonic god. Ordinary citizens displayed *Mein Kampf* in their homes in the place usually reserved for the Bible, and even addressed prayers to the Fuhrer, who often compared himself to Jesus or the promised Messiah. The torch-lit rituals, stirring songs, and goose-stepping in unison all unleashed a monstrous wave of ecstatic fervor to rid Germany of its non-Aryan contamination.

Even Nazi physicians found ways to dissociate their minds from the demands of their Hippocratic Oath—to serve all humankind and above all do no harm (Lifton 1986). They used their medical ethics to justify their grotesque medical experiments (de Zulueta 1994). "Of course I am a doctor and

I want to preserve life. And out of respect for human life, I would remove a gangrenous appendix from a diseased body. The Jew is a gangrenous appendix in the body of mankind" (Lifton 1986, p.16).

THE ECSTASIES OF THE SUICIDE BOMBERS

A bizarre scene occurred in the Wall Street Café near Haifa less than a month before September 11, 2001. Mohammed Mahmoud Nasr walked into the cafe and lifted his shirt to exhibit his belt of explosives to the waitress, "Do you know what this is?" he asked, lighting the fuse. (Koret 2001) She screamed and threw a menu at him; the owner threw a chair and they all ran. But by the time Nasr screamed *Allah Akhbar* and blew himself up, there was no one left to take with him. It must have seemed like a miracle that all the people in the café escaped.

It really was not a miracle. Apparently, wanting so much to display his "equipment" to the waitress prevented Nasr from successfully completing his act. When what was left of his genital area was examined by Israeli forensic pathologists, semen was detected on his skin, leading them to conclude that he had ejaculated just before blowing himself up. Nasr could have just walked in and detonated the bomb. But he did not do that. He needed to make a sexual statement first, like the act of a flasher: "See my big powerful stick of dynamite. I'm going to kill you with it" (Koret 2001). His need to flaunt his "equipment" to the waitress caused him to ejaculate, preventing successful completion of his act. The forensic pathologists said that a suicide bomber's genital area is often trussed in protective material "to prevent excessive damage to the precious cargo. One would not want to disappoint the virgins!" (Koret 2001).

Death and sex are powerfully linked in the minds of the suicide bombers. To understand the ecstasy of the suicide bomber, one must understand something of cult psychology, because terrorists have become in reality members of a destructive mind control cult. The systematic methods used to produce a fanatic is essentially the same as those used in Reverend Moon's Unification Church, Scientology, and other cults (Hassan 2001; Khan 2010). Thinking gets reduced to extremes of belief in which members are indoctrinated to exercise blind obedience to the charismatic leader. Up until several years ago, suicide bombers in Gaza went through an intense indoctrination in which they were put into a coffin and buried, and told that they are dead already. Their training capitalized on their chanting and praying at least five times a day, which helped them go into a trance state, confident of their redemption and their new identity as martyrs as they prepare to kill themselves and others (Hassan 2001).

The source of their rage is not only poverty and lack of opportunity, because only some are poor and uneducated. It is not only the existence of Israel and the occupation. They grow up filled with rage and feel compelled to inflict it upon others (deMause 1995; Khan 2010; Glazov 2001). As children, they are abandoned by their families to the madras's, fundamentalist boarding schools, where they experience brutal criticism and are disciplined with physical violence. Their experience of adolescence includes much sexual repression because they have no permitted sexual outlet. Children are taught to be vehemently opposed to pleasure, and so masturbation is prohibited. Not only are unmarried men forbidden to touch women; they are prohibited from even looking at them, and so the sexual abuse of boys in the madras's is common (Khan 2010).

The September 11 hijackers had lived within a very sexually arousing Western culture but their own beliefs prohibited them from finding sexual satisfaction. The man's orgasmic need is the primary factor in sexual expression in fundamentalist Islamic culture. Only married men have sexual privileges and they have nothing to do with mutuality but with pleasure through violent domination. Therefore Islam allows the man to have four wives at a time. It has been something of a secret to Western culture that in the absence of a female sexual partner, it is acceptable for a man to take a boy to use as a woman (Glazov 2001). A man sexually penetrating another male is considered a manifestation of male power that has nothing to do with homosexuality. It is simply a man "doing what men do," in much the same way that it becomes acceptable in prison. Although the culture does not stigmatize boys who are abused this way, these boys are left traumatized, with no culturally sanctioned means of seeking justice.

They are prone to idealize and mirror their teachers, through the development of mirroring and idealizing transferences (Khan 2010; Kohut 1971), and are eager to perform to please them. By brainwashing and rhetoric, their murderous rage toward these authority figures becomes displaced onto a symbolic authority such as the United States, the infidels, the Jews. In adolescence there is no debate or discussion of values or beliefs, and so the development of a personal identity is foreclosed (Erikson 1950). They are unable to reconcile themselves with the knowledge that they will not live forever, which produces all the more the need for a religion that believes in immortality. Becoming a suicide bomber is a perfect solution, a compromise formation serving multiple psychic functions, among which is the manic defense against the knowledge that ultimately, they will die. It gratifies their murderous rage at the same time that they achieve their ego ideal of martyrdom. Their previously meaningless lives become meaningful as they become immortal heroes, experiencing eternal ecstasies with seventy-two black-eyed virgins. And to top it off, there may be a financial bonus for their proud families, as much as $10,000, which in Gaza is tremendous wealth.

Having been sodomized, they reenact the trauma by becoming suicide bombers, using terror to induce in their victims the same sense of terror and despair they have known their whole lives, waging a holy war against those who enjoy the sinful activities that are prohibited to them (Bodansky 1999). It is a way for anally raped men to reenact that which had been done to them, a manic defense against the knowledge that they were raped. With a sense of vengeful entitlement, they violently penetrated the World Trade Centers' phallic towers, symbolically raping a world superpower for the entire world to see on television. And we saw the Palestinians too on television, dancing for joy in the streets as they watched the news. Suicide bombers require massive sacrifices of human flesh and blood, and even then they are not satisfied. They are insatiable addicts, requiring more and more to feed their blood lust.

An Egyptian psychiatrist interviewed on popular Iqraa Television beamed gleefully as he explained that Western civilization has no concepts of self-sacrifice and honor, which is why the infidels fail to understand that the suicide bomber experiences "the height of ecstasy and happiness" just at the moment when, "ten, nine, eight, seven, six, five, four, three, two, one, and then he presses the button to blow himself up" (Tell 2002).

JAILHOUSE CONVERSIONS

> A sudden shift in belief systems (usually finding Jesus, but also Allah and probably every other Deity) after a period of incarceration. Usually a ploy for leniency with the legal system. Oddly, given the separation of church and state that we're supposed to have in this country, it does sometimes seem to have a positive effect when going to talk to the judge/parole board. Everyone from your local meth dealer to Manuel Noriega, Dictator of Panama, have tried this one, making it one of the truly 'oldest ones in the book.'
>
> —Urban Dictionary, *Jailhouse Conversion*

Every inmate becomes familiar with the jailhouse conversion. Charles Colson, the first member of the Nixon administration to be incarcerated for Watergate-related charges, had a jailhouse conversion. So did Susan Atkins and Tex Watson, both of the Manson Family, and serial killer David Berkowitz, also known as "Son of Sam," found Jesus. There is also a movement to transform inmates into religious and political extremists, welcoming violent ideologies such as white supremacy, or *prison Islam*.

Even relentless publicity-seeker Paris Hilton, who had served a 45-day jail sentence, had a jailhouse conversion (Fowler 2007). She spent three days in jail for reckless driving, and because of an undisclosed medical condition, was released to home confinement. An irate judge sent her back to jail the following day, to the medical ward of a maximum-security detention center.

She had called her mother and, discovering that her mother was already on another line with reporter Barbara Walters, Hilton then called Barbara Walters herself, saying that her jailhouse experience has changed her deeply. She said that she was reading the bible and seeking God. "Now, I would like to make a difference. ... God has given me this new chance."

THE ECSTASIES OF A BORN-AGAIN KILLER

> The Great Goddess everywhere demands sacrifices, because the decisive moments in the life of the female —menstruation, deflowering, conception, and childbearing—are intimately bound up with a sacrifice of blood.
> —Erich Neumann, *The Great Mother: An Analysis of the Archetype*

Barbara Ehrenreich tells us that scholars consistently misrepresent the archaic goddesses by minimizing her more savage inclinations.

> Some of the earliest deities worshipped by humans were female, but they were hardly the nurturing 'earth mothers' imagined by so many later scholars, both male and female. The archaic goddess . . . was a huntress, a consumer of sacrificial offerings, and, most strikingly, an anthropo-morphized version of the predator beast" (Ehrenreich 1997, p. 97).

One of the most murderous predators was the Hindu goddess Kali, who wears a necklace of skulls, and carries a bloodied ax and a giant's severed head.. She is most demanding of blood sacrifices, especially "the human blood offered by frenzied, self-mutilating cult worshippers" (Ehrenreich 1997, p. 101). No wonder that she is often depicted with blood streaming from her mouth.

Kali's American double is Karla Faye Tucker, who committed the most brutal murders and became the first woman executed in Texas since the Civil War (Lowry 1998). According to Joseph Geringer's account, (2000), Karla's older sister Kari, a prostitute, as was Karla, wanted a sex orgy to celebrate her birthday. The party went on for three days, aided by beer, whisky, tequila, Placidyl, Dilaudid, Valium, Mandrax, coke, and bathtub speed. That night Karla, a "needle freak" (Levine 1974), who loved the feel of a needle in her arm as much as she loved violence, was shooting up coke when a fight broke out. She watched as her boyfriend Danny bludgeoned another man's head with a hammer. Her thighs tingled and she was drawn to it like a magnet. Karla grabbed a pick ax and sliced into the torso of Deborah Thornton. Deborah screamed and began to gurgle blood, a sound which angered Karla, so she tore into her again and again, in the chest, legs, stomach and shoulders. The more the body quivered, the more Karla struck, again and again. As Deborah's body turned to mush, blood splattered everywhere and onto Karla. She was ecstatic at hearing the whoosh of the axe, the squish of the blade penetrating Deborah's flesh. When she had finished with her, she finished off the other man with another twenty blows. Later Karla Faye bragged to friends that what she'd done had put her in the same league with the big boys.

By the time of her execution, Tucker had not only become born again, she had also become Texas's most controversial figure on any state's death row. She had become "the sweetheart of death row," redeemed and transformed into something of a goddess or saint. I can only assume that the bleakness of prison, a death sentence, and anticipation of burning in hell can readily be transformed into a manic defense, an omnipotent fantasy in which she was born-again into a new and ever-lasting life.

Karla's change was so dramatic that many came to love and respect her, believing that the sweetheart of death row had, as one lawyer claimed, left behind her evil self and had become someone new, good and as loving as a puppy (Lowry 1998). Not only was Karla penitent, she was pretty, sexy, and charming, having all the qualifications of a perfect sacrificial lamb and media star. She gave interviews on television talk shows and on Pat Robertson's Christian *700 Club*. She inspired many thousands worldwide to come to Jesus or to renew their relationship with him. Pope Paul II and television evangelist Pat Robertson pleaded for mercy for her. Even the families of some of her murdered victims did. Her born-again Christianity ignited debates all over the world over redemption and retribution on death row. Less than three weeks before her execution, Larry King asked on his television show what it felt like to be moving toward her execution. She said it was exciting. In the days before her execution she spoke to her friend and biographer, telling him that in Heaven she'll look different:

> She's as radiant as a heater, turned up high as she speaks. She plucks at the skin at her wrist. "This is not who we are," she says. "We are much more beautiful than this. And up there?" She points toward the ceiling. "I'll be in a glorious state. I'll be in a different form. But I'll recognize people I don't even know. I'll know people by name, even if I've never met them. . . . Oh, I'm going to be busy! A lot of people have asked me to take messages to their families and friends. I have a whole lot of people to say hello to." . . . She reads from the Bible, a description of Jesus making the way for others into Heaven (Lowry 1998, p. 69).

Tucker apologized to her victims' families: "I hope God will give you peace with this. I am going face to face with Jesus now. I love all of you very much. I will see you all when you get there. I will wait for you." After the lethal injection was administered, her supporters gathered together, rejoicing and singing of her ascension to heaven, as if she were the Virgin Mary. "Alleluia! Alleluia!"

Chapter Ten

Creative Ecstasies

Creativity—like human life itself—begins in darkness.
—Julia Cameron, *The Artist's Way: A Spiritual Path to Higher Creativity*

Artistic temperament sometimes seems a battleground, a dark angel of destruction and a bright angel of creativity wrestling.
—Madeleine L'Engle, *Love-Quotes.com*

Although Alice Flaherty had always written more than most people, she certainlyhad n o intention of writing a book when she was a neurology resident, working up to 110 hours a week. She took notes so compulsively that it managed to take over her life; the notes were transformed into her first book, *The Massachusetts General Hospital Handbook of Neurology* (Flaherty and Post 2000), described as the most widely used neurology text in its class. Then she became pregnant and gave birth to stillborn twin boys. She sank into a deep depression for ten days when suddenly she became wildly agitated and full of ideas, scribbling them on her arm while driving or on toilet paper while in the bathroom. Her writing had spiraled out of control, and had become hypermanic ecstasies of writing, a manic defense against her terrible sense of loss. She ricocheted daily between euphoria and terror.

> On good days, ideas would wake me at four in the morning, tendrils of words coiling around me like some heady perfume. It was as if a door had opened onto a hot wind from the tropics . . . On bad days, the words were like a charnel house through which I had to search for the bodies of people I loved. In either case, the desire to write was overpowering. I wrote during department meetings, when I should have been doing experiments, when I could have been with friends. The sight of a computer keyboard or a blank page gave me the same rush that drug addicts get from seeing their freebasing paraphernalia. . . The world was flooded with meaning, I believed I had unique access to

> the Kingdom of Sorrow, about which I had an obligation to enlighten my—very tolerant—friends and colleagues through essays and letters. While postpartum major depression occurs after one in ten deliveries, postpartum mania occurs after one in a thousand. . . .
> Why pathologize this and call it a disease? I could still do my normal job. But my writing *felt* like a disease: I could not stop, and it sucked me away from family and friends. Sensations outside of language dried up: music became irritating discord, the visual world grew faint. . . . While my hypergraphia felt like a disease, it also felt like one of the best things that has ever happened to me. It still does (Flaherty 2004, pp. 11–12).

The psychiatric unit where Alice Flaherty was hospitalized was the same one where she later became a neurological consultant. Diagnosed with bipolar illness, her wildly shifting moods were stabilized with the help of medication and her hypermanic writing calmed down (Flaherty 2004). Some people who suffer from bipolar disorder are what are known as "rapid cyclers," in which a period of depression or mania can, in some cases, last only a few minutes before the patient retreats back into the opposite mode. Rapid-cycling bipolar disorder, which seems to be what Flaherty has, is the most dangerous kind because the person is more likely to attempt suicide (Garcia-Amador, Colom, Valenti, Horga, and Vieta 2009) or kill himself unintentionally when acting on omnipotent grandiose beliefs.

The relationship between mood and creative productivity is a very complex one. Certainly, pathological conditions can produce wild ecstasies of writing, but at the same time, writing can be a healthy activity, arising from the evolutionary drive to communicate needs.

THE NATURE OF CREATIVITY

> If we had to say what writing is, we would have to define it essentially as an act of courage.
> —Cynthia Ozick

> Writers are not just people who sit down and write. They hazard themselves. Every time you compose a book your composition of yourself is at stake.
> —E. L. Doctorow

When we think of creativity, we tend to think of its products—a painting, poem, piece of music, or scientific discovery—but understanding the creative process itself is something that eludes us, despite the volume of material written about it by scientists and creative people themselves. It is commonly thought that the creative person works hard to solve a particular problem, but it is when that person is not consciously focused on the problem, such as when he is on vacation, or sleeping, or taking a walk that the creative solution mysteriously presents itself. It is also thought that the ordinary person may turn to painting, writing or other creative activity and finds that it has transformed the quality of his life (Rothenberg 1990). The focus here will be on writing rather than other media for two reasons, the first simply because the writer's creative world is most directly accessible to us because words are a more conceptual medium than form, sound, color, movement, or film. The second is because writing, along with my psychoanalytic work, are my primary creative media and so are the ones I have thought about the most and know best from the inside and outside.

Freud (1908) thought that the play of children and adult day dreaming were both creative processes, the main difference being that adults do not openly speak of their daydreams while children play openly.

> The opposite of play is not what is serious but what is real. In spite of all the emotion with which he cathects his world of play, the child distinguishes it quite well from reality; and he likes to link his imagined objects and situations to the tangible and visible things of the real world. This linking is all that differentiates the child's "play" from "phantasying."
>
> As people grow up, then, they cease to play, and they seem to give up the yield of pleasure which they gained from playing. . . . What appears to be a renunciation is really the formation of substitute or surrogate. In the same way, the growing child, when he stops playing, gives up nothing but the link with real objects; instead of playing, he now phantasies. He builds castles in the air and creates what are called daydreams (Freud 1908, pp. 144–45).

Csikszentmihzlyi (1997) told us that so much of that which is vital, human, and exciting comes about through creativity. While involved in creative work, we feel more alive than most any other time. Creativity is a central source of meaning in our lives, offering one of the most exciting models for living. It usually involves crossing the boundaries of domains (Csikszentmihzlyi 1997), for example neurology and writing, as Alice Flaherty has done.

Dictionaries defines creativity as bringing something new into being, which involves the ability to think in different domains and make the connections between them. Melanie Klein (1957) thought that one of the deepest anxieties in men and women relates to the capacity for creativity. Writer Katherine Anne Porter thought that for writers, courage was the first essential. Anxiety is inevitable, says Ralph Keyes (2003) in *The Courage to Write.* Many authors have begun writing a book, only to abandon it after years of work. This can happen out of anxiety, despair, frustration, ambition, inexperience, even previous success.

This is what happened to Michael Chabon. He was writing *Fountain City,* a sequel to his first novel, *The Mysteries of Pittsburgh,* but after five and a half years, feeling the book "erasing me, breaking me down, burying me alive, drowning me, kicking me down the stairs" (Kois 2011, p. 27), he stopped. That was in 1992. He wrote in the margin "A book itself threatens to kill its author repeatedly during its composition." He said that "Often when I sat down to work, I would feel a cold hand take hold of something inside my belly and refuse to let go. It was the Hand of Dread." The writer's life is not an easy one but when he fights back at the Hand of Dread, he can produce something marvelous. It is the combination of novelty and value that makes us both appreciate and envy the creative person's ability to play with thoughts, ideas, feelings, and images.

Envy can be such a destructive feeling, hurting not only the person who is envied but also the one who is envious. Writer Anne Lamott wrote about her hateful feeling toward other authors who were published. "But if you continue to write, you are probably going to have to deal with it, because some wonderful, dazzling successes are going to happen for some of the most awful, angry, undeserving writers you know—people who are, in other words, not you" (Lamott 1995, p. 122). When we are unaware of our envy of another's creativity, this creates an anxiety about our creative ambitions which can thwart our own creativity (Ellman 2000). When I became aware of my own envy of others' creativity, it began to free me up to use my creativity more fully (Farber 2005b). For many years, I had jotted down some ideas but did not have the confidence to develop them further. I read many professional papers, some written by people I knew. I envied them their status as published authors and did not like the hateful way my envy made me feel. But still, I never submitted anything I had written for publication. When I decided to get my PhD, the application process included an essay about why I wanted to get the doctorate, and I wrote that the primary motivation was to resolve a conflict or inhibition about writing professionally. *Feel the Fear and Do It Anyway* (Jeffers 1988), the title of a pop psychology book came to my mind. I had struggled with anxieties about writing over and over in my personal analysis, but I intuitively suspected that if I had to write lots of papers and a dissertation, that experience might get me to do some more self-analysis to face and resolve the conflict. It was the same thing Freud (1926) recommended to patients who were phobic; put yourself in the anxiety-provoking situation and observe the thoughts that emerge. A colleague had a paper published in a journal, and there I was, once again envious. Not only that, but I found her paper faulty so I sat down and wrote a long letter to the editor about it. To my great surprise, it was published in the next issue of the journal (Farber 1991). That was my first professional publication, a painless one, because when I sent it out, it was not with the intention of it being published (Farber 2005b). But once I had the experience of being published, that provided the confidence to submit work with the intention of getting it published. I had more work published and stopped hating published writers. I sometimes initiated contact with some writers whose work I admired, some of whom continue to be helpful to my writing career.

Creative people have brains that allow them to think and see in unusual ways, unconstrained by boundaries or stereotypes about what they can or cannot do (Andreason 2006). Even if they have a dominating passion; they grow throughout life, always exploring new interests that further develop their brains. They are richly and freely associational, tapping into thinking processes that are uncensored and do not involve a conscious organization of events into a linear account, which makes their brains unusually receptive and actively open to the external and inner world. Freud was a creative thinker and commented that often his writing reads more like short stories than serious science. "Like other neuropathologists, I was trained to employ local diagnoses and electro-prognosis, and it still strikes me myself as strange that the case histories I write should read like short stories and that, as one might say, they lack the stamp of serious science" (Freud 1893, p. 160f.).

When Freud began to use free association, he was following an obscure intuition which can be traced to Ludwig Borne, the first boyhood author in whose work Freud became absorbed (Freud 1920b; Jones 1953; Farber 2005a). At fourteen, he received a gift of Borne's collected works, the only books he kept from his adolescence. Many years later when he visited Père Lachaise, Borne's and Heine's graves were the only ones he visited (Jones 1953). Borne had written an essay in 1823, "The Art of Becoming an Original Writer in Three Days," which Freud took to heart and which also has become today's standard advice for writers (Cameron 1992; Farber 2005a).

> Here follows the practical prescription I promised. Take a few sheets of paper and for three days in succession write down, without any falsification or hypocrisy, everything that comes into your head. Write what you think of yourself, of your women, of the Turkish War, of Goethe, of the Fonk criminal case, of the Last Judgment, of those senior to you in authority—and when the three days are over you will be amazed at what novel and startling thoughts have welled up in you. That is the art of becoming an original writer in three days (Jones 1953, pp. 156-57).

Associational linkages occur in the association cortex, the same region found active during the randomly wandering free association process of psychoanalysis and psychoanalytic psychotherapy (Andreason 2006). This ability can be a blessing because it makes the creative person creative, but it can also be a curse, because it makes him vulnerable to brain disorders. Linkages of association have been found to be aided by REM sleep (Wagner, Gais, Haider, Verleger, and Born 2004). It is sound to advise someone in search of a solution to a problem to sleep on it. Often they will awaken with a solution. Some of this book was created this way, with awakening in the morning with the urge to rush to the computer with a new idea.

I have found that my creative patients can use psychotherapy differently from other patients, free associating more readily and more able to rapidly synthesize the opposing forces of their personalities in a way that is more difficult for those who are not creative. They often can achieve in fewer sessions what might require a greater number of sessions for someone else.

THEORIES OF CREATIVITY

> A creative writer is one for whom writing is a problem.
> —Roland Barthes, *Writing Degree Zero*

What Csikszentmihalyi (1991) tells us is that what seems to drive creative people is the pleasure gained by doing the work they do. Becoming rich or famous is a nice bonus, if it happens, but it is not what drives them to create. Creative people simply love what they do, because it produces an optimal experience which has been called *peak experience* (Maslow 1964) and *flow* (Csikszentmihalyi 1991). This experience was described in the same way, almost word for word, regardless of the different activities that produced it (Csikszentmihalyi 1991). Scientists, artists, athletes, religious mystics, and even ordinary working people described their most gratifying experiences with similar words, regardless of age, culture or gender.

Csikszentmihalyi (1991) found that nine main elements in creativity were mentioned repeatedly. First, the creative person knows clearly what he wants to do and how to do it. Second, what he does provides immediate feedback. The musician knows whether the note played is the right one; the writer knows when the words he selected and how they are put together are the right words. Third, his skills are on par with his challenges. Fourth, in a state of mindfulness, there is no distinction between his actions and his awareness. Fifth, without any effort, he excludes any distractions from consciousness. He is aware only of what is pertinent in the here and now. Sixth, there is no concern about failure, no anxiety. The creative person is too involved in what he is doing to think about failing or succeeding. Seventh, his self-consciousness disappears as his sense of self expands, and he emerges from the experience of flow with a stronger sense of self. Eighth, he loses any sense of time; several hours may pass in what seems like a few minutes. And last, the activity itself becomes an end in itself, not the means to an end.

Anne Lamott described the subjective experience superbly to students at her writing workshops, telling them that

> they may even go from wanting to have written something to just wanting to be writing, wanting to be working on something, like they'd want to be playing the piano or tennis, because writing brings with it so much joy, so much challenge. It is work and play together. . . . I also tell them that sometimes

> when my writer friends are working, they feel better and more alive than they do at any other time. And sometimes, when they are writing well, they feel that they are living up to something. It is as if the right words, the true words, are already inside them, and they just want to help them get out. . . . I want the people who come to my classes to have this feeling. too (Lamott 1995, xxix-xxxi).

Certain conditions are required for flow to occur (Csikszentmihalyi 1991). A problem to be solved may be assigned, which triggers the creative process, or a gap in the network of knowledge may reveal the goal, which is achieved by filling the gap. The goal is not so easily revealed for the creative person, because when the problem is a more creative one, what has to be done is not so clear. In cases like this, the creative person must develop some unconscious or intuitive means to tell him what to do. But when the creative person does not have specific performance goals to be met, how can he know, day in and day out, he is wasting his time or actually accomplishing something? It seems that those who keep on doing creative work have succeeded in taking the field's criteria of judgment and making it their own so that they can provide themselves with responses and not have to rely on experts to know how they are doing.

When these conditions occur, the creative process seems to happen serendipitously. Poet Mark Strand described it like this to Csikszentmihalyi:

> Well, you're right in the work, you lose your sense of time, you're completely enraptured, you're completely caught up in what you're doing, and you're sort of swayed by the possibilities you see in this work. If that becomes too powerful, then you get up, because the excitement is too great. You can't continue to work or continue to see the end of the work because you're jumping ahead of yourself all the time. The idea is to be so . . . so *saturated* with it that there's no future or past, it's just an extended present in which you're, uh, making meaning. And dismantling meaning, and remaking it. Without undue regard for the words you're using. It is meaning carried to a high order. It's not just essential communication, daily communication; it's a *total* communication. When you're working on something and you're working well, you have the feeling that there's no other way of saying what you're saying (Csikszentmihalyi 1997, p. 121).

One might conclude that flow and happiness are the same, but this is not so, says Csikszentmihalyi. The relationship is more complex.

> First of all, when we are in flow, we do not usually feel happy—for the simple reason that in flow we feel only what is relevant to the activity. Happiness is a distraction. . . . It is only after we get out of flow, at the end of a session or in moments of distraction within it, that we might indulge in feeling happy. . . . In the long run, the more flow we experience in daily life, the more likely we are to feel happy overall (Csikszentmihalyi 1997, p. 123).

Dean Simonton (1999) has proposed an evolutionary theory of creativity, suggesting that the genius is able to generate a diverse range of ideas, recombine them, and from them, choosing the "fittest" with which to proceed. In this evolutionary model, there are three stages of the development of creative ideas. In the first, the creator produces many different ideas, then the bad ideas are weeded out, either by the creator or critics. Then the surviving ideas, the fittest, generate new ideas, and the process repeats.

Psychoanalytic theories of creativity argue that creativity resides in the unconscious, with creative work serving to transform or sublimate excess libidinal energy into a more publicly acceptable, valued form (Freud 1908). Extending this theory, Ernst Kris (1952) argued that creativity requires a balance between primary and secondary process thinking. Primary process is concrete, associative, and irrational, the thought process of dreams, while secondary process is abstract, language-based, and logical. Some non-psychoanalytic researchers also use a two-process model of creativity, some referring to focused and unfocused attention, others, notably Csikszentmihalyi, refer to divergent and convergent thinking.

Kleinians, especially Hanna Segal, believe creativity is a response to the destructiveness and emptiness engendered by depression (Segal 1952).

> All artists aim at immortality; their objects must not only be brought back to life, but also life has to be eternal. And of all human activities art comes nearest to achieving immortality; a great work of art is likely to escape destruction and oblivion (Segal 1952, p. 207).

This seemed to be true for Freud, who, early on, knew how writing was of therapeutic benefit (Farber 2005a). He wrote a tremendous volume of material throughout his career, even while his body was ravaged with cancer. While he was absorbed in writing, he gained a desired space and freedom from the pain life imposed upon him, which helped him recover from the feelings of passivity and receptivity of his clinical hours (Mahony 2002; Farber 2005a). Alternating between darker and lighter moods, he said that he did some of his best writing when mildly depressed or in bad health, and had to learn to trust his moods (Flem 2003; Mahony 1987; Farber 2005a). Joyce Carol Oates, a most prolific author, said "I have forced myself to begin writing when I've been utterly exhausted, when I've felt my soul as thin as a playing card . . . and somehow the activity of writing changes everything." Hemingway said, far less poetically "When I don't write, I feel like shit" (Brand 1989; Farber 2005a p. 257; Flaherty 2004, p. 206).

We experience the world through our senses and so how the body feels and what it can do has the potential to be enjoyable and to produce the experience of flow. Walking, talking, singing, eating, speaking, writing, dancing all can produce flow (Csikszentmihalyi 1997). A recent Swedish study showed that the experience of flow is reflected in biological processes (de Manzano 2010; de Manzano, Theorell, Harmat, and Ulena 2010). Four studies based on three different methodologies were conducted, in which professional classical pianists were asked to play a musical piece five times and rate the state of flow after each performance. De Manzano and associates said that when arterial pulse pressure, breathing, head movements, and activity from certain facial muscles were measured for each performance, a "significant relation was found between flow and heart period, blood pressure, heart rate variability, activity of the *zygomaticus major* muscle, and respiratory depth (de Manzano 2010, p. 3 ; de Manzano, et al. 2010, p. 303)."

My own speculation about a theory of creativity is related to my thinking about ecstasy. To attain a state of ecstasy, it is likely that there occurs a process of tumescence and release (Laski 1961). There is a kindling of tension, increasing and building, at the same time that the frontal and temporal lobe circuits governing fear and anxiety increasingly shut down, resulting in a state in which no emotion is experienced, just sheer release from restraint. To go into the state of flow, which is not the same as ecstasy but may well lead to it, there is a gradual release from a state of anxiety or creative block, with the frontal and temporal lobe circuits steadily slowing down.

THE DRIVE TO WRITE

> The writer writes in order to teach himself, to understand himself, to satisfy himself; the publishing of his ideas, though it brings gratification, is a curious anticlimax.
>
> —Alfred Kazin

There are many writers, some with talent, and some without, who write because they love to write. Generating volumes of text is not enough to make it really creative; talent is needed to bring something new and of value into the world (Simonton 1999; Flaherty 2004). Talent plays a part in Simonton's selection stage, in which passages of poor quality are edited out. As Flaherty puts it, "the drive to write produces a first draft; it is the drive to write well that produces the second, third, the twentieth. . . a concept that includes, but is not limited to, everything from apt word choice to plot twists to philosophical insight to a sense of what will appeal to the audience" (Flaherty 2004, p. 54). Sometimes an outside editorial eye is needed, especially for writers who have the drive to write and do not know when to stop.

New writers tend to hug their words close to their chest and are so loathe to part with them that you might think editing is equivalent to maiming and mutilating their perfect newborn child. Having felt this way, I had considered writing a paper called "On Falling in Love with My Own Words." Years later, having had three whole chapters edited out of my first book as well as other big chunks of text, I am no longer so in love with my words, and can do a better job of editing.

The truly creative writer requires both the drive to create but talent as well, each of which is largely controlled by different regions of the brain (Flaherty 2004). It has become a popular notion that the right side of the brain was the source of creativity, producing a number of books with titles such as *Right Brain, Write On!* (Downey 1984). Then when *Drawing on the Right Side of the Brain* (Edwards 1979) was published a few years later, it became an instant bestseller, and the concept became even more popular. The problem with it, said Flaherty (2004), is that it was too simplified; it is true about painting and music, but in writing, it is the left hemisphere that is activated, along with the temporal lobes and limbic system, closely associated with right hemisphere functioning.

> the temporal lobes are important for producing literature, in part because they are necessary for understanding word meaning—and also Meaning in its philosophical senses. In addition, changes in the temporal lobes can produce hypergraphia. A second region of the brain that is surprisingly relevant to creative writing is the limbic system, the seat of emotion and drive . . . The limbic system connects more strongly to the temporal lobes than to any other region of the cortex. This strong link underlies the importance of of emotion and drive to creativity . . . —The limbic system also reflects the way mood swings can drive creativity. The temporal lobes and the limbic system appear to underlie the drive to seek beauty and meaning in nonliterary forms of artistic achievement as well. . . . (Flaherty 2004, pp. 4-5).

A study of frontal lobe activity in people doing creative work found that those who performed creatively had increased frontal lobe activity, while those whose performance was dull had decreased activity (Carlsson, Wend, and Risberg 2000). The limbic system is the source of dopamine, the brain chemical that is part of the reward system critical to all addictions (Volkow, Fowler, and Wang, 2004; Zuger 2011). Nora Volkow, the neuroscientist in charge of the National Institute on Drug Abuse said that "addiction is all about the dopamine" (Zuger 2011, p. D1), a concept which can help us to understand the addictive nature of the drive to write. The drive to write is not a core emotion like joy or fear and is not a biological drive in the way that hunger or sexual desire is; it is almost strong enough to be an instinct, growing out of the more basic drive to communicate (Flaherty 2004; Pinker 1995). Flaherty tells us that it is emotion, the powerful wish to communicate, that drives language. Psychotherapists and attuned mothers know that the way we use language can improve mood. When we use words to empathize with another, the listener's mood benefits. When we vent to someone, our mood benefits. (This is one reason that psychotherapy benefits both the patient and the psychotherapist.) Language has the power to worsen mood when the listener is the target of contempt or abuse. That childhood rhyme "Sticks and stones may break my bones but words will never harm me," is not at all correct. And when the drive to communicate is hindered, as, for example, an American who does not speak French moves to Paris or a writer suffers writer's block, powerful neural changes result (Flaherty 2004).

Neil Selinger retired at 54 from his law practice to do what he really wanted to do—write and do some volunteer work. He signed up for a writing class at Sarah Lawrence College. Two years later, amyotrophic lateral sclerosis (Lou Gehrig's disease) was diagnosed. He rapidly declined, going from cane to walker to wheelchair to almost complete immobility, to pureed food, losing his ability to speak. "As my muscles weakened, my writing became stronger. As I slowly lost my speech, I gained my voice. As I diminished, I grew. As I lost so much, I finally started to find myself" (Appelbome 2011, p. A14). His writing class eventually moved to his house. His recently published memoir, *A Sloan Product: A Memoir of a Lost Boy,* began when he was well and was finished when he still had the ability to type with one finger (Selinger 2011).

People who are suffering, whether it be from illness, loss, depression, post-traumatic stress, or narcissistic injury (insult to self-esteem), comprise the largest group of amateur writers (Flaherty 2004). "Suffering triggers limbic system and temporal lobe activity through their roles in emotion, and . . . increases the desire to write and communicate" (Flaherty 2004, p. 42). Numerous researchers, writers, and clinicians have found that writing can be therapeutic by promoting the ability to reflect about oneself (Bolton, Howlett, Lago and Wright 2004; Brand 1989; Freud 1908; Keyes 2008; Mallon 1986; Pennebaker 1991; de Salvo 1999; Farrow 1942; Farber 2005, 2007). Several studies have confirmed that writing on personally chosen subjects intensified positive emotions and diminished negative ones (Brand 1989). When students wrote about their most hurtful experiences and their feelings about them, their immune function improved, measured by a decrease in the number of doctor visits to a college health center (Pennebaker 1991).

Words are very powerful. Consider how God is said to have created the world; he spoke it into existence. "And God said, 'Let there be light; and there was light" (Genesis 1,3). When writers use words to bridge a sense of isolation, not only does the writer struggle to say it to others but to himself. Like the proverbial tree that falls in the forest and someone hears or sees it, putting it into words makes it real, whether the words are spoken or written (Farber 2005a). Patients suffering from alexithymia have great difficulty in putting their feelings into words (Taylor, Bagby, and Parker 1991; Taylor and Bagby 2005), which makes them detached or dissociated from their emotional selves (Clayton 2004).

Constructed writing tasks have been used as a therapeutic adjunct to treatment in eating disorders (Bolton, Howlett, Lago, and Wright, 2004; Schmidt, Bone, Hems, Lessem, and Treasure 2002). I began to introduce writing in my group therapy for women struggling with compulsive eating and body image issues, problems that are extremely resistant to traditional psychoanalytic treatment (Farber 1995a). All could do it readily in the group, but resisted writing when they were alone. It felt too lonely and made them too anxious to tolerate it. That led me to introduce it into the individual psychotherapy session of some alexithymic patients. It began when a patient in my eating disorder group asked during her individual session if she could write at that moment, saying that she would feel safer writing in my presence than writing alone. It was her idea, not mine, and because she seemed to know what she needed, I agreed to try it. I suggested she write about the particular problem we had been talking about; she was stuck there, and I sat there with her while she wrote. There was no hesitation at all, and five minutes of writing unleashed grief and facilitated the working through of unresolved mourning. Writing the words and seeing them on the page made the feelings real, and once they were written, then they could be spoken (Farber 2005a).

This worked well for several alexithymic patients, some with eating disorders, some who mutilated themselves or had some other psychosomatic disorder, who were used to using their bodies to speak of terrible past trauma. All these self-harm behaviors are action symptoms. It is easier for them to take action, to do something, than to speak of their emotions (Krueger 2002). Writing about their thoughts or feelings presented them with a compromise; it was doing something, a physical action, that led to thinking and then speaking about their feelings.

Another motivation for writing is the wish to be known and remembered. Some may write for an idealized reader (Farber 2005; Mallon 1986), who would read and accept without making judgments. Some may write to be remembered, even by those they may have never met. William Souter, a Scottish poet, wrote in his diary "Why do we wish to be remembered, even when none remain who looked upon our face. Surely, though it must retain an element of self-consideration, it is a last acknowledgment that we need to be loved; and, having gone from all touch, we trust that memory may, as it were, keep our unseen presence within the borders of day" (from William Soutar's diary, 1943, quoted by Mallon 1986, frontispiece). It is so gratifying when I hear from someone who has read something I have written, from a real person who calls or emails to connect with me, another real person. I know that as I get older, it is a comfort to know that my publications will remain after I am gone.

THE COMPULSION TO WRITE AND ENDLESSLY WRITE

> A creative artist works on his next composition because he is not satisfied with his previous one. When he loses a critical attitude toward his own work, he ceases to be an artist.
> —Dmitri Shostakovich

For some patients, writing can become the container for thoughts and feelings, can serve as a tool for further self-investigation, can ease the resistance to free association, lead one away from symptom formation, promote enhanced ego functioning, and can at times become a sublimation (Farber 2005). When suffering from post-traumatic stress, writing can express feelings and thoughts that had been dissociated. For example, Louise DeSalvo, an English professor and author of *Writing as a Way of Healing: How Telling Our Stories Transforms Our Lives*, experienced sexual abuse, the suicide of her sister, and other trauma. "We can write not to express feelings we don't have, but to discover what we might have felt if we hadn't been terrified" (DeSalvo 1999, p. 166).

But compulsive writing can also serve as a resistance to treatment. When the writer has an unconscious conflict about bringing forth his creation, he may continue to write obsessively and compulsively, not finishing it. Just as spoken free association can be used in the service of resistance, writing too can be used this way, and can become a solitary activity of obsessive rumination."It is critical to distinguish whether the patient's writing is object-directed and serves creative, self-observational functions or whether it is a resistant narcissistic withdrawal from object relations" (Farber 2005, p. 250). I have found that writer's block can be what Bergler (1954) called a kind of creative impotence or in my words, a form of psychic constipation. Two patients who were writers reported independently of each other that when they began to write after a period of being blocked, their bowel functioning improved and they felt more alive sexually (Farber 2005).

In the first chapter, you read about Dr. Susan Kavaler-Adler, who conducts workshops on the parallels between psychoanalytic practice and Argentine tango. The same Susan Kavaler-Adler is a psychoanalyst with a special interest in creativity, particularly writing, and has written about the problems writers may encounter. They may spend their lives compulsively driven to create and locked up in their work, with little meaningful interpersonal contact, a profile she calls the demon lover. She has given accounts of distinguished female writers (Sylvia Plath, Anais Nin, Emily Dickinson, Charlotte and Emily Bronte, and Edith Sitwell), who succumbed to the lure of the demon lover, and suffered terrible fates, including withdrawal from people and suicide. In her book, *The Compulsion to Create: Women Writers and Their Demon Lovers* (Kavaler-Adler 1993), she raises and explores the question of why some very talented women writers manage to heal themselves from the self-destructive relationship with their compulsion and why others fail. She asked several related and significant questions.

> Is the creative process freely motivated and interactive with interpersonal life? Or is it a closed system of compulsive repetition that may allow cathartic relief and even symbolic forms of emotional expression but that nevertheless defensively wards off interpersonal life? How may the power of the "creative urge" help people, especially woman, achieve healthy states of psychological integration? What developmental factors prevent this from occurring? Can the creative process become captive to a pathological mourning state, with its compulsive and addictive dynamics, leading necessarily to self-deterioration rather than self-development? Alternatively, can the creative endeavor promote a developmental mourning process that encourages self-development? (Kavaler Adler 2000, p. 1).

Kavaler-Adler believes that many creative people need to combine psychotherapy with the creative process to free themselves from the probability of remaining helplessly entrapped in isolated lives.

Writer Victoria Nelson (1993) tells us that at some point in their revision of a work, most writers experience a sense of closure and stop writing. But some writers revise obsessively, and these writers never experience closure, the work existing in an unhealthy symbiosis with the author. This impasse represents an incubation period that goes on too long, a retentive creative womb that postpones delivery too long. I tend to be one of those endless revisers, wanting to remain forever pregnant with the creative work. Creating a new life is the ultimate creative act. When pregnant with my son, I loved the feeling and did not mind the usual inconveniences that pregnant women complain about; they were just a small price to pay for the pleasure of being pregnant. When I did not go into labor at the expected time, my doctor thought that I had miscalculated although I knew I hadn't. I just didn't want my pregnancy to end. (My husband, who has absorbed some of the psychoanalytic lingo, started calling me *Retento*.) My physician, having determined that the placenta was doing its job, said he never saw a pregnant woman who did not ultimately go into labor and seemed not particularly concerned. I finally went into labor a full month after my due date. My son was born healthy but quite skinny, his skin wrinkled. I was told that post-mature infants often look as if they have lost weight in utero; most of the nutrition absorbed in the tenth month was benefitting his brain, because the rest of him was relatively finished. Looking back, I realize that I did little creative work during this time; bringing a whole new life into this world used my creativity in a very different way.

My first book, too, had post-mature syndrome. I really did not want the writing to end, and so I procrastinated submitting the final manuscript. I loved the process of writing even more than the idea of being published, which made me a bit anxious. My gynecologist recently told me that he has seen a number of women who loved being pregnant and delivered quite late.

As I write this section, I added it in before starting my final editing. I have started my final editing so many times, and in the process, find something I just *have* to revise, or I'll think of something to add to make the book *better.* This is part of the writer's craziness I struggle with. The other side of the coin is that editing is extraordinarily tedious and takes so much time that it feels as if I will never be able to finish it. I suppose I'll just get sick enough of editing that I'll just stop and that is how I will finish this book. I'm getting close.

MENTAL ILLNESS, ADDICTION, EPILEPSY AND CREATIVITY

Creativity and mental illness do not go hand in hand, as many seem to think. The link between the two is quite complex. The Greeks linked creativity to madness. So did the Romantic poets who glorified madness. Neuroscience has found that schizophrenics and those with bipolar disorder have a facility for making unusual associations that may seem bizarre to others; so do healthy people who are highly creative. In other words, the theories linking creativity with mental illness really imply mild illness or *psychotic traits*, rather than unremitting psychosis (Flaherty 2004). Research has found that creative abilities seem to run in the families of those with mental illness. The comments of Mark Strand, one of a number of exceptionally creative people interviewed by Csikszentmihali (1997), provides some food for thought.

> There have been lots of unfortunate cases of writers, painters, who have been melancholic, depressed, taken their own lives. I don't think it goes with the territory. I think those people would have been depressed, or alcoholic, suicidal, whatever, even if they weren't writing. I just think it's their characterological makeup. Whether that characterological makeup drove them to write or paint, as well as to alcohol or suicide, I don't know. I know there are an awful lot of healthy writers and painters who have no thoughts of suicide. I think it's a myth, by and large. It creates a special aura, a frailty, around the artist to say that he lives so close to the edge. He's so responsive to the world around him, so sensitive, so driven to respond to it, it's almost unbearable. That he must escape either through drugs, or alcohol, finally suicide, the burden of consciousness is so great. But the burden of consciousness is great for people who don't . . .want to kill themselves (Csikszentmihali 1997, pp. 73-74).

Transmission of the neurotransmitter dopamine is thought to play a role in creative thought and behavior (de Manzano, Cervenka, Karabanov, Farde, and Ullén 2010). When psychological tests designed to measure creativity were administered to 13 men and women who were both mentally healthy and highly creative, those who did well had certain brain chemistry features in common with schizophrenics, largely involving the dopamine communication system. The thalamus contains the greatest level of dopamine D2 receptors.

The thalamus and striatum of creative individuals are the brain regions that process and organize information before reaching conscious thought, and are also the areas involved in schizophrenia. When PET scans were used to determine the level of a dopamine D2 receptors in the thalamus and striatum of creative individuals, those with lower levels of dopamine D2 receptors in the thalamus scored higher on tests of divergent thinking, often producing a number of different solutions to a problem. This, combined with superior cognitive functions, could be the basis for the processes of production and selection which underlie real life creativity. Thus, although creative people may not have the ability to sort through information in their heads as well as normal people, this leaves them with a greater ability to make unusual connections and produce exceptional ideas. "In other words, thinking outside the box might be facilitated by having a somewhat less intact box" (de Manzano, Cervenka, et al. 2010, p. 6).

A whole generation of American poets were interested in the link between sanity and madness—Allen Ginsberg, Robert Lowell, Ted Roethke, Sylvia Plath, and Anne Sexton. And of course, depression and manic depression carry a high risk for suicide. Writer William Styron fell into a depression that led him to a flirtation with suicide, later concluding that many mental health professionals neither really recognize nor understand the nature of depression.

> When I was first aware that I had been laid low by the disease, I felt a need, among other things, to register a strong protest against the word "depression." Depression, most people know, used to be termed "melancholia," a word which appears in English as early as the year 1301 and crops up more than once in Chaucer, who in his usage seemed to be aware of its pathological nuances. "Melancholia" would still appear to be a far more apt and evocative word for the blacker forms of the disorder, but it was usurped by a noun with a bland tonality and lacking any magisterial presence, used indifferently to describe an economic decline or rut in the ground, a true wimp of a word for such a major illness. It may be that the scientist generally held responsible for its currency in modern times, a Johns Hopkins Medical School faculty member justly venerated—the Swiss-born psychiatrist Adolf Meyer—had a tin ear for the finer rhythms of English and therefore was unaware of the semantic damage he had inflicted by offering "depression" as a descriptive noun for such a dreadful and raging disease. Nonetheless, for over seventy-five years the word has slithered innocuously through the language like a slug, leaving very little trace of its intrinsic malevolence and preventing, by its very insipidity, a general awareness of the horrible intensity of the disease when out of control (Styron 1990, pp. 36-37).

Styron's psychiatrist did not understand what he was going through, and warned him to stay out of the psychiatric hospital because of the stigma. They met twice a week. There was little Styron could say to him except to try to describe his desolation. His doctor had little of value to say to him. He asked him if he was suicidal, and when Styron said he was, unfortunately, he did not inquire further. He did not know that everything around Styron had become transformed through his desperation into a potential means for suicide—the bathtub, where he could slash open his arteries, the attic rafters, serving as a hanging tree, the garage, where he could sit in his car inhaling carbon monoxide. "These thoughts may seem outlandishly macabre, a restrained joke—but they are genuine. . . . They are doubtless especially repugnant to healthy Americans, with their faith in self-improvement. . . Yet in truth such hideous fantasies, which cause well people to shudder, are to the deeply depressed mind what lascivious daydreams are to persons of robust sexuality" (Styron 1990, pp. 52-53).

When suicide has the promise of freeing someone from desolation, it presents the promise of an ecstatic glorious release. But when depression is milder, creativity can sometimes stand as a bulwark against a descent into psychosis or more severe depression (May 1975; Rothenberg 1990). Creativity had been that kind of protection for Freud. A heavy cigar smoker all his life, he had more than thirty surgeries to treat his oral cancer. In 1939 after his cancer was thought to be inoperable, Freud committed suicide. But earlier on, however, he wrote a tremendous volume of material, even while his body was ravaged with cancer. Or perhaps because his body was ravaged with cancer. He said that he did some of his best writing when mildly depressed or in bad health (Farber 2005a; Flem 2003; Mahony 2002).Writing had given him a needed space and freedom from the pain he suffered. I understand this well because this was true for me too. During my husband's cancer treatment, my anxiety drove me to write. And write. And write. The anxiety that can be immobilizing and which may keep around half of doctoral candidates from completing their dissertations helped me to complete mine. I retreated into my writing cocoon, a safe respite from endless rumination about whether chemotherapy was really killing the cancer cells or were they still growing. My mood not only improved but I became hypomanic. My manic defensive writing kept me going and was a blessing.

Some writers, however, lose their ability to regulate cycles of work and rest, consciousness and sleep, resorting to drugs or alcohol to help them get to sleep and to stimulants such as caffeine, amphetamines or cocaine to get them going again, ending up with multiple addictions. Writer Caroline Knapp wrote that she could identify with legions of drinking writers such as Tennessee Williams, William Styron, Carson McCullers, F. Scott Fitzgerald, Dylan Thomas, Eugene O'Neill, Dorothy Parker, Thomas Wolfe, William Faulkner, Ernest Hemingway, Theodore Roethke, and Jack London—those "dark and tortured souls, artists, people who lived life on a deeper plane than the rest of us, and drinking seemed like a natural outgrowth of their lives and work, both a product of and an antidote to creative angst" (Knapp 1996, pp. 15-16). Writer Erica Jong (2006) told how although alcohol took the edge off her depression, it also made the depression worse. When drug or alcohol abuse is combined with a mood disorder, it can be devastating, as it was for the wildly mercurial Welsh poet, Dylan Thomas, who died of the effects of alcoholism.

Rarely does a writer incubate his ideas or write well when intoxicated (Rothenberg 2001). Rather than serving as a muse to help produce creative work, alcohol interferes with creativity. So to sedate themselves, they began drinking during work-allotted hours, followed by anxiety after stopping, and subsequently drinking again to sedate those effects. The pattern was the same as for any alcoholic, but with one big difference; the writer or any artist, often carries out his creative pursuits in solitude, leading to drinking alone without interference from others (Rothenberg 2001). Rothenberg cautioned that although some authors, such as Hemingway, reputedly used alcohol to remove inhibitions, these reports must be taken with large grains of salt because of the tendency of well-known writers to develop to develop public tough-guy facades. For male writers, there may also be a wish to defy pervasive stereotypes of effeteness or, in some cases, to deny homosexual tendencies (Rothenberg 2001).

Some years ago I became so fascinated with the power of the creative process that I started a discussion group for writers.[1] I live in a suburb of New York City that is home to many creative people, and so when I put a small ad in the local newspaper, "Writers Wanted," I got many responses. I said that although I am a psychotherapist, I was not running this as a form of group therapy; I simply wanted the opportunity to get to know writers because I was very curious about the creative process involved in writing. I charged nothing. A man in his late forties joined, telling us that he had been a very well-paid corporate executive. He had made enough money that finally he could afford to do what he really wanted to do, and that was to retire and write novels. He was planning to do that. "Don't get me wrong. I'm not knocking money. But better than making money is to follow my bliss, and write. I'm grateful that making money is allowing me to do that." A woman in her fifties joined, someone I had met before, who had struck me as a timid mousey sort of person when I previously met her. In her writing she was strong and powerful, expressing a part of herself that she otherwise kept under wraps. A black man in his seventies joined, whom I had known because he and his wife had lived across the street from my home. I did not know him well, only that he was a retired Episcopal priest and editor of a small newspaper catering to the black community in the area. When he called, he surprised me by telling me that he had five completed fiction manuscripts sitting in his attic. He wanted to talk with other writers and find out what his next step was. He reminded me of myself at the time, too inhibited about daring to send anything out to be considered for publication

And then a few years later, a wonderful thing came into my life. A woman who was a photographer started a monthly meeting of artists and writers. I joined but could not identify myself as a writer, only as a psychotherapist with a great interest in the creative process who had always wanted to be a writer (Farber 2005b). The group met monthly; at each meeting, one member would present a current project, reading from a chapter he had written, demonstrating an innovative painting technique, and so on. A few even had well-established careers, with shows in galleries or books on the shelf at Barnes and Noble. The meetings were fascinating and fun, and I became friends with several very interesting people. I soon began to realize that maybe I was a writer after all, but an "in the closet" writer. Coming out as a writer was a strange process. I had begun very tentatively to identify myself as a writer, half expecting someone in the group to challenge me. "You're no writer! Who do you think you're fooling?" (Farber 2005b, p. 11). When I got my book contract for my first book, the support I received was wonderful. Finally, it was my turn to speak about my project, this book I was supposed to be writing but was not writing. Just signing the contract intimidated me so much that I could write nothing but a title and an outline. (I did not realize it but Csikszentmihalyi might have said that I was incubating.) I felt immobilized. The day before my presentation, I panicked. There was not even the beginning of a first chapter to tell them about. Would I open my mouth only to reveal myself publicly as a fraud or a liar? That thought was just what I needed to begin my first chapter the day before the presentation. Years of free association have made me pretty honest and straightforward, so the following day, I told them the story just as it happened, a true confession. To my surprise, they howled with laughter. It was the laughter of recognition. I then discovered that so many of them had thought of themselves as frauds early on too, and had the same difficulty in thinking of themselves as artists or writers. I had joined the fellowship. I suppose we all tended to believe in the myth that writing simply flows from inspiration, rather than, as Thomas Edison said, that creativity consists of one per cent inspiration and ninety-nine percent perspiration (Thomas Edison Quotes 1996).

Since that time, I have continued to write and have come to incorporate writing into the treatment of certain patients during their sessions, extending the concept of free association to be not only "the talking cure" but "the writing cure" as well (Farber 2005a). As Erica Jong said "Writing is the first antidepressant. It came before Prozac and Effexor. And it was cheaper." (Jong, 2006, p. 232).

Many writers enter psychoanalysis in order to overcome their writer's block, which has been understood by Edmund Bergler (1954) as creative impotence. His findings are derived from the analysis of 36 writers. He traces the drying up of creativity to an oral masochistic need for punishment for unconscious unacceptable wishes. Alice Flaherty's (2004) research into writer's block found that it is a frontal lobe process linked to depression and anxiety, both showing severe decreases in frontal lobe activity. Writer Victoria Nelson (1993) takes a different approach, regarding writer's block as a time when the writer is tuning in to preconscious material that may be standing in his way. Poet Stanley Kunitz said "The unconscious creates; the ego edits (Nelson1993, p. 2)", meaning that a part of the unconscious self is vetoing the program demanded by the conscious ego, defending the self from deeper knowledge that would be too threatening to know. A writer with an especially punitive conscience might benefit from some psychoanalytic psychotherapy to soften it, finding that his writer's block lessens. .

Traditionally the creative process has been depicted, as Csikszentmihalyi tells us, as happening in five steps (Csikszentmihalyi 1997). First there is a preparation stage, the engagement in a group of fascinating knotty issues that evoke interest. The second phase is an incubation phase, when ideas are stirred up. The third is insight, sometimes referred to as the "Aha!" moment. In real life, there may be a nonlinear process of several insights interspersed with periods of incubation, evaluation, and elaboration. Evaluation is when a decision must be made about whether the idea is important enough to follow it, and may be the most emotionally difficult portion of the process, because one feels most tentative and lacking in confidence. The last part is the explanation process, which is the hardest and takes a great deal of time. The period of incubation has a mysterious quality, which may be why it is often thought o be the most creative part of the process. This is the mysterious time, according to Freud (1910b, 1914), what the child may have felt, when witnessing his parents in the sexual act or when having ambivalent erotic emotions toward one parent.

The creative process requires the ability not only to tolerate being alone but to enjoy solitude. Novelist E. L. Doctorow described it as "going down to the rag bin of your mind and pulling up whatever you can find and somehow stitching it together, making a whole something out of little bits and pieces (Lahr 1998, p. 57)." It is little bit like making a patchwork quilt. It means that the psychologically healthy person can reach down into the dark place of his unconscious to create something new of aesthetic value in the transitional space between the unconscious and the conscious, and can then emerge intact and use conscious processes to edit that which he has created. This is a temporary dip down to the most primitive part of the mind, in which the bits and pieces are fashioned together into something new and of value. What Ernst Kris, an art historian before becoming a psychoanalyst, had to say is pertinent. Kris wrote about the creative process as a regression in the service of the ego (Kris 1952). He thought creative individuals were more flexible in terms of ego functioning and can use more primitive modes of functioning to gain access to preconscious thoughts for creative activity. Csikszentmihalyi reminds us that Freud (1908, 1914), thought that the child's natural curiosity about some sexual experience, such as witnessing his parents in the act of sex or his own ambivalent erotic feelings toward his mother, became so overwhelming that it became transformed into creative curiosity. For the artist, it may be interest in finding new forms of representation, thus displacing the search for hidden knowledge into a permissible curiosity. This process has elements in common with psychosis because of the closeness to the unconscious thought processes found in psychotic people, but it also is close to the dreams of normal people. It is, in fact, a healthy process that can help one define one's sense of self and clarify one's own thoughts and feelings. The state of absorption is a dissociated state of consciousness, a tendency found to develop from a disorganized attachment (Liotti 1995)..The tendency to absorption was found in two low-risk samples of young adults (N=136, N=308). In both studies, those participants whose parents experienced familial loss within two years of their birth showed elevated levels of absorption (Hesse and IJzendoorn 1998).

But when the fuzzy borders between the conscious, unconscious or dissociated states are too threatening, the person may need to medicate himself with drugs or alcohol in order to allow himself to descend into that threatening place to create. And when these borders dissolve too easily, the creative person may descend into madness. When Nancy Andreason (2006) studied creativity as faculty of the Iowa Writers' Workshop, she found that most had significant histories of mood disorders, such as depression and manic-depressive illness, a finding that was also documented by Kay Jamison (1995), who found that unipolar depression (depression without mania) is eight to ten times more likely to be found in writers, who are ten times more likely to suffer from manic depression, with poets a remarkable forty times more likely. When she examined the lives of well-known British painters, sculptors, playwrights, and poets, she found that thirty per cent had required treatment for mood disorders, compared to five percent in the general population, with poets struggling the most (Jamison1994). In *Touched with Fire*, Jamison (1994) concludes that there are some features of manic-depressive illness that could, under certain conditions, add profound depth, passion, and insight to artistic imagination. She quotes van Gogh as saying

> The more I am spent, ill, a broken pitcher, by so much more am I an artist—a creative artist . . . this green shoot springing from the roots of the old felled trunk, these are such abstract things that a kind of melancholy remains within

> us when we think that one could have created life at less cost than creating art (van Gogh 1958, p. 620).

I prefer to use the older term manic-depressive rather than the current term, bipolar illness, which does not capture the far more complex reality of the illness—the fluctuating and rapid cycling cycles of moods and energy levels as a backdrop to continually changing thoughts, behavior, and feelings. It spans the polarities of human experience, from the highest, most ecstatic highs to the lowest of the lows. Sometimes the passion to create can drive some people into the hypermanic (overly manic) state of ecstasy that characterizes manic-depressive illness, helping us to understand why Plato called creativity *the divine madness*. The word *mania* means excessive excitement, from which the word *maniac* is derived. Nowhere does the manic defense reign more supreme than in manic-depressive illness, in which the fear of giving it up can prevent patients from taking their mood-stabilizing medications. This an illness that can confer advantages on those who have it but make no mistake; it can destroy and kill in the process.

The overpowering desire to write is known to neurologists as *hypergraphia*, and was first called *the midnight disease* by Edgar Allan Poe and years later by Michael Chabon, referring to how the drive to write might strike late at night or in the earliest hours of the morning (Flaherty 2004). Although writing is anxiety-producing and takes guts, writers learn to live with the fear and write their way through it (Keyes 1996). Taking the risk generates a very pleasurable state in which they are so deeply absorbed that they lose sense of time, mood is elevated, thinking is fast, and sexuality is heightened. Virginia Woolf spoke of "the exalted sense of being above time and death which comes from being in a writing mood" (cited by Keyes 1996, p. 182). Many writers go into a trance-like state as they write, in which distractions disappear, and anxiety evaporates. After what seems like minutes, they may be surprised to find that they have been working for hours. This intense absorption is the state of being *in the zone* or *flow* (Csikszentmihalyi 1991), also experienced by firefighters, performers, and athletes. It comes to be experienced as a need (Farber 2005). Writer Isabel Allende compared a blank piece of paper to a clean sheet put on the bed for lovemaking, and said she found the process of writing so sensual, so ecstatic as to feel like an orgy (Keyes 1996). "Despite their bellyaching, most writers say that no other activity absorbs and arouses them as writing does. 'Writing is hell,' said William Styron with one breath, and with the next, 'I find that I'm simply the happiest, the placidest when I'm writing.' . . . Writers commonly note this mingling of sweet and sour in their calling, its yin and yang, terror and tingle" (Keyes 1996, p. 180).

Keyes (1996) notes that athletes call this state being in the zone, a trance-like- state probably due to natural opiates and endorphins flooding our bodies when we are under stress. They induce a state of intense concentration and play a role in sexual arousal, which may be why writers and adventurers alike so often use sexual imagery to describe the payoff for an encounter with danger, calling it arousing, orgiastic, even ecstatic. For writer Diane Ackerman,

> Reaching a state of ecstasy is rarely fun for those who seek adventure. Mountaineers enjoy being at the bottom and top of a peak far more than they like being in the middle. As they begin a climb, all is hope. At the end, relief and elation take over. In between, it's mostly slog and anxiety. Writers and mountain climbers share a lot in this regard. Like climbing a mountain, writing a book is exciting at the beginning, exhilarating at the end, but tedious, frustrating, and hair-raising in between. On bad days, book writers find they'd rather do anything than face their mountainous manuscript—especially during the third, fourth, or twentieth drafts. At the same time, fear mounts. Danger begins to feel overwhelming. "Consciousness of it generally strikes in the night when one wakes," wrote Catherine Drinker Bowen late in her career. "Actual physical sweating takes place, loud moans are rendered, and the question is put, 'Why in God's name did one undertake such a venture, such a presumptuous, enormous, unlikely book?" Why indeed? Because it's there? Like high-standard mountaineering, serious writing is seldom done as a lark. These pursuits are engaged in because one is compelled to do so; because of the challenge, the self-test, to confront, engage, and transcend fear (Keyes 1996, p. 182).

Writer Erica Jong (2006) succumbed to the temptation of sustaining the flow with alcohol, which seemed to work, at least at first, until she became an alcoholic. "At first it seems to deliver easy ecstasy. . . It promises everything but eventually imprisons you in the bottle itself. You write with great freedom but in the morning discover only gobbledygook" (Jong 2006 pp. 129-134). In reflecting on her experience, Jong said that that the people who crave ecstasy are the ones probably the least capable of moderation.

I think I have a touch of *the midnight disease*. I write a lot and find that it makes me happier than just about anything else. I am magnetically drawn to the computer, and the intention to write briefly about an idea that had struck me can easily turn into a roll of several hours. I can get so absorbed that I lose touch with physical needs, like eating and going to the bathroom. I have learned that I had to build in certain restraints to prevent a gift from becoming a curse that could ruin my life. I need to rein it in and still struggle to do so. I keep a kitchen timer next to my computer, set to tell me when it's time to stop. Even so, I have at times left some patients waiting at the door for me to buzz them in. My husband serves as an external restraint as well, sometimes calling out late at night, "Go to sleep, crazy lady." It is wonderful to see my work published, but it is the time when the writing flows that I treasure the most. It is like the flow of a good session in psychotherapy, my patient and me flowing in sync with each other.

CREATIVITY IN PSYCHOTHERAPY AND PSYCHOANALYSIS

The wish to find meaning in life is very strong in writers and. psychotherapists, who also want to find meaning in their work (Flaherty 2004). At its best, psychotherapy is a creative process for patient and therapist, a relationship in which both work together to create something new and of value, new ways of thinking, better self-esteem, new patterns of behavior (Rothenberg 1988).

Practicing psychotherapy and psychoanalysis is creative work. No matter how much training and experience a therapist has, if it is not used creatively, it is not worth much. Albert Rothenberg (1988) has studied the essence of creativity in scientific breakthroughs, artistic masterpieces, and the process of personality change in psychotherapy, and has found that the best therapists, from various disciplines, are scientific, rigorous, and consistent as well as intuitive and imaginative. He believes that the therapist's special sense of engaging in a worthy activity derives from its creative aspects, specifically from the paradoxical mixture of consistent rigor and free rein intuitiveness. According to Emanuel Hammer (1972), the creative psychoanalyst must allow himself to let go of his rationality. He must be flexible enough to feel excited, rather than anxious, when faced with something he does not understand, for which he has no theory at hand to rely on. Jean Sanville (1994) compares the process of psychoanalytic treatment with the child's play—imaginative, engaging, and spontaneous for both analyst and patient.

I have been struck by how many of my colleagues whose work I respect and admire work in an innovative, creative way and also are involved in creative activity outside their practice. I sent an email to several professional listservs I participate with, inquiring about this. Several wrote of the pleasure in creative play, not caring particularly about having or not having talent. One woman said "I paint, mostly in oils, and love that it's OK not to be good at it. Unlike my work with patients, it does not 'matter' and therefore can be pure play." Another psychotherapist wrote "When I turned 50, I decided I wanted to do something artistic that had nothing at all to do with psychoanalysis or psychology. So I learned to sing and eventually started performing, something I still do occasionally. I am not very good, but it gives me great pleasure." Another wrote

> I started cutting and welding steel after the birth of my only child at 44. When I was welding I couldn't worry about my kid or my job as a psychologist or I would blow the place up. It was actually a stress reducer to cut and weld metal. One thing led to another and the hobby morphed into gigantic steel sculptures which then changed into making sculptures out of resin and crushed glass with themes like the strength in fragility. Anyway, I find the creative process is a way of staying centered. In my art world I use a slightly different name so that I can keep my lives separate.

One man specializing in work with the seriously mentally ill has made three outstanding films about treatment of psychosis, is also a songwriter and has written plays. A woman plays flutes, djembe drums, and grows organic vegetables in a community garden. Another woman is a semi-retired opera singer, and continues to perform. Three women study and compete in ballroom dance. Another had her first career as a graphic designer and writer. One woman is a film critic. Another is a published author who makes jewelry. A man is a retired professor and psychotherapist who bakes bread and is an amateur photographer. Another man became the harmonica-playing leader of a group of musicians playing blues in local venues. One woman takes improvisation classes. A number sing in choirs or other choral groups. Another woman hosts a weekly mental health/wellness radio show. I love the fiber arts and have a floor loom and a few tapestry looms. I have made quilts, crewel and needlepoint pillows and wall hangings, hand-woven tapestries, and crocheted and knitted free-form wall hangings.

The area of dissociative disorders is ripe for creative innovations because the community of clinicians treating these patients is so diverse and the area is so new that clinicians are unusually receptive to new techniques. One man proposed a creative approach to the understanding and treatment of Dissociative Identity Disorder, and has published two papers on the subject, while a female therapist who experimented with different grounding techniques stumbled upon *zentangles* as a meditative doodle art.

> I tried it myself and found it was relaxing, fun and whimsical. My D. I. D. group loved it because it is adult and child friendly at the same time. Some clients liked the counting and repetition. You create patterns with individual strokes made with intention but the designs can be quite sophisticated and trust me, visual arts has not been part of my life so I was amazed at the results. I used it with an 82 year old who used to be an artist but now her hands shake. That just made the designs more interesting. Lots of the strokes are squiggly anyway. Check out the zentangle website. There are certified teachers but you can do it on your own. I hope to get the local teacher here to hold a class for therapists with the idea of something calming for themselves with the added bonus of being a tool for clients.

Another woman is an amateur photographer and quilter. A woman who loved ballet but was not allowed to take lessons as a child now takes lessons and loves dancing. Another makes stained glass. Some knit and crochet. "I knit and mostly crochet blankets. When I make blankets I like taking wool from the past and the present and stitching it all together." Another wrote that she makes pesto from the basil she grows and makes batches of sundried tomatoes which sit in a wonderful olive oil and herb marinade. Her friends look forward to gifts of jars filled with each throughout the year. In the fall she dries some herbs and plant others in pots and keep them in a sunny window through the winter until they are ready to be planted again outside. She loves to cook, and come up with new dishes. Several others cited being creative cooks. Others cited designing jewelry and forging metal, playing drums, writing fiction, poetry, plays, quilting, appliqué, belly dancing. One does a version of hula dance. One man teaches memoir writing to senior citizens, teaches poetry to children with special educational needs, and plays several musical instruments. Another leads men's experiential weekends. One man wrote that

"Folks at SUNY Upstate Medical University Department of Psychiatry and Behavioral Science here in Syracuse feel so strongly about creativity that they each year in April or May hold a free one day Creativity Conference, featuring professional and amateur artists of many types, clinicians who have creative bents, and clinicians who use creative arts in their practices."

One psychoanalyst who has been an avid amateur photographer for many years wonders if photography and psychoanalysis are similar in that both in a sense are a form of voyeurism. "We intrude either with lens or inquiry into the personal lives and minds of our patients. In both 'arts', are we not spectators to the lives of others as they unfold before our eyes?"

If bringing something new and of value into the world is the essence of creativity, many of my colleagues' activities were expressive, while some were real creative efforts. Whether or not they were really creative, being novel and having value is for the culture to decide. But the need for creative expression is clearly a powerful force in the lives of many clinicians.

OUR BEST CREATIVE MINDS SPEAK OUT ABOUT THEIR OWN MENTAL ILLNESS

> You may well ask what my experience has to do with the writing of normal people. The answer is that although my brain may have a screw loose, everyone has the same screw.
>
> —Alice Flaherty, *The Midnight Disease: The Drive to Write, Writer's Block, and the Creative Brain*

The intriguing relationship between creativity, mood disorders, and epilepsy is elaborated by the courageous personal disclosures of Lauren Slater, Kay Redfield Jamison, Marya Hornbacher, Jeanette Winterson, and Alice Flaherty. Slater, Jamison, and Flaherty have conveyed not only the subjective experience of their illness but their scientific thinking about them, helping me understand how the ecstasies produced by these illnesses can help us understand the pleasures and potential problems of relatively normal creative people.

For Jamison (2003), writing helped her conquer her illness, integrate the experience into her life, and write several books about it: *Touched with Fire:*

Manic Depressive Illness and the Artistic Temperament (1994), *An Unquiet Mind: A Memoir of Moods and Madness* (Jamison 1995), *Night Falls Fast: Understanding Suicide* (Jamison 1999) and *Exuberance: The Passion for Life* (2004). She also coauthored a textbook, *Manic-Depressive Illness* (Goodwin and Jamison 1990). In her memoir (Jamison 1995), Jamison wrote about her experience with her illness and her resistance to treatment. She knew something was very wrong with her in adolescence when she became transformed from an exuberant person into a psychotically depressed, delusional woman who wanted to end her life. Brought up in a very White Anglo-Saxon Protestant military world, where order and appearances were everything, she had no idea that she was ill or that there was treatment for her illness. Even if she had known that she had a treatable illness, it would not have been acceptable to be treated for it (Jamison 1995). Years later, after marrying and obtaining her doctorate in clinical psychology at the University of California in Los Angeles, she joined the faculty in the Department of Psychiatry. "I was hired as an assistant professor. . . got good parking for the first time in my life, joined the faculty club posthaste, and began to work my way up the academic food chain. I had a glorious—as it turns out, too glorious—summer, and within three months of becoming a professor, I was ravingly psychotic" (Jamison 1995, p. 63).

Her full-blown mania started out with feeling wonderful, enthusiastic, and having boundless energy. She went on shopping sprees, bringing home expensive jewelry, sexy clothing, even a dozen snakebite kits (cheaper by the dozen), because God had told her that an infestation of rattlesnakes was about to happen. She pounced upon twenty books published by Penguin; how wonderful to have her own personal penguin colony. She stayed up all night working round the clock; she couldn't follow the course of her own thinking.

Her marriage was falling apart, and she separated from her husband. She dated a colleague who thought she was manic-depressive and confronted her with the need to take lithium. It became terrifying to find that she did not have a mind to rely on any more. She was a psychologist and although she wanted help, was deeply embarrassed about having to seek it. She found herself doing what had previously been unthinkable because she realized she had no choice; if she did not get professional help she was likely to lose her job, her already rocky marriage, and her life (Jamison 1995).

Lithium had only recently been approved for use in mania when it was prescribed for her, and she was given a much higher dose than is usual today. She had terrible side effects but even worse was her self-denial (Jamison 1996). Although she knew very well that if manic-depressive illness remains untreated, it returns with a vengeance—more severely and more frequently, she was convinced that she was the exception that proves the rule. What was more to the point was that she clung ferociously to her manic ecstasies, like many other manic-depressives. Life seemed boring when she was "normal."

And so, she went on and off lithium for years. Having been raised in a world where she was expected to be totally self-reliant and not need anything resembling a crutch, it simply was not done.

When she was 28, she took a huge overdose of lithium to kill herself. Fortuitously, her phone rang and she picked it up. It was her brother calling to check on her. Each time she stopped taking her lithium, she became suicidally depressed. It took several such episodes before she could accept the reality that she needed both medication and psychotherapy.

> At this point in my existence, I cannot imagine leading a normal life without both taking lithium and having the benefits of psychotherapy. Lithium prevents my seductive but disastrous highs, diminishes my depressions, clears out the wool and webbing from my disordered thinking, slows me down, gentles me out, keeps me from ruining my career and relationships, keeps me out of a hospital, alive, and makes psychotherapy possible. But ineffably, psychotherapy heals. It makes some sense of the confusion, reins in the terrifying thoughts and feelings, returns some control and hope and possibility of learning from it all. Pills cannot, do not, ease one back into reality; they only bring one back headlong, careening, and faster than can be endured at times. Psychotherapy is a sanctuary; it is a battleground; it is a place I have been psychotic, neurotic, elated, confused, and despairing beyond belief. But, always, it is where I have believed—or learned to believe—that I might someday be able to contend with all of this.
>
> No pill can help me deal with the problem of not wanting to take pills; likewise, no amount of psychotherapy alone can prevent my manias and depressions. I need both. It is an odd thing, owing life to pills, one's own quirks and tenacities, and this unique, strange, and ultimately profound relationship called psychotherapy (Jamison1995, pp. 88-9).

Extended stages of depression, thinks Jamison, sometimes interrupted by manically intense and expansive periods, can guide us to a different kind of perspective, consideration, and articulation of the human condition. She has found that although creative work may be inspired by or even executed while in a mild or even a psychotic manic state, it may be shaped or partially edited while its creator is depressed, then put into final order when the creator is in a more normal state. What is critical is the interaction, tension, and transition between changing mood states, as well as the strength and discipline drawn from periods of health. In her memoir about the death of her second husband and her great effort to adjust to that loss (Jamison 2009), she wrote about the critical difference between grief and clinical depression, concluding that it is the process of mourning that returns us to life. "In grief, death occasions the pain. In depression, death is the solution to the pain" (Jamison 2009, p. 19). Jamison is grateful for the lithium that still works for her, stabilizing her moods, and greatly increasing her creativity, productivity, and capacity for happiness.

Because she was afraid that disclosing her illness would harm her career, she hid it from even her closest colleagues. She told her bosses, however, and received great support from them. Frederick K. Goodwin, MD, research professor of psychiatry at George Washington University, one of the few who knew of her illness and knew that she could understand it in a way he never could, asked her to join him in coauthoring the textbook *Manic-Depressive Illness: Bipolar Disorders and Recurrent Depression* (1990). It was only after its publication and that of *Touched with Fire*, in which she wrote about the link between creativity and manic depression, that Jamison decided to "come out" about her own illness by writing her memoir. Weary of hiding her secret, she began acting and feeling as if she had nothing to hide.

When I read Maria Hornbacher's first book, *Wasted: A Memoir of Anorexia and Bulimia* (Hornbacher 1998), I was struck by the compelling immediacy of the writing itself and how differently she wrote about her eating disorder compared to other accounts I had read. As a specialist in eating disorders, I had heard countless such accounts and Marya's struck me as having a hypermanic quality. I suspected that she might have manic depressive illness, which was confirmed ten years later after reading her book *Madness: A Bipolar Life* (Hornbacher 2008). It was published several years after she had been diagnosed with the most severe form of the illness, Type I rapid-cycling bipolar disorder. When a psychologist asked her about how fast she cycled (changed moods), she was surprised and confused. In her experience, the moods were random, coming and going without explanation, as did her bouts of starving herself, binging and purging, shopping and spending and one-night stands with men she did not remember meeting when she found herself in bed with them the next morning. All this addictive activity served as her best attempts at self-medication for an illness she did not know she had.

She had manias of writing, her words describing the early hypormania that felt like happiness, not at all like an illness, compared to the more intense, frenzied, even violent state known as hypermania.

> I'm a whirlwind of activity. I make phone calls, assign stories, juggle meetings, edit, interview, and write and write. . . .The other editors look at me a little strangely. There seems to be a concerted effort at this magazine to move as slowly as possible. People keep telling me to slow down. . . . I start at the magazine working thirty hours a week. That creeps up to forty, then fifty, sixty. By August 2003 it's eighty, and I'm whipping up and down the aisles between the cubicles at the office. I'm out late every night at openings and shows. I wake up at the crack of dawn to work on my novel, which is finally nearing completion, then race into work, where I move in fast-forward, delighted by the efficiency of my various systems, clicking along; answer the phone, assign the story, edit the piece, make the call, set up the interview—stopping briefly when someone comes over to talk to me, talking to them a

> million miles and dash out of the office for the lunch, dash back for the meeting, sit down at my desk, e-mail the writer, file the press releases, scribble the notes, get a little burst of energy and gallop down the hall, gallop back, crash into my chair, and slowly the office is emptying out, and I'm typing, and people are stopping by to say good night, and I'm typing, and I am humming under my breath, whole symphonies, all the parts, and I keep typing, and suddenly it's totally quiet. My head is humming. . . . It doesn't feel like mania. No, no, it's *happiness*, it's *energy*. Madness? This isn't madness. This is more fun than I've had in years. Why would I want to come down? This is just how it is now, this is how it's always *supposed* to be—I've hit my stride, and I didn't realize how painfully slow I'd been going before. Everything before, pshaw. That was nothing. Ladies and gentlemen, you've never seen anything like it. Watch *this* (Hornbacher 2008, pp. 164-167).

You read earlier about Lauren Slater, a Harvard-trained psychologist who practiced for eleven years before embarking on a full-time writing career. Her publications include *Welcome to My Country: A Therapist's Memoir of Madness* (Slater 1996), *Prozac Diary* (Slater, 1998), *Lying: A Metaphorical Memoir* (Slater 2001); *Love Works Like This: Travels Through a Pregnant Year* (Slater 2003), and *Opening Skinner's Box: Great Psychological Experiments of the 20th Century* (Slater 2004). In *Three Spheres* (Slater 2005), she wrote of visiting her new patient in the same psychiatric hospital where she herself had been a patient.

Before obtaining her professional training, she suffered from severe mental illness, including depression, anorexia, self-injury, and seizures, and was hospitalized several times. Whether or not she had temporal lobe epilepsy, she exhibited the personality characteristics of Geschwind Syndrome: the overpowering urge to write, a hyperphilosophical or hyperreligious emotional life, emotional volatility, including aggressive outbursts and altered sexuality, an extreme talkativeness caused by excessive attention to detail (Waxman and Geshwind 1974).

Slater was one of the first people to take Prozac after it had been released, before books and articles about it had appeared. She stayed on it for the next ten years. After starting Prozac, her depression lifted, and with it, she lost her intense desire to write. She wrote a little but only in her journal.

> Writing had always been essential to me, not the academic stuff of school, but the looser and loftier stuff of stories and poems (Slater 1998, p. 48). . . .
> It's been almost a year now since I've composed a short story or poem, I who always thought of myself as a writer, all tortured and intense. I can just manage this journal. So maybe I'm not a writer anymore. Maybe Prozac has made me into a nun, or a nurse, . . or worse. . . .
> Every morning, before work, I come to the blank page and look at it. It looks like winter. It is February in my mind. I think of the things people have said about the blank page, all the images. Sheet of snow. Anesthetized skin. To these images, I add my own: the white of Prozac powder, spread thin.

> Basically, good writing is intensity, pitch, sex. Raymond Carver used to say that sometimes, when he was deep into a poem, he would look down to find his hands cupping his balls. I've read that Prozac diminishes the sex drive, so it would stand to reason that if might diminish the by-products of that drive as well, the seduction of language, the cry inside a word. Used to write fast or not at all. Pre-Prozac, I had my days of silence, but they were punctuated by days of rapid flow, my eyes half closed, links of sentences slipping from me. I felt a pressure building, a bodily desire to utter, and then I came, unclasped. . . . Perhaps this journal represents my first attempts to love language differently, to write at lesser levels of arousal. I am not made ecstatic by these entries (Slater 1996, p. 91-92).

Although her writing diminished after being on Prozac, you would not know it from the volume of published material she has produced. Slater had no complaint about it. It seemed that the medication helped her get her intense desire to write under control, as it had done for Alice Flaherty. Given her very poor prognosis, Slater reflected on what helped her get back to a functional satisfying life.

> Mental health doesn't mean making the pains go away. I don't believe they ever go away. I do believe that nearly every person ... has the same warped impulses, the same scarlet id as the wobbliest of borderlines, the most florid of psychotics. Only the muscles to hold things in check. . . are stronger. I have not healed so much as learned to sit still and wait while the pain does its dancing work, trying not to panic or twist in ways that make the blades tear deeper . . . . (Slater 2005, p. 17).

Novelist Jeanette Winterson who has manic-depressive illness, said that creativity

> takes the heavy mass of our lives and transforms it back into available energy. Taking the mundane or the weighted, the overlooked or the too familiar, art is able to re-show us ourselves and ourselves in the world. Art holding up a mirror to life is commonly misunderstood as realism, but in fact it is recognition. We see through our own fakes, our own cover stories, we see things as they are, instead of how they look, or how we'd like them to be. (Winterson 2009).

Winterson believes that her creativity salvaged her otherwise hopeless childhood and helps her manage her illness without medication. She has produced nine novels and children's fiction. Her fascinating novel *Oranges Are Not the Only Fruit* (also made into a film), is the story of a girl named Jeanette, the adopted daughter of working-class evangelists in the North of England. Tender and funny, it tells of the wild side of rapture, or religious ecstasy and the power of love. Although fiction, it of course draws on her own experience.

> Then about two years ago, when I was finishing a novel—which is always a thin-skinned state—my lover left me, and I discovered some difficult-to-swallow facts about my adoption. Result? I fell off the edge of life.
> Trains pulled into the station and I couldn't board. Sometimes I couldn't cross the road. I couldn't work. I couldn't even think. All I could hold onto, like a rope, were the hundreds of lines of poetry I know by heart.
> One night, when I had been sitting outside in the pouring rain for hours, a soaked body lost at sea, I said, out loud, for no clear reason,
>
> > "My ties and ballasts leave me, my elbows rest in sea-gaps,
> > I skirt sierras, my palms cover continents,
> > I am afoot with my vision."
>
> That's from Walt Whitman's "Song of Myself," and I remembered in the night rain that Whitman wrestled with depression as though it were a dark angel.
> The flash-thought opened further into the Hebrew story of Jacob wrestling the angel. From that encounter there was a permanent wound, but also a blessing.
> I use that word on purpose. The French verb "blesser" means "to wound." Original etymologies from both Hebrew and Anglo-Saxon bind "bless" with a bloodying of some kind—the daubing of the lintel at Passover, the blood smear on the forehead or thigh of a new young warrior or temple initiate. Wounding—real or symbolic—is both mark and marker. It is an opening in the self, painful but transformative. (Winterson 2009)

Alice Flaherty learned a great deal from her bipolar illness, sparking her intense curiosity in the connection between mental illness and creativity. She went on to write a brilliant book, *The Midnight Disease: The Drive to Write, Writer's Block, and the Creative Brain* and to teach at Harvard Medical School. Learning from her personal experience, she understood quite well why many people with that illness fall so much in love with their mania that they refuse mood-stabilizing medication and put themselves at great risk for suicide.

So what does Flaherty's personal experience have to do with the writing of so-called normal people? "The answer" said Flaherty, "is that although my brain may have a screw loose, everyone has the same screw" (Flaherty 2004, p. 13). Her finding is supported by findings regarding the junction of the temporal and parietal lobes in out-of body-experiences (Blanke 2004; Blanke and Thut 2007). Flaherty's temporal lobe activity seems to have become magnified and altered by illness. She sees quite clearly the importance of temporal lobe activity for many driven to write who do not have epilepsy or major depression. "The pleasure of writing and the pain of its absence tells us something crucial about the motivation to write and the way it springs from our instinct to communicate. It is a feeling that is essential for our ability as writers and for our potential to interact as human beings" (Flaherty 2004, pp. 13-14). I have found that, although we may write to communicate with others but sometimes, even though it may not be our conscious intention, writing can be a way to communicate with ourselves.

> Certainly, writing is a search that may, like psychoanalysis, lead us into secret labyrinths where thoughts we never suspected are discovered, where ancient and forgotten fears thrust themselves, like stalagmites, into consciousness, where we catch glimpses of desires so evanescent that they scatter like cockroaches before the light. And always, the compulsion, the need, to know more (Shields and Howard 1999, p. 9).

When neuroscientists explored the relationship of the transmission of dopamine to creativity, they found that very creative but healthy people and people with schizophrenia have in common particular brain chemistry features, largely involving the dopamine communication system. Creative types had difficulty in sorting out or filtering information. This potentially disabling feature was also a blessing in disguise, because it enabled them to make innovative connections and generate unusual ideas. "In other words, thinking outside the box might be facilitated by having a somewhat less intact box." (de Manzano, Cervenka, Karabanov, Farde, and Ullen 2009, p. 6). When I read this article, it started to answer some very puzzling questions I had had about myself.

The expression "She can't walk and chew gum at the same time" may seem to be just another joke insulting someone's intelligence. Change it to "She can't walk and talk at the same time" and it describes me. I cannot walk and become absorbed in conversation at the same time. When walking with someone and becoming absorbed in conversation, my feet literally slow down, bringing me to a snail's pace, as if my feet have a mind of their own. Many years ago, while absorbed in discussion with a colleague while undergoing institute training, I almost caused us to miss our train in Grand Central Station. I cannot talk when I drive. I can listen to what a passenger says but had better not respond. When a friend invited me to sail on his boat and let me take the rudder, it was my first try. I did beautifully and enjoyed it, but when he and others started talking to me and I responded, I discovered that I couldn't sail while talking, and could have drowned us all. This difficulty in filtering information caused me profound humiliation professionally a few years ago in front of an audience of 300 people. Having researched and written about Attention Deficit/Hyperactivity Disorder (Farber 2010), I suspected that I had it. Unwilling to go to the expense of neuropsychological testing, I consulted a psychiatrist, who was not convinced that I had it. I did not want to use stimulant medication, and so he prescribed Wellbutrin, an antidepressant known to help with concentration. It had no effect at all on my ability to concentrate; I was not depressed and my mood remained the same. So I can only think that rather than having Attention Deficit/Hyperactivity

Disorder, my creative ability is facilitated by having a less intact box than "normal," or the same screw loose as Alice Flaherty, or both.

Some neurologists are coming to think that certain forms of early brain growth have positive effects at the same time that they can produce significant difficulties in brain function. It has been suggested that the astonishing skills of savants, although dormant in everyone, are not usually accessible without an unusual kind of brain impairment (Snyder, Mulcahy, Taylor, Mitchell, Sachdev, and Ganddevia 2003). In an attempt to replicate this brain impairment in healthy people, Snyder and associates stimulated their left fronto-temporal lobes with low frequency magnetic pulsations. Although it did not lead to major improvement in their artistic performance, it resulted in substantial stylistic changes in the drawings of four of the eleven participants. Their findings suggest that low frequency repetitive transcranial magnetic stimulation imitates this brain impairment by closing down part of the left fronto-temporal lobe. In addition, the research of Geschwind and others has found that, although the left hemisphere is dominant for many functions in most people, there are some people with relatively symmetrical brains; this unusual evenness might lead to significant differences in special abilities and special fields of difficulty (Geschwind and Galaburda 1988; West 1991).

So whether you say that having a somewhat less intact box helps one to think outside the box, or that having a screw loose helps one to write creatively, or that savant-like abilities exist in normal people, there seems to be a continuum from the supposedly normal to the bizarrely ill. In *An Anthropologist on Mars: Seven Paradoxical Tales* (Sacks 1996), Oliver Sacks presents us with several individuals with neurological *fascinomas*,[2] and in them, finds aspects of himself.

CREATIVE WRITING OF SCIENTIFIC PROSE

> Before writing a major paper, I make it a point to read papers or books by authors whose writing style I have a high regard for. This can be anything. . . classical fiction, scientific papers written during the Victorian period, etc. I find that this can favorably influence my own writing and erase the unfortunate memory of the numerous dry, badly written papers one inevitably has to read as background to the research one is presenting.
> —Prof. Kerry Emanuel, Massachusetts Institute of Technology

Ever since I wrote my doctoral dissertation in the dry, deadly academic style that was expected, I struggled to get away from it. Flaherty tells us why scientific writing *should* get away from it. The lack of metaphor or other figures of speech that sets scientific prose apart from literary prose might appear to be the main stylistic difference between scientific and literary writing but what also characterizes most scientific prose is that it is *so bad.*

Flaherty quoted British biologist Sir Peter Medawar, Nobel Laureate, who said "Broken English is the universal language of science" (Flaherty 2004, p. 226). Flaherty said that scientific writing has rejected style as being just a decorative presentation that obscures the truth. Scientific writing, said Flaherty, is weighty, boring, and dehumanizing. Using the passive voice gives it a false objectivity and dehumanizes it by removing all the actors. "It is never 'We injected the patients' but rather 'The patients were injected,' as if in the eventuality of a lawsuit, this would somehow protect the shadowy injectors" (Flaherty 2004, p. 227). There is an absence of emotion and metaphor. Metaphorical thinking, finding the similarities between dissimilar objects, underlies creativity in both artistic and scientific work, and there is little that is creative and vital in scientific writing.

When we write about a patient who tells us that her heart has been broken, it would not be at all helpful to write that her limbic drive wants to communicate her pain. Better to write that at that moment, she feels so bereft that she is sure her broken heart will never be put back together again.

NOTES

1. I am so grateful to Betsy Immershein for starting the Rivertowns Artists' and Writers' Group.
2. Fascinoma is medical slang for a fascinating case, usually involving a rare disease.

Chapter Eleven

Intervening with Those on the Road to Ecstasy

> Yes, I am my brother's keeper. I am under a moral obligation to him that is inspired, not by any maudlin sentimentality but by the higher duty I owe myself. What would you think me if I were capable of seating myself at a table and gorging myself with food and saw about me the children of my fellow beings starving to death.
> —Eugene V. Debs

When I was in post-graduate training, the late Gertrude Blanck, one of my favorite teachers, was teaching the concept of adaptation. A story she told stayed with me. She told of a man who came to her for treatment. He had had a very tough life. As an adolescent he stole food for his family because they were poverty-stricken, struggling to get by, leading to skirmishes with the law. He was in and out of juvenile detention facilities and had begun to think of himself as a thief. He began drinking too much. His mother had heard that the owner of a local bakery took all the baked goods that had not sold by the end of the day and left them outside the back door on a covered tray, for anyone to take. It was a simple, humane thing to do and cost nothing. He went there every evening, bringing home bread and pastry for his eagerly awaiting family. He began to think of the man who owned the bakery, whom he met only once when he came to pick up his supply, as a very kind, caring parent looking out for him. As a result, no matter what difficulties came his way, he felt that he could rise above them. Trudy Blanck called this his remarkable ability to adapt to his environment, and take from it what he could (Hartman 1939).

RESILIENCE CAN SURPRISE YOU

> The greatest good you can do for another is not just to share your riches but to reveal to him his own." —Benjamin Disraeli

Although Nietzsche may have said that whatever does not kill us makes us stronger, most of the empirical evidence offers little support for it. However, some research does show that adverse experiences may also foster subsequent resilience, resulting in advantages for mental health and well-being (Seery, Holman, and Cohen Silver 2010; Higgins 1994). Although those who have suffered a cruel past may be at risk for psychosis, Gina Higgins' (1994) study of people who created lives of hope and happiness despite having had brutal childhoods demonstrates the remarkable power of resilience, a concept related to adaptation.

Although resilience may be a quality or trait had by some, it makes more sense to regard it as an ongoing process in which an individual demonstrates a positive ability to cope with trauma, stress and adversity, resulting in the ability to use the adverse experiences for their steeling effect, allowing them to function far better than expected. It helps them complete the critical developmental tasks that face them as they grow (Higgins 1994). Unlike the term *survivor*, those who are resilient do more than get through or survive life's painful experiences; with the right kind of help, they can actually thrive.

Some of the individuals involved in the high-risk behavior that makes them inclined to seek ecstasy may be more resilient than you would expect. Their behavior has been the best means of survival they have been capable of, but despite the cruel past they have suffered, despite the trauma and victimization, it is essential that you regard them as more than survivors. They may well have a hidden capacity for adaptation and resilience that can develop over the life span, aided by the surrogate relationships which can become the light in a darkened life (Higgins 1994). If you allow yourself to remain open to the possibility, if you allow yourself to imagine it, you just might become that light in a darkened life

Even trauma researchers note that people react differently to the same stressful events and that some even respond relatively well. Clinical and empirical emphasis is now being placed on individuals whose functioning is not significantly compromised by major stress. Some of these people, in fact, demonstrate unusually good adaptive abilities that can evolve over the life span.

Between 1939 and 1942, Harvard recruited 268 of its strongest and most promising undergraduates to participate in the Grant Study, an innovative new study of the human life cycle. The originators of the program thought that medical research was too heavily weighted in the direction of pathology, and their intent was to chronicle the ways in which a group of the most capable individuals coped with their lives over the life span. The study was conceived of in 1937, when George Vaillant, the director of the study, was three years old (Vaillant1977). Vaillant's father killed himself in 1945, leaving eleven-year-old George traumatized. He had deep personal reasons for becoming a psychiatrist and later, for wanting to understand just how people adapt to painful life circumstances. Almost forty years after his father's suicide, Vaillant took the measure of the Grant Study men, and found that for many who came from painfully difficult childhoods, later love in life can be emotionally corrective. Vaillant posed essential questions about the individual differences in confronting life's stresses. How can we successfully change those patterns of behavior that make us miserable, unhealthy, and reckless? Why do some of us manage so well with what life hands us, while others, who have had similar advantages or disadvantages, cope poorly or not at all? The kind of defenses the men used played a major part in how well they adapted. Vaillant evaluated for each man which defense mechanisms in his repertoire were more adaptive than others, classifying them accordingly into four categories: psychotic, immature, neurotic, and mature. Human beings mature, according to Vaillant, by their adaptive processes and defense mechanisms evolving from lower to higher.

Similarly, Gina O'Connell Higgins (1994) came to the same conclusion when she studied what resilient adults have in common. She sought out resilient people in two studies, one in 1984 and another in 1992, finding forty subjects who were chosen for their extremes of past hurt and current health, employing human capacities that lie dormant or unamplified in many of us. As a group, she found that these resilient adults had IQs that were above average to superior; had exceptional talents, including creativity and other inner resources (and had developed many of them); obtained higher economic levels than their families of origin; demonstrated high levels of ego development; have sustained empathically close relationships in childhood, adolescence and adulthood, including those they formed with parental surrogates; frequently have siblings who are highly psychologically compromised; and they maintain strong political and social activism. From a more dynamic perspective, they remain fiercely committed to reflection, new perspectives, and ongoing therapy (Higgins 1994). Higgins found that resilience evolves over time. Even such conditions as schizophrenia and bipolar disorder, for which there is strong evidence of heritability, are molded by environmental influences and the brain's plasticity.

Resilience "best captures the active process of self-righting and growth that characterizes some people so essentially" (Higgins 1994, p. 1). A strength of the resilient, says Higgins, is the ability to acknowledge and experience significant psychological pain and still maintain their ability to *love well,* creating and sustaining relationships marked by much reciprocity and concern for the other as well as the self. They form and take part in relationships that can survive (or even thrive) on discord, disillusionment, frequent anger, and frustration when the needs of one or the other in the relationship are not met. These conflicts are actively and successfully negotiated throughout each relationship. They have a way of relating to others in a way that does not usually sacrifice the truth and understanding with which they perceive other people. They consistently and generally succeed in their efforts to recognize others' needs and characteristics and to distinguish them from their own.

Higgins found that some severely traumatized individuals have unexpected strengths and a capacity to love, despite being exposed to hatred. Resilience, she demonstrates, can be cultivated. Psychotherapists, teachers, counselors, and other surrogates should never underestimate their possible corrective impact on a child or adult. So many of the resilient said that their hope was continually bolstered by the sudden kindness of strangers, even for just brief moments, and integrated into the broader fabric of resilient faith over time. The gratitude with which the resilient recalled their surrogates was enormous. "Enormous reparative potential resides in the bread-and-butter basics of caring about the young and listening closely to their lives. You can do this in any capacity: babysitter, teacher, therapist, neighbor, relative, clergy, coach, butcher, baker, or candlestick maker" (Higgins 1994, p. 324).

Higgins found that most of her resilient subjects were in psychotherapy for prolonged periods of time. It should be no surprise that so many of the resilient turned out to become psychotherapists themselves. I am one of them. So are a number of respected colleagues. So is Gina Higgins, who said "At Harvard I once heard someone remark that all dissertations are veiled autobiographies. Perhaps this is true of all committed professional work, varying mostly in the transparency of the veil. I certainly know how hard are the quiet victories of a reclaimed life" (Higgins 1994, p. xviii). Many who become psychotherapists, physicians, and members of the clergy are wounded healers (Jung 1951) like the character House, from the television series of the same name. Dr. House's physical and emotional scars are both a burden and a driving force in his need to fix the problems of others. In fact, Jung wrote that only the wounded who have gotten well could heal effectively. The resilient capacities in ourselves and others are reparative mechanisms that can propel you forward at any phase in the life cycle.

Brenda, a psychologist in her forties, thinks one has to believe in something. The person most instrumental in her life was her grandmother, an uneducated peasant woman, who said that there was always something good, always something you can live for.

> I remember just loving to be around her, because she was the only really happy person I knew, and sort of modeling myself after her in that way . . . I got from her something I never got from either of my parents, which is that there is

> something out there. . . She died the same year my parents were divorced, (my brother was diagnosed schizophrenic and I began raising my sister because my parents became so depressed) . . . But in a funny way, it didn't matter . . . It's sort of like she kept on going. She didn't really die. . . . the part of her I needed didn't die.
> I came to believe there was sort of this *spirit*: there was something that maintains you (Higgins 1994, pp. 183-84).

Higgins also presents a portrait of a psychiatrist, happily married for twenty-eight years, who as a child was the victim of a satanic cult and forced to become a prostitute. Another subject, despite having been abused sexually by his mother and brutally beaten by his father as a child, became the director of a human service agency as an adult.

Do not underestimate the power of basic, humane interventions. When "I'm nobody. Who are you?" defines a sense of self as it did for Emily Dickinson, you can help patients start to feel that they are *somebody* simply by treating them as if they are. Higgins (1994) offered recommendations derived from her conclusions about what helped her subjects the most, as well as her own insights that informed her clinical and educational work. To them I add my own.

You will need to explain and amplify their past and present strengths, clarifying their adaptive strategies, acknowledging and celebrating how far and how well they have come. You will have to repeat this frequently. If they can't yet laugh, teach them how. A sixty-seven-year-old woman with a history of a severe eating disorder since infancy, a failure-to-thrive child, came into treatment with me. She did surprisingly well, thriving on the relationship. At one point she said to me "I don't know which does me the most good, the crying or the laughing" (Farber 2000). She had plenty to cry about but much to laugh about too. It is essential to honor the history of hope in their lives, looking for where the light was in these darkened lives, and where is it now? Were there surrogates or helpers along the way How did the surrogate shape what they internalized? Looking closely at their heroic figures, symbolic or real, will help them honor their own visions of who they are, who they might become, and how to get there. If there were none, know that you can become one. You need to be very curious about love, or the lack of it, in their lives. Be attuned to the quality of their relationships, especially in those who are too quiet or too eager to please.

For those of you who are teachers or guidance counselors, keep in mind that many resilient people found school to be the only safe place they found. It was predictable and reliable, and was tantamount to a therapeutic milieu, providing most of the coherence they encountered in their early years. You need to maintain a sense of wonder and respect for their overcoming so well. Don't be afraid to express frank admiration for what they have overcome. It may be the first time they have heard it, and it can make the difference between the glass being half empty or half full. Be openly caring for those you help; do not hide your caring under a veil of so-called neutrality. Be sure to remind them that they have done a good job of surviving, and now they can do more than survive their life. They can actually thrive.

A year ago I began treating Elise, a remarkably resilient woman raised by a neglectful father and a mentally ill mother who was emotionally and physically abusive, abandoning Elise and her sister for days on end. She took Elise to an endless stream of doctors for medical treatments of illnesses she never had. Apparently she had Munchausen by proxy syndrome, a hidden form oc child abuse. School was a safe haven for her and a place of kindness. She found every excuse to stay late. Working at two jobs, she put herself through college. She has turned out to be a devoted sister, wife, and extraordinary mother to her three children, and had started her own business. She is loved and respected in her community by neighbors, teachers, and other parents. When I heard about her history, it seemed to be a wonder that she was walking upright and I told her just that. I expressed my admiration for her, and told her that it seemed like a miracle that she was not an alcoholic or drug addict, or in and out of psychiatric hospitals, and asked how in the world this happened. Her response floored me. She had watched *Leave It to Beaver* and the *Bill Cosby Show* regularly as a child. She found in June and Ward Cleaver and in Dr.Cliff and Clair Huxtable models of how to behave to others, how to live in the world. She began to model her behavior on what she saw and heard on the television screen. Although it was quite remarkable, it of course, was not enough. She seemed to think she had to be perfect in every way, and had unrealistically unachievable aspirations that were making her unhappy. Her daughter too expected herself to be perfect, just like her mother, and was becoming depressed. When she witnessed her mother becoming very angry, it seemed to give her permission to be just like her mother that way too, and her depression began to lift. As we worked together, I kept pointing out to Elise her strength in coping with adversity, and along the way she has come to appreciate herself and value herself more. Just yesterday she was amazed to hear herself say that she was proud of herself.

We can serve as a surrogate parent for those who need one. The word *surrogate* comes from the Latin *surrogare,* meaning to choose in place of another. You might be surprised by how important your expression of concern can be to someone who may not have had anyone really concerned about him before, and how the simplest kindness can make you into a surrogate parent, with more influence and power than you might imagine.

When you touch the life of a damaged child or adult, never underestimate the power of your potential impact. It takes courage to be present to hear their grim stories. If you can bear hearing their stories, that itself provides hope that they too might bear the telling. As Judith Herman (1992) told us in *Trauma and Recovery*, anything less than bearing witness to the full catastrophe can be silencing, while your courage may lead them to relinquish their solitary, shameful pain.

Whether you are a psychotherapist, counselor, teacher, member of the clergy, neighbor, friend, or relative, this chapter and the next focus on how you can intervene with such people. One need not have specialized training to distill the essence of what is being said and use it creatively.

PROBLEMS IN SELF-CARE

The ability to care for oneself develops from the earliest phases of the parent child relationship, when the child's ability to care for and protect himself becomes internalized and developed through the experience of being cared for and protected by a nurturing parent (Freud 1913a; Freud 1966; Hartmann 1939;Khantzian and Mack 1983; Mahler, et al. 1975; Farber 2000). When one has not had such experiences, the ability to care for one's self does not develop optimally.

The ability to care for oneself includes an emotional investment in caring about or valuing the self. It requires that the person has enough self-esteem to feel himself to be worth caring for and protecting (Khantzian and Mack 1983; Farber 2000). It also includes the ability to anticipate dangerous situations and to respond to signal anxiety by protecting oneself, Further, it requires an ability to control impulses and forgo pleasures that may have harmful consequences, as well as a sense of gratification in mastering risky situations. It means having sufficient knowledge of the world and of oneself to allow one to survive in a threatening world, and an ability to assert oneself or be aggressive enough to protect oneself. It also means being able to choose significant others who will not threaten one's existence.

Part of the developmental task of adolescence is in becoming able to care for oneself, no easy task when seeking new and exciting experiences are features of adolescent behavior. Adolescents seek new, stimulating, and pleasurable experiences, often engaging in high-risk behavior without considering the consequences. The frontal cortex of the brain, which plays an essential central role in decision-making, does not become fully mature and functional until the mid or late twenties (Walsh and Bennett 2004; Kelley, Schochet, and Landry 2004).

The implications are clear enough. We must assume a protective caring stance with individuals involved in high-risk behavior, in order to protect them from themselves.

THE CRUX OF THE MATTER

> The turning point in the process of growing up is when you discover the core of strength within you that survives all hurt.
> —Max Lerner

When people are in crisis, they may not know that they are really at a crossroad in their life in which they can continue on the same risky path they have been taking, or they can take the other less travelled path. The crisis is really an opportunity in disguise. They will need someone to serve as a guide on this new road. Chances are, there may not have been anyone in his life who cared enough to do this, no safe and secure attachment to convey consistently the message that someone cares about them, that they are worth being cared for. This is what they are really hungry for. Hunger comes from a "self that has felt empty and lonely too long, that craves the feeling of living full, warm and juicy in one's own skin" (Farber 2000, p. 323). Ecstasy seekers, though they affect an air of bravado, are needy people in disguise. To deny one's neediness is to suffer "a disorder of the recognition of desire" (Ogden 1989, p. 214). When the hunger to live fully alive is thwarted, it may manifest itself in what has been called a hunger disease (Battegay 1991), referring to the emotional problems based on lack of self-esteem, in which people are driven to possess and consume people and/or things in an addictive manner. Whether they hunger for food, drugs, alcohol, money, clothing, power, sex, pain or suffering, no matter how much they get, it is not enough. The hunger is insatiable (Farber 2000).

When those who suffer from an addiction try to renounce it, doing so can upset a defensive structure in which the addiction was an integral part, leaving the person prone to relapsing to the use of another addictive-like behavior. Those compulsive eaters who have had weight loss surgery may become alcoholic (Buffington 2003; Hsu, Benotti, Roberts, Saltzman, Shikora, Rolls, and Rand 1998; Spencer 2006), while those who renounce alcohol may substitute another orally incorporative behavior (Wilson 1988). For example, in the film *Clean and Sober*, an older man, an abstinent alcoholic who has become a Twelve-Step sponsor, is waiting in a coffee shop to meet a younger man he is sponsoring. He is wolfing down a large piece of chocolate layer cake and washing it down with a chocolate ice cream soda. Having given up alcohol, he has turned increasingly to food to medicate himself for whatever ails him.

At rock bottom, both substance and behavioral addictions (Goodman 2008) are driven by the same need to block out psychic pain. When someone is in so much pain, the attention of a psychotherapist who can tolerate listening to the pain, and wants to understand it can be an enormously powerful experience, for the patient and for the therapist, and can be a turning point in the patient's life.

SEX PRODUCES ORGASMS; PERVERSIONS PRODUCE ECSTASY

There are good reasons to write here about the perversions. First, ecstasy seeking and the perversions are similar in ways that tend to make them resistant to treatment. Second, because orgasm and ecstasy are qualitatively different, when we compare the sexual experience of ordinary sex and ordinary orgasm with the experience of the perversions, this will help us understand why perversions can provide an ecstatic experience not usually attained during more ordinary sex.

In his endorsement on the back cover of Daniel Bergner's (2009) book on the perversions, George Packer wrote that Bergner's characters "live in erotic no-go zones where most of us would fear to tread. . . . the normal and perverse exist not in separate worlds but on a discomfiting, even threatening continuum." What may be a most powerful sexual experience for someone with a perversion is likely to leave the rest of us cold, puzzled at best, or frankly repulsed. The same thing is true about those who seek ecstatic experiences. The experience of ecstasy, like the perversions, stokes the flames of addiction.

When Stoller studied the perversions at the University of California in Los Angeles, it was an academic study of gender. Initially he referred to these people as specimens to be studied scientifically, then as he got to know them through his forays into West Hollywood's S & M community, he began to understand them as very real human beings, with all their ambiguities and contradictions

Most of us in the mental health field will rarely have the opportunity to treat someone for a perversion. We may treat people who come for treatment for some other presenting problem—anxiety, depression, relationship difficulties—and in the course of treatment, as the patient feels more comfortable with the therapist, may disclose that he practices a "different" kind of sexuality. If he gets the sense that the therapist regards this as psychopathology and is interested in treating him for it, chances are he will end the treatment quickly. Clinicians regard patients with psychopathology as suffering from it, but to those with perversions, it is not suffering they experience but exquisite ecstasy. Those who have tasted ecstasy will not want to be deterred in their quest for more, as the following case demonstrates.

Some time ago, Richard, a man in his late thirties, came to see me. He was a partner in a law firm, a career in which the dominant and controlling part of his personality prevailed, but his secret dissociated wish to be humiliated was taking over his life in a way that threatened his career and marriage.

He was visibly anxious as he told me that he had grown up in an affluent family that employed a housekeeper, and he began exposing himself to her and others since he was 16. He also made phone calls to cleaning women who had placed ads in the local paper, trying to hire them to clean his house. He was clear that the terms of employment included that he would be naked while they cleaned in his presence. While talking to them on the phone, he masturbated to orgasm.

Richard had been married for a year. Before getting married, he told his fiancée about his problem, then went into therapy for a few months, but stopped before his wedding, having convinced his fiancée that the problem was under control. He had found talking to his female therapist about his sexual acting out very exciting, and was concerned that I might be repelled to hear this. He had not told that therapist about it. I told him I was interested in hearing more, not repelled, and that any time he found talking to me or thinking about me exciting, it was essential that he tell me about it. The more secrets he kept about this were bound to sabotage his treatment.

He said he had considered contacting me sooner but was too reluctant to give up his unique pleasure. He called me when he did because it was becoming out of control. Richard was making daily calls to women he did not know, telling them that he wants to see their "tushy" and lick it. He had recently exposed himself to his neighbor's daughter. The more stressful his work was, the more he indulged these proclivities. Although he enjoyed sex with his wife, the phone calls produced more than orgasms; they produced ecstasy. He found himself having sexual fantasies about me a few times and when the thought intruded that he would have to tell me about them, they stopped.

He was afraid his wife would find out about what he did and that his professional position would be jeopardized. Just months before, a woman he had called identified him through Caller ID. Her husband called him and threatened him, which scared him. He was very ambivalent about being in treatment, especially when he found himself going for several days without any urge to call women and was beginning to have rather normal fantasies about kissing a female colleague on the mouth. Because his perversion was starting to lose its power over him, it was no surprise to me when he terminated treatment.

In trying to define the perversions, Stoller "came across the curious fact that women are not represented in most of the diagnoses of perversion; whatever their fantasies, women practice perversions less than men do" (Stoller 1992, p. 9). He came to understand, as did the late Louise Kaplan (1991), that women's erotic neuroses rarely take the form of the formally classified perversions. "How common are the little sadomasochisms of everyday life, covert but observable: the skin pinching, cuticle tearing, gum picking, colonic treatments, deep massage, hairpulling-dreamy-self-and-other-stimulations?" (Stoller, 1991, p. 23) I have found too that some women even get some perverse erotic pleasure in spending recklessly on clothing, shoplifting, or vomiting or mutilating themselves, usually while in a dissociated state (Farber 2000, 2008a, 2008b). You may recall the cases of erotic vomiting presented previously, serving as perversions in the way that Stoller (1985) defines them, as erotic forms of hatred. According to Kaplan (1991), self-mutilation, hair pulling, self-starvation, and bulimia as well as some of the normative female grooming and dressing behaviors are characterized as forms of female perversions with pronounced sadomasochistic and exhibitionistic elements that parody the feminine stereotyped models of submission and purity. These caricatures of female "virtues" serve to express hatred. "The pervert . . . is making hate" (Kaplan 1991, p. 40). Or to put it another way, "The basic rule is that perversions should never be taken for what they seem to be" (Kaplan 1991, p. 251). These female perversions are not as blatant and transparent as male perversions but nonetheless serve as enactments of past trauma. Disguised as they are, these behaviors would not qualify today as perversions, or paraphilias, as they are now called in the Diagnostic and Statistical Manual of Mental Disorders. Stoller (1991) presents a compelling case for using the word *perversion* precisely *because* of its nasty connotations. "*Perversion* is a sturdy word, throbbing with assumptions, while *paraphilia* is a wet noodle. . . . It is not only neutral; it is neutered, pithed. It does not contain the quality I believe the person we would call perverse finds essential. That quality is the sense of sin, of sinning" (Stoller 1985, p. 6). Embedded in the sin is the dissociated expression of hatred.

PREVENTIVE INTERVENTIONS

If we cannot successfully treat those openly seeking ecstasy, it is well worth thinking in terms of prevention for those with a taste for high-risk behavior. Because high-risk behavior is addictive in nature, those who are drawn to it are the ones most likely to spiral their way up into even riskier behavior. Because they are likely to minimize the extent of this behavior it is essential that you not take their descriptions of this behavior at face value. They probably drink a lot more and more frequently than they have disclosed, diet or starve themselves or binge and purge more severely than they have acknowledged. Their drug use may well be more than simply "recreational." Their casual sex may be more compulsive and unprotected than they have said. Their gambling or compulsive shopping or spending may be far greater than they have acknowledged. If you practice psychoanalytically, you and your patient cannot afford for you to allow the patient to tell this aspect of his story at his own more comfortable pace, the traditional psychoanalytic approach. With such patients we must take a more protective and active role, often a phase-oriented approach to treatment in which a "safety first, interpretations later" approach, as elaborated in my first book (Farber 2000), prevails.

THE HOLISTIC INQUIRY

Just as physicians would do well to inquire about their patients' emotional and psychological well-being, mental health professionals would do well to inquire at the outset about their patients' health and their general attitude toward it. This can help you determine how well or poorly developed is their instinct toward self-preservation. It also introduces the concept that the mind and body are connected (Freud 1913b; Khantzian and Mack[1] 1983).

If they are in good health, you would want to know how much they play a part in this by being proactive about their health. You would want to know when the last time was they had a medical examination. If they have certain health problems, do they tend to have a fatalistic or laissez-faire attitude about it, allowing events to take their own course? Or are they perhaps neglectful about their health? Or do they perhaps behave in a way that can result in harm toward themselves? Are they abusive toward themselves, overtly or covertly? With high-risk patients, we need to understand more about their attitude and spiritual beliefs about death and the afterlife (Farber, Jackson, et al. 2007; Schneidman 1994). Is the patient inclined to play a direct and intentional role in his own death, or a more ambivalent indirect, partial, covert, or unconscious role, or no significant role in his own death (Farber, Jackson, et al. 2007)? And what are his beliefs about what happens after death? Is there an afterlife? Reincarnation?

What this really is all about is attempting to prevent the development of that insidious kindling process that can easily spark the flames of addictive high-risk behavior. It is much easier to prevent a forest fire than to extinguish one that is raging out of control. At this time, an ambitious but not impossible therapeutic goal would be to cultivate the development of signal anxiety, experienced as a warning in the mind that that something bad is about to happen and you had better do something about it quickly (Freud 1926; Freud 1966).

ALCOHOLISM, COMPULSIVE EATING, AND BIPOLAR DISORDER

Let me give you an example of such an effort. Marty, a married man in his mid-forties with two children, came to see me around a month after he was discharged from a psychiatric hospital. Having engaged in white-collar criminal behavior, he was no longer allowed to practice law. His wife was filing for divorce and he no longer lived in the home they had shared, but in a small cottage on the property. His relationship with his two children was a disaster. On the day he was discharged from the hospital, he got a telegram from his wife that he had to pack up and move out. Suddenly, this formerly wealthy man had become homeless, with no choice but to move in with his parents, and become financially dependent on them.

He had been having affairs and binge drinking and eating for years. He had become so morbidly obese that he had had weight loss surgery several years before. He so depressed that he was thinking about ending his life. His mother knew of his depression but not his suicidal thinking, and suggested he speak with her friend, a clinical social worker. He did and on her advice, began an inpatient hospital assessment and treatment voluntarily. To his surprise, he was diagnosed as having Bipolar Disorder 1. It was also a relief, because it helped him to understand his binge eating and drinking as attempts to medicate himself for a condition he did not know he had. He began to understand some of the hypermanic ecstatic states he had had since adolescence. He attended daily Alcoholics Anonymous meetings and I referred him to a psychiatrist and to a bipolar support group. I suggested he read Marya Hornbacher's *A Bipolar Life* (2008).

He read how Hornbacher's mental illness manifested even earlier in childhood than his, and how she began drinking at age ten in an attempt to stabilize her moods. She too had an eating disorder, using her anorexic and bulimic behavior, as well as cutting herself, to regulate her moods. She was in and out of psychiatric hospitals, and had frequent promiscuous sex, before being diagnosed with childhood onset rapid cycling type 1 bipolar disorder. It took Hornbacher a long time to learn that she could not afford to drink, because of alcohol's powerful kindling effect on her illness. When she stopped drinking, she found that she had a chance for a life and did not have to remain a career mental patient, in and out of a revolving door of mental hospitals. Reading about Hornbacher served as a cautionary tale to Marty. Hearing the stories of those in his bipolar support group and AA who were struggling to manage their lives provided hope that he too might successfully manage his illness.

SELF-MUTILATION: "NOTHING TO GET SO CUT UP ABOUT"

Another effort was not successful, but it was not for lack of trying. Cat Stevens wrote the song, "First Cut Is the Deepest" in 1967.[2] The first time someone mutilates himself is the most difficult. After that it gets easier and easier, becoming the "new normal," especially if one's peers are doing it too. Marcie's mother had discovered disturbing scars on her fifteen-year-old daughter's arms, too many to be dismissed as accidents. It occurred to her that this just might be the self-mutilating behavior that she had been hearing about in the media. When confronted, Marcie acknowledged this to be true but insisted that it was no big deal; she could stop whenever she wanted, lots of kids were doing it.

Marcie ended up in my office, making it very clear that this was a total waste of her and my time and her parents' money. She agreed to tell me anything I wanted to know if this might get her mother off her back. She was sure she could convince me there really was nothing to worry about, and once convinced, I could convince her mother. According to Marcie, what it boiled down to is that it is much more comfortable to get rid of angry feelings with just a little slice of the razor blade than to walk around with all these pent-up angry feelings jumbled up inside and pressing to be released. She asked me "When you're leading a busy life, doesn't it make sense to have a quick and easy way to get rid of those feelings? It's like walking around with this big explosive fart inside you that can't get out."

I spoke in a way that told her I understood her dilemma, then said that if all it took to get rid of those feelings was to cut yourself, then doing it just once in your life should do the job for good. We could all do it. We *should* all do it. Doctors might even prescribe it. Insurance would even pay for it. By then we were both laughing. Then I told Marcie that the problem was that doing it just once does the job only for a short period of time, and then the angry feelings come back because they were never really gone in the first place. The cutting was only a temporary distraction from them. She agreed that this was true but so long as all she had to do was make a cut or two each time she felt like this, this was no problem, "no biggie." They were not deep, reckless cuts so what was the big deal? I told her that many people who cut themselves find that once they start to do it, they feel a need to do it more frequently (Russell and John 1999) and more recklessly and wondered if this might be true for her. She reluctantly acknowledged that it had become more frequent but not more reckless. I told her I thought it was only a matter of time before it becomes more dangerous, and explained how psychotherapy could help her develop the ability to regulate her intense anger so that it did not press so much to be discharged in this way. "Why bother," she said, "with psychotherapy which takes time, when just a little cut does the trick?" I repeated that if she continued, she would find herself cutting more deeply or wildly, and I'd hate to see that happen to her. That had not happened, she said angrily, and *would not* happen because she was totally and completely in control. In the way that adolescents have of thinking they are invulnerable, Marcie had no use for me. Although I had given her mother my opinion as well, she did not insist that Marcie return to see me. I never heard from her or her family again.

She agreed that this was true but so long as all she had to do was make a cut or two each time she felt like this, this was no problem, "no biggie." They were not deep, reckless cuts so what was the big deal? I told her that many people who cut themselves find that once they start to do it, they feel a need to do it more frequently (Russell and John 1999) and wondered if this might be true for her. She reluctantly acknowledged that it was. Hoping to sow the seeds for developing signal anxiety, I explained how psychotherapy might help her develop the ability to regulate her intense anger so that it did not press so much to be discharged in this way. I explained that she could develop other ways of expressing her anger. "Why bother," she said, "with psychotherapy which takes time, when just a little cut does the trick?" I went on to tell her that as people need to do it more frequently, they often find themselves cutting more deeply or wildly, and I'd hate to see that happen to her. That had not happened, she said angrily, and *would not* happen because she was totally and completely in control. In the way that adolescents have of thinking they are invulnerable, Marcie had no use for me. Although I had given her mother my opinion as well, unfortunately she did not insist that Marcie continue to see me. I never heard from her or her family again.

GOTH CULTURE

> Being Goth, for me, is seeing beauty, and its coming destruction, at the same time. . . It's the last dance as the walls are crumbling around you. . . .
> — Beatgrrl

Goth has been described as a subgenre of punk with a dark aesthetic, marked by distinctive clothing, makeup, and tastes in music (Young, Sweeting, and West, 2006). It began as a part of the punk rock scene. As punk rock began dying out, Goth endured by creating its own subculture, stimulated by fantasy and role playing games such as Dungeons & Dragons. Some American adolescents simply affect the look to distinguish themselves from mainstream youth while others become deeply absorbed in the dark beliefs and practices of the Middle Ages, becoming morbidly enthralled with death and pain. They may become attracted to the Goth subculture after feeling alienated in school, and find that this culture echoes these feelings. Goths tend to be nonviolent, pacifistic, passive, and tolerant (Hodkinson 2002).

Carolyn, a fifteen-year-old attending the alternative program in a local high school, was referred to me after she was discharged from a psychiatric hospital. She was in the school's alternative program because her strangeness was more accepted there than in the regular school program, where she was often ridiculed for her appearance. She was considerably overweight, in part a result of her compulsive eating and in part a result of mood-stabilizing and antidepressant medications. She wore a lot of black clothing and eye makeup, and foundation makeup that made her skin very pale. Her hair color changed from week to week, but always sported a streak or two of bright shades of pink, green, purple, or blue. She once arrived straight from school looking like a dominatrix from the S & M subculture, wearing a tightly laced corset that boosted and displayed her ample cleavage, and heavy black leather Shit Kicker boots. (Shit Kicker is a brand name, billed as "Made tough so you can stay tough.") I was amazed that she was allowed to come to school dressed like this. To Carolyn, her physical presentation was a way of expressing her individuality. To me, it seemed to express something dark and threatening lurking inside her. This smart, creative girl had had a flirtation with anorexia two years earlier and had been mutilating herself since she was eight, using thumbtacks or scissors on her right leg. Shortly before her hospitalization, she had cut her arm, using a razor blade, both for the first time, which scared her enough to tell her guidance counselor, who was instrumental in getting her admitted to the hospital. Her family was chaotic and at times violent, known to the local police, who had been called by neighbors numerous times. Her older brother, with whom she had her safest and most secure attachment, had gone off his medication for his bipolar disorder a year earlier. While Carolyn tried to protect her mother from his verbal abuse, he started to choke her. She managed to get away and ran out of the house. Although fearful of returning, she did come back but has been terrified of standing up to him ever since. She had lost the brother she knew and loved and had no one to rely on except her boyfriend, also a very disturbed person.

Outpatient therapy was not sufficient and she returned to the hospital's day treatment program. When discharged back to my care and her psychiatrist's, summer was starting and she wanted to find a job. More than anything she wanted to be a serving wench at the Renaissance Faire, but it was too far away. My aim in treatment was to help keep her alive until she was eighteen and could leave her family to go to college.

While treating Caroline, I was not aware of research that had been done on young people involved in this subculture. A recent longitudinal study was conducted of 1,258 people age 19, who were followed up since age 11, and found that current Goth identification was strongly associated with a lifetime incidence of self harm and attempted suicide (Young, Sweeting, et al 1996). Being female, having divorced or separated parents, smoking and any drug (not alcohol) use, and prior depression all predicted either self harm or a suicide attempt, with Goth identification remaining the single strongest predictor. Interestingly, it was found that becoming a Goth did not increase self-harm or suicidality, that "before these teens found a community that accepted their 'dark' interests . . . they were more prone to cut or otherwise harm themselves" (Perry and Szalavitz 2006, p. 189).

HUFFING, SNIFFING, DUSTING, AND BAGGING

For many involved parents who talk to their children about the risks of drugs, alcohol, and casual sex, it may not occur to them to tell them about the hazards of inhalant abuse because they may never have heard of it. Inhalant abuse, also known as huffing, sniffing, dusting and bagging, is a potentially deadly form of substance abuse. It is especially dangerous because kids think that all they are inhaling through their mouth or nose is air. They consider it to be a harmless way to get high, without the cost of drugs. Nothing could be further from the truth.

Inhalants are easily accessible, legal, everyday products that can be found in the home, school, or office— typewriter correction fluid, computer dusting spray, gasoline, propane, spray paint, air freshener, butane, felt-tip markers, cooking spray, aerosol whipped cream or other products, paint, and glue. They are "huffed" (sniffed) to create a high, affecting the brain forcefully and rapidly by preventing oxygen from reaching the lungs. When exposure to inhalants becomes chronic, it causes widespread damage to the brain and other parts of the nervous system. Poppers or amyl nitrate may be inhaled to enhance sexual pleasure, and have long been part of the club culture. Because the high is so brief, lasting only a few minutes, users may try to prolong it by inhaling continually over several hours, thus increasing the risk. Death can occur even with first-time use. Other risks include slurred speech, dizziness, confusion, hallucinations, delusions, headache, and nausea or vomiting. The suffocation can lead to brain damage, muscle spasms and tremors, addiction, liver, lung, and kidney problems, cognitive, hearing and vision damage, and heart attack. One in five American teens have used inhalants to get high, according to the the National Institute on Drug Abuse. When my son was around eight or nine, a new well-regarded babysitter, a teenage boy, stayed with him one evening. My son said that he had been sniffing repeatedly from a can of whipped cream, and was acting very weird. This was the first I had heard of huffing.

"DEAR ABBY, MY SISTER PLAYS THE CHOKING GAME AND I AM WORRIED"

In the past several years there have been media reports about kids who have died playing the *choking game*, which is also known as the *fainting game*, *space cowboy*, or *cloud nine*, referring to deliberately cutting off oxygen to the brain to induce temporary syncope and euphoria (Johnson 2007). The means to achieve oxygen deprivation can be strangulation and self-induced hypocapnia, the decrease of carbon dioxide levels in the blood (Center for Disease Control, 2008). Both can cause permanent brain damage or death. In strangulation, the method responsible for most reported fatalities, a rope, scarf, or belt or is tied around the neck, or hands or arms press the neck to compress the carotid artery, thus directly restricting blood flow to the brain. Self-induced hypocapnia, often called *riding a rocket,* involves hyperventilation (forced overbreathing) until dizziness, tingling, or light-headedness is experienced, followed by holding the breath. This may well cause a blackout but it is thought that the effect is increased if air pressure in the lungs is increased by holding the breath "hard," that is, a forced exhalation while not allowing any air to escape or by a bear hug by someone else. This hyperventilation produces an excessive eradication of carbon dioxide, with no significant additional amounts of oxygen able to be stored.

Someone who has experimented with self-induced hypocapnia wrote about it online:

Anyway what you do is:

- Squat down
- Take 20 DEEP and LONG breaths.
- On the last deep breath hold it and stand up slowly.
- Ask someone to give you a bear hug (without the knuckles into spine part) and squeeze tight.
- Observe.

> What happens is the squeezee goes limp. The squeezer has to be aware of this or you'll be dropped and probably get hurt, so make sure the squeezer puts you down slowly. Within 5 seconds or so, the squeezee will start to shake (as in like a seizure). The shaking will increase very rapidly. As soon as the squeezee starts shaking, the squeezer should lightly slap the squeezee to get him back into "conscious land." The whole process would take like 7-8 seconds, but for the squeezee, it *literally* feels like an eternity. So far nothing has happened. I don't know how safe it is because I don't know *what* it is. All people I've done it on came back to "life" within 10 seconds. There was one person that took like a minute and that scared my pants off, but he came back (had to actually violently slap him to get him back). So anyone know what this is, or has done this before, or has any info on it? (http://www.gamedev.net/topic/418004-self-induced-faintingblackingout- whole-life-flash-before-your-eyes/)

Not long ago, I read the following letter to *Dear Abby*, published in syndicated newspapers across the United States (Van Buren 2009).

> Dear Abby:
> During my visits at my dad's, I share a room with my stepsisters. They have made it clear they resent having to share their room with me, even though I have no choice about it.

> They play the choking game with some of their friends. When I refuse to participate, they put me down and call me chicken, but I'm not about to do something so dangerous.
> They have told me I'd better "mind my own business" and not say anything to their mom about it. I'm afraid if I do and I get them into trouble, they'll resent me more and make things even more difficult for me.
> On the other hand, I'd feel really guilty if I stay silent and something terrible happened to one or both of them. Should I tell their mom, even if it causes problems for me?
> Seattle Stepsister

> Dear Stepsister:
> I think you should tell your mother, and let her tell your father and his wife. The "choking game" isn't a game; it's extremely dangerous. It destroys brain cells and has been known to kill people. The practice can also be addictive, and when people do it alone and lose consciousness for the last time, the deaths are sometimes mistaken as suicides.

Unexplained marks on the neck, bloodshot eyes, ropes, scarves, or belts tied to bedroom furniture or doorknobs, bent closet rods, out-of-place leashes or bungee cords, bleeding under the skin or on the face, especially the eyelids, and talking about the choking game and disorientation can all be signs of a child participating in the choking game. If you hear about the choking game from someone you know or note any of the above signs, you might read him the Dear Abby letter and response, or tell him about sixteen-year-old Levi Draher. Levi was found clinically dead by his mother, hanging from a rope he had thrown across the frame of a bunk bed (Johnson 2007). Levi passed out faster than he could react and had a heart attack. He lay in a coma for three days, receiving anti-seizure drugs that he still takes. He told a high school audience "I died and I came back."

Alonza Womack found his sixteen-year-old son Nicholas unconscious in the basement of his home. He died three days later at the Westchester County Medical Center. Although the Medical Examiner's Office ruled his death a suicide by hanging, Nicholas's mother, Sylvia Womack, at first accepted what the police told her but then became quite certain it was not a suicide, but the result of the choking game. Nick, she said, was happy, well-liked, and enthusiastic about his future; he was a born entrepreneur with a future in business. His body was not found dangling feet from the ground as would be expected in an intentional suicide. "If he wanted to kill himself, he wouldn't have placed himself so close to the floor" (Howard 2010, p. 14A). Although the state police who responded to the scene say there was nothing to suggest anything other than intentional suicide, Alana Levine, MD, a spokesperson for the American Academy of Pediatrics, said that fatalities resulting from the choking game may be more common than is known because they resemble suicide. "I think it is a huge challenge because most of the time the behavior is done alone and people don't talk about it. So we don't really know how prevalent it is." Levine cited a 2008 study done by the Center for Disease Control, "Unintentional Strangulation Deaths from the 'Choking Game' among Youths Aged 6-19 Years." During 1995-2007, 82 probable deaths from the choking game were reported among young people.

In a more recent study of Oregon eighth-graders, around a third knew of someone playing the choking game, almost 3 percent had helped someone, and around 6 percent said they had played the "game." "We are just beginning to understand this behavior," said lead researcher Sarah Ramowski, MSW, an adolescent health policy and assessment specialist in the Oregon Department of Health. "What we found was that kids who have engaged in this behavior are much more likely to also have engaged in other health-risk behaviors, have mental health problems, have abused substances" (Reinberg 2010).

The choking game sometimes leads to autoerotic asphyxiation, using similar methods for purposes of a heightened sexual response. You may remember it in the film *Fatal Attraction*. It may be played by consenting partners or as an autoerotic form of masturbation, and was implicated in the death of actor David Carradine (Orloff 2009). A patient may casually drop a reference to autoerotic asphyxiation, meaning perhaps that that they find this titillating or that they may have done it. They may have seen the erotic scene from the film *Fatal Attraction*, in which Glen Close's character allows a man to wrap a scarf around her neck, cutting off her air supply, and has a powerful orgasm. Even if they insist that they would never try it, this is an opportunity to ask them what they know about it, what they have heard about it, saying that it can sound so exciting that lots of people imagine themselves trying it. It is also an opportunity for a bit of psychoeducation about how potentially deadly the practice can be.

SUMMING UP

We need to assume a protective stance and become parental surrogates with those patients who need to be protected from themselves. The development of a safe and secure attachment to someone who cares allows us to do that, and has the potential to become a corrective emotional experience (Alexander 1958; Bridges 2005; Farber 2000, 2002; Hartman and Zimberoff 2004). Just as a child's experience of being cared for and protected by a nurturing parent becomes internalized and develops into the ability to care for and protect himself (Farber 2000; Khantzian and Mack 1983), when a patient comes to feel really cared for another, this is a powerful experience which can alter his sense of personal identity. He can start to feel that he is someone worth caring about, which leads to wanting to take better care of himself. These corrective emotional experiences can build ego strength through overcoming shame, helplessness, and dissociation, while reclaiming worthiness and personal power. A sense of agency and effectiveness can develop. Helping someone to feel that he is somebody rather than nobody can help begin the process of developing a sense of personal identity (Hartman and Zimberoff 2004).

Our efforts will be successful with only some of the patients we try to help in this way. The gratification is in knowing we did what we could. For all the long, hard work involved in working with such difficult, worrisome, exasperating patients, when the effort is successful, it is enormously gratifying. But to have any success at all, the therapist must take the risk of caring.

NOTE

1. This is the same John Mack who was almost fired from his Harvard faculty position for publishing a book that took reports of alien abduction seriously.
2. "Nothing to Get So Cut up About" in the subheading above is borrowed from the title of an important work on self-mutilation, M. Simpson's *Self-Mutilation as Indirect Destructive Behavior: Nothing to Get So Cut up About*(Simpson 1980)

Chapter Twelve

Intersubjectivity and the Power of the Therapist's Affective Experience

> What each of us needs from the other . . . is at depth pretty much the same. We need to find in the other an affirming witness to the best that we hope we are, as well as an accepting and durable respondent to those worst aspects of ourselves that we fear we are.
>
> —James McLaughlin, "Touching Limits in the Psychoanalytic Dyad"

It is easy to lose sleep over patients who take terrible risks with their lives, something we cannot afford to do. They are intimidating to psychotherapists for good reason. Treating them may be a poor investment of time and emotional energy that is not likely to reap any rewards. They are difficult to treat; their treatment is likely to be quite stormy, and despite a therapist's best efforts they might end their life. This is a very real occupational hazard and so therapists may refuse to treat them.

It is only when we stick our necks out and risk letting ourselves feel intensely and passionately about them, that we might be truly effective in reaching them (Farber 2000, 2002; 2008a, 2008b). These patients seem to have developed a dissociated attachment to pain and suffering that is more intimate than any relationship they might have with another human being. Nevertheless, it is the therapist's passionate engagement with the patient that can shake him awake enough to get him to look at and think about how his use of dissociation puts him at risk for death (Farber, Jackson, et al. 2007). When confronted with this harsh reality, many patients are shocked at the risks they are taking and may become motivated to alter their behavior. Through the development of an attachment to the therapist, the patient may become more able to tolerate limits set for his protection. In fact, the therapist can use this attachment as leverage in the treatment, refusing to see the patient unless he begins to alter his behavior so that the therapist need *not* lose sleep. It is this attachment that may allow the patient to relinquish his attachment to pain and suffering that cries out for ecstatic release.

There is an all too real relationship between pathological dissociation, depression, alexithymia, and suicidality (Maarinen, Tanskanen, Honkalampi, Haatainen, Hintikka, and Viinamaki 2005). Despite the very real potential for their behavior to result in their death, their dissociation permits them to have a remarkably disturbing lack of anxiety about their own life-threatening behavior, leaving family, friends, and therapists to bear that burden (Farber, Jackson, et al. 2007). That imbalance must be shifted. Signal anxiety and the ability to anticipate danger are healthy defenses that are sorely deficient, resulting in severe deficits in their abilities to regulate their affect and somatic states and to care for themselves. It is paramount that treatment address the dissociative tendencies, something for which our professional training has not prepared us.[1]

A developmental line from irresponsibility to responsibility for the self grows out of the experiences the child has in the mother-infant dyad (A. Freud 1966; Khantzian, and Mack 1983). If the child has been well cared for by a loving and attuned mother (or caretaker), gradually the child develops the ability to care for and protect himself. In other words, the child internalizes the sense that he deserves to be protected and well cared for, and so comes to take good care of himself. In individuals who take grave risks with their lives, the capacity for self-care has been severely impaired or undeveloped. Not only do they fail to care for themselves and protect themselves from others, they fail to protect themselves from themselves (Farber 2000).

They are likely to be suffering from one or more serious disturbances that include post-traumatic stress disorder, a dissociative disorder, a mood or anxiety disorder, a behavioral or substance addiction, a personality disorder. Because dissociation is a common feature of post-traumatic stress disorder, approximately 30% of patients with PTSD will present with a dissociative disorder. However patients tend not to fit so neatly into subtype categories and may exhibit both types of responses at different times and in different contexts (Lanius and Hopper 2008).

AN INTEGRATED APPROACH TO TREATMENT

Because of serious difficulties in affect regulation, treatment should also have a strong dialectical component, integrating two seemingly paradoxical needs—the need to accept oneself as he is and at the same time, the need to change, a Zen Buddhism paradigm. This can be accomplished when the therapist uses a dialectical approach that is both supportive and mutative. This dialectic is central to Dialectical Behavioral Therapy (DBT), founded by Marsha Linehan (1993a, 1993b) for the treatment of patients with Borderline Personality Disorder, who often self-mutilate, have eating disorders, or make suicide attempts. Its objectives are to teach patients skills at interpersonal effectiveness, emotional regulation, distress tolerance, and mindfulness.

Dialectical thinking, however, is not unique to DBT. It is found in Kernberg's (1989) psychoanalytic psychotherapy approach as well in Tobin's (2000), Zerbe's (2008), and my integrated approach to treatment. In fact, Linehan said that the emphasis in DBT on behaviors that interfere with therapy is more like the psychodynamic emphasis on transference behaviors than to any aspect of standard cognitive behavioral therapies, and that "the most effective insights gained from treatment pertain to the patient's behaviors as they occur in the interactions with the therapist (Linehan 1993a, p. 268)." The dialectical approach is thus similar in this way to a relational way of conducting psychoanalytic psychotherapy. While developing a specialty in the treatment of eating disorders, I developed a dialectical approach on my own, out of the necessity of developing an integrated approach that fits the patient's unique needs. This occurred parallel to Linehan's conducting clinical trials at New York– Presbyterian Hospital in White Plains, before DBT became an evidence-based treatment modality.DBT continues to be adapted for use with different populations (Dimeff and Koerner 2007; Marra 2005; Astrachan-Fletcher and Maslar 2009). A number of DBT self-help workbooks can also be used by patients. Treatment will be enhanced by the creativity, flexibility, and perseverance of the therapist.

RISING TO THE CHALLENGE

Having taken on the challenge of treating very difficult high-risk patients, I have maintained the caution I have always used, and at the same time, I have increasingly trusted my intuition and improvisational ability. The concepts of improvisation and caution may seem to be at odds with each other, but I have found that paradoxically, one can enhance the other. When you improvise in treatment and continue to assess and adjust what you do, this *cautious improvisation* can work quite well.

For those who are inexperienced in treating dissociative patients, certain signs can be indicators of a dissociated state. If your patient seems to be "spacing out" in sessions or going somewhere else in his mind, if there is little eye contact, or he exhibits flat affect, or if there are discontinuities in the narrative, and shifts in and out of trance-like states, these are indicators of dissociation that need to be explored further (Farber 2008b). Dissociative processes serve a defensive function, acting as a shock absorber, circuit breaker, or mechanical diversion such that the mind's collection of content and experience can be pulled together in a way that maintains physiologic equilibrium and mental coherence. When there is an extreme post-traumatic response there may be little mental coherence. This is where we usually are when dissociative processes present themselves in the session

The first step is to interrupt the dissociative process and draw the patient's conscious attention to it, so that eventually he might become aware of doing this. Simply saying something like "You seemed to drift off somewhere. Where did your mind go?" demonstrates your interest in knowing, and might help to connect him to dissociated material, which then becomes available for discussion in the treatment.

A primary function of the therapist, according to Bowlby (1988), is to provide the patient with a safe and secure base of attachment (Farber 2008b) from which he can venture to explore the painful aspects difficulties of his life. Confiding in a supportive, empathic, and optimistic companion can make the journey possible. The process of change in psychoanalytic work requires an interpersonal space in which the threatening experience can play itself out, while the aroused painful affect can be managed. Process and outcome research in psychotherapy has found that success in treatment is correlated not with a specific technique or orientation but with the *fit* between patient and therapist, a factor related to attachment and the therapeutic alliance (Kroll 1993; Farber 2008b). Although the principle that the relationship between patient and therapist is the primary tool for change is central to the practice of psychotherapy, most of the literature has focused on understanding the patient's part of the relationship rather than the part each play (Edward and Bess 1998). The social work literature is markedly different, with the clinician engaging in a very present and real relationship with the client. Known in academic social work as "the clinical social work bible," *Casework: A Psychosocial Therapy* (Woods and Hollis 1990) describes how the psychosocial approach is used, whether it be in brief treatment, crisis intervention, or longer term intensive therapy. The therapist's characteristics of non-possessive warmth and concern, genuineness, empathy, and nonjudgmental acceptance all enhance the relationship; in intensive therapy especially, the social worker's self-awareness is crucial. Writing about self-disclosure in clinical social work, James Raines said that the concept of the therapist as a blank screen is an impossibility because "our personality exudes from everything we do or do not do!" (Raines 1996, p. 364).

Despite the traditional thinking about anonymity and neutrality on the part of the therapist in order not to interfere with the development of an adequate transference neurosis, seasoned and effective therapists kept finding that the disciplined use of their authentic selves resulted in noteworthy and rewarding results (Edward and Bess 1998). In a study designed to elicit from seasoned therapists of various disciplines and orientations what they thought was especially helpful to patients, social workers Coady and Wolgien found that what is most helpful is "being authentic and honest, . . . attending to impact of self, and using self-disclosure" (Coady and Wolgien 1996, p. 316). Although generally not acknowledged in the relational psychoanalytic literature, relational practice had its origins in social work, which has produced its own relational literature. The contributions of Arnd-Caddigan and Pozzuto (2008), Brandell (2010), Coady and Wolgien (1996); Edward and Bess (1998), and Goldstein, Miehls, and Ringel (2009) are only a few. Most recently clinical social worker Lynn Turner and psychologist Mary Wylie published "The Attuned Therapist: Does Attachment Theory Really Matter?" (Wylie and Turner 2011). Summing up Daniel Siegel's (1999) theory of how relationships and the brain interact to shape the people we are, Wylie and Turner describe how the whole self of the therapist must be attuned to the patient, not only understanding her feelings conceptually but feeling her feelings. "It must be a hands-on, body-on, mind-on therapy, in which the therapist's whole self vibrated like a tuning fork to every quiver in the client's being without, however, losing the basic emotional stability that the client needed to regulate his or her runaway emotions" (Sykes and Turner 2011, p. 25).

ATTUNEMENT AND ATTACHMENT-BASED PSYCHOTHERAPY

Isakower's (1992a, 1992b) concept of the joint participation of patient and analyst within the analytic setting is that it is a unique *analyzing instrument*. The patient follows the fundamental rule of free association, while the analyst listens with free-floating attention, alternating as speaker and listener, sharing. When both have arrived at comparable, but not equivalent states of partial ego regression, similar to a sleep or trance state, involuntary thoughts, images, and perceptions become available to each. The patient's free association and the analyst's free-floating attention are the two halves of the analyzing instrument, a kind of reciprocal free association. Empathy is a significant factor in the analyst's functioning. His communication to the patient of his thoughts, images, or perceptions is often reciprocated by the patient, thus facilitating the emergence, understanding, and interpretation of the patient's fantasy or memory communications to the analyst.

When high-risk symptoms predominate in trauma-related symptomotology, treatment will require a phase-oriented attachment–based treatment (Farber 2000; Howell 2005; Pearlman and Courtois 2005; Steele, van der Hart, and Nijenhuis 2005). The first phase focuses on symptom reduction and stabilization, the second on the treatment of traumatic memories, and the third on integration of dissociated parts of the personality, rehabilitation, and development of intimate relationship.

Attachment-based psychotherapy incorporates both the principles of attachment theory and the knowledge of neuroscience (Siegel 1999). It is the psychotherapist's attunement to those "critical micromoments of interaction" (Siegel 1999, p.290) "with the patient—including tone of voice, facial expression, posture, motion, eye gaze—that reveal states of mind that are otherwise hidden.

Wylie and Turner (2011) sum up and apply Siegel's theory to the relationship that is optimally established in psychotherapy. "The mind emerges from the activity of the brain, whose structure and function are directly shaped by interpersonal experience" (Siegel 1999, p.1). Although there are no formal protocols for doing attachment-based psychotherapy, certain principles upon which most attachment–based therapists would agree are:

> Insecure, ambivalent, avoidant, or disorganized early attachment experiences are real events which can substantially and destructively shape a client's emotional and relational development . . .The attachment pattern learned in early childhood experiences will play out in psychotherapy. . . . The right brain/ limbic (unconscious, emotional, intuitive) interaction of the psychotherapist and client and to his/her own internal triggers is critical to effective therapy. . . Reparative enactments of early attachment experiences, co-constructed by therapist and client, are fundamental to healing. (Wylie and Turner 2011, p. 25)

As Wylie and Turner (2011) say, this is not a psychotherapy for the faint of heart. The therapist is a fellow traveler who resonates with the patient's sadness, anger, and anxiety. He must not recoil from the intensity of the patient's experience but must provide, through tone of voice, eye contact, expression, posture, and words, the steadiness to keep the patient feeling understood, safely held, and supported.

Many of those with high-risk behavior may have a depersonalization disorder or other dissociative disorder, the result of either shock trauma, resulting from physical or sexual abuse, loss of a parent in childhood, etc., or relational trauma, which is associated with the caregiver's maltreatment or gross insensitivity in early life (Farber 2008b). Those with dissociative disorders have, a disorganized or traumatic attachment pattern (Main and Solomon, 1986; Main and Morgan 1996; Farber 2008b). Schilder described depersonalization as early as 1928.

> To the depersonalized individual the world appears strange, peculiar, foreign, dream like. Objects appear at times strangely diminished in size, at times flat. Sounds appear to come from a distance. The tactile characteristics likewise, seem, strangely altered, but the patients complain not only of the changes in their perception, but their images appear to be altered. Patients characterize their imagery as pale, colourless, and some complain that they have altogether lost the power of imagination. The emotions, likewise, undergo marked altera-

> tion. Patients complain that they are experiencing neither pain or pleasure; love and hate have perished with them. They experience a fundamental change in their personality, and the climax is reached with their complaints that they have become strangers to themselves. It is as though they were dead, lifeless, mere automatons. The objective examination of such patients reveals not only an intact sensory apparatus but also an intact emotional apparatus. All these patients exhibit natural affective reactions in their facial expressions, attitudes, etc, so that it is impossible to assume that they are incapable of emotional response. (Schilder 1928, p. 120)

We can understand the attachment disorder in the following way. When the caretaker, who is meant to protect the child fails to protect him or preys upon him instead, this presents the child with the impossible dilemma of wanting to be comforted by the caretaker while being terrified of being annihilated by the caretaker. This annihilation anxiety (Hurvich 2003) causes the child to freeze in a trance-like stillness, the beginning of a tendency toward dissociation (Farber 2008b; Perry, et al.. 1995; Blakely, Baker, and Vigilante 1995).

Those with a disorganized attachment suffer from an out of control stream of consciousness dominated by flashbacks and dissociated fragments of early frightening memories of the attachment figure, accompanied by intense anxiety and anger.

So much of attachment-based therapy is intuitive, played out in enactments, through which patient and therapist create together a coherent story which helps the patient make sense of his inner turmoil (Wylie and Turner 2011). This connection happens through a relational unconscious, in which one unconscious mind communicates with the other's unconscious mind, a dissociated form of communication (Schore and Chefetz 2005; Bromberg 1998, 2006).

THE THERAPIST AS TUNING FORK:

REVISITING THE CONCEPTS OF NEUTRALITY, ABSTINENCE, AND ANONYMITY

Some psychotherapists who have had no training in psychotherapy fly by the seat of their pants, without any theory to base their work on. I used to look down on them, thinking that my training in classical analytic theory and technique and ego psychology was the better way. But I have since discovered that flying by the seat of their pants may work for some therapists, if they are talented, attuned, and intuitive enough, even when they have no theory to serve as a guide to treatment. By no means am I suggesting that we do away with training. When the freedom to improvise is combined with good non-authoritarian training, it can be a winning combination.

Classical psychoanalytic theory is grounded in drive theory and the principles of neutrality, abstinence, and anonymity (Freud 1911-15), which guide the psychotherapist toward restraint of self rather than active use of self. When these principles are followed mindlessly, the result resembles a *New Yorker* cartoon version of psychoanalysis. The blank screen concept (Freud 1912) means that the analyst's personality should not enter into the consulting room. This detached manner can be readily experienced as a repetition of the trauma of having emotionally uninvolved parents. Many clinicians think it an error when the therapist is *not* a blank screen upon which the patient can transfer his feelings about other important people in his life, claiming that in such cases, the transference cannot be analyzed. My years of clinical experience have told me that when the therapist does not project a blank screen persona, transference forms nonetheless. If the patient experiences the blank screen therapist as detached and uncaring, that is what the therapist is communicating and is not transference.

Above all else, the patient-therapist relationship is a relationship between two real people, and the therapist's warmth, humor, and anger are all part of his personality. When the therapist uses his personality judiciously and creatively, he can work intuitively, transparently, and pragmatically.

Owen Renik (2003) challenged the status quo in psychoanalysis, commenting on how little psychoanalytic principles of technique have evolved since the early days of psychoanalysis, that in the effort to maintain a psychoanalytic identity, analysts have clung too tenaciously to established practices based on received wisdom.

> Standardization, in this sense, does not mean rigidity. It goes without saying that any generalization we might propose remains open to revision and review. As a matter of fact, in my opinion, something we very much need to standardize is an experimental approach to psychoanalytic technique. It's striking how little our principles of technique have evolved since the early days of psychoanalysis. I think that in our efforts to maintain what is called a "psychoanalytic identity," we have clung too tenaciously to established practices based on received wisdom. . . . psychoanalysts have tended to insist on certain procedures that we believe distinguish us from other therapists, make us special—frequency of visits, use of the couch, a stance of personal anonymity, etc. I think that psychoanalysts have been insufficiently open to the possibility that some of these procedures are not actually useful in many—or even any—cases. That's the kind of standardization we don't need (Renik 2003, pp. 51-52).

A few years later, he published a provocatively titled book, *Practical Psychoanalysis for Therapists and Patients* (Renik 2006).

> By now, the term *practical psychoanalysis* has become an oxymoron. The way psychoanalytic treatment is generally conducted, it is extremely *im*practical: it

> doesn't serve the needs of the vast majority of potential patients. Understandably, people who seek the help of mental health caregivers want a therapy that will provide maximum relief from emotional distress as quickly as possible. Most clinical psychoanalysts offer instead a lengthy journey of self-discovery during which too much concern with symptom relief is considered counterproductive. "Self-awareness" is the main goal; symptom relief is of secondary importance and is expected to arrive, if at all, only after a while. . . . No surprise, then, that psychoanalysis has come to be regarded by the public at large as an esoteric practice that promotes a self-involved escape from real life, rather than a treatment method that helps the patient live real life more happily (Renik 2006, p. 1).

The analyst's authentic engagement with the patient is a complex question at the center of psychoanalytic controversies today (Bucci 2007a). Freud went through many changes in his thinking about the analyst's engagement, moving gradually from his earlier view that the treatment required a whole human relationship to a later view of the analyst's engagement as a hazard to the treatment (Bucci 2007a). He had difficulty with the Christian concept of *agape,* described by C. S. Lewis (1991) as the highest level of love known to humanity—a selfless love, passionately committed to the well-being of the other, regarding it as unrealistic, challenging it as a practical norm for everyday behavior, although he thought the concept retained its validity as an ideal (Meissner 2003). Freud saw psychoanalysis not only as a procedure for investigating mental processes and a method of treatment but as a collection of information leading to a new scientific discipline. Bergmann said:

> If we follow this line of thought, we can say that any method of treatment that is based on the data collected by the analytic method deserves to be called psychoanalysis. The ideal method of treatment chosen should be based on our psychoanalytic understanding of our patients' personality structure and how most profitably to approach them. We must lose the fear that obsessed Freud that the gold of psychoanalysis will be diluted by some copper of psychotherapy . . . Orthodoxy of any kind forces us to live on the capital accumulated by previous generations, and this is the enemy of creativity. (Bergmann 1999, pp. 282-87)

Psychoanalysis has always accounted for the patient's subjectivity constantly being expressed within the clinical situation, largely in ways of which he is unaware. More recently, we have begun to acknowledge that the same is true of the analyst. Adopting an intersubjective perspective in psychoanalysis or psychoanalytic psychotherapy means giving up "the myth of isolated mind" (Stolorow and Atwood 2002; Renik 2004, 2006, 2007). Levine and Friedman (2000) wrote of an "irreducible subjectivity" in the therapeutic encounter, placing the analytic relationship at the center of the analytic process in which the emotional life of the analyst is joined to that of the patient.

The concept of abstinence means that the therapist avoids gratifying the patient's transference wishes (Freud 1915), often interpreted as abstaining from touching the patient other than an introductory handshake at the initial meeting, socializing etc. There are times, however, when a pat on the shoulder, a brief hug, or taking the patient's hand is just the humane thing to do. But we have so many taboos about touch that make this unthinkable for some therapists. The meaning of touch in treatment can only be understood within the intersubectivity of the relationship. Touch is our first medium of communication, our first language (Montagu 1971; Pines 1980). When used sensitively and judiciously, touch can enhance the therapeutic alliance. North America seem has become a touch-deprived culture, in which therapists become touch-phobic, and nursery school teachers are afraid to hold a crying child in their arms (Farber 2000). Because there have been harmful boundary violations by psychotherapists such as sexual involvement with the patient, or because of the tendency of patients who have been sexually abused to overreact with anxiety to touch, many clinicians have become phobic about all touch, to the detriment of their patients' treatment.

Over the past decade or so, there has been a corresponding movement away from the classical principles toward an interactive vision of the analytic situation that makes the analytic relationship, with its powerful, reciprocal affective currents, crucial to the therapeutic action. "Practical psychoanalysis means remaining open-minded with regard to theory, holding nothing as axiomatic; and it means retaining an experimental approach to technique—that is, searching for whatever way of working together with a given patient seems to make progress toward the desired goals of treatment" (Renik 2006, p. 3).

THE DISSOCIATIVE RESPONSE AS A FORM OF COMMUNICATION

> I have never managed to give a better description than this of the strange state of mind in which one knows and does not know a thing at the same time. —Sigmund Freud, *Studies on Hysteria*

Although Freud was wary about passion in his personal life and mysticism in his professional life, his younger colleague Ferenczi was discovering something about mental telepathy that the odd practices of the psychics helped him think about (Phillips 1995). This is something psychoanalysis only recently has begun to look at, specifically in the work of Philip Bromberg and Wilma Bucci. Ferenczi found that at times his free associations to what the patient was saying seemed to replicate what the patient was saying to him, as if he were holding some of the patient's thoughts which the patient could not allow himself to think (Phillips 1995). For Melanie Klein, too, who introduced the concept of projective identification (1946, 1952), it was a form of communication, the earliest form of empathy, based on getting a person to put himself in another's shoes by feeling what the other cannot allow himself to feel.

> The patient could evoke in the analyst, as though by thought transference, the disowned parts of himself. . . . And it was obvious to Ferenczi that if this was true, then it was going to be a two-way traffic: it couldn't only be the patient doing this to the analyst; it must also be the analyst doing it to the patient. This made psychoanalysis a rather more reciprocal venture than Freud's resolutely scientific, quasi-medical model could allow (Phillips 1995, p. 22).

Ferenczi was referring to dissociated states of consciousness, which Freud initially acknowledged but then dismissed. Despite this, Freud had a profound interest in the uncanny, the occult, and "thought transference" (Freud 1919, 1922, 1925, 1933, 1941a, 1941b). He corresponded continually with Ferenczi and Jung about his conviction that telepathic thought transference was real and clinically important (Mayer 2001). Because pathological dissociation is a reaction to trauma, the nature of the analytic relationship took on a new and special significance, and analysts such as Ferenczi, Balint, Sullivan, Fairbairn, Bion, and Kohut, representing different analytic schools of thought, all struggled with the question of how dissociation shapes the analytic relationship and its effectiveness (Bromberg 1998). In *Psychoanalysis and the Occult*, Devereaux (1953) cited 235 papers on telepathic experiences and psychoanalysis. Apparently unaware of Bromberg's new paradigm, Mayer commented "It is notable that almost never has the reporting analyst revealed to a patient the fact that some communication between the two of them has struck the analyst as telepathic. . . . And if only one party in the communication is considering its nature, our ability to learn about what it entailed will necessarily be limited" (Mayer 2001, p. 632). In a revolutionary departure in technique, Bromberg promotes speaking openly about this with the patient (Bromberg 1998). Although his concept was quite similar to Ferenczi's, it was remarkably different in revealing to the patient the "telepathic" nature of the communication between them.

PROJECTIVE IDENTIFICATIONS AND ENACTMENTS

> All human love is a dramatic enactment of the wild, reckless, unquenchable undrainable love that powers the universe. If death is everywhere and inescapable, then so is love, if we but knew it. We can begin to know it through each other. . . So when you ask me why I cannot love you more calmly, I answer that to love you calmly is not to love you at all.
> —Jeanette Winterson, *The PowerBook*

Effective treatment frees the patient to develop toward higher levels of integration than those already reached. The therapist can serve as both a new and real object in the patient's life, the source of a corrective emotional experience (Farber 2000). Optimally the therapist represents a higher level of ego and self organization, and a higher level of being and relating (Loewald 1960). More recent understandings of the concept include understanding transference-countertransference relations in terms of the container and the contained (Bion 1962). That is, the therapist is understood to be a container, with the capacity to contain, tolerate, and ultimately interpret the patient's projective identifications (Rosenfeld 1987).

This is a tall order. In order to do this, the therapist must be able to allow the patient his chaotic regressions, while maintaining an optimism that these regressions will ultimately give way to healthier progressions (Boyer 1997). The therapist must be able to tolerate the introjection of whatever the patient is projecting into him while observing it without reacting severely. At the same time, the patient is introjecting the kindness and acceptance that the therapist is providing. This is the essential element, the therapist's capacity to observe how both he and the patient feel and act, to evaluate what goes on between them, assessing his own somatic sensations and thoughts. When both patient and therapist can enter into various degrees of reverie and intersubjective play, this can generate a potential, transitional space in which creativity can occur (Boyer 1997, 1999). This can be an extremely difficult thing to do, taxing the limits of the therapist's emotional resources.

Treatment can be comprised of the numerous struggles between patient and therapist known as enactments. An enactment is any mutual action within the patient/analyst relationship that arises in the context of difficulties in countertransference work (Bateman 1998). In enactments, patients get stuck in repeating and repeating the same experience, like dreaming the same dream over and over again. The literature on enactment considers it to be a powerful two-person phenomenon occurring between patient and therapist which is powered by projective identification, a primitive defense to which we all can regress in certain situations but one which is especially prominent in those with borderline personalities or dissociative disorders.

Projective identification is an unconscious process by which the patient, unable to contain an unacceptable affect or quality within himself, dissociates it from himself and projects it into the therapist (Klein 1946, 1952). It seems to occur as if an invisible projectile missile whistles silently across the boundaries separating the patient's own self state from the therapist's, landing directly in the therapist. The therapist may find himself reacting intensely to the patient as if he were controlled by some powerful puppeteer. There is an abrupt rupture in the working alliance, which both patient and therapist experience as being the consequence of the other's behavior, creating a crisis. The therapist may experience it as the patient's provocative tantrum while the patient may regard it as the therapist's inexplicably "losing it" or going crazy. The therapist's response has the potential to destroy the treatment or it can even serve as a corrective emotional experience. It is as if, in one way, the patient is communicating that the analyst must somehow lose his mind in order to know the patient's (Bromberg 1991).

An enactment can serve as a turning point in which the growth, not only of the patient but the therapist as well, depends upon which road is taken. In an enactment the boundary between what is personal and what is professional becomes dramatically permeable, allowing for the deepest and most enduring self-growth to occur (Bromberg 1998, 2006). When the therapist becomes swept up into the enactment, his private and subjective experience can serve to hold to the patient's dissociated experience, and can serve as the conduit through which his dissociated experiences can be accessed linguistically. This means that countertransference provides an opportunity for solving an emotional problem, providing that the analyst can achieve the psychological separation from the patient and from his own emotional experience, which seems at the time very real and objectively justified by the situation. "The analyst's ability to make creative use of this disorganized state of relatedness, while keeping his own center of subjectivity without inflicting it on the patient, is the heart of this part of the work" (Bromberg 1998, p.138). When this occurs, an internal linking will occur through an intersubjective field in which fantasy, perception, thought, and language all play a part. When the therapist is open and above-board and does not hide behind so-called objective interpretations of reality that mask their subjective origin, this makes it possible for the patient to risk gradually reclaiming that which had been previously dissociated. The patient begins to awaken from the dissociative state as if from a dream (Bromberg 2006). As this process continues, feelings of personal authenticity and vitality increase.

PASSION: A PECULIAR KIND OF LOVE

> Passion, it lies in all of us, sleeping. . . waiting. . . and though unwanted. . . unbidden."
>
> —Joss Whedon, screenwriter and executive producer

Joss Whedon (2010) said that passion is the source of our finest moment. Passion is the therapist's ongoing process of integrating and using his most basic and primal emotions, and is different from countertransference, which usually precedes passion (Bion 1963; Billow 2000). The analyst's integration and use of his primal feelings of love, hate, and curiosity serve as a central organizer of meaning in the analytic interaction (Bion 1963; Billow 2000). These feelings involve pain, and if they remain unintegrated or dissociated in the thinking process, the analyst can become stuck in repetitive transference-countertransference experiences without establishing fresh meaning. In other words, although passion is an internal process, it takes place within an intersubjective context. "Passion," said Bion, "is evidence that two minds are linked" (Bion 1963, p 13). Passion intensifies living in the here-and-now, and may include interludes of terror, dread, and confusion. In evoking such primitive elements, passion animates the analyst's thinking by achieving a heightened emotional awareness of himself, the links, the other, and the relationship (Billow 2000).

When the patient is unable to develop emotional meaning, he projects raw emotional experience into the analyst, who must serve as a container for it. Using primary processes such as free association, images, and dreams as well as secondary processes, the analyst gathers and deciphers the patient's disowned emotionality, and gradually presents it to the patient, transformed into words (Billow 2000). An important cognitive dimension of this containing function involves states of reverie, which also demands what Renik (1996) calls *irrational emotional involvement.* In reverie, the analyst uses dreamlike and irrational elements of his mind in order to understand and further develop the the patient's and his own unformulated thoughts and feelings (Bion 1962; Billow 2000). A passionate interpretation propels the painful process of separating from a prior cognitive-emotional state of being.

It is important to understand that containing is not only something the analyst does but something the patient does too. Just as an infant becomes a container, using reverie to receive and interpret the mother's thoughts and feelings, only some of which she may understand, the patient intuits and perceives aspects of the analyst's personality, including some of which the analyst may not be conscious. In this way, containing becomes a two-way communicative process (Billow 2000). It is through this intersubjective relationship, especially those passionate moments in that relationship, that the patient begins to emerge from his dissociation. These moments become engraved in the brain of both patient and therapist, although differently for each. The word *passion* brings to mind the word *love*, two words, which used together, would make many psychoanalysts uncomfortable in thinking about their patients. Do some psychoanalysts love their patients, or some of them? Recently, Lawrence Friedman addressed the provocative question of whether "there might be a universal and peculiarly psychoanalytic something in The analyst's feelings that deserves the name of love . . . (Friedman 2005b, p. 385)." Freud wrote to Jung about this on December 12, 1906, letting him know that he could say what he was going to say only to a few select colleagues.

> It is not possible to say anything to a hostile public; accordingly I have kept certain things that might be said concerning the limits of the therapy and its mechanisms to myself, or spoken of them in a way that is intelligible only to

> the initiate. . . Essentially, one might say, the cure is effected by love (McGuire 1994, p.10).
>
> It is especially impressive that some analysts have been willing to even contemplate general loving feelings toward patients, given that the possibility of affective responses toward patients made them squirm for years, for obvious reasons.
>
> The technical model of psychoanalysis is a paradox: the analyst is supposed to be an objective observer, but one whose inner responses are in important ways uncontrolled and freely *moved* by the patient's impact. Theory seems to forbid and require detachment (Friedman 2005a, p. 350).

If the analyst were to really settle into a love relationship in the ordinary sense, the patient's freedom would be at risk, since love is, to varying degrees, necessarily "confining and demanding of the beloved" (Friedman 2005b, p. 386) and would not be the idealized love for which the patient yearns, a love which does not want or demand anything (Bucci 2007b). The love which does not want or demand anything is as close to a selfless love that anyone will ever have or give.

> It's a love heightened by obstacles, taboos, and impossibilities . . . That makes it all the more delectable. The therapist is like a knight who must prove his devotion by *not* lying down with his lady (or man). That was, after all, the final and truest test of a knight's love, if he could steal into his lady's chamber and climb into bed beside her, while her naked body appealed to all his normal . . . appetites, without laying a hand on her. In therapy, the patient lies down—literally or figuratively—and is more naked than naked, more exposed than mere nudity could ever reveal. The therapist proves his devotion by not responding sexually. His quest is to restore what has been lost or stolen from the castle of her self-regard. It is a difficult task, which they both construe as a journey fraught with obstacles and danger and strife. There are dragons to slay. There are whirlwinds to tame. There are enemies without. There are monsters within (Ackerman 1995, p. 326).

I think that it is this peculiar kind of psychoanalytic love that patients Really seek, even when they seem to want parental or erotic love. They find it "in those indelible moments when the patient is moved or shaken by the therapist's passion and discovers that the therapist can weather the storm, that the patient can begin to know that he can find safety, trust, and love in another person (Farber 2000, p. 461)." The therapist's passion must be harnessed and redirected, and sublimated and transformed into something greater (Loewald 1988). And he must be able to do that with all his patients, becoming what Diane Ackerman called a "serial lover"! "If they are any good, they are serial lovers (Ackerman 1994, p. 323)." My clinical experience has repeatedly told me that this kind of psychoanalytic love is felt most acutely by patients and therapist when they have been "through the wars" together, and lived to tell each other the tale.

The new work in the neurosciences on mirror neurons brings the authenticity of the analyst's response to the fore in a new way. "The analyst must experience real activation, longing, suffering, vulnerability; must really care; must really feel attacked, not in an "as if" sense; the analyst's experience must be real in the moment" (Bucci 2007b, p. 323). It is this that patients truly seek, and its absence is felt as the absence of real love. This is shown in the research on mirror neurons, neurons that fire when a person acts and also when it observes the same action performed by another, thus mirroring the behavior of the other, as though the observer were itself acting (Rizzolati, Fogassi, et al. 2001). Mirror neurons allow us to understand facial expressions and respond appropriately, feeling empathy for real others and characters in fiction. So when the analyst feels real longing, suffering, and vulnerability, even though it may be dissociated and communicated nonverbally, the patient will know the authenticity of the analyst's feelings.

INTUITION AND IMPROVISATION

> Psychoanalysis began, then, as a kind of virtuoso improvisation within the science of medicine; and free association—the heart of psychoanalytic treatment—is itself ritualized improvisation. . . . With the invention of psychoanalysis, —or rather, with the discovery of what he called the unconscious—Freud glimpsed a daunting prospect: a profession of improvisers.
> —Adam Phillips, *On Kissing, Tickling, and Being Bored*

For treatment to become a real help to the patient in living his life in a more satisfying and less dangerous way, the therapist must have a certain flexibility to use his intuition and be able to improvise. None of Freud's theories is engraved in stone. From the beginning, psychoanalysis had no texts, no institutes, no training analysts, no rhetoric. The first practitioners made it up as they went along (Phillips 1994). Anna O. coined the term "the talking cure" to describe Freud's improvisational free-association technique that relieved her of her hysterical symptoms. Freud, a neurologist, wanted to be regarded as part of a community of scientists. But his improvisation was more like what the artists and writers did than what the scientists did, making psychoanalysis difficult to place. This may be one of its unique virtues. "Nor need it be a cause for dismay-despite the splits and synthesizing of theories. . . in contemporary psychoanalysis—that psychoanalysis can be a circus with many acts" (Phillips 1994, pp. 3-4).

Drawing on cutting-edge neuroscience and psychology, Malcolm Gladwell (2005) tells us about the power of intuition, how we think without thinking, about choices made in the blink of an eye. This does not mean abandoning the classical psychoanalytic principles. It means that we must think about them in an open-minded way, not as sacred cows to be revered blindly.

WALKING ABOUT IN DREAM TIME, FOLLOWING A TRAIL OF BREADCRUMBS

The more clinically experienced I became, the more comfortable I began to feel working in an improvisational way, before I had the words or theory to explain it (Farber 2000). I was pleased to read what Adam Phillips had to say about this: "A psychoanalyst . . . has to learn how not to know what he is doing and to go on doing it (Phillips 1995, p. xiv)."

When I began working with Jean fourteen years ago, I knew little about the dissociative processes operating in projective identification and enactments (Bromberg 1998, 2006) or about disorganized attachments (Blizard 2003; Liotti 1995; Main and Morgan 1996). Through a painful process of "blood, sweat, and tears," I came to understand what I later read about in Bromberg's work, that I had to focus on the dissociative processes before trying to work with intrapsychic conflict, and that difficult enactments can serve as needed corrective emotional experiences. Bromberg noted that "there was a large group of my patients to whom what seemed most important was their being allowed to show who they were by being it rather than telling it. . . They needed to be a mess with me, for me to know them I had to be part of the mess in some way that I could feel internally (Bromberg 1998, p. 25).

The account of Jean's treatment will show you how a patient can begin to move from a dissociative mode serving manic defensive functions and manifesting a disorganized attachment pattern to a more interpersonally connected and reflective mode. It will also illustrate how my own dissociated expression of rage was a pivotal point in the treatment. It got me to know my limits as to what I would tolerate from her. It gave Jean the opportunity to know my mind in a new way and gave me the opportunity to know hers more fully, and become more empathically attuned to her.

"Attunement is a rhythmic encounter that is entirely dependent upon being present in the moment. Empathically attuned clinicians are like microtonal tuning forks. They resonate with a variety of emotional pitches and will resonate with nuanced shifting of emotional tone. This resonance forms the basis of dissociative attunement" (Hopenwasser 2008, p. 357) an implicit knowing of information within the therapeutic relationship that might or might not be available for mindful awareness. In a patient with a dissociative disorder, the shifts in ego states may be so rapid and nonlinear that they are impossible to follow, making it impossible to reflect upon them as they occur. When this occurs, it is very difficult to stay empathically attuned. But in dissociative attunement, the therapist patient pair "can resonate in a syncopated rhythm that allows for an embodied connection, despite much mental confusion" (Hopenwasser 2008, p. 358). That is, dissociative attunements are self-emergent moments in which multiple self-states are shared by means other than projection. And sometimes, says Hopenwasser, dissociative attunement can, paradoxically, appear to be misattunement, as she reminds us that empathy is not always warm, fuzzy, and compassionate.

When Jean, a married mother of two, came to see me, she had an advanced degree and responsible job in her chosen profession but nonetheless, had never developed a sense of competence. She was disorganized, bouncing checks, overcharging credit cards, and cancelling appointments at the last minute. What was most difficult for me was that she tormented and criticized me relentlessly. She made it a point of denigrating social workers, a sore point for me. In my years of hospital practice, social workers were often treated as "hand-maidens to the physicians," a denigration of clinical social workers endemic to many psychologists as well. "Don't you social workers read the tea leaves or throw the I Ching?" Jean taunted me, suggesting that social workers don't know what they are doing, that it is a laughable profession for which no one has any respect. I was unprepared for anything like this and tolerated it far too long.

Interestingly, she *knew* I was a social worker when she called for the initial appointment. Among her insurance plan's list of participating therapists, I was listed with other social workers but was the only one with a PhD. She could have chosen a PhD psychologist but she did not. Her husband was insistent that I was a fraud, and that I could not possibly have a PhD. He wanted her to terminate treatment with me. I had to point to my diploma on the wall and asked if she thought it was a fake. I came to understand later that her choice was a compromise formation (Freud 1923, Moore and Fine1990), but a dissociated one, joining the PhD's higher status with the social worker's lower status. A compromise formation is an attempt to solve a conflict between the id, ego, and superego, providing some acceptable degree of expression for each competing part (Freud 1923b, 1926). So if Jean wanted to have someone to persecute and look down upon, choosing a social worker allowed her to do that. And if she wanted to get started with a competent therapist, and in her mind, it was those with PhDs who were most competent, her dissociated compromise was to choose a social worker with a PhD. Her dissociation allowed her to keep the nature of this compromise a secret from herself. I later discovered that secrets were precious to her, *especially* those she kept from herself. She kept it a secret from herself how she sometimes shoplifted, drove much too fast, and tolerated her husband's emotional and sexual abuse.

She had trouble shopping for clothes because she had never developed her own taste or style, and had always dressed as her mother had. She often pointed out some new article of clothing she was wearing, asking if I thought it was all right. I found myself wanting to care for her and feeling a bit like a mother hen. But at times she harshly criticized my clothing and office furnishings. When I got dressed in the morning, if it was a day she was coming in, I'd anticipate what nasty remark she would make about my clothing. It was becoming unbearable. I suggested that when she was feeling the impulse to attack me, to tell me about the impulse so that we could talk about it instead of her acting on it. She could not or would not do this. One day she came in, took a look at me, and said "You actually *bought* that outfit you're wearing?" I had to restrain myself from saying that at least, I had *paid* for it and had not stolen it. I began telling myself, as if it were a mantra, that some patients are capable of provoking their own murder. I felt preyed upon and enjoyed fantasies of revenge, and struggled not to act on them.

The mantra did not work very well. One day I was having lunch when I was shocked to hear her voice, dripping with venom. "Enjoying your salad—on my time?" I looked up to see her hovering over me and immediately realized that I had forgotten her appointment and had gone out for lunch instead. She had gone to my office and when no one answered the doorbell, she got in her car and tracked me down. I felt humiliated and exposed. (At the time, I was not at all able then to consider the length to which Jean had gone in order to find me because I might actually have some value to her). I did not know what to say or how to explain myself. All I could do was apologize. I told her that when she came in for her next session in two days that I hoped by then to understand what had led me to forget her appointment. She clearly relished catching me in the act.

Two days later she sat down and asked with a little smirk if I had figured it out yet. Yes, I had. I told her that I realized that I had not allowed myself to know how furious I was at her for the way she treated me; forgetting her appointment was a wakeup call that I had disconnected myself from my rage. I heard my voice tremble in rage as I told her I would no longer tolerate her disrespect and contempt. My best advice was to find herself another therapist whom she *could* respect, a psychologist with a PhD, because it was not good for her to be in treatment with a therapist for whom she had no respect and it obviously was not good for me.

I thought I was getting rid of her. I wanted to. She shocked me when she began to sob. She told me how much she valued our work together and did not want to jeopardize it. I was stunned to hear her say that no other therapist had been able to get through to her as I had. She was very grateful that I had told her what I had; she said that she had been wondering how long I could tolerate her hateful treatment of me. It seemed that not only setting a limit with her but the passion with which I expressed it had a profound effect, awakening something alive and vital in her.

An idea that had special appeal to Martin Bergmann (1999) came to have special appeal to me too, that genuine insight is accompanied by a sense of surprise for both patient and therapist. It lead me to reread Winnicott's (1958) paper on hate in the countertransference, which resonated as it never before had. Also, what Bromberg said is especially apropos here: " . . . it is as if the patient is communicating that the analyst must somehow 'lose' his mind in order to know the patient's" (Bromberg1998, p. 138).

Jean then told me about a male teacher in high school to whom she is forever grateful. He took her aside one day after class and told her that if she continued to treat people the way she treated her classmates she would end up all alone in life. No one would want to be with her. She realized that he cared enough to tell her this. She told me that her vicious tongue had always been a problem, ruining potential friendships before they even had a chance. She had already been feeling safe and secure with me but this incident was the glue that cemented the bond. She begged me to continue with her and I agreed, with the stipulation that she begin to assume some further responsibility for maintaining our relationship, which was a two-way street. She agreed to try.

The discrepancy between the real person that the therapist is and the patient's expectations of the therapist, based on expectations from the past, can provide a new emotional experience that is corrective (Alexander 1958). This powerful incident seemed to have been one of a series of corrective emotional experiences that occurred between us. But as Renik said "As far as corrective emotional experiences are concerned, an analyst never knows ahead of time exactly where he or she needs to go or how to get there, In that sense, an analyst is flying blind" (2006, p. 39).

I learned the hard way that traditional psychoanalytic technique would not work with Jean, who had both a severe depersonalization disorder and post-traumatic stress disorder. If she had ever developed a sense of self, it had been lost. (I discovered only recently that only tentative treatment recommendations for depersonalization disorder had been proposed (Neziroglu 2010; Simeon 2004; Simeon and Abugel 2008)[2] What to do? There was nothing else to do but improvise.

I followed June's lead, literally and metaphorically, as she walked around the room in something of a trance-like state. It was a dreamlike journey that reminded me of the Australian film *Walkabout,* in which a teenage girl and her younger brother, abandoned by their father, were forced to make their way across the outback, where they met a young Aboriginal man who was on his *walkabout.* A walkabout is a transitional phase of life where one discovers if he can survive on his own. Although they could not speak to him because they did not speak the same language, they somehow found ways to communicate. And so it was with June and me. I learned to speak her language and I walked with her in a strange dreamy state of mind that I later learned was called a reverie (Ogden 1994, 1997; Bion 1962), and oddly enough, at times we connected.

It went something like this. The door to my playroom had been left ajar and Jean peeked in quickly, secretively, as if it were forbidden. "That's where I work with young children," I said. Not a secret. She then let her gaze linger on the toys, dollhouse, crayons. I said "It looks like you would like to play." (Retrospectively I remembered that as a child she had enjoyed playing with her mother before her mother became so mentally ill, but I was not conscious of that during the session.) She entered my office, eyes darting up, down, sideways, scanning hypervigilantly for what had changed the slightest bit about the room or me since last time. . . my desk, envelopes, mail, from whom, what, what, what? Her eyes darted down to my feet, then up. I noticed and she noticed that I had. She laughed, her secret exposed. "My feet," I said. "Your shoes. They're new. I haven't seen you wear them before. . . You take care of yourself. You went shopping. They're nice. Maybe I'll get a pair like that too." (She was free associating! Something good was happening.) I came to understand later that by being like me, she was unwittingly trying to mitigate her envy of me by converting our differences into similarities, an unconscious tactic described by Boris (1994). More laughter, giggles. "We'll be like the Bobbsey twins (a children's book series)." Then a secret sideways glance at the title of the book sitting next to me. I held the book up, cover facing her. "Here, this is what I'm reading" I said. She laughed (secret exposed again!), asked if it is good, and said that maybe she would read it too. I said that she seemed to like to do what I did and seemed to think my way is the way it should be. She replied that if I'm reading something it must be good to read; and what I'm wearing must be the right thing to wear. Her eyes went to the wall. An abrupt shift in tone, agitated. "You need a paint job. Why don't you get it painted? What will people think?" "I don't know," I said and asked her what *she* thought about it. "I think that you don't care enough about what things look like. If the walls look shabby, people will think you are a shabby therapist. . . . (Becoming very indignant) . . . And what's more, your plants are withering outside. They look terrible; you don't take care of them. If you take care of your patients the way you take care of your plants, people will think you are a terrible therapist." I responded "If you need a gardener, you don't look for a therapist." Jean laughed, paused and tossed back "If you need a therapist, you don't look for a gardener. Is this one of those Zen poems, you know, the sound of one hand clapping or whatever?" We both laughed.

She is quiet, relaxed. But suddenly, she became agitated again and panicked. Her eyes darted to my wire spindle memo holder, with memo papers pierced by its sharp point. Her voice was shrill: "That should not be here. Why do you have it? What do you do with it?" Speaking slowly, in contrast to her rapid speech, I asked her what she *thought* I might do with it. She did not know but said it was not safe. "Get rid of it. I don't like it here." I asked if perhaps she thought that I might stick myself with it? Or her? "Who knows what you might do!" I responded that she seemed frightened that I might hurt myself all of a sudden or that I might hurt her. I suspected that this traced back to feeling that her mother, who had cut herself and had been hospitalized repeatedly for depression, was cutting Jean out of her life. "Yes, you never know what someone might do. Never!"

When I had time to think about it later, it became clear that this was a post-traumatic stress disorder response. Kroll's description of the borderline/PTSD patient's reactivity captured it beautifully, and for this reason I repeat it. Jean seemed to suffer

> from the inability to turn off a stream of consciousness that has become its own enemy, comprised of actual memories of traumatic events, distorted and fragmented memories, intrusive imageries and flashbacks, dissociated memories, unwelcome somatic sensations, negative self-commentaries running like tickertape through the mind, fantasied and feared elaborations from childhood of the abuse experiences, and concomitant strongly dysphoric moods of anxiety and anger. Much that the adult PTSD/borderline patient does, in and out of therapy, is a response to, or an attempt to terminate or modify, the intolerable presence of this stream of consciousness (Kroll 1993, p. xv.).

But at the time I was operating intuitively, without the benefit of Kroll's knowledge. I said slowly and deliberately "We've known each other quite awhile now. Do you *really* think I might stick myself or stick you with it?" She was very anxious, and leaned forward, "You could; you might; it's possible. How can I know what to expect?" I said that of course *anything* is within the realm of possibility, but please, use your mind and *think* for a minute. Do you *really* think I would? Silence a moment, then no, she did not think I would. She relaxed visibly, then asked if I wanted her to leave. "You're always sure I want to get rid of you. Maybe you're having a nasty thought about wanting to get rid of me?" A moment later, she stood up, saying she had to go to the bathroom. "Before you leave the room, can you tell me what you're thinking or feeling, what's making you feel you have to go this very moment?" "No, I'm on a diet, I drink a lot of water, I have to pee a lot. And I have to go right now." She darted out to the bathroom and returned moments later, a slight smile on her face. "I'm back. Surprised?" "No, I'm used to you running away for a bit and then returning. It seems to make you feel better." "Yes, sometimes I just have to get away from you. It's too much. When I can get away from you, then I can come back." This too had been a secret and was no longer . . . . I told her that I was glad that she did come back and glad that she told me how she needed to get away from me and I wondered too if maybe she wanted to get rid of me by peeing me down the toilet? "What an absolutely disgusting thing to say! . . . (long pause as she thought about it). Do you *really* think so?" I shrugged: "It's a thought." A moment of silence passed before a slow smile crept across her face, and she said "Now, wouldn't it be wonderful if we *could* pee people away?" And so in this telepathic communication, Jean taught me how to taste the many flavors of pain from which she suffered. And so we began to explore the many ways she has invented to keep herself from knowing what she really knows, how her dissociation allows her to disavow what she knows to be true.

What Boyer (1997) wrote about reverie was true of my relationship with Jean. I had to be a container, with the capacity to tolerate, contain, and interpret Jean's projective identifications (Rosenfeld 1987). In order to do this, the therapist must be able to allow the patient his chaotic regressions, while maintaining an optimism that these regressions will ultimately give way to healthier progressions. The therapist must be able to tolerate the introjection of whatever the patient is projecting into him while observing it without reacting crudely. At the same time the patient is introjecting the therapist's kindness and acceptance. This is the essential element, being able to observe how you feel and act and how the patient feels and acts, to evaluate what goes on between you and the patient, assessing your own somatic sensations and overt thoughts. Both patient and therapist enter into various degrees of reverie and intersubjective play, generating a space that is a very powerful link to the patient's dissociated space. The patient's ability to move from dissociation to conflict is dependent on whether or not the therapist can relate to several selves at the same time, and maintain an authentic dialogue with each (Bromberg 1998). Through this process relational bridges are built between self-experiences that could not formerly be contained in a relationship with the same person.

Thomas Ogden (1997) has found that the analyst can make use of his own and patient's overlapping states of reverie, making reverie a personal and private event and an intersubjective one at the same time. It is an experience that takes the most mundane and personal of shapes and is made up of the stuff of ordinary life.

> Reveries are things made out of lives and the world that the lives inhabit... . . (they are about) people: people working, thinking about things, falling in love, taking naps . . . They are our ruminations, daydreams, fantasies, bodily sensations, fleeting perceptions, images emerging from states of half-sleep, tunes and phrases that run through our minds . . . " (Ogden 1997, p.568).

All along, Jean's husband insisted that she end her treatment with me, and she kept trying to keep it a secret that she was defying him. Jean has managed to safeguard her treatment. She soon began dressing more in my style and had her hair styled in a similar way. If she saw a book I was reading, she would get the same book and read it, a real twinship transference (Kohut 1971). As she began to disclose more of her husband's emotional and sexual sadism and her shame at tolerating it, I began to understand that he was a very angry man who probably experienced some ecstatic release through his eroticized rage. Jean was not looking for ecstasy but it seemed that he was, and she was part of the trip.

What alarmed me so much about Jean was her readiness to tolerate his abusive and dangerous sadistic practices. She feared he would leave her if she did not, and so she tolerated it by doing what she knew so well, going into a self-induced trance state that allowed her mind to disconnect itself from what her body was enduring. She made herself into a non-person by depersonalizing. Many years before she trusted me enough to tell me about this, she told me something that I came to understand more fully: "He puts his venom in me and I have no choice but to spew it out onto you." It also became clear that she felt compelled to repeat the trauma she experienced at his hands and to reenact it with me, but playing the active sadist rather than the masochistic victim. Better to be the torturer than the one being tortured.

She once called me to ask what I thought about his wanting to "play around" with putting a rope around her neck during sexual activity; he had told her it made for a fantastic orgasm. I had to silence the impulse to ask if she was out of her mind but on second thought it would not have been so bad if I had. I have had to tell her very emphatically numerous times that she was endangering her life, and although I wanted to stop her, I could not. I told her that I did not think that her husband consciously wanted to kill her, but conscious or not, by playing possum and lying there as if dead, she made it possible for it to happen. It would not have been the first time that someone died during sadomasochistic sex (Litman and Swearingen 1996). I told her most forcefully that I did not want to have to testify against him at a murder trial. Just a bit earlier, the media had been publicizing a case of a physician who murdered his wife by throwing her out of his private plane into the ocean. I was shocked to discover that she was a clinical social worker whom I had known professionally, so it was all too real to me that killing one's wife does not necessarily happen only in mystery novels or some very removed sphere or galaxy. It was quite real and could really happen to Jean.

I continued to be amazed to discover that she was far more dissociative than I had known. She walked around in her disembodied state, eating more and more. I saw her weight go up and down. On some level she too knew how disconnected she was from herself. Recently she told me that from the beginning of treatment, she had kept a journal in which she recorded things I had said that she knew were valuable for her to think about, because in another dissociated state, she'd be likely to blot them out. She wanted to protect herself from herself. And she wanted to protect me from herself. And I think it meant a great deal to her that I *wanted* to protect her.

A continual theme in her treatment was that she knew that I really did not want her there. If she had to cancel a session, she was certain that I was glad that I did not have to see her. She was certain that even though I said all the right things and acted as if I were glad to see her, it was all an act. She had difficulty beginning her sessions, remaining for them, and ending them, often getting up abruptly to leave because she suddenly was sure I did not want her there. She was testing me to see whether I really wanted her there and at the same time, I think she wanted to see if I could stand for her to go. That would be proof that I did not need her to fill in my gaps and spaces. As Harold Boris said, "That we can stand for our patients to leave us at any time, in any condition, is a minimal condition for being in practice" (Boris 1994, p. 182).

I discovered that she sniffed out certain books to read that could lead her deeper to a place in herself where she needed to go. Although she was not consciously aware of this, she needed me to go there with her and so she left a trail of bread crumbs for me to follow. She would bring in a book she was reading and tell me something about it, and I would get a copy, start to read it, and then we talked about what the book had to do with her. This happened a number of times, creating a shift, from her reading books I had read, to my reading books she had read. (I appreciated that we shared some of the same taste for books.) One of them was Aimee Bender's novel, *The Particular Sadness of Lemon Cake* (Bender 2010) Rose's mother knew that nine-year-old Rose loved sour food, and so she made a lemon birthday cake for her. At first it was delicious, but then suddenly it began to taste hollow, and her mouth filled with the taste of smallness and shrinking. Rose began to know that her usually happy, competent mother tasted of despair and desperation. Jean had begun to communicate with me in the way she knew best, and I continued to learn the language.

Although I do not routinely give my cell phone number to patients, I gave it to Jean so that she could feel that she could reach me when she needed to. Occasionally she would call me when she was feeling confused or in an extreme anxiety state, and a few moments of such contact helped her to calm down. Occasionally just listening to my recorded voice was enough, and she would hang up. At times when she sent me a payment, she would include a note. This is one of them: "I think of you often and always have a piece of you with me—based on our work together—and your capacity to have reached me and connected in a very powerful way—through my fragmentation and anxiety." It seemed that the distance provided by a note allowed her to acknowledge her need for the relationship, something too difficult to do in person.

There were times when she stayed away from treatment out of a wish to feel that she did not need me and perhaps to test whether I could stand for her to go, but after awhile she would then find herself far more dissociated and engaging in more high-risk behavior that frightened her, and she would return. Usually she left some belonging of hers in my office, representing some dissociated part of herself, which she would eventually come back to reclaim. She began to develop the courage to stand up for herself to her husband, drawing a line between what was and what was not acceptable behavior from him. My having drawn the line with her had enabled her to do the same with him. She has begun to develop a capacity to experience intrapsychic conflict, although her intruding dissociative states make it difficult for her to maintain it. She has discovered that when her husband is away from home, she can relax and live more in the present. When she is with him at home, she drifts off into her depersonalized state. She has become aware too that she drinks more when they are together because alcohol helps her depersonalize even more. She is considering filing for divorce. A delightful sense of vitality and humor has emerged from her. We have been able to joke together about how years ago she had tracked me down like a dog and found me eating my countertransference lunch. Never would I have imagined that I would find myself feeling so fond of her.

I discovered accidentally that when I had given her a copy of text about her for my first book (Farber 2000), seeking her permission to include them, although her initial reading had gotten her quite upset, subsequent readings were quite helpful to her in looking at her dissociated self-states through my eyes, and was actually quite therapeutic. It also brought up the subject of envy, the critical element in the negative therapeutic reaction and which may explain some of the difficulty in engaging the hard-to-reach (Klein 1957; Boris 1994; Ellman 2000). Jean made a derisive comment about my having a book published. I suggested that perhaps she felt envious of me for distinguishing myself in this way. She thought a moment and said that she guessed the difference between us was that I had written a book and she had not. This was an acknowledgment of my achievement, and something of a turning point, because it was a thoughtful recognition of my value, whereas envy may be our most primitive recognition of that value (Boris 1994). Boris reminded us that the Latin word for envy is *invidia* or nonsight. "Dante represented the envious . . . their eyes sewn shut with leaden wire envy" (Boris 1994, p. xx). Envy, said Adam Phillips, is a kind of radar, a sixth sense, with the analyst a sitting target for the patient's envy (Boris 1994). "Envy is what in some measure the have-nots feel toward the haves. It arises out of a state of mind in which we scrutinize what others have in order to compare to what we ourselves possess" (Boris 1994, p. xv). Because envy is so often one-sided and isolating, it makes one who is filled with envy feel deficient, defective, hateful and humiliated (Boris 1994). No one can tolerate being caught being envious. Jean must have felt envious at the outset of our work together, and she let the hatred fly. When someone can acknowledge it in herself, this can free up her own ambition and creativity. Guilt about these envious feelings often leads to profound inhibitions and masochistic behavior. Carolyn Ellman (2000) suggests that by interpreting a woman's fear of her destructive envy, one can free her to enjoy her own sexuality, to find appropriate ways to express her aggression, and also to be more creative. This proved to be true of Jean.

Recently she reluctantly acknowledged that despite her provocative behavior, and irregular treatment schedule, I have consistently been there for her; oddly enough, what she said was that I have consistently been there for her, *to a fault.* Puzzled, I commented that this sounded like a complaint and wondered what she meant. She could not explain it. I have come to think of this statement, along with how she began her treatment, in terms of envy and the manic defense. If I have been there so consistently *to a fault,* that means she has little to complain about me and must acknowledge my value to her. Her manic defensive relationship to me was characterized by control, triumph, and contempt, which dominated the beginning of our relationship. They defended against the depressive feelings of valuing me and feeling dependent upon me. In that critical moment when I told her to find another therapist, I punctured her manic defense by confronting her with the reality that I would not tolerate her contempt, and she had to acknowledge that she needed me, something difficult to fully acknowledge even now.

THE ECSTASY OF ONENESS AND THE RAGE OF TWONESS

> A sense of bodily separateness is the heartbreak at the centre of all human existence, and that for various reasons some people experience it in a more drastic way than others. How it is dealt with seems to affect the development of the whole personality.
>
> —Frances Tustin, *The Protective Shell in Children and Adults*

Although I was not successful in my effort with Marcie, the self-mutilating adolescent I wrote about in the previous chapter, several other cases involving self-mutilation had a very positive outcome, including the case of Joanie, a brilliant thirty-year-old research scientist. She had cut and burned herself since she was ten, had a psychiatric hospitalization in college, and despite several psychotherapies, her cutting continued (Farber 2008a, 2008b). It continued in her marriage with her husband's knowledge, until he finally insisted she stop because he could no longer stand it. She feared losing him. A year later she began treatment with me because although she had not begun cutting herself again, it was all she could think about, the only thing she really wanted, like an alcoholic gone sober, a "dry drunk." Her impulses to cut seemed to be always with her. There was a little voice inside her, a dissociated voice that said, "Go ahead, do it. It'll make you feel so much better. He doesn't have to know." Although sorely tempted, she was afraid that if she gave in to the impulses at all she would lose control, and that was the dilemma that brought her to seek psychotherapy. Very doubtful that a soft science such as psychotherapy could help her, but feeling desperate, she made an appointment, insisting that her husband come with her because she expected to be too upset by the end of the consultation to drive herself home.

From the beginning, the treatment felt like magic to her and to me too. The scientist in her wanted to understand how and why the "magic" worked. The dissociated part of herself that wanted to cut almost overwhelmed her but fortunately, the part of her that wanted to understand and be understood was even greater, explaining in part why she did so well in treatment.

Joanie was my first patient who mutilated herself, and I began seeing her shortly before completing my first book. The truth was that although I was quite experienced in treating people with eating disorders, I had never treated someone who self-mutilated, at least, not to my knowledge, and was somewhat anxious about it. That's how we began, with an anxious patient and anxious therapist. Not an auspicious beginning.

In that initial consultation, after hearing briefly about her psychiatric history, I asked what part of her body she usually cut or burned. She gestured toward her left forearm, covered by a long sleeve. Wanting to evaluate the severity of her self-harm, I asked if I could see what she had done. She pulled up the sleeve and I saw an almost horizontal grid of white lines, the color indicating that they were old scars. I put my hand out and asked if I might touch it. She nodded. I stroked her arm lightly, then let my hand rest there a moment. Although I had known what to expect, seeing this directly was a shock. I muttered "Look what you did to yourself." When I looked up, I saw tears welling up in her eyes.

I learned of serious problems since early childhood. Joanie had been told that she was conceived accidentally. Her father did not want a child, with whom he would have to compete for his wife's attention. Joanie had been a *cork child* (Tustin 1986; McDougall 1980), accustomed to plugging up the emptiness of her mother's depression. She recalled lying in her crib, scared because the doll that she slept with had fallen to the floor. She knew better than to call out for either parent to retrieve it. And so she slept very poorly and was always tired. If she did call out, her mother would not get up to fetch her doll but would instead get up and take Joanie into bed with her. She wanted Joanie all to herself.

When Joanie was older and could not sleep, her mother would readily get into her bed and spend the rest of the night there, or she would bring Joanie into her parents' bed, displacing her angry father, who went to sleep in Joanie's bed. Joanie felt safe and could fall asleep next to her mother's warm body until she was five or six, which is when the tickling started. What Adam Phillips (1994) has to say about tickling is quite relevant.

> . . . the adult's tickling of the child is an obviously acceptable form of sensuous excitement between parents and children in the family. The child who will be able to feed himself, the child who will masturbate, will never be able to tickle himself. It is the pleasure he cannot reproduce in the absence of the other. . . .
> Helpless with pleasure, and usually inviting this helplessness, the child, in the ordinary, affectionate, perverse scenario of being tickled, is wholly exploitable. . . Through tickling, the child will be initiated in a distinctive way into the helplessness and disarray of a certain primitive kind of pleasure, dependent upon the adult to hold and not exploit this experience. And this means to stop at the blurred point, so acutely felt in tickling, at which pleasure becomes pain, and the child experiences an intensely anguished confusion; because the tickling narrative, unlike the sexual narrative, has no climax. It has to stop, or the real humiliation begins. . .
> The *Oxford English Dictionary* cites . . . the following: "In unstable equilibrium, easily upset or overthrown, insecure, tottering, crazy." Other definitions describe a range of experience from incredulity to incontinence. The word speaks of the precarious, and so of the erotic. To tickle is, above all, to seduce (Phillips 1994, pp. 9-10).

Being tickled by her mother was nothing new. Often she tickled Joanie until she wet herself. But this time was different. Joanie began to cry no, no, stop—and got hysterical when suddenly her mother held her down and fondled her genitals, saying that they should get naked together. Joanie's mind went blank; she froze. After this, she never called out to her mother at night. She stayed up reading with the lights on, or curled up on the floor with the dog. They did, however, continue bathing together until Joanie entered adolescence, when Joanie wanted to bathe alone. She actually had to lock the bathroom door to keep her mother out. Once her mother even picked the lock to get in.

Joanie grew up determined that she would never have a baby for fear that she would abuse her child. When she married and had problems in her marriage and was angry at her husband, she would cut herself. As she told me more about how cutting had helped her to feel better, it was a great relief to her to discover that I wanted to understand this. "Why do I do this?" she asked, to which I responded that although the reasons were not yet clear, I was sure that underneath it all there was a "method to her madness" which might become clearer in time.

For Joanie, it seemed that the infantile wishes both to merge with and separate from her mother's body created an intolerable tension (Blanck and Blanck 1974; Kernberg 1975), from which dissociation came to serve as A temporary escape. When the caretaker who is meant to protect the child preys upon him instead, this presents the child with an impossible quandary, creating a disorganized attachment (Blizard 2003; Main and Morgan 1996; Farber 2008a, 2008b). What does a child do when she needs comfort from her mother but at the same time is petrified of being annihilated by her? She freezes in a trance-like stillness, the beginning of a tendency toward dissociation (Perry, Blakely, Baker, and Vigilante 1995). Dissociation is what also allowed her to protect her father from her rage by enacting her violent wishes toward him on her own body instead. When he made a suicide gesture when Joanie was ten and her mother began paying more attention to him than to Joanie, she soon began sticking herself with pins and then cutting herself.

Although Joanie was not autistic, she had autistic traits, which Frances Tustin's studies of autistic children helped me to understand. (Farber 2008a). Tustin (1990) concluded that the autistic child could not tolerate the sense of his body being separate from his mothers' body because he experiences his skin as if it were the mother's, and so a sudden rupture in the mother-child relationship is experienced as part of his skin being ripped away, leaving a black hole on the body's surface (Tustin 1980, 1992). The black hole is experienced as a "hard" sensation, and so the child uses hard autistic objects, such as fingernails, pins, or razor blades, to soothe himself by plugging up the hole. Tustin (1992) also found that in autistic children, sensation-generating activities can merge ecstasy and rage in a discharge so explosive that the boundaries between self and other disappear.

From the outset, I suggested that when feeling the urge to cut herself, that she call me instead, explaining that this might tide her over through the hardest times until her next appointment. I explained that of course I might not be able to speak with her when she called but I would call back as soon as I could. It took quite awhile for her to do this because she had difficulty imagining that anyone might ever pay attention to her need for comfort because her earliest needs for comfort were not heeded. Her mother, it seemed, needed Joanie to comfort her.

After the first session, the impulse to cut herself receded and so did her schizoid dissociated quality (Farber 2000; 2008a; 2008b). Her parents had negated, ignored, or demeaned her thoughts and feelings, and so in time she came to understand that the regular and reliable experience of being listened to, taken seriously, and then coming to understand the connections between her thoughts, feelings, behavior and relationships was the recipe for "magic."

As she stopped enacting violent wishes on her own body, these wishes were brought into the transference relationship with me and analyzed. There were recurrent violent, chaotic dreams in which often she was being burned with cigarettes or molested by a woman. Often I was the woman molesting her, as her mother had done. Sometimes she dreamed she was in my house, snuggling in bed with me. In her mind I alternated between holding her tenderly and abusing her as her mother had done.

She had dreams of being in bed with her husband and having an orgasm, and then he turned into her mother. There were dreams and hypnogogic hallucinations about the thing that lurked near her crib, wanting to kill her. When she got shampoo in her eyes and they burned, images of the thing lurking near her crib formed on her eyelid, as if it were a projection screen. When she remembered that her father told her that children are very "beatable," she came to realize the thing lurking near her crib was her father, wanting to kill her as soon as she was born, maybe before.

Once during her treatment, Joanie cut herself "accidentally" while slicing vegetables. I asked her to tell me how it happened. She said that she did not realize what she had done until she heard a "ping" sound. "A 'ping'sound?" I asked, puzzled because cutting oneself with a knife does not really make a sound. Yes, a ping sound, she said. "Was it really a 'ping' sound," I asked, "or was it, perhaps, a 'ping' feeling, a sensation?" At this she gasped, shocked, "Yes, that's what it was, a ping feeling, like a mild electric current running through my body." She had kept it a secret from herself that her not so accidental accident had given her a secret little 'ping" ecstasy. Exploring further, we discovered that she had been so enraged at her husband that she could not stand it. Cutting herself "accidentally" did not really "count" as cutting herself. It was a secret little dissociated ping ecstasy, a momentary collapse into the autistic world of sensation dominated experience (Tustin 1990), a manic defense against the depression and anxiety of being so abruptly separated from her mother.

Then there were two other times when she tried to hurt herself. My husband's medical crisis rendered me not as attuned to her as she was accustomed to, and disrupted our regular schedule. Distraught and anxious, I had less ability than usual to contain the dissociative self states that Joanie forced into my mind (Bromberg 1998). When I could not contain and reflect on my countertransferential anger at her, she responded by somehow managing to slam herself (not just her hand) in the door of her car. In fact, she did it twice in two weeks. Like an autistic child, Joanie had experienced our twoness too quickly and abruptly. She came to realize how enraged she was at me but had dissociated these intolerable feelings. Like the cutting "accident," slamming herself in the car door was not cutting herself so it didn't count.

We came to understand together that she was enacting on her body the unbearable ecstasy of oneness and tantrum of twoness. She even came to understand why I had become angry at her, and could acknowledge how angry she had been with me, how she felt she was competing with my husband for my attention, just as her father had competed with her for her mother's attention. Even more amazing to her was that each of us could become angry with the other, that we could talk about it together, and it was alright. Nothing terrible happened. She was finding that the connection we had through language was becoming better than autistic withdrawal and sensation. Even though I was not the perfect therapist she had imagined me to be, I was, as Winnicott (1965) said about mothers, *good enough.* And several other people in her life, she discovered, imperfect as they were, were good enough too.

She began to grieve over that which she never had in her life, over what she once had but lost, over what might have been but was never to be, and over what happened to her that should not have happened. She incorporated writing into her treatment (Farber 2005) and I directed her to a course, "Writing as a Way of Healing." To her surprise, an unexpected bonus was that she found that even her scientific writing had improved. Colleagues commented on how lively it was, not dry at all. The proverbial half-empty glass had begun to fill. As Tustin said, "Insight into the pathological states associated with the agonizing experiences of bodily separateness . . . can seem like a baptism of fire. However, if this fiery baptism is survived and the autistic scales fall from our eyes, thinking becomes clearer, and a sense of individual identity is more firmly established" (Tustin 1990, pp. 166-67).

Joanie's relationship with her husband improved, and to her surprise and mine, she found herself wanting to have a baby. Although I suggested that they postpone this decision until we had ample time for her to further consider it in our work together, she and her husband decided that she would stop using birth control, which she understood as an acting out of her wish to be independent of and separate from me. She soon became pregnant, but had a miscarriage. Her grief was profound, and we were both struck by her ability to tolerate it. Despite her anxiety about losing another baby, she soon became pregnant again, and the anxiety continued through the first trimester. Then amidst the excitement of tracking the fetal development, there were occasional revisiting and further working through of past trauma.

She has become a devoted mother, committed to meeting her infant's needs even when it required a painful revisiting and further working through of her own difficult past (Benedek 1959). Gradually, she realized that she wanted to raise her daughter amidst her large extended family, and so Joanie and her husband decided to move back to the area where they were both from and where her parents still live, several hundred miles away. She knew this would entail her having to develop a new relationship with her parents. This leave-taking, while only a partial one, became a deeply emotional process for us both, happy and sad. Finally she blurted out, "I could not be doing this if it were not for you. And I've wanted for so long to tell you how grateful I am. But I was afraid of telling you, for fear that you would need and expect more and more of this from me, that you would need me to adore you." And as soon as she said it, she knew she was talking about her mother, whom Joanie had told repeatedly that she was the very best mother in the whole wide world. In the process of moving, once again, Joanie's skin began speaking for her, erupting suddenly and dramatically in hives, trying to communicate something to her about her anxiety about the impending geographic separation from me and decision to live near her parents.

Treatment continued by telephone successfully for the past few years. Joanie had a second baby and has come to accept that although her relationship with her parents has improved, they will never be the parents she had wanted them to be (Farber 2000, 1998a, 2008b). There has been no need to continue the treatment, and so it has stopped. From time to time, I receive photos of her with her children, and news of how she is. When I found a funny message in a fortune cookie that was pertinent to her struggle, I sent it to her; she has it framed on the wall of her office. Once, after I presented this case to a group of colleagues, one of those present said, in a tone of wonder or astonishment "You loved her; you really loved her!" I could only plead that I was "guilty as charged."

HOPE IS THE THING WITH FEATHERS

To end, I will say that we need to work creatively and intuitively, improvising when necessary, to use the attachment we develop to these patients, and theirs to us, on their behalf. The therapeutic action involves communicating a sense of hope and safety within a therapeutic relationship that includes lively, at times passionate exchanges, revitalizing for both patient and therapist (Farber 2006; Helm 2004). The therapist's empathy, affective attunement and other forms of connectedness can serve as a corrective emotional experience, offering hope to the patient that relationships can be different from what he experienced in the past. A passionate enactment or interpretation propels the painful process of separating from a prior cognitive-emotional state of being (Billow 2000), and can provide hope, one of the most powerful feelings that the therapist can engender in the patient. It is only when someone who plays recklessly with life and death comes to feel deeply attached to another that he can begin to give up the attachment to pain and suffering and the promise of release that ecstasy provides. Poet Emily Dickinson said it best.

> Hope is the Thing with feathers
> That perches in the soul
> And sings the tune without the words,
> And never stops at all (Dickinson 1891, p. 27).

NOTES

1. The website of the International Society for the Study of Trauma and Dissociation provides guidelines for assessment and treatment of patients with dissociative disorders as well as professional training in treatment of chronic complex trauma, child and adolescent trauma and dissociation, basic and advanced training in adult dissociative disorders in face-to-face and online formats. http://www.isst-d.org/
2. Kings College of London at the Institute for Psychiatry at the Maudsley Hospital has a depersonalization research unit with a listing of research articles on depersonalization disorder.

References

ABC News. (2008). Defence workers trained by 'cult.' December 2, 2008. http://www.abc.net.au/news/2008-04-02/defence-workers-trained-by-cult/2390174. Downloaded January 1, 2012.

Ackerman, D. (1990). *A natural history of the senses.* New York: Vintage Books.

———. (1995). *A natural history of love.* New York: Vintage.

———. (1999). *Deep play.* New York: Random House.

———. (2004). *An alchemy of mind: The marvel and mystery of the brain.* New York: Scribner

Akhtar, S. (2001). *Three faces of mourning: Melancholia, manic defense, and moving on.* Lanham, MD: Jason Aronson.

Aleksander, I. (2011, March 20). Look who's meditating now. *New York Times.*

Alexander, F. (1958). *The scope of psychoanalysis.* New York: Basic Books.

Allison, J. (1967). Adaptive regression and intense religious experiences. *Journal of Nervous & Mental Disease, 145*(6), 452-63.

Ambrose, P. (1976, September 3). Spinning into an early grave? *The Morning News* http://www.themorningnews.org/archives/my_life_in_the_times/spinning_into_an_early_grave.php

American Psychiatric Association. (1994). *Diagnostic and statistical manual of mental disorders* (5th ed.). Washington, DC: American Psychiatric Association.

Ames, L. (2002, January 19). A onetime crack addict finds a new high in his life as an author. *New York Times,* p. 14.

Anda, R, Felitti, V., Bremner, J., Walker, J., Witfield, C., Perry, B., Dube, S., & Giles, W. (2006). The enduring effects of abuse and related adverse experiences in childhood: A convergence of evidence from neurobiology and epidemiology. *European Archives of Psychiatry and Clinical Neuroscience, 256*(3), 174-86.

Anderson, P., & Nghiem, H. (2009). *Psychiatric disorders, sexual trauma linked to urinary tract symptoms.* Medscape Medical News. http://cme.medscape.com/viewarticle/711427?src=cmemp&uac=130263DV.

Andreason, N. (2006). *The creative brain: The science of genius.* New York: Plume.

Angier, N. (1994, May 24). Mother's milk found to be potent cocktail of hormones. *New York Times,* C1.

Anzieu, D. (1980). Skin ego. In S. Lebovici & D. Widlocher (Eds.), *Psychoanalysis in France* (pp. 17-32). New York: International Universities Press.

———. (1990). *Psychic envelopes.* New York: Brunner/Mazel.

Appelbaum, S. (1978). *Out in inner space: A psychoanalyst explores the new therapies.* New York: Anchor Press.

Appelbome, P. (2011, March 7). Loss of speech evokes the voice of a writer. *New York Times.*

Appignanesi, R., & Zarate, O. (2004). *Introducing Freud*. Thriplow, Royston, UK: Icon Books.

Apollon, W., Bergeron, D., & Cantin, L. (2002). *After Lacan: Clinical practice and the subject of the unconscious*. Albany: State University of New York Press.

Armstrong, K. (2000). *The battle for God*. New York: Knopf.

Arnd-Caddigan, M., & Pozzuto, R. (2008). Use of self in relational clinical social work. *Clinical Social Work Journal, 36*(3), 235-43.

Asia Society. (2002). Interview with Sudhir Kakar. http://asiasociety.org/countries-history/religions-philosophies/interview-sudhir-kakar.

Associated Press (2007a, March 13). Family says Jeni committed suicide. *Washington Post*, retrieved March 13, 2007.

Associated Press (2007b, June 29). Coroner's report: Jeni was mentally ill. *Washington Post*, retrieved July 8, 2011.

Astrachan-Fletcher, E., & Maslar, M. (2009). *The dialectical behavior therapy skills workbook for bulimia: Using DBT to break the cycle and regain control of your life*. Oakland, CA: New Harbinger.

Austin, D. (1998). *Zen and the brain*. Cambridge: Massachusetts Institute of Technology Press.

Axelrod, T. (2010, October 22). Hitler exhibit opens, with Jewish applause. *The Jewish Week*, 42.

Babbie, E. (1977). Est in prison. *American Journal of Corrections, 39*(6), 22-25.

Bachar, E., Latzer, Y., Canetti, L., Gur, E., Berry, E., & Bonne, O. (2002). Rejection of life in anorexic and bulimic patients. *International Journal of Eating Disorders, 31*(1), 43-48.

Baglio, M. (2009). *The rite: The making of a modern exorcist*. New York: Doubleday.

Balmer, R. (1993). *Mine eyes have seen the glory: A journey into the evangelical subculture in America*. New York: Oxford University Press.

Baker, D. (2008). *A blue hand: The Beats in India*. New York: The Penguin Press.

Baker-Pitts, C. (2009). Under the knife: Women and cosmetic surgery. Workshop at American Association for Psychoanalysis in Clinical Social Work conference, New York, February 27.

Barthes, R. (1977). *Writing degree zero*. New York: Hill and Wang.

Bataille, G. (1985). *Visions of excess: Selected writings, 1927–1939*. University of Minnesota Press.

Bateman, A. (1998). Thick- and thin-skinned organisations and enactment in borderline and narcissistic disorders. *International Journal of Psycho-Analysis, 79*, 13-25.

Battegay, R. (1991). *Hunger diseases*. Lewiston, NY: Hogrefe and Huber.

Baumeister, R. (1997). *Evil: Inside human violence and cruelty*. New York: W.H. Freeman.

Baxandall, R., & Gordon, L. (2001). *Dear sisters: Dispatches from the women's liberation movement*. New York: Basic Books.

Beaudoin, T. (1998). *Virtual faith: The irreverent spiritual quest of Generation X*. San Francisco: Jossey-Bass.

Begley, S. (2001, May 7). Religion and the brain: In the new field of "neurotheology," scientists seek the biological basis of spirituality. Is God all in their brains? *Newsweek*, 50-57.

Beiler, R. (2009). After jailhouse conversion, Madoff to join ministry of televangelist Kenneth Copeland. http://blog.sojo.net/blogs/2009/04/01/after-jailhouse-conversion-madoff-join-ministry-televangelist-kenneth-copeland.

Bell, R. (1985). *Holy anorexia*. Chicago: University of Chicago Press.

Benbadis, S. (2005). The problem of psychogenic symptoms: Is the psychiatric community in denial? *Epilepsy and Behavior, 1*(148), 9-14.

———. (2006). The EEG in nonepileptic seizures. *Journal of Clinical Neurophysiology, 23*(4), 340-52.

Bender, A. (2010). *The particular sadness of lemon cake*. New York: Doubleday.

Benedek, T. (1959). Parenthood as a developmental phase. In *Psychoanalytic investigations: Selected papers, 1973* (pp. 377-407). New York: Quadrangle.

Benson, A. (2000). *I shop, therefore I am: Compulsive consumption and the search for self*. Northvale, NJ: Jason Aronson.

Bergler, E. (1954). *The writer and psychoanalysis*. New York: Brunner.

Bergmann, M. (1992). *In the shadow of Moloch: The sacrifice of children and its impact on western religions.* New York: Columbia University Press.

———. (1998). Asking for Freud's blessing. In C. Ellman, S. Grand, M. Silvan, & S. Ellman (Eds.), *The modern Freudians: Contempory psychoanalytic technique* (pp. 269-98). Northvale, NJ: Jason Aronson.

Bergner, D. (2009a, January 25). What do women want? A new generation of postfeminist sexologists is trying do discover what ignites female desire. *New York Times Magazine,* pp. ST 26-52.

———. (2009b). *The other side of desire: Four journeys into the far realms of lust and longing.* New York: Ecco.

Bion, W. (1962). *Learning from experience.* London: Heinemann.

———. (1963). *Elements of psycho-analysis.* New York: Jason Aronson.

Blake, W. (1973). William Blake. In L. Bredvold, A. McKillop, & L. Whitney (Eds.), *Eighteenth century poetry and prose* (3d ed) (pp. 1450-1458, 1475). New York: The Ronald Press.

Blakeslee, S., & Blakeslee, M. (2007). *The body has a mind of its own: How body maps in your brain help you do (almost) everything better.* New York: Random House.

Blanke, O. (2004). Out of body experiences and their neural basis. *British Medical Journal, 329,* 1414-15.

Blanke, O., Landis, T., Spinelli, L., & Seeck, M. (2004). Out-of-body experience and autoscopy of neurological origin. *Brain, 127*(2), 243-58.

Blanke, O., & Thut, G. (2007). Inducing out-of-body experiences. In S. Della Sala (Ed.), *Tall tales about the mind and brain: Separating fact from fiction* (pp. 425-39). New York: Oxford University Press.

Blos, P. (1962). *On adolescence: A psychoanalytic interpretation.* New York: Free Press.

———. (1967). The second individuation process of adolescence. *Psychoanalytic Study of the Child, 22,* 162-86.

Blum, D. (1997). *Sex on the brain: The biological differences between men and women.* New York: Viking.

Blumenthal, J. (2010). Madoff's jailhouse conversion reminds Bogle of Blodget. *Philadelphia Business Journal.* http://www.bizjournals.com/philadelphia/blogs/law/2010/04/madoffs_jailhouse_conversion_reminds_bogle_of_blodget.html.

Bodansky, Y. (1999). *Bin Laden: The man who declared war on America.* Roseville, CA: Prima Publishing.

Bollas, C. (1992). *Being a character: Psychoanalysis and self experience.* New York: Hill and Wang.

———. (1997). *Freely associated: Encounters in psychoanalysis with Christopher Bollas, Joyce McDougall, Michael Eigen, Adam Phillips, Nina Coltart,* ed. A. Molino. London: Free Association Books.

Bolton, G., Howlett, S., Lago, C., & Wright, J. (Eds.) (2004). *Writing cures: An introductory handbook of writing in counselling and pychotherapy.* New York and East Sussex: Brunner/Routledge.

Bond, M. (1976). Psychological and psychiatric aspects of pain. In J. Howells (Ed.), *Modern perspectives in the psychiatric aspects of surgery* (pp. 109-38). New York: Brunner/Mazel.

Bor, D. (2010). The mechanics of mind reading. *Scientific American Mind, 21,* 52-57.

Bordo, S. (1997). The body and the reproduction of femininity. In K. Conboy, N. Medina, & S. Stanbury (Eds.), *Writing on the body: Female embodiment and feminist theory* (pp. 90-110). New York: Columbia University Press.

Boris, H. (1994). *Envy.* Northvale, NJ: Jason Aronson.

Bowlby, J. (1988). *A secure base: Parent-child attachment and healthy human development.* New York: Basic Books.

———. (1969). *Attachment and loss* (vol. 1). New York: Basic Books.

Boyer, B. (1997). The verbal squiggle game in treating the seriously disturbed patient. *Psychoanalytic Quarterly, 66*(1), 62-81.

———. (1999). *Counter-transference and regression.* Northvale, NJ: Jason Aronson.

Brand, A. G. (1989). *The psychology of writing: The affective experience (contributions in psychology).* New York: Greenwood Press.

Brandell, J. (2010). *Theory and practice in clinical social work.* New York: Sage.

Bratman, S. (2004). *Health food junkies: Orthorexia nervosa—the health food eating disorder.* New York: Broadway.

Breslau, K. (2002, June 2). The "sextasy" craze: Clubland's dangerous party mix: Viagra and ecstasy. *Newsweek.* http://www.highbeam.com/doc/1G1-94715682.html.

Breuer, J. (1893). Studies on hysteria (theoretical). *Standard edition* (pp. 183-251). London: Hogarth Press.

Breuer, J., & Freud, S. (1895). On the psychical mechanism of hysterical phenomena: A preliminary communication. *Standard edition* (pp. 2, 1-17). London: Hogarth Press.

Bridges, N. (2005). Activating the corrective emotional experience. *Journal of Clinical Psychology, 62*(5), 551-68.

Brizendine, L. (2006). *The female brain.* New York: Broadway Books.

Brisman, J., & Siegel, M. (1984). Bulimia and alcoholism: Two sides of the same coin. *Journal of Substance Abuse Treatment, 1,* 113-18.

Brody, J. (2008). Health "facts" you only thought you knew. *New York Times,* July 22.

Bromberg, P. (1991). On knowing one's patient inside out: The aesthetics of unconscious communication. *Psychoanalytic Dialogues, 1*(4), 399-402.

———. (1998). *Standing in the spaces: Essays on clinical process, trauma, and dissociation.* Hillsdale, NJ: Analytic Press.

———. (2006). *Awakening the dreamer: Clinical journeys.* Hillsdale, NJ: Analytic Press.

———. (2008). "Grown-up" words: An interpersonal/relational perspective on unconscious fantasy. *Psychoanalytic Inquiry, 28*(2), 131-250.

Bronfen, E. (1998). *The knotted subject: Hysteria and its discontents.* Princeton, NJ: Princeton University Press.

Brumberg, J. (1997). *The body project: An intimate history of American girls.* New York: Random House.

Brunet, A., Holowka, D., & Laurence, J. (2001). Dissociation. In M. Aminoff & R. Daroff (Eds.), *Encyclopedia of the neurological sciences.* San Diego: Academic Press.

Bry, A. (1976). *Est (Erhard seminars training): 60 hours that transform your life.* New York: Avon.

Bryant, R, O'Donnell, M., Creamer, M., McFarlane, A., & Silove, D. (2011). Posttraumatic intrusive symptoms across psychiatric disorders. *Journal of Psychiatric Research, 45*(6), 842-47.

Buber, M. (1970). *I and thou.* Walter Kaufman (Trans.). New York: Charles Scribner's Sons.

Bucci, W. (2007a). Dissociation from the perspective of multiple code theory. Part I: Psychological roots and implications for psychoanalytic treatment. *Contemporary Psychoanalysis, 43*(2), 165-84.

———. (2007b).Dissociation from the perspective of multiple code theory. Part II: The spectrum of dissociative processes in the psychoanalytic relationship. *Contemporary Psychoanalysis, 43*(3), 305-26.

Buckley, P., & Galanter, M. (1979). Mystical experience, spiritual knowledge, and a contemporary ecstatic religion. *British Journal of Medical Psychology, 52,* 281-89.

Buffington, C. (2003). Food addiction. *Beyond change.* http://www.beyondchange-obesity.com/obRes.html.

Bugliosi, V. (1974). *Helter skelter: The true story of the Manson murders.* New York: W.W. Norton.

Burt, V., & Rudolph, M. (2000). Treating an Orthodox Jewish woman with obsessive-compulsive disorder: Maintaining reproductive and psychologic stability in the context of normative religious rituals. *American Journal of Psychiatry, 157,* 620-24.

Butterfield, S. (1999). *Amway: The cult of free enterprise.* Cambridge, MA: South End Press.

Bynum, C. (1999). *Holy feast and holy fast: The religious significance of food to medieval women.* Berkeley: University of California Press.

Cameron, J. (1992). *The artist's way: A spiritual path to higher creativity.* Los Angeles: Tarcher.

Campbell, J. (1972). *The hero with a thousand faces*. Princeton: Princeton University Press.
Carey, B. (2006). A neuroscientific look at speaking in tongues. *New York Times Magazine*, November 7, p. F5.
———. (2011a, Jan. 4). On road to recovery, past adversity provides a map. *New York Times*, p. D5.
———. (2011b, Jan. 6). Journal to publish paper on ESP. Psychologists sense outrage. *New York Times*, pp.A1-A3.
Carlsson, I., Wend, P., & Risberg, J. (2000). On the neurobiology of creativity: Differences in frontal activity between high and low creative subjects. *Neuropsychologia, 38*(6), 873-85.
Carmichael, J. (1992). *The birth of Christianity: Reality and myth.* New York: Barnes & Noble.
Carroll, R. (2002). Near-death experience (NDE). The skeptic's dictionary.http://skepdic.com/nde.html.
Castaneda, C. (1972). *The teachings of Don Juan: A Yaqui way of knowledge*. Berkeley: University of California Press.
Centers for Disease Control. (2008). Unintentional strangulation deaths from the "choking game" among youths aged 6-19 years. http://www.cdc.gov/mmwr/preview/mmwrhtml/mm5706a1.htm.
Chamberlain, L. (1998). An introduction to chaos and nonlinear dynamics. In L.Chamberlain & M. Butz (Eds.), *Clinical chaos: A therapist's guide to nonlinear dynamics and therapeutic change* (pp. 3-14). Philadelphia: Brunner/Mazel
Chatoor, I. (1989). Infantile anorexia nervosa: A developmental disorder of separation and individuation. *Journal of the American Academy of Psychoanalysis, 17*(1): 43-64.
Chemtob, C., Nomura, Y., & Abramovitz, R. (2008). Impact of conjoined exposure to the World Trade Center attacks and to other traumatic events on the behavioral problems of preschool children. *Pediatrics and Adolescent Medicine, 162*(2), 126-33.
Chopra, D., Sharma, H., & Triguna, B. (1991). Letter from New Delhi (Maharishi Ayur-Veda: Modern insights into ancient medicine. *Journal of the American Medical Association, 265*, 2633-37.
Christensen, C. (1963). Religious conversion. *Archives of General Psychiatry, 9*(3), 207-16.
Cirves, S. (2010). A story about runner's high.http://www.runaddicts.net/stories/a-story-about-runners-high.
Clark, A., & Chalmers, D. (2010). The extended mind. In A. Clark & D. Chalmers (Eds.), *The extended mind.* Cambridge: MIT Press.
Clasen, S. (2008). Making modern-day martyrs using medieval methods. http://www.odan.org/tw_making_modern_martyrs.htm.
Clayton, K. (2004). The Interrelatedness of disconnection: The relationship between dissociative tendencies and alexithymia. *Journal of Trauma & Dissociation, 5*(1), 77-101.
Clement, C. (1994). *Syncope: The philosophy of rapture*. Minneapolis: University of Minnesota Press.
Cline, A. (2003). Terri Schiavo's medical facts and history: Bulimia, coma, brain death in Terri Schiavo. www.About.com: Agnosticism, Atheism.
Coady, N., & Wolgien, C. (1996). Good therapists' views of how they are helpful. *Clinical Social Work Journal, 24*(3), 311-22.
Cohen, S., & Stern, G. (2001, April 22). Inside the world of Opus Dei. *The Journal News.*
Conway, F., & Siegelman, J. (1995). *Snapping: America's epidemic of sudden personality change* (2d ed). New York: Stillpoint Press.
Coren, S., & Hewitt, P. (1998). Is anorexia nervosa associated with elevated rates of suicide? *American Journal of Public Health, 88*, 1206-7.
Covington, D. (1995). *Salvation on Sand Mountain: Snake handling and redemption in southern Appalachia*. New York: Addison-Wesley.
Csikszentmihalyi, M. (1991). *Flow: The psychology of optimal experience*. New York: HarperCollins.
———. (1997). *Creativity: Flow and the psychology of discovery and invention.* New York: Harper Perennial.
Cuneo, M. (2001). *American exorcism: Expelling demons in the land of plenty*. New York: Doubleday.

Cutting, L. (1997). *Memory slips: A memoir of music and healing*. New York: HarperCollins.
Damasio, A. (1999). *The feeling of what happens: Body and emotion in the making of consciousness*. New York: Harcourt, Brace.
Dass, R. (1971). *Remember, be here now* Santa Fe: Hanuman Foundation.
———. (2000). *Still here: Embracing aging, changing, and dying*. New York: Riverhead Books.
De Bellis, M., Lefter, L., Trickett, P., & Putnam, F. (2004). Urinary catecholamine excretion in sexually abused girls. *Journal of American Academy of Child and Adolescent Psychiatry, 33*(3), 320-7.
de Graaf, J., Wann, D., & Naylor, T. (2002). *Affluenza: The all-consuming epidemic*. San Francisco: Berrett-Koehler Publishers.
Deikman, A. (1972). Deautomatization and the mystic experience. In C. Tart (Ed.), *Altered states of consciousness* (pp. 24-46). Garden City, NY: Doubleday.
de Manzano, O. (2010). Biological mechanisms of creativity and flow. Stockholm: Karolinska Institute
de Manzano, O., Karabanov, I., Karabanov, A., Farde, L., & Ullén, F. (2010). Thinking outside a less intact box: Thalamic dopamine D2 receptor densities are negatively related to psychometric creativity in Healthy individuals. *PLoS ONE, 5*,5.http://www.plosone.org/article/info%3Adoi%2F10.1371%2Fjournal.pone.0010670.
de Manzano, O., Theorell, T., Harmat, L., & Ulléna, F. (2010). The psychophysiology of flow during piano playing. *Emotion, 10*(3), 301-11.
De Salvo, L. (1999). *Writing as a way of healing: How telling our stories transforms our lives* Boston: Beacon Press.
Descartes, R. (1999). *Discourse on method and meditations on first philosophy*. New York: Hackett.
———. (2003). *Treatise of man*. New York: Prometheus Books.
Detrick, B. (2010, Dec. 26). Salvia takes a starring role. *New York Times*, ST1-ST5.
Deutsch, F. (1959). *On the mysterious leap from the mind to the body*. New York: International Universities Press.
Diamond, L. (2009). *Sexual fluidity: Understanding women's love and desire*. Cambridge, MA: Harvard University Press.
Diaz de Chumaceiro, C. (1993). Richard Wagner's life and music: What Freud knew. In S. Feder, R. Karmel, & G. Pollack (Eds.), *Psychoanalytic explorations in music, Second Series* (pp. 249-78). Madison, CT: International Universities Press.
Dickens, C. (2010). *A tale of two cities*. Calgary: Qualitas Classics.
Dickinson, E. (1891). *Poems* (2d series) M. L. Todd & T. W. Higgins (Eds.). Boston: Little, Brown.
———. (1892). *Poems*. M. L. Todd & T.W. Higgins (Eds.). Boston: Little, Brown.
———. (1924). *The complete poems*. Boston: Little, Brown.
———. (1982). *Collected poems of Emily Dickinson*. New York: Avenel Books.
Dlin, B. (1976). The experience of surviving death. In J. Howells (Ed.), *Modern perspectives in the psychiatric aspects of surgery* (pp. 713-29). New York: Brunner/Mazel.
Doidge, N. (2007). *The brain that changes itself: Stories of personal triumph from the frontiers of brain science*. New York: Penguin.
Douglas, M. (2002). *Natural symbols*. New York: Taylor and Francis.
Downey, B. (1984). *Right brain—write on! Overcoming writer's block and achieving your creative potential*. New York: Prentice Hall Trade
Dubner, S. (1998). *Turbulent souls: A Catholic son's return to his Jewish family*. New York: Avon.
Duncan, R., Oto, M., Martin, E., & Pelosi, A. (2006). Late onset psychogenic nonepileptic attacks. *Neurology, 66*(11), 1620-21.
Durkheim, E. (1965). *The elementary forms of the religious life*. New York: Free Press.
Easton, D., & Liszt, C. (1995). *The topping book: Getting good at being bad*. San Francisco: Greenery Press.
———. (1996). *The bottoming book: How to get terrible things done to you by wonderful people*. San Francisco: Greenery Press.

Edmundson, M. (2007). *The death of Sigmund Freud: The legacy of his last days*. New York: Bloomsbury.

Edwards, B. (1979). *Drawing on the right side of the brain*. Los Angeles: J. P. Tarcher.

Edwards, J., & Bess, J. (1998). Developing effectiveness in the therapeutic use of self. *Clinical Social Work Journal, 26*(1), 89-105.

Eftychiadis, A., & Marketos, S. (1999). Saint Marina: The protectress of nephrology. *American Journal of Nephrology, 19*, 107-10.

Ehrenreich, B. (1997). *Blood rites: Origins and history of the passions of war*. New York: Henry Holt.

———. (2007). *Dancing in the streets: A history of collective joy*. New York: Metropolitan Books.

———. (2009). *Bright-sided: How the relentless promotion of positive thinking has undermined America*. New York: Metropolitan Books.

Eigen, M. (1999). *The psychoanalytic mystic*. Binghamton, NY: ESF.

———. (2001). *Ecstasy*. Middletown, CT: Wesleyan University Press.

Eisenberger, N., Liebman, M., & Williams, K. (2003). Does rejection hurt? An fMRI study of social exclusion. *Science, 302*, 290.

Eisler, R. (1995). *Sacred pleasure: Sex, myth, and the politics of the body*. San Francisco: HarperSanFrancisco.

Eliade, M. (1958). *Rites and symbols of initiation: The mysteries of birth and rebirth*. New York: Harper & Row.

———. (1959). *The sacred and the profane*. New York: Harper & Row.

Elkins, D. (1998). *Beyond religion: 8 alternative paths to the sacred: A personal program for building a spiritual life outside the walls of traditional religion*. Wheaton, IL: Quest Books.

Elliott, C. (2003). *Better than well: American medicine meets the American dream*. New York: W.W. Norton.

Ellman,C. (2000). The empty mother: Women's fear of their destructive envy. *Psychoanalytic Quarterly, 69*(4), 633-57.

Erikson, E. (1950). *Childhood and society*. New York: W.W. Norton.

Erikson, M. (1972). A special inquiry with Aldous Huxley into the nature and character of various states of consciousness. In C. Tart (Ed.), *Altered states of consciousness* (pp. 47-74). Garden City, NY: Doubleday.

Eugenides, J. (2007). *Middlesex*. New York: Picador.

Etkin, T., Pittinger, C., Polan, J., & Kandel, E. (2005). Toward a neurobiology of psychotherapy: Basic science and clinical applications. *Journal of Neuropsychiatry and Clinical Neuroscience, 17*, 145-58.

Faber, R. (1992). Money changes everything: Compulsive buying from a biopsychosocial perspective. *American Behavioral Scientist, 35*(6), 809-19.

Fairfield, K., & Fletcher, R. (2002). Vitamins for chronic disease prevention in adults: Scientific review. *Journal of the American Medical Association, 287*, 3116-26.

Farber, S. (1991). A Response to "The emotional consequences of physical child abuse" by Annaclare Van Dalen. *Clinical Social Work Journal, 19*(1), 95-98.

———. (1995). A psychoanalytically informed understanding of the association between binge-purge behavior and self-mutilating behavior: A study comparing binge-purgers who self-mutilate severely with binge-purgers who self-mutilate less severely or not at all. Doctoral Dissertation. New York University School of Social Work. Published by UMI Dissertation Services.

———. (1997a). Self-medication, traumatic reenactment, and somatic expression in bulimic and self-mutilating behavior. *Clinical Social Work Journal, 25*(1), 87-106.

———. (1997b, March 7). Letter to the editor: This life matters. *Rivertowns Enterprise*, p. 20.

———. (2000). *When the body is the target: Self-harm, pain, and traumatic attachments*. Northvale, NJ: Jason Aronson.

———. (2003). Ecstatic stigmatics and holy anorexics, medieval and contemporary. *Journal of Psychohistory, 31*(2), 183-204.

———. (2005a). Free association reconsidered: The talking cure, the writing cure. *Journal of the American Academy of Psychoanalysis and Dynamic Psychiatry, 33*(2), 249-73.

———. (2005b). Write, write, write! Or feel the fear and do it anyway. *National Membership Committee on Psychoanalysis Newsletter,* Winter/Spring, pp. 3-12.

———. (2006). The inner predator: Trauma and dissociation in bodily self-harm. Invited presentation at New Orleans American Psychological Association Panel "Trauma: Obvious and hidden: Possibilities for treatment," August 10.

———. (2007). Book review of *The writing cure: How expressive writing promotes health and emotional well-being,* ed. Stephen L. Lepore & Joshua M. Smyth. *Journal of the American Academy of Psychoanalysis and Dynamic Psychiatry, 35*(1), 162-65.

———. (2008a). Autistic and dissociative features in eating disorders and self-mutilation. *Modern Psychoanalysis, 33*(1), 23-49.

———. (2008b). Dissociation, traumatic attachment, and self-harm (eating disorders and self-injury). *Clinical Social Work Journal, 36*(1), 63-72.

———. (2010). The comorbidity of eating disorders and attention-deficit hyperactivity disorder. *Eating Disorders: The Journal of Treatment & Prevention, 18*(1), 81-89.

Farber, S., Jackson, C., Tabin, J., & Bachar, E. (2007). Death and annihilation anxieties in anorexia nervosa, bulimia, and self-mutilation. *Psychoanalytic Psychology, 24*(2), 289-30.

Farrow, E. (1942). *A practical method of self-analysis enabling a person to remove unreasonable fears and depression from his mind.* London: George Allen & Unwin.

Favazza, A. (1996). *Bodies under siege: Self-mutilation and body modification in culture and psychiatry*, 2d ed. Baltimore: Johns Hopkins University Press.

Febos, M. (2010). *Whip smart: A memoir*. New York: Thomas Dunne Books.

Federal Bureau of Investigation. (2011). *Common fraud schemes: Pyramid schemes.* http://www.fbi.gov/scams-safety/fraud/fraud#pyramid. Downloaded September 25, 2011.

Fernandez-Marina, R. (1961). The Puerto Rican syndrome: Its dynamics and cultural determinants. *Psychiatry, 24*, 79-82

Ferracuti, S., & Sacco, R. (1996). Dissociative trance disorder: Clinical and Rorschach findings in ten persons reporting demon possession and treated by exorcism. *Journal of Personality Assessment, 66*(3), 525-39.

Fessler, D. (2002). Starvation, serotonin, and symbolism: A psychobiocultural perspective on stigmata. *Mind and Society, 6*(3), 81-96.

Firlik, K. (2007). *Another day in the frontal lobe: A brain surgeon exposes life on the inside.* New York: Random House.

First, M. (2005). Desire for amputation of a limb: Paraphilia, pychosis, or a new type of identity disorder. *Psychological Medicine, 35*, 919-28.

Fisher, H. (2009). *Why him? Why her? Finding real love by understanding your personality type*. New York: Henry Holt.

Flaherty, A. (2004). *The midnight disease: The drive to write, writer's block, and the creative brain*. New York: Houghton Mifflin.

———. (2005). Frontotemporal and dopaminergic control of idea generation and creative drive. *The Journal of Comparative Neurology, 493*(1), 147-53.

Flaherty, A., & Post, N. (2000). *The Massachusetts General Hospital handbook of neurology* (2d ed.). Philadelphia: Lippincott Williams & Wilkins.

Flanagan, B. (1993). *Bob Flanagan: Super-masochist*. A. Juno & V. Vale (Eds.). San Francisco: RE/Search Publications.

Flannery, T. (1999). *Throwim way leg: Tree-Kangaroos, possums, and penis gourds—on the track of unknown mammals in wildest New Guinea.* New York: Atlantic Monthly Press.

Flem, L. (2003). *Freud the man: An intellectual biography*. Susan Fairchild (Trans.). New York: Other Press.

Foucault, M. (1977). *The history of sexuality: Volume 1: An introduction*. New York: Vintage Books.

———. (1996). An ethics of pleasure. In *Foucault live*, S. Lotringer (Ed.). New York: Semiotexte(e).

Fowler,R. (2007). Paris Hilton jailhouse conversion? Ray Fowler.org: Thoughts on God and life from a Christian perspective. http://www.rayfowler.org/2007/06/13/paris-hilton-jailhouse-conversion/.

Fox, M. (2005, Sept. 25). Tobias Schneebaum, chronicler and dining partner of cannibals, dies. *New York Times*. http://www.nytimes.com/2005/09/25/obituaries/24schneebaum.html?pagewanted=all .

———. (1997). *Confessions: The making of a post-denominational priest*. San Francisco: Harper San Francisco.

Francis, L., & Robbins, M. (2003). Personality and glossolalia: A study among male evangelical clergy. *Journal of Pastoral Psychology, 51*(5), 391-96.

Frederick, C. (2007). *Est: Playing the game the new way*. Miami: Synergy International of the Americas, Ltd.

French, C., Santomauro, J., Hamilton, V., Fox, R., & Thalbourne, M. (2008). Psychological aspects of the alien contact experience. *Cortex, 44*(10), 1387-95.

Frenken, R. (2000). Childhood and fantasies of medieval mystics. *The Journal of Psychohistory* 28: 150-72.

Freud, A. (1966). *The writings of Anna Freud, Volume 2: The ego and the mechanisms of defense*. New York: International Universities Press.

Freud, S. (1893). Some points for a comparative study of organic and hysterical motor paralyses. *Standard edition*. London: Hogarth Press. 1: 157-72.

———. (1895). Miss Lucy R. *Standard edition* 2: 106-24.

———. (1896). The Aetiology of hysteria. *Standard edition* 3: 191-221.

———. (1900). The interpretation of dreams. *Standard edition* 4: 1-610.

———. (1905). Three essays on the theory of sexuality. *Standard edition* 7: 135-243.

———. (1908). Creative writers and daydreaming. *Standard edition* 9: 143-53.

———. (1910a). Five lectures on psychoanalysis. *Standard edition* 11: 7-56.

———. (1911-1915). Papers on technique. *Standard edition* 12: 89-171.

———. (1912). Recommendations to physicians practising psycho-Analysis. *Standard edition* 12: 109-20.

———. (1913a). Totem and taboo. *Standard edition* 13: 1-162.

———. (1913b). Theme of the three caskets. *Standard edition* 12: 289-301.

———. (1914). The Moses of Michelangelo. *Standard edition* 13: 209-38.

———. (1915). Observations on transference love. *Standard edition* 12: 157-74.

———. (1917). Introductory lectures on psychoanalysis, part III. *Standard edition* 16: 243-463.

———. (1919). The uncanny. *Standard edition* 17: 217-56.

———. (1920a). Beyond the pleasure principle. *Standard edition* 18: 7-64.

———. (1920b). A note on the prehistory of the technique of analysis. *Standard edition* 18: 263-65.

———. (1921). Group psychology and the analysis of the ego. *Standard edition* 18: 67-143.

———. (1922a). Dreams and telepathy. *Standard edition* 18: 197-220.

———. (1923a). The two classes of instincts. *Standard edition* 19: 40-47.

———. (1923b). The ego and the id. *Standard edition* 20: 3-66.

———. (1923c). A seventeenth century demonological neurosis. *Standard edition* 19: 69-105.

———. (1925). Some additional notes on dream interpretation as a whole. *Standard edition* 19: 125-38.

———. (1926). Inhibitions, symptoms, and anxiety. *Standard edition* 20: 87-174.

———. (1927). The future of an illusion. *Standard edition* 21: 1-56.

———. (1930). Civilization and its discontents. *Standard edition* 21: 64-145.

———. (1933). Dreams and occultism. *Standard edition* 22: 31-56.

———. (1939). Moses and monotheism. *Standard edition* 23: 7-137.

———. (1941b). Psychoanalysis and telepathy. *Standard edition* 18: 177-93.

———. (1960). Letter to R. Rolland, 19 January 1930. In *The letters of Sigmund Freud*. New York: Basic Books.

Friedman, L. (2005a). Is there a special psychoanalytic love? *Journal of the American Psychoanalytic Association, 53*(2), 349-75.

———. (2005b). Response to Martha Nussbaum. *Journal of the American Psychoanalytic Association, 53*(2), 385-88.

Friedman, R. (2010, Aug. 31). Lasting pleasures, robbed by drug abuse. *New York Times*, p. D5.

Frost, R., & Steketee, G. (2010). *Stuff: Compulsive hoarding and the meaning of things*. New York: Mariner Books.

Frye, M. (1932). Do not stand at my grave and weep. http://www.findagrave.com/cgi-bin/fg.cgi?page=dfl&GRid=9749178.

Gaines, C., & Butler, G. (1982). *Yours in perfect manhood, Charles Atlas: The most effective fitness program ever devised.* New York: Simon & Schuster.

Galanter, M. (1999). *Cults: Faith, healing and coercion*. New York: Oxford University Press.

Gallese, V., & Goldman, A. (1998). Mirror neurons and the simulation theory of mind-reading. *Trends in Cognitive Science, 2*(12), 493-501.

Gans, E. (2000). The body sacrificial. In *The body aesthetic: From fine art to body modification* (pp. 159-78). Ann Arbor: University of Michigan Press.

Ganzel, G., Kim, P., Glover, G., & Temple, E. (2008). Resilience after 9/11: Multimodal neuroimaging evidence for stress-related change in the healthy adult brain. *Neuroimage, 40*(2), 788-95.

Garcia-Amador, M., Colom, F., Valenti, M., Horga, G., & Vieta, E. (2009). Suicide risk in rapid cycling bipolar patients. *Journal of Affective Disorders, 117*(1-2), 74-78.

Gardner, M. (2000). The second coming. In *Did Adam and Eve have navels?: Discourses on reflexology, numerology, urine therapy, and other dubious subjects* (pp. 288-96). New York: W.W. Norton.

Gates, K. (2005, Dec. 12). Eat me! A weekend among suburban cannibals. *The Village Voice*. http://www.villagevoice.com/2005-12-06/people/eat-me/.

Georgiadis, J., Kortekaas, R., Kuipers, R., Nieuwenburg, A., Pruim, J., Reinders, A., & Holsteg, G. (2006). Regional cerebral blood flow changes associated with clitorally induced orgasm in healthy women. *European Journal of Neuroscience, 24*(11), 3305-16.

Geringer, J. (2000). Karla Faye Tucker: Texas' controversial murderess. http://www.crimelibrary.com/classics3/tucker/ .

Geschwind, N. & Galaburda, A. (1988). *Cerebral dominance: The biological foundations*. Cambridge: Harvard University Press.

Ginsberg, A. (1956). *Howl and other poems*. San Francisco: City Lights Books.

———. (2001). *Spontaneous mind: Selected interviews, 1958-1996.* D. Carter (Ed.). New York: Penguin.

Girard, R. (1977). *Violence and the sacred*. Baltimore: Johns Hopkins University Press.

Gladwell, M. (2000). *The tipping point: How little things can make a big difference*. New York: Little, Brown.

———. (2005). *Blink: The power of thinking without thinking*. New York: Little, Brown.

Glass, M., Kirsch, L., & Parris, F. (1977). Psychiatric disturbances associated with Erhard seminars training: I. A report of cases. *American Journal of Psychiatry, 134*(3), 245-47.

Glazov, J. (2001). The sexual rage behind Islamic terror.http://www.frontpagemagazine.com/columnists/glazov/glazov10-04-01.htm.

Gleick, J. (1987). *Chaos: Making a new science*. New York: Viking.

Goldberg, L. (1993). Guidelines for therapists. In M. Langone (Ed.), *Recovery from cults* (pp. 232-50). New York: W. W. Norton.

———. (1997). A psychoanalytic look at recovered memories, therapists, cult leaders, and undue influence. *Clinical Social Work Journal, 25*(1), 71-86.

Goldhagen, D. (1997). *Hitler's willing executioners: Ordinary Germans and the Holocaust*. New York: Vintage.

Goldman, A. (1992). *The search for God at Harvard*. New York: Random House.

Goldstein, E., Miehls, D., & Ringel, S. (2009). *Advanced clinical social work practice: Relational principles and techniques*. New York: Columbia University Press.

Goldstein, J. (2009). *Hysteria complicated by ecstasy: The case of Nanette Leroux*. Princeton, NJ: Princeton University Press.

Goodman, A. (2008). Neurobiology of addiction: An integrative review. *Biochemical Pharmacology, 75*(1), 266-322.

Goodwin, F., & Jamison, K. (1990). *Manic-depressive illness: Bipolar disorders and recurrent depression*. New York: Oxford University Press.

Gordon, K. (2004). The tiger's stripe: Some thoughts on psychoanalysis, gnosis, and the experience of wonderment. *Contemporary Psychoanalysis, 40*, 5-45.

Gosink, P., & Jumbelic, M. (2000). Autoerotic asphyxiation in a female. *American Journal of Forensic Medicine and Pathology, 21*(2), 114-18.

Green, A. (1986). The dead mother. In *On private madness* (pp. 142-73). London: Hogarth Press.

Greenberg, D., & Shefler, G. (2002). Obsessive compulsive disorder in ultra-orthodox Jewish patients: A comparison of religious and non-religious symptoms.*Psychology and Psychotherapy: Theory, research and Practice, 7*(5), 123-30.

Greenfield, R. (1975). *The spiritual supermarket: An account of gurus gone public in America*. New York: Dutton.

Greif, J., & Hewitt, W. (1996). First international collegiate body art project. Presented at Barnard College, October 22.

Greif, J., Hewitt,W., & Armstrong, M. (1999). Tattooing and body piercing: Body art practices among college students. *Clinical Nursing Research, 8*(4), 368-85.

Grieshaber, K. (2010, Oct. 26). German foreign ministry willingly assisted in Holocaust, report finds. *Journal News*, p.12A.

Griffiths, M. (1995). *Adolescent gambling*. New York: Routledge.

Grimes, R. (1995). *Readings in ritual studies*. New York: Prentice Hall.

Groddeck, G. (1923). *The book of the it*. New York: New American Library.

Gross, J. (2006). *Neighbors: The destruction of the Jewish community in Jedwabne, Poland*. Princeton, NJ: Princeton University Press.

Grossman,W. (1991). Pain, aggression, fantasy, and concepts of sadomasochism. *Psychoanalytic Quarterly, 60*(1), 22-51.

Grossman,C., & Grossman, S. (1965). *The wild analyst: The life and work of George Groddeck*. New York: Dell.

Grotstein, J. (1979). Demoniacal possession, splitting, and the torment of joy: A psychoanalytic inquiry into the negative therapeutic reaction, unanalyzability, and psychotic states. *Contemporary Psychoanalysis, 15*(3), 407-53.

Grüsser, S., Plöntzke, B., Albrecht, U., & Mörsen, C. (2007, Jan. 19). The addictive potential of lottery gambling. *Journal of Gambling Issues, 19*, 19-29.

Guner.F. -2010). The arts desk. Q&A: Adam Phillips. http://www.theartsdesk.com/index.php?option=com_k2&view=item&id=1339:adam-phillips-interview&Itemid=23.

Gura, T. (2008). Addicted to starvation. *Scientific American Mind*, June/July, pp. 60-67.

Hahn, L. & Tapper, A. (2004). Phish phans give phinal phreylach pharewell to band. *The Jewish Daily Forward*. http://www.forward.com/articles/5160/.

Hamill, P. (1997). *Snow in August*. New York: Warner Vision Books.

Hammer, E. (1972). The creative process in psychoanalytic treatment. *Journal of Contemporary Psychotherapy, 4*(2), 81-86.

Harden, C. (1997). Pseudoseizures and dissociative disorders: A common mechanism involving traumatic experiences. *Seizure, 6*, 151-55.

Harrison, K. (1994). *Exposure: A novel*. New York: Warner Books.

Harrison, T. (1996). *Stigmata: A medieval mystery in a modern age*. New York: Penguin.

Hartman, D. & Zimberoff, D. (2004). Corrective emotional experience in the therapeutic process. *Journal of Heart-centered Therapies, 7*(2), 3-84.

Hartmann, H. (1939). *Ego psychology and the problem of adaptation*. New York: International Universities Press.

Hassan,S. (2001). Suicide bombers and cult psychology. http://www.freedomofmind.com/sep11_01.htm.

Hay, D., & Morisy, A. (1978). Reports of esctatic, paranormal, or religious experience in Great Britain and the United States: A comparison of trends. *Journal for the Scientific Study of Religion, 17*(3), 255-68.

Hebb, D. (1949). *The organization of behavior*. New York: Wiley.

Heckler, R. (1994). *Waking up alive: The descent, the suicide attempt & the return to life*. New York: G.P. Putnam.

Hedges, L. (1983). *Listening perspectives in psychotherapy*. New York: Jason Aronson.

———. (1994). *In search of the lost mother of infancy*. Northvale, NJ: Jason Aronson.

Hegi, U. (1994). *Stones from the river*. New York: Simon & Schuster.

———. (1997). *Tearing the silence: On being German in America*. New York: Simon & Schuster.

Helm, F. (2004). Hope is curative. *Psychoanalytic Psychology, 21*(4), 554-66.

Herman, J. (1992). *Trauma and recovery: The aftermath of violence, from domestic abuse to political terror*. New York: Basic Books.

Hernstrom,M. (2010). *The pain chronicles: Cures, myths, mysteries, prayers, diaries, brain scans, healing, and the science of suffering*. New York: Picador.

Hersch, P. (1998). *A tribe apart: A journey into the heart of American adolescence*. New York: Fawcett.

Hicinbothem, G. J., & Lester, D. (2006). Body modification and suicidal behavior. *Death Studies, 30*, 351-63.

Higgins, G. (1994). *Resilient adults: Overcoming a cruel past*. San Francisco: Jossey-Bass.

Hilburn, R. (1992, Feb. 9). Dylan Now. *Los Angeles Times Magazine*. http://www.punkhart.com/dylan/interviews/latimes.2-9-92.html.

Hill, A. A. (1972). Tattoo renaissance. In G. Lewis (Ed.), *Side-saddle on the golden calf: Social structure and popular culture in America* (pp. 245-49). Pacific Palisades: Goodyear.

Hill, D., & Saroka, K. (2010). Sonic patterns, spirituality and brain function. *NeuroQuantology, 8*(4), 509-16.

Hitt, J. (2001,Aug. 26). A confederacy of sauces: Once again, the Civil War has pitted brother against brother. This time, it's over barbecue. *New York Times Magazine*, pp. 28-31.

Hodkinson, P. (2002). *Goth: Identity, style and subculture*. Oxford: Berg Publishers.

Hoffman, A., & Hoffman, A. (2000).*To America with love: Letters from the underground*. Los Angeles: Red Hen Press.

Hollander, E. (1993) Obsessive-compulsive spectrum disorders: An overview. *Psychiatric Annals, 23*(7), 355-58.

Holmes, J. (1996). *Attachment, intimacy, autonomy: Using attachment theory in adult psychotherapy*. Northvale, NJ: Jason Aronson.

Hopkins, L. (2006). *False self: The life of Masud Khan*. New York: Other Press.

Hopenwasser, K. (2008). Being in rhythm: Dissociative attunement in therapeutic process. *Journal of Trauma & Dissociation,9*(3), 349-67.

Hornbacher, M. (1998). *Wasted: A memoir of anorexia and bulimia*. New York: HarperFlamingo.

———. (2008). *Madness: A bipolar life*. New York: Houghton Mifflin Harcourt.

Howell, E. (2005). *The dissociative mind*. Hillsdale, NJ: The Analytic Press.

Hsu, L., Benotti, J., Roberts, S., Saltzman, E., Shikora, S., Rolls, R. & Rand, W. (1998). Nonsurgical factors that influence the outcome of bariatric surgery: A review. *Psychosomatic Medicine, 60*, 338-46.

Hughes, J., Smith, T., Kosterlitz, H., Fothergill, L., Morgan, B. & Morris, H. (1975). Identification of two related pentapeptides from the brain with potent opiate agonist activity. *Nature, 18*(258), 577-80.

Hurvich, M. (2003). The place of annihilation anxieties in psychoanalytic theory. *Journal of the American Psychoanalytic Association, 51*(2), 579-616.

Huxley, A. (2009). *The doors of perception and heaven and hell*. New York: Harper Perennial Modern Classics

Incalterra, L., & Henderson, T. (2011, Jan. 15). Shooting draws scrutiny of herb. *The Journal News*, pp. 1A-8A.

Isakower, O. (1992a). The analyzing instrument in the teaching and conduct of the analytic process. *Journal of Clinical Psychoanalsis, 1*,181-222.

Isakower, O. (1992b). Chapter four: The analyzing instrument: Further thoughts. *Journal of Clinical Psychoanalysis,1*, 200-3.

Jacobs, A. J. (2007). *The year of living biblically: One man's humble quest to follow the Bible as literally as possible*. New York: Simon & Schuster.
Jacobs, D. (1988). Evidence for a common dissociative-like reaction among addicts. *Journal of Gambling Studies, 4*(1), 27-37.
James, W. (1890). *The principles of psychology*. New York: Cosimo Classics.
———. (1985). *The varieties of religious experience: A study in human nature*. New York: Penguin.
———. (2007). *The principles of psychology* (vol. 2). New York: Cosimo Classics.
———. (1994). *Touched with fire: Manic depressive illness and the artistic temperament*. New York: Free Press.
———. (1995). *An unquiet mind: A memoir of moods and madness*. New York: Random House.
———. (1999). *Night falls fast: Understanding suicide*. New York: Knopf.
———. (2004). *Exuberance: The passion for life*.New York: Knopf.
———. (2009). *Nothing was the same: A memoir*. New York: Knopf.
Jancin, B. (2005). Piercings and tattoos possibly linked to suicidality; here's the question: Is body modification a marker for increased risk, or a sort of substitute activity? *Clinical Psychiatry News*, August. http://findarticles.com/p/articles/mi_hb4345/is_8_33/ai_n29203176/
Janet, P. (1907). *The major symptoms of hysteria*. London: Macmillan.
J.B. (1993). Letter to the editor. *Piercing Fans International Quarterly, 41*, 32-33.
Jeffers, S. (1988). *Feel the fear and do it anyway*. New York: Ballantine Books.
Jilek, W., & Jilek-Aali, L. (1978). Initiation in Papua New Guinea: Psychohygienic and ethnopsychiatric aspects. *Papua New Guinea Medical Journal, 21*(3), 252-63.
Johnson, K. (2007, March 28). Back from the dead, teenager casts light on a shadowy game. *New York Times*, pp. A1-A14.
———. (1996). *Unfortunate emigrants: Narratives of the Donner party*. Logan: Utah State University Press.
Johnson, R. (1989). *Ecstasy: Understanding the psychology of joy*. San Francisco: HarperSanFrancisco.
Jones, E. (1953). *The life and work of Sigmund Freud: Volume 1: The formative years and the great discoveries, 1856-1900*. New York: Basic Books.
———. (1955). *The life and work of Sigmund Freud: Volume 2: Years of maturity, 1901-1919*. New York: Basic Books.
———. (1957). *The life and work of Sigmund Freud: Volume 3: The last phase, 1919-1939*. New York: Basic Books.
Jong, E. (1998). *What do women want? Bread, roses, sex, power*. New York: HarperCollins.
———. (2006). *Seducing the demon: Writing for my life*. New York: Jeremy P. Tarcher.
Joseph, B. (1982). Addiction to near-death. *International Journal of Psychoanalysis, 63*, 449-56.
Jourdain, R. (1997). *Music, the brain, and ecstasy: How music captures our imagination*. New Yorl: Harper Paperbacks.
Jung, C. (1951). *Fundamental questions of psychotherapy*. Princeton, NJ: Princeton University Press
———. (1957). *Mysterium coniunctionis* (2d ed.), R. F. C. Hull (Trans.). Princeton, NJ: Princeton University Press.
———. (1961). *Memories, dreams, reflections*. New York: Vintage Books.
Kagan, J. (1994) *Galen's prophecy: Temperament in human nature*. New York: Basic Books
———. (2007). *What is emotion?: History, measures, and meanings*. New Haven: Yale University Press
Kakar, S. (1982). *Shamans, mystics, and doctors: A psychological inquiry into India and its healing traditions*. New York: Knopf.
———. (1991). *The analyst and the mystic: Psychoanalytic reflections on religion and mysticism*. Chicago: University of Chicago Press.
———. (2003). *Ecstasy*. New York: Overlook TP.
Kaplan, L. (1991). *Female perversions*. New York: Doubleday.

Karasu, T. B. (2011). *Gotham chronicles*. Lanham, MD: Rowman & Littlefield.

Kavaler-Adler, S. (2000). *The compulsion to create: Women writers and their demon lovers*. New York: Other Press.

Kavaler-Adler, S., & Sowchek, E. (2003). It takes two to tango: A special workshop on Argentine tango, psychoanalysis, and the intersubjectivity dimension of both. Downloaded September 3, 2006. kavaleradler.com/Argentine_Tango_and_Psychoanalysis.htm.

Kelley, A., Schochet, T., & Landry, C. (2004). Risk taking and novelty seeking in adolescence: Introduction to part I. *Annals of the New York Academy of Sciences, 1021*, 27-32.

Kennedy, J. F. (1962, Sept. 14). John F. Kennedy America's Cup yacht crews speech. http://home.comcast.net/~ceoverfield/sea.html.

Kernberg, O. (1975). *Borderline conditions and pathological narcissism*. New York: Jason Aronson.

———. (1986). Institutional problems of psychoanalytic education. *Journal of the American Psychoanalytic Association, 34*, 799-834.

———. (1992a). Robert Stoller's contribution to contemporary psychoanalysis. *Los Angeles Psychoanalytic Bulletin*, Winter, pp. 24-27.

———. (1992b). *Aggression in personality disorders and perversions*. New Haven, CT: Yale University Press.

Kernberg, O., Selzer, M., Koenigsberg, H., Carr, A., & Appelbaum, A. (1989). *Psychodynamic psychotherapy of borderline patients*. New York: Basic Books.

Kerr, J. (1993). *A most dangerous method: The story of Jung, Freud, and Sabina Spielrein*. New York: Analytic Press.

Kessler, D. (2010). *The end of overeating: Taking control of the insatiable American appetite*. New York: Rodale

Keyes, R. (1996). *The courage to write: How writers transcend fear*. New York: Henry Holt.

Khan, A. (2010). Psychological makeup of a Muslim suicide bomber. Presentation to International Cultic Studies Association conference. Fort Lee, NJ, July 3.

Khan, M. (1989). *The long wait and other psychoanalytic narratives*. New York: Summit Books.

Khantzian, E. (1985). The self-medication hypothesis of addictive disorders: Focus on heroin and cocaine dependence. *American Journal of Psychiatry, 142*(11), 1259-64.

Khantzian, E., & Mack, J. (1983). Self-preservation and the care of the self: Ego instincts reconsidered. *Psychoanalytic Study of the child, 38*, 209-32.

Kifner, J. (2008, April 28). Columbia's radicals of 1968 hold a bittersweet reunion. *New York Times*. http://www.nytimes.com/2008/04/28/nyregion/28columbia.html?sq=columbia%201968&st=nyt&adxnnl=1&scp=1&pagewanted=2&adxnnlx=1324837047-hu8NdlidUteBW/TKtFMHkA.

Kinetz, E. (2006, Sept. 26). Is hysteria real? Brain images say yes. *New York Times*, pp. F1-F4.

Kirsch, M., & Glass, L. (1977). Psychiatric disturbances associated with Erhard seminars training: II. additional cases and theoretical considerationsychiatric disturbances associated with Erhard seminars training: I. A report of cases. *American Journal of Psychiatry 134*, 1254-58.

Kirsner, D. (2009). *Unfree Associations: Inside psychoanalytic institutes*. Lanham, MD: Jason Aronson.

Klam, M. (2001, Jan. 21). Experiencing ecstasy: MDMA is different from all the drugs that came before it—which explains why it has become the fastest-growing illegal substance in America. *New York Times Magazine*, pp. 8-79.

Klein, M. (1935). A contribution to the psychogenesis of manic-depressive states. *International Journal of Psycho-Analysis, 16*, 145-74.

———. (1946). Notes on some schizoid mechanisms. *International Journal of Psycho-Analysis, 27*, 99-110.

———. (1952). The origins of transference. In *Envy and gratitude, 1946-1963* (pp. 48-56). New York: Free Press.

———. (1957). Envy and gratitude. In *Envy and gratitude, 1946-1963* (pp. 176-235). New York: Free Press.

———. (1964). *Contributions to psychoanalysis*. New York: McGraw-Hill.

Klinghoffer, D. (1998). *The Lord will gather me in: My journey to Jewish Orthodoxy*. New York: Free Press.

Knapp, C. (1996). *Drinking: A love story*. New York: Dial Press.

Kohut, H. (1971).*The analysis of the self: A systematic approach to the psychoanalytic treatment of narcissistic personality disorders*. New York: International Universities Press.

———. (1977).*The restoration of the self New York*: International Universities Press.

Kois, D. (2011, March 6). Why do writers abandon novels? *New York Times Book Review*, p. 27.

Komisaruk, B., Beyer-Flores, C., & Whipple, B. (2006). *The science of orgasm*. Baltimore: Johns Hopkins University Press.

Konrath, S., O'Brien, E., & Hsing, C. (2011). Changes in dispositional empathy in American college students over time: A meta-analysis. *Personality and Social Psychology Review, 152*, 180-98.

Koret, R. (2001, Aug. 16). Sexual fantasies of a suicide bomber. *Israeli Insider*. http://www.israelinsider.com/views/articles/views_0108.htm.

Kornfield, J. (2000). *After the ecstasy, the laundry: How the heart grows wise on the spiritual path*. New York: Bantam.

Kosfeld, M., Heinrichs, M., Zak, P., Fischbacher, U., & Fehr, E. (2005). Oxytocin increases trust in humans. *Nature, 435*(2), 673-76.

Krakauer, S. (2001). *Treating dissociative identity disorder: The power of the collective heart*. Philadelphia: Routledge.

Krakow, A. (1994). *The total tattoo book*. New York: Warner Books.

Kramer, P. (1993). *Listening to Prozac* (vol. 1). New York: Viking.

Kraus, J. (2000). Sensitization phenomena in psychiatric illness: Lessons from the kindling model. *Journal of Neuropsychiatry and Clinical Neurosciences, 12*, 328-43, 343.

Krick, F., & Koch, C. (2004). Consciousness and neurosurgery. *Neurosurgery, 55*(2), 273-82.

Kris, E. (1952). *Psychoanalytic explorations in art*. New York: International Universities Press.

———. (1956). The recovery of childhood memories in psychoanalysis. *Psychoanalytic Study of the Child, 11*, 54-88.

Kroll, J. (1993). *PTSD/ Borderlines in therapy: Finding the balance*. New York: W.W. Norton.

Kross, E., Berman, M., Mischel,W., Smith, E., & Wager, T. (2011). Social rejection shares somatosensory representations with physical pain. *Proceedings of the National Academy of Sciences,108*(15), 6270-75.

Krueger, D. (1988). On compulsive shopping and spending: A psychodynamic inquiry. *American Journal of Psychotherapy, 22*(4), 574-84.

Krueger, D. (1989). *Body self and psychological self: Developmental and clinical integration in disorders of the self*. New York: Brunner/Mazel.

Kubler-Ross E. (1997). *On death and dying*. New York: Scribner.

La Barre, W. (1969). *They shall take up serpents: Psychology of the southern snake-handling cult*. New York: Schocken Books.

Lachmann, F., & Beebe, B. (1997). The contribution of self-and mutual regulation to therapeutic action: A case illustration. In M. Moskowitz, C. Monk, C. Kaye, & S. Ellman (Eds.), *The neurobiological and developmental basis for psychotherapeutic intervention* (pp. 91-121). Northvale, NJ: Jason Aronson.

Lahr, J. (1998). Skeleton of the new: The story behind the scenes of "Ragtime." *New Yorker, 73*, 56-60.

Lambert, K., and Lilienfeld, S. 2007. Brain stains. *Scientific American Mind*, Oct./Nov., 46-53.

Lamott, A. (1995). *Bird by bird: Some instructions on writing and life*. New York: Anchor.

———. (1999). *Traveling mercies: Some thoughts on faith*. New York: Anchor Books.

Langone, M. (1993). Helping cult victims: Historical background. In M. Langone (Ed.), *Recovery from cults: Help for victims of psychological and spiritual abuse* (pp. 22-47). New York: W.W. Norton.

Lanius, R., & Hopper, J. (2008). Reexperiencing hyperaroused and dissociative states in posttraumatic stress disorder. *Psychiatric Times 25*(13). http://www.psychiatrictimes.com/display/article/10168/1348751.

La Plante, E. (1993). *Seized: Temporal lobe epilepsy as a medical, historical, and artistic phenomenon*. New York: HarperCollins.

Lappe, M. (1996). *The body's edge: Our cultural obsession with skin*. New York: Henry Holt.

Largo, M. (2010). *God's lunatics: Lost souls, false prophets, martyred saints, murderous cults, demonic nuns, and other victims of man's eternal search for the divine*. New York: Harper Paperbacks.

Lasch, C. (1979) *The culture of narcissism*. New York: W. W. Norton.

Laski, M. (1961). *Ecstasy: A study of some secular and religious experiences*. Los Angeles: Jeremy P. Tarcher.

———. (1980). *Everyday ecstasy*. London: Thames and Hudson.

Lattin, D. (2010). *The Harvard psychedelic club: How Timothy Leary, Ram Dass, Huston Smith, and Andrew Weil killed the fifties and ushered in a new age for America*. New York: HarperOne

Lawrence, L. (1990). The psychodynamics of the compulsive shopper. *American Journal of Psychoanalysis, 50*(1), 67-70.

Lawson, D. (1996). *So you want to be a shaman*. London: Godsfield Press.

Leary, T., Metzner, R., & Alpert, R. (1964). *The psychedelic experience: A manual based on the Tibetan book of the dead*. New York: University Books.

Lehrer, J. (2007). *Proust was a neuroscientist*. New York: Houghton Mifflin Harcourt

Lesser, W. (1995, Feb. 19). Book review. *An anthropologist on Mars: Seven paradoxical tales by Oliver Sacks*. *New York Times*. http://www.nytimes.com/1995/02/19/books/everybody-is-peculiar.html?pagewanted=all&src=pm.

Levine, D. (1974). "Needle freaks": Compulsive self-injection by drug users. *American Journal of Psychiatry, 131*(3), 297-300.

Levine, H., & Friedman, R. (2000). Intersubjectivity and interaction in the analytic relationship. *Psychoanalytic Quarterly, 69*(1), 63-92.

Levine, P. (1997). *Waking the tiger: Healing trauma: The innate capacity to transform overwhelming experiences*. Berkeley: North Atlantic Books.

Levitin, D. (2006). *This is your brain on music: The science of a human obsession*. New York: Dutton.

Lewis, C. S. (1991). *The four loves?* New York: Houghton Mifflin.

Lewis-Fernández, R., Garrido-Castillo, P., Bennasar, M., Parrilla, E., Laria, A., Ma, G., & Petkova, E. (2002). Dissociation, childhood trauma, and *ataque de nervios* among Puerto Rican psychiatric outpatients. *American Journal of Psychiatry,159*, 163-65.

Liebowitz, M. (1983). *The chemistry of love*. New York: Little, Brown.

Lifton, R. (1986). *The Nazi doctors: A study in the psychology of evil*. London: Papermac.

Lilienfeld, S., & Arkowitz, H. (2011). Can people have multiple personalities? *Scientific American Mind*, Sept./Oct., 64-65.

Lilienfeld, S., & Lynn, S. (2004). Dissociative identity disorder. In S. Lilienfeld, S. Lynn, & J. Rohr (Eds.), *Science and pseudoscience in clinical psychology* (pp. 109-41). New York: Guilford Press.

Linehan, M. (1993a) *Cognitive-behavioral treatment of borderline personality disorder*. New York: Guilford.

———. (1993b) *Skills training manual for treating borderline personality disorder*. New York: Guilford.

Liotti, G. (1995). Disorganized/disoriented attachment in the psychotherapy of the dissociative disorders. In S. Goldberg, R. Muir, & J. Kerr (Eds.), *Attachment theory: Social, developmental, and clinical perspectives* (pp. 343-63). Hillsdale, NJ: Analytic Press.

Litman, R., & Swearingen, C. (1996). Bondage and suicide. In J.Maltsberger & M. Goldblatt (Eds.), *Essential papers on suicide* (pp. 243-58). New York: New York University Press.

Loa Zavala, N. (2010). The expulsion of evil and its return: An unconscious fantasy associated with a case of mass hysteria in adolescents. *The International Journal of Psychoanalysis, 91*(5), 1157-78.

Loewald, H. (1960). On the therapeutic action of psychoanalysis. *International Journal of Psycho-Analysis, 41*, 16-33.

———. (1988). *Sublimation: Inquiries into theoretical psychoanalysis*. New Haven, CT: Yale University Press.

Loewenthal, K., & Grady, B. (1997). Features associated with speaking in tongues (glossolalia). *British Journal of Medical Psychology, 70*(2), 186-91.

Lowry, B. (1998). The good bad girl. *New Yorker, 73*, 60-69.

Ludwig, A. (1972). Altered states of consciousness. In C. Tart (Ed.), *Altered states of consciousness* (pp. 11-24). Garden City, NY: Doubleday.

Maaranen, P., Tanskanen, A., Honkalampi, K., Haatainen, K., Hintikka, J., & Viinamaki, H. (2005). Factors associated with pathological dissociation in the general population. *Australian and New Zealand Journal of Psychiatry, 39*(5), 387-94.

Mack, J. (1994). *Abduction: Human encounters with aliens*. New York: Scribner.

———. (2008). *Passport to the cosmos: Human transformation and alien encounters* (commemorative edition). Largo, FL: Kunati.

MacKendrick, K. (1999). *Counterpleasures*. Albany: State University of New York Press.

Mahler, M., Pine, F., & Bergmann, A. (1975). *The psychological birth of the human infant: Symbiosis and individuation*. New York: Basic Books.

Mahony, P. (1987). *Freud as a writer*. New Haven, CT: Yale University Press.

———. (2002). Freud's writing: His (w)rite of passage and its reverberations. *Journal of the American Psychoanalytic Association, 50*(3), 895-907.

Main, M., Kaplan, N., & Cassidy, J. (1985). Security in infancy, childhood, adulthood: A move to the level of representation. In J. Bretherton & E. Waters (Eds.), *Monographs of the society for research in child development* (pp. 66-104). Chicago: University of Chicago Press.

Main, M., & Morgan, H. (1996). Disorganization and disorientation in infant strange behavior: Phenotypic resemblance to dissociative states. In L. Michelson & W. Ray (Eds.), *Handbook of dissociation: Theoretical, empirical and clinical perspectives* (pp. 107-38). New York: Plenum.

Main, M., & Solomon, J. (1986). Discovery of a new, insecure-disorganized disoriented attachment pattern. In T. Brazelton & M. Yogman (Eds.), *Affective development in infancy* (pp. 65-124). Norwood, NJ: Ablex.

Mallon, T. (1986). *A book of one's own: People and their diaries*. New York: Penguin Books.

Marks, I., & Nesse, R. (1994). Fear and fitness: An evolutionary analysis of anxiety disorders. *Ethology and Sociobiology, 15*, 247-61.

Marra, T. (2005). *Dialectical behavior therapy in private practice*. Oakland, CA: New Harbinger Publications.

Martin, P., Dole, A., Langone, M., & Wiltrout, J. (1992). Post-cult symptoms as measured by the MCMI before and after residential treatment. *Cultic Studies Journal, 9*(2), 219-50.

Maslow, A. (1964). *Religions, values, and peak-experiences*. New York: Viking.

———. (1971). *The farther reaches of human nature*. New York: Viking.

May, R. (1975). *The courage to create*. New York: W. W. Norton.

Mayer, E. (2001). On "Telepathic dreams?" Unpublished paper by Robert J. Stoller. *Journal of the American Psychoanalytic Association, 49*(2), 629-57.

———. (2007). *Extraordinary knowing: Science, skepticism, and the inexplicable powers of the human mind*. New York: Bantam.

McDougall, J. (1980). A child is being eaten: Psychosomatic states, anxiety neurosis and hysteria—a theoretical approach II: The abysmal mother and the cork child—a clinical illustration. *Contemporary Psychoanalysis, 16*, 417-59.

———. (1992). *A plea for a measure of abnormality*. New York: International Universities Press.

Medwick, C. (1999). *Teresa of Avila: The progress of a soul*. New York: Knopf.

Meissner, W. W. (2003). *The ethical dimension of psychoanalysis: A dialogue*. State University of New York Press.

Melton, G. (1998). *Encyclopedia of American religions*. New York: GaleGroup/McGrath.

Merkin, D. (1997). *Dreaming of Hitler*. New York: Crown Publishers.

Merkur, D. (1989). Unitive experiences and the state of trance. In M. Idel & B. McGinn (Eds.), *Mystical Union and monotheistic faith* (pp. 125-153). New York/London: Macmillan and Collier Macmillan.

Merkur, D. (2006). Interpreting numinous experiences. *Social Analysis, 50,* 204-23.
———. (1994). *Approaching hysteria.* Princeton: Princeton University Press.
Milkman, H., & Sunderwirth, S. (1987). *Craving for ecstasy: The consciousness and chemistry of escape.* New York: Lexington Books.
Mollon, P. (2000). *Freud and false memory syndrome.* Duxford, Cambridge, UK: Icon Books.
Montagu, A. (1971). *Touching: The human significance of the skin.* New York: Harper & Row.
Moody, R. (1946) Bodily changes during abreaction. *The Lancet, 248*(6435), 934-35.
———. (2001). *Life after life: The investigation of a phenomenon—survival of bodily death.* New York: HarperOne.
Moore, B., & Fine, B. (1990). *Psychoanalytic terms and concepts.* New Haven, CT: The American Psychoanalytic Association and Yale University Press.
Morgan, H. (1990). Dostoevsky's epilepsy: A case report and comparison. *Surgical Neurology, 33*(6), 413-16.
Morinis, A. (1985). The ritual experience: Pain and the transformation of consciousness in ordeals of initiation. *Ethos, 13,* 150-74.
Morris, D.B. (1991). *The culture of pain.* Berkeley: University of California Press.
Mostofsky, E., Maclure, M., Sherwood, J., Tofler, G., Muller, J., & Mittleman, M. (2012). Risk of acute myocardial infarction after death of a significant person in one's life: The determinants of MI onset study. *Circulation American Heart Association.* Published online January 9. http://circ. Ahajournals.org/content/early/2012/01/09/CIRCULATIONAHA.111.061770. Abstract
Myers, J. (1995). Nonmainstream body modification: Genital piercing, branding, burning, and cutting. In T. Weinberg (Ed.), *S & M: Studies in dominance and submission* (pp. 151-193). Amherst, NY: Prometheus Books.
Name withheld (1997). Dead teen's friend urges parents to reach out. *Rivertowns Enterprise,* March 27, pp. 2-21.
Nelson, J. (2005). *Seeing through tears: Crying and attachment.* New York: Brunner-Routledge.
Nelson, K. (2011). *The spiritual doorway in the brain: A neurologist's search for the God experience.* New York: Dutton Adult.
Nelson , K., Mattingly, M., Lee, S., & Schmitt, F. (2006). Does the arousal system contribute to near death experience? *Neurology, 66,* 1003-9.
Nelson , K., Mattingly, M., & Schmitt, F. (2007). Out-of-body experience and arousal. *Neurology, 68*(10), 794-95.
Nelson, V. (1993). *On writer's block.* New York: Houghton Mifflin.
Ness, R., & Wintrob, R. (1980). The emotional impact of fundamentalist religious participation: An empirical study of intragroup variation. *American Journal of Orthopsychiatry, 50*(2): 302-15.
Neumann, E. (1963). *The great mother: An analysis of the archetype.* Princeton, NJ: Princeton University Press.
Neumeister, L. (2009, August 26). Alleged Madoff mistress tells "what made Bernie tick." *Journal News,* 4B.
New York Times (2000). 235 Sect members reported in suicide by fire in Uganda. March 19. http://www.nytimes.com/2000/03/19/world/235-sect-members-reported-in-suicide-by-fire-in-uganda.html. Downloaded July 6, 2009.
Newberg, A., & d'Aquili, E. (1994). The near death experience as archetype: A model for "prepared" neurocognitive processes. *Anthropology of Consciousness, 5*(4), 1-15.
———. (2000). The creative brain/the creative mind. *Zygon, 35*(1), 53-68.
———. (2001). *Why God won't go away: Brain science and the biology of belief.* New York: Ballantine Books.
Newberg, A., & Waldman, R. (2010). *How God changes your brain: Breakthrough findings from a leading neuroscientist.* New York: Ballantine Books.
Newberg, A., Wintering, N., Morgan, D., & Waldman, M. (2006). The measurement of regional cerebral blood flow during glossolalia: A preliminary SPECT study. *Psychiatry Research, 48*(1), 67-71.
Newman, J. (2010, October 28). A strange, green journey. *New York Times,* E1-E10.

New York Times Magazine (1997). Making a joyful noise: Rev. Matthew Fox hopes his sweaty rave masses will change the way we pray, raving my religion. June 22.

Neziroglu, F., Donnelly, K., & Simeon, D. (2010). *Overcoming depersonalization disorder: A mindfulness and acceptance guide to conquering feelings of numbness and unreality*. Oakland, CA: New Harbinger.

Nickell, J. (2000). Stigmata: In imitation of Christ. *Skeptical Inquirer* .http://www.findarticles.com/cf_0/m2843/4_24/63693003/print.jhtml.

Nir, S. (2011, January 9). For dancers, "Black Swan" is a cautionary tale. *New York Times*, p. ST5.

Norris, J. (1988) *Serial killers: The growing menace.* New York: Bantam.

———. (2007, December 3). Postcard from padre: Pio's ride. *The New Yorker,* 43.

Northrup, C. (1998). *Women's bodies, women's wisdom: Creating physical and emotional health and healing* (rev. ed.). New York: Bantam.

Nuland, S. (1995). *How we die: Reflections on life's final chapter*. New York: Vintage Books.

Oates, J. (2010). A widow's story: The last week of a long marriage. *The New Yorker*, 70-79.

Ode, K. (2009, August 10). Bringing bipolar into the light. *Star Tribune*. http://www.startribune.com/lifestyle/52683772.html?elr=
KArks7PYDiaK7DUHPYDiaK7DUiacyKUnciatkEP7DhUr.

Ogden, T. (1989). *The primitive edge of experience*. Northvale, NJ: Jason Aronson

———. (1994). Playing, dreaming, and interpreting experience. In M. Fromm & B. Smith (Eds.), *The facilitating environment: Clinical applications of Winnicott's theory* (pp. 255-78). Madison, CT: International Universities Press.

———. (1996). *Subjects of analysis*. Northvale, NJ: Jason Aronson.

———. (1997). Reverie and interpretation. *Psychoanalytic Quarterly, 66(*4), 567-95.

Orenstein, P. (2002, Feb. 10). Staying clean: Patrick, Mike, and Sharon are drug addicts who have been in legal trouble. Voters and experts want them in rehab rather than in jail. But will treatment really keep them off drugs? *New York Times Magazine*, 34-75.

Orloff, B. (2009). David Carradine died of accidental asphyxiation. *People*. http://www.people.com/people/article/0,20289267,00.html.

Orwell, G. (1949). *1984*. London: Penguin Books.

Otto, R. (1923). *The idea of the holy*. New York: Oxford University Press

Papolos, D., & Papolos, J. (1999). *The bipolar child.* New York: Broadway Books.

Pearlman, P., & Courtois, C. (2005). Clinical applications of the attachment framework: Relational treatment of complex trauma. *Journal of Traumatic Stress, 18*(5), 449-59.

Pennebaker, J. (1991). *Opening up: The healing power of confiding in others*. New York: Avon.

Peres, J., Newberg, A., Mercante, J., Simao, M., Albuquerque, V., Peres, M., & Nasello, A. (2007). Cerebral blood flow changes during retrieval of traumatic memories before and after psychotherapy: A SPECT study. *Psychological Medicine 37*, 1481-91.

Perry, B., Pollard, R., Blakeley, T., Baker, W., & Vigilante, D. (1995). Childhood trauma, the neurobiology of adaptation, and "use-dependent" development of the brain: How "states" become "traits." *Infant Mental Health Journal*, *16*(4), 271-91.

Perry, B., & Szalavitz, M. (2006). *The boy who was raised as a dog: And other stories from a child psychiatrist's notebook—What traumatized children can teach us about loss, love, and healing.* New York: Basic Books.

Persinger, M. (1983). Religious and mystical experiences as artifacts of temporal lobe function: a general hypothesis. *Perceptual and Motor Skills*, *57*, 1255-62.

———. (1993). Transcendental meditation (tm) and general meditation are associated with enhanced complex partial epileptic-like signs: Evidence for "cognitive" kindling? *Perceptual and Motor Skills, 75*, 80-82.

———. (2001). The neuropsychiatry of paranormal experiences. *Journal of Neuropsychiatry and Clinical Neuroscience*, *13*(4), 515-24.

Persinger, M., Carrey, N., & Suess, L. (1980). *TM and cult mania*. Hanover, MA: Christopher Publishing House.

Phillips, A. (1994). *On kissing, tickling and being bored: Psychoanalytic essays on the unexamined life*. Cambridge, MA: Harvard University Press.

———. (1995). *Terrors and experts*. Cambridge, MA: Harvard University Press.
———. (1996). The influence of suggestion on suicide: Substantive and theoretical implications of the Werther effect. In J. Maltsberger & M. Goldblatt (Eds.), *Essential papers on suicide*. (pp. 290-313). New York: New York University Press.
Phillips, H. (2006). Hooked: Why your brain is primed for addiction. *New Scientist*. http://www.newscientist.com/channel/being-human/mg19125661.200-hooked-why-your-brain-is-primed-for-addiction.html.
Pines, D. (1980). Skin communication: Early skin disorders and their effects on the transference and counter-transference. *International Journal of Psychoanalysis, 61*, 315-23.
Pinker, S. (1995). *The language instinct: How the mind creates language*. New York: Perennial.
Piper, Jr., A. (2008). Multiple personality disorder: Witchcraft survives in the twentieth century. In S. Lilienfeld, J. Ruscio, & S. Lynn (Eds.), *Navigating the mindfield: A guide to separating science from pseudoscience in mental health* (pp. 249-68). Amherst, NY: Prometheus Books.
Polhemus, T. (1988). *Body styles*. Luton, Beds: Lennard Publishing.
Pollack, A. (2010, October 29). With safety concerns growing, F.D.A. rejects another diet pill. *New York Times*, A1-B4.
Post, R., & Weiss, S. (1998). Sensitization and kindling phenomena in mood, anxiety, and obsessive-compulsive disorders: the role of serotonergic mechanisms in illness progression. *Biological Psychiatry, 44*(3), 193-206.
Poulain, A. (1912). Mystical stigmata. *The Catholic Encyclopedia*, XIV.http://www.newadvent.org/cathen/14294b.htm.
Pressman, S. (1993). *Outrageous betrayal: The real story of Werner Erhard from est to exile*. New York: St. Martins Press.
Prothero, S. (2003). *American Jesus*. New York: Farrar, Straus and Giroux.
Proust, M. (2007). *Swann's way: In search of lost time, Vol.1*. C. K. Scott Moncrieff and Terence Kilmartin (Trans.). New York: Vintage.
Putnam, F. (1992). Discussion: Are alter personalities fragments or fiction? *Psychoanalytic Inquiry, 12*, 95-111.
Quinodoz, D. (1997). *Emotional vertigo: Between anxiety and pleasure*. New York: Routledge.
Raines, J. (1996). Self-disclosure in clinical social work. *Clinical Social Work Journal, 24*(4), 357-75.
Rarick, E. (2008). *Desperate passage: The Donner party's perilous journey west*. New York: Oxford University Press.
Raubolt, R. (2007). *Power games: Influence, persuasion, and indoctrination in psychotherapy training*. New York: Other Press.
Read, K., & Purse, M. (2005). The "kindling" model in bipolar disorder.http://bipolar. About.com/cs/brainchemistry/a/0009_kindling1.htm.
Reinberg, R. (2010). Deadly 'choking game' still common among kids.http://www.dentalplans.com/articles/46602/deadly-choking-game-still-common-among-kids.html.
Renik, O. (2003). Standards and standardization. *Journal of the American Psychoanalytic Association, 51*, 43-55.
———. (2004). Intersubjectivity in psychoanalysis. *International Journal of Psycho-analysis, 85*, 1053-56.
———. (2006). *Practical psychoanalysis for therapists and patients*. New York: Other Press.
Reynolds, S. (1995). *The rapture of Canaan*. New York: Berkley Books.
Rhoades, G., & Sar, V. (Eds.). (2006). *Trauma and dissociation in a cross-cultural perspective: Not just a North American phenomenon*. New York: Routledge.
Ring, K. (1993). *The Omega project: Near-death experiences, UFO encounters, and mind at large*. New York: Quill.
Rivers, J., & Frankel, V. (2008). *Men are stupid . . . and they like big boobs: A woman's guide to beauty through plastic surgery*. New York: Pocket.
Rizzolatti, G., Fogassi, L., & Gallese, V. (2001). Neurophysiological mechanisms underlying the understanding and imitation of action. *Nature Reviews Neuroscience, 2*, 661-70.

Rizzuto, A. (1985). Eating and monsters: A psychodynamic view of bulimarexia. In S. Emmett (Ed.), *Theory and treatment of anorexia nervosa and bulimia* (pp. 194-210). New York: Brunner/Mazel.

———. (1998). *Why did Freud reject God? A psychodynamic interpretation.* New Haven, CT: Yale University Press.

Roffman, J., Marci, C., Glick, D., Dougherty, D., & Rauch, S. (2005). Neuroimaging and the functional neuroanatomy of psychotherapy. *Psychological Medicine, 35*(10), 1385-98.

Roiphe, A. (2011). *Art and madness: A memoir of lust without reason.* New York: Nan A. Talese

Rolland, R. (1929). *The life of Ramakrishna*. Calcutta: Advaita Ashrama.

Rosenfeld, H. (1987). *Impasse and interpretation.* London: Tavistock.

Rothenberg, A. (1988). *The creative process of psychotherapy.* New York: W. W. Norton.

———. (1990). *Creativity and madness: New findings and old stereotypes.* Baltimore: Johns Hopkins University Press.

———. (2001). The muse in the bottle. In J. Petrucelli & C. Stuart (Eds.), *Hungers and compulsions: The psychodynamic treatment of eating disorders and addictions* (pp. 245-61). Northvale, NJ: Jason Aronson.

Ruffin, C. B. (1982). *Padre Pio: The true story.* Huntington, IN: Our Sunday Visitor.

Russell, P., & John, J. (1999). Self-injurious behavior: A kindling phenomenon? *Pediatric Rehabilitation, 3*(1), 1-4.

Ruthven, M. (1989). *The divine supermarket: Shopping for God in America.* Westminster, MD: Arbor House.

Sacks, O. (1987). *The man who mistook his wife for a hat: And other clinical tales.* New York: Perennial Library.

———. (1996). *An anthropologist on mars: Seven paradoxical tales.* New York: Vintage.

———. (2007). *Musicophilia: Tales of music and the brain.* New York: Knopf.

Saks, E. (2007). *The center cannot hold: My journey through madness.* New York: Hyperion.

Samarin, W. (1972). *Tongues of men and angels: The religious language of Pentacostalism.* New York: Macmillan.

Sanders, C. (1989). *Customizing your body: The art and culture of tattooing.* Philadelphia: Temple University Press.

Sanville, J. (994). *The playground of psychoanalytic therapy,* Hillsdale, NJ: Analytic Press.

Sarno, J. (1991). Healing back pain: The mind-body connection. New York: Warner Books.

———. (1999). *The mindbody prescription: Healing the body, healing the pain.* New York: Warner Books.

———. (2006). *The divided mind: The epidemic of mindbody disorders.* New York: Regan Books.

Savage, D. (1996, Nov. 12). Savage Love. *The Village Voice*, p. 121.

Scaer, R. (2005). *The Trauma spectrum: Hidden wounds and human resiliency.* New York: W. W. Norton.

Schachter, J. (1997). *Human resiliency.* New York: W. W. Norton.

The body of thought: Psychoanalytic considerations on the mind-body. *Psychoanalytic Psychotherapy, 11*(3), 211-9.

Schilder, P. (1928). *Depersonalization: Introduction to a psychoanalytic psychiatry.* Nervous and mental disease monograph series No. 50. New York: Nervous and Mental Disease Publishing Company.

Shaw, D. (2003). Traumatic abuse in cults: A psychoanalytic perspective. *Cultic Studies Review, 2*(2), 101-31.

Schneebaum, T. (1969). *Keep the river on your right.* New York: Grove Press.

Schneidman, E., Farberow, N., & Litman, N. (1994). *The psychology of suicide: A clinician's guide to evaluation and treatment.* Northvale, NJ: Jason Aronson .

Schochet, J. (1990). *Chassidic dimensions: Themes in Chassidic thought and* practice (mystical dimension, vol. 3). New York: Kehot Publication Society

Schore, A. (1997). Interdisciplinary developmental research as a source of clinical models. In M. Moskowitz, C. Monk, C. Kaye, & S. Ellman (Eds.), *The neurobiological and developmental basis for psychotherapeutic Intervention* (pp. 1-71). Northvale, NJ: Jason Aronson.

Schore, A., & Chafetz, R. (2005). The dissociative self: Integrating neuroscience and clinical practice: mind and body in the treatment of psychological trauma. International Society for the Study of Dissociation Conference. Torrance, CA, February 11.

Sebold, A. *The lovely bones*. New York. Little, Brown.

Segal, K. 1952). Psychoanalytical approach to aesthetics. *International Journal of Psychoanalysis, 33*, 196-207.

Selinger, N. (2011). *A Sloan product: A memoir of a lost boy. N*ew York: World Audience.

Selzer, R. (1996). *Mortal lessons: Notes on the art of surgery*. New York: Harcourt Brace.

———. (2001a). *Confessions of a knife*. East Lansing: Michigan State University Press.

Selzer, R. (2001b).

Schmidt, U., Bone, G., Hems, S., Lessem, J., & Treasure, J. (2002). Structured therapeutic writing tasks as an adjunct to treatment in eating disorders. *European Eating Disorders Review, 10*(5), 299-315.

Schwartz, B. (1960). Ordeal by serpents, fire, and strychnine. *Psychiatric Quarterly, 34*, 405-29.

Schweinsburg, A. Brown, S., & Tapert, S. (2008). The influence of marijuana use on neurocognitive functioning in adolescents. *Current Drug Abuse Review, 1*(1), 99-111.

Scott, D. (1998). Rites of passage in adolescent development: A reappreciation. *Child & Youth Care Forum, 27*(5), 317-35.

Scott, G. (2002). *The complete idiot's guide to shamanism*. New York: Penguin.

Seery, M., Holman, A., & Cohen Silver, R. (2010). Whatever does not kill us: Cumulative lifetime adversity, vulnerability, and resilience. *Journal of Personality and Social Psychology, 99*(6), 1025-41.

Segal, H. (1974). *Introduction to the work of Melanie Klein* (2d ed.). New York: Basic Books.

———. (1952). Psychoanalytical approach to aesthetics. *International Journal of Psychoanalysis, 33*, 196-207.

Sharp, C., & Freeman, C. (1993). The medical complications of anorexia nervosa. *British Journal of Psychiatry, 162*, 452-62.

Shaw, D. (2005). Madness and evil: An insider's view of the Sullivanian Institute. A review essay of *the Sullivanian Institute/Fourth Wall community: The relationship of radical individualism and authoritarianism,* by Amy B. Siskind. *Contemporary Psychoanalysis, 41*(4), 765-73.

Shear, J. (2006). *Experience of meditation: Experts introduce the major traditions*. St. Paul: Paragon House.

Shengold, L. (1979). Child abuse and deprivation: Soul murder. *Journal of the American Psychoanalytic Association, 27*(3), 533-59.

———. (1989). *Soul murder: The effects of childhood abuse and deprivation*. New Haven, CT: Yale University Press.

———. (2000). *Soul murder revisited: Thoughts about therapy, hate, love, and memory*. New Haven, CT: Yale University Press.

Shields, C., & Howard, B. (1999). *A celibate season*. New York: Penguin Books.

Shorter, E. (1992). *From paralysis to fatigue: A history of psychosomatic illness in the modern era*. New York: Free Press.

Shorto, R. (1999). *Saints and madmen: Psychiatry opens its doors to religion*. New York: Henry Holt.

Showalter, E. (1997). *Hystories: Hysterical epidemics and modern culture*. New York: Columbia University Press.

Shree Ma (2001). Swamiji in the fire. *Devi Mandir newsletter,* January. http://www.shreemaa.org/drupal/.

Shulman, A. (1995). *Drinking the rain: A memoir*. New York: Farrar Strauss Giroux.

Siegel, d. (1999). *The developing mind: How relationships and the brain interact to shape who we are*. New York: Guilford Press.

Sierra, M. (2009). *Depersonalization: A new look at a neglected syndrome*. New York: Cambridge University Press.

Simeon, D. (2004). Depersonalisation disorder: A contemporary overview. *CNS Drugs, 18*(6), 343-54.

Simeon, D., & Abugel, J. (2008). *Feeling unreal: Depersonalization disorder and the loss of the self.* New York: Oxford University Press.

Simeon, D., Stanley, B., Frances, A., Mann, J., Winchel, R., & Stanley, M. (1992) Self-mutilation in personality disorders: Psychological and biological correlates. *American Journal of Psychiatry, 149*, 221-26.

Simonton, D. (1999). *Origins of genius: Darwinian perspectives on creativity.* New York: Oxford University Press.

Simpson, M. (1980). Self-mutilation as indirect self-destructive behavior: "Nothing to get so cut up about . . . ." In N. Farberow (Ed.), *The many faces of suicide: Indirect self-destructive behavior* (pp. 257-83). New York: McGraw-Hill.

Singer, M., & Lalich, J. (1996). *Crazy therapies: What are they? Do they work?* New York: Jossey-Bass.

Singer, M., & Ofshe, R. (1990). Thought reform programs and the production of psychiatric casualties. *Psychiatric Annals, 20*, 188-93.

Siskind, A. (2003). *The Sullivan Institute/Fourth Wall community: The relationship of radical individualism and authoritarianism.* New York: Praeger Books.

Skolnick, A. (1991). Maharishi Ayur-Veda: guru's marketing scheme promises the world eternal 'perfect health.' *The Journal of the American Medical Association, 266*(13), 1741-46.

Slater, L. (1998). *Prozac diary.* New York: Random House.

———. (1996). *Welcome to my country: A therapist's memoir of madness.* New York: Anchor/Doubleday.

———. (2001). *Lying: A metaphorical memoir.* New York: Penguin.

———. (2003). *Love works like this: Travels through a pregnant year.* New York: Random House.

———. (2004). *Opening Skinner's box: Great psychological experiments of the twentieth century.* New York: W. W. Norton.

———. (2005). Three spheres. In L. Gutkind (Ed.), *In fact: The best of creative nonfiction* (pp. 3-24). New York: W. W. Norton.

Small, G. (1983). Mass hysteria. *Western Journal of Medicine,142*(5), 682-83.

Small, G., & Borus, G. (1983). Outbreak of illness in a school chorus—Toxic poisoning or mass hysteria? *New England Journal of Medicine, 308*(11), 632-35.

Small, G., & Vorgan, G. (2010). *The naked lady who stood on her head: A psychiatrist's stories of his most bizarre cases.* New York: William Morrow.

Snyder, A., Mulcahy, E., Taylor, J., Mitchell, J., Sachdev, P., & Ganddevia, S. (2003). Savant-like skills exposed in normal people by suppressing the left fronto-temporal lobe. *Journal of Integrative Neuroscience, 2*, 149-58.

Solomon, R., & Corbit, J. (1974). An opponent-process theory of motivation, Part 1. Temporal dynamics of affect. *Psychological Review, 81*(2), 119-45.

Spencer, J. (2006, July 18). "I drank the way I ate": Swapping addictions. *Wall Street Journal*, D1-3.

Spitz, R. (1945). Hospitalism: An inquiry into the genesis of psychiatric conditions in early childhood. *Psychoanalytic Study of the Child, 1*, 53-74.

———. (1946). Hospitalism: A followup report. *Psychoanalytic Study of the Child, 1*, 53-74.

Stace, W. (1960). *Mysticism and philosophy.* London: Macmillan.

Steele, K., van der Hart, O., & Nijenhuis, E. (2005). Phase-oriented treatment of structural dissociation in complex traumatization: Overcoming trauma-related phobias. *Journal of Trauma & Dissociation, 6*(3), 11-53.

Steinberg, M., & Schnall, M. (2001). *The stranger in the mirror* New York: Harper Paperbacks.

Starkman, R., Steinitz, Y., & Stern, Y. (2010, October 10). German Jewish leader welcomes Hitler exhibition in Berlin. Haaretz.com

Stolorow, R., & Atwood, G. (2002). *Contexts of being: The intersubjective foundations of psychological life.* New York: Routledge.

Stoller, R. (1985). *Observing the erotic imagination.* New Haven: Yale University Press.

———. (1991). *Pain and passion: A psychoanalyst explores the world of S & M.* New York: Plenum Press.

———. (1992). *Presentations of gender*. New Haven, CT: Yale University Press.

Strassman, R. (2000). *DMT: The spirit molecule: A doctor's revolutionary research into the biology of near-death and mystical experiences.* New York: Park Street Press

Strassman, R., Wojtowicz, S., Luna, L., & Frecska, E. (2008). *Inner paths to outer space: Journeys to alien worlds through psychedelics and other spiritual technologies*. New York: Park Street Press.

Strauch, B. (2004). *The primal teen: What the new discoveries about the teenage brain tell us about our kids.* New York: Anchor.

Strong, M. (1998). *A bright red scream*. New York: Viking.

Styron, W. (1990). D*arkness Visible: A memoir of madness*. New York: Random House.

Suspension (2002). http://www.suspension.org/faq.htm. Downloaded 03/07/2003.

Swift, J. (1996). *A modest proposal and other satirical works*. Mineola, NY: Dover Publications.

Szimhart, J. (2009). Razor's edge indeed: A deprogrammer's view of harmful cult activity. *Cultic Studies Review*, *8*(3), 231-65.

Tart, C. (1972). Introduction. In C. Tart (Ed.), *Altered states of consciousness* (pp. 1-8). Garden City, NY: Doubleday.

———. (1998). Investigating altered states of consciousness on their own terms: A proposal for the creation of state-specific sciences. *Ciencia e Cultura (Journal of the Brazilian Association for the Advancement of Science), 50*(2/3), 103-16.

Taylor, G. (1978). Demoniacal possession and psychoanalytic theory. *British Journal of Medical Psychology, 51*, 53-60.

Taylor, G., & Bagby, R. (2005). New trends in alexithymia research. *Psychotherapy and Psychosomatics, 73*, 68-77.

Taylor, G., Bagby, R., & Parker, J. (1991). The alexithymia construct: A potential paradigm for psychosomatic medicine. *Psychosomatics, 32*(2), 153-64.

Tell, D. (2002, June 12). The baby face of hate. *Weekly Standard.* http://www.weeklystandard.com/Content/Public/Articles/000/000/001/355bqppp. Asp.

Teresa of Avila. (1988). *The life of Saint Teresa of Avila by herself.* J. M. Cohen (Trans.). New York: Penguin Classics.

Terr, L. (1973). Children of Chowchilla: A study of psychic trauma. *Psychoanalytic Study of the Child, 34*, 547-623.

———. (1987). Childhood trauma and the creative product. *Psychoanalytic Study of the Child.* 42: 545-72.

———. (1989). Terror writing by the formerly terrified: A look at Stephen King. *Psychoanalytic Study of the Child, 44*, 369-90.

———. (1990). *Too scared to cry. New* York: Harper and Row.

———. (1994). *Unchained memories: True stories of traumatic memories lost and found.* New York: Basic Books.

The Holy Bible (1991). King James Version. New York: Ballantine.

Thomas Edison Quotes (1996). http://www.thomasedison.com/quotes.html, Downloaded April 7, 2006.

Thompson, M., Callaghan, P, Hunt, G., Cornish, J., & McGregor, S. (2007). A role for oxytocin and 5-HT1A receptors in the prosocial effects of 3,4 methylenedioxymethamphetamine ("ecstasy"). *Neuroscience, 146*(2), 509-14.

Thornhill, R, & Thornhill, N. (1992). The evolutionary psychology of men's coercive sexuality. *Brain and Behavioral Sciences, 15*(3), 363-421.

Tickle, P. (1997). *God-Talk in America*. New York: Crossroad Publishing Company.

Tobin, D. (2000). *Coping strategies therapy for bulimia nervosa.* Washington, DC: American Psychological Association.

Torgoff, M. (2004). *Can't find my way home: America in the great stoned age, 1945-2000.* New York: Simon & Schuster.

Torgovnick, M. (1996). *Primitive passions: men, women, and the quest for ecstasy*. New York: Knopf.

Torrey, R. (1901). *How to promote and conduct a successful revival.* Ada, MI: Revell.

Tustin, F. (1990). *The protective shell in children and adults*. London: Karnac.

Twenge, J., & Campbell, W. (2009). *The Narcissism epidemic: Living in the age of entitlement.* New York: Free Press.

Vaillant, G. (1977). *Adaptation to life.* Boston: Little, Brown.

Vale, V., & Juno, A. (1989). *Modern primitives: An investigation of contemporary adornment and ritual—tattoo, piercing, scarification.* San Francisco: Re/Search Publications.

Van Buren, A. (2009, October 7). Dear Abby: Choking game can't be ignored. *The Buffalo News.* http://www.buffalonews.com/opinion/columns/dearabby/story/820321.html?imw=Y.

van der Hart, O., Lierens, R., Goodwin, J. (2006). Jeanne Fery: A sixteenth century case of dissociative identity disorder. *Journal of Psychohistory, 24*(1), 18-35.

van der Hart, O., & Witztum, E. (2009). Dissociative psychosis. In A. Moskowitz, I. Schäfer, & M. Dorahy (Eds.), *Psychosis, Trauma and dissociation: Emerging perspectives on severe psychopathology* (pp. 257-59). London: John Wiley & Sons.

van der Kolk, B. (1988). The trauma spectrum: The interaction of biological and social events in the genesis of the trauma response. *Journal of Traumatic Stress 1*(3), 273-90.

———. (1989). The compulsion to repeat the trauma: Re-enactment, revictimization, and masochism. *Psychiatric Clinics of North America, 12*(2), 389-411.

———. (1994). The body keeps the score: Memory and the evolving psychobiology of post-traumatic stress. *Harvard Review of Psychiatry, 1,* 253-65.

van Gennep, A. (2004). *The rites of passage.* New York: Routledge.

van Gogh, V. (1958). *The complete letters of Vincent van Gogh* (vol. 2). Boston: New York Graphic Society.

Volkow, N., Fowler, J., Wang, J. (2004). The addicted human brain viewed in the light of imaging studies: Brain circuits and treatment strategies. *Neuropharmacology, 47,* 3-13.

Volkow, N., Fowler, J., Wang, J., Swanson, J., & Telang, F. (2007). Dopamine in drug abuse and addiction: Results of imaging studies and treatment implications. *Archives of Neurology, 64*(11), 1575-79.

Volkow, N., Chang, L., Wang, G., Fowler, J., Leonido-Yee, M., Franceschi, D., Sedler, M., Gatley, J., Hitzemann, R., Ding, Y., Logan, J., Wong, C., & Miller, E. (2001). Association of dopamine transporter reduction with psychomotor impairment in methamphetamine abusers. *American Journal of Psychiatry, 158,* 377-82.

Wallin, D. (2007). *Attachment in psychotherapy.* New York: Guilford Press.

Walsh, D., & Bennett, N. (2004). *Why do they act that way? A survival guide to the adolescent brain for you and your teen.* New York: Free Press.

Walsh, B., & Rosen, P. (1988). *Self-mutilation.* New York: Guilford Press.

Wagner, U., Gais, S., Haider, H., Verleger, R., & Born, J. (2004). Sleep inspires insight. *Nature, 427*(6972), 352-55.

Watson, S. (1995). *The birth of the Beat generation: Visionaries, rebels, and hipsters, 1944-1960.* New York: Pantheon Books.

Waxman, S., & Geschwind, N. (1974). Hypergraphia in temporal lobe epilepsy. *Neurology, 24,* 629-36.

Weinstein, S. (2009). *Madoff's other secret: Love, money, Bernie, and me.* New York: St. Martin's Press.

Weiss, B. (1988). *Many lives, many masters: The true story of a prominent psychiatrist, his young patient, and the past-life therapy that changed both their lives.* New York: Simon & Schuster.

West, T. (1991). *In the mind's eye: Creative visual thinkers, gifted dyslexics, and the rise of visual technologies.* Buffalo: Prometheus Books.

Whedon, J. (2010). Passion. www.Thinkexist.com/Whedon. Downloaded May 7, 2010.

Wieder, H., & Kaplan, E. (1969). Drug use in adolescents-psychodynamic meaning and pharmacogenic effect. *Psychoanalytic Study of the Child, 24,* 399-431.

Whitlock, F., & Hynes, J. (1978). Religious stigmatization: An historical and psychophysiological inquiry. *Psychological Medicine, 8,* 185-202.

Wild, B., Erb, M., & Bartels, M. (2001). Are emotions contagious? Evoked emotions while viewing emotionally expressive faces: Quality, quantity, time course and gender differences. *Psychiatry Research, 102*(2), 109-24.

Wilentz, A. (2002, May 6). The Middle East war at home: Crisis for American Jews. *New York Magazine*, 35, 26-101.

Wilson, I. (1988). *The bleeding mind: An investigation into the mysterious phenomenon of stigmata*. London: Weidenfield and Nicholson.

Winchel, R., & Stanley, M. (1991) Self-injurious behavior: A review of the behavior and biology of self-mutilation. *American Journal of Psychiatry, 148*(3), 307-17.

Wilson, C. P. (1988). Bulimic equivalents. In H. Schwartz (Ed.), *Bulimia: Psychoanalytic treatment and theory* (pp. 489-522). Madison, CT: International Universities Press.

Winnicott, D. (1953). Transitional objects and transitional phenomena. *International Journal of Psycho-Analysis, 34*(4), 510-16.

———. (1965). *The maturational processes and the facilitating environment*. New York: International Universities Press.

———. (1971). *Playing and reality*. New York: Basic Books.

———. (1975a). The manic defense. In *Through paediatrics to psycho-analysis* (pp. 129-44). New York: Basic Books.

———. (1975b). Mind and its relation to the psyche-soma. In *Through paediatrics to psycho-analysis* (pp. 243-54). New York: Basic Books.

Winterson, J. (2009, October 17). In Praise of *The crack-up*: A novelist peers through darkness to find glittering gems in writing and art. *Wall Street Journal*. http://online.wsj.com/article/SB10001424052748704322004574475654003711242.html#articleTabs%3Darticle.

Woods, M., & Hollis, F. (1990). *Casework: A psychosocial therapy*. New York: McGraw-Hill.

Woods, S., Carlson, J., & McGlashan, T. (2020). DSM-5 and the 'psychosis risk syndrome': The DSM-5 proposal is better than DSM-IV. *Psychosis: Psychological, Social and Integrative approaches, 29*(3) , 187-90.

Wylie, M., & Turner, L. (2011, March/April). The attuned therapist: Does attachment theory really matter? *Psychotherapy Networker*, pp. 18-49.

Yates, A. (1991). *Compulsive exercise and the eating disorders: Toward an integrated theory of activity*. New York: Brunner/Mazel.

Yaryura-Tobias, J., & Neziroglu, F. (1978) Compulsions, aggression and self-mutilation: A hypothalamic disorder. *Orthomolecular Psychiatry, 7*, 114-17.

Yaryura-Tobias, J., Neziroglu, F., & Kaplan, S. (1995) Self-mutilation, anorexia, and dysmenorrhea in obsessive- compulsive disorder. *International Journal of Eating Disorders, 17*(1), 33-38.

Young, S., Sweeting, H., & West, P. (2006). Prevalence of deliberate self-harm and attempted suicide within contemporary Goth youth subculture: Longitudinal cohort study. *British Medical Journal, 332*(549), 1058-61.

Zalewski, D. (2001, March 27). Once, in the jungle. *New York Times Magazine*. pp. 54-57.

Zaretsky, E. (1999). An unpublished letter from Freud on female sexuality: Translated with an introduction by Eli Zaretsky. *Gender and Psychoanalysis, 4*(1), 99-104.

Zerbe, K. (2008). *Integrated treatment of eating disorders: Beyond the body betrayed*. New York: W. W. Norton.

Zuger, A. (2011, June 14). A general in the drug war. *New York Times*, pp. D1-D4.

Zulueta, F. (1994). *From pain to violence: The traumatic root of destructiveness*. Northvale, NJ: Jason Aronson.

Index

About the Author

Sharon Klayman Farber, PhD, is a board-certified diplomate in clinical social work in private practice of psychotherapy and psychoanalysis with children, adolescents, and adults in Hastings-on-Hudson, New York. She is the founder of Westchester Eating Disorders Consultation Services and runs a group for women with eating problems. She has taught at medical and social work schools, training institutes, and the Cape Cod Institute, and she is an invited speaker in the United States and abroad.

Farber is the author of several journal articles and *When the Body Is the Target: Self-Harm, Pain, and Traumatic Attachments* (Jason Aronson, 2000). Farber loved to write and wanted to be a writer long before obtaining the professional training to do the work she loves, and she enjoys writing about it. She also enjoys teaching other professionals to write scientific prose that is engaging, transparent, and accessible to other professionals as well as the untrained reader. She runs a group and teleseminar for clinicians who want to write for publication.